决胜美国高考ACT系列备考丛书

非官方指南

（上册）

主编 李现伟 田新笑

内容提要

本书共分为三部分，包含ACT考试科学、数学和写作部分的官方指南疏理和真题解析，其中加入了官方指南所没有解释明确的信息和内容。本书适合国内备考ACT考试的学生以及广大英语学习爱好者使用。

图书在版编目(CIP)数据

ACT非官方指南.上册/李现伟.田新笑主编.—上海:上海交通大学出版社,2016

ISBN 978-7-313-14904-6

Ⅰ.①A… Ⅱ.①李…②田… Ⅲ.①英语—高等学校—入学考试—美国—自学参考资料 Ⅳ.①H31

中国版本图书馆CIP数据核字(2016)第090805号

ACT非官方指南(上册)

主　　编：李现伟　田新笑

出版发行：上海交通大学出版社

邮政编码：200030

出 版 人：韩建民

印　　制：上海春秋印刷厂

开　　本：787mm×1092mm　1/16

字　　数：870千字

版　　次：2016年8月第1版

书　　号：ISBN 978-7-313-14904-6/H

定　　价：93.00元

地　　址：上海市番禺路951号

电　　话：021-64071208

经　　销：全国新华书店

印　　张：31.25

印　　次：2016年8月第1次印刷

决胜美国高考系列备考丛书

总　　序

（一）

和田老师相识多年，同乡之谊和同行间的惺惺相惜使我们下定决心打造这一系列的书籍，包括从新 SAT、ACT、SSAT、TOEFL、IELTS、GRE、SAT2、AP 到 IB、Alevel、留学申请等一系列丛书，2016 年年初第一期出版的书共 9 本，涵盖 ACT 书籍 4 本、新 SAT 书籍 5 本。

我从小在农村长大，深知升学是离开农村这个生活环境的唯一道路。因为饱尝农活的艰辛，经历过被束缚在土地上的无奈，幸亏有亲戚朋友的帮助以及自己虽天资愚笨但还足够勤奋，我一路还算优秀顺利：考到复旦，读书，然后工作。这虽然带有非常现实的功利主义，但确实是这个时代很多农村出来的“80 后”的真实写照。改革的红利促进了低龄出国潮的兴起，“90 后”以及“00 后”开始经营自己的人生，留学读书少了彼时容闳的拓荒气质、小说人物方鸿渐的镀金目的、20 世纪 70 年代的国家主义、90 年代的精英主义，此时更多是一种自由主义的选择。

自由是很美妙的。复旦读书时，我阴差阳错入读了公共卫生学院，然后一系列的不利因素使我曾经一度想放弃再重新参加高考，然而每当回到老家看到三间瓦房下父母黝黑的脸庞，我又熬了 5 年，终于以 GPA 垫底的成绩毕业。彼时的我除了普通话稍微标准一些，再无长处可循，所以走向新东方从事教师职业实属无奈。但是因为普通话不标准刚一开始我只能教授词汇。似乎是为了报复自己，我硕士读了北大与中欧商学院，都没有正常毕业，然而在我看来，却没有任何遗憾，因为这种自由的选择比名校光环和过时的知识重要得多。当然，每念及白花的钱可以在农村给父母盖座像模像样的洋房，也甚是心痛，然而这就是呼吸自由空气的代价。

其实此时出国读书再成为邵亦波、曾子墨、陈欧的概率已经大大降低，统计上的大数定律已经慢慢开始起作用，那我们为什么还要出国读书？“Because it is there”，就像很多登珠穆朗玛峰的人回答别人的提问一样，或者说，这种问题只能有后验主义的回答。出国读书是我们这个时代所赋予的自由选择，也是我们变得更加优秀的途径之一。优秀是一种自由赋予的权利，所以也容易形成习惯。

所以，我们希望这套丛书以及相配套的线上视频音频、题库资源和线下培训课程等能够培养学生优秀的学习习惯。正如你口语能力的真正提高不在于托福口语考得的高分，而是在英语国家生活和学习了一段时间之后慢慢习得的纯正的语言习惯。所以，我们在本系列书的基础上，推出更多的沉浸性的阶梯式资源，期望能够为广大学子在学习英语的道路上贡献力量。

加油吧，去享受这个时代赋予你的自由！

加油吧，去追逐自由空间里优秀的自己！

加油吧，去创造更多自由、更多的卓越！

李现伟

2016 年 1 月于上海宝山

(二)

十多年前我踏入了留学考试培训行业,见证了不同出国留学考试(TOEFL、IELTS、SAT、ACT、GMAT、GRE)的发展变革,同时,数万青少年考生备考的激情和为实现求学梦想而飞跃重洋的坚定决心一直鼓励着我在这个劳动和智力双密集的行业里耕耘。

我给自己拟过一个微信名——种稻。这个带有农活儿色彩的词汇部分描述了我的少年时代(不过那时候我们家是种麦),部分描述了我这十几年的教学活动。我像辛勤的老农一般一节节课讲到现在,成就了众多的考生,也成就了自己对教学的感悟和经验积累。凭着教学所积累的经验,我开始了教育培训行业的管理、咨询、教师培训等一些列工作,我会从个别经验里面凝炼出抽象的模型,这个凝炼过程所带来的认知能力的迁移,使得我愿意做好同领域其他模块的事情。

我与李现伟老师是多年的同事,也是同乡。他是教育培训界异常勤奋的劳模和专家。我们一直关注着本行业和相关考试的动态和发展趋势,都参加过各种北美留学考试,而且都取得过优异的成绩,一直活跃在教育培训界的讲台和管理咨询岗位上。本系列书籍是我们多年教学培训的心得总结和精华。

从某种意义上讲,我们可以把出国考试按照考试性质分为语言水平类测试和能力水平类测试。但是,在中国做出国考试类培训都不能回避二语教学的概念。所以,很多时候我们在进行能力水平类测试培训的时候会花很大精力在学员语言能力的培训上,因为几乎所有的测试都离不开语言作为其载体,也就是说,要在出国考试里取得上佳成绩,首先要过语言关。学习语言本来就是一个潜移默化的过程。但是,在短期内学习一门外语,并且各方面都要学好并非易事。如果能够对出国考试培训或者学习过程有清晰的规划,明确自己在备考过程中需要做哪些具体工作,这个过程就会变得容易得多。

能力类考试(SAT、ACT、GMAT、GRE)一般的内容模块构成是:阅读、数学、语法、写作。这些模块本质上还是以语言为载体,因此语言学习、培训的具体行为要求大致相同,只不过需要加入语法的部分:做题、核对答案、分析错题、改正错题、明确语法点和考点、测试、速度训练等。需要指出的是这些还只是备考模块的部分具体行为,整体上还有模考、单词学习、以考代练、个性化学习方案制定和执行等模块,在此不一一赘述。

但是,能力类考试跟语言类测试也有明显的区别:难度较大、词汇量大、思维挑战性大。但是,表面上,西方人所设计的能力类考试一方面考查人类应该具备的输入或输出信息的能力;本质上,这类考试意在测试人类基本的理性思考能力、思辨力、严谨性,甚至还有缜密程度。笔者不揣浅陋,试着对这些能力模块进行部分解构,见下表:

能力模块	具体能力解构
解释	明确、释义、描述、转化、抽象词简化、态度理解、演绎、精确
举例	修辞目的、示例、示例化、证据、循证
分类	归类、归入、定性、定义
总结	概括、归纳、抽象化、观点理解、选项的归纳总结
推理	断定、结论、外延推理、内向推理、预判、细节词汇暗示性推理、修辞性语言
比较	对比、比较、对应、配对、类比
归因	解构、因果逻辑、由果及因、由因到果

（续表）

能力模块	具体能力解构
思辨	命题、命题的多种暗示、最优选项、概念细微差异和边界
决策	判断、带有时间限制的决定
情感	坚持、优秀的习惯、对语言中感性成分的理性判断、元认知能力（对学习的反思）

这些能力模块有个别还比较抽象，需要在具体备考过程中悉心体会、努力训练。说来有趣，几乎所有能力类考试到最后考的都是“细致！细致！细致！”。丁肇中先生曾提到，他发现J粒子的过程犹如某个中国一线城市下了一场大雨，其中有个红色雨滴，被他找到了。丁先生用切身经历告诉我们“细致”是一种能力，相应地，“粗心”也就不是一种理由，而是能力还没到，或者还没有被训练出来。我在讲座中常常提到一个“普通”的英文单词“consume”。我写下：“buy”“purchase”“use”“eat”“drink”“waste”这些词语，然后问，这其中哪些可以用来解释“consume”。问到最后，大家说其实都可以。这就是没有达到能力考试中词汇含义严谨度的学习要求。其实“buy”的本质意思是“交换（exchange，trade，barter）”而“consume”的本质意思是“使用（use）”，可以在某些语境里被理解为“eat”“drink”“waste”等等。实际上，每一次能力类考试中真正的难题并不多，但难题就成了区分高分段和中等分数的分界线。所以，“细致”这种能力或者精神是想要取得能力类考试高分的必要条件。

以上能力模块需要考生在备考过程中进行有针对性的训练，有时需要接受前辈考生或者老师的指导。明确了具体的考试、能力模块，接下来就是选择专业的备考材料。材料的准确性、练习的量和仿真度直接决定了备考的效果。多年来，社会上出现了无数的备考资料，有很多的材料或者备考建议都流于空泛，或者过度偏离真实考试，对考生帮助不大。本着对考试本质的精研态度，为考生提供实质性的帮助心理，我跟李现伟老师夜以继日、废寝忘食地编撰了本系列书籍，希望能够实实在在地帮助到广大考生。

最后回到我的微信名字——种稻。实际上这个名字的谐音是“中道”，不偏不倚。怡然自得、从容无碍一直是很多人追求的人生境界，当然也是我对生活的坚持和追求。最后也祝愿所有读者都能如愿以偿地获得自己务实坚强、张弛有度的人生状态。

田新笑

2016年1月于上海浦东

编写说明

➢ 本书内容简介

《ACT 非官方指南(上册)》包括科学、数学和写作 3 大部分。其中每部分都有对应的知识点和考点的梳理,有解题技巧和方法论的讲解。在每个科目的后面都附有科目所对应的历年真题的解析和讲解。其中,科学部分的真题原文可到 www. act. org 网站查看,并对照本书使用。2015 年 ACT 的写作部分有了改革,本书紧跟考试改革步伐,对新 ACT 写作进行了详尽地剖析和技巧方法的讲解。

➢ 本书特色介绍

本书详细分解了 ACT 考试的每个科目,并且倾情分享了每个科目的考点归纳和解题技巧,解析部分更是能够详尽地分析考点和答案的对应关系,使得考生备考事半功倍,提高效率。写作部分除了有方法论和技巧的讲解,还配有权威范文 20 套,以及范文的精讲精析。每个部分除了题目解析之外还配备一定量的练习,考生在学习方法的同时,还可以进行实战练习。

➢ 延伸学习建议

《ACT 非官方指南(上册)》和《ACT 非官方指南(下册)》是一个完整的体系,学习者要逐步地学习这两册书籍。同时,考生需要了解:

ACT 对学生阅读/处理信息的速度提出了很大的挑战,但是这种快速阅读能力也必须基于考生对于词汇的熟悉度和理解的准确性,也就是说,考生要从原来的短期快速背诵单词的观念中解脱出来,进入到单词深度学习的行为中。我们的"学习单词"理念安排是:先通过《ACT 真题核心词汇 3 600 词基础达标版》积累单词,然后再通过《ACT 真题词汇精选和长难句 60 套》巩固单词。

编者的水平和能力有限,书中若有批漏不当之处在所难免,请广大读者指正。

目　　录

第一部分

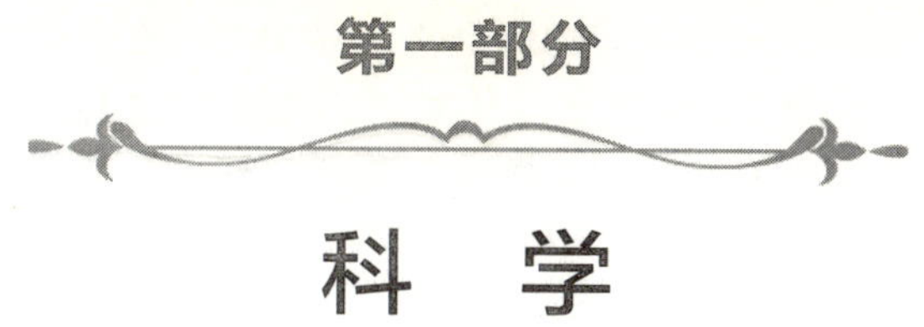

科　学

一、科学总论

（一）学科综述

1. ACT 科学基本情况

ACT 科学在 ACT 考试标准化分数的最后一项，总分是 36 分，其中包含 7 篇文章，需要在 35 分钟内完成累计 40 道题目（试卷代码 72 之前），新的北美方面的试卷是 6 篇文章，需要在 35 分钟内完成累计 40 道题（试卷代码 72 之后），其中包含 3 类文章：data representations（数据展示）、research summaries（研究概要）、conflicting viewpoints（对立观点）。

2. 科学部分的考察重心在于以下几个方向

（1）科学类文章的速读能力。

（2）数据的读取分析能力。

（3）图形的趋势判断、综合预测能力。

（4）数据、图形中隐藏结论的推测能力。

（5）综合信息推断结论的能力。

3. 科学部分考察会涉及以下学科内容

（1）生物大项：cell biology（细胞生物学）、botany（植物学）、zoology（动物学）、microbiology（微生物学）、ecology（生态学）、genetics（遗传学）。

（2）化学大项：properties of matter（物质的构成）、acids and bases（酸和碱）、thermochemistry（热化学）、chemical equation & rate（化学反应方程式和速率）、organic chemistry（有机化学）。

（3）物理大项：mechanics（力学）、fluid mechanics（流体力学）、optics（光学）、atomic physics（原子物理学）、thermodynamics（热力学）、electromagnetism（电磁学）。

（4）宇宙学/地理学大项：geology（地质学）、archaeology（考古学）、meteorology（气象学）、oceanography（海洋学）、astronomy（天文学）、environmental science（环境科学）。

4. 科学考试总体主观描述

科学（science）部分是体现 ACT 与 SAT（Old SAT）之间最主要区别的一个部分，**科学部分旨在考察学生的逻辑推理能力**，这在 Old SAT 中体现的不是很多，而且科学部分文章的载体都是缩略版的科学实验，前沿的科学研究成果，符合美国最新推行的 STEM（Science，Technology，Engineering，Mathematics，代表科学、技术、工程、数学）政策，将科学与技术体现在文章中，用数据读取、图形分析、结论揭示、未来预测等不同的题型来考察学生的逻辑思维能力，从这一点来看，和 Subjects Test(SAT II)是有本质区别的，ACT 总体是一个“evidence-based reading”(基于证据的阅读)，就是说 ACT 科学几乎会将所有题目的出题源和答案检索范围都放在文章中，所以在 ACT 科学部分中就需要极其**特殊的阅读方式和检索信息能力**，当然找到信息后的逻辑推理能力也是非常非常重要的，不然题目也不太容易做得对。所以，一句话概括，ACT 科学就是一门用看起来很复杂的科学信息来考察考生逻辑推理能力的考试。

(二) ACT 前期准备内容(授课前)

1. ACT 科学学科单词(汇编)

词汇永远都是任何考试的基础，这里的科学词汇我们是用词频统计软件对于所有 ACT 现存试题进行词频筛选得出的一本单词手册。

2. ACT 科学背景知识手册(汇编)

ACT 科学部分就算知道了单词意思但是对中文的专业词汇也不一定能够快速地理解内涵，那就需要不同于课内教科书大包大揽那样的具有专项优越性的背景知识手册。不需要理解计算过程，需要理解清楚概念即可。

3. ACT 长难句解析(汇编)

ACT 部分前面两块是基础中的基础，真正到了考试中能够决定你能不能快速高效的完成试题还是需要非常强的阅读能力，阅读能力又体现在对于长句子、难句子的拆分和理解，这一块能够很好地帮助我们快速做题。

4. ACT 科学文章的预习

不用做题，只是单纯地需要拿出 2～3 套真题看一下所有文章的基础架构、题目的基础架构、数据表示(data representations)类型的文章的结构、研究总结(research summaries)类文章的结构、相反观点(conflicting viewpoints)类文章的结构，也要关注数据题、读图题、推理题的句式以及提问方式。

(三) ACT 科学图表出现规律

1. 基本图形

(1) 数据图：柱状图、饼图、折线图、曲线图、散点图。

(2) 示意图：分区图、实验装置图、实验原理图、模型图。

2. 图形考察重点

标题、自变量轴/因变量轴、单位、图形的复合、趋势判断、图形的预测。

3. 图形识读方法

(1) 读图的标题、横轴、纵轴、图注、自变量/因变量的相对变化趋势。

(2) 注意图的转折点、极大值和极小值。

(3) 找到两条或多条曲线的交点。

(4) 表格类信息注意标题和文字信息，观察数据变化趋势。

4. 难点

图形的复合：只有能够共一条轴的图形才能够复合，并且基本要是一类图形才可以。

(四) ACT 总体做题方法

由题目中给出的定位词回到文章中定位，第一定位词往往是图 1 这类点出考点的范围限定词，第二定位词是斜体或文章中重点提到的科学概念专有名词，第三类定位词应该是单位或者横轴纵

轴等图形上展示出的内容，综上都无法定位的话，把这题目当作常识题来做，即不需要参考文章中的部分内容，用自己的知识储备来做(一般 40 道题目中每次会出现 1～3 题常识题)。

(五) ACT 题目类型及各类题型应对策略(精)

1. Data Representations(数据展示)

1) 数据定位及判断

(1) 直接查找：这类题目考察如何直接读图，直接由定位词找到限定条件即可。

(2) 数据比较：这类题目考察对于两个或者两组及以上数据的数值比较，找清楚想要比较的数据的参数即可。

(3) 数据排序：这类题目考察对于某一特定参数的排序，看清排序的参数以及次序非常重要，并且一定要快速识别这类题目。

2) 数据之间的关系

(1) 作图题：这类题目考察是否能够快速将文章中给出的数据用图形表示出来，注意选项中给出的图形横轴、纵轴，以及大趋势的判断。

(2) 趋势变化题：这类题目考察图或表两种不同图形的数据变化趋势，一般出题方式就是随着 A 的增大，B 怎么变化。注意看清楚题目的提问方式，有很多种不同的英文表述，比较趋势类的题目非常好做，但是极其容易犯视觉错误。

(3) 推理题大类

① 总结题：直接问关于文章中某一处内容的相关问题，定位准确，阅读没有障碍，直接回答即可。

② 判断题：题目一般在前半句给出一句陈述或推理作为这道题目需要判断的原始句子，后面的问题会问文章中的数据是否与这句表述一致，这种类型的题目前半句就是结论，后面就是需要验证，看清楚表述就可以。

③ 总结题：题目一般在前半句会给出一句新的条件，一般对于做题是有用的，需要结合给出的这句话和文章中给出的数据来做出一个新结论的推断，这类题目比较难的地方在于给出的选项中有可能并不是主旨类大的结论，有可能正确选项就是一个微小的点，需要注意。

④ 预测题：题目一般给出比较粗的条件，需要你结合整篇文章(包含文中的数据和结论)做出一个结论的预测，这类题目综合性很强，需要结合文章主旨来推断，data representations 类的文章一般考察的不是非常多。

2. Experiment 类文章

1) 实验设计考察

(1) 实验目的题：这类题目考察对于实验主要目的的把握，也会考察每一个分实验和主要实验目的的串联关系。注意一开始读文章时看清整个实验的实验目的。

(2) 步骤理解题 & 实验用具题：这类题目考察对于实验步骤的理解，需要对于整个实验进程有一个大体上的把握，注意步骤表述的文字那里会有部分小词的提示。实验用具题目一定会在文章中告知使用的器材或者直接用文字表述告知你器材的连接方式，注意看清文章。

(3) 实验变量题：这类题目考察对于实验中变量的区分，注意自变量和因变量的概念定义，不要受混淆变量的干扰。

(4) 实验对比：对于做了同样处理的实验结果或者过程之间的对比，这类题目一般用在控制变量法的实验中，注意比较清楚做了相同处理措施的实验才能够进行比较。

(5) 实验对照：对照实验(control experiment)是在国外的科学研究中经常需要进行的一种实验方法，就是对于有一组实验对象完全不做任何实验措施，让其自由发展，用来和做实验的组进行对照,以判断研究变量对于实验是否有正向或者逆向的影响。

(6) 去除干扰题:这类题目主要考察能够熟练判断如何去除实验干扰或者如何调整实验来达到最小化误差,这类题目记清楚实验环境、前实验对象、实验产物,在这三者之间寻找答案。

2) 实验结果类

(1) 公式题:这类题目考察能够将文章中的一些数据用一个公式来表述,直接定位到文章中描述到公式的地方即可。

(2) 实验结论推理题

① 总结题:直接问关于文章中某一处内容的相关问题,定位准确,阅读没有障碍,直接回答即可。

② 判断题:题目一般在前半句给出一句 statement 或 inference 作为这道题目需要判断的原始句子,后面的问题会问文章中的数据是否与这句表述一致,这种类型的题目前半句就是结论,后面就是需要验证,看清楚表述就可以。

③ 总结题:题目一般在前半句会给出一句新的条件,一般对于做题是有用的,需要结合给出的这句话和文章中给出的数据来做出一个新结论的推断,这类题目比较难的地方在于给出的选项中有可能并不是主旨类大的结论,有可能正确选项就是一个微小的点,需要注意。

④ 预测题:题目一般给出比较粗的条件,需要你结合整篇文章(包含文中的数据和结论)做出一个结论的预测,这类题目综合性很强,需要结合文章主旨来推断,data representation 类的文章一般考察的不是非常多。

3. Conflicting Viewpoints(对立观点)

(1) 这类文章全部都是推理题,分为以下 3 大类:(1)单一观点题(只关于一个人的观点)(2)多观点题(两个或者多个人之间的观点的比较)(3)简介&综述题目(一种问 introduction 部分内容;另外一部分就是问整个文章,结合信息做一个推理)

(2) 具体题型如下

① 总结题:直接问关于文章中某一处内容的相关问题,定位准确,阅读没有障碍,直接回答即可。

② 判断题:题目一般在前半句给出一句陈述或推理作为这道题目需要判断的原始句子,后面的问题会问文章中的数据是否与这句表述一致,这种类型的题目前半句就是结论,后面就是需要验证,看清楚表述就可以。

③ 总结题:题目一般在前半句会给出一句新的条件,一般对于做题是有用的,需要结合给出的这句话和文章中给出的信息做出一个新结论的推断,这类题目比较难的地方在于给出的选项中有可能并不是主旨类大的结论,有可能正确选项就是一个微小的点,需要注意。

④ 预测题:题目一般给出比较粗的条件,需要你结合整篇文章(包含文中的数据和结论)做出一个结论的预测,这类题目综合性很强,需要结合文章主旨来推断,数据表示类的文章一般考查得不是非常多。

(六) 科学总体做题思路

1. 数据类型文章(3×4 分钟)

Step 1　看图表数据,看清楚单位、图像变化趋势。

Step 2　由题目中的关键词入手,带入到文章中定位,找到关键词。

Step 3　判断题目类型直接做题。

Tips　不用看文章。

2. 研究类型文章(3×5 分钟)

1）Study 类型(数据重点)

Step 1 找到文章主要讲的那个科学概念或科学模型，这是行文的主线。

Step 2 辨别每一个 study 下的主要内容(不需要细读)，有图先看图，帮助理解主线内容即可(数据是这类题目的核心)。

Step 3 由题目看考察题目类型回到原文中 2～3 句话检索信息。

Step 4 判断清晰，做对题目。

2）实验类型

Step 1 找到文章实验的总实验目的

Step 2 搞清楚每一个分实验的总体研究目的以及和总实验目的之间的关系。

Step 3 判断题目类型检索信息，做对题目。

3. Viewpoints 类型文章(1×6.5 分钟)

Step 1 分类文章题目类型(单观点、多观点、简介 & 综述题)，标注出关于哪些人的观点。

Step 2 读 introduction 部分内容找到总的讨论主题。

Step 3 分开观点阅读做对应观点后的题目，比如读一个观点 1，将有关观点 1 的单观点题做完。

Step 4 全部单观点题目做完后做多观点题。

Step 5 判断综述 & 简介题目推理类型后，回到全文中检索信息来完成题目。

Session 1 生物 1

本章主要介绍 ACT 科学测试生物科目中的细胞生物学、植物学和动物学三大分支学科，并通过解析例题，以及相应的练习题明确这三门学科的考试形式、考试重点和相关词汇。

(一) 学科背景

ACT 科学测试主要考察和重点考察科学推理能力，了解相应的学科知识可以快速理解文章内容，提高解题速度。

1. 学科综述

1）细胞生物学(Cell Biology)

细胞生物学旧称细胞学(cytology)，是研究细胞的形态结构、生理机能、细胞周期、细胞分裂、细胞凋亡，以及各种胞器及信息传递路径的学科。

2）植物学(Botany)

植物学是一门研究植物形态解剖、生长发育、生理生态、系统进化、分类，以及与人类关系的综合性科学，是生物学的分支学科。

3）动物学(Zoology)

动物学作为生物学的一大分支，研究范围涉及动物的形态、生理构造、生活习性、发展及进化史、遗传及行为特征、分布，以及与环境间的相互关系。

2. 学科背景知识

1）细胞生物学

细胞生物学研究范围专注在生物学的微观下与分子层次。细胞生物学研究包括极大的多样性的单细胞生物，如细菌和原生动物，以及在多细胞生物如人类、植物和海绵的许多专门的细胞。

细胞生物学的一个重要组成部分是研究由蛋白质移动到细胞内不同的地方,或从细胞不同的地方分泌的分子机制。大多数蛋白质是由粗面内质网(RER)的核糖体合成的。核糖体含有的核糖核酸(RNA),它装配和连接的氨基酸制造蛋白质。在细胞质内以及在内质网(RER)内,它们可以被单独地或群组地找到。这个过程被称为蛋白质的生物合成。

2) 植物学

植物学是生物学的分支学科。研究植物的形态、分类、生理、生态、分布、发生、遗传、进化等。目的在于开发、利用、改造和保护植物资源,让植物为人类提供更多的食物、纤维、药物、建筑材料等。

植物学有下面 4 个主要领域:

(1) 形态学研究植体(由细胞到器官各个层次)的结构及形状。

(2) 生理学研究植物功能,与生物化学及生物物理学密切相关。

(3) 生态学研究生物与环境间的交互作用,在某些方面与生理学相近。

(4) 系统学研究植物的鉴定和分类。

3) 动物学

动物学是揭示动物生存和发展规律的生物学分支学科。它研究动物的种类组成、形态结构、生活习性、繁殖、发育与遗传、分类、分布移动和历史发展,以及其他有关的生命活动的特征和规律。

动物门类繁多,作为学科也极其复杂,但综合起来,其研究方法不外乎以下几种。

(1) 描述法:即通过观察,将动物外形、内部结构、生活习性及经济和学术意义用文字和图形如实记录下来。

(2) 比较法:通过动物间的系统比较,推究异同,认识它们之间的内在联系,从而得出规律。

(3) 实验法:在人为条件下,用物理的、化学的和生物学的方法对动物的生活和生命活动现象进行观察,以揭示动物生活和生命活动的本质。实验法往往和比较法同时进行。

(二) 学科单词

ACT 科学要求有一定的阅读量,文章中涉及大量的专业词汇,了解这些专业词汇的意思有助于理解文章和题意。以下是三门学科常见的专业词汇,考生需要熟悉单词的意思,以便在考试中能更准确地理解文章内容。

1. 细胞生物学

英文	中文释义	英文	中文释义
metazoan	多细胞动物	metaphase	中期
protozoan	原生动物	base pair	碱基对
membrane	薄膜	restriction enzyme	限制酶
cilia	纤毛	neuromuscular	神经肌肉的
flatworm	扁形虫	synaptic terminal	突触末端
colony	群落	axon	轴突
flagellum	鞭毛	motor end plate	运动终板
hydra	水螅	plasma	等离子体
pigment	色素	synaptic cleft	突触间隙
acetone	丙酮	vesicle	泡;囊
methanol	甲醇	neuron	神经元
mitotic/mitosis	有丝分裂的	botulin	肉毒毒素
telophase	末期	myosin	肌球蛋白

2. 植物学

英文	中文释义	英文	中文释义
reproduce	繁殖	decompose	分解
macronutrient	大量营养素	maturity	成熟
porphyrin	卟啉	chlorophyll	叶绿素
enzyme	酶	photosynthesis	光合作用
Deficiency	缺乏;不足	eukaryotic	真核的
hybrid	杂种	tare	测定皮重、自重
contral	对照物	chloroplast	叶绿体
correlation	关联	mitochondria	线粒体
compost	堆肥	lysosome	溶酶体

3. 动物学

英文	中文释义	英文	中文释义
amphibian	两栖类的	cyst	包囊
egg-laying	产卵的	trematode	吸虫
hatch	孵化	abnormality	畸形;变态
dissolved oxygen	溶解氧	teratogen	畸胎剂
carp	鲤鱼	retinoid	类视色素
saturation	饱和	hind limb	后肢
monomorphic	单一形态	aquatic	水栖的
dimorphic	二态的	metamorphose	变态
tadpole	蝌蚪	Parasitize	寄生于
morphological	形态学的	deer tick	鹿虱

(三)例题解析

本节选取了三门学科的真题进行详细的解析,帮助考生迅速了解考试的形式、内容和解题思路。

1. 细胞生物学(Cell Biology)

1)例题练习 1

(55C　Passage IV)

所有的多细胞生物可以被归结为后生动物。大多数的后生动物是双边对称的(他们的左半边和右半边几乎是相同的)。生物学家们认为,在大约 6 亿年前,后生物从原生动物(单细胞生物)演变而来,但是他们对这是如何发生的产生了分歧。生物学家们提出了 3 个理论。

Cellularization Theory(细胞化理论)

一些生物学家认为,后生动物是从多核的原生动物(有多个细胞核的原生动物)演变而来的。当两个相邻的细胞核之间形成薄膜时,分裂的细胞成形了。后来,纤毛(用来移动的毛状结构)从每一个细胞中生长出来。这些纤毛状的原生生物祖先随后演变成水生动物和与现代扁形虫相似的双边对称的后生动物。最后,其他的后生生物从这些扁形虫一样的生物中演变出来(见图 1)。

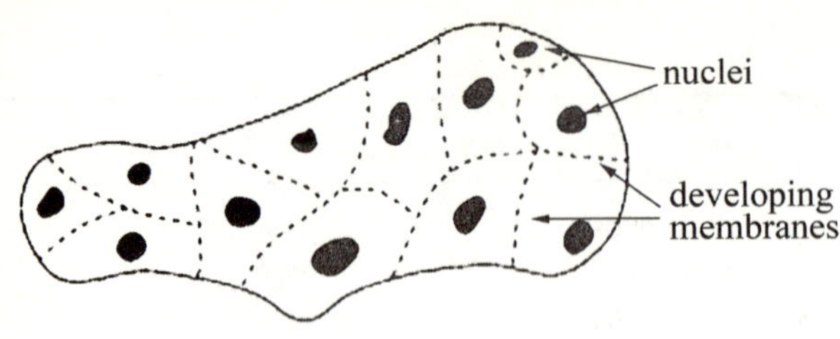

ancestral multinucleated protozoan

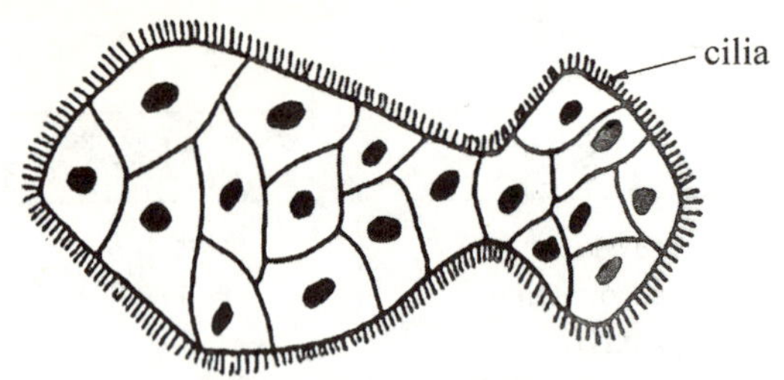

first flatworm-type metazoan

图 1

Colonial Theory(菌落理论)

其他的一些生物学家提出,许多原生动物聚集在一起形成一个空心的球,或者叫做菌落。这个菌落演变成最初的后生动物。菌落的每一个细胞都有一个用来移动的鞭毛(可移动的尾状物)。最初,部分细胞非常适合再生,并且这些细胞变成了后生动物的可再生细胞。最初的后生动物是水生动物,有鞭毛的放射对称的有机体(身体部分围绕一个中心对称排列,就像现代的水母)。所有后来的后生动物都是从这些水母状的有机体演变而来的(见图 2)。

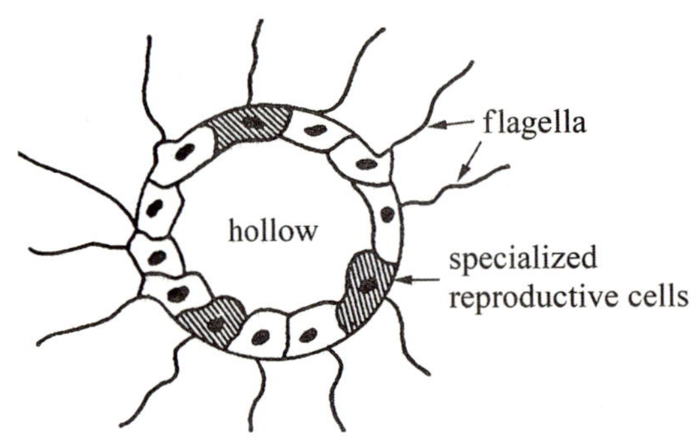

ancestral protozoan colony
(cross section through spherical colony)

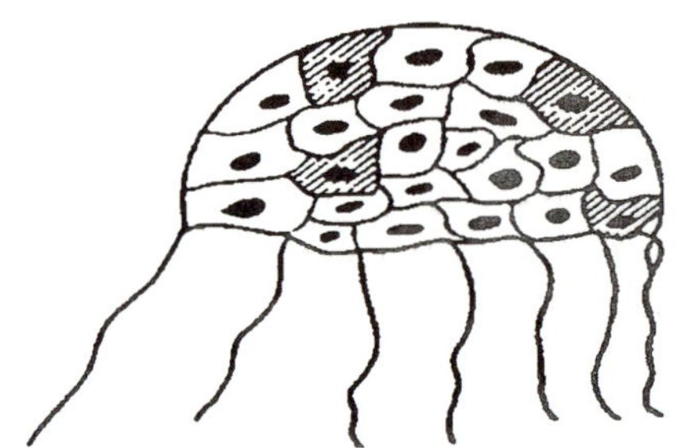
first jellyfish-like metazoan

图 2

Separate Line Theory(分离线理论)

这个理论的支持者认为,2 个分离的原生动物排成线型产生后生动物。放射对称的后生动物是从有鞭毛的、菌落状的原生生物进化而来。放射对称的后生生物是从有纤毛的多核的原生生物进化而来。这些最初的后生生物分别是水母状的生物和扁形虫状的生物。这两个原生生物组之间的关系不大,这两个组中的水生生物的演变是相互独立的并且发生在不同的时期。

(1) 例题练习 1.1

The Cellularization Theory does NOT include the hypothesis that the earliest metazoans were:

F. ciliated.

G. aquatic.

H. hollow.

J. bilaterally symmetrical.

【考点分析】

- 观点(理论)冲突类文章,此题为单一观点题。
- 抓住定位词 *The Cellularization Theory*,直接定位到第二段部分,题目考察 *The Cellularization*

Theory 不包括的假设。

● 根据第二段句子的描述“Later，cilia（hairlike structures），used for movement，grew from each cell. These ciliated protozoan ancestors then evolved into aquatic，bilaterally symmetrical metazoans similar to modern flatworms”，下划线三个单词一一对应三个选项，由此可知正确答案为 **H**。

（2）例题练习 1.2

The development of which of the following characteristics is addressed in the passage by the Colonial Theory but NOT by the Cellularization Theory?

A．Body symmetry

B．Ciliated tissues

C．Multinucleated cells

D．Reproductive cells

【考点分析】

● 观点（理论）冲突类文章，此题为多观点冲突题。

● 抓住定位词 *The Cellularization Theory & the earliest metazoans*，直接定位到第二段和第三段部分，题目考察 *The Cellularization Theory* 不包括的特点。

● 用排除法，根据上一题，直接可以排除 A、B 选项；根据第二段句子的描述“Some biologists believe that metazoans evolved from multinucleated protozoans（protozoans with many nuclei）”排除 C 选项，由此可知正确答案为 **D**。

● 同时 **D** 选项对应句子为“Initially，some of these cells were better suited for reproduction，and-these became the reproductive cells of the metazoan.”。

（3）例题练习 1.3

Supporters of all 3 theories would agree with the conclusion that the first metazoans：

F．evolved from protozoans.

G．are older than the first protozoans.

H．had many nuclei in each cell.

J．were radially symmetrical.

【考点分析】

● 观点（理论）冲突类文章，此题为综合观点题。

● 抓住定位词 *all 3 theories & the first metazoans*，需要直接阅读全文，题目考察 *the conclusion that the first metazoans*。

● 根据第一段句子描述“Biologists agree that metazoans evolved from protozoans（single-celled organisms）over 600 million years ago，but they do not agree on how this occurred”，由此可知正确答案为 **F**。

● 综合全文来看，G 选项只有第二个理论明显提及，第二个理论没有阐述 H 选项，J 选项只符合最后一个理论。

（4）例题练习 1.4

Which of the following types of organisms，if present today，would provide the most support for the Colonial Theory?

A．Flagellated protozoans living in dense colonies

B．Flagellated protozoans living in hollow colonies

C．Ciliated protozoans living in dense colonies

D．Ciliated protozoans living in hollow colonies

【考点分析】

● 观点(理论)冲突类文章,此题为单一观点题。

● 抓住定位词 *the Colonial Theory*,直接定位到第三段部分,题目考察最支持 *the Colonial Theory* 的结构证据。

● 根据第二段句子的描述"Other biologists suggest that many protozoans grouped together into a hollow ball, or colony.",排除选项 A、C,根据"The first metazoans were aquatic, flagellated, radially...",排除选项 D,由此可知正确答案为 **B**。

● 还可以根据 Figure 2 来作答,根据图中所示,明显具备 hollow 和 flagella 元素,故可以得出正确答案。

(5) 例题练习 1.5

Assuming that the Separate Line Theory is correct, which of the following conclusions can be made about modern hydras, which are radially symmetrical, and modern flukes, which are bilaterally symmetrical?

F. Hydras and flukes evolved from radially symmetrical metazoans.

G. Hydras and flukes evolved from bilaterally symmetrical metazoans.

H. Hydras and flukes are more closely related to each other than to protozoans.

J. Hydras and flukes are only distantly related through protozoans.

【考点分析】

● 观点(理论)冲突类文章,此题为单一观点题。

● 抓住定位词 *the Separate Line Theory*,直接定位到最后一段,题目考察对此理论的理解。

● 根据最后一段中句子的描述"Proponents of this theory argue that 2 separate protozoan lines led to metazoans. Radially symmetrical metazoans evolved from flagellated, colonial protozoans. Bilaterally symmetrical metazoans evolved from ciliated, multinucleated protozoans"和题干得出 F、G 是错误选项,根据最后一段中句子的描述"The 2 protozoan groups were only distantly related to each other",由此可知正确答案为 **J**,H 选项文章中未提及。

(6) 例题练习 1.6

Which of the following questions is raised by the Colonial Theory, but is NOT answered in the passage?

A. Why did the first flatworm-like metazoans have cilia?

B. Why were some colonial cells better suited for reproduction?

C. How could 2 lines of metazoans evolve from protozoans?

D. How were multinucleated cells transformed into cells with single nuclei?

【考点分析】

● 观点(理论)冲突类文章,此题为综合信息题。

● 抓住定位词 *the Colonial Theory & NOT answered in the passage*,可知是以第三段为主,并且结合全文,考察对 *the Colonial Theory* 的理解以及全文把控。

● 直接看选项,A 选项题眼 *the first flatworm-like metazoans have cilia*,明显可知为第一个理论内容,文章中"Later, other metazoans evolved from these flatworm-like creatures (see Figure 1)."为依据;B 选项题眼为 *reproduction*,为 *the Colonial Theory* 提到的内容,文章中"Initially, some of these cells were better suited for reproduction, and these became the reproductive cells of the metazoan."为依据,提出了此观点,但全文中未给出解释,所以 **B** 为正确答案;C 选项明显可知由第三种理论提出,文章中"Proponents of this theory argue that 2 separate protozoan lines led to

metazoans. ”为依据，并且从第二段可知与第二种理论无关；D 选项文章未涉及。

(7) 例题练习 1.7

Proponents of all 3 theories would agree with which of the following, conclusions about the evolution of metazoans?

F. Bilaterally and radially symmetrical metazoans evolved at different times.

G. The first metazoan was a jellyfish-like organism with flagella.

H. The evolution of metazoans led to the extinction of protozoans.

J. Bilaterally symmetrical metazoans are more advanced than radially symmetrical metazoans.

【考点分析】

- 观点(理论)冲突类文章，此题为综合观点题。
- 抓住定位词 *Proponents of all 3 theories*，考察对全文的掌握。
- 排除法来做，先看 F 选项，从最后一段最后一句可以找到支持，同时另外两种理论也未就此进行反驳，故而 F 选项应为正确；G 选项为第二个理论观点，根据文章中“The first metazoans were aquatic, flagellated, radially symmetrical organisms (body parts arranged symmetrically around a central point, as in modern jellyfish)”，可找到依据，但从第二段可知，第一个理论支持 *flatworm-like* 结构，与 G 选项不同；H、J 选项全文并未提及。

2) 知识拓展 1

[后生动物]

后生动物(metazoa)是除原生动物外所有其他动物的总称(后生动物亚界)。动物界除原生动物门以外的所有多细胞动物门类的总称。其特征是体躯由大量形态有分化、机能有分工的细胞构成；与群体原生动物的兼有营养和生殖功能的细胞不同，其生殖细胞和营养细胞有明显的分化；依体制形态的对称情况，后生动物可分为不对称动物(多孔动物门)、辐射对称动物(腔肠动物门、栉水母动物门、棘皮动物门；后者的对称是次生的，栉水母和某些珊瑚是左右辐射对称)和两侧对称动物(其他所有门类)。

后生动物系来自原生动物的祖先已毫无疑问，但什么样的原生动物是其祖先则议论很多。大致可分：

(1) 是多核原生动物的细胞分化结果(纤毛虫类起源说，认为从多核纤毛类产生原始的扁形动物，腔肠动物是由此而来的次生性动物)。

(2) 从老的学说来看，认为是从团藻那样的鞭毛虫群体演化而来。在这两种学说中，一般认为前者的论据不足，赞成后者的人比较多。后者的论点认为，这种群体构造是后生动物没有变化的胚芽；构成群体中的个体，按照极轴产生构造上的变化；分化成营养个员和生殖个员；在形成群体的过程中，特别类似于海绵动物的个体发生；后生动物的雄性生殖细胞保持着鞭毛虫的形态等等。

2. 植物学(Botany)

1) 例题练习 2

(57B Passage I)

除草剂可以用来控制杂草的生长。如果后一种庄稼被种在包含之前的剩余的除草剂的土壤中时，一种除草剂可能对一种庄稼非常安全但是可能对另一种庄稼造成伤害。我们进行了两个实验来研究这个影响。

Experiment 1 实验 1

一个植物学家在 90 个罐子中装了第一种土壤。其中 10 个罐子中没有加入除草剂。剩余的罐子按每组 10 个分组，每一组加入 10、20、50 或 100 ppm 的除草剂 A 和 B。所有其他的因素都是相同的。每一个罐子中种下 10 个杂化的种子。40 天之后，这些植物被连根拔起，用烤箱烘干并且称重。结果显示在表 1 中。

Table 1

Herbicide dose (ppm)	Average mass of plants (g)	
	Herbicide A	Herbicide B
10	14.1	15.6
20	12.4	13.7
50	9.3	12.1
100	5.5	9.3

Note: average plant mass in untreated soil was 16.0 g

Experiment 2 实验 2

实验 1 用 90 罐种类 1 的土壤和 90 罐种类 2 的土壤重复进行。用同样的除草剂计量和杂化种子。其他所有的因素都保持相同。40 天之后,植物的高度被测量出来。结果显示在表 2 中。

Table 2

Herbicide dose (ppm)	Average height of plants (cm)			
	Soil type 1		Soil type 2	
	Herbicide A	Herbicide B	Herbicide A	Herbicide B
10	46.3	49.0	50.3	52.5
20	42.0	47.0	44.4	47.0
50	34.1	39.4	40.6	42.3
100	19.6	22.7	30.9	36.4

Note: Average plant height in untreated soil type 1 was 50.6 cm; average plant height in untreated soil type 2 was 52.7 cm.

Information on the two soil types used is given in Table 3.

Table 3

Soil type	pH	Organic matter (%)	Clay (%)
1	6.9	5.0	16.3
2	6.2	9.5	7.9

(1) 例题练习 2.1

The results of Experiment 2 indicate that, at every herbicide dose, average plant height was lowest under which of the following conditions?

A. Herbicide A and Soil Type 1
B. Herbicide B and Soil Type 1
C. Herbicide A and Soil Type 2
D. Herbicide B and Soil Type 2

【考点分析】

- 数据表述类文章,此题为数据比较题。
- 抓住定位词实验 2,直接定位到第二个实验,题目考察最低值(*lowest*)。
- 根据实验 2 中的表 2,直接比较得出正确答案为 **A**。

(2) 例题练习 2.2

Which of the following sets of plants served as the control in Experiment 1?

F. Plants grown in untreated soil

G. Plants grown in soil treated with 10 ppm of Herbicide A

H. Plants grown in soil treated with 10 ppm of Herbicide B

J. Plants grown in soil treated with 100 ppm of Herbicide A

【考点分析】

- 数据表述类文章,此题为数据对照题。
- 抓住定位词实验 1,直接定位到第 1 个实验,题目考察实验对照组。
- 根据实验 1 中表 1(以下为截图),直接查找得出正确答案为 **F**。

Note: average plant mass in untreated soil was 16.0 g

- 同时根据文章第二段"A botanist filled 90 pots with Soil Type 1. No herbicide was added to the soil in 10 pots. The other pots were divided into groups of 10 and the soil in each group was treated with 10, 20, 50, or 100 ppm of either Herbicide A or B"也可看出正确答案。

(3) 例题练习 2.3

Which of the following best explains why the herbicides were applied to the soil instead of directly onto the corn plants?

A. Corn plants are not affected when herbicides are applied directly on them.

B. Corn plants usually die immediately upon application of herbicides.

C. The experiments were testing how herbicides present in the soil affect corn growth.

D. The experiments were testing how soil pH affects corn growth.

【考点分析】

- 数据表述类文章,此题为实验设定题,一般都在前言中可以得出答案。
- 抓住关键词 *why the herbicides were applied to the soil instead of directly onto the corn plants*,直接定位到第一段。
- 根据第一段中"Herbicides are used to control the growth of weeds. An herbicide that may be used safely with one crop species may damage another crop if the latter crop is planted in soil containing residual amounts of the herbicide from an earlier application"可以知道是需要使用在土壤中然后作用到庄稼的生长的,选项 C 为正确答案,而选项 A 和 B 表述的内容,试验中并没有给出,所以不正确,而选项 D 中所说到的 pH 值,在实验中同一种土壤 pH 恒定,故而不正确。

(4) 例题练习 2.4

Assume that there is a direct correlation between plant height and plant mass. If Experiment 1 were repeated using Soil Type 2, one would predict that the average plant mass would be lowest under which of the following conditions?

F. Herbicide A at 20 ppm

G. Herbicide B at 50 ppm

H. Herbicide A at 100 ppm

J. Herbicide B at 100 ppm

【考点分析】

● 数据表述类文章,此题为数据关联题。

● 抓住定位词实验 1 和土壤类型,直接定位到表 1 和表 2,同时题目给出了一个假设即植物的高度和植物的重量成正比,考察最低值(*lowest*)。

● 从两个表格中可以看到实验 1 中给出的是植物重量,实验 2 中给出的是植物高度,根据当高度和重量成正相关时,实验一相当于实验二的 Type 1 部分,题目考察的是类型 2 部分,根据表 2 可知可以知道在用 Herbicide A at 100 ppm 时植物高度最低,即对应重量最小,得出正确答案为 **H**。

(5) 例题练习 2.5

Assume that a second corn hybrid was grown in soil treated with varying doses of a third herbicide (Herbicide C). Based on the results of the experiments, what prediction, if any, about the effect of Herbicide C on the growth of this second corn hybrid can be made?

A. Herbicide C would have no effect on the growth of these plants.

B. Herbicide C would interfere with plant growth, but only at doses above 50 ppm.

C. Herbicide C would interfere with plant growth at low doses, but have no effect at high doses.

D. No prediction can be made on the basis of the results.

【考点分析】

● 数据表述类文章,此题为数据推理题。

● 抓住关键词 *Assume & a second corn hybrid & Herbicide C*,可知此题为推理题,题目要求我们根据文章中实验来推倒,第三种药剂对这一种植物的影响。

● 纵观全文,根本无法找到能给这个假定实验做对照的实验数据组,所以我们并不能推导出作用关系,所以根据实验结果,根本无法推理,得出正确答案为 **D**。

(6) 例题练习 2.6

To investigate the impact of soil acidity alone on the effect of the herbicides on corn growth, the botanist should design experiments using soils of:

F. varying pH, percent organic matter, and percent clay.

G. varying pH and percent organic matter, but identical percent clay.

H. varying pH and percent clay, but identical percent organic matter.

J. varying pH, but identical percent organic matter and identical percent clay

【考点分析】

● 数据表述类文章,此题为推理(变量关系题)题。

● 抓住关键词 *the impact of soil acidity alone*,题目考察土壤酸度的影响,很明显变量为 pH 值,不考察土壤构成,那么土壤的其他成分需要固定,可知正确答案为 **J**。

2) 知识拓展 2

[除草剂]

除草剂(herbicide)是指可使杂草彻底地或选择性地发生枯死的药剂,又称除莠剂,用以消灭或抑制植物生长的一类物质。其中的氯酸钠、硼砂、砒酸盐、三氯醋酸对于任何种类的植物都有枯死的作用,其作用受除草剂、植物和环境条件三因素的影响。按作用分为灭生性和选择性除草剂,选择性除草剂特别是硝基苯酚、氯苯酚、氨基甲酸的衍生物多数都有效。

除草剂可按作用方式、施药部位、化合物来源等多方面分类。

按使用方法分类:

(1) 茎叶处理剂:将除草剂溶液兑水,以细小的雾滴均匀地喷洒在植株上,这种喷洒法使用的除

草剂叫茎叶处理剂，如盖草能、草甘膦等。

（2）土壤处理剂：将除草剂均匀地喷洒到土壤上形成一定厚度的药层，当杂草种子的幼芽、幼苗及其根系接触吸收而起到杀草作用，这种作用的除草剂，叫土壤处理剂，如西玛津、扑草净、氟乐灵等，可采用喷雾法、浇洒法、毒土法施用。

（3）茎叶、土壤处理剂：可作茎叶处理，也可作土壤处理，如阿特拉津等。

3. 动物学(Zoology)

1）例题练习 3

（57B　Passage IV）

Because amphibian eggs lack a hard outer shell, their DNA can be damaged by exposure to ultraviolet (UV) radiation in sunlight. Table 1 lists the egg-laying behavior of 7 amphibian species and the species' relative ability to repair DNA damage caused by exposure to UV radiation.

Table 1

Amphibian	Relative ability to repair DNA damage	Egg-laying behavior	Exposure of eggs to sunlight
A	<0.1	Egg buried	None
B	<0.1	Eggs laid under cover	low
C	0.1	Eggs laid in relatively deep water	moderate
D	0.2	Eggs laid in relatively deep water	moderate
E	0.3	Eggs laid in shallow water	high
F	0.5	Eggs laid in shallow water	high
G	1.0	Eggs laid in shallow water	high

Figure 1 shows the percent of eggs that survived to hatching in the lab for these 7 species after exposure to unfiltered sunlight or to sunlight from which the UV radiation had been filtered out.

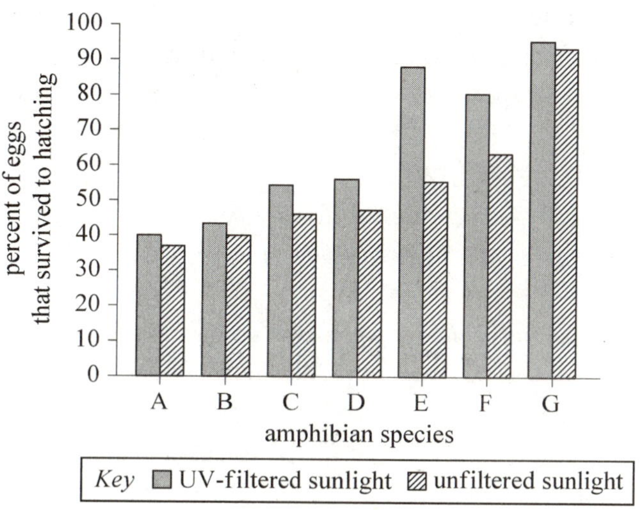

Figure 1

Figure 2 shows predicted UV levels over time in 4 geographic regions that have amphibian populations.

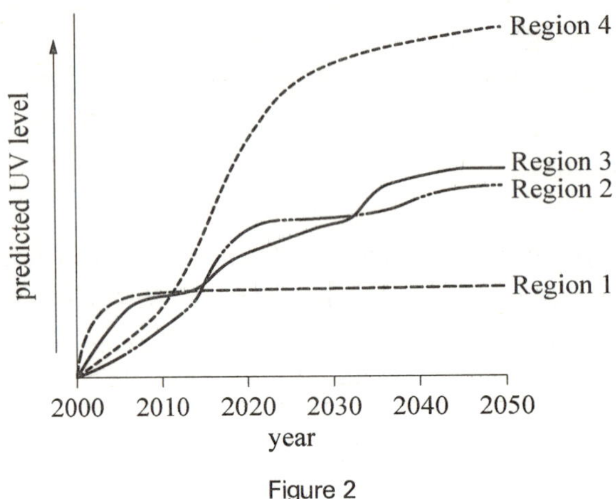

Figure 2

(1) 例题练习 3.1

Based on the information in Figure 1, eggs from which species are most likely to survive prolonged exposure to sunlight?

A. Species A　　B. Species C　　C. Species F　　D. Species G

【考点分析】

- 数据表述类文章,此题为数据比较题。
- 抓住定位词图 1,题目考察 *most likely to survive prolonged exposure to sunlight*。
- 根据图 1 中数据可以看出,在光下 egg 存活百分比最高的是物种 G,所以直接得出正确答案为 **D**。

(2) 例题练习 3.2

According to the data in Figure 1, which species showed the greatest difference between the percent of eggs that survived to hatching after exposure to unfiltered sunlight and the percent of eggs that survived to hatching after exposure to UV-filtered sunlight?

F. Species A　　G. Species C　　H. Species E　　J. Species G

【考点分析】

- 数据表述类文章,此题为数据比较题。
- 抓住定位词图 1,题目考察 *the greatest difference between*....。
- 根据图 1 中数据可以看出,对比值最大的物种为 E,当然可以知道正确答案为 **H**。

(3) 例题练习 3.3

Researchers recently discovered a new amphibian species that lays its eggs under cover. Based on the data in Table 1, the researchers would predict that this species' relative DNA-repair ability is most likely:

A. less than 0.1.　　B. greater than 0.1 and less than 0.3.

C. greater than 0.3 and less than 0.7.　　D. greater than 0.7.

【考点分析】

- 数据表述类文章,此题为数据推理题。

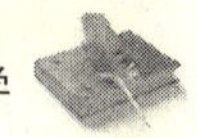

● 抓住定位词表 1，题目考察 *a new amphibian species that lays its eggs under cover & relative DNA-repair ability*。

● 根据表 1 中，不论物种，先将光照等级分类，我们可以看出大趋势是光照强度越大，修复能力越强，结合新物种的蛋是 under cover，对应的光强是 low，在此光强下物种 B 的修复能力是<0.1，推理可得，新物种的修复能力也应该是<0.1，故正确答案为 **A**。

(4) 例题练习 3.4

According to the information in Table 1, for all the species shown, as the exposure of eggs to sunlight increases the relative ability to repair DNA damage generally:

F. decreases only.　　G. increases only.

H. decreases, then increases.　　J. increases, then decreases.

【考点分析】

● 数据表述类文章，此题为数据推理(数据间关系)题。

● 抓住定位词表 1，题目考察当 *the exposure of eggs to sunlight increases* 时，*the relative ability to repair DNA damage* 的变化趋势。

● 根据表 1 中，不论物种，先将光照等级分类，我们可以看出大趋势是光照强度越大，修复能力越强，直接比较得出正确答案为 **G**。

(5) 例题练习 3.5

Based on the data in Table 1 and Figure 1, amphibians that had the lowest percent of eggs that survived to hatching when exposed to unfiltered sunlight tend to:

A. bury their eggs.　　B. lay their eggs under cover.

C. lay their eggs in deep water.　　D. lay their eggs in shallow water.

【考点分析】

● 数据表述类文章，此题为数据比较题。

● 抓住定位词表 1 和图 1，题目考察 *the lowest percent of eggs that survived to hatching*。

● 根据图 1 中，在 unfiltered sunlight 条件下，物种 A 的百分比最低，同时结合表 1 中物种 A 的 egg-laying behavior 是 eggs buried，可以得出正确答案为 **A**。

2) 知识拓展 3

[两栖动物]

两栖动物(amphibia)包括所有生没有卵壳的卵，拥有四肢的脊椎动物。两栖动物的皮肤裸露，表面没有鳞片，毛发等覆盖，但是可以分泌黏液以保持身体的湿润；其幼体在水中生活，用鳃进行呼吸，长大后用肺兼皮肤呼吸。两栖动物可以爬上陆地，但是不能一生离水，因为可以在两处生存，称为两栖。它是脊椎动物从水栖到陆栖的过渡类型。现在大约有 3 000 多种两栖动物。两栖动物是冷血动物。

两栖动物繁殖时需要水，因为它们的卵要生在水里。刚从卵里出来的幼体形态似鱼(如蝌蚪)用鳃呼吸，有侧线，依靠尾鳍游泳。然后经变态(metamorphosis)才能上陆生活。一般来说，它们最后会离开水，但是并非所有两栖动物都是这样。

它们成长过程中最明显的是长出四条腿在陆地上行走，另外还有：身体分为头、躯干、尾和四肢四部分；鱼鳃改为别的呼吸器，如肺；皮肤变为可以交换气体的器官；眼睛加了活动性眼睑，下眼睑连有瞬膜(但某些鲨鱼已有瞬膜)；在蛙蟾类的眼后常有一圆形鼓膜(tympanic membrance)覆盖在中耳(middle ear，或称鼓室 tympnic cavity)外壁，内接耳柱骨(columella)，并出现耳咽管(eustachian tube)。

(四) Practice 实战练习

1) Practice 4

(63C　Passage I)

在某些溶液中,甜菜细胞经历薄膜破裂,使细胞释放出甜菜花青苷(一种红色的色素)。AS 薄膜破裂越多,就释放越多的甜菜花青苷。我们通过计算被溶液吸收的光量(在某一个特定的波长)来决定甜菜花青苷释放的量。当溶液中甜菜花青苷的浓度增加时,吸收的光的量也增加。

为了决定被溶液吸收的光的量,光可以直接穿过溶液的样品到达探测器。

By measuring the amount of light that hits the detector, the amount of light absorbed by the sample can be determined (see Figure 1).

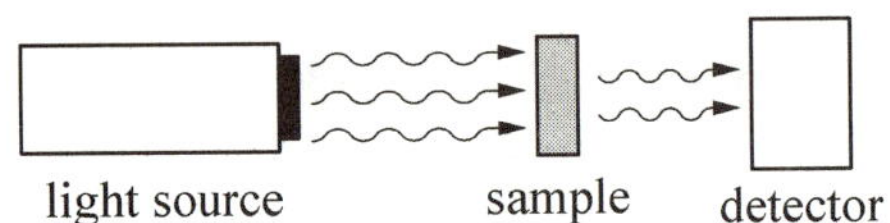

Figure 1

Experiment 1

For each of 9 trials, a student placed a beet section (2 cm×2 cm×1 cm) in 100 mL of water at a specific temperature for 10, 20, or 30 min. The student then removed a sample of the solution and determined its absorbance (see Table 1).

Table 1

Trial	Temperature (℃)	Time (min)	absorbance
1	25	10	0.12
2	25	20	0.14
3	25	30	0.16
4	50	10	0.31
5	50	20	0.37
6	50	30	0.43
7	75	10	0.62
8	75	20	0.71
9	75	30	0.82

Experiment 2

Experiment 1 was repeated, except that in each trial an acetone/water solution was used instead of water and the temperature was kept constant at 250℃ (see Table 2).

Table 2

Trial	Acetone concentration (% by volume)	Time (min)	Absorbance
10	10	10	0.31
11	10	20	0.38
12	10	30	0.45
13	30	10	0.69
14	30	20	0.76
15	30	30	0.86
16	50	10	0.82
17	50	20	0.90
18	50	30	0.96

Experiment 3

Experiment 2 was repeated, except that in each trial a methanol/ water solution was used instead of an acetone/water solution (see Table 3).

The student then determined the absorbance of water, of acetone, and of methanol. Each had an absorbance of 0.00.

Table 3

Trial	Methanol concentration (% by volume)	Time (min)	Absorbance
19	10	10	0.15
20	10	20	0.18
21	10	30	0.20
22	30	10	0.21
23	30	20	0.24
24	30	30	0.26
25	50	10	0.29
26	50	20	0.33
27	50	30	0.36

(1) Practice 4.1

Suppose that in Experiment 3 a beet section had been placed in a solution that was 40% methanol by volume for 20 min. The absorbance of the sample from the resulting solution would most likely have been closest to which of the following?

A. 0.15　　B. 0.30　　C. 0.45　　D. 0.60

(2) Practice 4.2

Based on the results of Experiment 2, which of the following additional trials would have resulted in an absorbance closest to 0.80?

F. 10% acetone for 15 min G. 10% acetone for 25 min

H. 30% acetone for 25 min J. 30% acetone for 35 min

(3) Practice 4.3

The results of Experiment 1 are most consistent with which of the following conclusions about the effects of temperature on membrane disruption and absorbance? Higher temperatures resulted in:

A. greater membrane disruption and higher absorbances.

B. greater membrane disruption and lower absorbances.

C. less membrane disruption and higher absorbances.

D. less membrane disruption and lower absorbances.

(4) Practice 4.4

The student concluded that at a given concentration, acetone causes more membrane disruption than does methanol. Is this conclusion supported by the results of Experiments 2 and 3?

F. No, because at each concentration tested, more betacyanin was released in the acetone solution than was released in the methanol solution.

G. No because at each concentration tested, less betacyanin was released in the acetone solution than was released in the methanol solution.

H. Yes, because at each concentration tested, more betacyanin was released in the acetone solution than was released in the methanol solution.

J. Yes, because at each concentration tested, less betacyanin was re eased in the acetone solution than was released in the methanol solution.

(5) Practice 4.5

Suppose that in Experiment 1, betacyanin concentration was directly proportional to absorbance. Accordingly, the betacyanin concentration in the sample in Trial 7 was most likely twice as great as the betacyanin concentration in the sample in:

A. Trial 3. B. Trial 4. C. Trial 5. D. Trial 6.

(6) Practice 4.6

In Experiment 1, the student directly varied 2 independent variables and measured how these changes affected the value of the dependent variable. Which of the following lists an independent variable and the dependent variable in Experiment 1?

Independent variable	Dependent variable
F. absorbance water	concentration
G. water concentration	methanol concentration
H. methanol concentration	temperature
J. temperature	absorbance

2) Practice 5

(52C Passage VI)

Most plants require specific substances known as minerals to grow and reproduce. The following table provides a list of the minerals essential to flowering plants and a description of their functions. The first seven listed are called macronutrients, since they are present in large quantities

in the plants. The other minerals are called micronutrients because they are often present in trace amounts. The number of pounds of each mineral required to grow 100 bushels of corn is also depicted in the table.

Element	Amount needed to grow 100 bushels of corn (1bs)	Function
Macronutrients: Calcium	50	Influences permeability of menbranes; component of pectic salts in middle lamellae and necessary for cell wall formation; activator for several enzymes
Iron	2	Activation of porphyrins to form hemes which are contained in cytochromes, peroxidases, catalases, and some other enzymes
Magnesium	50	Structural component of chlorophyll; cofactor for many enzymes involved in carbohydrate metabplism
Nitrogen	160	Structural component of amino acids, nucleic acids, many hormones and coenzymes, etc.
Potassium	125	Essential to a vast number of plant functions, but its exact role is not well understood
phosphorus	40	Structural component of nucleic acids, phospholipids, ATP, coenzymes, etc.
Sulfur	75	Structural component of some amino acids, vitamins, and enzymes, etc.
Micronutrients: Boron	0.06	Function unknown; may play a role in translocation of sugar; perhaps necessary for utilization of calcium in cell wall formation.
Copper	Trace	Structural component of many enzymes that catalyze oxidation reaction
Chlorine	0.06	Function unknown
Manganese	Trace	Cofactor for many enzymes involved in cellular respiration, photosynthesis, and nitrogen metabolism
Molybdenum	Trace	Structural component of the enzyme that reduces nitrate to nitrite; essential for fixation of nitrogen and nitrogen-fixing bacteria
Sodium	0.06	Function unknown
Zinc	Trace	Necessary for synthesis of tryptophan (a precursor of auxin); component of the enzyme that catalyzes the decomposition of carbonic acid to CO_2 and H_2O; may be a cofactor for some enzymes involved in the oxidation of carbohydrates

(1) Practice 5.1

According to the information presented in the table, flowering plants require iron in order to:

A. fix nitrogen. B. activate porphyrins.

C. utilize calcium. D. synthesize chlorophyll

(2) Practice 5.2

A scientist hypothesized that some minerals are required in minute quantities and are used as components of enzymes by flowering plants. The data for which of the following minerals would support this hypothesis?

F. Calcium G. Phosphorus H. Sodium J. Zinc

(3) Practice 5.3

A botanist in South America found a new variety of corn identical to the type described in the table with the exception that it utilizes copper, instead of iron, in activating porphyrins. Approximately how many pounds of copper would you predict would be required to grow 100 bushels of this new corn?

A. 0.3 lb B. 2.0 lb C. 4.0 lb D. 50.0 lb

(4) Practice 5.4

Which of the following conclusions about the mineral requirements of flowering plants is consistent with the data presented in the table?

F. Plants require larger amounts of minerals than are available in the soil.

G. Plants require some minerals whose functions remain unknown.

H. Deficiencies of certain minerals have little, if any, effect on plant growth.

J. The addition of minerals to the soil in the form of fertilizer results in a smaller yield of corn.

(5) Practice 5.5

A researcher using the table concluded that minerals used as components of enzymes and as cofactors for enzymes are required in very small amounts. This is supported by the information given for all of the following elements EXCEPT:

A. magnesium. B. manganese. C. molybdenum. D. zinc.

3) Practice 6

(61F Passage I)

Frog eggs develop into tadpoles, which then metamorphose into adult frogs. Recently, reported observations of frogs with morphological abnormalities (usually a missing or malformed hind limb) have increased in many localities. Four hypotheses attempt to explain this increase.

Hypothesis 1 假设 1

Tadpoles are commonly parasitized by *trematodes*, flatworms that burrow into the tadpoles, causing cysts to form. The presence of cysts during tadpole development can cause morphological abnormalities in the adult frog. Thus, increases in *trematode* populations most likely account for the recent increase in morphological abnormalities.

Hypothesis 2 假设 2

Due to industrial pollution, Earth's ozone layer has thinned. This process has led to an increase in the amount of ultraviolet (UV) radiation reaching Earth's surface. UV radiation can directly cause abnormalities in frog eggs by producing mutations in the DNA that controls frog development UV radiation can also indirectly cause abnormalities in frog eggs by chemically transforming certain pollutants into teratogens, chemicals that cause developmental abnormalities.

Hypothesis 3 假设 3

Certain pesticides contain a class of compounds called *retinoids*. Frogs naturally produce *retinoids*, but at high concentrations, *retinoids* cause mutations in frog eggs. These mutations later result in morphological abnormalities. Many of these mutations affect genes that control hind limb development. Thus, the recent increase in morphological abnormalities is probably due to an increase in *retinoids* from pesticides.

Hypothesis 4 假设 4

Tadpoles and frogs are prey for many aquatic predators, including fish, turtles, and wading birds such as herons. Predator attacks are not always completely successful; many result in injured frogs and tadpoles. Permanent injuries in tadpoles and frogs could later appear to be developmental abnormalities. Thus, increases in predator populations most likely account for the recent increase in morphological abnormalities.

(1) Practice 6.1

Which 2 hypotheses argue that the recent increase in morphological abnormalities in frogs is the result of human activities?

A. Hypotheses 1 and 4 B. Hypotheses 2 and 3
C. Hypotheses 2 and 4 D. Hypotheses 3 and 4

(2) Practice 6.2

All 4 hypotheses propose that the factors causing morphological abnormalities in frogs are present in the:

F. pesticides used by farmers. G. environment in which the frogs live.
H. UV radiation produced by the Sun. J. bodies of the organisms that prey on frogs.

(3) Practice 6.3

Which 2 hypotheses propose that direct contact between tadpoles and another organism results in morphological abnormalities in frogs?

A. Hypotheses 1 and 4 B. Hypotheses 2 and 3
C. Hypotheses 2 and 4 D. Hypotheses 3 and 4

(4) Practice 6.4

An artificial pond was created. The following were added to the pond: trematodes, UV-induced teratogens, retinoids, frog predators, tadpoles, and materials necessary for tadpole development. The frequency of morphological abnormalities in frogs was very high. This finding best supports which, if any, of the 4 hypotheses, and why?

F. Hypothesis 1, since it shows that the morphological abnormalities are caused by parasitism by trematodes.

G. Hypothesis 2, since it shows that the morphological abnormalities are the result of DNA mutations caused by teratogens.

H. Hypothesis 3, since it shows that the morphological abnormalities are caused by the presence of retinoids.

J. None of the 4 hypotheses is best supported, because the result does not indicate which factor caused the morphological abnormalities.

(5) Practice 6.5

Normal adult frogs were captured, tagged, and released into a pond. After 2 months the frogs were recaptured and examined. Five percent of these frogs showed morphological abnormalities, such as missing hind limbs. These results best support which hypothesis?

A. Hypothesis 1 B. Hypothesis 2 C. Hypothesis 3 D. Hypothesis 4

(6) Practice 6.6

Supporters of Hypothesis 4 would most likely argue that the frequency of morphological abnormalities in frogs would be lowest in which of the following types of aquatic communities?

F. Those with fish, turtles, and wading birds

G. Those with fish and turtles, but without wading birds

H. Those with fish and wading birds, but without turtles.

J. Those without fish, turtles, and wading birds

(7) Practice 6.7

A biologist has argued that some of the factors cited in both Hypothesis 1 and Hypothesis 2 are combining to cause the increase in the morphological abnormalities in frogs. Which of the following findings about trematodes, if true, would best support this view?

A. Trematodes are highly sensitive to injury from UV light

B. Trematodes are immobilized by teratogens.

C. Exposure to UV light increases trematode populations.

D. Exposure to UV light improves frogs' resistance to trematode parasitism.

Answers for Practice 4 - 6

Practice 4　B H A H B J

Practice 5　B J B G A

Practice 6　B G A J D J C

Session 2　生物 2

本章主要介绍 ACT 科学测试生物科目中的微生物学、生态学和遗传学三大分支学科,并通过解析例题,以及相应的练习题明确这三门学科的考试形式、考试重点和相关词汇。

(一)学科背景

ACT 科学测试主要考察和重点考察科学推理能力,了解相应的学科知识可以快速理解文章内容,提高解题速度。

1. 学科综述

1) 微生物学(Microbiology)

微生物学是研究微生物的一门学科。微生物包括病毒、原核生物和简单的真核生物。很多病原(像是造成植物病害的四大病原:病毒、真菌、线虫、细菌)都可以算是广义的微生物。

2) 生态学(Ecology)

生态学是德国生物学家恩斯特·海克尔于 1866 年定义的一个概念:生态学是研究生物体与其周围环境(包括非生物环境和生物环境)相互关系的科学。

3) 遗传学(Genetics)

遗传学是研究生物的遗传与变异的科学,研究基因的结构、功能及其变异、传递和表达规律的学科。遗传学中的亲子概念不限于父母子女或一个家族,还可以延伸到包括许多家族的群体,这是群体遗传学的研究对象。

2. 学科背景知识

1) 微生物学

微生物学是生物学的分支学科之一。它是在分子、细胞或群体水平上研究各类微小生物(细菌、放线菌、真菌、病毒、立克次氏体、支原体、衣原体、螺旋体原生动物以及单细胞藻类)的形态结

构、生长繁殖、生理代谢、遗传变异、生态分布和分类进化等生命活动的基本规律，并将其应用于工业发酵、医学卫生等领域的科学。

微生物特点：

①体积小、比表面积大；②吸收多、转化快；③生长旺、繁殖快；④适应强、易变异；⑤分布广、种类多；⑥易于变异，产生突变。

2）生态学

生态学是德国生物学家恩斯特·海克尔于1866年定义的一个概念：生态学是研究生物体与其周围环境（包括非生物环境和生物环境）相互关系的科学。目前已经发展为“研究生物与其环境之间的相互关系的科学”。环境包括生物环境和非生物环境，生物环境是指生物物种之间和物种内部各个体之间的关系，非生物环境包括自然环境：土壤、岩石、水、空气、温度、湿度等。

生态学是生物学的一个分支，生物学的研究对象向微观和宏观两个方面发展，生态学是向研究宏观方向发展的分支，是以生物个体、种群、群落、生态系统直到整个生物圈作为它的研究对象。生态学是将生物群落和其生活的环境作为一个互相之间不断地进行物质循环和能量流动的整体来进行研究。

3）遗传学

遗传学是研究生物体的遗传和变异的科学，是生物学的一个重要分支。现代遗传学，其目的是寻求了解遗传的整个过程的机制，遗传单位遵守简单的统计学规律，这些遗传单位现在被称为基因。

基因位于DNA上，而DNA是由四类不同的核苷酸组成的链状分子，DNA上的核苷酸序列就是生物体的遗传信息。天然DNA以双链形式存在，两条链上的核苷酸互补，而每一条链都能够作为模板来合成新的互补链。这就是生成可以被遗传的基因的复制方式。

基因上的核苷酸序列可以被细胞翻译以合成蛋白质，蛋白质上的氨基酸序列就对应着基因上的核苷酸序列。这种对应性被称为遗传密码。DNA上的一个基因的改变可以改变其编码的蛋白质的氨基酸，并可能改变此蛋白质的结构和功能，进而对细胞甚至整个生物体造成巨大的影响。

（二）学科单词

ACT科学要求有一定的阅读量，文章中涉及大量的专业词汇，了解这些专业词汇的意思有助于理解文章和题意。以下是三门学科常见的专业词汇，考生需要熟悉单词的意思，以便在考试中能更准确地理解文章内容。

1. 微生物学

英文	中文释义	英文	中文释义
biotic index	生物指数	fungi	真菌
larvae	幼虫	disinfectant	消毒剂
fertilizer	肥料	antiseptics	杀虫剂
fermentation	发酵	alcohol	酒精
pathway	途径；路径	microbial flora	微生物菌丛
lactose	乳糖	microorganism	微生物
broth	液体培养基	aqueous	水的；含水的
phenol red	酚红	tincture	酊剂
synergism	协同作用	assay	化验
bacteria	细菌	glucose	葡萄糖
generation time	世代时间	cell	细胞
metabolism	新陈代谢		

2. 生态学

英文	中文释义	英文	中文释义
measurement	测量	rangeland	牧场
illumination	光照	slope	斜坡
high-salt	高盐的	sprinkler	洒水器
osmosis	渗透	depression	洼地;凹坑
vacuole	液泡	soil	土壤
cytoplasm	细胞质	shrimp	小虾
genome	基因组	lipid	脂质
genotype	基因型	carbonhydrate	碳水化合物
allele	等位基因	porosity	多孔性
seedling	幼苗	void ratio	孔隙比
nutrient	营养的	succession	演替
variable	变量	shrub	灌木丛

3. 遗传学

英文	中文释义	英文	中文释义
hydrogen	氢	ovule	胚珠
denature	变性	weevil	象鼻虫
random coil	无规卷曲	cone	松果
synthesis	合成	arginine	精氨酸
meiosis	减数分裂	precursor	先驱
chromosome	染色体	autosomal	正染色体
crossover	杂交	receptor	受体
plasmid	质体	strand	股;线
replicate	复制	organism	生物体
donor	供体	eukaryote	真核细胞
fruit fly	果蝇	yeast	酵母
zamia	泽米属植物	cellular	细胞的
pollination	授粉	gene expression	基因表现

(三)例题解析

本节选取了三门学科的真题进行详细的解析,帮助考生迅速了解考试的形式、内容和解题思路。

1. 微生物学(Microbiology)

1)例题练习 1

(OG4　Passage I)

Two measures of water quality are the number of Escherichia coli bacteria present and the biotic index, BI (a numerical value based on the type, diversity, and pollution tolerance of aquatic invertebrate animals). Both of these measures can be affected by water flow.

E. coli levels that are above 100 colonies formed per 100 mL of water indicate reduced water quality. Figure 1 shows the E. coli levels on 5 collection days at Sites 1 and 2 in a river.

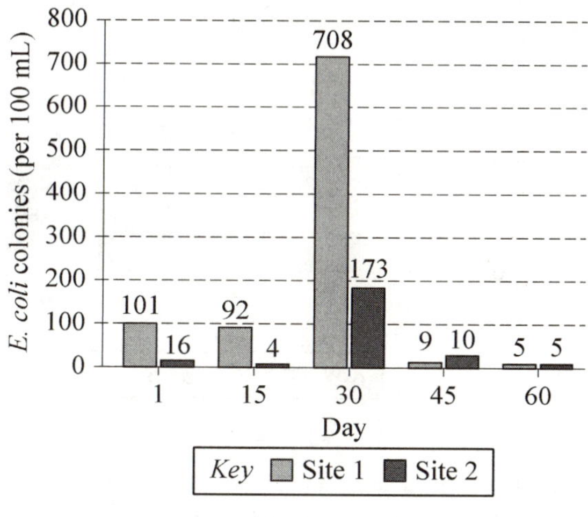

Figure 1

Table 1 shows how water quality rating varies with BI. Table 2 shows the average BI of each site during the collection period.

Table 1

BI	Water quality rating
≥3.6	Excellent
2.6 to 3.5	Good
2.1 to 2.5	Fair
1.0 to 2.0	poor

Table 2

Location	Average BI
Site 1	6.3
Site 2	2.5

Figure 2 shows the water flow at each site on the 5 collection days.

(1) 例题练习 1.1

If an E. coli level of over 400 colonies formed per 100 mL of water is unsafe for swimming, on which of the following collection days and at which site would it have been unsafe to swim?

A. Day 1 at Site 1

B. Day 30 at Site 1

C. Day 1 at Site 2

D. Day 30 at Site 2

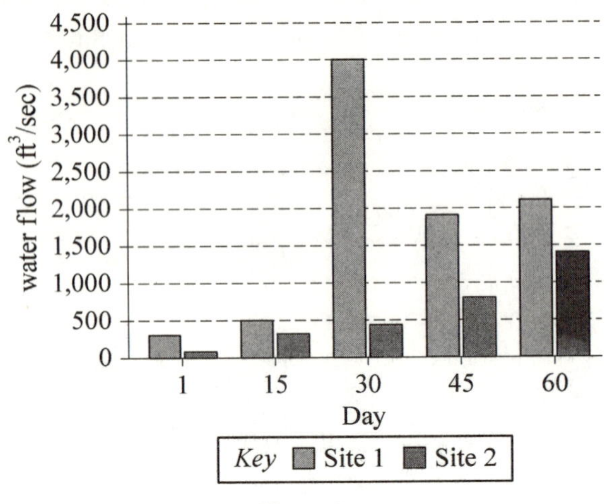

Figure 2

Figures adapted from Stephen C. Landry and Michele L. Tremblay, "State of the Upper Merrimack 1995 - 1997: A River Quality Report." © 2000 by Upper Merrimack River Local Advisory Committee.

【考点分析】

- 数据表述类文章,此题为数据查找题。
- 抓住关键词 *E. coli* (*level of over 400 colonies*),可以得知考察的是 Figure 1,当然从文章第二段也可以找到解题点。
- 题目设定的值是高于 400 colonies formed per 100 mL 是危险的,根据 Figure 1 中数据可以看到只有 site 1 在 day 30 时这个值达到 708,由此可知正确答案为 **B**。

(2) 例题练习 1.2

Based on Figures 1 and 2, consider the average water flow and the average E. coli level for Site 1 and Site 2 over the collection period. Which site had the higher average water flow, and which site had the higher average E. coli level?

	Higher water flow	Higher E. coli level
F.	Site 1	Site 1
G.	Site 1	Site 2
H.	Site 2	Site 1
J.	Site 2	Site 2

【考点分析】

- 数据表述类文章,此题为数据题。
- 抓住定位词图 1 和图 2,题目考察 *Which site had the higher average water flow, and which site had the higher average E. coli level* 。
- 根据图 1 中数据可以看出 E. coli level 指标 Site 1 明显大于 Site 2,根据图 2 中可以看出 water flow 指标也是 Site 1 明显大于 Site 2,由此可知正确答案为 **F**。

(3) 例题练习 1.3

As water quality improves, the number of stone fly larvae (a type of aquatic invertebrate) increases. Students hypothesized that more stone fly larvae would be found at Site 1 than at Site 2. Are the data presented in Table 2 consistent with this hypothesis?

A. Yes; based on BI, Site 1 had a water quality rating of good and Site 2 had a water quality

rating of poor.

B. Yes; based on BI, Site 1 had a water quality rating of excellent and Site 2 had a water quality rating of fair.

C. No; based on BI, Site 1 had a water quality rating of poor and Site 2 had a water quality rating of good.

D. No; based on BI, Site 1 had a water quality rating of fair and Site 2 had a water quality rating of excellent.

【考点分析】

- 数据表述类文章,此题为数据对比题。
- 抓住关键词表 *2 & water quality*,题目考察表二中数据是否支持学生假设。
- 根据表 2 可得,Site 1 和 Site 2 的 BI 值分别为 6.3 和 2.5,同时据表 1 数据可知,BI 值对应 water quality,分别为 excellent 和 fair,Site 1 water quality 优于 Site 2,根据题目中给出信息,水质高的 stone fly larvae 数量高,由此可知正确答案为 **B**。

(4) 例题练习 1.4

Which set of data best supports the claim that Site 1 has lower water quality than Site 2?

F. Figure 1   G. Figure 2   H. Table 1   J. Table 2

【考点分析】

- 数据表述类文章,此题为数据推理题。
- 抓住关键词 *support & Site 1 has lower water quality than Site 2*,考察哪组数据支持 Site 1 有更低的 water quality。
- 根据关键词 *water quality*,我们搜索对应信息,文章中第二段第一句"E. coli levels that are above 100 colonies formed per 100 mL of water indicate reduced water quality",据图 1 所得,Site 1 该项指标高于 Site 2 ,并且 Day 1 和 Day 30 的数值均高于 100,由此可知正确答案为 **F**。

(5) 例题练习 1.5

Suppose large amounts of fertilizer from adjacent fields begin to enter the river at Site 1. The BI of this site will most likely change in which of the following ways? The BI will:

A. increase, because water quality is likely to increase.

B. increase, because water quality is likely to decrease.

C. decrease, because water quality is likely to increase.

D. decrease, because water quality is likely to decrease.

【考点分析】

- 数据表述类文章,此题为实验假设题。
- 抓住关键词 *BI* ,同时题干给出 *Suppose large amounts of fertilizer from adjacent fields begin to enter the river at Site 1*.
- 根据题干的假设,大量肥料在 Site 1 进入河流,肥料增加,那么微生物等细菌都会增加,可以肯定E. coli 必定会增加,进而导致水质变差,根据表 1 数据,水质变差,相应的 BI 值也会下降,由此可知正确答案为 **D**。

2) 知识拓展 1

[大肠杆菌]

大肠杆菌(escherichia coli,通常简写:E. coli)是人和动物肠道中最著名的一种细菌,主要寄生于大肠内,约占肠道菌中的 1%。是一种两端钝圆、能运动、无芽孢的革兰氏阴性短杆菌。除某些菌型能引起腹泻外,一般不致病,能合成维生素 B 和 K,对人体有益。

在水净化和污水处理领域,因大肠杆菌在粪便中数量极多,故常用为检查水源是否被粪便污染的标志,其测量标准为大肠菌群指数。此外大肠杆菌多数情况下无害,不会从实验室“逃脱”而伤害人类。利用大肠杆菌作为粪便污染的指示物也可能产生误导性的结论,因为其他环境如造纸厂中,大肠杆菌也可大量存在。

大肠杆菌的一个株是具有某些能和其他株区分开的特征的族群。不同的大肠杆菌菌株生活在不同动物中,因此我们可以通过其判断粪便来源于人或者鸟类等。通过突变,新的大肠杆菌菌株不断出现,其中一些可能对宿主动物造成损害。尽管对于大多数健康成年人,这样的菌株可能只引起一场腹泻,或者根本没有症状,但对于幼儿、大病初愈的人或者进行某些药物治疗的人来说,陌生的菌株可能引起严重疾病甚至死亡。大肠杆菌 O157:H7 就是一个毒性很强的菌株。

大肠杆菌是现代生物学中研究最多的一种细菌,作为一种模式生物,其基因组序列已全部测出。用分子生物学方法在大肠杆菌得出的结论可用于其他生物的研究。此外,在生物工程中,大肠杆菌被广泛用于基因复制和表达的宿主。

2. 生态学(Ecology)

1) 例题练习 2

(55C　Passage V)

降雨后,由于植物(草、树叶和树枝)的影响和动物的践踏,牧场的沉积物会产生流失(腐蚀)。科学家使用面积相同且略有倾斜的两小块土地进行了两次实验。实验使用了含沙量完全不同的两种土壤。土壤 1 的含沙量是 60%,而土壤 2 的含沙量是 25%。实验中使用喷洒装置模拟了降雨。值得注意的是,首先在受压土壤收集雨水,如动物蹄印中的雨水,之后雨水从其中溢出并腐蚀土壤。沉积物流失的测量方式是测量一小时降雨后首测土地每平方米雨水的克数(克/每平方米)。

Experiment 1 实验 1

实验中,实验人员使用具有不同网格大小的纱窗来模拟植被。每英寸网格的数目越多,纱窗模拟植被的效果就越好。一块实验地没有进行遮盖,而另一块实验地则由不同网格尺寸的纱窗遮盖。表 1 展示了每块实验地的沉积物流失的情况。

Table 1

soil	Sediment runoff (g/m^2) with a simulated vegetation cover of:			
	0%	30%	50%	70%
1	947	751	572	492
2	378	331	291	200

Experiment 2 实验 2

实验中,实验人员模拟动物践踏的方式是:使用一只重达 500 公斤的奶牛在这两块土壤类型不同的实验地中来回践踏,一直到蹄印的覆盖面积达到一块地的 30% 和另一块地的 60% 为止。除此之外,每个土壤类型的实验地额外留出一块没有受到践踏的土地。实验人员使用第一个实验中的方法模拟了降雨。表 2 展示了动物蹄印中储存雨水的深度,其单位为厘米。表 3 展示了因腐蚀而引起的沉积物流失。

Table 2

Soil	Water stored (cm) in hoofprints on plot that was:		
	0% trampled	30% trampled	60% trampled
1	0	0.67	0.79
2	0	0.65	0.52

Table 3

Soil	Sediment runoff (g/m^2) from plot that was:		
	0% trampled	30% trampled	60% trampled
1	347	730	801
2	282	307	311

Tables adapted from G. Gifford and M. Savabi, "Effects of Simulated Canopy Cover and Animal Disturbances on Rill and Interrill Erosion." © 1989 by the American Water Resources Association.

(1) 例题练习 2.1

Which of the following assumptions was made in the design of Experiment 1?

A. All soils will show the same amount of erosion under the same conditions.

B. Sprinklers do not adequately simulate actual rainfall.

C. Grass is more important than trees in preventing sediment runoff.

D. Simulated plant cover acts like natural plant cover in protecting the soil from erosion by water.

【考点分析】

● 实验总结类文章，此题为实验目的题。

● 抓住定位词 *Experiment 1*，直接定位到第一个实验，根据阅读第二段可以得出，实验 1 是研究 sediment runoff 与 simulated vegetation cover 的关系。同时结合前言部分第一句话，土壤流失受植被和动物踩踏的影响，那么很显然，实验 1 是基于模拟植被覆盖对于土壤的保护类似于自然植被覆盖，才能用模拟植被来做实验，很显然正确答案为 **D**。

(2) 例题练习 2.2

According to the results of Experiments 1 and 2, one can minimize soil erosion by:

F. increasing plant cover, decreasing the amount of trampling, and using land covered with Soil 2.

G. increasing plant cover, decreasing the amount of trampling, and using land covered with Soil 1.

H. decreasing plant cover, increasing the amount of trampling, and using land covered with Soil 2.

J. decreasing plant coyer, decreasing the amount of trampling, and using land covered with either soil.

【考点分析】

● 实验总结类文章，此题为实验结果题。

● 抓住定位词实验 1 和 2,考察实验的结果,从而进行推导。

● 先看实验 1,根据实验 1 也就是表 1 数据得出植物覆盖率越大,土壤流失程度越低,同时同等覆盖率下 Soil 1 土壤流失比 Soil 2 严重;再看实验 2,表 2 中显示踩踏越多,土壤流失越严重,同等情况下 Soil 1 流失更严重,所以可以得出为了减少流失,需要增大植被覆盖量,减少踩踏,采用第二种土壤,很明显正确答案为 **F**。

(3) 例题练习 2.3

If Experiment 2 were repeated using a different soil containing 50% sand, which of the following would be the expected water storage in soil hoofprints and sediment runoff on a plot subjected to 60% trampling?

A. 0.89 cm water stored; 321 g/m^2 sediment runoff

B. 0.86 cm water stored; 932 g/m^2 sediment runoff

C. 0.71 cm water stored; 700 g/m^2 sediment runoff

D. 0.56 cm water stored; 295 g/m^2 sediment runoff

【考点分析】

● 实验总结类文章,此题为实验假设题。

● 抓住关键词实验 2 和 *soil containing 50% sand & 60% trampling* 直接定位到实验 2,根据 60% trampling 可以得出 Soil 1 的 water stored 为 0.79,sediment runoff 为 801,Soil 2 的 water stored 为 0.52,sediment runoff 为 311。而前言部分“Soil 1 contained 60% sand and Soil 2 contained 25% sand”,结合题目中给出的 soil containing 50%,可以得出第三种土壤的取值应该介于 1 和 2 的数值之间,water stored 指标选项 C、D 都符合,而第二项指标只有 C 符合,因此正确答案为 **C**。

(4) 例题练习 2.4

In Experiment 2, after 30% trampling, water stored in the two soil types was similar, but sediment runoff was not. Which of the following statements is the most likely explanation for the difference in sediment runoff?

F. Water stored in hoofprints has a significant relationship to sediment runoff.

G. Water in soil hoofprints evaporates before it can erode the soil.

H. A soil with a smaller percent sand is less susceptible to erosion than soil with a higher percent sand.

J. Sediment carried from higher areas of the plot is trapped in soil depressions.

【考点分析】

● 实验总结类文章,此题为实验结果题。

● 抓住关键词 *Experiment 2 & 30% trampling*,题目考察 *after 30% trampling*, *water stored in the two soil types was similar*, *but sediment runoff was not* 的原因。

● 在实验 2 中,前提为 30% trampling 的情况下,Soil 1 和 Soil 2 的不同点在于“Soil 1 contained 60% sand and Soil 2 contained 25% sand”,所以最合理的解释是含沙量小的土壤不太容易土壤流失,而这个也属于基本常识,所以不会错,很明显正确答案为 **H**。

(5) 例题练习 2.5

If Experiment 1 were repeated using a soil containing 50% sand with 70% plant cover, which of the following would be closest to the expected sediment runoff from this soil?

A. 175 g/m^2 B. 200 g/m^2

C. 425 g/m^2 D. 500 g/m^2

【考点分析】

● 实验总结类文章，此题为实验结果题。

● 抓住关键词实验 1 和 *a soil containing 50% sand with 70% plant cover*，题目考察此种 soil 的 sediment runoff。

● 在实验 1 中，前提为 70% plant cover 的情况下，Soil 1 和 Soil 2 的 sediment runoff 分别为 492 和 200，结合前言部分"Soil 1 contained 60% sand and Soil 2 contained 25% sand"，可知新的 soil 的 sediment runoff 应该介于 1 和 2 的值之间，根据这个来判断，很明显正确答案为 **C**。

(6) 例题练习 2.6

To further investigate the effect of vegetation cover on soil erosion, the scientists should repeat Experiment:

F. 1, using plots planted with different grasses.

G. 1, using no window screen.

H. 2, using plots with steeper slopes.

J. 2, using a third soil type.

【考点分析】

● 实验总结类文章，此题为实验设计题。

● 抓住关键词 *the effect of vegetation cover*，根据关键词结合文章内容可以知道实验 1 的研究内容与此相关。所以是重复进行实验 1，排除选项 H 和 J，其次题目给出的实验目的是深入研究植被覆盖对土壤流失的影响，那么必然与覆盖率和植被种类相关，同时实验 1 中本身已经研究了覆盖率不同的情况，那么只剩下植被种类，很显然正确答案为 **F**。

2) 知识拓展 2

[水土流失]

水土流失(也被称为侵蚀作用或土壤侵蚀)是自然界的一种现象，是指地球的表面不断受到风、水、冰融等外力的磨损，地表土壤及母质、岩石受到各种破坏和移动、堆积过程以及水本身的损失现象，包括土壤侵蚀及水的流失。狭义的"水土流失"是特指水力侵蚀地表土壤的现象，使水土资源和土地生产力受到破坏和损失，影响到人类和其他动植物的生存。

水土流失可能是由于自然环境引起的，譬如地势陡峭，突发大量降水，或者地质变化。但更多的是由于人类活动导致的，譬如过度放牧，开垦土地，砍伐森林、开矿筑路，炸山采石等。流失侵蚀可能由水流、冰移或风吹而发生。

水土流失是在湿润或半湿润地区，由于植被破坏严重导致的。如果是在干旱地区的植被破坏，会导致沙尘暴或者土地荒漠化，而不同于水土流失。因为植被破坏严重，再加上雨水和地表水的冲刷，导致水土流失。增加植被覆盖率，可以保持水土，也就能防止水土流失的发生。

3. 遗传 Genetics

1) 例题练习 3

(OG2 Passage VI)

A polypeptide molecule is a chain of amino acids. A protein consists of 1 or more polypeptides. A protein's shape is described by 3 or 4 levels of structure.

1. The primary structure of a protein is the sequence of amino acids in each polypeptide.

2. The secondary structure of a protein is the local folding patterns within short segments of each polypeptide due to hydrogen bonding (weak chemical bonds).

3. The tertiary structure is the folding patterns that result from interactions between amino acid side chains (parts of an amino acid) in each polypeptide. These folding patterns generally

occur across greater distances than those associated with the secondary structure.

4. The quaternary structure is the result of the clustering between more than 1 folded polypeptide.

A protein can adopt different shapes, and each shape has a relative energy. Lower-energy shapes are more stable than higher-energy shapes, and a protein with a relatively high-energy shape may denature (unfold) and then renature (refold), adopting a more stable shape. A protein that is almost completely denatured is called a random coil. Random coils are unstable because they are high-energy shapes; however, some can renature, adopting more stable shapes.

Two scientists discuss protein shape.

Scientist 1

The active shape (the biologically functional shape) of a protein is always identical to the protein's lowest-energy shape. Any other shape would be unstable. Because a protein's lowest-energy shape is determined by its primary structure, its active shape is determined by its primary structure.

Scientist 2

The active shape of a protein is dependent upon its primary structure. However, a protein's active shape may also depend on its process of synthesis, the order (in time) in which the amino acids were bonded together. As synthesis occurs, stable, local structures form within short segments of the polypeptide chain due to hydrogen bonding. These local structures may be different than the local structures associated with the protein's lowest-energy shape. After synthesis, these structures persist, trapping the protein in an active shape that has more energy than its lowest-energy shape.

(1) 例题练习 3.1

According to the passage, protein shapes with relatively low energy tend to:

A. be random coils.
B. lack a primary structure.
C. become denatured.
D. maintain their shape.

【考点分析】

- 观点冲突类文章,此题为综合信息题。
- 抓住定位词 *the passage*。
- 此种题目一般先看前言部分,多数可从前言得出答案。根据"Lower-energy shapes are more stable than higher-energy shapes",直接得出正确答案为 **D**。

(2) 例题练习 3.2

The information in the passage indicates that when a protein is completely denatured, it still retains its original:

F. primary structure,
G. secondary structure,
H. tertiary structure,
J. quaternary structure.

【考点分析】

- 观点冲突类文章,此题为综合信息题。
- 抓住定位词 *the passage*。
- 此种题目一般先看前言部分,多数可从前言得出答案。根据"The primary structure of a protein is the sequence of amino acids in each polypeptide",结合"A protein that is almost completely denatured is called a random coil. Random coils are unstable because they are high-

energy shapes; however, some can renature, adopting more stable shapes",推出得出正确答案为 **F**。

(3) 例题练习 3.3

Scientist 2's views differ from Scientist 1's views in that only Scientist 2 believes that a protein's active shape is partially determined by its:

A. quaternary structure.
B. amino acid sequence.
C. process of synthesis.
D. tertiary folding patterns.

【考点分析】

- 观点冲突类文章,此题为多观点冲突题。
- 抓住关键词 *only Scientist 2 believes*。
- 根据第四段"its active shape is determined by its primary structure",结合第五段"The active shape of a protein is dependent upon its primary structure. However, a protein's active shape may also depend on its process of synthesis",故正确答案为 **C**。

(4) 例题练习 3.4

A student has 100 balls. The balls are various colors. The student chooses 15 balls and aligns them in a row. The spatial order in which the balls were placed corresponds to which of the following levels of structure in a protein?

F. Primary structure
G. Secondary structure
H. Tertiary structure
J. Quaternary structure

【考点分析】

- 观点冲突类文章,此题为综合信息题。
- 抓住关键词 *aligns them in a row*。
- 纵观全文,在前言部分,介绍了 4 种蛋白质结构,根据"The primary structure of a protein is the sequence of amino acids in each polypeptide",直接得出正确答案为 **F**。

(5) 例题练习 3.5

Suppose proteins are almost completely denatured and then allowed to renature in a way that allows them to have their lowest-energy shapes. Which of the following statements about the proteins is most consistent with the information presented in the passage?

A. If Scientist 1 is correct, all of the proteins will have their active shapes.

B. If Scientist 1 is correct, all of the proteins will have shapes different than their active shapes

C. If Scientist 2 is correct, all of the proteins will have their active shapes.

D. If Scientist 2 is correct, all of the proteins will have shapes different than their active shapes.

【考点分析】

- 观点冲突类文章,此题为综合信息题。
- 抓住关键词 *denatured and then allowed to renature & lowest-energy shapes*。
- 第四段中科学家 1 认为"The active shape (the biologically functional shape) of a protein is always identical to the protein's lowest-energy shape ... a protein's lowest-energy shape is determined by its primary structure",第五段中科学家 2 认为"The active shape of a protein is dependent upon its primary structure. However, a protein's active shape may also depend on its process of synthesis ... After synthesis, these structures persist, trapping the protein in an active

shape that has more energy than its lowest-energy shape”,可以推断出正确答案为 **A**。

(6) 例题练习 3.6

Which of the following diagrams showing the relationship between a given protein's shape and its relative energy is consistent with Scientist 2,s assertions about the energy of proteins, but is NOT consistent with Scientist 1's assertions about the energy of proteins?

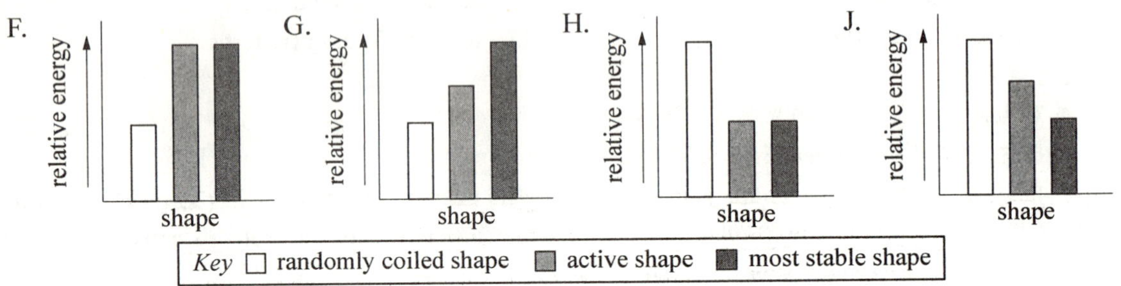

【考点分析】

● 观点冲突类文章,此题为单一观点画图题。

● 抓住定位词 *Scientist 2*。

● 根据第五段最后“After synthesis, these structures persist, trapping the protein in an active shape that has more energy than its lowest-energy shape”,同时结合前言部分“Lower-energy shapes are more stable than higher-energy shapes”,可以直接排除错误选项,得出正确答案为 **J**。

(7) 例题练习 3.7

Scientist 2 says that a protein may be trapped in a moderately high-energy shape. Which of the following findings, if true, could be used to counter this argument?

A. Once a protein has achieved its tertiary structure, all of the folding patterns at the local level are stable.

B. Enough energy is available in the environment to overcome local energy barriers, driving the protein to its lowest-energy shape.

C. During protein synthesis, the secondary structure of a protein is determined before the tertiary structure is formed.

D. Proteins that lose their tertiary structure or quaternary structure also tend to lose their biological functions.

【考点分析】

● 观点冲突类文章,此题为单一观点题。

● 抓住定位词 *Scientist 2*,题目说科学家 2 认为蛋白质可以保持相对高能量的形态,如何反驳此观点?

● 纵观全文,并不能直接得出答案,根据基础知识,蛋白质加热,一定会变性,最终形成低能量的稳定形态。第一级结构不发生变化,可以得出正确答案为 **B**。

● 分析选项,A 为支持此种观点,故不能用来反驳;C 同样与此观点一致,不正确;D 选项内容不正确。

2) 知识拓展 3

[基因]

基因一词来自希腊语,意思为“生”。是指携带有遗传信息的 DNA 序列,是控制性状的基本遗

传单位亦即一段具有功能性的DNA序列。基因通过指导蛋白质的合成来表达自己所携带的遗传信息,从而控制生物个体的性状表现。人类约有2万至2.5万个基因。染色体在体细胞中是成对存在的,每条染色体上都带有一定数量的基因。一个基因在细胞有丝分裂时有两个对列的位点,称为等位基因,分别来自父与母辈。按照其控制的性状,又可分为显性基因和隐性基因。

基因与脱氧核苷酸的关系:

(1) 基因的基本组成单位是脱氧核苷酸。

(2) 基因中脱氧核苷酸的排列顺序称为遗传信息。

(3) 基因中脱氧核苷酸的排列顺序的多样性决定了基因的多样性。

基因与DNA的关系:

(1) 基因是有遗传效应的DNA片段,每个DNA分子上有许多个基因。一个DNA分子上的碱基总数大于该DNA分子上所有基因上的碱基数之和。

(2) 基因具有遗传效应是指其能控制生物的性状。基因是控制生物性状的结构和功能的基本单位,特定的基因控制特定的性状。

基因与染色体的关系:

(1) 基因在染色体上呈线性排列。

(2) 染色体是基因的主要载体,但不是唯一载体,如粒线体、叶绿体中也有少量的DNA,也是基因的载体。

[蛋白质结构&蛋白质变性]

蛋白质结构是指蛋白质分子的空间结构。蛋白质的分子结构可划分为四级,以描述其不同的方面:

(1) 一级结构:组成蛋白质多肽链的线性氨基酸序列。

(2) 二级结构:依靠不同氨基酸之间的C═O和N—H基团间的氢键形成的稳定结构,主要为α螺旋和β折叠。

(3) 三级结构:通过多个二级结构元素在三维空间的排列所形成的一个蛋白质分子的三维结构。

(4) 四级结构:用于描述由不同多肽链(亚基)间相互作用形成具有功能的蛋白质复合物分子。

蛋白质变性(protein denaturation)是指蛋白质在某些物理和化学因素作用下其特定的空间构象被改变,从而导致其理化性质的改变和生物活性的丧失,这种现象称为蛋白质变性。

变性作用是蛋白质受物理或化学因素的影响,改变其分子内部结构和性质的作用。一般认为蛋白质的二级结构和三级结构有了改变或遭到破坏,都是变性的结果。能使蛋白质变性的化学方法有加强酸、强碱、重金属盐、尿素、丙酮等;能使蛋白质变性的物理方法有加热(高温)、紫外线及X射线照射、超声波、剧烈振荡或搅拌等。

天然蛋白质的空间结构是通过氢键等次级键维持的,而变性后次级键被破坏,蛋白质分子就从原来有序的卷曲的紧密结构变为无序的松散的伸展状结构(但一级结构并未改变)。

(四) 实战练习 Practice

1) Practice 4

(55C　Passage VII)

细菌,霉菌和病毒(微小有机体)能够引起疾病和感染。消毒剂是用在无生命的物体上来杀死或者阻止微生物生长的化学药剂。杀菌剂是用在皮肤上用来杀死或阻止微生物生长的化学药剂。Several groups of disinfectants and antiseptics are depicted in Table 1.

Table 1

Groups	Chemical agent	Effective against	Mechanism of action	Preferred use
Alcohols	Ethanol	Bacteria, fungi, viruses	Cell disruption, stops protein function, cleaning	Skin antiseptic and thermometer disinfectant
Halogen	Iodines	Bacteria, fungi, some viruses	Stops protein function	Skin antiseptic
Halogen	Chlorines	Bacteria, fungi, viruses	Stops protein function	Water disinfectant; disinfectant used on dairy, restaurant, and household equipment
Heavy metals	Mercurochrome, merthiolate	Bacteria	Stops protein function	Skin antiseptic
Quaternary ammonium compounds	Zephiran, cepacol	Bacteria, fungi, viruses	Cell disruption, stops protein function	Skin antiseptic; disinfectant for instruments, utensils, and rubber goods
Detergents	Soaps, surfactants	Bacteria, fungi, viruses	Cleansing, decreases, surface tension	Mechanical removal of microorganisms by scrubbing

The chemical agents that make up disinfectants and antiseptics can be dissolved either in alcohol (forming a tincture) or water (forming an aqueous solution). The effectiveness of a variety of antiseptics against the normal microbial flora of the skin is shown in Figure 1.

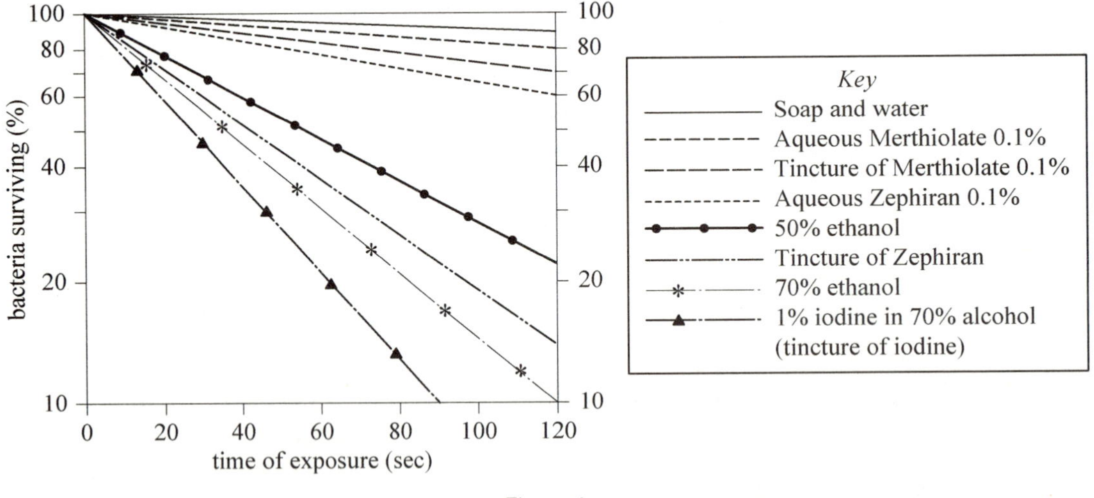

Figure 1

Table and Figure adapted from Tortora, Funke, and Case, Microbiology: An Introduction. © 1989 by The Benjamin/ Cummings Publishing Company.

(1) Practice 4.1

According to the passage, the most effective antiseptic against microorganisms is the one that leaves the:

F. lowest percentage of surviving microorganisms in the longest time of exposure.

G. lowest percentage of surviving microorganisms in the shortest time of exposure.

H. highest percentage of surviving microorganisms in the longest time of exposure.

J. highest percentage of surviving microorganisms in the shortest time of exposure.

(2) Practice 4.2

According to the information presented in Table 1 and Figure 1, what conclusion about the use of alcohol as an antiseptic may be reached?

A. Dissolving chemical agents in alcohol increases their effectiveness as antiseptics.

B. Using 70% ethanol is ineffective as an antiseptic.

C. Increasing the concentration of alcohol decreases its overall effectiveness as an antiseptic.

D. The mechanism of action for alcohol as an antiseptic is unknown.

(3) Practice 4.3

Is the statement "tinctures, are more effective against microorganisms than aqueous solutions of the same antiseptic" supported by the information presented in Figure 1, and why?

F. Yes, because tincture of Merthiolate is more effective against microorganisms than aqueous is aqueous Merthiolate.

G. Yes, because 70% ethanol is more effective against microorganisms than is tincture of Zephiran.

H. No, because soap and water is more effective against microorganisms than is 50% ethanol.

J. No, because aqueous Zephiran is more effective against microorganisms than is tincture of Zephiran.

(4) Practice 4.4

After you thoroughly wash your hands with plain soap and water for 2 minutes, your hands probably carry:

A. the same number of bacteria as before; most are dead.

B. the same number of bacteria as before; most are still alive.

C. fewer bacteria than before; most are dead.

D. fewer bacteria than before; most are still alive.

(5) Practice 4.5

According to Figure 1, if a researcher prepared a disinfectant solution of 60% alcohol, the time of exposure required to kill 90% of the bacteria present would be:

F. 60 to 80 sec.　　G. 80 to 100 sec.

H. 100 to 120 sec.　　J. greater than 120 sec.

2) Practice 5

在盐分高的环境中,西红柿生长缓慢。导致这种效果主要有两个原因:

1. 水在植物细胞的细胞质和盐分高环境之中通过渗透作用产生的净移动。

2. 细胞质 Na^+ 浓度的增高。

拟南芥这种植物还有一种逆向转运蛋白基因(AtNHX1)。这个基因的产物醋酸乙烯(VAC)可促进植物液泡对细胞质 Na^+ 进行吸收。

一位研究人员创建了四组在基因上相同的西红柿(L1 - L4)。研究人员隔离了拟南芥的逆向转运蛋白基因,并将该基因的两个相同复制品融入到了 L1 的基因组。实验人员为每组西红柿使用不同的 AtNHX1 等位基因，在 L2 和 L3 重复上述的过程，从而 L1、L2 和 L3 拥有不同基因型的 AtNHX1。之后，这位研究人员进行了一个实验。

Experiment

四组西红柿中每一组的 50 个籽苗在 10 升营养液中生长 80 天。这 10 升营养液含有水、12 克的化肥和 3 克氯化钠，每 5 天对这些营养液进行更换。80 天后，研究人员对平均高度、平均质量(不含果实)和平均果实质量(单测)进行测量(见表 1)。

Table 1

3 g of NaCl/10 L nutrient solution			
Line	Height (cm)	Mass (kg)	Fruit mass (kg)
L1	124	1.2	2.1
L2	128	1.2	2.0
L3	120	1.2	2.1
L4	124	1.2	2.0

This process was repeated except the 10 L nutrient solution contained 60 g of NaCl instead of 3 g of NaCl (see Table 2).

Table 2

60 g of NaCl/10 L nutrient solution			
Line	Height (cm)	Mass (kg)	Fruit mass (kg)
L1	119	1.1	1.9
L2	121	1.1	1.9
L3	61	0.4	1.1
L4	63	0.5	1.0

The process was repeated again except the 10 L nutrient solution contained 120 g of NaCl instead of 3 g of NaCl (see Table 3).

Table 3

120 g of NaCl/10 L nutrient solution			
Line	Height (cm)	Mass (kg)	Fruit mass (kg)
L1	118	1.0	1.8
L2	115	1.0	1.7
L3	34	0.2	0
L4	36	0.3	0

Tables 1 – 3 adapted from Hong-Xia Zhang and Eduardo Blumwald, "Transgenic Salt-Tolerant

Tomato Plants Accumulate Salt in Foliage But Not in Fruit." © *2001 by Nature Publishing Group*.

(1) Practice 5.1

One plant produced no fruit and had a height of 21 cm. Which of the following most likely describes this plant?

F. It was from L2 and was grown in a 10 L nutrient solution containing 60 g of NaCl.

G. It was from L2 and was grown in a 10 L nutrient solution containing 120 g of NaCl.

H. It was from L4 and was grown in a 10 L nutrient solution containing 60 g of NaCl.

J. It was from L4 and was grown in a 10 L nutrient solution containing 120 g of NaCl.

(2) Practice 5.2

During osmosis, water migrates through a semipermeable barrier. The osmosis referred to in the passage occurs through which of the following structures?

A. Chromosomes B. Nuclear envelope

C. Cell membrane D. Rough endoplasmic reticulum

(3) Practice 5.3

For each line, as the concentration of salt in the nutrient solutions increased, average plant mass:

F. increased only. G. decreased only.

H. increased, then decreased. J. decreased, then increased.

(4) Practice 5.4

Which of the following was an independent variable in the experiment?

A. Whether a line received AtNHX1 B. Whether a tomato plant was used

C. Plant mass without fruit D. Plant height

(5) Practice 5.5

Suppose the data for all of the plants were plotted on a graph with height on the x-axis and mass (without fruit) on the y-axis. Suppose also that the best-fit line for these data was determined. Which of the following would most likely characterize the slope of this line?

F. The line would not have a slope, because the line would be vertical.

G. The slope of the line would be zero.

H. The slope of the line would be negative.

J. The slope of the line would be positive.

(6) Practice 5.6

The researchers included 1 of the 4 lines to serve as a control. This line was most likely which one?

A. L1 B. L2 C. L3 D. L4

3) Practice 6

在减数分裂前期的第一阶段,同源染色体频繁交换,这种过程称为染色体交叉。因此,同源染色体上的基因进行重组,并沿染色体形成新的等位基因组合(见图 1)。

homologous chromosomes before crossing over occurs

a *b* | *a* *b* *A* *B* | *A* *B*

crossing over

a *b* | *a* *b* *A* *B* | *A* *B*

homologous chromosomes after crossing over occurs

a *b* | *A* *b* *a* *B* | *A* *B*

Figure 1

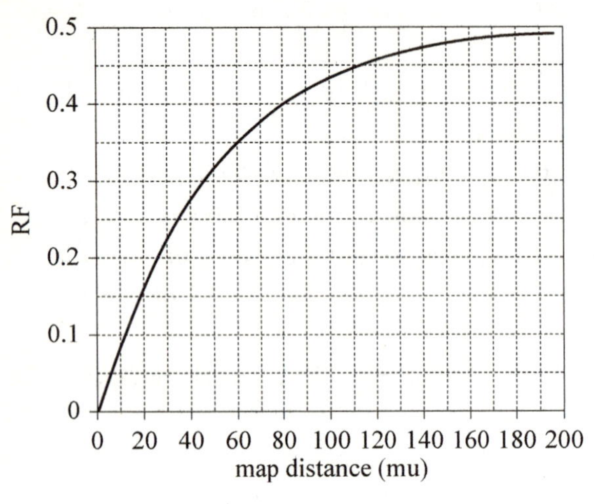

Figure 2

因为随着两种基因间染色体的图距增加(沿染色体的距离,单位为图距单位),重组频率也进行了提高,所以重组频率可用来估算染色体上基因之间的图距。然而,由于两个基因间图距的增加,复合交叉的可能性也随之增加。负荷交叉可明显减小两个基因间的重组频率,导致重组频率值低估图距的发生。为了减小这种影响,研究人员使用了定位函数,从而以重组频率为基础,改善两个基因间图距的估算(见图 2)。

四位研究人员进行了一系列的实验以确定染色体上不同基因对的重组频率。他们使用了定位函数来确定每个基因对间的图距。表 1 展示了此实验结果。

Table 1

Genes	RF	Map distance (mu)
A and B	0.165	20
B and C	0.226	30
A and D	0.122	14

之后,这四位研究人员的每一位都提出了一个与表 1 中实验结果相符的模型。每个模型展示了基因是如何沿着染色体进行定位的(见图 3)。每个模型正确地假定了基因的长度短到在计算基因间图距时可以忽略不计。

之后,研究相同染色体和基因的第五位研究人员确定基因 A 和基因 C 之间的基因图距为 0.091。

Researcher	Model
1	D A B C
2	A D B C
3	DC A B
4	C A D B

Figure 3

(1) Practice 6.1

All 4 models agree on the map distance between which of the following pairs of genes?

F. Genes A and B　　G. Genes A and C

H. Genes B and D　　J. Genes C and D

(2) Practice 6.2

According to Figure 2, if 2 genes are separated by 70 mu, the RF of those 2 genes is most likely closest to which of the following?

A. 0.377　　B. 0.477　　C. 0.577　　D. 0.677

(3) Practice 6.3

If Researcher 2's model is correct and an additional gene, Gene G, is 8 mu from Gene B and 14 mu from Gene D, then Gene G is most likely between:

F. Genes A and B.　　G. Genes A and D.

H. Genes B and C.　　J. Genes B and D.

(4) Practice 6.4

The result of the mapping experiment performed by the fifth researcher for Genes A and C is consistent with the models proposed by which 2 researchers?

A. Researchers 1 and 3　　B. Researchers 1 and 4

C. Researchers 2 and 3　　D. Researchers 3 and 4

(5) Practice 6.5

Based on the information provided, crossing over occurs during the process that leads directly to the formation of which of the following?

F. Neurons　　G. Skin cells　　H. Erythrocytes　　J. Gametes

(6) Practice 6.6

Which researcher's model proposes that Genes C and D are separated by 64 mu?

A. Researcher 1's　　B. Researcher 2's

C. Researcher 3's　　D. Researcher 4's

(7) Practice 6.7

Genes R and T are separated by 10 mu on 1 chromosome. An organism has alleles R and T on 1 chromosome and alleles r and t on the homologous chromosome. If a single crossover occurred between these 2 genes as shown in Figure 1, the genotype of Genes R and T for the 2 chromatids involved in the crossover would be:

F. Rt and rT.　　G. RT and rt　　H. Rr and Tt.　　J. RR and TT.

Answers for Practice 4-6

Practice 4　G A F D J

Practice 5　J C G A J D

Practice 6　F A H D J A F

Session 3　地球学/宇宙学 1

本章主要介绍 ACT 科学测试地球学/宇宙学科目中的地质学、考古学和气象学三大分支学科，并通过解析例题，以及相应的练习题明确这三门学科的考试形式、考试重点和相关词汇。

(一) 学科背景

ACT 科学测试主要考察和重点考察科学推理能力，了解相应的学科知识可以快速理解文章内容,提高解题速度。

1. 学科综述

1) 地质学(Geology)

地质学是对地球的起源、历史和结构进行研究的学科。主要研究地球的物质组成、内部构造、外部特征、各圈层间的相互作用和演变历史。

2) 考古学(Archaeology)

考古学(archaeology 或 archeology),对于过去人类社会的研究,主要透过重建与分析古代人们的物质文化与环境资料,包括器物、建筑、生物遗留与文化地景。

3) 气象学(Meteorology)

气象学是把大气当作研究的客体,从定性和定量两方面来说明大气特征的学科,集中研究大气的天气情况和变化规律和对天气的预报。

2. 学科背景知识

1) 地质学

地质学是一门探讨地球如何演化的自然哲学,地质学的产生源于人类社会对石油、煤炭、金属、非金属等矿产资源的需求,由地质学所指导的地质矿产资源勘探是人类社会生存与发展的根本源泉。地质学是研究地球的物质组成、内部构造、外部特征、各层圈之间的相互作用和演变历史的知识体系。

地壳是一个极其复杂的研究对象,不但具有复杂的物质成分,不同的化学性质、物理性质和各式各样的结构方式,而且在漫长的时间和广大的空间内,又都受到了一系列物理作用、化学作用甚至生物作用等综合地质作用的影响,不断地发生着错综复杂的物理和化学变化。

2) 考古学

考古学的任务在于根据古代人类通过各种活动遗留下来的物质资料,研究人类古代社会的历史。实物资料包括各种遗迹和遗物,它们多埋没在地下,必须经过科学的调查发掘,才能被系统地、完整地揭示和收集。因此,考古学研究的基础在于田野调查发掘工作。

考古学研究的对象是实物。主要是物质的遗存,或者说是遗物与遗迹。而这些遗存应该是古代人类的活动遗留下来的。考古学的研究集中在对过去的研究上,包括过去文化所遗留下来的各种资料。所以它的研究对象是属于一定时间以前的古代。

3) 气象学

第一位建立气象学的学者是古希腊哲学家亚里士多德。在他的专著《气象汇论》中,他最先叙述和粗浅地解释了风、云、雨、雪、雷、雹等天气现象,而这本书是世界上最早的气象书籍。直到 18~19 世纪,由于物理学和化学的发展,以及气压、温度、湿度和风等测量仪器的陆续发明,使大气科学研究由单纯的描述进入了可以定量分析的阶段。1820 年,德国人布德兰绘制了第一张地面天气图,开创了近代天气分析和预报方法。1835 年,法国人科利奥里提出风偏转的概念;1857 年荷兰人白贝罗提出风和气压的关系,他们的概念都成为大气动力学和天气分析的基础。

研究的方法主要有四种,分别为观测研究、理论研究、数值模式研究及实验研究。

(二) 学科单词

ACT 科学要求有一定的阅读量,文章中涉及大量的专业词汇,了解这些专业词汇的意思有助于理解文章和题意。以下是三门学科常见的专业词汇,考生需要熟悉单词的意思,以便在考试中能更准确地理解文章内容。

1. 地质学

英文	中文释义	英文	中文释义
plateau	高原	lithosphere	岩石圈
lava	火山岩	crust	地壳
molten	融化的	oceanic	海洋的
plume	岩浆柱	ocean ridge	洋脊
mantle	地幔	abyssal	深海的
stream	川流	trench	海沟
infiltration	渗透	back-arc basin	弧后盆地
earthquake	地震	hydrothermal vent	深海热泉
fault zone	断裂带	till	冰碛
crack	裂缝	bedrock	基岩
active fault	活性断层	resistivity	电阻率
radon gas	氡气	eruption	喷发
foreshock	前震	silica	二氧化硅
seismograph	地震仪	hollow tube	空心管

2. 考古学

英文	中文释义	英文	中文释义
volcanism	火山活动	rock formation	岩层
aerosol	悬浮微粒	mudstone	泥岩
acid rain	酸雨	skeleton	骨骼
ozone	臭氧	sandstone	砂岩
equator	赤道	snail	蜗牛
ice sheet	冰原	radiocarbon dating	放射性碳年代测定
glacier	冰川;冰河的		
circulation	环流	whorl	螺纹
oxidize	氧化	carnivorous	食草的
carbonate	碳酸盐	reptile	爬行动物
deposit	沉淀;沉淀物	spine	脊椎
velocity	速度	vertebrae	椎骨
hazy	有薄雾的	projection	凸出物
solidify	凝固	lizard	蜥蜴
sail	背鳍	anatomy	结构;构造

3. 气象学

英文	中文释义	英文	中文释义
wavelength	波长	dew point	露点温度
infrared	红外线的	cloud layer	云层
mesopause	中间层顶	ceilometer	云高测量仪
mesosphere	中间层	cloud cover	云量
stratosphere	平流层	flux	通量

(续表)

英文	中文释义	英文	中文释义
troposphere	对流层	cosmic	宇宙的
thermosphere	热电离层	high cloud	高云
weather instrument	气象仪	low cloud	低云
atmosphere	大气层	rain cloud	雨云
air mass	气团	cloud droplet	云滴
relative abundance	相对丰度	cumulus cloud	积云
ionosphere	电离层	seed	在(云中)播散干冰使人工降雨

(三) 例题解析

本节选取了三门学科的真题进行详细的解析,帮助考生迅速了解考试的形式、内容和解题思路。

1. 地质学(Geology)

1) 例题练习 1

(OG1　Passage I)

溢流玄武岩高原占据了地球表面的很大一部分面积,其表面覆盖着厚厚的硬化熔岩。科学家假定熔岩的大量流出形成了这些高原,而这些熔岩是由熔融物羽流从地球深处升起而导致的。

Study 1 研究 1

一个典型羽流的模型是使用计算机生成的。研究人员假定羽流的"顶端"的熔融物到达表面后产生了溢流玄武岩高原。图 1 展示了计算机生成的羽流及其直径,以及羽流顶端到达地球表面的时间(单位:百万年)。

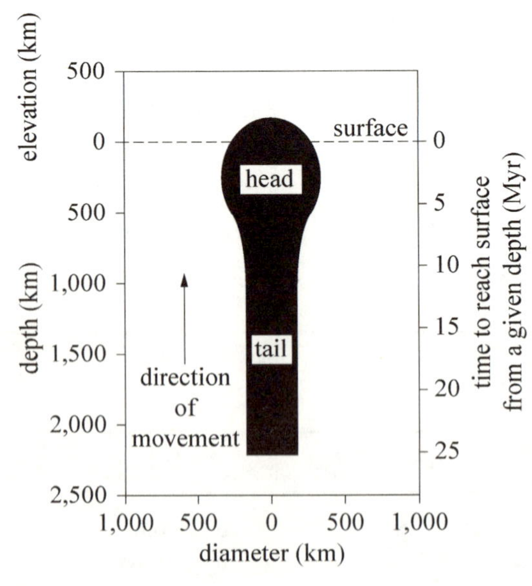

Figure 1

图片来自 R. I. Hill 等人的研究资料《地幔羽和大陆构造》。© 1992,美国科学发展协会出版。

Study 2 研究 2

研究人员研究了四个溢流玄武岩高原(A～D)。研究人员估算了每个高原区域的熔岩量(单位:立方千米)和熔岩的平均厚度。研究人员还估算了每个高原上熔岩的形成时间、速度(单位:立方千米/每年)。表 1 展示了研究结果。

Table 1

Plateau	Age (Myr)	Lava volume (km^3)	Lengthe of time lava was produced (Myr)	Rate of lava production (km^3/yr)
A	60	2 000 000	1.6	1.25
B	67	1 500 000	1.3	1.2
C	135	1 440 000	1.2	1.2
D	192	2 125 000	1.7	1.25

表 1 来自 Mark A. Richard 等人的研究资料《溢流玄武岩和热点轨道:地幔羽顶端和末端》。© 1989,美国科学发展协会出版。

Study 3 研究 3

科学家发现海洋生物三次大灭绝的时间和三个溢流玄武岩高原形成的时间相似(5 500 万年、6 600万年和 1.33 亿年)。科学家认为在形成这些高原的过程中,大量的熔岩和气体可能是导致这些海洋生物灭绝的罪魁祸首。

(注释:所有这些时间有 ± 100 万年的误差)。

(1) 例题练习 1.1

If the plume model in Study 1 is typical of all mantle plumes, the scientists would generalize that the heads of plumes are:

A. approximately half the diameter of the tail.

B. approximately twice the diameter of the tail.

C. the same diameter as the tail.

D. half as dense as the tail.

【考点分析】

- 实验总结类文章,此题为实验结果题。
- 抓住定位词 *Study 1*,直接定位第一个实验,题目问 *the heads of plumes*。
- 根据 Figure 1 中,我们可以看到头的直径约为 500 km,尾的直径约为 250 km,很明显倍数关系是 2 倍,结合选项可知正确答案为 **B**。

(2) 例题练习 1.2

The scientists in Study 3 hypothesized that the larger the volume of lava produced, the larger the number of marine organisms that would become extinct. If this hypothesis is correct, the formation of which of the following plateaus caused the largest number of marine organisms to become extinct?

F. Plateau A　　G. Plateau B　　H. Plateau C　　J. Plateau D

【考点分析】

- 实验总结类文章,此题为实验假设题。

● 抓住定位词 *Study 3 & the volume of lava produced*，题干给出的假设是 *that the larger the volume of lava produced, the larger the number of marine organisms that would become extinct*。

● 根据 Study 3 描述"Scientists found that 3 large extinctions of marine organisms had ages similar to those of the formation of 3 of the flood basalt plateaus; 58 Myr, 66 Myr, and 133 Myr"，纵观全文 Study 2 的 Table 1 中给出了 Plateau A、B、C、D 的信息，对比可知，实验 3 中给出的三个 plateaus 数据，非常靠近 A、B、C 的 Age，同时 D 的 volume of lava produced 是四个中最大的，我们完全可以推断第四个发生在 D 附近，结合选项可知正确答案为 **J**。

(3) 例题练习 1.3

Based on the results of Study 2, a flood basalt plateau that produced lava for a period of 1.8 Myr would most likely have a lava volume:

A. between 1,440,000 km^3 and 1,500,000 km^3.

B. between 1,500,000 km^3 and 2,000,000 km^3.

C. between 2,000,000 km^3 and 2,125,000 km^3.

D. over 2,125,000 km^3.

【考点分析】

● 实验总结类文章，此题为实验推断题。

● 抓住定位词 *Study 2*，直接定位到第三段部分和 *Table 1*，题目考察 *a flood basalt plateau that produced lava for a period of 1.8 Myr*。

● 根据表格中我们可以看到 Length of time lava was produced 的变化趋势是先降低后增加，所以 1.8 应该出现在 1.7 后面，同时随着时间变化，Lava volume 的变化趋势是也是先降低后增加，并且两组数据最大值对应最大值，借此推断 1.8 时，Lava volume 的值应该大于 2 125 000，由此可知正确答案为 **D**。

(4) 例题练习 1.4

According to Study 2, which of the following statements best describes the relationship, if any between the age of a flood basalt plateau and the length of time lava was produced at that plateau?

F. As the age of a plateau increases, the length of time lava was produced increases.

G. As the age of a plateau increases, the length of time lava was produced decreases.

H. As the age of a plateau increases, the length of time lava was produced increases, and then decreases.

J. There is no apparent relationship between the age of a plateau and the length of time lava was produced.

【考点分析】

● 实验总结类文章，此题为实验结果题。

● 抓住定位词 *Study 2*，直接定位到第三段部分和 *Table 1*。

● 考察两组数据间的关系，直接看表格数据，根据表格来看 the age of a flood basalt plateau 依次递增时，Length of time lava was produced 是先减后增，F、G、H 选项均不符合，由此可知正确答案为 **J**。

(5) 例题练习 1.5

Which of the following graphs best represents the relationship between the age of a flood basalt plateau and the rate of lava production?

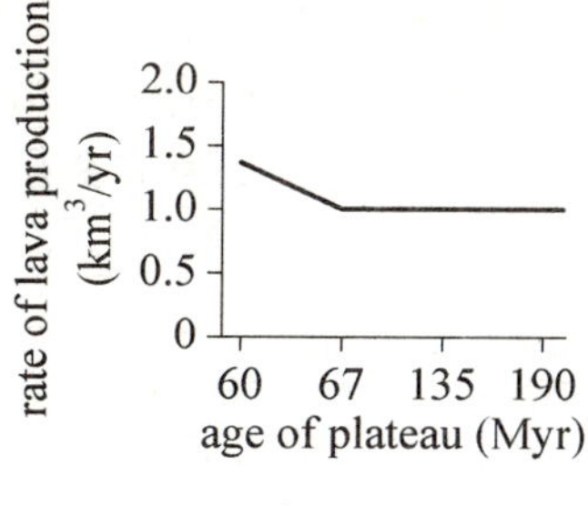

A.

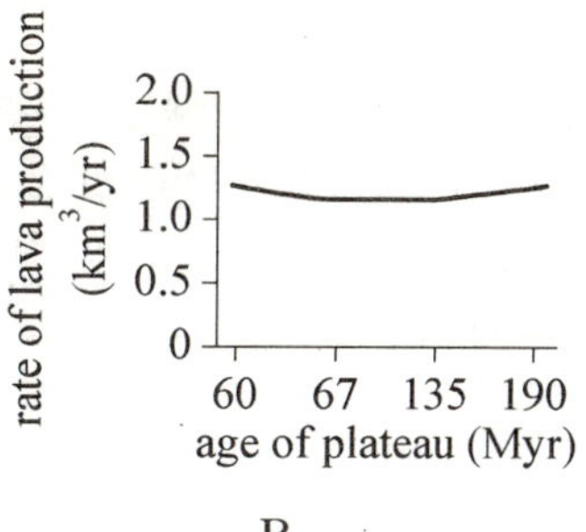

B.

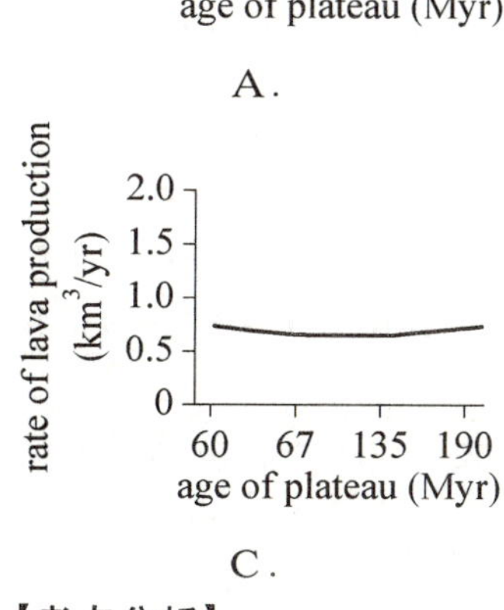

C.

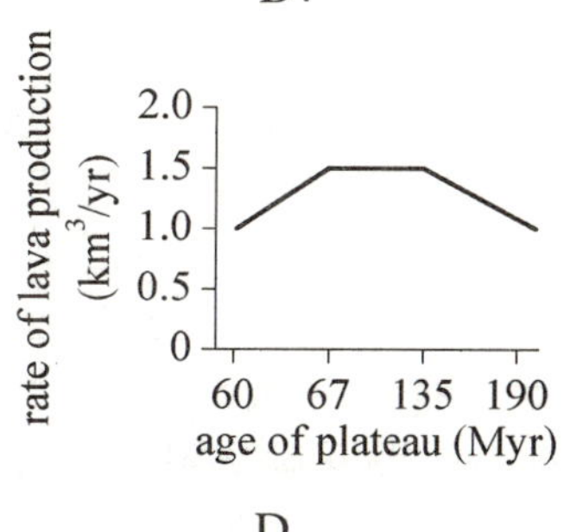

D.

【考点分析】

- 实验总结类文章,此题为实验结果画图题。
- 抓住定位词 *the age of a flood basalt plateau and the rate of lava production*,题目考察两者关系。
- 看到选项,横坐标是 age of plateau,直接看到 Table 1,找到对应 rate 的数值,根据表格可知正确答案为 **B**。

(6) 例题练习 1.6

If the hypothesis made by the scientists in Study 3 is correct, evidence would most likely be found of another extinction of marine organisms that occurred around:

F. 77 Myr ago. G. 192 Myr ago. H. 250 Myr ago. J. 314 Myr ago.

【考点分析】

- 实验总结类文章,此题为实验假设题。
- 抓住定位词 *Study 3*,假设实验 3 正确,题目考察 another extinction of marine organisms 发生的时间。
- 根据最后一段,三个发生灭绝的时间分别是 58、66、133 Myr,对应到表格 1 中,分别是 A、B、C 附近数值,据此推断,第四个应该发生在 D 附近,由此可知正确答案为 **D**。

2) 知识拓展 1

[玄武岩]

玄武岩(basalt),洋壳主要组成,是一种地下岩浆从火山中喷出或从地表裂隙中溢出凝结形成的火成岩,也是地球陆壳和月球月陆的重要组成物质。

玄武岩的主要成分是硅铝酸钠或硅铝酸钙,二氧化硅的含量大约是 45%~52%,还含有较高的氧化铁和氧化镁,是一种细粒致密的黑色岩石。由于喷发时产生大量气孔,有时是大孔如杏仁状构造,后来中间常被其他矿物充填。玄武岩岩浆的黏度小,易于流动,形成很大的覆盖层,常形成广大的熔岩台地,所以分布很广。

玄武岩根据其成分不同可以分为拉斑玄武岩、碱性玄武岩、高铝玄武岩;按其结构不同可分为气孔状玄武岩、杏仁状玄武岩、玄武玻璃;按其充填矿物不同可分为橄榄玄武岩、紫苏辉石玄武岩等。

没有被风化的玄武岩是黑色或暗绿色的致密岩石,由于其凝结后产生六方晶体节理,被风化后形成六方柱状,风化厉害可以形成黄褐色的玄武土,如果进一步被雨水淋滤,除去二氧化硅形成铝土矿。有的玄武岩气孔中还充填有铜、钴、硫磺等矿物。

2. 考古学(Archaeology)

1)例题练习 2

(OG3 Passage V)

科学家讨论了两种导致 2.5 亿年前 90%海洋生物灭绝的原因。

科学家 1

这些海洋生物灭绝的原因是大陆溢流的火山作用,这种作用导致火山喷发持续了 100 万年,产生了 200 万立方千米的熔岩。火山喷发导致大量的含硫气体(四氧化硫)进入空气之中。这些气体与空气中的水蒸气结合,从而产生了酸雨,之后酸雨在全球范围降落,毒害了水中的许多生物。四氧化硫也损坏了大气中的臭氧,使高强度的紫外线射向地球表面。

火山爆发也向大气中释放了大量的二氧化碳。大气中二氧化碳等级的升高提高了海洋表面海水二氧化碳的含量,使二氧化碳达到了可以使许多海洋生物中毒的等级。二氧化碳含量的增加也引起了气候变暖,减少了地球两极和赤道之间的温度差,因此海洋环流减少,海水变得缺少氧气。

科学家 2

这些海洋生物灭绝的原因是富有二氧化碳的深海水的翻转。

2.5 亿年前,地球上没有大陆冰盖。现如今,大陆冰盖促进降低海水表面的温度,冰盖下降,驱使海洋进行垂直环流。2.5 亿年前,因为海洋没有这样的环流形成,所以海水停滞不前且缺乏氧气。

生活在海水表面的光合生物移除大气中的二氧化碳,将其转换为有机物质。这种有机物质沉入海底,之后通过氧化形成二氧化碳。因此,深海里二氧化碳含量的等级急剧提升,而大气中二氧化碳含量继续下降,这种现象导致了气候变冷。冰川和冰盖快速形成,从而降低了海水表面的温度,海洋开始垂直环流。深海中的海水升到了海洋表面,释放了积累已久的二氧化碳,明显地增加了大气和海洋表面的二氧化碳浓度。过量的二氧化碳毒害了许多海洋生物。

(1) 例题练习 2.1

Which of the following statements best explains why Scientist 1 mentioned ultraviolet light?

A. High levels of ultraviolet light are beneficial to many living things.

B. High levels of ultraviolet light are harmful to many living things.

C. Ultraviolet fight helps create ozone in the atmosphere.

D. Ultraviolet light helps create CO_2 in the atmosphere.

【考点分析】

- 观点冲突类文章,此题为单一观点题。
- 抓住定位词 *Scientist 1*,直接定位到第一种观点,题目考察 *ultraviolet light* 提到原因。
- 根据“SO_4-containing aerosols also helped break down ozone in the atmosphere, permitting high levels of ultraviolet light to reach the surface”可以直接排除 C、D 选项,同时结合“The extinctions were caused by continental flood volcanism, a massive volcanic eruption lasting 1 million years that produced 2 million km^3 of lava. The eruption sent large amounts of sulfate-containing (SO_4) aerosols into the air”,直接比较得出正确答案为 **B**。

(2) 例题练习 2.2

Large amounts of SO_4-containing aerosols in the atmosphere are known to reflect some of the

incoming solar radiation back into space, which results in a lowering of the surface temperature. Based on the information provided, this finding would most likely weaken the viewpoint (s) of:

F. Scientist 1 only.
G. Scientist 2 only.
H. both Scientist 1 and Scientist 2.
J. neither Scientist 1 nor Scientist 2.

【考点分析】

● 观点冲突类文章,此题为综合观点题。

● 抓住定位词 *SO_4-containing aerosols*,题目给出信息 *SO_4-containing aerosols* 会降低温度。

● 先看科学家 1 的观点,"The eruption sent large amounts of sulfate-containing (SO_4) aerosols into the air. ... The increased levels of also caused climatic warming that decreased the temperature difference between the poles and the equator, thus slowing ocean circulation and causing ocean water to become oxygen-poor",结合起来必然削弱科学家 1 的观点,而科学家 2 根本未提到 SO_4,故而不受影响,直接得出正确答案为 **F**。

(3) 例题练习 2.3

Scientist 2 would most likely state that the vertical circulation that is present in most of the oceans today is maintained, at least in part, by the presence of:

A. high levels of CO_2 in the air.
B. active volcanoes around the Pacific Ocean rim.
C. ice sheets in Earth's polar regions.
D. marine organisms in deep ocean waters.

【考点分析】

● 观点冲突类文章,此题为单一观点题。

● 抓住定位词 *Scientist 2 & vertical circulation*。

● 根据"Glaciers and ice sheets grew rapidly, cooling the ocean surface waters such that vertical circulation of the ocean began",推断得出正确答案为 **C**。

(4) 例题练习 2.4

Both scientists would most likely agree that the ocean water was, or became, oxygen-poor when which of the following events occurred?

F. Ocean water circulation reversed its usual direction.
G. Ocean water circulation slowed, stopped, or was absent.
H. Oceanic organisms dramatically increased the available oxygen in the ocean water.
J. Oceanic organisms used up all the available CO_2 in the ocean water.

【考点分析】

● 观点冲突类文章,此题为综合观点题。

● 抓住定位词 *ocean water*。

● 根据"...thus slowing ocean circulation and causing ocean water to become oxygen-poor"和"Since this circulation was absent 250 Ma, the ocean water was stagnant and oxygen poor"综合,可以得出正确答案为 **G**。

(5) 例题练习 2.5

According to the information provided, radioactive dating of volcanic rocks created during the continental flood vulcanism described by Scientist 1 would show the rocks to be about how many million years old?

A. 1　　B. 50　　C. 100　　D. 250

【考点分析】

● 观点冲突类文章,此题为单一观点题。

● 抓住定位词 *Scientist 1*。

● 根据"an event 250 million years ago (Ma) in which 90% of all marine species became extinct.... The extinctions were caused by continental flood volcanism, a massive volcanic eruption lasting 1 million years that produced 2 million km^3 of lava",推断得出正确答案为 **D**。

(6) 例题练习 2.6

SO_4-containing aerosols are produced today in large quantities by human activity. Scientist 1 would most likely predict that the climatic effect in an area where large amounts of SO_4-containing aerosols are put into the atmosphere would be a decrease in the:

F. amount of ultraviolet light reaching Earth's surface in that area.

G. average pH of rainfall in that area.

H. amount of rainfall in that area.

J. average wind speed in that area.

【考点分析】

● 观点冲突类文章,此题为单一观点题。

● 抓住定位词 *Scientist 1*。

● 根据"The eruption sent large amounts of sulfate-containing (SO_4) aerosols into the air. The aerosols combined with water vapor in the air to produce acid rain that fell worldwide and poisoned many bodies of water",结合常识(酸雨有毒,并且 pH 值低于普通雨水)得出正确答案为 **G**。

(7) 例题练习 2.7

Inorganic carbonates are rocks formed from calcium carbonate ($CaCO_3$) that precipitate out of ocean surface waters which have much higher than normal levels of dissolved CO_2. If scientists found large deposits of inorganic carbonates that had formed around 250 Ma, this discovery would most likely support the viewpoint (s) of:

A. Scientist 1 only.

B. Scientist 2 only.

C. both Scientist 1 and Scientist 2.

D. neither Scientist 1 nor Scientist 2.

【考点分析】

● 观点冲突类文章,此题为综合观点题。

● 抓住关键词 CO_2。

● 根据全文信息,对于科学家 1 和 2 来说 CO_2 含量影响都非常大,所以综合全篇得出正确答案为 **C**。

2) 知识拓展 2

[化石]

化石是存留在岩石中的古生物遗体、遗物或生活痕迹,最常见的是骸骨和贝壳等。

化石是古代生物的遗体、遗物或遗迹埋藏在地下变成的跟石头一样的东西。研究化石可以了解生物的演化并能帮助确定地层的年代。保存在地壳岩石中的古动物或古植物的遗体或表明有遗体存在的证据都谓之化石。从太古宙(34 亿年前)至全新世(1 万年前)之间都有化石出现。

简单地说,化石就是生活在遥远过去的生物的遗体或遗迹变成的石头。在漫长的地质年代里,地球上曾经生活过无数的生物,这些生物死亡后的遗体或是生活时遗留下来的痕迹,许多都被当时的泥沙掩埋起来。在随后的岁月中,这些生物遗体中的有机质分解殆尽,坚硬的部分如外壳、骨骼、枝叶等与包围在周围的沉积物一起经过石化变成了石头,但是它们原来的形态、结构(甚至一些细

微的内部构造)依然保留着;同样,那些生物生活时留下的痕迹也可以这样保留下来。我们把这些石化了的生物遗体、遗迹就称为化石。从化石中可以看到古代动物、植物的样子,从而可以推断出古代动物、植物的生活情况和生活环境,可以推断出埋藏化石的地层形成的年代和经历的变化,可以看到生物从古到今的变化等等。

实体化石是由古生物遗体本身的全部或部分(特别是硬体部分)保存下来而形成的。在能够避开空气氧化作用和细菌腐蚀作用的特别适宜的情况下,有些生物的遗体能够比较完好地保存而没有显著的变化。如西伯利亚冻土中发现的第四纪猛犸象、波兰发现的迄今所知的最完整的脊椎动物化石——1 万年前落入沥青湖的披毛犀,以及树脂化石(如琥珀)。

3. 气象学(Meteorology)

1)例题练习 3

(OG1 Passage IV)

Certain layers of Earth's atmosphere absorb particular wavelengths of solar radiation while letting others pass through. Types of solar radiation include X rays, ultraviolet light, visible light, and infrared radiation. The cross section of Earth's atmosphere below illustrates the altitudes at which certain wavelengths are absorbed. The arrows point to the altitudes at which solar radiation of different ranges of wavelengths is absorbed. The figure also indicates the layers of the atmosphere and how atmospheric density, pressure, and temperature vary with altitude. 地球大气层中的某些层吸收了某些特定波长的太阳辐射,其他波长的太阳辐射可轻松通过大气层,其中包括 X 光、紫外线、可见光和红外线。下面的地球大气层横截面展示了大气层吸收不同波长太阳辐射的高度。该图也展示了大气层的各层情况,以及大气密度、压力和温度随着高度变化的变化。

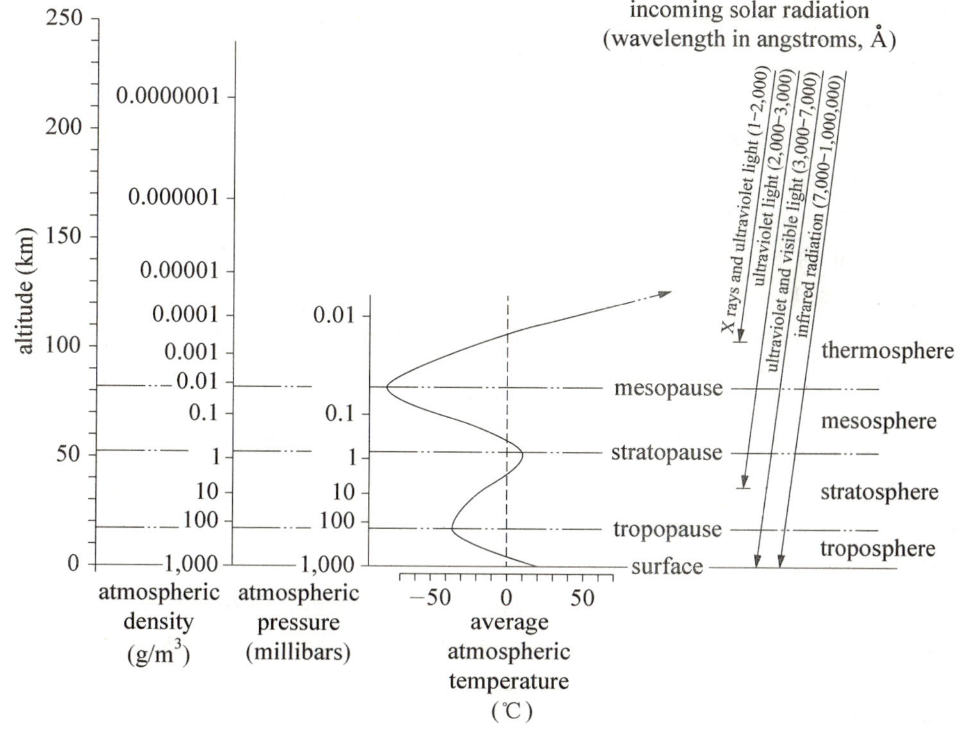

Note: 1 Å = 1 × 10⁻¹⁰ meters.

Flgure adapted from Arthur Strahler. *The Earth Sclences*. © 1963 by Harper and Row.

(1) 例题练习 3.1

According to the data provided, at what altitude is the upper boundary of the thermosphere located?

F. 150 km

G. 200 km

H. 250 km

J. The upper boundary is not included on the figure.

【考点分析】

- 数据分析类文章,此题为数据查找题。
- 抓住关键词 *upper boundary*。
- 根据 Figure 中可以看到并未给出上边界,所以正确答案为 **J**。

(2) 例题练习 3.2

The ozone layer selectively absorbs ultraviolet radiation of 2,000 – 3,000 Å wavelengths. According to this information and the data, which atmospheric layer contains the ozone layer?

A. Troposphere　　B. Stratosphere

C. Mesosphere　　D. Thermosphere

【考点分析】

- 数据分析类文章,此题为数据查找题。
- 抓住关键词 *ultraviolet radiation of 2,000 –3,000 Å wavelengths*。
- 直接查找 Figure 中数据,可以看到此范围波长在 Stratosphere,所以正确答案为 **B**。

(3) 例题练习 3.3

The information provided in the figure indicates that the air temperature in the troposphere is LEAST likely to be influenced by which of the following wavelengths of energy?

F. 1,500 Å　　G. 4,500 Å　　H. 6,000 Å　　J. 7,000 Å

【考点分析】

- 数据分析类文章,此题为数据查找题。
- 抓住关键词 *troposphere*。
- 直接查找 Figure 中数据,可以看到 troposphere 内波长范围是 3 000～7 000、7 000～1 000 000,对比出正确答案为 **F**。

(4) 例题练习 3.4

On the basis of the information in the figure, one could generalize that atmospheric pressure in each atmospheric layer increases with:

A. decreasing temperature.　　B. increasing temperature.

C. decreasing altitude.　　D. increasing altitude.

【考点分析】

- 数据分析类文章,此题为数据对比题。
- 抓住关键词 *atmospheric pressure*。
- 结合选项,选项分两种内容,一种是 temperature,从 Figure 中看到随着气压增加,温度降、增、降、增,不是直接的线性关系,A、B 排除,另一种是 altitude,随着气压增加,altitude 降低,正确答案为 **C**。

(5) 例题练习 3.5

Atmospheric boundaries are at a higher than usual altitude above areas that get more direct

solar radiation. Based on this information and the data provided, which of the following predictions about atmospheric boundaries would most likely be true if Earth received less solar radiation than it presently does?

F. The tropopause, stratopause, and mesopause would all increase in altitude.

G. The tropopause, stratopause, and mesopause would all decrease in altitude.

H. The tropopause and stratopause would increase in altitude, but the mesopause would decrease in altitude.

J. The tropopause would decrease in altitude, but the stratopause and mesopause would increase in altitude.

【考点分析】

- 数据分析类文章,此题为数据假设题。
- 题目给出信息:Atmospheric boundaries are at a higher than usual altitude above areas that get more direct solar radiation.
- 根据题目假设 Earth received less solar radiation than it presently does,那么所有的 boundary 都会在一个比目前低的高度,正确答案为 **G**。

2) 知识拓展 3

[大气层]

大气层(atmosphere),地球就被这一层很厚的大气层包围着。大气层的成分主要有氮气,占 78.1%;氧气,占 20.9%;氩气,占 0.93%;还有少量的二氧化碳、稀有气体(氦气、氖气、氩气、氪气、氙气、氡气)和水蒸气。大气层的空气密度随高度而减小,越高空气越稀薄。大气层的厚度大约在 1 000千米以上,但没有明显的界限。整个大气层随高度不同表现出不同的特点,分为对流层、平流层、中间层、暖层和散逸层,再上面就是星际空间。

对流层在大气层的最低层,紧靠地球表面,其厚度大约为 10~20 千米。对流层的大气受地球影响较大,云、雾、雨等现象都发生在这一层内,水蒸气也几乎都在这一层内存在,还存在大部分的固体杂质。这一层的气温随高度的增加而降低,大约每升高 1 000 米,温度下降 5~6℃;动、植物的生存,人类的绝大部分活动,也在这一层内,因为这一层的空气对流很明显,故称对流层。

对流层以上是平流层,大约距地球表面 20~50 千米。平流层以上是中间层,大约距地球表面 50~85 千米,这里的空气已经很稀薄,突出的特征是气温随高度增加而迅速降低,空气的垂直对流强烈。中间层以上是暖层,大约距地球表面 100~800 千米,最突出的特征是当太阳光照射时,太阳光中的紫外线被该层中的氧原子大量吸收,因此温度升高,故称暖层。散逸层在暖层之上,为带电粒子所组成。

(四) 实战练习 Practice

Practice 4

(52C Passage I)

一位地质学家进行了三项研究,从而评估水进入和离开湖泊的速度,以及其对湖泊水容量的影响。水进入湖泊称为进水,而水离开湖泊称为出水。这些研究历时 5 年。

Study 1 研究 1

这位地质学家测量了进水的两个主要来源:降雨和湖水流入。这位地质学家用了 5 年的时间定期地对每个进水的来源进行了测量。通过这些测量,他计算了每年的平均降水总量为 260×10^6 立方米。表 1 展示了他的测量结果。

Table 1

Type of inflow	Average inflow (m^3/yr)
Inflowing streams	200×10^6
Rainfall on lake	60×10^6

Study 2 研究 2

水离开湖泊的方式主要是通过湖水流出、蒸发和深入到湖底的岩石之中。这位地质学家用了 5 年的时间定期地对这三种过程进行了测量。此外,一家水务公司用水泵将水从湖中抽出,以供附近的几个小区使用。在研究期间,这家水务公司向地质学家给出了水泵的抽水速度。计算后的总出水量为 300×106 立方米/年。每个过程的平均出水量见表 2。

Table 2

Type of outflow	Average outflow (m^3/yr)
Outflowing streams	100×10^6
Evaporation	50×10^6
Infiltration	60×10^6
Pumping	90×10^6

Study 3 研究 3

这位地质学家在湖中央安装了一台水深度记录仪,并在这 5 年中每月定期读取测试数值。每年,他算出这些数值的平均数,得出湖面每年平均降低 10 厘米。

(1) Practice 4.1

If dams were constructed to effectively stop the escape of water by outflowing streams, which of the following is most likely?

A. Total outflow would equal total inflow.

B. Total outflow and lake volume would both probably increase.

C. Total outflow and lake volume would both probably decrease.

D. Total outflow would decrease and lake volume would increase.

(2) Practice 4.2

If the area had experienced a lack of rainfall during the five-year study period, how would this have affected the results?

F. Total outflow would be higher.

G. Total inflow would be lower.

H. Infiltration would be higher.

J. All results would be unaffected by the drought.

(3) Practice 4.3

Which of the following generalizations about the lake's water balance can be made based on the results of the studies?

A. For any lake, total water outflow always exceeds total water inflow.

B. The number of inflowing streams exceeds the number of outflowing streams.

C. If the rates of water entering and leaving a lake are not balanced, lake depth will change.

D. A lake cannot have both inflowing and outflowing streams and maintain a constant volume.

(4) Practice 4.4

Would the geologist have obtained more accurate results if the investigation period was decreased from five to two years?

F. Yes, because there would be less chance of human error in the measurements.

G. Yes, because there would be fewer variables to consider.

H. No, because abnormally high or low measurements would distort the averages.

J. No, because water movement in and out of the lake is slow.

(5) Practice 4.5

Which of the following assumptions was made in all three studies?

A. The three studies were done at different five-year periods.

B. The lake is underlain by rock that water cannot infiltrate.

C. Total inflow and outflow were constant during the investigation.

D. All significant inflows and outflows of water were identified.

(6) Practice 4.6

Based on the results of the studies, the geologist concludes that lake volume decreased annually. Which of the following would help support that conclusion?

F. Determining if rainfall rate increased annually.

G. Determining if the surface area of the lake decreased annually.

H. Repeating the same studies on a different lake.

J. Repeating the depth measurements on a different lake.

2) Practice 5

(52C Passage II)

Fossil footprints of dinosaurs can be used to identify the type, size, speed, and gait of these animals. Determination of gait (the manner of moving on foot) is based on comparisons with speeds at which modern animals walk and run. Geologists performed the following studies to help estimate this information for some ancient footprints.

Study 1(研究 1)

A 68-million-year-old fossil trackway was discovered in a rock formation that consisted of alternating layers of mudstone and sandstone. A trackway is a path or trail commonly used by groups of animals. In the top mudstone layer, five sets of tracks were exposed that belonged to several species of two-legged dinosaurs. The tracks were oriented in the same direction and were formed at approximately the same time. Geologists concluded that two sets were made by meat-eating dinosaurs and the other three sets by plant-eaters. Measurements of the foot length and stride length (distance between successive footprints) of each set of dinosaur tracks were taken at the trackway.

Study 2(研究 2)

A geologist measured the skeletons of meat-eating and plant-eating dinosaurs in a museum. Table 1 shows the leg length, foot length, and ratio of leg length to foot length for those museum specimens.

Table 1

Dinosaur	Leg length (m)	Foot length (m)	Ratio
Large meat-eater	3.25	0.78	4.2 : 1
Small meat-eater A	1.33	0.31	4.3 : 1
Large plant-eater B	0.69	0.17	4.1 : 1
Large plant-eater	2.46	0.68	3.6 : 1
Small plant-eater	0.44	0.12	3.7 : 1

Study 3(研究 3)

The leg length of the five dinosaurs from Study 1 was estimated using the data from Study 2. Their estimated speed was then calculated from modern animals that have stride-length-to-leg-length ratios similar to those of dinosaurs. Table 2 shows the calculated leg length, calculated speed, and gait of the dinosaurs.

Table 2

Dinosaur	Leg length (m)	Speed (m/sec)	Gait
Meat-eater 1	2.60	2.0	Walk
Meat-eater 2	0.22	3.5	Run
Plant-eater 1	1.60	4.8	Run
Plant-eater 2	0.14	4.3	Run
Plant-eater 3	0.13	3.0	run

(1) Practice 5.1

A geologist hypothesized that speed is related to, the cold - or warm-bloodedness of an animal and that warm-blooded animals usually move at higher speeds. If this is true and some dinosaurs were known to be warm-blooded, which dinosaur in Study 3 was most likely warm-blooded?

A. Meat-eater 1

B. Meat-eater 2

C. Plant-eater 1

D. Plant-eater 3

(2) Practice 5.2

Based on the information provided by the three studies, one can make the generalization that if:

F. speed is known, the type of dinosaur can be determined.

G. stride length and leg length are known, a dinosaur's speed can be estimated.

H. leg-length-to-foot-length ratio is known, the weight of the dinosaur can be calculated.

J. the type of food a dinosaur ate is known, its gait can be determined.

(3) Practice 5.3

The information gathered in Study 2 was necessary because it:

A. showed the exact species of the dinosaurs in Study 1.

B. allowed the geologist to estimate the speed of the dinosaurs in Study 3.

C. determined the age of the fossil trackway discovered in Study 1.

D. helped to identify the rock types in the formation of Study 1.

(4) Practice 5.4

A fossil trackway is found in an exposed sandstone layer that is less than 20 million years old. The tracks belong to a large flightless bird. Would Studies 1, 2 and 3 need to be modified to estimate the speed of this bird?

F. Yes, because measurements should be done on museum skeletons of fossil flightless birds.

G. Yes, because Study 1 used more than one set of tracks.

H. No, because birds are thought to be the ancestors of dinosaurs.

J. No, because the bird would have a speed that falls within the range of those of the dinosaurs in Table 2.

(5) Practice 5.5

Another section of the trackway, 100 m farther down the path from the first site, is discovered. All five sets of tracks can be seen and are measured as in Study 1. It is found that Meat-eater 1 now has a speed of 4.6 m/sec, while the other speeds stayed the same. Which of the following conclusions is NOT consistent with the new data?

A. Meat-eater 1 has changed gaits from walking to running.

B. Meat-eater 1 will overtake the other four dinosaurs.

C. Plant-eater 1 is in the least danger of being overtaken by Meat-eater 1.

D. Plant-eater 3 is in the most danger of being overtaken by Meat-eater 1.

(6) Practice 5.6

Which of the following alterations to the method of Study 2 would have made the results of Study 3 more accurate?

F. Measuring the skeletons of dinosaurs that belong to species of dinosaurs other than those in Study 1.

G. Measuring the skeletons of more specimens of the same species as those in Study 1.

H. Measuring only the foot length of modern animals of various types.

J. Measuring the foot length of the small front feet of two-legged dinosaurs.

3) Practice 6

(55C Passage VI)

Earth's atmosphere consists of various gases and suspended liquid and solid matter. The atmosphere can be divided into layers based on air temperature and/or composition. Figure 1 shows the layers of the atmosphere, the altitude of the layer boundaries, in kilometers (km), and the air pressure, in millibars (mb), at those boundaries. Figure 2 shows the average air temperature, in degrees Celsius (℃), in arctic (cold) and tropical (warm) air asses at various altitudes. Table 1 shows air pressure and temperature readings from weather instruments carried into the stratosphere by balloons on 2 separate days.

Layer of atmosphere	Altitude (km)	Air pressure (mb)
	500	1.9×10^{-9}
	400	3.4×10^{-9}
thermosphere ionosphere F2		
	190	3.4×10^{-7}
F1	140	3.4×10^{-6}
E	90	3.4×10^{-3}
80 km D	72	3.4×10^{-2}
mesosphere		
	50	3.4
chemosphere ozonosphere		
stratosphere	32	10.8
	11	301
troposphere		
surface	0	1,013

Figure 1

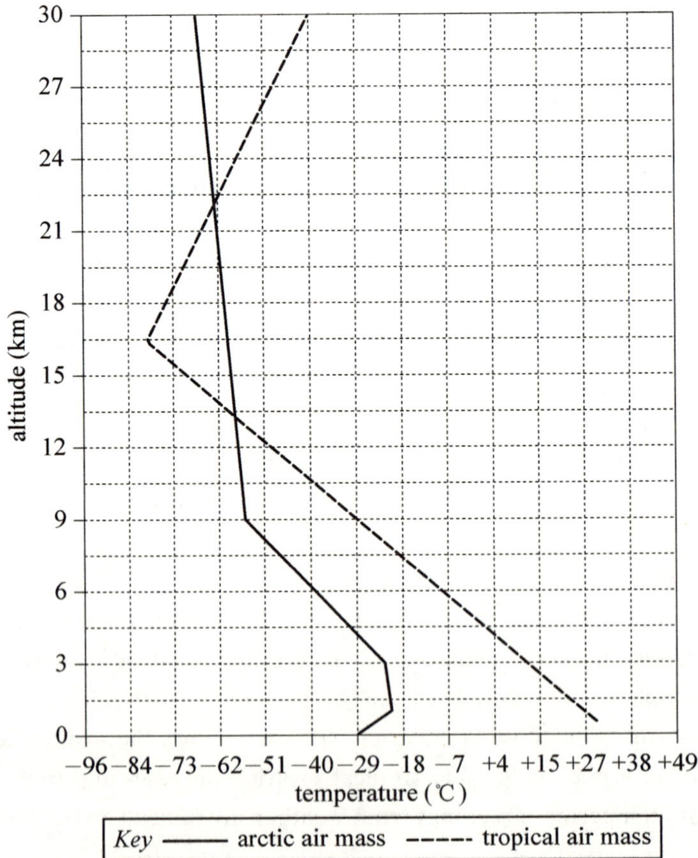

Figure 2

Table 1

Air pressure (mb)	Altitude (km)	Temperature (℃) readings on:	
		Day 1	Day 2
1 000	0	2	25
900	0.9	0	15
700	2.9	−17	6
600	4.2	−25	−2
500	5.6	−30	−12
400	7.2	−40	−20
300	9.1	−50	−32
250	11.4	−50	−50
200	13.7	−48	−58

(1) Practice 6.1

According to Figure 2, at approximately which of the following altitudes would a weather instrument measuring air temperature be unable to distinguish between tropical and arctic air masses?

A. 12.0 km B. 13.5 km C. 15.5 km D. 16.5 km

(2) Practice 6.2

According to Figure 1, several atmospheric layers overlap one another. Which of the following describes atmospheric layers that share part of a common altitude range?

F. Stratosphere and mesosphere G. Stratosphere and thermosphere

H. Mesosphere and thermosphere J. Mesosphere and chemosphere

(3) Practice 6.3

According to Figure 1 and Table 1, if the weather instruments rose above 13.7 km, the air pressure would most likely:

A. increase to more than 1,000 mb. B. stay at 200 mb.

C. decrease to less than 200 mb. D. decrease to 1,000 mb.

(4) Practice 6.4

According to Figure 1, a weather instrument reading an air pressure of 5 mb is most likely in which of the following layers?

F. Troposphere G. Ozonosphere H. Mesosphere J. Ionosphere

(5) Practice 6.5

According to Table 1, which of the following statements best describes the relationship between altitude and air temperature?

A. The air temperature decreased with increasing altitude on Day 1 only.

B. The air temperature increased with increasing altitude on Day 1 only.

C. The air temperature decreased with increasing altitude on Day 2 only.

D. The air temperature increased with increasing altitude on Day 2 only.

Answers for Practice 4 - 6

Practice 4　D G C H D G

Practice 5　C G B F B G

Practice 6　B J C G C

Session 4　地球学/宇宙学 2

本章主要介绍 ACT 科学测试地球学/宇宙学科目中的海洋学、天文学和环境科学三大分支学科,并通过解析例题,以及相应的练习题明确这三门学科的考试形式、考试重点和相关词汇。

(一) 学科背景

ACT 科学测试主要考察和重点考察科学推理能力,了解相应的学科知识可以快速理解文章内容,提高解题速度。

1. 学科综述

1) 海洋学(Oceanography)

海洋学是研究海洋的自然现象、性质及其变化规律,以及开发利用海洋的知识体系。是地球科学和地理学中的自然地理学的组成部分。

2) 天文学(Astronomy)

天文学是观察和研究宇宙间天体的学科,它研究天体的分布、运动、位置、状态、结构、组成、性质及起源和演化,是自然科学中的一门基础学科。

3) 环境科学(Environment Science)

环境科学是一门研究人类社会发展活动与环境演化规律之间相互作用关系,寻求人类社会与环境协同演化、持续发展途径与方法的科学。

2. 学科背景知识

1) 海洋学

海洋科学是研究海洋的自然现象、性质及其变化规律,以及与开发利用海洋有关的知识体系。它的研究对象是占地球表面 71%的海洋,包括海水、溶解和悬浮于海水中的物质、海洋中的生物、海底沉积和海底岩石圈,以及海面上的大气边界层和河口海岸带等。海洋科学的研究领域十分广泛,其主要内容包括对海洋的物理、化学、生物和地质过程的基础研究,海洋资源开发利用,以及海上军事活动等的应用研究。

海洋中发生的各种自然过程,在不同程度上同大气圈、岩石圈和生物圈都有耦合关系,并且同全球构造运动以及某些天文因素密切相关,这些自然过程本身也相互制约,彼此间通过各种形式的物质和能量循环结合在一起,构成一个具有全球规模的、多层次的海洋自然系统。

2) 天文学

天文学所研究的对象涉及宇宙空间的各种物体,大到月球、太阳、行星、恒星、银河系、河外星系以至整个宇宙,小到小行星、流星体以至分布在广袤宇宙空间中的大大小小尘埃粒子。天文学家把所有这些物体统称为天体。地球也是一个天体,不过天文学只研究地球的总体性质而一般不讨论它的细节。另外,人造卫星、宇宙飞船、空间站等人造飞行器的运动性质也属于天文学的研究范围,可以称之为人造天体。

太阳系(solar system)是由太阳、8 颗大行星、66 颗卫星,以及无数的小行星、彗星及陨星组成的。行星由太阳起往外的顺序是:水星(Mercury)、金星(Venus)、地球(Earth)、火星(Mars)、木星

(Jupiter)、土星(Saturn)、天王星(Uranus)和海王星(Neptune)。

3）环境科学

环境科学是一门研究环境的地理、物理、化学、生物四个部分的学科。它提供了综合、定量和跨学科的方法来研究环境系统。由于大多数环境问题涉及人类活动，因此经济、法律和社会科学知识往往也可用于环境科学研究。

在宏观上，环境科学要研究人与环境之间的相互作用、相互制约的关系，要力图发现社会经济发展和环境保护之间协调的规律；在微观上，要研究环境中的物质在有机体内迁移、转化、蓄积的过程及其运动规律，对生命的影响和作用机理，尤其是人类活动排放出来的污染物质。

（二）学科单词

ACT 科学要求有一定的阅读量，文章中涉及大量的专业词汇，了解这些专业词汇的意思有助于理解文章和题意。以下是三门学科常见的专业词汇，考生需要熟悉单词的意思，以便在考试中能更准确地理解文章内容。

1. 海洋学

英文	中文释义	英文	中文释义
calcite	碳酸钙	phytoplankton	浮游植物
marine	海洋的	silicic acid	硅酸
dissolve	溶解	Inorganic phosphorus	无机磷
seafloor	海底	equator	赤道
sediment	沉积	subarctic	亚北极的；近北极的
saturation	饱和	cod	鳕鱼
precipitate	沉淀	cliff	悬崖
calcareous ooze	钙质软泥	shoreline	海岸线

2. 天文学

英文	中文释义	英文	中文释义
comet	彗星	hot spot	热点
orbital period	轨道周期	latitude	纬度
ecliptic plane	黄道面	ultramafic	超镁铁的
inclination	轨道倾角	dissipate	散逸
telescope	望远镜	upper atmosphere	高层大气
gravitationalfield	重力场	arcsecond	弧秒；角秒
solar system	太阳系	angular size	角距大小
lunar	月亮的	revolve	旋转；回转
orbit	轨道	elongation	距角
rotation	自转	perihelion	近日点
asteroid	小行星	aphelion	远日点
crater	陨石坑	semimajor axis	半长轴
boggy	似沼泽的	escape velocity	逃逸速度；宇宙速度
fragment	碎片	orbital speed	轨道速度

3. 环境科学

英文	中文释义	英文	中文释义
toxic	有毒的	needle	针叶
carbon monoxide	一氧化碳	combustion	氧化
concentration	浓度	chamber	房间
volume	体积	soak	浸透
atmospheric	大气层的	ignite	点燃
hose	橡胶管	flame	火焰
tailpipe	排气管	crown	树冠
inject	注射	foliage	树叶
chromatograph	色谱仪	resemble	相像
interval	间隔	clearing	林中空地
coliform	大肠菌	insectivore	食虫类
tributary	支流	frugivore	食果动物
hummingbird	蜂鸟		

(三)例题解析

本节选取了三门学科的真题进行详细的解析,帮助考生迅速了解考试的形式、内容和解题思路。

1. 海洋学(Oceanography)

1)例题练习 1

(OG2　Passage V)

一些海洋虾是垂直迁徙物种。对于垂直迁徙物种,大部分种群白天处于生活深度范围的底部,夜间处于深度范围的顶部。表 1 展示了 3 种垂直迁移虾类的生活深度范围及其水分、蛋白质、脂肪和碳水化合物,以及 3 种非迁移深海虾。图 1 展示了不同海洋深度的水温和氧分压。

Table 1

Species	Depth range (m)	Water content (% wet weight)	% ash-free dry weight		
			Protein	Lipid	Carbohydrate
Vm 1	300 - 600	77.5	62.8	23.8	0.7
Vm 2	10 - 400	76.6	53.4	16.4	0.8
Vm 3	75 - 400	79.5	60.5	14.7	0.7
Nm 1	500 - 1 100	75.9	36.9	36.1	0.5
Nm 2	500 - 1 000	72.8	35.8	49.0	0.5
Nm 3	650 - 1 000	72.8	35.8	49.0	0.5

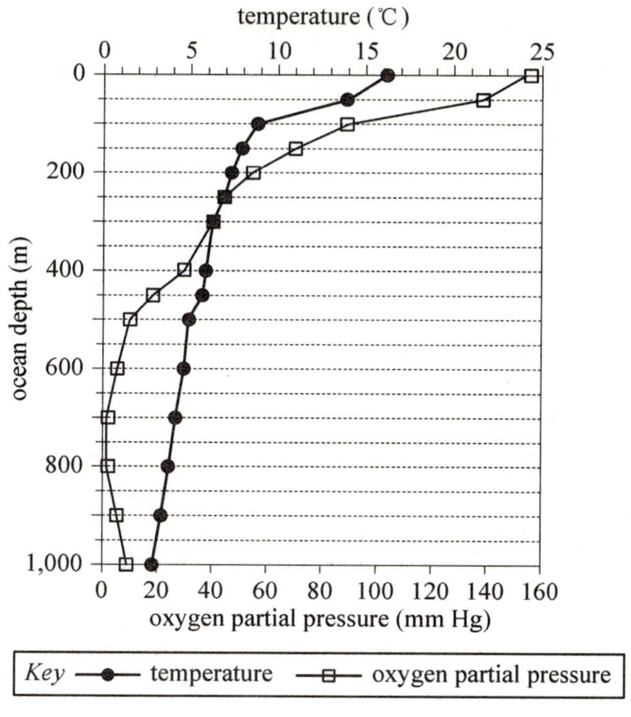

Figure 1

(1) 例题练习 1.1

Based on the information in Table 1, one would conclude that vertically migrating shrimp have a higher, percent content of:

A. protein than lipid.

B. lipid than protein.

C. carbohydrate than lipid.

D. carbohydrate than protein.

【考点分析】

- 数据分析类文章,此题为数据对比题。
- 抓住关键词 *Table 1*,题目问 vertically migrating shrimp have a higher, percent content of。
- 根据 Table 1 中,我们可以看到,对于 vertically migrating shrimp 来说,protein 百分比大于 carbohydrate,lipid 百分比也大于 carbohydrate,protein 大于 lipid,结合选项可知正确答案为 **A**。

(2) 例题练习 1.2

On the basis of the information given, one would expect that, compared to the vertically migrating shrimp species, the nonmigrating shrimp species:

F. have a greater water content.

G. have a lower percent lipid content.

H. can tolerate higher water temperatures.

J. can tolerate lower oxygen partial pressures.

【考点分析】

- 查看 Table 1 第 3 列,可以看出 nonmigrating shrimp (Nm 1, 2, 3)的 water content 都小于 vertically migrating shrimp (Vm 1, 2, 3),故 F 错误。
- 同理查看 Table 1 第 5 列,可得出 G 错误。

● H、J 结合了 Table 1 和图 1 的信息。图 1 和 Table 1 的桥梁是 depth，查看 Table 1 第 2 列可知 Nm 生活的 depth 大于 Vm。又从图 1 中可看出 depth 的大小与 water temperature 和 oxygen partial pressure 均成反比。故 Nm 可以承受 lower water temperature 和 oxygen partial pressure，故 H 错，J 正确。

(3) 例题练习 1.3

Assume that shrimp of a newly discovered species of vertically migrating shrimp were captured at night at a minimum depth of 200 m. Assume that only temperature limits the range of this species. Based on the information in Figure 1, one would predict that the maximum water temperature these shrimp could survive in would be：

A. 3.5℃. B. 7.5℃. C. 12.5℃. D. 15.5℃.

【考点分析】

● 此题为数据图表信息提取题

● 最小深度为 200 m，意思是它只能生活在 200 m 以下。又从图 1 中可看出水深与温度成反比，所以 200 m 以下的水域温度都低于 200 m 处温度。又题中告知温度是影响生活范围的唯一因素，故它能适应的最高温度是 200 m 处的温度。在图 1 中查看实心点曲线可得 200 m 的温度是 7.5℃，所以 B 正确。

2) 知识拓展 1

[海洋生态系统]

海洋生态系统(marine ecosystems)是海洋中由生物群落及其环境相互作用所构成的自然系统，生态系(Ecosystem)一词，系英国 A. G. 坦斯利于 1935 年提出。

由海洋生物群落和海洋环境两大部分组成，每一部分又包括有众多的要素。这些要素主要有 6 类：

(1) 自养生物，为生产者，主要是具有绿色素的能进行光合作用的植物，包括浮游藻类、底栖藻类和海洋种子植物；还有能进行光合作用的细菌。

(2) 异养生物，为消费者，包括各类海洋动物。

(3) 分解者，包括海洋细菌和海洋真菌。

(4) 有机碎屑物质，包括生物死亡后分解成的有机碎屑和陆地输入的有机碎屑等，以及大量溶解有机物和其聚集物。

(5) 参加物质循环的无机物质，如碳、氮、硫、磷、二氧化碳、水等。

(6) 水文物理状况，如温度、海流等。

大洋环流和水团结构是海洋的一个重要特性，是决定某海域状况的主要因素。由此形成各海域的温度分布带——热带、亚热带、温带、近极区(亚极区)和极区等海域；暖流和寒流海域；水团的混合；水团的垂直分布和移动；上升流海域等。这些都对海洋生物的组成、分布和数量有重要影响。

2. 天文学(Astronomy)

1) 例题练习 2

(OG4 Passage V)

Introduction 前言

彗星是围绕太阳运行的冰和尘埃的复杂混合物。根据其轨道周期可分为长周期彗星和短周期彗星。

长周期彗星轨道周期超过 200 年，起源于我们太阳系内的奥尔特云，很多冰体的球行壳体离太阳的平均距离为 40 000 A. U.(1 A. U. = 地球距离太阳的平均距离)。长周期彗星从各个方向接近太阳。

短周期彗星轨道周期为 200 年或更短，其轨道平面与地球公转黄道平面的倾角为 30 度或更小。这些平面的构成如图 1 所示。

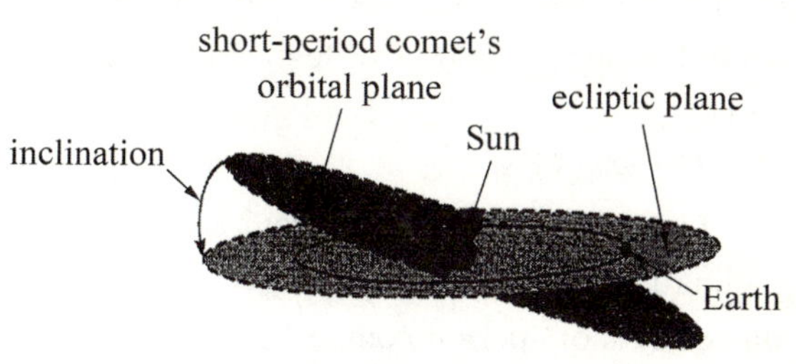

Figure 1

两位科学家对于短周期彗星的起源提出了他们的观点。

Scientist A 科学家 A

太阳系内的短周期彗星起源于一个狭窄的环形区，称为柯伊伯带（KB）。柯伊伯带与黄道平面倾角很小，距离太阳的距离在 30 A. U. 到 50 A. U. 之间。柯伊伯带包含数以亿计的冰体，冰体直径在 10～30 千米之间。这些彗星的目标太小，在地球上的望远镜很难清晰辨认。这些望远镜可以收集到作为柯伊伯带一部分的稍大的冰体的间接证据，而不是清晰的图像。短周期彗星轨道与黄道平面的很小的倾角与短周期彗星起源于柯伊伯带的观点一致。人们发现附近的其他星体与围绕他们的冰体有同样的来源。

Scientist B 科学家 B

柯伊伯带并不存在。短周期彗星曾经是长周期彗星。一些长周期彗星太靠近巨行星（如木星），受巨行星的重力场影响，被迫改变轨道，轨道周期短于 200 年。这些改变后的轨道与黄道倾角很小。大多数短周期彗星与巨行星的轨道平面的夹角很小，反过来，与黄道平面的倾角也很小。

（1）例题练习 2.1

Which of the following generalizations about comets is most consistent with Scientist B's viewpoint?

A. Long-period comets cannot become short-period comets.

B. Short-period comets cannot become long-period comets.

C. Long-period comets can become short-period comets.

D. No long-period comets or short-period comets orbit the Sun.

【考点分析】

- 观点冲突类文章，此题为单一观点题。
- 抓住定位词 *Scientist B* 。
- 根据“The KB does not exist. Short-period comets were once long-period comets”直接得出正确答案为 C。

（2）例题练习 2.2

Scientist A would most likely suggest that a new telescope more powerful than previous telescopes be used to search which of the following regions of space for objects in the KB?

F. The region 100,000 A. U. beyond our solar system

G. The region 30 A. U. to 50 A. U. from the Sun at an angle of 90° with respect to the ecliptic plane

H. The region 30 A. U. to 50 A. U. from the Sun at angles of 0° to 30° with respect to the ecliptic plane

J. The region closely surrounding the planet Jupiter

【考点分析】

- 观点冲突类文章，此题为单一观点题。
- 抓住定位词 *Scientist A*。
- 根据“The KB has a small inclination with respect to the ecliptic plane and is located in the

solar system between 30 A. U. and 50 A. U. from the Sun”,结合前言“Short-period comets have orbital periods of 200 yr or less, and their orbital planes have inclinations 30° ”,直接得出正确答案为 **H**。

(3) 例题练习 2.3

Given the information about short-period comets in the introduction, which of the following inclinations with respect to the ecliptic plane would most likely NOT be observed for the orbital planes of short-period comets?

A. 5° B. 15° C. 30° D. 45°

【考点分析】

- 观点冲突类文章,此题为简介题。
- 抓住定位词 *introduction*。
- 根据“Short-period comets have orbital periods of 200 yr or less, and their orbital planes have inclinations 30°...”,推断得出正确答案为 **D**。

(4) 例题练习 2.4

According to Scientist B, which of the following planets in our solar system is most likely capable of changing the orbit of a long-period comet over time?

F. Mercury G. Earth H. Mars J. Saturn

【考点分析】

- 观点冲突类文章,此题为单一观点题。
- 抓住定位词 *Scientist B*。
- 根据“Short-period comets were once long-period comets. Some long-period comets pass close enough to the giant planets (for example, Jupiter) to be influenced by the gravitational fields of the giant planets and are forced into orbits with orbital periods less than 200 yr”,综合信息可知解题关键为 giant planet,此处考察常识,在太阳系内有 4 颗气态巨行星:木星、土星、天王星和海王星。可以得出正确答案为 **J**。

(5) 例题练习 2.5

Comet Hailey currently has an orbital period of 76 yr. According to the information provided, Scientist B would most likely currently classify Comet Hailey as a:

A. short-period comet that originated in the Oort Cloud.

B. short-period comet that originated in the KB.

C. long-period comet that originated in the Oort Cloud.

D. long-period comet that originated in the KB.

【考点分析】

- 观点冲突类文章,此题为单一观点题。
- 抓住定位词 *Scientist B*。
- 根据“The KB does not exist. Short-period comets were once long-period comets”,结合前言“Short-period comets have orbital periods of 200 yr or less ”,直接得出正确答案为 **H**。

(6) 例题练习 2.6

Based on Scientist A's viewpoint, the “much larger icy bodies” in the KB most likely have diameters of:

F. less than 10 km. G. between 10 km and 20 km.

H. between 20 km and 30 km. J. greater than 30 km.

【考点分析】

- 观点冲突类文章，此题为单一观点题。
- 抓住定位词 *Scientist A*。
- 根据"The KB contains billions of icy bodies with diameters between 10 km and 30 km. These comet-size objects are too small to be clearly discerned at that distance with telescopes located on Earth's surface. Such telescopes have gathered indirect evidence, but not clear images, of much larger icy bodies that are part of the KB"，得出正确答案为 **J**。

(7) 例题练习 2.7

Suppose a study of 1 nearby star revealed that it had no spherical shell of material similar to the Oort Cloud surrounding it. How would this discovery most likely affect the scientists' viewpoints, if at all?

A. It would weaken Scientist A's viewpoint only.

B. It would strengthen Scientist B's viewpoint only.

C. It would strengthen both scientists' viewpoints.

D. It would have no effect on either scientist's viewpoint.

【考点分析】

- 观点冲突类文章，此题为综合观点题。
- 抓住关键词 *the Oort Cloud*。
- 根据全文信息，两位科学家的观点都未涉及到此内容，所以综合全篇得出正确答案为 **D**。

2）知识拓展 2

［八大行星］

八大行星特指太阳系的 8 颗行星，按照离太阳的距离从小到大，它们依次为水星(Mercury)、金星(Venus)、地球、火星(Mars)、木星(Jupiter)、土星(Saturn)、天王星(Uranus)、海王星(Neptune)。八大行星自转方向多数也和公转方向一致。只有金星和天王星两个例外。金星自转方向与公转方向相反。而天王星是在轨道上横滚的。而曾经被认为是"九大行星"之一的冥王星于 2006 年 8 月 24 日被定义为"矮行星"。八大行星的通常记法是：水金地火木土天海。行星定义：一是必须围绕恒星运转的天体；二是质量足够大，能依靠自身引力使天体呈圆球状；三是其轨道附近没有其他物体。

以行星表面岩质划分：

(1) 类地行星(又称岩质行星)：即水星、金星、地球和火星，表面是岩石固体。

(2) 类木行星(又称气体行星)：即木星、土星、天王星和海王星，主要成分是气体。

气态巨行星(Gas Giant)，有时称为类木行星(Jovian planet)，是不以岩石或其他固体为主要成分构成的大行星。在太阳系内有 4 颗气态巨行星：木星、土星、天王星和海王星。许多环绕恒星的系外行星已经被证实是气态巨行星。

3. 环境科学(Environment Science)

1）例题练习 3

大气中一氧化碳的浓度高于 0.1%时是有毒的。城市区域内，汽车是大气中一氧化碳的主要来源。天气越冷，一氧化碳浓度越高。一系列研究提出在汽车启动的前 15 分钟，在低温环境中比高温环境中排放更多的一氧化碳。学生做了下列实验研究该假设。

Experiment 1 实验 1

将一根软管连接到汽车的排气管上。启动引擎，将废气收集在一个塑料袋中。用注射器从废气中取出 1 毫升样本，将其注射到气相色谱仪中，色谱仪是将混合气体分离成各组成部分的仪器；比较废气和已知一氧化碳浓度确定废气中一氧化碳的体积百分比。废气每 2 分钟收集一次。来自

4 辆汽车的废气样本在外部温度为 − 9℃时测试。结果如表 1 所示。

Table 1

Time after starting (min)	Percent of CO in the exhaust at − 9℃			
	1978 model X	1978 model Y	1996 model X	1996 model Y
1	3.5	3.2	1.2	0.3
3	4.0	3.7	1.0	1.2
5	4.5	7.5	1.5	2.5
7	3.6	10.0	1.0	3.0
9	3.2	9.1	0.5	2.6
11	3.1	8.0	0.5	2.0
13	3.0	7.0	0.5	2.0
15	2.9	7.0	0.4	1.8

Experiment 2 实验 2

来自同样车的废气使用实验一相同的程序在外界温度为 20℃测试(见表 2)。

Table 2

Time after starting (min)	Percent of CO in the exhaust at 20℃			
	1978 model X	1978 model Y	1996 model X	1996 model Y
1	2.0	0.8	0.3	0.2
3	2.8	2.0	0.5	1.0
5	3.4	6.0	0.5	1.5
7	1.5	7.0	0.3	0.8
9	1.3	7.0	0.3	0.5
11	1.0	6.5	0.1	0.3
13	1.0	5.0	0.1	0.3
15	0.9	4.8	0.1	0.2

(1) 例题练习 3.1

Do the results from Experiment 1 support the hypothesis that, at a given temperature and time, the exhaust of newer cars contains lower percents of CO than the exhaust of older cars?

F. Yes; the highest percent of CO was in the exhaust of the 1996 Model Y.

G. Yes; both 1996 models had percents of CO that were lower than those of either 1978 model.

H. No; the highest percent of CO was in the exhaust of the 1978 Model Y.

J. No; both 1978 models had percents of CO that were lower than those of either 1996 model.

【考点分析】

● 实验总结类文章，此题为实验结果题。

● 抓住关键词 *Experiment 1*。

● 根据实验 1 中结果也就是表 1 中数据可以看出 1966 年的 Model X、Y 均比 1978 年对应的百分比要小，显然实验结果支持假设，得出正确答案为 **G**。

(2) 例题练习 3.2

A student, when using the gas chromatograph, was concerned that CO_2 in the exhaust sample may be interfering in the detection of CO. Which of the following procedures would best help the student investigate this problem?

A. Filling the bag with CO_2 before collecting the exhaust

B. Collecting exhaust from additional cars

C. Injecting a sample of air into the gas chromatograph

D. Testing a sample with known amounts of CO and CO_2

【考点分析】

● 实验总结类文章，此题为实验设计题。

● 抓住关键词 *CO_2 in the exhaust sample may be interfering in the detection of CO*。

● 直接根据题干推断，文章中的实验都是要检测 CO 的百分比，由于 CO_2 可能会影响 CO 的检测，那么我们需要确定此种可能性，为了解决这个问题，我们有必要去检测一个已知两种气体百分比的样本，这样可以获得 CO 的百分比是否会受影响，所以正确答案为 **D**。

(3) 例题练习 3.3

Based on the results of the experiments and the information in the table below, cars in which of the following cities would most likely contribute the greatest amount of CO to the atmosphere in January? (Assume that the types, numbers, and ages of cars used in each city are approximately equal.)

City	Average temperature (F) for january
Minneapolis	11.2
Pittsburgh	26.7
Seattle	39.1
San diego	56.8

F. Minneapolis G. Pittsburgh H. Seattle J. San Diego

【考点分析】

● 实验总结类文章，此题为实验结果题。

● 抓住关键词 *the results of the experiments*。

● 直接看到试验中两个表格数据，很明显 Table 1 的数据均高于 Table 2，同时表一设定温度 −9度，表格为 20 度，结合题干表格，正确答案为 **F**。

(4) 例题练习 3.4

In Experiment 1, which of the following factors varied?

A. The method of sample collection

B. The volume of exhaust that was tested

C. The year in which the cars were made

D. The temperature at which the engine was started

【考点分析】

● 实验总结类文章,此题为题。

● 抓住关键词 *Experiment 1*。

● 最简单的方法,用排除法,从实验 1 中可以看出 A、B、D 选项明显不是变量,所以正确答案为 **C**。

(5) 例题练习 3.5

Many states require annual testing of cars to determine the levels of their CO emissions. Based on the experiments, in order to determine the maximum percent of CO found in a car's exhaust, during which of the following times after starting a car would it be best to sample the exhaust?

F. 1 - 3 min   G. 5 - 7 min.   H. 9 - 11 min   J. 13 min or longer

【考点分析】

● 实验总结类文章,此题为实验结果题。

● 抓住关键词 *the maximum percent of CO*。

● 根据表格中数据中可以看到最大值出现在第五分钟或者第七分钟,据此推断要得到最大值,需在这个时间段中间来测量,所以正确答案为 **G**。

(6) 例题练习 3.6

How would the results of the experiments be affected, if at all, if the syringe contents were contaminated with CO-free air? (The composition of air is 78% N_2, 21% O_2, 0.9% Ar, and 0.1% other gases.) The measured percents of CO in the exhaust would be:

A. higher than the actual percents at both -90℃ and 20℃.

B. lower than the actual percents at -9℃, but higher than the actual percents at 20℃.

C. lower than the actual percents at both -9℃ and 20℃.

D. the same as the actual percents at both -9℃ and 20℃.

【考点分析】

● 实验总结类文章,此题为实验假设题。

● 抓住关键词 *if the syringe contents were contaminated with CO-free air*。

● 根据题干,假设收集的气体被污染了,并且是加入了不包含 CO 的气体,那么很显然在气体中 CO 所占比例变小了,而且此种影响与温度无关,所以正确答案为 **C**。

2) 知识拓展 3

[环境污染]

由于人们对工业高度发达的负面影响预料不够,预防不力,导致了全球性的三大危机:资源短缺、环境污染、生态破坏。环境污染指自然或人为地向环境中添加某种物质而超过环境的自净能力,从而产生危害的行为(或由于人为的因素,环境受到有害物质的污染,使生物的生长繁殖和人类的正常生活受到有害影响)。由于人为因素使环境的构成或状态发生变化,环境素质下降,从而扰乱和破坏了生态系统和人类的正常生产和生活条件的现象。

按环境要素分:大气污染、土壤污染、水体污染。

按属性分:显性污染,隐性污染。

按人类活动分:工业环境污染、城市环境污染、农业环境污染。

按造成环境污染的性质来源分:化学污染、生物污染、物理污染(噪声污染、放射性污染、电磁波污染等)固体废物污染、液体废物污染、能源污染。

(四) 实战练习 Practice

1) Practice 4

(57B Passage V)

海岸悬崖的岩石和沉积物常常因海浪侵蚀而流失。图 1 表明悬崖的组成成分、悬崖高度，以米为单位；和 1880—1970 年海岸线截面平均高潮面(MHWM)的净变化，以米为单位。平均高潮面的负变化表明了岩石或沉积物的净损失，净正变化表明沉积物的净增加。

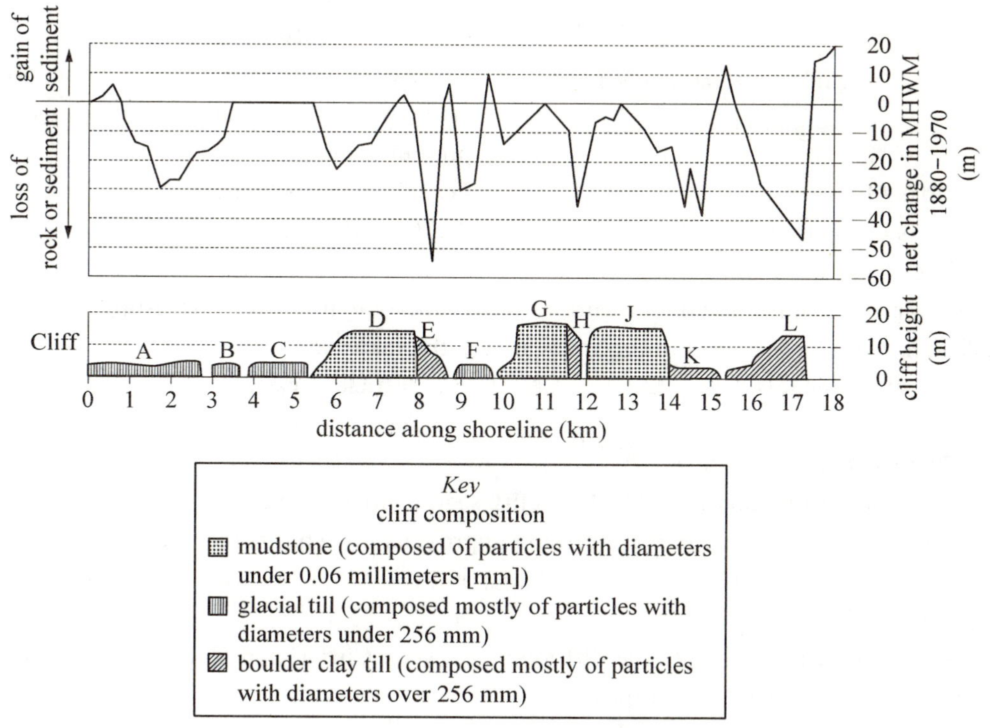

Figure 1

Table 1 shows the percentage of a year that vertical sections of a cliff are exposed to wave erosion.

Table 1

Cliff section height (m)	Percentage of a year cliff section is exposed to wave erosion
0.0 - 0.05	52.0
0.5 - 1.0	37.0
1.0 - 1.5	21.0
1.5 - 2.0	9.5
2.0 - 2.5	3.9
2.5 - 3.0	1.7
3.0 - 3.5	0.8
3.5 - 4.0	0.5

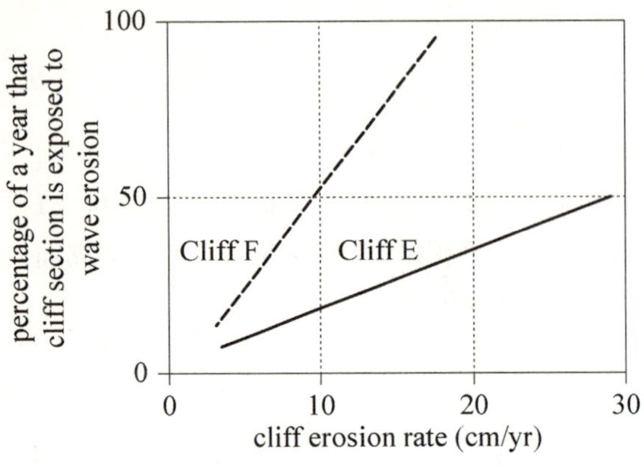

Figure 2

Figure 2 shows Cliff E and F erosion rates, in cm/yr as they relate to percentage of a year that a cliff section is exposed to wave erosion.

Figures and Table adapted from D. Jones and A. Williams Statistical Analysis of Factors Influencing Gliff Erosion Alonq a Section of the West Wales Coast, U.K." © 1991 by John Wilev and Sons, Ltd.

(1) Practice 4.1

According to Figure 1, at a distance of 12 km along the shoreline, cliffs of what composition are present if any?

F. Cliffs of glacial till
G. Cliffs of boulder clay till
H. Cliffs of mudstone
J. No cliffs are present.

(2) Practice 4.2

According to the information in Figure 1, one property that was used to distinguish the various materials that compose the cliffs in the study area is the materials':

A. particle diameters.
B. particle density.
C. color.
D. age.

(3) Practice 4.3

Based on the information in Table 1, a cliff section with a height of 4.0 – 4.5 m above the zero baseline would be exposed to wave erosion approximately what percentage of a year?

F. 10%
G. 2%
H. 0.8%
J. 0.3%

(4) Practice 4.4

According to Figures 1 and 2, the difference between Cliff E and Cliff F erosion rates could best be explained by a difference in the:

A. composition of the 2 cliffs.
B. force of waves on the 2 cliffs.
C. distance of the 2 cliffs along the shoreline.
D. annual rainfall on the 2 cliffs.

(5) Practice 4.5

According to Table 1, which of the following figures best represents the relationship between the height of a cliff section and the percentage of a year that a cliff section is exposed to wave erosion?

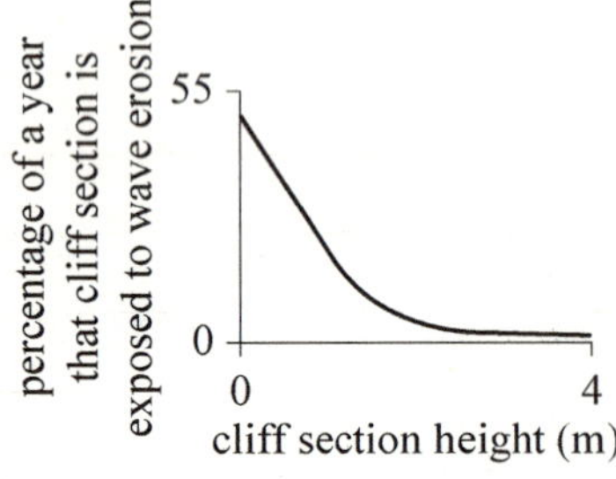

F.

percentage of a year that cliff section is exposed to wave erosion
55
0
0
4
cliff section height (m)

G.

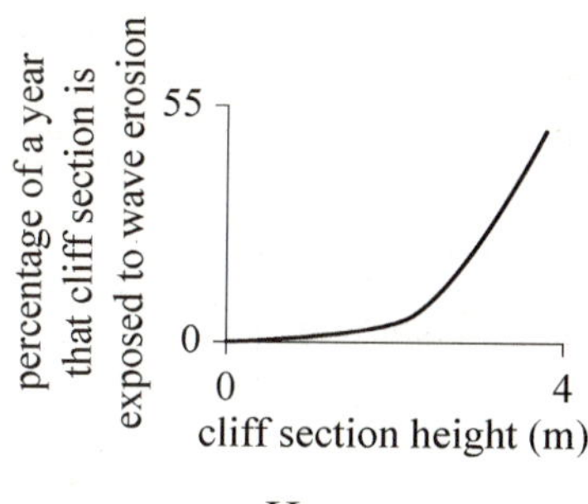

H.

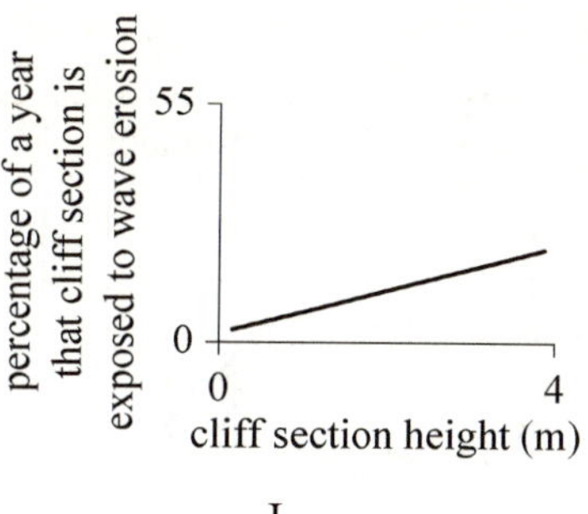

J .

2）Practice 5

（63E　Passage VII）

如图 1 所示，行星在椭圆轨道上围绕太阳运动。

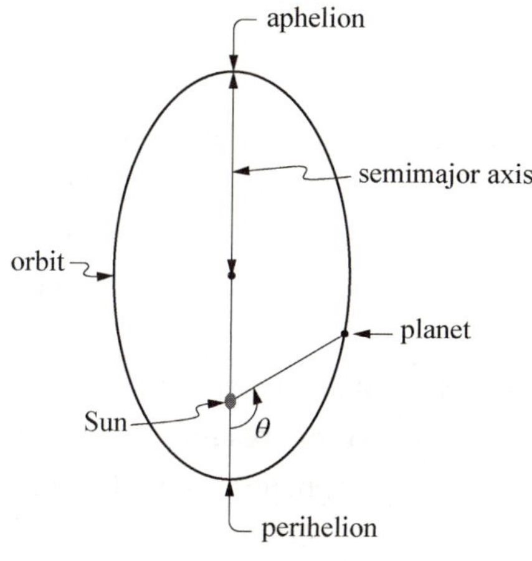

Figure 1

椭圆的离心率描述了它的伸长率；椭圆越狭长，离心率越大。半长轴是椭圆长的一半。

近日点（角 $\theta = 0^\circ$）是轨道上最靠近太阳的点；远日点（$\theta = 180^\circ$）是离太阳最远的点。行星的速度随着 θ 的变化而变化。对于不同的离心率和半长轴行星的速度与 θ 成反比，如图 2 所示。

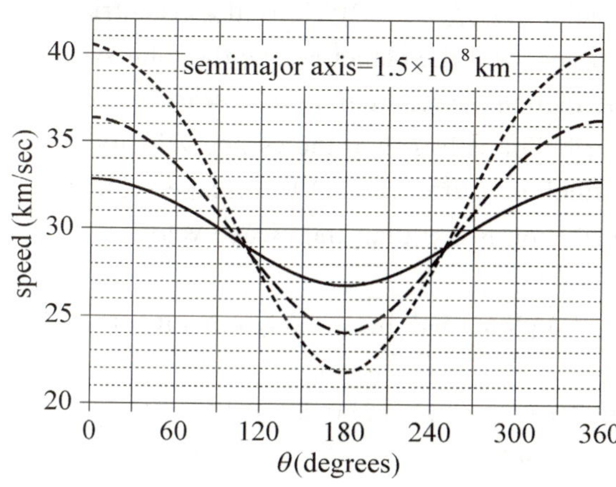

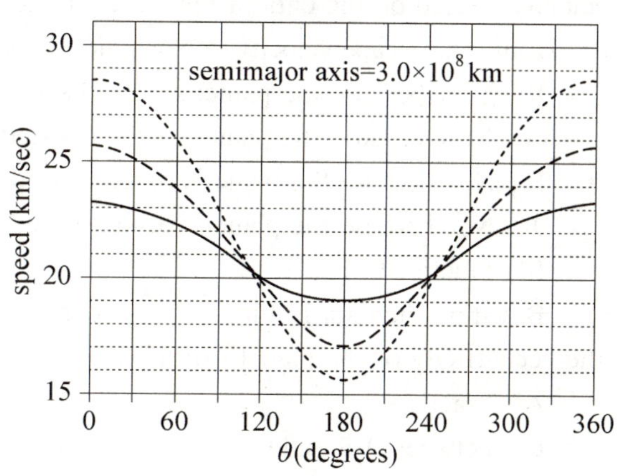

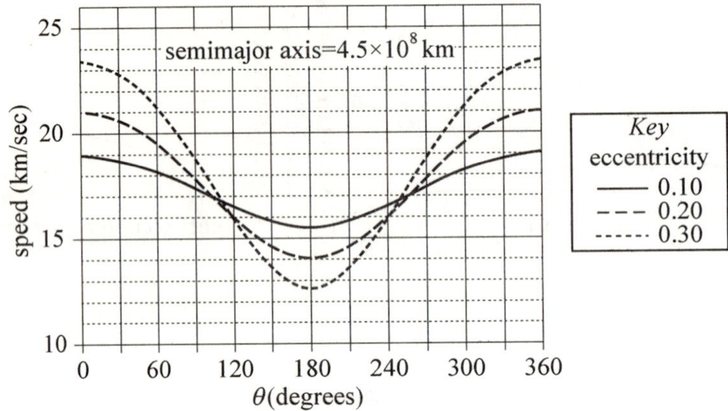

Figure 2

(1) Practice 5.1

Consider a planet as it travels from $\theta=0^\circ$ to $\theta=359^\circ$ in an orbit with a semimajor axis of 1.5×10^8 km and an eccentricity of 0.10. Based on the data in Figure 2, how many times does the planet have a speed of 30 km/sec as it travels between those 2 angles?

F. One time G. Two times H. Three times J. Four times

(2) Practice 5.2

Based on the data in Figure 2, how does the speed of a planet change while it moves from perihelion to aphelion and while it moves from aphelion to perihelion?

Perihelion to aphelion	Aphelion to perihelion
A. speed increases	speed increases
B. speed increases	speed decreases
C. speed decreases	speed increases
D. speed decreases	speed decreases

(3) Practice 5.3

A planet will escape from the solar system if its orbital speed is greater than the escape velocity. Based on the data in Figure 2, if the semimajor axis is 1.5×10^8 km, the eccentricity is 0.10, and the escape velocity at perihelion is 44.2 km/sec, will the planet escape the solar system?

F. Yes, because the planet's orbital speed at perihelion is greater than the escape velocity.

G. Yes, because the planet's orbital speed at perihelion is less than the escape velocity.

H. No, because the planet's orbital speed at perihelion is greater than the escape velocity.

J. No, because the planet's orbital speed at perihelion is less than the escape velocity.

(4) Practice 5.4

Based on the data in Figure 2, the orbital speed of a planet will most likely remain constant if the eccentricity of the planet's orbit is:

A. exactly 0. B. between 0.1 and 0.5.

C. between 0.5 and 0.9. D. exactly 1.

(5) Practice 5.5

Based on the data in Figure 2, for a planet in an orbit around the Sun with a semimajor axis of

3.0×10^8 km and an eccentricity of 0.05, the speed at $\theta=0°$ will be：

F. less than 23 km/sec.
G. between 23 km/sec and 26 km/sec.
H. between 26 km/sec and 28 km/sec.
J. greater than 28 km/sec.

3）Practice 6

两个研究测验在地球大气含氧气超过21%的晚古生代，森林火灾是如何燃烧的。

在试验中使用现代树类中的南洋杉树叶和松树木屑和松针，这是最近接古生代森林的标准树种。

Study 1 研究 1

10 毫克南洋杉树叶在大气氧含量为20%时以400℃/min 加热。在加热期间，大多数样本每2秒测量一次。这些程序在大气含氧量为35%的第二次试验时重复。每次试验使用10克纸代替南洋杉树叶重复试验(见图1)。物质损失比与燃烧率成正比。

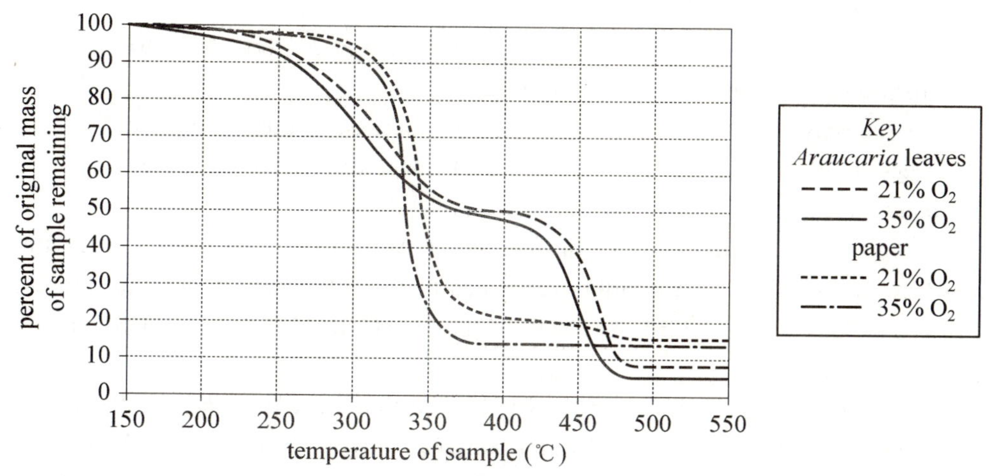

Figure 1

Study 2 研究 2

在每次试验中，75厘米长的燃烧室中填满来自松树的木屑或松针。每份木屑或松针样本已经脱水，然后吸水到西药的含水量。向燃烧室不断提供氧气和氮气混合气体。样本在燃烧室中的端口1点燃。

对于样品完全燃烧的试验，记录火焰的蔓延率。这些试验表明了森林火灾失去控制地燃烧的条件。记录试验中在燃烧室中的火焰在样本完全燃尽之前自己熄灭为燃烧失败(F)(见表1)。

Table 1

Water content of：		Flame spread rate (cm/min) in an atmosphere containing：			
		16% O_2	21% O_2	28% O_2	35% O_2
Dowels	2%	2.48	2.76	3.92	5.00
	12%	F	1.45	2.49	3.09
	23%	F	F	F	2.73
	61%	F	F	F	F

(续表)

Water content of:		Flame spread rate (cm/min) in an atmosphere containing:			
		16% O_2	21% O_2	28% O_2	35% O_2
Needles	2%	18.75	20.69	37.50	39.30
	12%	17.24	19.43	22.61	28.08
	23%	F	15.00	18.22	22.86
	61%	F	F	F	F

Note: %O_2 was by volume

Figure and table adapted from Richard Wildman et al., "Burning of Forest Materials under Late Paleozoic High Atmospheric Oxygen Levels," © 2004 by the Geological Society of America.

(1) Practice 6.1

According to the results of Study 2, as O_2 content increased from 16% to 35%, the flame spread rate for dowels having a water content of 2%:

A. increased only.
B. increased, then decreased.
C. decreased only.
D. decreased, then increased.

(2) Practice 6.2

According to the results of Study 1, the sample of Araucaria leaves heated in an atmosphere containing 35% O_2 lost mass most rapidly over which of the following temperature ranges?

F. 275℃ to 325℃ G. 325℃ to 375℃ H. 375℃ to 425℃ J. 425℃ to 475℃

(3) Practice 6.3

Suppose that the needles and wood of a type of tree that existed in the late Paleozoic era and closely resembled modern Pinus trees had water contents above 65% by weight. Based on Study 2, would a tree of that type have burned completely in an atmosphere containing 28% O_2 by volume and in an atmosphere containing 35% O_2 by volume, respectively?

	28% O_2	35% O_2
A.	No	Yes
B.	No	No
C.	Yes	No
D.	Yes	Yes

(4) Practice 6.4

Suppose that in an additional trial in Study 2, needles having a water content of 10% by weight had been burned in an atmosphere containing 28% O_2 by volume. Based on the results of Study 2, the flame spread rate recorded for that trial would most likely have been:

F. less than 18.22 cm/min.
G. between 18.22 cm/min and 22.61 cm/min.
H. between 22.61 cm/min and 37.5 cm/min.
J. greater than 37.5 cm/min.

(5) Practice 6.5

Consider a Paleozoic forest fire burning out of control in a stand of trees that closely resembled modem Pinus trees. Based on the results of Study 2 for an atmosphere containing 28% O_2 and an

atmosphere containing 35% O_2, is it more likely that the crown fire (fire spreading through the live foliage of trees) or the surface fire (fire spreading through the trees just above the ground) would have spread faster?

A. The crown fire, because the flame spread rates for needles were much lower than the corresponding rates for dowels.

B. The crown fire, because the flame spread rates for needles were much higher than the corresponding rates for dowels.

C. The surface fire, because the flame spread rates for needles were much lower than the corresponding rates for dowels.

D. The surface fire, because the flame spread rates for needles were the same as the corresponding rates for dowels.

(6) Practice 6.6

In Study 1, the paper sample heated in an atmosphere containing 21% O_2 had lost approximately what percent of its original mass by the time the temperature reached 350℃?

F. 20%　　G. 40%　　H. 60%　　J. 80%

Answers for Practice 4 - 6

Practice 4　J A J A F

Practice 5　G C J A F

Practice 6　A J B H B H

Session 5 化学 1

本章主要介绍ACT科学测试化学科目中的物质的构成、酸和碱和热化学三大分支学科，并通过解析例题，以及相应的练习题明确这三门学科的考试形式、考试重点和相关词汇。

(一) 学科背景

ACT科学测试主要考察和重点考察科学推理能力，了解相应的学科知识可以快速理解文章内容，提高解题速度。

1. 学科综述

1) 物质的构成(Properties of Matter)

基础化学，研究物质的成分。

2) 酸和碱(Acids and Bases)

研究pH值。

3) 热化学(Thermochemistry)

化学热力学的一个分支。中学化学中用“化学反应中的能量变化”来简单地介绍该内容。它用各种量热方法准确测量物理的、化学的以及生物的过程的热效应，从而根据热效应来研究有关现象及规律性。

2. 学科背景知识

1) 酸和碱

酸，电离时生成的阳离子全部是氢离子(H^+)的化合物叫做酸，25℃时，其稀溶液的**pH值小于7**。酸是一类化合物的统称。酸在化学中狭义的定义是，在水溶液中电离出的阳离子全部都是氢离子的化合物。由阿伦尼乌斯提出,此理论即为阿伦尼乌斯酸碱理论。广义定义是,能够接受电子对的物质。

碱,其水溶液的 **pH 值大于 7**。在水溶液中电离出的阴离子全部是氢氧根离子(今理论认为,电离时能吸收质子的物质为碱性,阴离子全为 OH^- 的为碱类,统称碱),与酸反应形成盐和水。碱的更广义的概念是指提供电子的物质,或是接受质子的物质。

2) 热化学

热化学的测量曾对物理化学的发展起过重要作用。热化学的数据(如燃烧热、生成热等)在热力学计算、工程设计和科学研究等方面都具有广泛的应用。热化学是研究物理和化学过程中热效应规律的学科。是化学的一支,也是物理学中热学在化学中的应用。

化学反应热效应:当生成物与反应物温度相同时,化学反应过程中的吸收或放出的热量。化学反应热效应一般称为反应热。注意必须具备以下条件才是化学反应热效应:

(1) 生成物的温度和反应物的温度相同,避免将使生成物温度升高或降低所引起的热量变化混入到反应热中。

(2) 只做体积功不做其他功。

(二) 学科单词

ACT 科学要求有一定的阅读量,文章中涉及大量的专业词汇,了解这些专业词汇的意思有助于理解文章和题意。以下是三门学科常见的专业词汇,考生需要熟悉单词的意思,以便在考试中能更准确地理解文章内容。

1. 酸和碱

英文	中文释义	英文	中文释义
nitrite	亚硝酸盐	isotope	同位素
ion	离子	parameter	参数
discoloration	褪色	ice core	冰芯
compound	混合物	glacial	冰川的;冰河的
solution	溶液	pore water	孔隙水
dilute	稀释	fen	沼泽
absorbance	吸收率	conductivity	导电率
soluble	可溶的	water table	地下水位
solute	溶质	bog	泥沼
mole	摩尔	peat layer	泥炭层
sucrose	蔗糖	solidify	凝固
sodium chloride	氯化钠;食盐	potassium	钾
boiling point	沸点	dry ice	干冰
freezing point	冰点	property	属性

2. 热化学

英文	中文释义	英文	中文释义
titrant	滴定标准液	calorimeter	热量计
probe	探针	sodium bromide	溴化钠

（续表）

英文	中文释义	英文	中文释义
acetic	醋;乙酸	peroxide	过氧化氢
titration	滴定法	formic acid	甲酸
dye	染料	oxidation	氧化
base	碱	induction period	诱导期;感应期
basic	碱性的	antioxidant	抗氧化剂
acid	酸性的	biodiesel	生物柴油
indicator	指示剂	colorimeter	色量计
well plate	孔板	vial	药水瓶
cluster	丛;簇	deicer	除冰剂
hydroxyl	羟基	compressive strengt	抗压强度
molar	摩尔的		

（三）例题解析

本节选取了三门学科的真题进行详细的解析，帮助考生迅速了解考试的形式、内容和解题思路。

1. 物质的构成(Properties of Matter)

1）例题练习 1

（OG1 Passage VII）

我们经常将包含亚硝酸离子的盐加入到肉类中来阻止由空气或细菌增长引起的褪色。亚硝酸离子的使用是有争议的，因为研究表明亚硝酸离子与癌症有关。学生进行了 2 个实验来计算亚硝酸离子的等级。

Experiment 1 实验 1

准备了四种溶液，每种溶液中都包含了不同量的亚硝酸钠(一种盐)。向溶液中加入一种有色的试剂，与亚硝酸离子结合形成一种紫色化合物能够强烈的吸收特定波长的光，并且每种溶液都被稀释到 100 mL。以同样的方式准备一种溶液，不加入任何亚硝酸钠。用色量计(用来计算一种选定波长的光被样品吸收的量)来计算每种溶液的吸收率。我们通过将每个读数减去空白溶液的吸收率来得到正确的结果(见表 1 和图 1)。

Table 1

Concentration of NO_2^- (ppm*)	Measured absorbance	Corrected absorbance
0.0	0.129	0.000
1.0	0.282	0.153
2.0	0.431	0.302
4.0	0.729	0.600 0
8.0	1.349	1.220

* ppm is parts per million

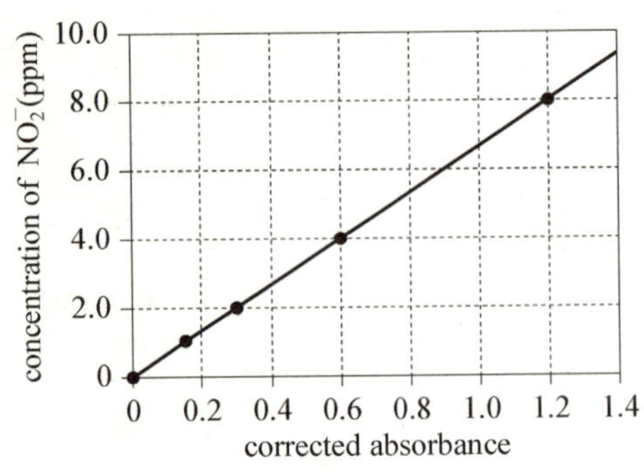

Figure 1

Experiment 2 实验 2

将 100 g 的肉样品放入一个盛有 50 mL 水的搅拌器中,并且将混合物过滤。然后用水冲洗搅拌器和剩余的肉,将冲洗的水过滤,并且将液体加入到样品溶液中去。加入有色的试剂并且将溶液稀释到 100 mL。这个过程重复几次,并且计算每个溶液的吸收率(见表 2)。

Table 2

Meat	Corrected absorbance	Concentration of NO_2^- (ppm)
Hot dog	0.667	4.4
Bologna	0.561	3.7
Ground turkey	0.030	0.2
Ham	0.940	6.2
Bacon	0.773	5.1

(1) 例题练习 1.1

Based on the results of Experiment 1, if the concentration of NO_2^- in a solution is doubled, then the corrected absorbance of the solution will approximately:

A. remain the same. B. halve. C. double. D. quadruple.

【考点分析】

- 实验总结类文章,此题为实验结果题。
- 抓住关键词 *Experiment 1 & if the concentration of NO_2^- in a solution is doubled*。

(2) 例题练习 1.2

A sample of pastrami was also measured in Experiment 2 and its corrected absorbance was determined to be 0.603. Which of the following correctly lists bologna, bacon, and pastrami in decreasing order of NO_2^- concentration?

F. Bologna, bacon, pastrami G. Pastrami, bacon, bologna

H. Bologna, pastrami, bacon J. Bacon, pastrami, bologna

【考点分析】

- 实验总结类文章,此题为实验结果题。
- 抓住关键词 *Experiment 2*。
- 题干给出的 pastrami 的 corrected absorbance 是 0.603,然后定位到第二个表格,Bologna 和 Bacon 的 corrected absorbance 分别为 0.561 和 0.773,将三组数据从高到低排序,即可得出答案,

由此可知正确答案为**J**。

(3) 例题练习 1.3

Based on the results of Experiment 1, if a solution with a concentration of 1.5 ppm NO_2^- had been tested, the corrected absorbance would have been closest to which of the following values?

A. 0.15　　B. 0.23　　C. 0.30　　D. 0.36

【考点分析】

- 实验总结类文章，此题为实验设计题。
- 抓住关键词 *a different coloring agent that produces a different color when it binds with NO_2^-*。
- 先要知道 coloring agent 的作用，根据文章信息"A coloring agent was added that binds with NO_2^- to form a purple compound that strongly absorbs light of a specific wavelength, and each solution was diluted to 100 mL. A blank solution was prepared in the same manner, but no $NaNO_2$ was added. A colorimeter device that measures how much light of a selected wavelength is absorbed by a sample was used to measure the absorbance of each solution"，由此可知正确答案为**J**。

(4) 例题练习 1.4

Based on the results of Experiments 1 and 2, if the measured absorbances for the meats tested in Experiment 2 were compared with their corrected absorbances, the measured absorbances would be:

A. higher for all of the meats tested.

B. lower for all of the meats tested.

C. lower for some of the meats tested, higher for others.

D. the same for all of the meats tested.

【考点分析】

- 实验总结类文章，此题为实验结果题。
- 抓住关键词 *corrected absorbances VS measured absorbances*。
- 根据表格 1 中数据可知，每一组数据中 corrected absorbances $<$ measured absorbances，由此可知正确答案为**A**。

(5) 例题练习 1.5

If some of the water-soluble contents found in all of the meats tested in Experiment 2 absorbed light of the same wavelength as the compund formed with NO_2^- and the coloring agent, how would the measurements have been affected? Compared to the actual NO_2^- concentrations, the NO_2^- concentrations apparently measured would be:

F. higher.

G. lower.

H. the same.

J. higher for some of the meats, lower for others.

【考点分析】

- 实验总结类文章，此题为实验假设题。
- 抓住关键词 *absorbed light of the same wavelength as the compund formed with NO_2^- and the coloring agent*。
- 根据题目信息我们可以知道，由于 water-soluble contents 吸收同样的波长，那么测量结果肯定会升高，由此可知正确答案为**F**。

2. 酸和碱(Acids and Bases)

1) 例题练习 2

酸碱滴定实验是一个将精确体积的滴定标准液(酸或碱溶液)加入到一个已知体积的样品溶液(碱或酸溶液,相对的)中的技术。显示这个过程可以通过向样品溶液中加入酸碱指示剂(一种可以在特定的 pH 值范围之间变色的物质)或者计算样品溶液的导电率。导电率(单位为 kS/cm)是对一种物质导电能力的度量。

我们进行了两个滴定实验,一种实验为 0.10 M 的氢氧化钠(NaOH)溶液和 0.001 0 M 氯化氢(HCl)溶液,另一种实验为 0.10 M 的氢氧化钠(NaOH)溶液和 0.001 0 M 的醋酸溶液(M 是每升溶液中酸或碱的摩尔数)。所有的溶液都是水溶液。另外,还要使用一种叫做"nitrazine yellow"的指示剂溶液。"nitrazine yellow"在 pH 值小于 6.0 时为黄色,pH 值大于 7.0 时为蓝色。

Experiment 1(实验 1)

将一滴 nitrazine yellow 溶液加入到盛有 100.0 mL 的 HCl 溶液的烧瓶中。一个用来测量导电率的探针放在溶液中。每次向 HCl 溶液中加入少量的 NaOH 溶液。每次加入 NaOH 溶液后,搅拌 HCl 溶液,然后记录溶液的颜色和导电率(见图 1)。

Experiment 2(实验 2)

将实验 1 重复,除了将 HCl 溶液替换为醋酸溶液之外全部相同(见图 2)。

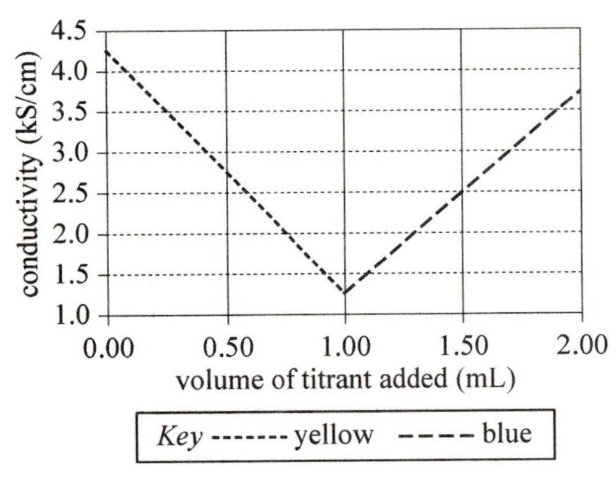

Figure 1

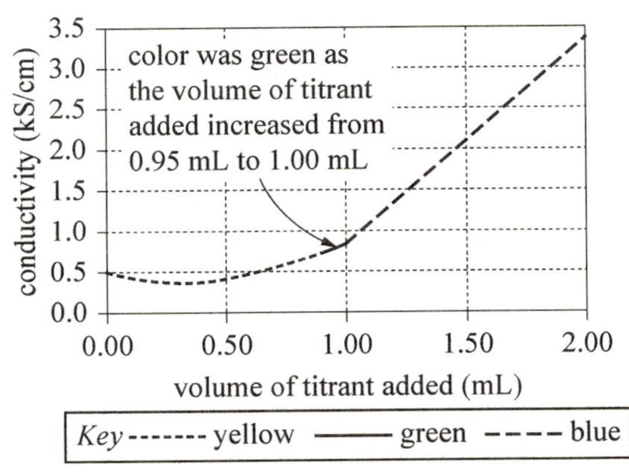

Figure 2

Figures adapted from J. West Loveland, "Conductance and Oscillometry," in Gary D. Christian and James E. O'Reilly, eds., Instrumental Analysis, 2nd ed.© 1986 by Allyn and Bacon, Inc.

(1) 例题练习 2.1

In Experiment 1, the sample solution was yellow at which of the following values for the volume of titrant added?

F. 0.80 mL　　G. 1.20 mL　　H. 1.60 mL　　J. 2.00 mL

【考点分析】

- 实验总结类文章,此题为实验结果题。
- 抓住定位词 *Experiment 1*。
- 直接定位到第 1 个实验,根据 Figure 1 中来看,当滴定液加入小于 1.00 mL 的时候,溶液一直是 yellow,很显然正确答案为 **F**。

(2) 例题练习 2.2

In Experiment 2, the sample solution was neutral at which of the following values for the volume of titrant added?

A．0.50 mL　　B．1.00 mL　　C．1.50 mL　　D．2.00 mL

【考点分析】

● 实验总结类文章，此题为实验结果题。

● 抓住定位词 *Experiment 2*。

● 直接定位到第 2 个实验，根据 Figure 2 中来看，当滴定液加入为 0.95～1.00 mL 的时候，溶液颜色是 green，很显然此时 pH 值约为 7，溶液为中性，正确答案为 **B**。

(3) 例题练习 2.3

In Experiment 1, if 2.30 mL of titrant had been added to the sample solution, the conductivity would most likely have been:

F．less than 0.80 kS/cm.

G．between 0.80 kS/cm and 2.30 kS/cm.

H．between 2.30 kS/cm and 3.80 kS/cm.

J．greater than 3.80 kS/cm.

【考点分析】

● 实验总结类文章，此题为实验结果题。

● 抓住定位词 *Experiment 1*。

● 直接定位到第 1 个实验，根据 Figure 1 中来看，当滴定液加入 1.00 mL 以后，溶液开始变 blue，并且这之后随着滴定液的加入，conductivity 的值也随着递增，当加入 2.00 mL 时，conductivity 的值约为 3.8 左右，那么当加入 2.3 mL 滴定液时，数值还要大。很显然正确答案为 **J**。

(4) 例题练习 2.4

In Experiment 2, which solution was the titrant solution and which solution was the sample solution?

A．acetic acid　　NaOH

B．HCl　　NaOH

C．NaOH　　acetic acid

D．NaOH　　HCl

【考点分析】

● 实验总结类文章，此题为实验用具题。

● 抓住定位词“实验 2”。

● 直接定位到第 2 个实验，根据“Experiment 1 was repeated, except that the acetic acid solution was used instead of the HCl solution ”，同时根据实验 1 可知，滴定液为 NaOH，很显然正确答案为 **C**。

(5) 例题练习 2.5

In Experiments 1 and 2, the probe that was placed in the sample solution most likely did which of the following?

F．Cooled the solution to its freezing point

G．Heated the solution to its boiling point

H．Detected the concentration of nitrazine yellow in the solution

J．Passed an electrical current through a portion of the solution

【考点分析】

- 实验总结类文章,此题为实验用具题。
- 抓住定位词 *Experiment 1 and 2*,关键词为 *the probe*。
- 先定位到第一个实验,根据"A probe that measures conductivity was placed in the solution",很显然正确答案为 **J**。

(6) 例题练习 2.6

A chemist claimed that in Experiment 2, the pH of the sample solution was greater at a value of 0.2 mL of titrant added than at a value of 1.8 mL of titrant added. Do the results of Experiment 2 support this claim?

A. No; at a value of 0.2 mL of titrant added, the sample solution was yellow, and at a value of 1.8 mL of titrant added, the sample solution was blue.

B. No; at a value of 0.2 mL of titrant added, the sample solution was blue, and at a value of 1.8 mL of titrant added, the sample solution was yellow.

C. Yes; at a value of 0.2 mL of titrant added, the sample solution was yellow, and at a value of 1.8 mL of titrant added, the sample solution was blue.

D. Yes; at a value of 0.2 mL of titrant added, the sample solution was blue, and at a value of 1.8 mL of titrant added, the sample solution was yellow.

【考点分析】

- 实验总结类文章,此题为实验结果题。
- 抓住定位词 *Experiment 2*。
- 直接定位到第二个实验,根据 Figure 2 中来看,当滴定液加入为 0.2 mL 的时候,溶液颜色是 yellow,结合前言可知此时 pH 值小于 6.0,当滴定液加入为 1.8 mL 时,溶液是 blue,此时 pH 值大于 7,综合可知前种情况 pH 小于后者,实验结果不符合题干的观点,很显然正确答案为 **A**。

2) 知识拓展 2

[酸碱中和滴定]

酸碱中和滴定,是用已知物质量浓度的酸(或碱)来测定未知物质的量浓度的碱(或酸)的方法。实验中用甲基橙、甲基红、酚酞等做酸碱指示剂来判断是否完全中和。酸碱中和滴定是一种化学测量方法,系以强酸或强碱滴定碱或酸溶液,由滴定曲线图或指示剂颜色变化判定滴定终点,它可以粗略地测定出未知溶液的浓度。它是一种早期的测定未知溶液浓度的方法。

原理:酸碱指示剂的变色。人们在实践中发现,有些有机染料在不同的酸碱性溶液中能显示不同的颜色。于是,人们就利用它们来确定溶液的 pH。这种借助其颜色变化来指示溶液 pH 的物质叫做酸碱指示剂。

酸碱指示剂一般是有机弱酸或有机弱碱。它们的变色原理是由于其分子和电离出来的离子的结构不同,因此分子和离子的颜色也不同。在不同 pH 的溶液里,由于其分子浓度和离子浓度的比值不同,因此显示出来的颜色也不同。例如,石蕊是一种有机弱酸,它是由各种地衣制得的一种蓝色色素。

3. 热化学(Thermochemistry)

1) 例题练习 3

我们用一个炸弹热量计来测量一个物质在氧气中燃烧所放出的热量(见图 1)。通过在炸弹热量计中的水的温度的改变来计算释放出的热量,测量的单位为千焦(kJ)。表 1 显示了在炸弹热量计中不同物质燃烧所放出的热量。表 2 显示了不同量的蔗糖燃烧放出的热量。表 3 显示了不同化合物燃烧所释放出的热量。

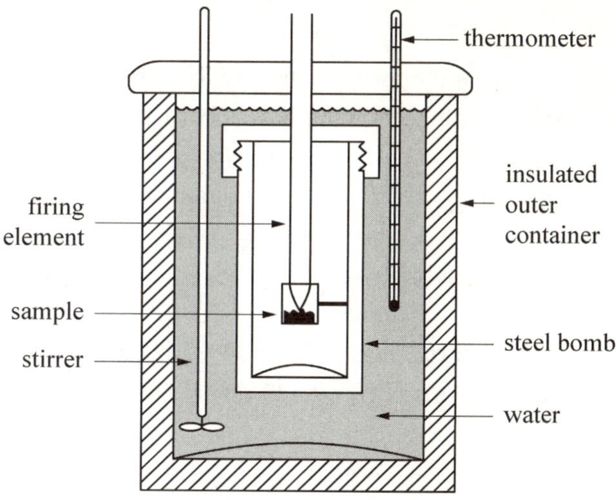

Figure 1

Figure 1 adapted from Antony C. Wilbraham, Dennis D. Staley, and Michael S. Matta, Chemistry. © 1995 by Addison-Wesley Publishing Company, Inc.

Table 1

Food	Mass (g)	Change in water temperature (℃)	Heat released (kJ)
Bread	1.0	8.3	10.0
Cheese	1.0	14.1	17.0
Egg	1.0	5.6	6.7
Potato	1.0	2.7	3.2

Table 1 adapted from American Chemical Society, ChemCom: Chemistry in the Community. © 1993 by American Chemical Society.

Table 2

Amount of sucrose (g)	Heat released (kJ)
0.1	1.6
0.5	8.0
1.0	16.0
2.0	32.1
4.0	64.0

Table 3

Chemical compound	Molecular formula	Mass (g)	Heat released (kJ)
Methanol	CH_3OH	0.5	11.4
Ethanol	C_2H_5OH	0.5	14.9
Benzene	C_6H_6	0.5	21.0
Octane	C_8H_{18}	0.5	23.9

(1) 例题练习 3.1

According to Tables 1 and 2, as the mass of successive sucrose samples increased, the change in the water temperature produced when the sample was burned most likely:

F. increased only. G. decreased only.

H. increased, then decreased. J. remained the same.

【考点分析】

● 数据表述类文章,此题为数据推理题。

● 抓住定位词 *Tables 1 and 2*。

● 先看 Table 1,从中我们可以看到温度改变越大,热量释放越多,然后看 Table 2,可知质量越大,热量释放越多,据此可得出以下关系:只有越大,热量释放越多,温度改变越大,直接得出正确答案为 **F**。

(2) 例题练习 3.2

Which of the following graphs best illustrates the relationship between the heat released by the foods listed in Table 1 and the change in water temperature?

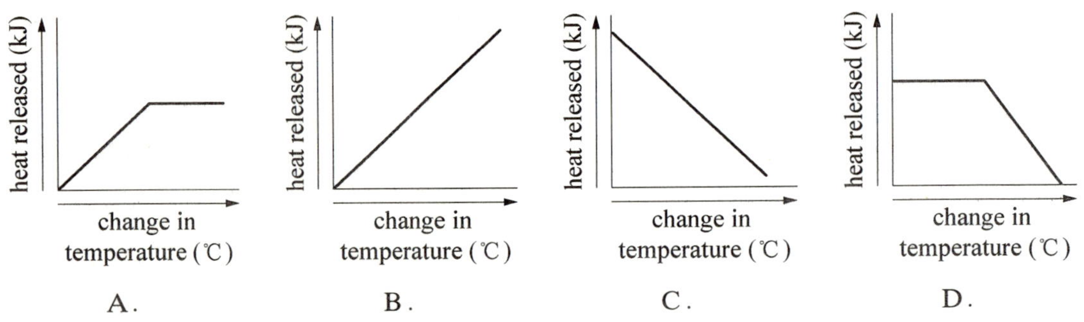

【考点分析】

● 数据表述类文章,此题为数据查找与之对应关系题。

● 抓住定位词 *Table 1*。

● 先看 Table 1,从中我们可以看到温度改变越大,热量释放越多,直接得出两者关系为正比例,很显然正确答案为 **B**。

(3) 例题练习 3.3

Based on the data in Table 2, one can conclude that when the mass of sucrose is decreased by one-half, the amount of heat released when it is burned in a bomb calorimeter will:

F. increase by one-half. G. decrease by one-half.

H. increase by one-fourth. J. decrease by one-fourth.

【考点分析】

● 数据表述类文章,此题为数据查找题。

● 抓住定位词 *Table 2*。

● 先看 Table 2,从中我们可以看到质量增加多少倍,热量释放也增加多少倍,所以很快得出正确答案为 **G**。

(4) 例题练习 3.4

Which of the following lists the foods from Tables 1 and 2 in increasing order of the amount of heat released per gram of food?

A. Potato, egg, bread, sucrose, cheese B. Sucrose, cheese, bread, egg, potato

C. Bread, cheese, egg, potato, sucrose　　D. Sucrose, potato, egg, bread, cheese

【考点分析】

- 数据表述类文章,此题为数据对比题。
- 抓住定位词 *Tables 1 and 2*。
- 先看 Table 1,我们将释放热量从低到高排序,得到 potato, egg, bread, cheese 序列,再看 Table 2,找到对应质量的 sucrose 释放的热量为 16 kJ,大于 bread 的小于 cheese 的,故正确答案为 **A**。

(5) 例题练习 3.5

Based on the information in Tables 1 and 2, the heat released from the burning of 5.0 g of potato in a bomb calorimeter would be closest to which of the following?

F. 5 kJ　　G. 10 kJ　　H. 15 kJ　　J. 20 kJ

【考点分析】

- 数据表述类文章,此题为数据查找之关系题。
- 抓住定位词 *Tables 1 and 2*。
- 先看 Table 1,表中所列为质量为 1 g 的各种食物燃烧释放的热量和温度改变,然后看 Table 2,从表中可以看到燃烧物的质量和释放的温度基本上成正比例关系,那么从表一中得出 1 g 的 potato 然后放热 3.2 kJ,那么可知 5 g potato 释放的热量约为此数据的 5 倍,约为 16 kJ,可得出正确答案为 **H**。

2) 知识拓展 3

[燃烧]

燃烧是一种放热发光的化学反应,其反应过程极其复杂,游离基的链锁反应是燃烧反应的实质,光和热是燃烧过程中发生的物理现象。发生燃烧必须具备三个条件,即可燃物、助燃物(氧化剂)、达到燃烧点。

燃烧的一般性化学定义:通常情况下,燃烧是一种发光、发热、剧烈的氧化反应。燃烧是可燃物跟助燃物(氧化剂)发生的一种剧烈的、发光、发热的化学反应。燃烧的广义定义:燃烧是指任何发光发热的剧烈的化学反应,不一定要有氧气参加。比如金属钠(Na)和氯气(Cl_2)反应生成氯化钠(NaCl),该反应没有氧气参加,但是属于剧烈的发光发热的化学反应,同样属于燃烧范畴。(注:核燃料"燃烧",轻核的聚变和重核的裂变都是发光、发热的"核反应",而不是化学反应,不属于燃烧范畴。)

化学变化中的爆炸指物质在有限的空间,瞬间急剧氧化或分解反应产生大量的热和气体,并以巨大压力急剧向四周扩散和冲击而发生巨大响声的现象。可燃气体、蒸气或粉末与空气组成的混合物遇火源能发生爆炸的浓度称爆炸极限,其最低浓度称为爆炸下限,最高浓度称为爆炸上限。低于下限的遇明火既不爆炸也不燃烧,高于上限的,虽不爆炸,但可燃烧。

(四) 实战练习 Practice

1) Practice 4

对水中存在的氧的同位素的研究能够给我们关于当地天气的线索。将雨、雪或冰中的同位素 ^{16}O和^{18}O 的比例与标准样品中^{18}O 和^{16}O 的比例相比较。标准样品有已知的参数测量的值。样品比例与标准比例的比较称为 O－18 指数($\delta^{18}O$)。我们用下面的公式来计算 $\delta^{18}O$。

$$\delta^{18}O=\frac{\left(\frac{^{18}O}{^{16}O}\right)_{sample}-\left(\frac{^{18}O}{^{16}O}\right)_{standard}}{\left(\frac{^{18}O}{^{16}O}\right)_{standard}}\times 1\,000$$

科学家进行了 3 个研究来检查北极和南极冰川中的冰的 $\delta^{18}O$ 值并且了解了那里过去的气候情况。

Study 1 研究 1

将容器分别放置在北极 25 个不同地点的冰川上来收集降雪。在一年的周期中每 2 周收集一次容器中的降雪，并分析 ^{16}O 和 ^{18}O。图 1 显示了每个月的 ^{18}O 值和平均气温。

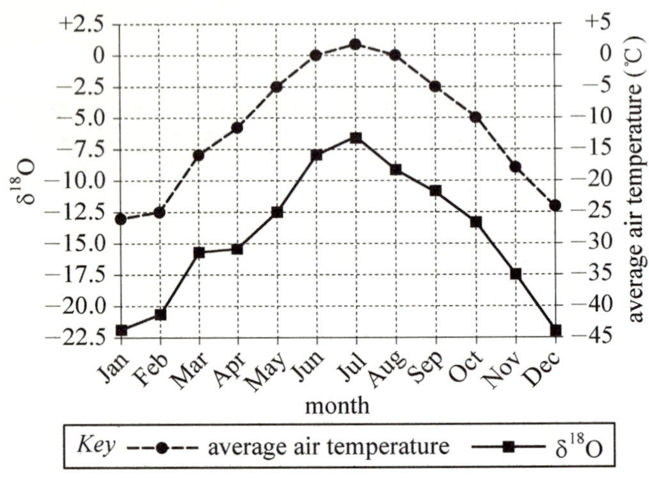

Figure 1

Study 2 研究 2

在研究 1 中北极 25 个地点，每个地点钻了一个 500 m 垂直深度的冰芯。每一个冰芯代表了这个位置在过去 100 000 年中冰川的聚集。从冰川的表面开始，沿着冰芯的长度每隔 10 m 取样。这些样品用来分析 ^{18}O 和 ^{16}O 的值。较大的 ^{18}O 值表明在这个时期的相对气温要比 $\delta^{18}O$ 值小的时期的气温更温暖。图 2 显示了样品中计算的 $\delta^{18}O$ 平均值。

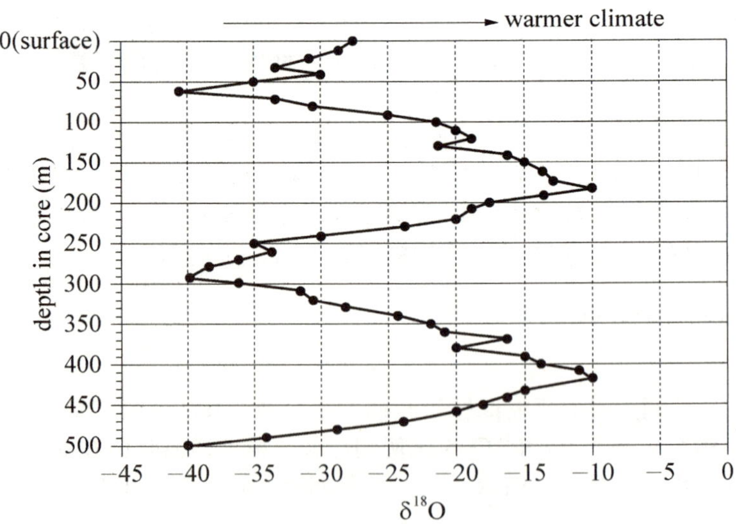

Figure 2

Study 3 研究 3

将研究 2 中的过程在南极的 25 个地区重复进行。用一个 300 m 的冰芯来代表这个位置过去 100 000 年的冰川聚集。图 3 显示了样品中计算的^{18}O的平均值。

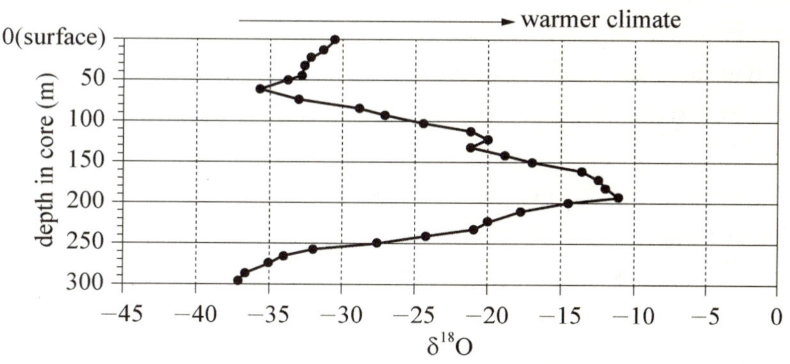

Figure 3

(1) Practice 4.1

According to Study 1, average air temperatures in the Arctic were closest for which of the following pairs of months?

A. January and March
B. March and September
C. May and September
D. October and December

(2) Practice 4.2

According to Study 1, which of the following best describes the relationship between the $\delta^{18}O$ of the Arctic snow samples and the average monthly air temperatures? As the average monthly air temperatures increased, then decreased, the $\delta^{18}O$:

F. increased only.
G. increased, then decreased.
H. decreased only.
J. decreased, then increased.

(3) Practice 4.3

Which of the following statements best describes why sites, in the Arctic and Antarctic were chosen for these studies? These sites had to have:

A. average air temperatures below −25℃ year-round.
B. glaciers present at many different locations.
C. several months during the year in which no precipitation fell.
D. large areas of bare soil and rock present.

(4) Practice 4.4

According to Study 2, the ice found in the Arctic core at depths between 150 m and 200 m was formed during a period when the climate in the Arctic was most likely:

F. somewhat cooler than the present climate in the Arctic.
G. the same as the present climate in the Arctic.
H. the same as the present climate in the Antarctic.
J. somewhat warmer than the present climate in the Arctic.

(5) Practice 4.5

According to Studies 2 and 3, 100,000 years of ice accumulation was represented by a 500 m core in the Arctic and a 300 m core in the Antarctic. Which of the following statements best explains why the ice cores were different lengths? The average rate of glacial ice accumulation over that time period in the Arctic:

A. was greater than the rate in the Antarctic.

B. was the same as the rate in the Antarctic.

C. was less than the rate in the Antarctic.

D. could not be determined with any accuracy.

(6) Practice 4.6

According to the information provided, a sample that had a calculated $\delta^{18}O$ of zero had a $^{18}O/^{16}O$ value that compared in which of the following ways to the $^{18}O/^{16}O$ value of the standard sample? The sample's $^{18}O/^{16}O$ ratio was:

F. of the $^{18}O/^{16}O$ ratio of the standard.

G. the same as the $^{18}O/^{16}O$ ratio of the standard.

H. 1 times larger than the $^{18}O/^{16}O$ ratio of the standard.

J. twice as large as the $^{18}O/^{16}O$ ratio of the standard.

2) Practice 5

A typical acid-base indicator is a compound that will be one color over a certain lower pH range but will be a different color over a certain higher pH range. In the small range between these pH ranges—the transition range—the indicator's color will be an intermediate of its other 2 colors. Students studied 5 acid-base indicators using colorless aqueous solutions of different pH and a well plate (a plate containing a matrix of round depressions—wells—that can hold small volumes of liquid).

Experiment 1

The students added a pH = 0 solution to 5 wells in the first column of the well plate, then added a pH = 1 solution to the 5 wells in the next column, and so on, up to pH = 7. Next, they added a drop of a given indicator (in solution) to each of the wells in a row, and then repeated this process, adding a different indicator to each row. The color of the resulting solution in each well was then recorded in Table 1.

(B = blue, G = green, O = orange, P = purple, R = red, Y = yellow).

Table 1

Indicator	Color in solution with a pH of:							
	0	1	2	3	4	5	6	7
Metanil yellow	R	R	O	Y	Y	Y	Y	Y
Resorcin blue	R	R	R	R	R	P	P	B
Curcumin	Y	Y	Y	Y	Y	Y	Y	Y
Hessian Bordeaux	B	B	B	B	B	B	B	B
Indigo carmine	B	B	B	B	B	B	B	B

Experiment 2

Experiment 1 was repeated with solutions that had a pH of 8 or greater (see Table 2).

Table 2

Indicator	Color in solution with a pH of :						
	8	9	10	11	12	13	14
Metanil yellow	Y	Y	Y	Y	Y	Y	Y
Resorcin blue	B	B	B	B	B	B	B
Curcumin	O	R	R	R	R	R	R
Hessian Bordeaux	B	R	R	R	R	R	R
Indigo carmine	B	B	B	B	G	Y	Y

Experiment 3

Students were given 4 solutions (Solutions 1 - IV) of unknown pH. The well plate was used to test samples of each solution with 4 of the 5 indicators (see Table 3).

Table 3

Indicator	Color in solution:			
	I	II	III	IV
Metanil yellow	Y	Y	Y	O
Resorcin blue	B	B	R	R
Curcumin	R	R	Y	Y
Indigo carmine	B	Y	B	B

Tables adapted from David R. Lide, ed., CRC Handbook of Chemistry and Physics, 78th ed. © 1997 by CRC Press LLC.

(1) Practice 5.1

One way Experiment 2 differed from Experiment 3 was that in Experiment 2:

A. the solutions to which indicators were added were of known pH.

B. the solutions to which indicators were added were of unknown pH.

C. metanil yellow was used.

D. metanil yellow was not used.

(2) Practice 5.2

Based on the description of the well plate and how it was used, the empty well plate would most likely have been which of the following colors?

F. Black G. Blue H. Red J. White

(3) Practice 5.3

Based on the results of Experiments 1 and 2, which of the following is a possible transition range for curcumin?

A. pH = 3.9 to pH = 7.3 B. pH = 4.2 to pH = 6.6

C. pH = 7.4 to pH = 8.6 D. pH = 8.4 to pH = 9.5

(4) Practice 5.4

A chemist has 2 solutions, one of pH = 1 and one of pH = 6. Based on the results of Experiments 1 and 2, could indigo carmine be used to distinguish between these solutions?

F. No; indigo carmine is blue at both pH = 1 and pH = 6.

G. No; indigo carmine is blue at pH = 1 and is yellow at pH = 6.

H. Yes; indigo carmine is blue at both pH = 1 and pH = 6.

J. Yes; indigo carmine is blue at pH = 1 and is yellow at pH = 6.

(5) Practice 5.5

A student claimed that Solution III has a pH of 7.3. Arc the results of Experiments 1 - 3 consistent with this claim?

A. No, because in Solution III metanil yellow was yellow.

B. No, because in Solution III resorcin blue was red.

C. Yes, because in Solution III metanil yellow was yellow.

D. Yes, because in Solution III resorcin blue was red.

(6) Practice 5.6

Based on the results of Experiments 1 - 3, which of Solutions I - IV has the lowest pH?

F. Solution I　　G. Solution II

H. Solution III　　J. Solution IV

3) Practice 6

Pore water is water in the pores of subsurface material. Pore water chemistry in 2 wetlands-a fen and a bog was studied during a 1990 summer drought and again the next summer, which had normal rainfall. The primary water supplies for fens and bogs are, respectively, ground-water and rainfall. Figure 1 shows the methane CH_4 gas concentration in the pore water at various depths in the fen and the bog. Figures 2 and 3 show the pore water conductivity (which is directly proportional to the concentration of dissolved ions) and pH at various depths in the fen and the bog, respectively. Also shown are the locations of the water table, the peat (partially decomposed plant material) layer, and the mineral soil layer.

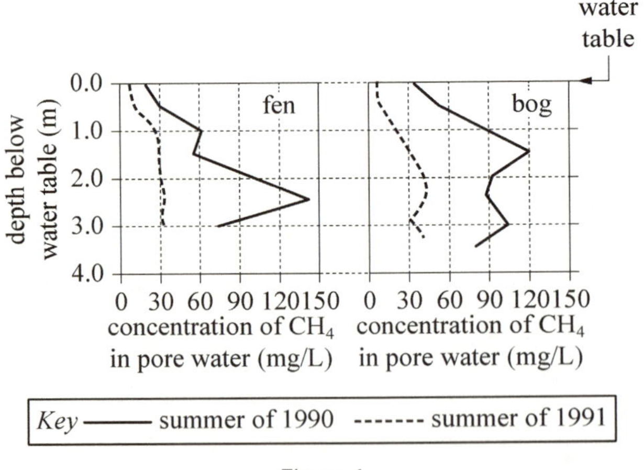

Figure 1

(1) Practice 6.1

According to Figure 2, the conductivity of fen pore water in 1990 at a depth of 2.5 m was closest to which of the following?

A. 350 μmho/cm　　B. 475 μmho/cm　　C. 600 μmho/cm　　D. 725 μmho/cm

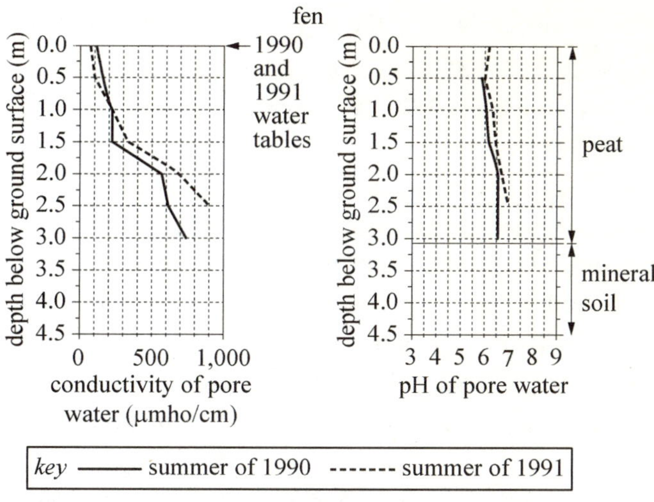

Figure 2

Note: Mineral soil is composed mainly of mineral matter.

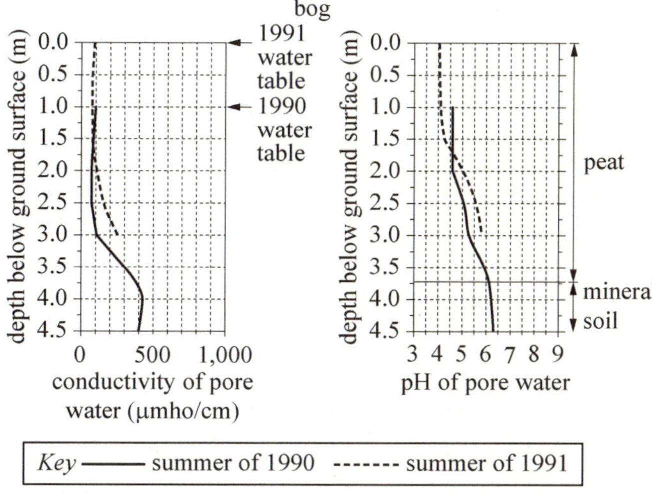

Figure 3

Note: Mineral soil is composed mainly of mineral matter.

(2) Practice 6.2

Based on Figure 2, if the pH of pore water in the fen at a depth of 2.7 m had been measured in the summer of 1991, it would most likely have been closest to which of the following?

F. 4.0　　G. 5.5　　H. 7.0　　J. 8.5

(3) Practice 6.3

Which of the following is the most likely explanation for the difference in the depth of the bog water table in the 2 years?

A. The amount of groundwater discharged to the bog was higher during the drought, and therefore the bog received more water than normal.

B. The amount of groundwater discharged to the bog was higher during the drought, and therefore the bog received less water than normal.

C. The amount of rainfall received by the bog was higher during the drought, and therefore the bog' received more water than normal.

D. The amount of rainfall received by the bog was lower during the drought, and therefore the bog received less water than normal.

(4) Practice 6.4

If the data in Figures 2 and 3 are typical of fens and bogs in general, one would most likely make which of the following conclusions about the peat layer in a fen and in a bog?

F. The peat layer in both a fen and a bog is completely above the water table at all times.

G. The peat layer in both a fen and a bog is completely below the water table at all times.

H. The peat layer in a fen is thicker than the peat layer in a bog.

J. The peat layer in a fen is thinner than the peat layer in a bog.

(5) Practice 6.5

According to Figure 1, the average concentration of CH_4 over the depths from 0.0 m to 3.0 m was higher during the summer of:

A. normal rainfall than during the summer of drought in both wetlands.

B. normal rainfall than during the summer of drought in the fen only.

C. drought than during the summer of normal rainfall in both wetlands.

D. drought than during the summer of normal rainfall in the bog only.

Answers for Practice 4 - 6

Practice 4　C G B J A G

Practice 5　A J C F B J

Practice 6　C H D J C

Session 6　化学 2

本章主要介绍 ACT 科学测试化学科目中的化学方程式、化学反应速率和有机化学三大分支学科，并通过解析例题，以及相应的练习题明确这三门学科的考试形式、考试重点和相关词汇。

(一) 学科背景

ACT 科学测试主要考察和重点考察科学推理能力，了解相应的学科知识可以快速理解文章内容，提高解题速度。

1. 学科综述

1) 化学方程式和反应速率(Chemical Equation & Rate)

化学方程式，也称为化学反应方程式，是用化学式表示化学反应的式子。化学方程式反映的是客观事实。因此书写化学方程式要遵守两个原则：**一是必须以客观事实为基础；二是要遵守质量守恒定律。**

化学反应速率就是化学反应进行的快慢程度(平均反应速率)，用单位时间内反应物或生成物的物质的量来表示。在容积不变的反应容器中，通常用单位时间内反应物浓度的减少或生成物浓度的增加来表示。

2) 有机化学(Organic Chemistry)

有机化学是研究有机化合物及有机物质的结构、性质、反应的学科，是化学中极重要的一个分支。有机化学研究的对象是以不同形式包含碳原子的物质，又称为碳化合物的化学。

2. 学科背景知识

1）化学反应

分子分解成原子，原子重新排列组合生成新物质的过程，称为化学反应。在反应中常伴有发光、发热、变色、生成沉淀物等，判断一个反应是否为化学反应的依据是反应是否生成新的物质。

按反应物与生成物的类型分四类：化合反应、分解反应、置换反应、复分解反应；按电子得失可分为：氧化还原反应、非氧化还原反应。

用化学式（有机化学中有机物一般用结构简式）来表示物质化学反应的式子，叫做化学方程式。化学方程式不仅表明了反应物、生成物和反应条件。同时，化学计量数代表了各反应物、生成物物质的量关系，通过相对分子质量或相对原子质量还可以表示各物质之间的质量关系，即各物质之间的质量比。

2）化学反应速率

影响化学反应速率的因素：主要因素包括反应物本身的性质，外界因素：温度、浓度、压强、催化剂、光、激光、反应物颗粒大小、反应物之间的接触面积和反应物状态。另外，X 射线、γ 射线、固体物质的表面积与反应物的接触面积、反应物的浓度也会影响化学反应速率。

表示方法：用单位时间内反应物或生成物的物质的量、浓度的变化来表示。

在容积不变的反应容器里，通常用单位时间内反应物物质的量的变化或生成物物质的量的变化来表示。不管用哪种物质表示，均为正值。

3）有机化学

有关有机化合物或有机物质结构的研究包括用光谱、核磁共振、红外光谱、紫外光谱、质谱或其他物理或化学方式来确认其组成的元素、组成方式、实验式及化学式。有关性质的研究包括其物理性质及化学性质，也需评估其化学反应性，目的是要了解有机物质在其纯物质形式（若是可能的话），以及在溶液中或是混合物中的性质。有机反应的研究包括有机物质的制备（可能是有机合成或是其他方式），以及其化学反应。

有机化学研究的范围包括碳氢化合物，也就是只由碳和氢组成的化合物，化合物中也有可能还会参与其他的元素，包括氢、氮、氧和卤素，还有诸如磷、硅、硫等元素。

（二）学科单词

ACT 科学要求有一定的阅读量，文章中涉及大量的专业词汇，了解这些专业词汇的意思有助于理解文章和题意。以下是三门学科常见的专业词汇，考生需要熟悉单词的意思，以便在考试中能更准确地理解文章内容。

1. 化学方程式

英文	中文释义	英文	中文释义
plunger	活塞泵	barium	钡
droplet	液滴	magnesium	镁
mass	质量	strontium	锶
reaction	反应	sulfuric acid	硫酸
corrode	腐蚀	beaker	烧杯
hydroxide	氢氧化物	filtration	过滤
inhibitor	抑制剂；抗化剂	chromate	铬酸盐
coating	涂层；覆盖层	fluorine	氟
catalyst	催化剂	induction	感应
electronegativity	电负性	container	容器
electronegative	带负电的	substrate	基质

2. 化学反应速率

英文	中文释义	英文	中文释义
Amylase	淀粉酶	iodine	碘
buffer solution	缓冲溶液	reactant	反应物
iodine	碘酒	trypsin	胰岛素;胰蛋白
starch	淀粉	casein	酶
maltose	麦芽糖	potassium	酪蛋白
refrigerant	制冷剂	permanganate	高锰酸钾
propellant	推进剂	exothermic	发热的
constant	恒定的	endothermic	吸热的
lubricate	润滑	ammonium	铵
limiting reagent	限量试剂	thermogravimetric	热重量的
dehydrate	脱水		

3. 有机化学

英文	中文释义	英文	中文释义
polymer	高分子	flammable	可燃的
solvent	溶剂	brittle	易碎的
polystyrene	聚苯乙烯	cation	正离子;阳离子
synthesize	合成	anion	阴离子;负离子
hydrocarbon	碳氢化合物	dissociate	离解
propane	丙烷	covalent	共价的
butane	丁烷	urea	尿素
pentane	戊烷	hygroscopic	吸湿的
carboxylic	羧基的	isomer	同分异构物

(三)例题解析

本节选取了三门学科的真题进行详细的解析,帮助考生迅速了解考试的形式、内容和解题思路。

1. 化学方程式和反应速率(Chemical Equation & Rate)

1)例题练习 1

(52C—Passage IV)

钡(Ba)、钙(Ca)、镁(Mg)和锶(Sr)作为二价离子 M^{2+} 存在在他们的化合物中(Mg^{2+}、Ca^{2+} 等)。当这些离子的溶液与存在负二价离子 X^{2-}(硫酸盐、碳酸盐等)的溶液混合,如果正离子和负离子组合形成不溶于水的盐 MX,那么这些盐就会沉淀(形成固体)。

$$M^{2+}\,(\text{solution}) + X^{2-}\,(\text{solution}) \longrightarrow MX\ (\text{solid})$$

下表概述了一些由硝酸盐和含有相同浓度的负二价离子 X^{2-} 的溶液混合的结果。

	Barium	Calcium nitrate	Magnesium nitrate	Strontium nitrate
Sulfuric acid (H_2SO_4)	White precipitate	No reaction	No reaction	White precipitate
Sodium carbonate (Na_2CO_3)	White precipitate	White precipitate	No reaction	White precipitate
Ammonium oxalate [$(NH_4)_2C_2O_4$]	White precipitate	White precipitate	No reaction	White precipitate
Potassium chromate (K_2CrO_4 in acid)	Yellow precipitate	No reaction	No reaction	No reaction

(1) 例题练习 1.1

The addition of sulfuric acid to calcium nitrate results in "no reaction." In terms of what the chemist observes in the reaction beaker, "no reaction" takes place when:

F. a white solid forms.

G. a yellow solid forms.

H. the solution changes color.

J. no solid forms and the solution does not change color.

【考点分析】

● 数据表述类文章,此题为数据推理题。

● 抓住关键词 *no reaction*。题目说将 sulfuric acid 加入到 calcium nitrate 结果是 no reaction。

● 看向表格,不同的反应结果有 no reaction,还有不同颜色的沉淀物,可见得知结果为没有反应时,至少应该是没有沉淀物生成,同时根据常识推断,如果溶液本身颜色发生变化,也不可能写成 no reaction。由此可知正确答案为 **J**。

(2) 例题练习 1.2

An unknown solution containing salts of two of the four elements barium, calcium, magnesium, and strontium gives no reaction with sulfuric acid. Based on the table, the unknown solution probably contains:

A. barium and calcium ions.

B. barium and strontium ions.

C. calcium and magnesium ions.

D. magnesium and strontium ions.

【考点分析】

● 数据表述类文章,此题为数据查找题。

● 抓住关键词 *no reaction with sulfuric acid*。

● 直接看向表格,找到对应 sulfuric acid 的行数,与之反应结果为 no reaction 的为 Calcium nitrate 和 Magnesium nitrate,由此可知正确答案为 **C**。

(3) 例题练习 1.3

A student was given a solution that contained only one metallic ion, which was either Sr^{2+} or Ca^{2+}. The student was told to run one test with only one reagent (a substance used to identify or produce other substances) to identify the ion. Which one of the following reagents should the student use to correctly identify the ion?

F. Sulfuric acid

G. Sodium carbonate

H. Ammonium oxalate　　　　J. Potassium chromate

【考点分析】

● 数据表述类文章,此题为数据查找题。

● 抓住关键词 *either* Sr^{2+} *or* Ca^{2+}。

● 看向表格,找到这两者离子与不同溶液发生反应之后对应的反应物,根据给出信息可知只有在与硫酸发生反应时,结果可观察出不同,这样才能区分到底是哪种离子。由此可知正确答案为 **F**。

(4) 例题练习 1.4

Based on the table, which of the following experimental results confirms that an unknown solution contains magnesium nitrate ions only?

A. No reaction in sulfuric acid

B. No reaction in sulfuric acid followed by no reaction in potassium chromate solution

C. No reaction in potassium chromate followed by a white precipitate in sodium carbonate solution

D. No reaction in ammonium oxalate followed by a white precipitate in sodium carbonate solution

【考点分析】

● 数据表述类文章,此题为数据查找分析题。

● 抓住关键词 *magnesium nitrate ions only*。

● 看向表格,magnesium nitrate 和不同溶液发生反应后,仅与碳酸钠产生沉淀,其他均为无反应。由此可知正确答案为 **D**。

(5) 例题练习 1.5

A solution contains a mixture of equal concentrations of barium, calcium, magnesium, and strontium ions. The procedure that would best separate the ions by precipitation (followed by filtration) would be to add X^{2-} ion solutions in which of the following orders?

F. Sulfate, chromate, carbonate, oxalate　　G. Carbonate, sulfate, oxalate, chromate

H. Oxalate, sulfate, carbonate, chromate　　J. Chromate, sulfate, oxalate, carbonate

【考点分析】

● 数据表述类文章,此题为数据推理题。

● 抓住关键词 *A solution contains a mixture of equal concentrations of barium, calcium, magnesium, and strontium ions*。

● 根据题干可知,需要将四种离子一一分开来,根据反应结果来看,加入不同的离子,有的有沉淀,有的没有沉淀生成,那么要一一区分的话,就必须第一种加入的溶液只和其中一种离子产生沉淀,就能分离出一种离子。根据表格数据来看,第一应加入 Chromate,这样可以分离出 barium,然后加入 sulfate,可分离出 strontium,以此类推,可知正确答案为 **J**。

2) 例题练习 2

Aluminum water-based paints (AWPs) contain aluminum (Al) flakes that give surfaces a shiny, metallic appearance. If the flakes corrode, a dull coating of aluminum hydroxide forms on them:

(铝基于水的漆(AWPs)包含铝薄片,能够使表面光亮,有金属的外观。如果薄片腐蚀,会形成稳定的氢氧化铝涂层。)

$$2Al + 6H_2O \text{——} 2Al(OH)_3 + 3H_2$$

Table 1 shows the volume of H_2 gas produced over time (at 25℃ and 1 atm) from 100 mL samples of freshly made AWPs 1 – 3 in 3 separate trials. AWPs 1 – 3 were identical except that each had a different concentration of DMEA, an AWP ingredient that increases pH.

Table 1

AWP	pH of AWP	Volume (mL) of H_2 produced by:			
		Day 2	Day 4	Day 6	Day 8
1	8	4	33	81	133
2	9	21	187	461	760
3	10	121	1 097	2 711	4 480

The AWP 3 trial was repeated 4 times, but for each trial, the sample had the same concentration of 1 of 4 corrosion inhibitors (see Figure 1).

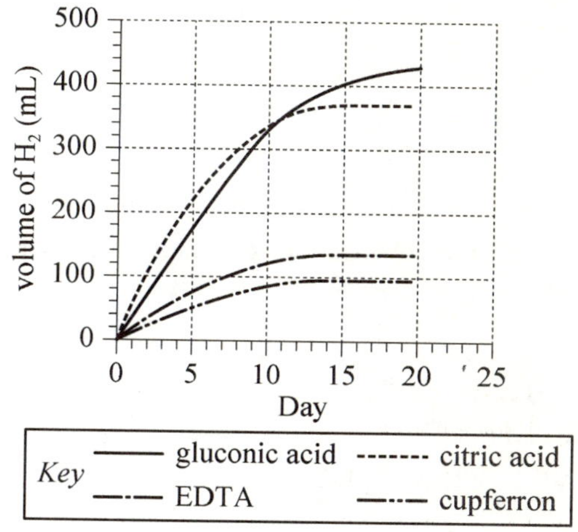

Figure 1

Figure 1 adapted from Bodo Müller, "Corrosion inhibitors for Aluminum." © 1995 by Division of Chemical Education, Inc., American Chemical Society.

(1) 例题练习 2.1

Based on Table 1, which of the following graphs best shows how the volume of H_2 produced by AWP 2 changed over time?

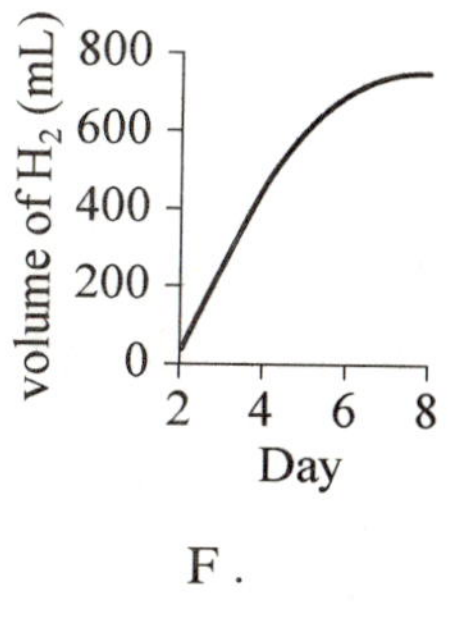

F.

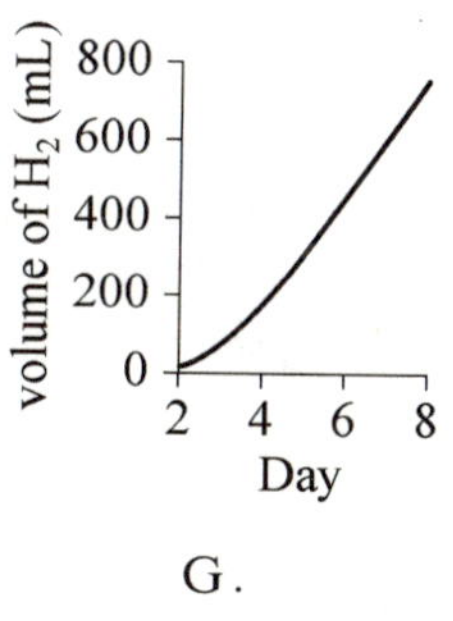

G.

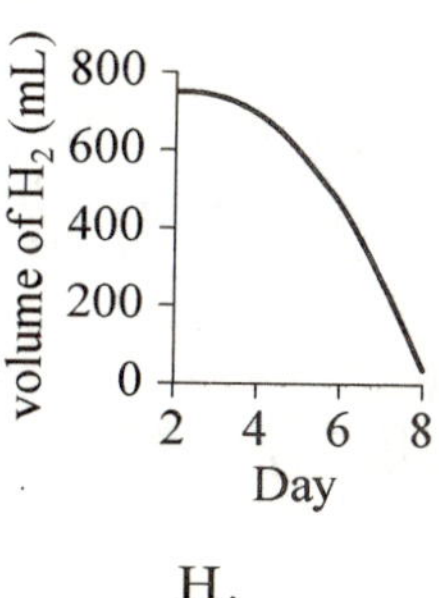

H.

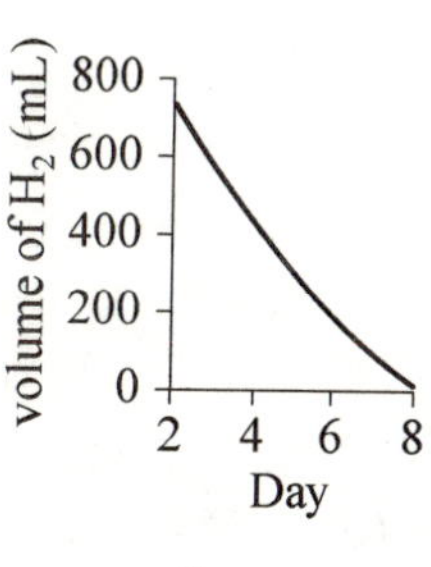

J.

【考点分析】

● 数据表述类文章,此题为数据关系画图题。

● 抓住关键词 *Table 1 & the volume of H_2 produced by AWP 2 changed over time*。

● 看向 Table 1,锁定 *AWP 2* 这行,时间变量为 2、4、6、8,对应的氢气体积分别为 21、187、461、760,很明显速率是越来越快,据此对应到选项,可知正确答案为 **G**。

(2) 例题练习 2.2

Based on Table 1, if the volume of H_2 produced by Day 10 from the AWP 1 sample had been measured, it would most likely have been:

A. less than 133 mL.
B. between 133 mL and 461 mL.
C. between 461 mL and 760 mL.
D. greater than 760 mL.

【考点分析】

● 数据表述类文章,此题为数据推理题。

● 抓住关键词 *Table 1 & AWP 1 & Day 10*。

● 直接看向 Table 1 ,找到对应 AWP 1 的行数,Day 2、4、6、8 对应的数值分别为 4、33、81、133,间距分别为 29、48、52,可知由 Day 8 到 Day 10 间距肯定大于 52,仅凭这些无法得出答案,我们看向 AWP 2 与 133 数值相近的为 187,两天后变为 461,并且通过比较得知 AWP 2 产生氢气速率快于 AWP 1,由此可知 Day 10 的数值远小于 461,据此推断出正确答案为 **B**。

(3) 例题练习 2.3

According to Table 1, what volume of H_2 was produced by AWP 1 from the time the volume was measured on Day 6 until the time the volume was measured on Day 8?

F. 52 mL
G. 81 mL
H. 133 mL
J. 214 mL

【考点分析】

● 数据表述类文章,此题为数据查找题。

● 抓住关键词 *Table 1 & AWP 1*。

● 直接看向 Table 1,AWP 1 的 Day 6 和 Day 8 对应数值分别为 81 和 133,中间间距为 52,由此可知正确答案为 **F**。

(4) 例题练习 2.4

In the trials represented in Table 1 and Figure 1, by measuring the volume of H_2, the experimenters were able to monitor the rate at which:

A. H_2O is converted to Al.

B. Al is converted to H_2O.

C. Al is converted to $Al(OH)_3$.

D. $Al(OH)_3$ is converted to Al.

【考点分析】

● 数据表述类文章,此题为背景知识题。

● 抓住关键词 *measuring the volume of H_2*。

● 虽然题干感觉需要我们定位到文章中去查找数据,但是其实是常识题,就考化学反应中原子的去向,水分子不可能转变成 Al, A 选项错误,反之亦然,B 选项错误,根据化学反应式可知 $Al(OH)_3$是生成物。由此很快可知正确答案为 **C**。

(5) 例题练习 2.5

Consider the volume of H_2 produced by Day 2 from the AWP 3 sample that contained no corrosion inhibitor. Based on Table 1 and Figure 1, the AWP 3 sample containing EDTA produced

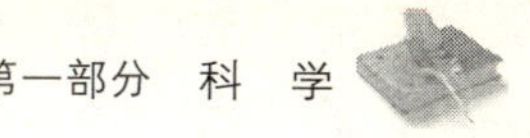

approximately the same volume of H_2 by which of the following days?

F. Day 1　　G. Day 4　　H. Day 7　　J. Day 10

【考点分析】

● 数据表述类文章，此题为数据查找题。

● 抓住关键词 *Table 1 and Figure 1*。

● 先看 Table 1，可得 volume of H_2 produced by Day 2 from the AWP 3 sample 是 121 mL，题目需求的是在 Figure 1 中 AWP 3 containing EDTA 在哪天氢气体积约为此值，我们直接找到 Figure 1 中对应曲线，找到对应点，可知正确答案为 **J**。

3）知识拓展 1

［催化剂］

在化学反应里能改变反应物的化学反应速率（既能提高也能降低），而本身的质量和化学性质在化学反应前后都没有发生改变的物质叫催化剂（也叫触媒）。据统计，约有 80%～85%的化工生产过程中使用过催化剂，如氨、硫酸、硝酸的合成，乙烯、丙烯的聚合。

催化剂自身的组成、化学性质和质量在反应前后不发生变化；它和反应体系的关系就像锁与钥匙的关系一样，具有高度的选择性（或专一性）。一种催化剂并非对所有的化学反应都有催化作用，例如二氧化锰在氯酸钾受热分解中起催化作用，加快化学反应速率，但对其他的化学反应就不一定有催化作用。某些化学反应并非只有唯一的催化剂，例如，在氯酸钾受热分解中能起催化作用的还有氧化镁、氧化铁和氧化铜等，氯酸钾制取氧气时还可用红砖粉或氧化铜等做催化剂。

人们利用催化剂，可以改变化学反应的速率，这被称为催化反应。大多数催化剂都只能加速某一种化学反应，或者某一类化学反应，而不能被用来加速所有的化学反应。催化剂并不会在化学反应中被消耗掉。不管是反应前还是反应后，它们都能够从反应物中被分离出来。不过，它们有可能会在反应的某一个阶段中被消耗，然后在整个反应结束之前又重新产生。

3. 有机化学（Organic Chemistry）

1）例题练习 3

碳氢化合物包含碳原子（C）和氢原子（H），他们之间以化学键（化学键在化学记号中用短直线表示）相结合。碳原子之间以化学键相连形成线型的、分支的或者环形的结构（例子见表 1）。表 2 列出了这些碳氢化合物的沸点。表 3 列出了他们的密度（质量与体积之比）。

Table 1

Number of carbon atoms	Name	Structure		
		linear	branched	cyclic
3	propane	$H_3C-CH_2-CH_3$	none	H_2C-CH_2 \ / CH_2
4	butane	$H_3C-CH_2-CH_2-CH_3$	$H_3C-CH-CH_3$ | CH_3	H_2C-CH_2 | | H_2C-CH_2
5	pentane	$H_3C-CH_2-CH_2-CH_2-CH_3$	$H_3C-CH-CH_2-CH_3$ | CH_3	H_2C-CH_2 | | H_2C CH_2 \ / CH_2

(续表)

Number of carbon atoms	Name	Structure		
		linear	branched	cyclic
6	hexane	$H_3C—CH_2—CH_2—CH_2—CH_2—CH_3$	$H_3C—CH—CH_2—CH_2—CH_3$ $\quad\ \ \vert$ $\quad CH_3$	CH_2 $H_2C \quad CH_2$ $H_2C \quad CH_2$ CH_2
7	heptane	$H_3C—CH_2—CH_2—CH_2—CH_2—CH_2—CH_3$	$H_3C—CH—CH_2—CH_2—CH_2—CH_3$ $\quad\ \ \vert$ $\quad CH_3$	$H_2C—CH_2$ $H_2C \quad CH_2$ $H_2C \quad CH_2$ CH_2

Table 2

Number of carbon atoms	Boiling point (℃)		
	Linear	Branched	Cyclic
3	−42	None	−33
4	0	−12	12
5	36	28	49
6	69	60	81
7	98	90	118

Table 3

Number of carbon atoms	Density (g/cm^3)		
	Linear	Branched	Cyclic
3	0.59	None	0.72
4	0.60	0.55	0.73
5	0.63	0.62	0.75
6	0.66	0.65	0.78
7	0.68	0.68	0.81

(1) 例题练习 3.1

According to Table 2, by approximately how many degrees does the boiling point of a linear hydrocarbon differ from that of a branched hydrocarbon with the same number of carbon atoms?

A. 50℃ B. 100℃ C. 200℃ D. 300℃

【考点分析】

- 数据表述类文章,此题为数据推理题。
- 抓住定位词 *Tables 2*。

● 从题目中可知，要求的是两种结构的沸点的差值，先看 Table 2，对应差值分别为 12、8、9、8，计算平均值，可知答案约为 10，据此可知正确答案为 **B**。

(2) 例题练习 3.2

According to Tables 1 and 3, which hydrocarbon has the lowest density?

F. Linear propane　　G. Branched butane

H. Branched pentane　　J. Cyclic heptane

【考点分析】

● 数据表述类文章，此题为数据对比题。

● 抓住定位词 *Tables 1 and 3 & the lowest density*。

● 根据 Table 3，最小值为碳原子数为 4 个，为 branched 结构，找到 Table 1，对应为 butane，据此可知正确答案为 **G**。

(3) 例题练习 3.3

For each type of structure, what is the relationship between number of carbon atoms to the boiling point and density? As the number of carbon atoms increases, the boiling point:

A. increases but the density decreases　　B. decreases but the density increases

C. decreases but the density decreases　　D. increases but the density increases

【考点分析】

● 数据表述类文章，此题为数据查找之数据间关系题。

● 抓住关键词 *the relationship between number of carbon atoms to the boiling point and density*。

● 根据文章解题的数据在 Table 2、3，先看 Table 2，当碳原子数增加时，同一种结构下，沸点是增加的，再看 Table 3，当碳原子数增加时，同一种结构下，密度亦是增加的，据此可知正确答案为 **D**。

(4) 例题练习 3.4

According to Table 3, how do the structures of butanes (4 carbon atoms) correspond to their density?

F. The cyclic butane has a higher density than the linear and the linear has a higher density than the branched.

G. The cyclic butane has a higher density than the branched and the branched has a higher density than the linear.

H. The branched butane has a higher density than the linear and the linear has a higher density than the cyclic.

J. The branched butane has a higher density than the cyclic and the cyclic has a higher density than the linear.

【考点分析】

● 数据表述类文章，此题为数据对比题。

● 抓住定位词 *Tables 3 & 4 carbon atoms*。

● 根据 Table 3，碳原子数为 4 个时，linear 结构密度为 0.60，branched 结构密度为 0.55，cyclic 结构密度为 0.73，对比可知正确答案为 **F**。

(5) 例题练习 3.5

Which hydrocarbons in Table 2 are gases at 10℃?

A. All the linear, branched, and cyclic hydrocarbons containing at least 5 carbon atoms

B. The cyclic butane plus all the linear, branched, and cyclic hydrocarbons containing at least 5 carbon atoms

C. The linear and cyclic propanes and the linear, branched, and cyclic butanes

D. The linear and cyclic propanes and the linear and branched butanes

【考点分析】

- 数据表述类文章，此题为数据查找题。
- 抓住定位词 *Tables 2 and gases at 10℃* 。
- Table 2 数据表示的是沸点温度，结合常识可知，在 10 度时要是气体，那么必须沸点低于 10 度，符合条件的数值一目了然，对应 Table 1 中名称，据此可知正确答案为 **H**。

(四) 实战练习 Practice

1) Practice 4

(OG3　Passage VI)

在特定的情况下，氢气和氧气混合会形成水(H_2O)。学生们做了一下的实验来研究水是如何形成的。

Experiment 1 实验 1

一个安装了点火装置的厚壁的气体注射器中充满了 20 mL 的氢气(H_2)和 10 mL 的氧气(O_2)，如图 1 所示。

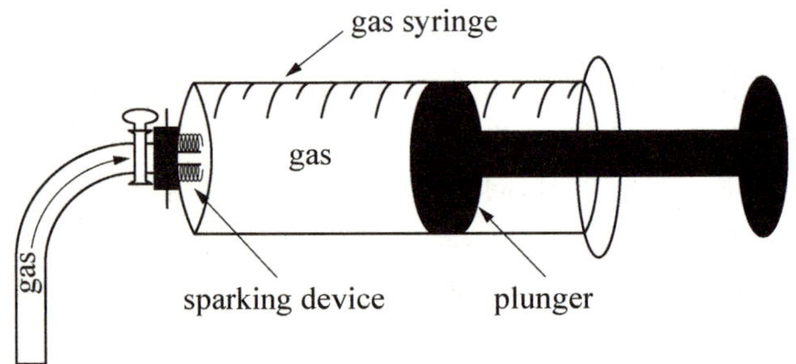

Figure 1

将注射器的活塞固定，并点燃气体。注射器中发生了化学反应，形成水的液滴。然后释放活塞。使注射器中的气体恢复到室温和常压，并记录最后气体的体积。如果注射器中还有剩余的气体，再分析决定其组成。用不同体积的气体重复做这个过程，并将结果记录在表 1 中。因为我们知道在相同的气压和温度下，相同分子数量的不同气体占据的体积是相同的。下面的方程式：

$$2H_2 + O_2 \longrightarrow 2H_2O$$

Table 1

Trial	Volume (mL)			
	Initial H_2	Initial O_2	Final H_2	Final O_2
1	20	10	0	0
2	20	20	0	10
3	20	30	0	20
4	10	20	0	15
5	40	20	0	0
6	50	20	10	0

Experiment 2 实验 2

在图 2 的装置中，氢气流经炙热的氧化铜(CuO)，产生水蒸气。用氯化钙($CaCl_2$)来吸收水蒸气。

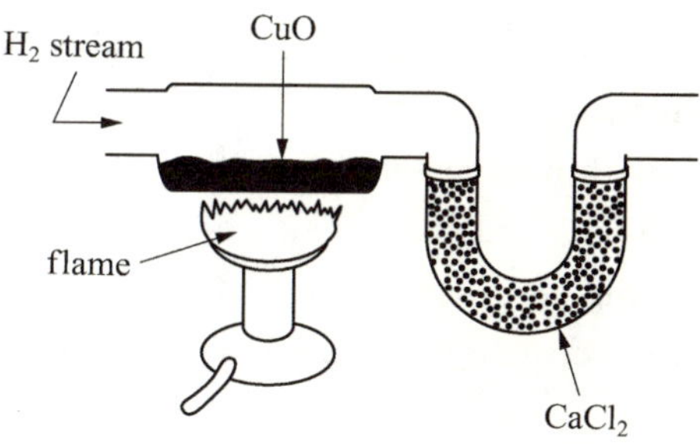

Figure 2

包含氧化铜和氯化钙的试管质量的改变可以用来计算氢气与氧化铜反应产生的水的体积。得出每个 CuO 反应会产生 1 个水分子。

$$CuO + H_2 \longrightarrow Cu + H_2O$$

(1) Practice 4.1

In Trial 1 of Experiment 1, after the reaction had taken place, but before the syringe plunger was unlocked, one would predict that, compared to the pressure in the syringe before the spark, the pressure in the syringe after the spark was:

A. lower, because the overall amount of gas decreased.

B. lower, because the overall amount of gas increased.

C. higher, because the overall amount of gas decreased.

D. higher, because the overall amount of gas increased.

(2) Practice 4.2

If 50 mL of H_2 and 50 mL of O_2 were reacted using the procedure from Experiment 1, the final volume of O_2 would most likely be:

F. 0 mL G. 10 mL H. 15 mL J. 25 mL

(3) Practice 4.3

Which of the following assumptions about the chemical reactions in Experiment 1 were made before the final measurements were taken?

A. Excess O_2 must be present for water to form.

B. Only hot CuO will react with H_2.

C. H_2 is not absorbed by $CaCl_2$.

D. Each reaction had run to completion.

(4) Practice 4.4

When nitrogen gas (N_2) is reacted with H_2 under certain conditions, the following reaction occurs:

$$N_2 + 3H_2 \longrightarrow 2NH_3$$

Based on the results of Experiment 1, if 10 mL of N_2 were completely reacted with 40 mL of H_2 at the same pressure and temperature, what volume of H_2 would remain unreacted?

F. 0 mL　　G. 10 mL　　H. 20 mL　　J. 30 mL

(5) Practice 4.5

Which of the following, if it had occurred, would probably NOT have caused an error in interpreting the results of Experiment 2?

A. Using H_2 contaminated with nonreactive impurities

B. Using CuO contaminated with reactive impurities

C. H_2O escaping without being absorbed by the $CaCl_2$

D. Other reactions occurring between CuO and H_2 that produced different products

2) Practice 5

酶在消化过程中作为一种催化剂(在化学反应中能够加快反应速率但是其本身并不消耗的化合物)。在消化过程中胰蛋白酶能够使蛋白质分解成更小的亚单位。一位学生调查了温度、潜伏期和 pH 值对酶活性的影响。

Experiment 1 实验 1

在 11 个试管中的每一个试管中加入 6 mL 的酪蛋白(一种蛋白质)溶液。在 1 到 10 号试管的每个试管中加入 1 mL 的胰蛋白酶溶液。11 号试管中加入 1 mL 不带胰蛋白酶的水。在不同的温度下,试管放在水槽中进行搅拌,并且培养(加热)0～15 分钟。加热过后,在每个试管中加入 0.1 mL 的氯化钙溶液。氯化钙使反应停止并且与蛋白质形成不会被胰蛋白酶破坏的沉淀(固体)。将沉淀从试管中移除并干燥。通过测量沉淀物的质量(mg)来决定每一个试管中蛋白质剩余的量。结果显示在表 1 中。

Table 1

Tube	Temperature of water bath (℃)	Amount of trypsin (mL)	Incubation time (min)	Mass of precipitate (mg)
1	25	1	0	3.0
2	25	1	5	2.4
3	25	1	10	2.0
4	25	1	15	1.7
5	30	1	5	2.4
6	30	1	10	1.4
7	30	1	15	0.5
8	35	1	5	0.1
9	35	1	10	0.1
10	35	1	15	<0.1
11	35	0	5	3.0

Experiment 2 实验 2

在 6 个试管中各加入 6 mL 的酪蛋白溶液和 1 mL 的胰蛋白酶溶液。调整试管的 pH 值,使每个试管的 pH 值不同。将每一个试管中的溶液搅拌并在 25℃条件下加热 10 分钟。按照实验 1 的方法来决定每个试管中蛋白质相对的量。结果显示在表 2 中。

Table 2

Tube	pH	Mass of precipitate (mg)
12	4	2.8
13	6	2.5
14	8	2.0
15	10	2.3
16	12	2.6
17	14	2.9

(1) Practice 5.1

In Experiment 1, which of the following conditions allowed the large amount of precipitate to form in Tube 11?

A. Higher temperature
B. Higher pH
C. Lack of casein
D. Lack of trypsin

(2) Practice 5.2

In which of the following ways are the designs of Experiments 1 and 2 different?

F. A larger volume of trypsin solution per test tube was used in Experiment 1 than in Experiment 2.

G. Temperature was varied in Experiment 1 but held constant in Experiment 2.

H. Incubation time remained constant in Experiment 1 but was varied in Experiment 2.

J. The pH of the solutions in the tubes varied in Experiment 1 but not in Experiment 2.

(3) Practice 5.3

Which of the following hypotheses about the effects of pH on trypsin activity is best supported by the results of Experiment 2? As the pH of the solutions increases from 4 to 14, the effectiveness of trypsin:

A. increases only.
B. decreases only.
C. increases, then decreases.
D. stays the same.

(4) Practice 5.4

Suppose that $CaCl_2$ had been added immediately to Tube 16 with no incubation time allowed. Based on the results of Experiment 1, one would predict that the amount of precipitate formed would have been approximately:

F. 2.0 mg.
G. 2.3 mg.
H. 2.6 mg.
J. 3.0 mg.

(5) Practice 5.5

In which of the following tubes was the greatest amount of protein broken down by trypsin?

A. Tube 1
B. Tube 3
C. Tube 8
D. Tube 10

(6) Practice 5.6

According to the results of both experiments, one would predict that the LEAST amount of precipitate would be formed if tubes were incubated for 12 min under which of the following conditions?

F. 25℃ at pH of 4
G. 25℃ at pH of 8
H. 30℃ at pH of 4
J. 30℃ at pH of 8

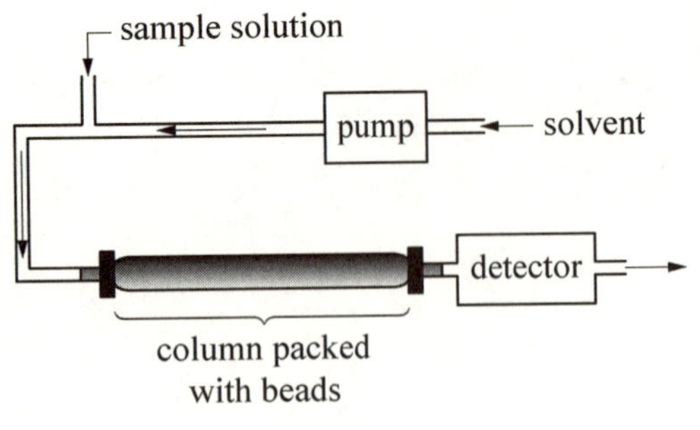

Figure 1

3）Practice 6

尺寸排阻色谱法(SEC)可以用来分离由多聚分子组成的溶液。在尺寸排阻色谱法中，将由多聚分子形成的样品溶液注射到溶剂中。然后将样品流经一段圆柱体，圆柱体中装满了包含很多微小的孔的珠子(见图 1)。

Smaller molecules easily diffuse into the pores. Larger molecules do not as easily diffuse into the pores, or are larger than the pores. Therefore, smaller molecules spend more time in the column than do larger molecules, causing the components of the mixture to separate. As solvent containing a component of the mixture exits the column through the detector, a peak is plotted versus time (starting from injection). The portion of solvent corresponding to a peak is called a fraction. The time corresponding to the top of a peak is the fraction's retention time (RT). The RT corresponds to the average molecular mass (AMM) of the molecules in that fraction. The shape of the peak reflects the distribution of molecular masses of the molecules in the fraction.

Experiment 1

Polystyrene is a polymer made up of identical sub-units. Five types of polystyrene (P1 – P5) were dissolved together in a solvent. The AMM of P1 – P5 is given in Table 1. The range of molecular masses for each of P1 – P5 was amu of the AMM.

Table 1

Polystyrene	AMN(amu*)
P1	800
P2	4 000
P3	10 000
P4	50 000
P5	200 000

* amu = atomic mass unit

A sample of the solution was injected into an SEC apparatus. Each fraction was analyzed as it exited the apparatus (see Figure 2).

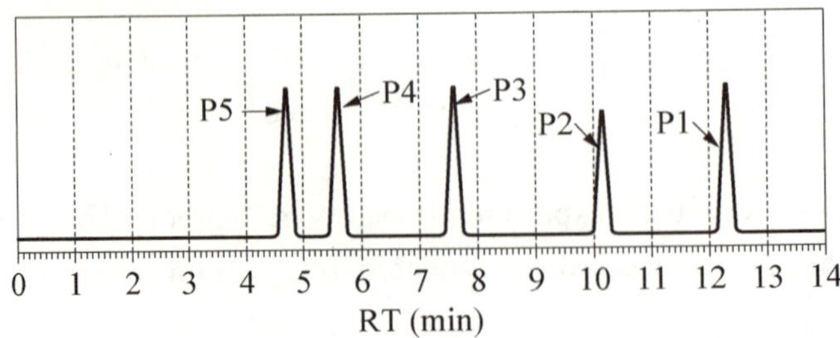

Figure 2

Experiment 2

Chemists used 3 different methods to synthesize polystyrenes, forming polystyrene mixtures M1, M2, and M3, respectively.

Each of M1 - M3 was then analyzed as in Experiment 1 (see Figure 3).

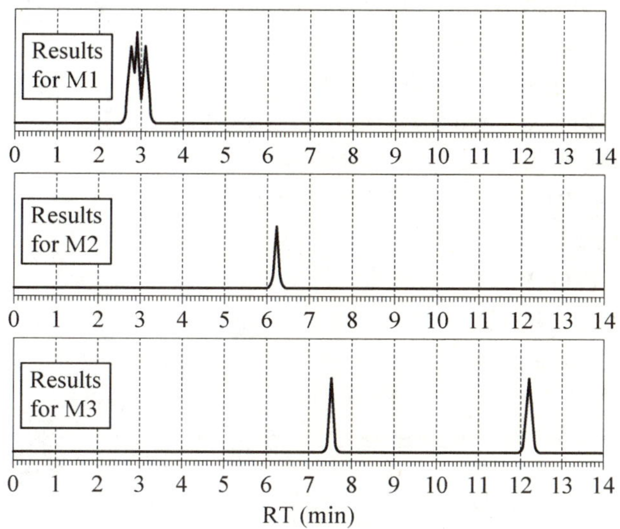

Figure 3

(1) Practice 6.1

Based on the results of Experiments 1 and 2, M3 is most likely which polymer (s) from Experiment 1?

A. P1 only

B. mixture of P1 and P3 only

C. mixture of P3 and P5 only

D. mixture of P2, P4, and P5 only

(2) Practice 6.2

In Experiment 1, the molecules of which of the following polymers spent the longest amount of time in the column?

F. P1 G. P2 H. P4 J. P5

(3) Practice 6.3

Based on the results of Experiments 1 and 2, which of the following ranks P4, P5, and M2 from smallest AMM to largest AMM?

A. P4, P5, M2 B. P5, M2, P4 C. M2, P4, P5 D. M2, P5, P4

(4) Practice 6.4

In Experiment 1, on average, did P3 molecules or P4 molecules more easily diffuse into the pores of the beads while in the column of the SEC apparatus?

F. P3 molecules, because they have a larger AMM.

G. P3 molecules, because they have a smaller AMM.

H. P4 molecules, because they have a larger AMM.

J. P4 molecules, because they have a smaller AMM.

(5) Practice 6.5

In which, if any, of the mixtures synthesized for Experiment 2 is the average mass of the molecules in the mixture most likely greater than 200,000 amu?

A. M1　　B. M2

C. M3　　D. Neither M1, M2, nor M3

(6) Practice 6.6

How does the number of molecules in a 1 g sample of P2 compare to the number of molecules in a 1 g sample of P4? The number of P2 molecules is:

F. less, because P2 has a larger AMM than does P4.

G. less, because P2 has a smaller AMM than does P4.

H. greater, because P2 has a larger AMM than does P4.

J. greater, because P2 has a smaller AMM than does P4.

Answers for Practice 4 - 6

Practice 4　H A J D G A

Practice 5　D G C J D J

Practice 6　B F C G A J

Session 7　物理 1

本章主要介绍 ACT 科学测试物理科目中的力学、流体力学和光学三大分支学科,并通过解析例题,以及相应的练习题明确这三门学科的考试形式、考试重点和相关词汇。

(一) 学科背景

ACT 科学测试主要考察和重点考察科学推理能力,了解相应的学科知识可以快速理解文章内容,提高解题速度。

1. 学科综述

1) 力学(Mechanics)

力学是一门独立的基础学科,是有关力、运动和介质(固体、液体、气体和等离子体),宏、细、微观力学性质的学科,研究以机械运动为主,及其同物理、化学、生物运动耦合的现象。

2) 流体力学(Fluids Mechanics)

流体力学是力学的一门分支,是研究流体(包含气体、液体及等离子体)现象以及相关力学行为的科学。

3) 光学(Optics)

光学是研究光的行为和性质的物理学科。光是一种电磁波,在物理学中,电磁波由电动力学中的麦克斯韦方程组描述;同时,光具有波粒二象性,需要用量子力学表达。

2. 学科背景知识

1) 力学

力学是一门基础学科,同时又是一门技术学科。它研究能量和力以及它们与固体、液体及气体的平衡、变形或运动的关系。力学可粗分为静力学、运动学和动力学三部分,静力学研究力的平衡或物体的静止问题;运动学只考虑物体怎样运动,不讨论它与所受力的关系;动力学讨论物体运动和所受力的关系。现代的力学实验设备,诸如大型的风洞、水洞,它们的建立和使用本身就是一个综合性的科学技术项目,需要多工种、多学科的协作。

人们在日常劳动中使用杠杆、打水器具等,逐渐认识物体受力及平衡的情况。古希腊时代,阿

基米德曾对杠杆平衡、物体重心位置、物体在水中受到的浮力等做了系统研究，确定它们的基本规律，初步奠定了静力学，即平衡理论的基础。

2）流体力学

流体力学是连续介质力学的一们分支，是以宏观的角度来考虑系统特性，而不是微观地考虑系统中每一个粒子的特性。流体力学（尤甚是流体动力学）是一个活跃的研究领域，其中有许多尚未解决或部分解决的问题。流体动力学在数学上非常复杂，最佳的处理方式是利用电脑进行数值分析。

流体力学假设所有流体满足以下的假设：

（1）质量守恒

（2）能量守恒

（3）动量守恒

（4）连续体假设

3）光学

光学是物理学的重要分支学科。也是与其他应用技术相关的学科。狭义来说，光学是关于光和视见的科学，“optics”一词早期只用于跟眼睛和视见相联系的事物。而今天常说的光学是广义的，是研究从微波、红外线、可见光、紫外线直到X射线和γ射线的宽广波段范围内的电磁辐射的产生、传播、接收和显示，以及与物质相互作用的科学，着重研究的范围是从红外到紫外波段。它是物理学的一个重要组成部分。

光学主要是研究光的现象、性质与应用，包括光与物质之间的相互作用、光学仪器的制作。光学通常研究红外线、紫外线及可见光的物理行为。因为光是电磁波，其他形式的电磁辐射，例如X射线、微波、电磁辐射及无线电波等也具有类似光的特性。

（二）学科单词

ACT科学要求有一定的阅读量，文章中涉及大量的专业词汇，了解这些专业词汇的意思有助于理解文章和题意。以下是三门学科常见的专业词汇，考生需要熟悉单词的意思，以便在考试中能更准确地理解文章内容。

1. 力学和流体力学

英文	中文释义	英文	中文释义
frictionless	无摩擦的	pendulum	钟摆
acceleration	加速	oscillate	周期性摆动
scale	秤	stopwatch	秒表
force	力	sphere	球体
clockwise	顺时针的	kinetic energy	动能
dial	表盘；刻度盘	mechanical energy	机械能
spring	弹簧	potential energy	势能
compression	压缩	conserved	守恒的
trajectory	轨迹	vacuum	真空
launcher	发射器	helium	氦
mount	安装	motion	运动
viewfinder	取景器	law	定理；定律
emit	发射	diethyl ether	乙醚
pulse	脉冲	vapor pressure	蒸气压
land	着陆	buret	滴定管

2. 光学

英文	中文释义	英文	中文释义
stopcock	旋塞阀	density	密度
nonane	壬烷	solid	固体
microscope	显微镜	furnace	熔炉
objective lens	物镜	fraction	分馏部分
magnification	放大率	residue	残渣
resolution	分辨率	emission	排放
slide	载玻片	particulate	微粒
radiation	辐射能	dioxin	二恶英
capacitor	电容器	incinerator	焚烧炉
deflect	偏斜;偏转	polarity	极性
total solar eclipse	日全食	adsorbent	吸附剂
lead	铅	elute	洗提
vaporize	蒸发	soapy water	肥皂水

(三)例题解析

本节选取了三门学科的真题进行详细的解析,帮助考生迅速了解考试的形式、内容和解题思路。

1. 力学(Mechanics)

1)例题练习 1

学生通过使用两个相同的台秤来研究力,秤 A 和秤 B,它们当中的其中一个显示在图 1 中。每一个秤的平台的重量可以忽略不计。当一个力(例如由重力产生的力)作用在平台的表面,刻度盘上指针绕着零刻度顺时针旋转。旋转的量与力的大小成正比。

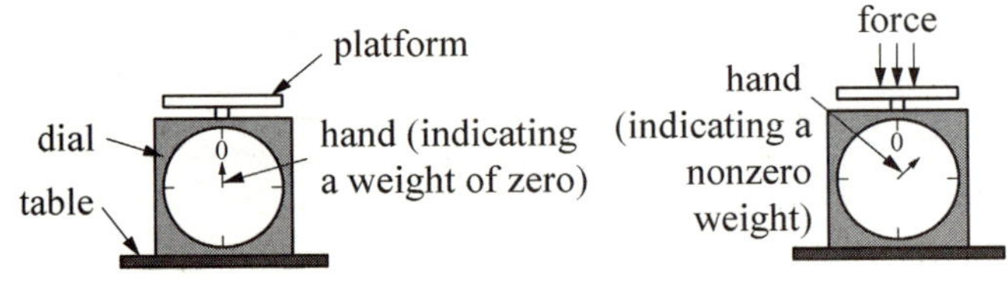

Figure 1

Study 1 研究 1

在做实验 1~3 之前,学生将秤 A 和秤 B 的刻度的读数设置成零。在每一个实验中,秤 A 放在秤 B 的上方(见图 2)。在试验 1 中,秤 A 的平台上没有放置任何重量;在试验 2 中,秤 A 的平台上放置了 5.0 牛顿(N)的重量;在试验 3 中,秤 A 的平台中放置了 10.0 牛顿(N)的重量。图 2 显示了三个试验的刻度盘上的读数。

Study 2 研究 2

学生们在每个秤上都放了一支铅笔,并且在铅笔的上方放置了一块板,板在两个秤之间距离为 0.4 m。在进行实验 4~6 之前,学生们将秤 A 和秤 B 的刻度调为零(见图 3)。

在每一个实验中,将 10.0 N 的重量放置在平板上,其与秤 B 上面的铅笔的距离不同。在试验 4 中,重量距离铅笔有 0.10 m;在试验 5 中,重量距离铅笔有 0.2 m;在试验 6 中,重量距离铅笔有 0.3 m。三个实验刻度盘上的读数显示在图 4 中。

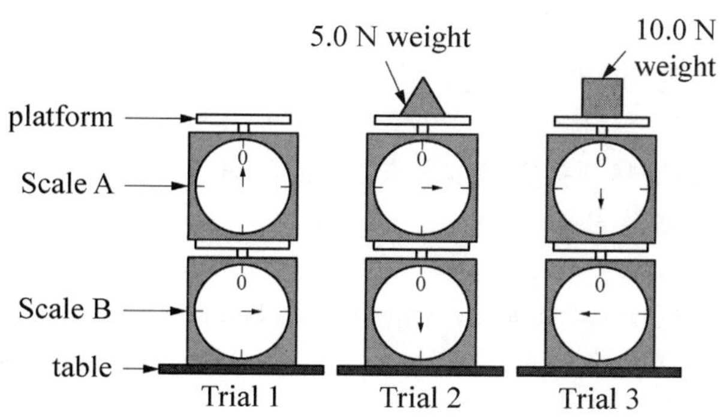

Figure 2

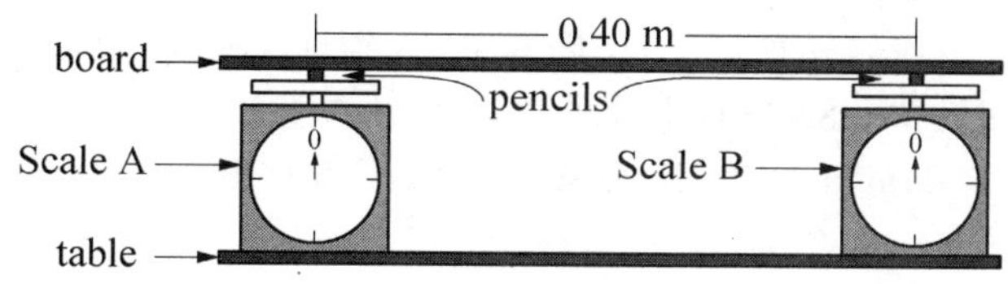

Figure 3

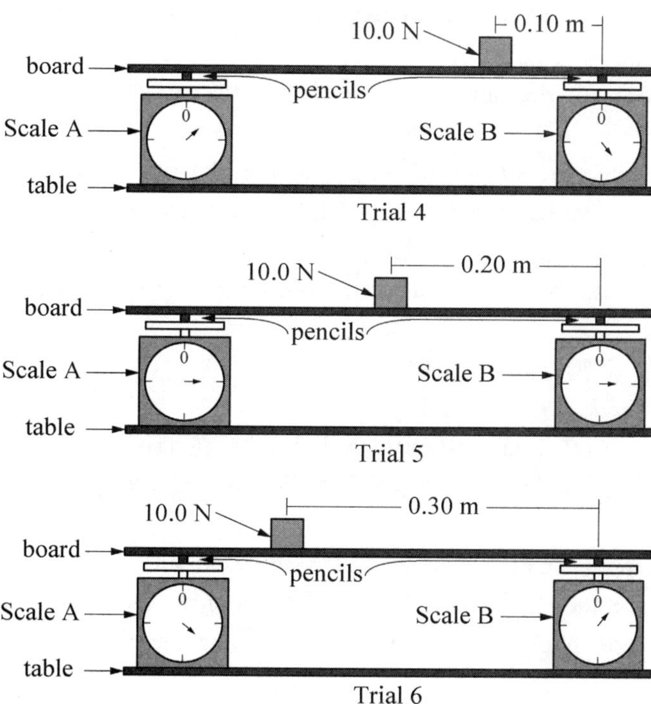

Figure 4

(1) 例题练习 1.1

In which of the trials in Study 2, if any, was the force of the 10.0 N weight equally distributed between Scales A and B?

A. Trial 4　　B. Trial 5　　C. Trial 6　　D. None of the trials

【考点分析】

● 实验总结类文章,此题为实验结果题。

● 抓住定位词 *Study 2*。

● 直接定位到 Study 2,直接根据实验结果来看,在 Trial 5 中重物离两边距离一样,再者可根据指针来判断,由此可知正确答案为 **B**。

(2) 例题练习 1.2

Based on the results of Trials 1 and 2, Scale A and Scale B each weighed:

F. 2.5 N. G. 5.0 N. H. 7.5 N. J. 10.0 N.

【考点分析】

● 实验总结类文章,此题为实验结果题。

● 抓住定位词 *Study 1 & Trials 1 and 2*。

● 直接定位到 Study 1,我们先看向 Trial 1, Scale A 指针指向 0,Scale B 指针顺时针 90°,再看 Trial 2,Scale A 指针顺时针 90°,Scale B 指针顺时针 180°,A 上放着重 5 N 的重物,由此可判断顺时针 90°,代表 5 N,那么结合 Trail 1 可知,Scale A 重 5 N,而 A 和 B 一样,由此可知正确答案为 **A**。

(3) 例题练习 1.3

Assume that whenever a weight was placed on a scale's platform, a spring inside the scale was compressed. Assume also that the greater the added weight, the greater the amount of compression. Was the amount of potential energy stored in Scale A's spring greater in Trial 1 or in Trial 3?

A. In Trial 1, because the amount of weight on the platform of Scale A was greater in Trial 1.

B. In Trial 1, because the amount of weight on the platform of Scale A was less in Trial 1.

C. In Trial 3, because the amount of weight on the platform of Scale A was greater in Trial 3.

D. In Trial 3, because the amount of weight on the platform of Scale A was less in Trial 3.

【考点分析】

● 实验总结类文章,此题为实验结果题。

● 抓住定位词 *in Trial 1 or in Trial 3*。

● 直接定位到 Study 1,在 Trial 1 中 Scale A 上无重物,在 Trial 3 中 Scale A 上放置 10 N 的重物,明显 Trial 3 中 A 所受力大于 Trial 1 中,结合题干可知正确答案为 **C**。

(4) 例题练习 1.4

In a new study, suppose Scale A were placed upside down atop Scale B, so that the platform of Scale A rested directly on the platform of Scale B. Which of the following drawings best represents the results that would most likely be obtained for this arrangement?

F.

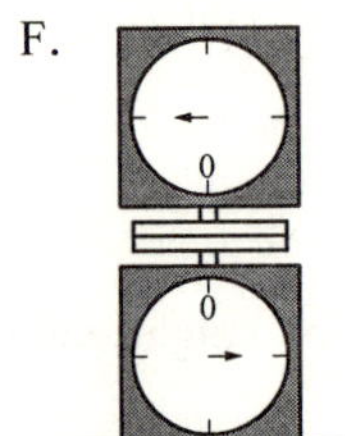

G.

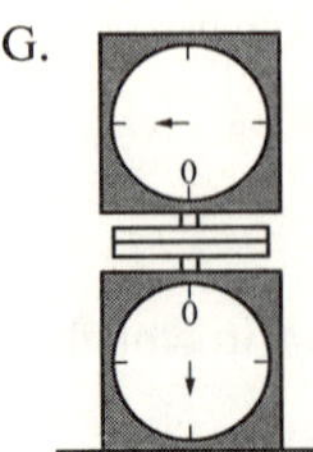

H.

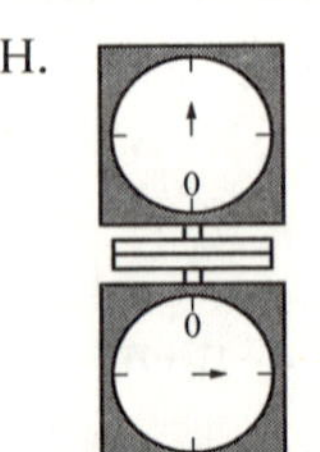

J.

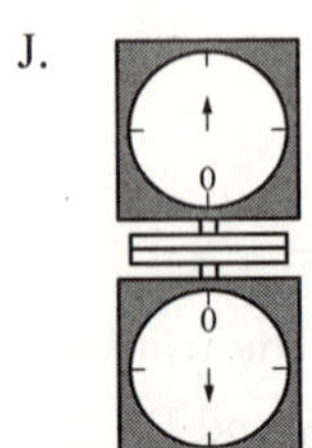

【考点分析】

● 实验总结类文章，此题为实验设计题。

● 抓住关键词 *Scale A were placed upside down atop Scale B*。

● 题干假设 A 倒置在 B 上，问指针指向情况，根据前面题目，我们已知每个 Scale 重 5 N，当 A 倒置时，需要承受自身重量，那么指针将与 0 刻度线成 90°，而 B 因为受力不变，所以指针仍然指向 90°，同时由于 A 倒置，所以 0 刻度线朝下，所以 A 的指针是从 0 刻度线开始，顺时针旋转 90°，由此可知正确答案为 **F**。

(5) 例题练习 1.5

In Study 2, as the distance between the 10.0 N weight and the pencil on Scale B increased, the amount of force exerted on the surface of Scale B's platform:

A. remained the same.
B. increased only.
C. decreased only.
D. varied, but with no general trend.

【考点分析】

● 实验总结类文章，此题为实验结果题。

● 抓住定位词 *Study 2*。

● 直接定位到 Study 2，题目考察重物与 Scale B 的距离和 Scale B 受力大小的关系，根据实验结果，Trail 4 中距离最小受力最大，Trail 6 中距离最大受力最小，Trail 5 居中，由此可知正确答案为 **C**。

(6) 例题练习 1.6

Which of the following statements most likely describes an important reason for setting the dial readings of both scales to zero after Study 1, prior to each of Trials 4 - 6?

F. To add the weights of the scales to each weight measurement
G. To add the weights of the board and pencils to each weight measurement
H. To subtract the weights of the scales from each weight measurement
J. To subtract the weights of the board and pencils from each weight measurement

【考点分析】

● 实验总结类文章，此题为实验用具题。

● 抓住定位词 *prior to each of Trials 4 -6*。

● 我们直接定位到 Study 2，文章说“Prior to each of Trials 4 - 6, the students set the dial readings of Scales A and B to zero (see Figure 3)”，直接看向 Figure 3，图中指针都指向 0，但是 A 和 B 上面放置着 board 和 pencils，常识来说，这两样都是有重量的，之所以清 0，是为了后续实验中指针不受这两个物体重量的影响，据此可知正确答案为 **J**。

2) 知识拓展 1

[重力]

由于地球的吸引而使物体受到的力，叫做重力。方向总是竖直向下，不一定是指向地心的(只有在赤道和两极指向地心)。地面上同一点处物体受到重力的大小跟物体的质量 m 成正比，同样，当 m 一定时，物体所受重力的大小与重力加速度 g 成正比，用关系式 $G=mg$ 表示。通常在地球表面附近，g 值约为 9.8 N/kg，表示质量是 1 kg 的物体受到的重力是 9.8 N。(9.8 N 是一个平均值：在赤道上 g 最小，$g=9.79$ N/kg；在两极上 g 最大，$g=9.83$ N/kg。N 是力的单位，字母表示为 N，1 N大约是拿起两个鸡蛋的力。)

物体的各个部分都受重力的作用。但是，从效果上看，我们可以认为各部分受到的重力作用都集中于一点，这个点就是重力的等效作用点，叫做物体的重心(center of gravity)。

超重:物体对支持物的压力(或对悬绳的拉力)大于物体所受重力的现象叫做超重。

失重:物体对支持物的压力(或对悬绳的拉力)小于物体所受重力的现象叫做失重。

2. 流体力学(Fluids Mechanics)

1) 例题练习 2

当一种易挥发的液体在一个封闭容器中时,液体表面蒸发(形成蒸气)的速度和凝结(重新形成液体)的速度相等。在平衡状态下(当蒸发速率和凝结速率相等时),蒸气作用引起的力叫做蒸气压力,可以用水银来测量,单位为(mm Hg)。学生们做了一下的实验来研究蒸气压力和沸点。

Experiment 1 实验 1

在烧瓶中放了 5 mL 的水,然后加热直到它沸腾。将一个包含温度和压力传感器的两洞瓶塞塞入烧瓶中。当烧瓶在冰槽中冷却到 0℃时,记录下液体的温度和蒸气压。用酒精和乙醚重复进行这个过程(见 Figure 1)。

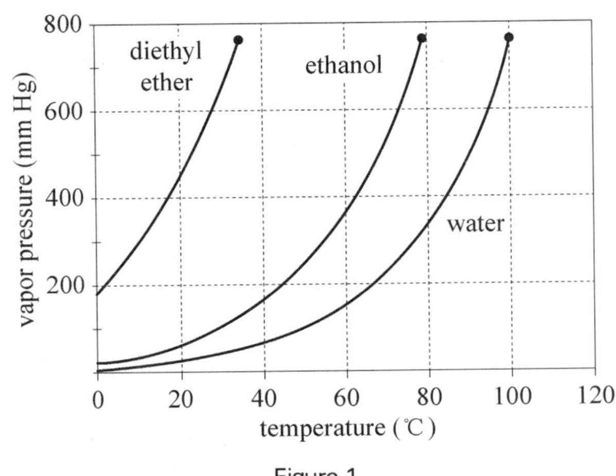

Figure 1

Figure adapted from Henry F. Holtzclaw William R. Robinson, and William H. Nebergall, College Chemistry With Qualitative Analysis, 7th ed. © 1984 by D. C. Heath and Company.

Experiment 2 实验 2

将含有 100 mL 水的烧杯加热到大气压力(760 mm Hg)。在水沸腾了 1 分钟之后,记录下温度。用酒精和乙醚重复进行这个过程(见表 1)。

Table 1

Liquid	Boiling point (℃)
Water	100.0
Ethanol	78.5
Diethyl ether	34.6

Experiment 3 实验 3

在烧瓶中放入 100 g 水的样品并且在室温(20℃)下将 0.1 mole 的不挥发的物质溶解到水中去。测量这个溶液的蒸气压,同时测量含有 0.2 mole 和 0.3 mole 物质的溶液的蒸气压。用酒精和乙醚重复进行这个过程(见表 2)。

Table 2

Amount added (mole)	Vapor pressure (mm Hg) at 20℃ for:		
	Water	Ethanol	Diethyl ether
0	17.5	43.9	442.2
0.1	17.2	43.1	434.4
0.2	16.9	42.4	426.8
0.3	16.6	41.7	419.5

(1) 例题练习 2.1

A student claimed that liquids with higher molecular masses boil at higher temperatures than liquids with lower molecular masses. Do the results of Experiment 2 and the information in the table below support his claim?

Liquid	Molecular mass (g/mole)
Water	18
Ethanol	46
Diethyl ether	74

A. Yes; diethyl ether has the highest molecular mass and the highest boiling point.

B. No; diethyl ether has the highest molecular mass and the lowest boiling point.

C. Yes; water has the lowest molecular mass and the lowest boiling point.

D. No; water has the lowest molecular mass and the lowest boiling point.

【考点分析】

- 实验总结类文章,此题为实验结果题。
- 抓住定位词 *Experiment 2*。
- 直接定位到 Experiment 2,从 Table 1 中可以看到,沸点从低到高分别为 Water、Ethanol、Diethyl ether,题干给出的信息,这三者的分子质量排序是从低到高,结合选项内容可知正确答案为 **B**。

(2) 例题练习 2.2

Based on the results of Experiment 1, diethyl ether will have a vapor pressure of 100 mm Hg when it is at a temperature:

F. greater than 100℃.

G. between 50℃ and 100℃.

H. between 0℃ and 50℃.

J. less than 0℃.

【考点分析】

- 实验总结类文章,此题为实验结果题。
- 抓住定位词 *Experiment 1*。
- 直接定位到 Experiment 1,找到 Figure 1 中当 vapor pressure 为 100 mm Hg 时 diethyl ether 对应的温度,从图中可以看到,并没有对应的温度值,结合温度从左至右是升高的,根据曲线走向,可以判断出 100 mm Hg 时温度低于 0,可知正确答案为 **J**。

(3) 例题练习 2.3

Is the statement "If the amount of a nonvolatile substance dissolved in a liquid is increased, the vapor pressure will increase" supported by the results of Experiment 3?

A. No; as the amount of substance dissolved was increased in all 3 liquids, the vapor pressure for all 3 liquids stayed the same.

B. Yes; as the amount of substance dissolved was increased in all 3 liquids, the vapor pressure for 2 of the 3 liquids increased.

C. No; as the amount of substance dissolved was increased in all 3 liquids, the vapor pressure for all 3 liquids decreased.

D. Yes; as the amount of substance dissolved was increased in all 3 liquids, the vapor pressure for all 3 liquids increased.

【考点分析】

- 实验总结类文章,此题为实验结果题。
- 抓住定位词 *Experiment 3*。
- 直接定位到 Experiment 3,从 Table 2 中可以看到,随着摩尔数增加,三种流体的 vapor pressure 都会减少,结合题干可知题干观点错误,正确答案为 **C**。

(4) 例题练习 2.4

Based on the results of Experiment 3, if 0.5 mole of the nonvolatile substance were dissolved in 100 g of diethyl ether, the vapor pressure, in mm Hg, of the solution would most likely be closest to:

F. 405.　　G. 415.　　H. 440.　　J. 455.

【考点分析】

- 实验总结类文章,此题为实验结果题。
- 抓住定位词 *Experiment 3*。
- 直接定位到 Experiment 3,从 Table 2 中可以看到,摩尔数每增加 0.1(从 0~0.3),diethyl ether 的 vapor pressure 减少量依次为 7.8、7.8、7.3,据此可以判断,当摩尔数再增加 0.2 时,减少量约为 15 左右,0.3 时,数值是 419.5,减去减少量,得答案约为 404.5,结合选项内容可知正确答案为 **F**。

(5) 例题练习 2.5

Which of the following best represents the apparatus that was being used as the computer recorded the results of Experiment 1?

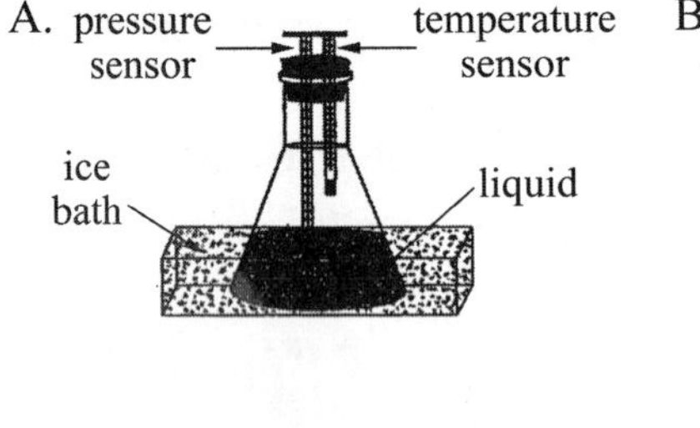

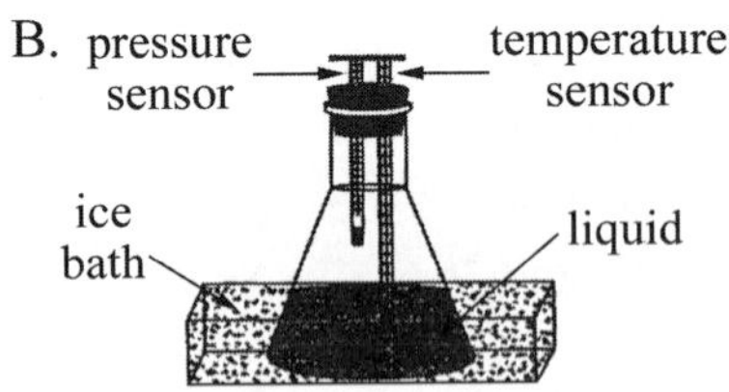

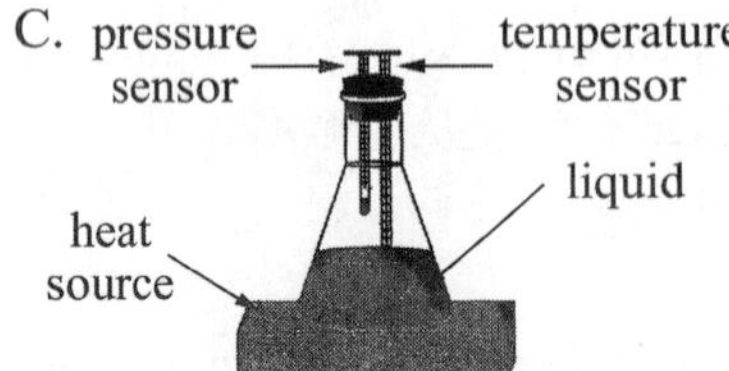

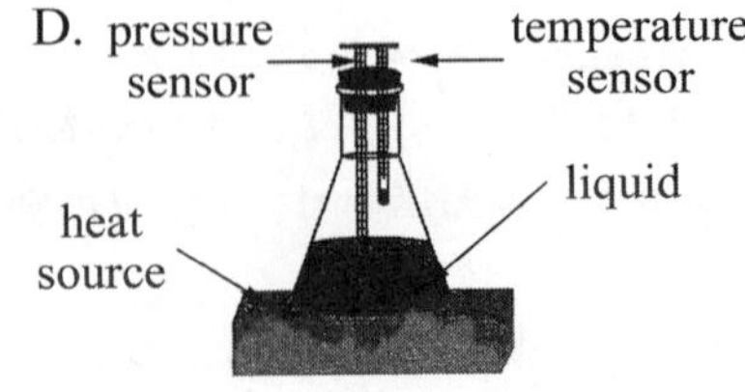

【考点分析】

● 实验总结类文章，此题为实验用具题。

● 抓住定位词 *Experiment 1*。

● 直接定位到 Experiment 1，根据“A 5 mL sample of water was placed in a flask, then heated until it boiled. A 2-hole stopper containing temperature and pressure sensors was inserted into the flask. The temperature of the liquid and its vapor pressure were recorded by computer as the flask was cooled in an ice bath to 0℃. The procedure was repeated using ethanol and diethyl ether (see Figure 1)”，阅读此段话可知 flask 是浸在 ice bath 的，直接排除 C、D，而测量蒸气压的话必须 pressure sensors 和蒸气接触，同理测量流体温度，温度计必须浸入流体，很显然正确答案为 **B**。

(6) 例题练习 2.6

According to the results of Experiments 1 and 2, which of the following tables best shows the vapor pressures of the boiling liquids in Experiment 2?

F.

Water	100 mm Hg
Ethanol	78 mm Hg
Diethyl ether	35 mm Hg

G.

Water	35 mm Hg
Ethanol	78 mm Hg
Diethyl ether	100 mm Hg

H.

Water	100 mm Hg
Ethanol	100 mm Hg
Diethyl ether	100 mm Hg

J.

Water	760 mm Hg
Ethanol	760 mm Hg
Diethyl ether	760 mm Hg

【考点分析】

● 实验总结类文章，此题为实验结果题。

● 抓住定位词 *Experiments 1 and 2*。

● 从题干我们得知需要求解的内容是三种流体在沸点时的蒸气压，根据 Table 1 中内容可以获知各流体的沸点，根据沸点，我们在 Figure 1 中找到对应的点，可以看到三种流体在沸点时蒸气压基本一致，在 700～800 mm Hg 之间，结合选项内容可知正确答案为 **J**。

2) 知识拓展 2

[蒸气压]

一定外界条件下，液体中的液态分子会蒸发为气态分子，同时气态分子也会撞击液面回归液态。这是单组分系统发生的两相变化，一定时间后，即可达到平衡。平衡时，气态分子含量达到最大值，这些气态分子撞击液体所能产生的压强，简称蒸气压(vapor pressure)。蒸气压反映溶液中有少数能量较大的分子有脱离母体进入空间的倾向，这种倾向也称为逃逸倾向。在饱和状态时，湿空气中水蒸气分压等于该空气温度下纯水的蒸气压。对于液体，从蒸气压高低可以看出蒸发速率的大小。具有较高蒸气压的物质通常说其具有挥发性。

任何物质的蒸气压都随着温度非线性增加，它们之间的关系可以用克劳修斯-克拉佩龙方程描述。随着温度的升高,物质蒸气压随之升高直到足以克服周围大气的压强从而在物质本体内的任何位置发生气化而产生大量气泡。这一现象叫做沸腾,而这个温度叫做此压强下的沸点。物质的常压沸点就是此物质的饱和蒸气压等于一个标准大气压时候的温度。需要注意的是在较深液体中发生的沸腾所需温度会高于较浅液体中的沸腾,因为除了大气压强外还需要克服液体自身深度所造成的压强。对于溶液,请用拉乌尔定律。

当液体的蒸气压达到外压时,液体即产生沸腾现象,此时的温度即在该外压下该液体的沸点。以水为例,一个大气压(101.325 kPa)下,若水温达到 100℃,此时水的蒸气压正好是一个大气压,水开始沸腾,100℃ 即是一个大气压下水的沸点。

3. 光学(Optics)

1) 例题练习 3

一位学生用带有 4 个物镜的显微镜进行了 3 项活动。

Activity 1 活动 1

这个学生通过每个物镜观察了 4 个载玻片(A、B、C 和 D)。每一个载玻片上涂了两条细线。对每一个物镜,学生决定是否可以看清两条分离的线或者是否他们模糊成一张图片。结果显示在表 1 中。

Table 1

slide	Objective Lens:			
	1	2	3	4
A	I	I	I	I
B	I	I	I	II
C	I	I	II	II
D	I	II	II	II

Note: II indicates lines appeared separate; I indicates lines blurred together.

Activity 2 活动 2

学生准备了上面有 0.1 mm 长的细线的载玻片。这个长度定义为物体的大小。接下来,她通过每个物镜观察载玻片,并估计线的长度。这个估计的长度称为图像尺寸。最后,她通过下面的公式计算了每一个物镜的放大率:

$$M = \text{image size} \div \text{object size}.$$

数据显示在表 2 中。

Table 2

Objective Lens	Image size (mm)	*M*
1	4	40
2	10	100
3	20	200
4	40	400

Activity 3 活动 3

每一个物镜的数值孔径（*NA*）被印在显微镜上。*NA* 决定了能够看到多少细节并且它与分辨率相关（*R*）。*R* 定义为两个物体之间显得分离的最小距离。因此，分辨率较小的物镜能够比分辨率较高的物镜更加清晰的显示样品。分辨率 *R* 可以从下面的公式计算得出：

$$R = \lambda \div 2(NA)$$

λ 为光的波长，单位为纳米（nm），用来观察物体。

学生计算了每一个物镜的分辨率 *R*，假设光的波长为 550 nm。数据显示在表 3 中。

Table 3

Objective Lens	*NA*	*R*（nm）
1	0.10	2 750
2	0.25	1,100
3	0.40	688
4	0.65	423

(1) 例题练习 3.1

If the student had viewed the slide used in Activity 2 through a fifth objective lens and the image size with this objective lens was 30 mm, the *M* associated with this objective lens would have been:

F. 30. G. 100. H. 300. J. 1 000.

【考点分析】

- 实验总结类文章，此题为实验假设题。
- 抓住定位词 *Activity 2 & image size 30 mm*。
- Activity 2 中，根据实验结果给出了一个很重要的公式：*M* = image size ÷ object size. 而 object size 为 0.1 mm，现在从假设得知 image size 为 30 mm，代入公式可得 *M* 值，简单计算得出正确答案为 **H**。

(2) 例题练习 3.2

Based on the results of Activity 2, the combination of which of the following lines and objective lenses would result in the greatest image size?

A. A 0.7 mm line viewed through Objective Lens 1

B. A 0.6 mm line viewed through Objective Lens 2

C. A 0.5 mm line viewed through Objective Lens 3

D. A 0.4 mm line viewed through Objective Lens 4

【考点分析】

- 实验总结类文章，此题为实验结果题。
- 抓住定位词 *Activity 2*。
- Activity 2 中，根据实验结果给出了一个很重要的公式：*M* = image size ÷ object size，得出 image size = *M* × object size，现在题目要求 image size 最大值，一一计算选项 *M* 值，即可得出答案，根据公式计算得出 A 选项值为 28，B 为 60，C 为 100，D 为 160，很明显正确答案为 **D**。

(3) 例题练习 3.3

When viewing Slide C in Activity 1, the student was able to discern 2 distinct lines with how many of the objective lenses?

F. 1　　G. 2　　H. 3　　J. 4

【考点分析】

- 实验总结类文章,此题为实验结果题。
- 抓住定位词 *viewing Slide C in Activity 1*。
- Activity 1 中观察 Slide C,根据 Table 1 实验结果直接可以看到 objective lens 为 1、2 时可观察到 1 条线,为 3、4 时可观察到两条线,直接得出正确答案为 **G**。

(4) 例题练习 3.4

Which of the following equations correctly calculates R (in nm) for Objective Lens 2, using light with a wavelength of 425 nm?

A. $R = 425 \div 2(0.10)$

B. $R = 425 \div 2(0.25)$

C. $R = 0.10 \div 2(425)$

D. $R = 0.25 \div 2(425)$

【考点分析】

- 实验总结类文章,此题为实验结果题。
- 抓住定位词 R (*in nm*)。
- 根据定位词可知需要根据 Activity 3 中公式来求,根据公式 $R = \lambda \div 2(NA)$,而 Lens 2 的 NA 为 0.25,题干给出 λ 也就是波长值为 425,代入可得正确答案为 **B**。

(5) 例题练习 3.5

Another student calculated the R of a fifth objective lens as described in Activity 3. He determined that for this fifth objective lens, $R = 1\,830$ nm. Accordingly, the NA of this lens was most likely closest to which of the following values?

F. 0.15　　G. 0.25　　H. 0.35　　J. 0.45

【考点分析】

- 实验总结类文章,此题为实验结果题。
- 抓住定位词 *Activity 3* & $R = 1\,830$ nm。
- Activity 3 中,根据公式 $R = \lambda \div 2(NA)$ 可知,$NA = \lambda \div 2R$,代入数值,可以求得 NA 约为 0.15,得出正确答案为 **F**。

(6) 例题练习 3.6

Activity 1 and Activity 2 differed in that in Activity 1:

A. 4 different slides were used.

B. 4 different objective lenses were used.

C. the wavelength of the light was varied.

D. the object sizes were greater than the image sizes.

【考点分析】

- 实验总结类文章,此题为实验用具对比题。
- 抓住定位词 *Activity 1 and Activity 2*。
- 综合观察两个实验可以看到实验 1 中有四种 Slide,而实验 2 中就唯一一个,而 Objective lens 一样都用了 4 个,据此可知正确答案为 **A**。

2) 知识拓展 3

[物镜]

物镜是由若干个透镜组合而成的一个透镜组。组合使用的目的是为了克服单个透镜的成像

缺陷，提高物镜的光学质量。显微镜的放大作用主要取决于物镜，物镜质量的好坏直接影响显微镜映像质量，它是决定显微镜的分辨率和成像清晰程度的主要部件，所以对物镜的校正是很重要的。

物镜主要参数包括：放大倍数、数值孔径和工作距离。

(1) 放大倍数是指眼睛看到像的大小与对应标本大小的比值。它指的是长度的比值而不是面积的比值。例：放大倍数为 100，指的是长度是 1 μm 的标本，放大后像的长度是 100 μm，要是以面积计算，则放大了 10 000 倍。显微镜的总放大倍数等于物镜和目镜放大倍数的乘积。

(2) 数值孔径也叫镜口率，简写 *NA* 或 *A*，是物镜和聚光器的主要参数，与显微镜的分辨力成正比。干燥物镜的数值孔径为 0.05～0.95，油浸物镜(香柏油)的数值孔径为 1.25。

(3) 工作距离是指当所观察的标本最清楚时物镜的前端透镜下面到标本的盖玻片上面的距离。物镜的工作距离与物镜的焦距有关，物镜的焦距越长，放大倍数越低，其工作距离越长。例：10 倍物镜上标有 10/0.25 和 160/0.17，其中 10 为物镜的放大倍数；0.25 为数值孔径；160 为镜筒长度(单位 mm)；0.17 为盖玻片的标准厚度(单位 mm)。10 倍物镜有效工作距离为 6.5 mm，40 倍物镜有效工作距离为 0.48 mm。

(四) 实战练习 Practice

1) Practice 4

一条较重的链条放在一张没有摩擦力的桌子上方，其中长度为 Y_0 悬挂在桌子的边缘，如图 1 所示。整个链条的长度为 L。当释放链条后，它会沿着边缘滑落，如图 2 所示。

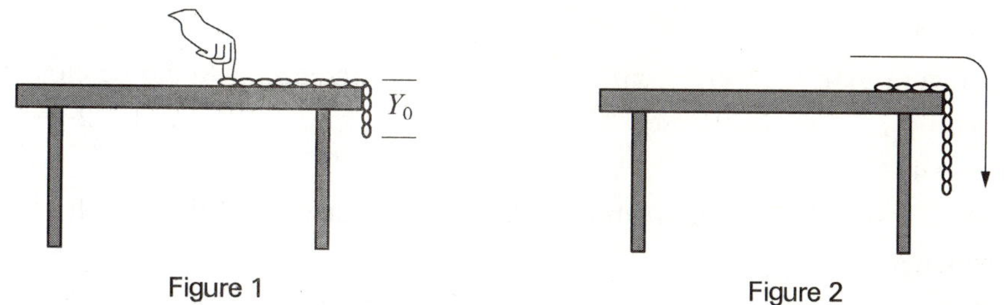

Figure 1　　Figure 2

记下落的时间为链条完全从桌子上滑落的时间。木星、地球和月球上滑落的时间记录在图 3 中。在 3 种星球表面上相对于链条长度的滑落时间记录在图 4 中。表 1 显示了在这些星球表面的重力加速度。

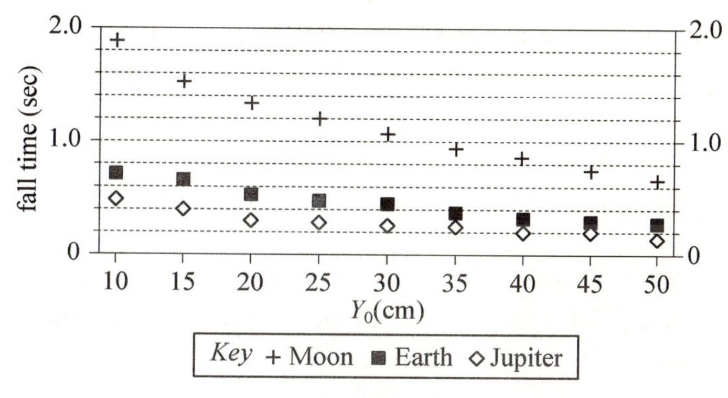

Figure 3

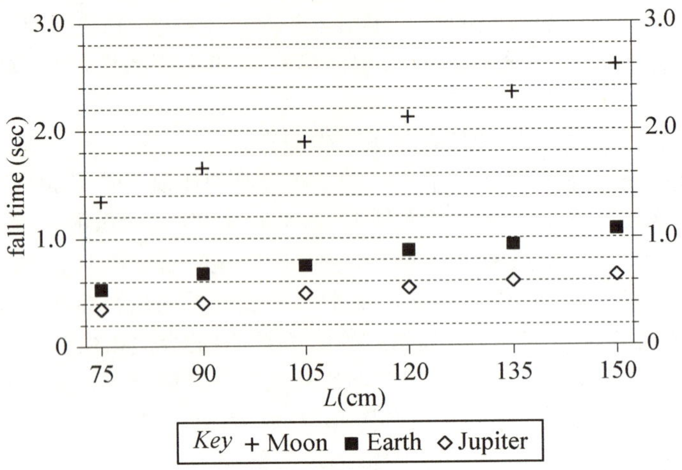

Figure 4

Table 1

Planet or moon	Acceleration due to gravity at surface of planet or moon (m/sec^2)
Jupiter	24.9
Earth	9.8
Moon	1.6

(1) Practice 4.1

Based on Figure 3, if Y_0 were 5 cm, the fall time on the Moon would be closest to:

F. 0.4 sec. G. 0.8 sec. H. 1.9 sec. J. 2.3 sec.

(2) Practice 4.2

According to Figure 4, the chain with $Y_0 = 20$ cm will have a fall time on the Moon of 2.0 sec if L is approximately:

A. 75 cm. B. 94 cm. C. 113 cm. D. 135 cm.

(3) Practice 4.3

Before the chain was released, the horizontal length of the chain on the tabletop equaled:

F. $L+Y_0$. G. $L-Y_0$. H. Y_0 J. L.

(4) Practice 4.4

Suppose the chain represented in Figure 3 has a 0.7 sec fall time at Earth's surface. For the same chain to have a 0.7 sec fall time at the Moon's surface, Y_0 at the Moon's surface would have to be approximately:

A. 35 cm greater than at Earth's surface. B. 35 cm less than at Earth's surface.

C. 47 cm greater than at Earth's surface. D. 47 cm less than at Earth's surface.

(5) Practice 4.5

The acceleration due to gravity on the surface at the planet Neptune is approximately 11.7. Based on Figure 3, a chain's fall time, calculated for Neptune's surface and a given Y_0, would be:

F. less than its fall time at Jupiter's surface.

G. greater than its fall time at Jupiter's surface, and less than its fall time at Earth's surface.

H. greater than its fall time at Earth's surface, and less than its fall time at the Moon's

surface.

J . greater than its fall time at the Moon’s surface.

2) Practice 5

液体的压强 P_L与在液体表面下面的深度 D 和液体的密度ρ 有关。如果水槽中的液体与空气相连，在深度 D 下的整体压强 P_T为在深度 D 下的液体压强 P_L加上大气压强 P_A。

表 1 列出了在 25℃下 4 种液体的密度 ρ，单位为千克每立方米（kg/m^3）。

Table 1

Liquid	ρ (kg/m^3)
Carbon tetrachloride	1 580
Ethanol	786
Ethylene glycol	1 130
Water	997

图 1 显示了，在深度 D 为 10 m 的情况下，液体压强 P_L（in kilopascals，kPa）相对于液体密度 ρ（1 kPa = 10^3 Pa = 10^3 newtons/m^2）的图像。图 2 显示了在 25℃下，某一天水槽中水（与大气相连）的压强 P_L相对于深度 D 的图像。

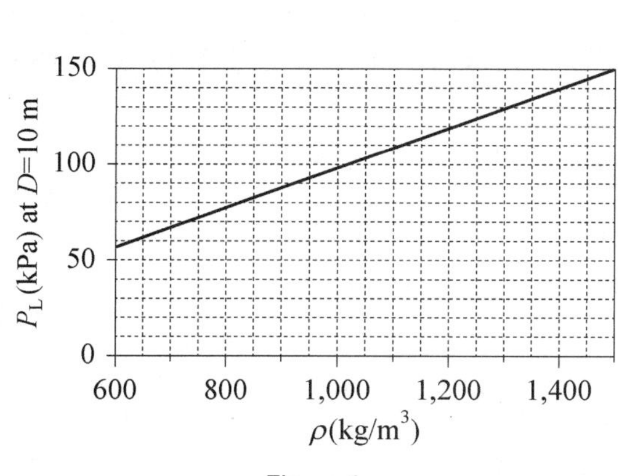

Figure 1

Figure 2

(1) Practice 5.1

What is the correct ranking of the liquids listed in Table 1, from the liquid with the least density at 25℃ to the liquid with the greatest density at 25℃?

F. Carbon tetrachloride, ethanol, ethylene glycol, water

G. Carbon tetrachloride, ethylene glycol, water, ethanol

H. Water, ethanol, carbon tetrachloride, ethylene glycol

J . Ethanol, water, ethylene glycol, carbon tetrachloride

(2) Practice 5.2

Based on Table 1 and Figure 1, compared to P_L at D = 10 m in 25℃ ethanol, P_L at D = 10 m in 25℃ carbon tetrachloride will be approximately:

A. 1/4 as great. B. 1/2 as great. C. 2 times as great. D. 4 times as great.

(3) Practice 5.3

Based on Table 1, the mass of 3 m^3 of ethylene glycol at 25℃ would be closest to which of the following values?

F. 1,130 kg G. 2,260 kg H. 3,390 kg J. 4,520 kg

(4) Practice 5.4

Based on Figure 2, the relationship between P_L (in kPa) and D (in m) for the water in the tank is best represented by which of the following equations?

F. $P_L = 9.8 \times D$ G. $P_L = D \div 9.8$ H. $P_L = 19.6 \times D$ J. $P_L = D \div 19.6$

(5) Practice 5.5

Based on Figure 2, on the particular day, 20 m below the surface of the water in the open tank, P_L plus P_A was closest to which of the following values?

F. 100 kPa G. 200 kPa H. 300 kPa J. 400 kPa

3) Practice 6

Solar cycles are periodic variations in the Sun's brightness.

Table 1 contains the date of onset for, and duration of, recent solar cycles; the time from a cycle's onset until the Sun reached solar maximum (the maximum brightness for that cycle); and the number of sunspots at solar maximum.

Table 1

Solar cycle number	Date of onset of cycle (month, year)	Duration of cycle (years)	Time from onset of cycle to solar maximum (years)	Number of sunspots at solar maximum
1	December 1878	11.3	5.0	75
2	March 1890	11.8	3.8	88
3	January 1902	11.6	4.0	64
4	August 1913	10.0	4.0	105
5	August 1923	10.1	4.7	78
6	September 1933	10.4	3.6	119
7	February 1944	10.2	3.3	152
8	April 1954	10.5	3.9	201
9	October 1964	11.7	4.1	111
10	June 1976	10.3	3.5	165
11	September 1986		2.8	158
Average		10.8	3.9	120

Figure 1 shows the number of sunspots and the Sun's brightness at a particular wavelength for part of one cycle.

For the same cycle, Figure 2 shows the number of proton events, when the Sun emitted much higher than average numbers of protons (positively charged particles).

(1) Practice 6.1

The most likely reason that the data in Table 1 for Cycle 11 are incomplete is that:

F. the omitted value was probably too small to be included in Table 1.

G. the omitted value was probably too large to be included in Table 1.

H. the Sun s surface contained no sunspots during that cycle.

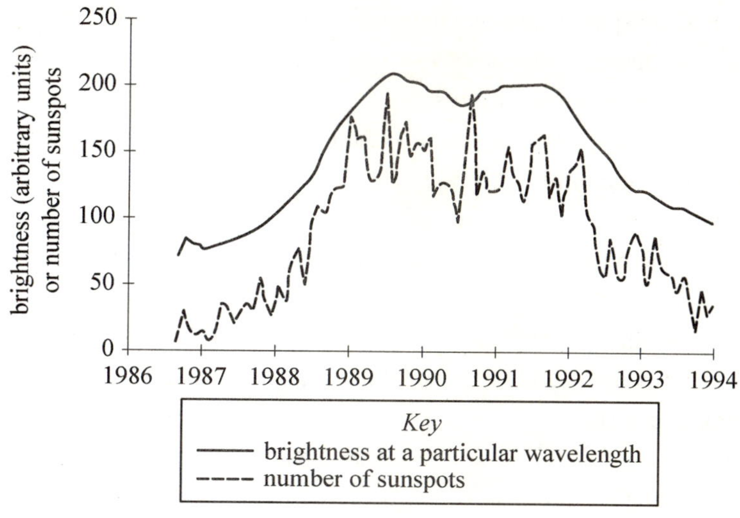

Figure 1

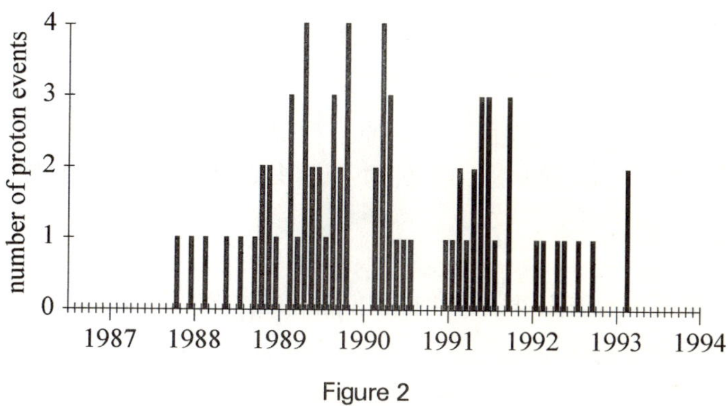

Figure 2

J. Cycle 11 was still in progress at the time Table 1 was made.

(2) Practice 6.2

According to Figure 2, the highest number of proton events in 1990 was measured during the month of:

A. January. B. March. C. September. D. November.

(3) Practice 6.3

According to Figures 1 and 2, for the 7-year span between 1987 and 1994, proton events occurred most frequently when:

F. the Sun's brightness was above 90 units and the number of sunspots was below 90.

G. the Sun's brightness was below 90 units and the number of sunspots was above 90.

H. both the Sun's brightness and the number of sunspots were above 90.

J. both the Sun's brightness and the number of sunspots were below 90.

(4) Practice 6.4

Based on Figure 1, which of the following hypotheses best relates the number of sunspots to the Sun's brightness at the particular wavelength?

A. The number of sunspots is highest when the Sun is near its maximum brightness.

B. The number of sunspots is lowest when the Sun is near its maximum brightness.

C. The number of sunspots is highest both when the Sun is near its maximum brightness and when the Sun is near its minimum brightness.

D. The number of sunspots is lowest both when the Sun is near its maximum brightness and when the Sun is near its minimum brightness.

(5) Practice 6.5

Based on Table 1, the onset of Cycle 21 will most likely occur during which of the following intervals?

F. After 1950, but before 2000　　G. After 2050, but before 2100

H. After 2150, but before 2200　　J. After 2250, but before 2300

Answers for Practice 4 - 6

Practice 4　J C G A G

Practice 5　J C H A H

Practice 6　J B H A G

Session 8　物理 2

本章主要介绍 ACT 科学测试物理科目中的原子物理学、热力学和电磁学三大分支学科，并通过解析例题，以及相应的练习题明确这三门学科的考试形式、考试重点和相关词汇。

(一) 学科背景

ACT 科学测试主要考察和重点考察科学推理能力，了解相应的学科知识可以快速理解文章内容，提高解题速度。

1. 学科综述

1) 原子物理学(Atomic Physics)

原子物理学是研究原子的结构、运动规律及相互作用的物理学分支。它主要研究:原子的电子结构、原子光谱、原子之间或与其他物质的碰撞过程和相互作用。

2) 热力学(Thermodynamics)

热力学是研究热现象中物质系统在平衡时的性质和建立能量的平衡关系，以及状态发生变化时系统与外界相互作用(包括能量传递和转换)的学科。

3) 电磁学(Electromagnetism)

电磁学是物理学的一个分支，起源于近代。广义的电磁学包含电学和磁学，但狭义来说是一门探讨电性与磁性交互关系的学科。主要研究电磁波、电磁场以及有关电荷、带电物体的动力学等。

2. 学科背景知识

1) 原子物理学

原子物理学是研究原子的结构和性质及原子与电磁辐射和其他原子相互作用的科学。

光谱是研究原子物理学的重要途径之一。不同元素原子光谱中谱线的发现和深入研究标志着原子物理学的开端。谱线是指光谱中细锐的峰，出现于受激发的原子[辐射或热激发的离子(参见火焰)]或发光自由原子(自由原子是指气体或蒸汽状态下存在的原子，与其他原子距离足够远，相互作用可以忽略)。

原子是从宏观到微观的第一个层次，是一个重要的中间环节。物质世界这些层次的结构和运

动变化是相互联系、相互影响的，对它们的研究缺一不可，很多其他重要的基础学科和技术科学的发展也都要以原子物理为基础。

2）热力学

热力学是研究热现象中物态转变和能量转换规律的学科；它着重研究物质的平衡状态与准平衡态的物理、化学过程。热力学定义许多宏观的变量（像温度、内能、熵、压强等），描述各变量之间的关系。热力学描述数量非常多的微观粒子的平均行为，其定律可以用统计力学推导而得。

热力学可以总结为四条定律。热力学第零定律定义了温度这一物理量，指出了相互接触的两个系统、热流的方向。热力学第一定律指出内能这一物理量的存在，并且与系统整体运动的动能和系统与环境相互作用的势能是不同的，区分出热与功的转换。热力学第二定律涉及的物理量是温度和熵。熵是研究不可逆过程引入的物理量，表征系统通过热力学过程向外界最多可以做多少热力学功。热力学第三定律认为，不可能透过有限过程使系统冷却到绝对零度。

3）电磁学

由于摩擦起电现象，静电和静磁现象很早就被人类发现。库仑定律是静电学中的基本定律，其主要描述了静电力与电荷电量成正比，与距离的平方成反比关系。法国物理学家夏尔·奥古斯丁·库仑于1784年至1785年间进行了他著名的扭秤实验，其实验的主要目的就是为了证实静电力的平方反比律，因为他认为“假说的前一部分无需证明”，也就是说他已经先验性地认为静电力必然和万有引力类似，和电荷电量成正比。

在奥斯特发现电流的磁效应之后，法国物理学家让-巴蒂斯特·毕奥和费利克斯·萨伐尔进一步详细研究了载流直导线对周围磁针的作用力，并确定其磁力大小正比于电流强度，反比于距离，方向垂直于距离连线，这一规律被归纳为著名的毕奥-萨伐尔定律。

（二）学科单词

ACT科学要求有一定的阅读量，文章中涉及大量的专业词汇，了解这些专业词汇的意思有助于理解文章和题意。以下是三门学科常见的专业词汇，考生需要熟悉单词的意思，以便在考试中能更准确地理解文章内容。

1. 单词表1

英文	中文释义	英文	中文释义
atomic nuclei	原子核	voltage	电压
proton	质子	apparatus	装置、设备
neutron	中子	linear	线性的
decay	衰减	pulley	滑轮
electron jump	电子跃迁	stopper	用塞子塞住
nuclear fusion	核聚变	capillary	毛细管的
containment vessel	保护壳；安全壳	graduated	有刻度的
magnetic force	磁力	ethanol	乙醇
magnetic field	磁场	syringe	注射器
deuterium	氘	nitrogen	氮
tritium	氚	methane	甲烷
laser light	激光	copper	铜
nucleus	核	nickel	镍
charged	带电的	brass	黄铜
photon	光子	particle	粒子
buoyant	有浮力的	molecule	分子

2. 单词表 2

英文	中文释义	英文	中文释义
joule	焦耳	conduction	传导
blackbody	黑体	thermal equilibrium	热平衡
evaporate	蒸发	thermal	热的;热量的
condense	冷凝	bubble point	始沸点;起泡点
vapor	蒸汽	resistance	电阻
flask	烧瓶	capacitor	电容器
manometer	压力计	alternating current	交流电
hexane	己烷	microfarad	微法拉
dropper	滴管	output voltage	输出电压
mercury	水银	frequency	频率
thermometer	温度计	farad	法拉(电容单位)
metal rod	金属棒	viscosity	黏稠
insulated	绝缘的	ampere	安培
configuration	配置;布局	electrical conductor	导电体
insulator	绝缘体	variable	变量
thermal	热的;热量的	rheostat	变阻器

(三) 例题解析

本节选取了三门学科的真题进行详细的解析,帮助考生迅速了解考试的形式、内容和解题思路。

1. 原子物理学(Atomic Physics)

1) 例题练习 1

原子核可以由一些符号的组合来表示:

$$^{A}_{Z}X$$

Z 表示的是元素 X 的原子核中质子的数目,A(等于 Z 加上中子的数目)表示的是相同原子核的质量数。例如,$^{12}_{6}C$ 代表的是碳原子核内有 6 个质子和 6 个中子;$^{14}_{6}C$ 代表的是碳的另一种同位素(种类),有 6 个质子和 8 个中子组成。

原子核经历 3 种放射性衰变。表 1 列出了 3 种衰变释放出的粒子。图 1 显示了一系列的放射性衰变,称为铀系,该衰变从铀 238 衰变开始。

Table 1

Type of radioactive decay	Particle emitted	Symbol of emitted particle
Alpha	Helium nucleus	$^{4}_{2}He$
Beta	Electron	e^{-}
Gamma	Gamma ray photo	γ

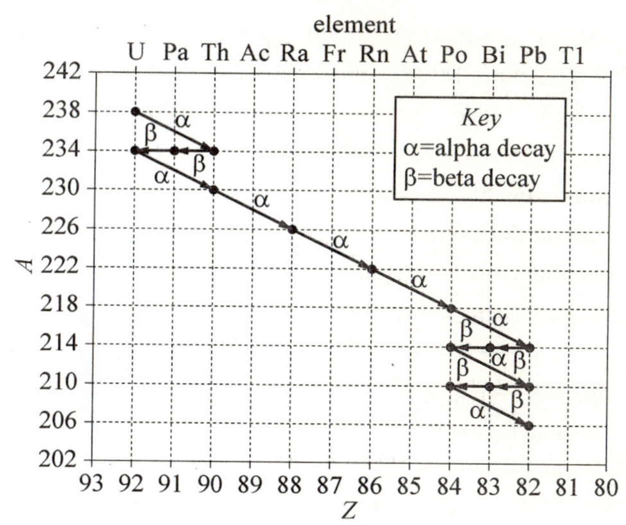

Figure 1

(1) 例题练习 1.1

Which of the following symbols correctly represents the isotope of radium (Ra) that is part of the radioactive decay sequence plotted in Figure 1?

F. $^{88}_{226}\mathrm{Ra}$　　G. $^{226}_{226}\mathrm{Ra}$　　H. $^{88}_{88}\mathrm{Ra}$　　J. $^{226}_{88}\mathrm{Ra}$

【考点分析】

- 数据表述类文章,此题为数据查找题。
- 抓住定位词 *Figure 1*。
- 直接定位到 Figure 1,找到 Ra 元素对应的坐标值,*A* 值为 226,*Z* 值为 88,结合文章中原子书写方式,可知正确答案为 **J**。

(2) 例题练习 1.2

How many neutrons, if any, does a nucleus of the isotope of helium listed in Table 1 contain?

A. 0　　B. 1　　C. 2　　D. 3

【考点分析】

- 数据表述类文章,此题为数据查找题。
- 抓住定位词 *Table 1*。
- 直接定位到 Table 1,找到$^{4}_{2}\mathrm{He}$,可知 *A* 值为 4,*Z* 值为 2,结合文章给出信息,我们知道质子数为 *Z*,*A* 为质子数和中子数之和,简单求解可知正确答案为 **C**。

(3) 例题练习 1.3

Based on Figure 1, if a nucleus of $^{230}_{90}\mathrm{Th}$ underwent beta decay, which of the following nuclei would be produced?

F. $^{230}_{230}\mathrm{Pa}$　　G. $^{230}_{92}\mathrm{Pa}$　　H. $^{91}_{91}\mathrm{Pa}$　　J. $^{230}_{91}\mathrm{Pa}$

【考点分析】

- 数据表述类文章,此题为数据推理题。
- 抓住定位词 *Figure 1 & beta decay*。
- 直接定位到 Figure 1,观察图中 beta decay,可以发现此衰变后,新原子的 *A* 值不变 *Z* 值加 1,那么经过一次衰变后,会变成 91,根据质子数 91,可找到对应原子为找到 Pa,可知正确答案为 **J**。

(4) 例题练习 1.4

A sample of spent nuclear reactor fuel contains a mixture of a uranium isotope, $^{235}_{92}U$, and a plutonium isotope, $^{239}_{94}Pu$. Based on Table 1 and Figure 1, if one of the isotopes is produced by the radioactive decay of the other isotope, which of the following best explains how the mixture was formed?

A. $^{235}_{92}U$ underwent alpha decay, producing $^{239}_{94}Pu$.

B. $^{239}_{94}Pu$ underwent alpha decay, producing $^{235}_{92}U$.

C. $^{235}_{92}U$ underwent beta decay, producing $^{239}_{94}Pu$.

D. $^{239}_{94}Pu$ underwent beta decay, producing $^{235}_{92}U$.

【考点分析】

- 数据表述类文章,此题为数据推理题。
- 抓住定位词 *Table 1 and Figure 1*。
- 题中给出两种原子,我们来分析下区别,可以看到两者 A 值相差 4,Z 值相差 2,对比 Table 1 中三种衰变,明显题目符合 Alpha 衰变,排除 C、D 选项,同时结合 Figure 1,可知经过一次 Alpha 衰变,A 值减 4,Z 值减 2,可知正确答案为 **B**。

(5) 例题练习 1.5

Suppose the $^{4}_{2}He$ nucleus emitted during an alpha decay and the e^- emitted during a beta decay have the same kinetic energy. Which of the 2 particles is moving at the higher speed?

F. The $^{4}_{2}He$ nucleus, because it is more massive than the e^-.

G. The $^{4}_{2}He$ nucleus, because it is less massive than the e^-.

H. The e^-, because it is more massive than the $^{4}_{2}He$ nucleus.

J. The e^-, because it is less massive than the $^{4}_{2}He$ nucleus.

【考点分析】

- 数据表述类文章,此题为数据推理题。
- 抓住关键词 *the same kinetic energy*。
- 我们知道动能公式为 $E=\frac{1}{2}mV^2$,同时根据文章背景得知氦原子质量远远大于电子质量,那么很显然当动能一致时,电子速度更快,结合这些信息可知正确答案为 **J**。

2) 知识拓展 1

[放射性衰变]

绝大多数的核素是不稳定的,它们会自发的蜕变,变成另一种核素,同时放出各种射线,这就叫做放射性衰变,其中包括 α、β、γ 等衰变。

能自发地放射各种射线的同位素称为放射性同位素。放射性同位素射出各种射线而发生核转变的过程称为放射性衰变。衰变前的放射性同位素称为母体,衰变过程中产生的新同位素称为放射成因同位素,或叫作子体。

放射性同位素衰变方式主要有:

(1) α 衰变:原子核自发地放射出 α 粒子而转变成另一种核的过程叫做 α 衰变。对于天然放射性同位素而言,只有质量数 A 大于 140 的重原子核才能产生 α 衰变,特别是原子序数 Z 大于 82 和质量数 A 大于 209 的放射性同位素,都以 α 衰变为主。α 衰变的通式为:$X(Z, A) \rightarrow Y(Z-2, A-4)+\alpha$.

(2) β 衰变:β 粒子有正、负电子之分,放出正电子的称 β+ 衰变,放出负电子的为 β- 衰变。

(3) K 轨道电子捕获:原子核从核外 K 层捕获一个轨道电子的过程称为轨道电子捕获。K 捕

获和β衰变所产生的子体是相同的，究竟发生那一类衰变，取决于衰变前后能量的变化。

(4) γ衰变：γ射线是从原子核内部放出的一种电磁辐射，常伴随α或β射线产生。γ衰变的母体和子体是同种同位素，只是原子核内部能量状态不同而已。γ衰变亦可称为同质异能跃迁。

(5) 核裂变：重核分裂成两个或几个中等质量的碎片，同时发射出中子和能量的过程称为原子核裂变。

2. 热力学(Thermodynamics)

1）例题练习 2

固体、液体和气体在被加热时经常膨胀。科学家进行了 3 个实验来研究不同物质的膨胀。

Experiment 1 实验 1

图 1 中的装置用来测量由不同金属制成的相同长度的金属线的膨胀。在每一个试验中，金属线被连上电压，经过一系列的滑轮，然后被附上重量。金属线的温度可以通过改变提供的电压大小来改变。膨胀的量与最后滑轮旋转的量成正比。结果显示在图 1 中。

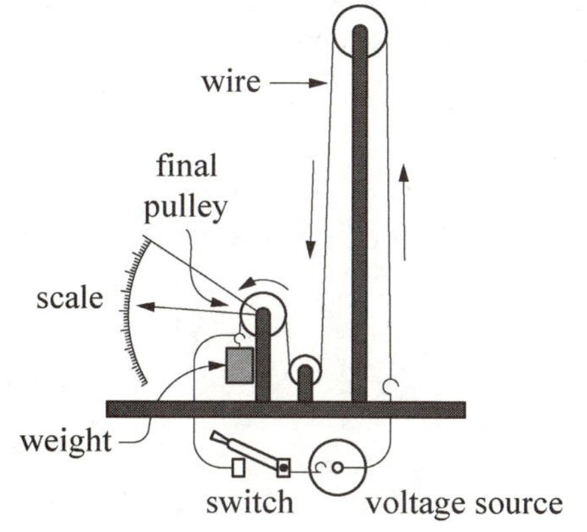

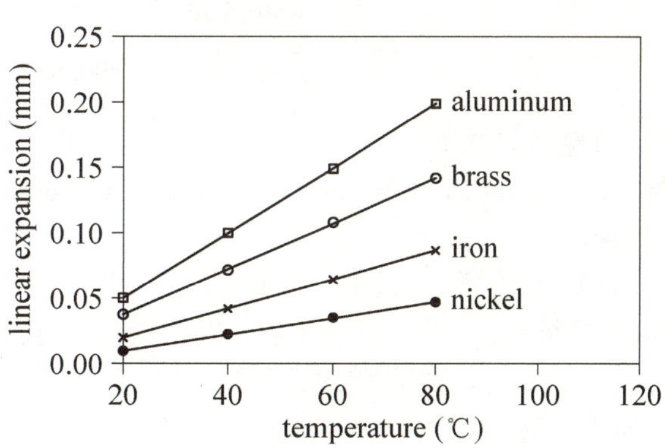

Figure 1

Experiment 2 实验 2

液体的样品放置在一个被瓶塞塞住的试管中，瓶塞上安装了一个有刻度的毛细管，然后将试管放置在一个可控温度的水槽中(见图 2)。在不同的温度下测量毛细管中液体上升的量。图 2 显示了 3 种液体的结果。

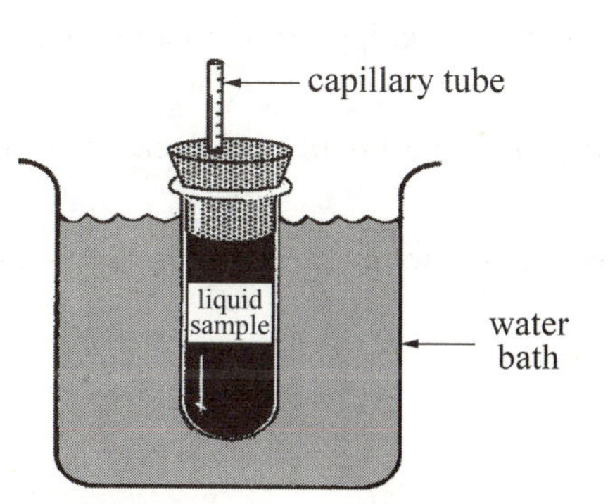

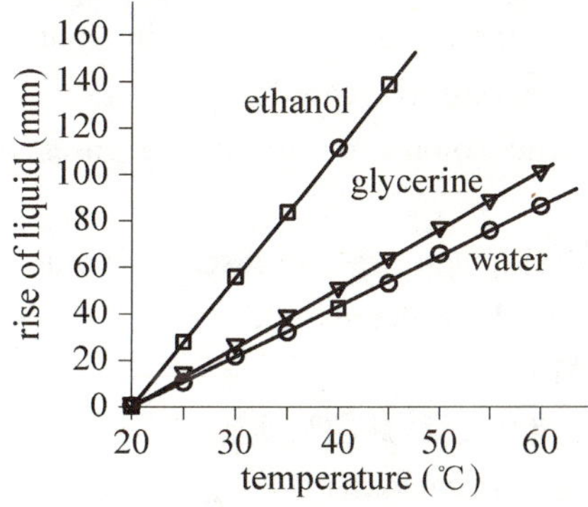

Figure 2

Experiment 3 实验 3

一个气体注射器中有 20 mL 的样品气体,在常温下(20℃)将注射器放置在温度可控的水槽中(图 3)。测量当温度增加时 3 种气体的体积变化。结果显示在图 3 中。

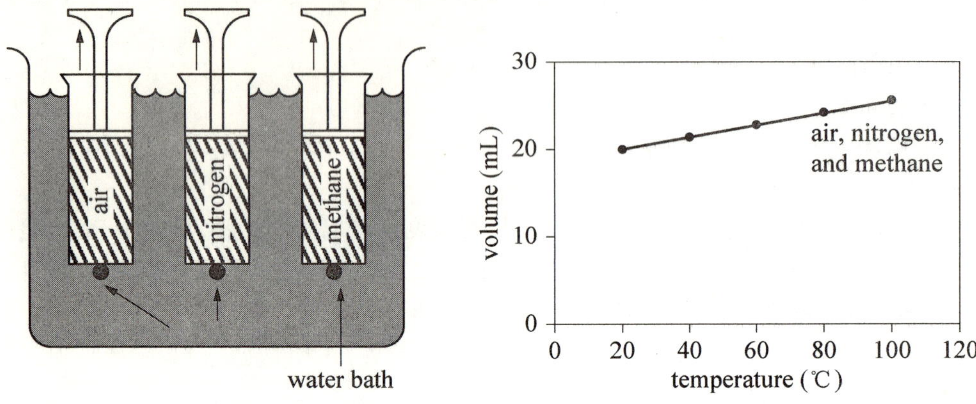

Figure 3

(1) 例题练习 2.1

In Experiment 2, at which of the following temperatures did all of the liquids tested have the same volume?

F. 20℃　　G. 30℃　　H. 40℃　　J. 50℃

【考点分析】

- 实验总结类文章,此题为实验结果题。
- 抓住定位词 *Experiment 2*。
- 直接定位到 Experiment 2,从 Figure 2 中可以看到,三条线在 20℃ 相交,很明显此时三者体积一致,正确答案为 F。

(2) 例题练习 2.2

A scientist has hypothesized that as the temperature of a gas is increased at constant pressure, the volume of the gas will also increase. Do the results of Experiment 3 support his hypothesis?

A. Yes; the volume of all of the gases tested in Experiment 3 increased as temperature increased.

B. Yes; although air decreased in volume when the temperature increased, nitrogen and methane volumes both increased.

C. No; the volume of all of the gases tested in Experiment 3 decreased as temperature increased.

D. No; although air increased in volume when the temperature increased, nitrogen and methane volumes both decreased.

【考点分析】

- 实验总结类文章,此题为实验假设题。
- 抓住定位词 *Experiment 3*。
- 题干的假设是恒定压力下,气体的温度增加,气体的体积也将增加。直接定位到 Experiment 3,从 Figure 3 中可以看到,3 种气体的体积随着温度增加而增加,很明显符合题干假设,正确答案为 A。

(3) 例题练习 2.3

Based on the results of Experiment 1, if an engineer needs a wire most resistant to stretching when it is placed under tension and heat, which of the following wires should she choose?

F. Aluminum G. Brass

H. Iron J. Nickel

【考点分析】

- 实验总结类文章,此题为实验结果题。
- 抓住定位词 *Experiment 1*。
- 题干要求找一种最能对抗压力和高温的绳子,我们先定位到 Experiment 1,从 Figure 1 中可以看到,4 种不同材质的绳子,在温度变高时绳子都有不同程度的拉伸,其中 nickel 拉伸度最小,也最稳定,所以正确答案为 **J**。

(4) 例题练习 2.4

Based on the results of Experiment 3, if a balloon was filled with air at room temperature and placed on the surface of a heated water bath, as the temperature of the water increased, the volume of the balloon would:

A. increase only. B. decrease only.

C. decrease, then increase. D. remain the same.

【考点分析】

- 实验总结类文章,此题为实验结果题。
- 抓住定位词 *Experiment 3*。
- 直接定位到 Experiment 3,从 Figure 3 中可以看到气体体积随着温度升高而增加,很显然正确答案为 **A**。

(5) 例题练习 2.5

The scientists tested a copper wire of the same initial length as the wires tested in Experiment 1. At 80℃, the linear expansion of the wire was 0.12 mm. Based on the results of Experiment 1, which of the following correctly lists 5 wires by their length in the apparatus at 80℃ from shortest to longest?

F. Aluminum, brass, copper, iron, nickel

G. Aluminum, copper, brass, iron, nickel

H. Nickel, iron, copper, brass, aluminum

J. Nickel, iron, brass, copper, aluminum

【考点分析】

- 实验总结类文章,此题为实验结果题。
- 抓住定位词 *Experiment 1*。
- 直接定位到 Experiment 1,从 Figure 1 中可以看到,在 80℃时,可以查找出 aluminum 的长度增加约为 0.20 mm,brass 约为 0.14 mm,iron 约为 0.08 mm,nickel 约为 0.04 mm,结合题目 copper 为 0.12,排序出来可知正确答案为 **H**。

(6) 例题练习 2.6

If Experiment 1 had been repeated using a heavier weight attached to the brass wire, which of the following figures best shows the comparison between the results of using the heavier weight and the original weight on the brass wire?

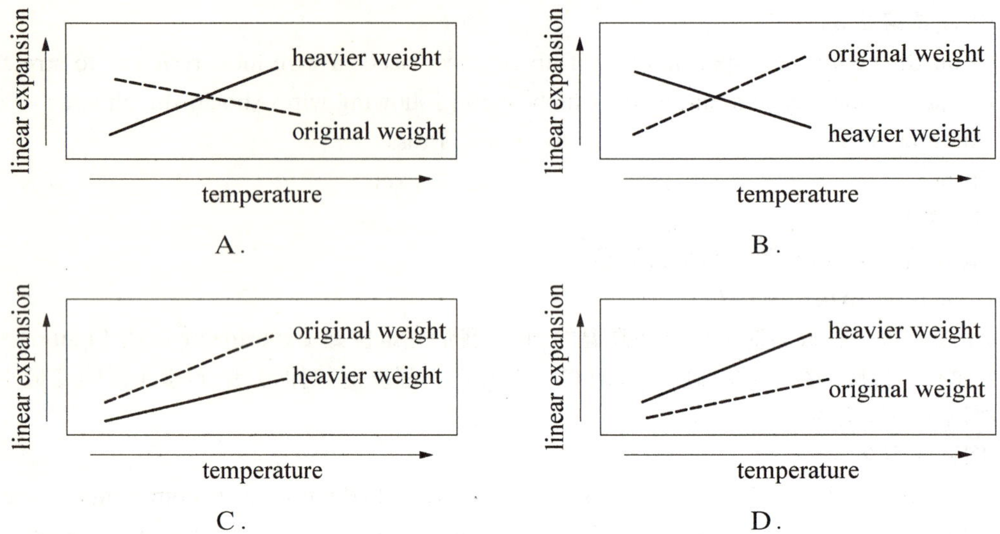

【考点分析】

- 实验总结类文章,此题为实验(设计)结果题。
- 抓住定位词 *Experiment 1*。
- 直接定位到 Experiment 1,根据实验结果可知,随着温度上升,绳子长度增加,而当重物增加重量时也就表示绳子上受的力加大,拉伸量必然比之前的要大,因为正确答案为 **D**。

3. 电磁学(Electromagnetism)

1) 例题练习 3

表 1 和表 2 概括了一些关于 1 m 长的铝线和铜线电阻的信息,相应的,这些线有不同的直径。铝线和铜线的电阻(单位为欧姆)限制了电流的大小并且使电能转化为热能。表 3 报告了在 20℃下不同长度的直径为 0.10 mm 的铝线的电阻,单位为欧姆。

Table 1

Diameter of aluminum wires (mm)	Resistance (ohms) at:		
	0℃	20℃	50℃
0.08	5.20	5.64	6.31
0.10	3.27	3.55	3.97
0.16	1.29	1.40	1.57
0.20	0.81	0.88	0.99

Table 2

Diameter of copper wires (mm)	Resistance (ohms) at:		
	0℃	20℃	50℃
0.08	3.17	3.44	3.85
0.10	1.99	2.16	2.42
0.16	0.79	0.86	0.96
0.20	0.50	0.54	0.60

Table 3

Length of 0.10-mm-diameter aluminum wire (m)	Resistance (ohms) at 20℃
1	3.55
2	7.10
4	14.20
10	35.50

(1) 例题练习 3.1

To determine if metal type affects resistance, the resistance of a copper wire with a diameter of 0.16 mm at a temperature of 0℃ should be compared to the resistance of:

A. an aluminum wire with a diameter of 0.16 mm at 0℃.

B. an aluminum wire with a diameter of 0.16 mm at 20℃.

C. a copper wire with a diameter of 0.08 mm at 0℃.

D. a copper wire with a diameter of 0.16 mm at 20℃.

【考点分析】

- 数据表述类文章,此题为背景常识题。
- 题干指出想要知道金属种类对电阻是否有影响。
- 那么根据常识我们知道,变量是金属种类,而其他应该保持不变,很显然正确答案为 **A**。

(2) 例题练习 3.2

Based on the information in Table 3, one would predict that a 20-m length of aluminum wire with a 0.10-mm diameter would have a resistance of:

F. 16 ohms. G. 25 ohms. H. 34 ohms. J. 71 ohms.

【考点分析】

- 数据表述类文章,此题为数据推理题。
- 抓住定位词 *Table 3*。
- Table 3 中,给出了对应长度下的对应电阻值,根据数据我们可以看出,长度与电阻值成正比,当长度增加多少倍,电阻亦增加多少倍,简单计算得出正确答案为 **J**。

(3) 例题练习 3.3

Could an experimenter calculate the density (mass/volume) of aluminum from a single table provided in the passage?

A. No, because the mass of only the aluminum wire is known.

B. No, because the mass is not given for any of the wires.

C. Yes, because both the mass and the volume of each wire can be calculated.

D. Yes, because the density is already given in the tables.

【考点分析】

- 数据表述类文章,此题为逻辑推理题。
- 抓住关键词 *density* (*mass/volume*)。
- 纵观整篇文章和实验数据,均没有提到任何有关质量的内容,所以不能得出,正确答案为 **B**。

(4) 例题练习 3.4

According to the data in Tables 1 and 2, which of the following sets of conditions would lead to the lowest resistance through 1 m of wire?

F. Aluminum wire, small diameter, high temperature

G. Copper wire, small diameter, low temperature

H. Copper wire, large diameter, low temperature

J. Copper wire, large diameter, high temperature

【考点分析】

- 数据表述类文章,此题为数据对比题。
- 抓住定位词 *Tables 1 and 2 & the lowest resistance*。
- 结合 Table 1 & 2,可以得到相同直径的铝丝/铜丝,温度越低电阻越小;而相同温度下,同一种材质时,直径越大,电阻越小;而当直径相同、温度相同时,铜丝电阻更小,得出正确答案为 **H**。

(5) 例题练习 3.5

Which of the following graphs best represents the relationship between diameter and resistance for wires made of aluminum?

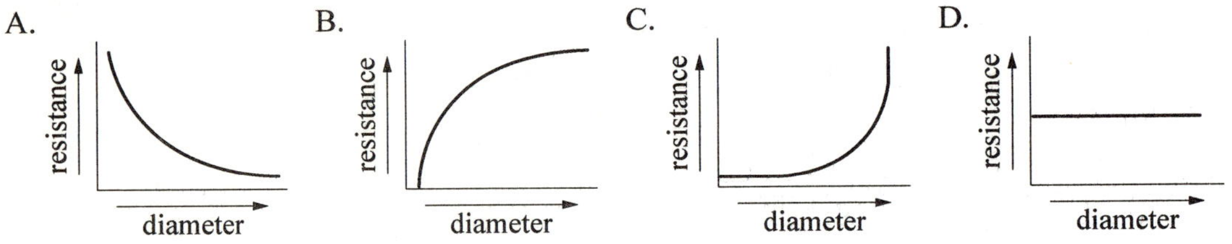

【考点分析】

- 数据表述类文章,此题为数据查找画图题。
- 抓住定位词 *diameter and resistance for wires made of aluminum*。
- 很明显数据都在 Table 1 中,直接根据表格数据作图便可得答案,正确答案为 **A**。

2) 知识拓展 2

[电阻]

电阻(Resistance,通常用"*R*"表示),是一个物理量,在物理学中表示导体对电流阻碍作用的大小。导体的电阻越大,表示导体对电流的阻碍作用越大。不同的导体,电阻一般不同,电阻是导体本身的一种特性。电阻将会导致电子流通量的变化,**电阻越小,电子流通量越大,反之亦然。而超导体则没有电阻。**

电阻虽然定义为 1 伏电压产生一安电流则为 1 欧电阻,但电压、电流并不是决定电阻的因素。电阻元件的电阻值大小一般与温度、材料、长度,还与横截面积有关,衡量电阻受温度影响大小的物理量是温度系数,其定义为温度每升高 1℃时电阻值发生变化的百分数。电阻的主要物理特征是变电能为热能,也可说它是一个耗能元件,电流经过它就产生内能。电阻在电路中通常起分压、分流的作用。对信号来说,交流与直流信号都可以通过电阻。

各种金属导体中,银的导电性能是最好的,但还是有电阻存在。20 世纪初,科学家发现某些物质在很低的温度时,如铝在 1.39 K(−271.76℃)以下,铅在 7.20 K(−265.95℃)以下,电阻就变成了零。这就是超导现象,用具有这种性能的材料可以做成超导材料。科学家已经开发出一些"高温"超导材料,它们在 100 K(−173℃)左右电阻就能降为零。

(四) 实战练习 Practice

1) Practice 4

(63D　Passage VI)

核聚变是原子核的结合,并且可以用来产生能量。不同的原子核含有不同数目的质子(带简单

正电荷的粒子)和中子(不带电粒子)。

一个保护壳中盛有氘(含有一个质子和一个中子)和氚(含有一个质子和两个中子)的原子核混合物。(密度 n 为每立方厘米内原子核的数目;高密度能够增加原子核碰撞的频率。)原子核碰撞、融合,并且释放出巨大的能量。因为相似电荷的粒子相互排斥,所以要是两个原子核离得足够近来融合就需要将原子核加速到非常高的速度,需要消耗能量。而且,能量被消耗能够防止原子核撞击保护壳的内壁,一旦撞击到内壁原子核会丢失速度。

为了使核聚变产生的能量比消耗的能量更多,温度必须在很短的时间 τ 内维持在 4×10^7 K 以上,并且 n 和 τ 的产生必须超出 10^{14} nuclei/cm^3(称为劳森准则)。

下面讨论了两种关于限制(阻止原子核碰撞撞击到容器的内壁)和产生原子核聚变的方法。

The Magnetic Confinement Method 磁场限制法

用一个磁力场来压缩氘和氚原子核的气体。因为过大的气体密度会导致磁场弯曲,使得气体逃出限制并且撞击到保护壳上,所以允许的最大密度为 10^{14} nuclei/cm^3。因此,为了满足劳森准则,需要在大约 1 秒维持温度为 10^8 K。

The Laser Confinement Method 激光限制方法

一个包含氘和氚原子的小球会受到激光脉冲的影响,产生出密度为 10^{23} nuclei/cm^3 的气体。激光脉冲可以用来在 10^{-9} 秒内压缩和加热气体至 10^8 K。可惜一些激光能量会被气体反射而不是被气体吸收。

目前,磁场限制方法产生的功率(单位时间内产生或消耗的能量)与消耗的功率之比要比激光限制法高得多。但是,由于小球内高密度的原子核,激光限制法产生的功率要比磁场限制法高的多。

(1) Practice 4.1

Both confinement methods consume large amounts of energy in order to:

A. cause fusion between nuclei.
B. increase the distances between nuclei.
C. decrease the speed of the nuclei.
D. decrease the charges oh the nuclei.

(2) Practice 4.2

According to the passage, for the Magnetic Confinement Method approximately what is the value of τ?

F. 10^{-10} sec
G. 10^{-5} sec
H. 1 sec
J. 10 sec

(3) Practice 4.3

For both confinement methods, fusing deuterium nuclei is difficult because the nuclei have identical:

A. charges.
B. masses.
C. speeds.
D. weights.

(4) Practice 4.4

To increase the probability that nuclei will collide, a goal of both methods is to:

F. decrease the temperature inside the containment vessel.
G. decrease the density of nuclei in the containment vessel.
H. increase the density of nuclei in the containment vessel.
J. increase the number of neutrons in the nuclei.

(5) Practice 4.5

A comparison of the densities of the deuterium/tritium gas for the two methods shows that the:

A. Magnetic Confinement Method typically produces higher densities.

B. Laser Confinement Method typically produces higher densities.

C. Laser Confinement Method never produces higher densities.

D. two methods usually produce equal densities.

(6) Practice 4.6

In the Laser Confinement Method, laser light is used to:

F. cool the deuterium and tritium nuclei.

G. exert pressure on the deuterium and tritium nuclei.

H. illuminate the walls of the containment vessel.

J. heat the walls of the containment vessel.

(7) Practice 4.7

For a new method of confinement, the product of n and τ is about 10^{13} sec/cm^3. Which of the following changes would be most likely to bring the new method into compliance with Lawson's criterion?

A. A large decrease in n and a small increase in τ

B. A small increase in n and a large decrease in τ

C. Large decreases in both n and τ

D. Large increases in both n and τ

2) Practice 5

(OG2　Passage IV)

黑体是可以吸收所有撞击到它的辐射的物体。黑体同样可以释放出所有波长的辐射;释放出的辐射叫做黑体辐射。给定波长的黑体辐射的亮度取决于黑体的温度。对于一个黑体,亮度相对于波长的图像称为黑体曲线。下图显示了在 3 种不同的温度下,相同黑体的黑体曲线。

(Note: 1 watt = 1 joule per second; joule is a unit of energy. At wavelengths above 25×10^{-6} m, the brightness of the blackbody at each temperature continues to decrease.)

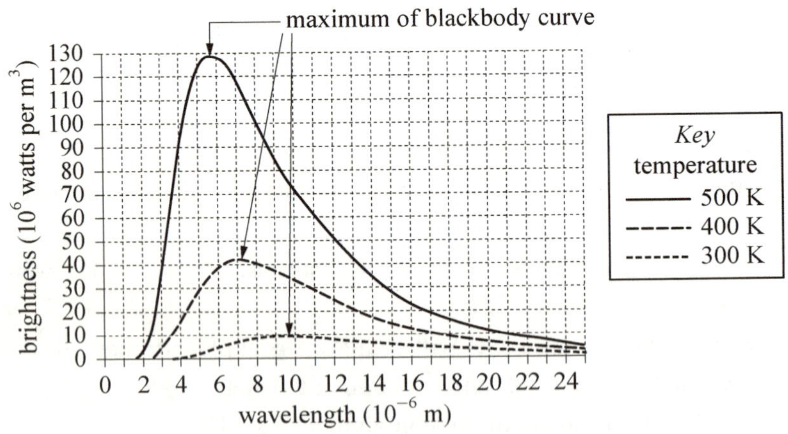

(*Note: 1 watt = 1 joule per second; joule is a unit of energy. At wavelengths above 25×10^{-6} m, the brightness of the blackbody at each temperature continues to decrease.*)

(1) Practice 5.1

The area under each blackbody curve gives the total amount of energy emitted every second by 1 m^2 of the blackbody. Which of the following correctly ranks the 3 curves, from greatest to least, according to the total amount of energy emitted every second by 1 m^2 of the blackbody at the

wavelengths shown?

F. 300 K, 400 K, 500 K
G. 300 K, 500 K, 400 K
H. 400 K, 500 K, 300 K
J. 500 K, 400 K, 300 K

(2) Practice 5.2

Based on the figure, at a temperature of 300 K and a wavelength of 30×10^{-6} m, the brightness of a blackbody will most likely be:

A. less than 5×10^{-6} watts per m^3.
B. between 5×10^{-6} watts per and 40×10^{-6} watts per m^3.
C. Between 40×10^{-6} watts per and 130×10^{-6} watts per m^3.
D. greater than 130×10^{-6} watts per m^3.

(3) Practice 5.3

The radiation emitted by a star can be represented by the radiation from a blackbody having the same temperature as the star's visible surface. Based on the figure, which of the following sets of blackbody curves best represents stars of equal diameter with surface temperatures of 3,000 K, 6,000 K, and 9,000 K?

F.

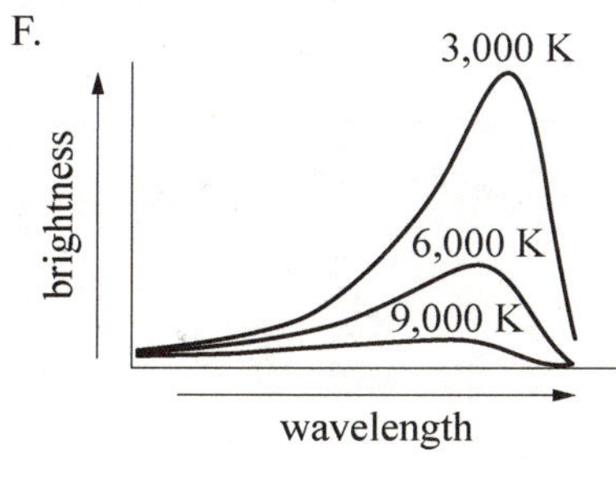

G.

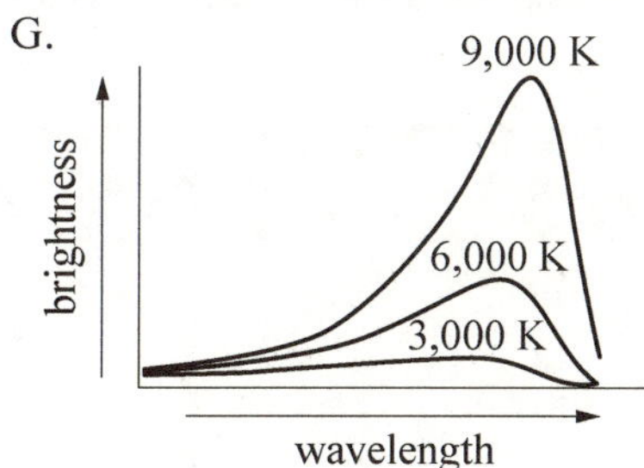

H.

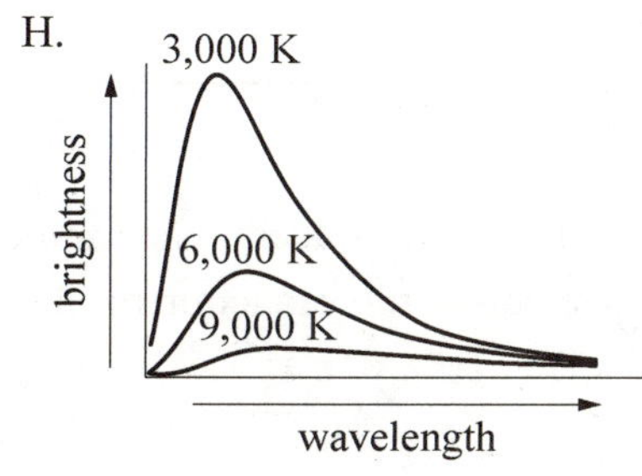

J.

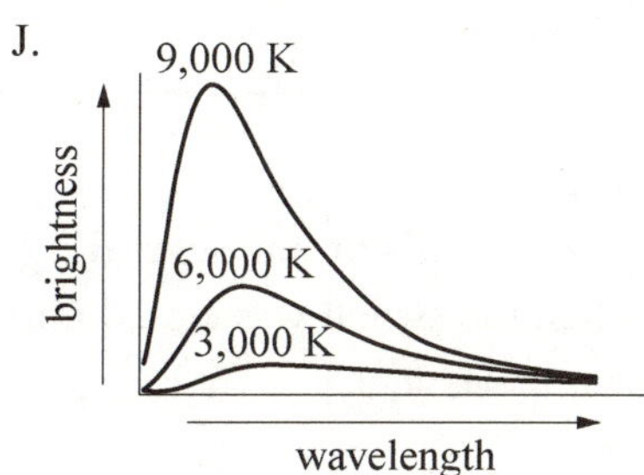

(4) Practice 5.4

Based on the figure, the maximum of the blackbody curve will equal 75×10^{6} watts per m^3 when the temperature of the blackbody is closest to:

A. 250 K.
B. 350 K.
C. 450 K
D. 550 K.

(5) Practice 5.5

The frequency of radiation increases as the radiation's wavelength decreases. Based on this information, over all wavelengths in the figure, as the frequency of the radiation from a blackbody increases, the brightness of the radiation:

F. increases only,
G. decreases only.
H. increases, then decreases.
J. decreases, then increases.

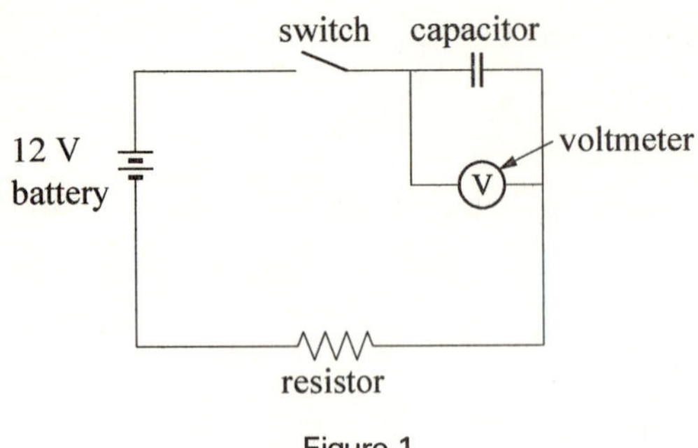

Figure 1

3) Practice 6

(61C—Passage III)

An electrical circuit contained a 12 - volt (V) battery, a resistor (a device that resists the flow of electricity), a capacitor (a device that stores electrical charge and electrical energy), a voltmeter (an instrument for measuring volt-age), and a switch, as shown in Figure 1.

Some students studied the behavior of the circuit.

Experiment 1

The students used a 1×10^7 ohm (Ω) resistor and a capacitor with a capacitance of 1×10^{-6} farad (F). (Capacitance is a measure of the maximum amount of electrical charge and electrical energy a capacitor can store.) The capacitor was initially uncharged. At time zero, the students simultaneously closed the switch and started a stopwatch. At time zero and at 12 sec intervals thereafter, they recorded the voltage across the capacitor. Their results are shown in Table 1.

Table 1

Time (sec)	Voltage across capacitor (V)
0	0.0
12	8.4
24	10.9
36	11.7
48	11.9
60	12.0

Experiment 2

Using the 1×10^7 resistor and several different capacitors, the students determined the length of time from when the switch was closed until the voltage across the capacitor reached 6 V. Their results are shown in Table 2.

Table 2

Capacitance ($\times 10^{-6}$F)	Time to reach 6 V across capacitor (sec)
1.2	8.3
0.6	4.2
0.3	2.1
0.1	0.7

Experiment 3

The students conducted the same procedure described in Experiment 2, except that they used a constant capacitance of 1×10^{-6} F and several different resistors. Their results are shown in Table 3.

Table 3

Resistance ($\times 10^7 \Omega$)	Time to reach 6 V across capacitor (sec)
0.75	5.2
0.50	3.5
0.25	1.7

(1) Practice 6.1

In Experiment 1, the time constant of the circuit was the time required for the voltage across the capacitor to reach approximately 7.6 V. The time constant of the circuit used in Experiment 1 was:

F. less than 12 sec. G. between 12 sec and 24 sec.

H. between 24 sec and 36 sec. J. greater than 36 sec.

(2) Practice 6.2

If, in Experiment 2, a 1.5×10^{-6} capacitor had been used, the time required for the voltage across the capacitor to reach 6 V would have been closest to:

A. 4.2 sec. B. 7.0 sec. C. 10.5 sec. D. 15.0 sec.

(3) Practice 6.3

The main purpose of Experiment 3 was to determine how varying the:

F. battery's voltage affected the resistor's resistance at a given time.

G. capacitor's capacitance affected the time required for the voltage across the capacitor to reach a set value.

H. capacitor's capacitance affected the voltage across the battery at a given time.

J. resistor's resistance affected the time required for the voltage across the capacitor to reach a set value.

(4) Practice 6.4

Based on Figure 1, to measure the voltage across the resistor only, which of the following circuits should one use?

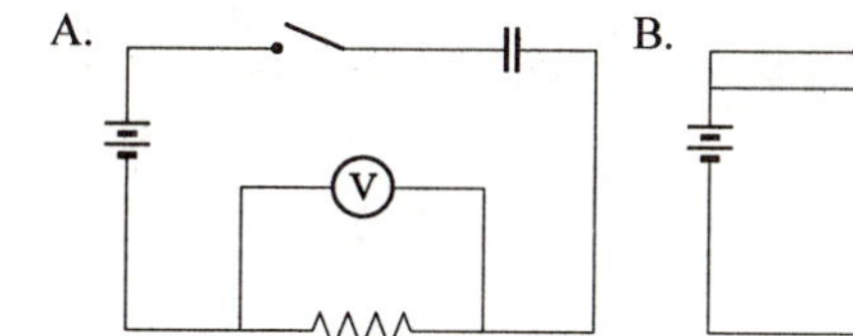

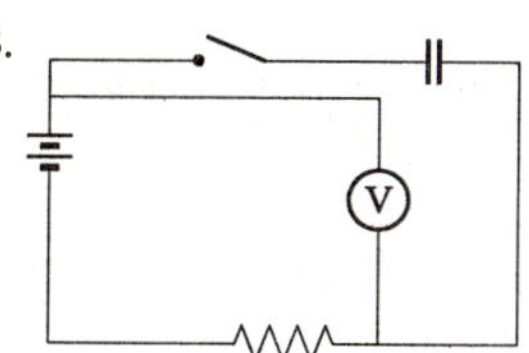

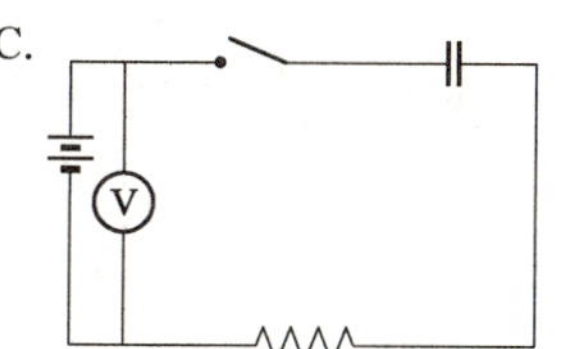

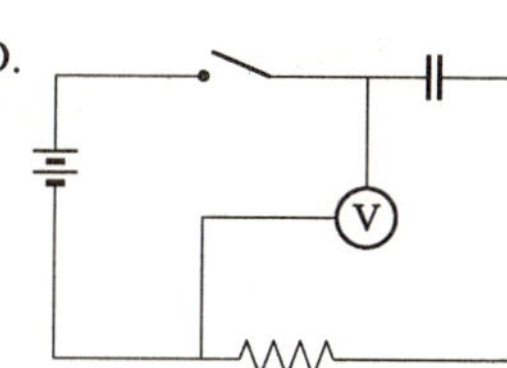

(5) Practice 6.5

Consider a circuit like that shown in Figure 1. Based on Experiments 2 and 3, the voltage across the capacitor will reach a given value in the shortest amount of time if the circuit contains which of the following capacitances and resistances, respectively?

F. 0.1×10^{-6} F, 0.3×10^{7} Ω G. 0.1×10^{-6} F, 1.0×10^{7} Ω

H. 1.2×10^{-6} F, 0.3×10^{7} Ω J. 1.2×10^{-6} F, 1.0×10^{7} Ω

(6) Practice 6.6

Consider the following hypothesis: In a circuit arranged as in Figure 1 containing a battery, a capacitor, and a constant resistance, as capacitance increases, the time required to reach a given voltage across the capacitor increases. Do the experiments support this hypothesis?

A. Yes; in Experiment 1, as capacitance increased, the time required to reach a given voltage increased.

B. Yes; in Experiment 2, as capacitance increased, the time required to reach a given voltage increased.

C. No; in Experiment 1, as capacitance increased, the time required to reach a given voltage decreased.

D. No; in Experiment 2, as capacitance increased, the time required to reach a given voltage decreased.

Answers for Practice 4 - 6

Practice 4　A H A H B G

Practice 5　J A J C H

Practice 6　F C J A F B

二、解析

31B 解析

[**Passage I**]

1. 答案:B

   题干:判断只产生黑猫后代的亲本性状。

   定位:Table 3

   解析:从 Table 3 中可以看出,黑猫对应的基因型为 XbXb 和 XbY,所以亲本的基因型中能含有 B 基因。

2. 答案:H

   题干:判断杂交体 1 后代中黑猫比例。

   定位:Table 1

   解析:从 Table 1 中可以看出,黑猫为 14 只,占 29 只后代的比例为 50%。

3. 答案:C

   题干:判断最能表示杂交体 2 后代分布的柱状图。

   定位:Table 2

   解析:根据 Table 2 中后代数目判断。

4. 答案:F

   题干:判断 XBY 基因型的后代比例。

   定位:Table 2、3

   解析:从 Table 3 中可以看出,XBY 对应的性状为橙色黑猫,数量为 12 只,在 60 只后代中所占比例为 20%。

5. 答案:D

题干：判断两个实验中亲本的区别。
定位：Table 1、2
解析：在实验 1 中，亲本为橙色公猫和黑色母猫，杂交多次；实验 2 中，亲本为杂色母猫和黑色公猫，杂交多次。

6. 答案：J
题干：判断母猫所有可能的性状。
定位：Table 3
解析：从 Table 3 中可以看出，母猫对应的基因型可以为 XBXB、XbXb 和 XBXb，所以母猫的性状可以为橙色、黑色和杂色。

7. 答案：A
题干：判断子代的性状。
定位：Table 3
解析：题目中给定的亲本基因型可产生 XBXB 和 XBY 的子代基因型，对照 Table 3 可知子代性状全部为橙色。

[**Passage II**]

8. 答案：A
题干：判断研究者的说法在实验中属于哪一环节。
定位：无
解析：研究者的理论在组织实验前提出，即为假说。

9. 答案：D
题干：判断实验目的。
定位：Figure 1
解析：从 Figure 1 中可以看出，实验关心的是两种不同 strain 的生长速度。

10. 答案：H
题干：判断哪个长度可能是在第 180 天 Strain A 中雌性的长度。
定位：Figure 2
解析：Figure 2 中代表 Strain A 的是虚线柱体，只出现在 23～32 mm 的范围。

11. 答案：D
题干：判断哪两种鱼的长度在 150 天和 180 天之间保持不变。
定位：Figure 1
解析：Figure 1 中最下方两条曲线在此范围内保持水平。

12. 答案：F
题干：比较在第 180 天时雌性鱼与雄性鱼的平均长度。
定位：Figure 1
解析：通过计算，在 180 天时雌性鱼的平均长度为 25 mm，雄性鱼的平均长度为 17.5 mm。

13. 答案：B
题干：判断实验中需要控制的变量。
定位：Figure 1
解析：实验关心的是基因在不同种鱼生长速度方面的作用，所以需要控制试验中鱼摄入的食物数量。

14. 答案：F

题干：判断 Strain B 中鱼的长度从 20 mm 到 25 mm 范围内数量的变化。
定位：Figure 2
解析：Figure 2 中代表 Strain B 的实心柱体在此范围内先升高后降低。

[**Passage III**]

15. 答案：D
题干：判断在 280 秒时衰变的 N 所占的比例。
定位：Figure 2
解析：从 Figure 2 下方的曲线可以得出。
16. 答案：G
题干：判断$^{15}_{8}$O 所含有的质子数目。
定位：Table 1
解析：从 Table 1 中可以看到，左下角的数字即为原子中的质子数目。
17. 答案：C
题干：判断$^{15}_{8}$O 有 50%衰减所用的时间。
定位：Figure 1
解析：从 Figure 1 下方的曲线可以得出。
18. 答案：J
题干：判断 X 衰变为 Y 的过程中 X 与 Y 含量的变化。
定位：Figure 1、2
解析：比较 Figure 1 和 2 可以看出，O 衰变为 N 时，O 的比例减小，N 的比例增加。所以 X 衰变为 Y 时，X 减少 Y 增加。
19. 答案：B
题干：判断衰变之后原子中质子数目的变化。
定位：Table 1
解析：从 Table 1 可以看出，每次衰变之后，质子数目都减少一个。

[**Passage IV**]

20. 答案：G
题干：判断哪个学生认为糖水有最高的 BP。
定位：最后一句
解析：从最后一句可以看到，第三个学生认为糖水因为有最大的粘度所以有最高的 BP，而其他两个同学认为糖水和盐水的 BP 相同。
21. 答案：C
题干：判断哪个学生认为向水中加盐会提高溶液的 BP。
定位：Student 3、4
解析：从 Student 3 的论述中可以看到，通过向水中加盐或者糖，会提高溶液的粘稠度从而提高 BP。
22. 答案：G
题干：判断哪个选项符合 Student 2 的观点。
定位：Student 2
解析：从 Student 2 的论述中可以看到，他认为糖水和盐水有着相同的 BP，并且要比纯水的

BP 低。

23. 答案：

题干：缺失

24. 答案：G

题干：判断化学家的说法与哪个学生的解释一致。

定位：Student 2、3

解析：从 Student 2 的论述中可知，他认为加入糖会使糖水的 BP 低于纯水，那么可推理知加入更多糖会导致比纯水的 BP 更低，与化学家说法一致。

25. 答案：A

题干：比较盐水和糖水的粘稠度。

定位：Student 3

解析：从 Student 3 的论述中可以看到，第三个学生认为糖水有更大的粘稠度，所以 NaCl 对水粘稠度的提升要低于蔗糖。

[**Passage V**]

26. 答案：G

题干：判断 2003 年东北部湖泊的 SO_4^{2-} 含量。

定位：Figure 3

解析：从图中可以看到，2002 年的含量高于 80 低于 100，趋势也是逐渐减少，所以 2003 年含量约为 85。

27. 答案：C

题干：判断生物能在哪个湖泊生存。

定位：Figure 2、3

解析：从图中可以看到，1996 年 Upper Midwest 的湖泊 pH 值高于 6.5，Northeast 的湖泊 pH 值约为 5.5，所以生物在两个湖泊中都能存活。

28. 答案：A

题干：判断当 SO_4^{2-} 含量降低时，湖泊 pH 值的变化趋势。

定位：Figure 2

解析：从图中可以看到，pH 值对应的曲线是单调递增的。

29. 答案：D

题干：判断“在 1982 到 1996 年间中西部地区 SO_2 排放量的降低导致了 SO_4^{2-} 含量的升高”的正确性。

定位：Figure 1、2

解析：从图 1 中可以看到，SO_2 的排放量逐年减少，而图 2 中 SO_4^{2-} 的含量也逐年减少。

30. 答案：F

题干：判断在 1990 年的湖水中加入哪一年的湖水会让 pH 下降。

定位：Figure 3

解析：从图 3 中可以看到，1990 年的湖水 pH 值约为 5.4，pH 值逐年增长，所以为了让 pH 值下降，需要混合入 pH 值更小的湖水，即 1990 年之前的湖水。

52C 解析

[**Passage I**]

1. 答案:D

解析:由于题干意思是要修建水坝防止水流走,故流出量将减少,而流入量不会受到影响,从而使水的总量增加。所以正确答案是 D。A、B、C 均应排除,因为流入量取决于降雨和河流输送,不会由于水坝的建成而改变。

2. 答案:G

解析:由题干,该区域 5 年内缺少降雨,而降雨是 inflow 的一大来源,则水流入量相对降低,流出量不受影响。所以正确答案是 G。

3. 答案:C

解析:A 选项过于绝对,排除;B 选项,流入径流数大于流出径流数,无法从题目中得到相关信息,排除;C 选项,若河流的流入量与流出量不平衡,水体深度将改变,正确;D 选项,错误,若流入量与流出量相等可达到动态平衡,使水体保持一定容量。

4. 答案:H

解析:地质学家得到的结果是河流深度平均年际变化,若只测定两年很有可能由于这两年情况比较特殊而使平均值结果不可靠,选择 H。F、G 应排除,因为测量次数越多,人为误差的影响会随样本量的增加而减小。J 错误,流速与测定时间无关。

5. 答案:D

解析:A、B、C 三项均无法由题中信息推出。D 项正确,因为 3 个研究都用到了水体流入量或流出量的计算,而这隐含的假设就是题中表格里的种类全面,包含了所有重要的 inflows 和 outflows。

6. 答案:G

解析:由题干,河流容量逐年降低,支持该结论的情况不可能是降雨量增加,故排除 F;河流表面面积减少可能造成容量减少,G 选项正确。H、J 错误,因为不同河流存在差异,不具有可比性。

[**Passage II**]

7. 答案:C

解析:由题干信息,温血动物通常移动速度更快,而研究 3 中速度最快的为食草动物 1(plant-eater 1),故选择 C 选项。

8. 答案:G

解析:本题可用排除法作答。仅从速度无法辨别恐龙种类,排除 A;腿足长比例与体重关系无法从原文中得知,排除 H;恐龙的食性与步态无关,排除 J。由 study 3 的第二句可知步长和腿长可估算恐龙速度,正确选项为 G。

9. 答案:B

解析:由 study 3 的首句即可得,study 1 是由 study 2 的数据估算而出,而 study 3 又用到了 study 1 的结论,故 study 2 间接贡献了 study 3 的结果,选 B。

10. 答案:F

解析:由于题干中发现的是一种大型鸟的路径,其与恐龙的身体特征、形态都有较大差异,若要

得到它的速度，必须先知道其腿长等数据，故选 A。

11. 答案：B

解析：由题干可知，食肉动物 1 的速度增加到了 4.6 m/s，可能是因为：A 选项步态改变，正确；B 选项食肉动物 1 将会超过其他 4 种恐龙，错误，因为其中食草动物 1 的速度更快，不会被超过；C 选项食草动物 1 被超过的危险最低，正确；D 选项食草动物 3 被超过的危险最大，正确，因为其速度相对最慢。要求选不符合新数据的选项，故选 B。

12. 答案：G

解析：由于 study 1 是由 study 2 的数据估算而出，而 study 3 又用到了 study 1 的结论，若在 study 2 中使用更多类似的恐龙样本，会间接地使 study 3 更加精确，故选择 G 选项。

[**Passage III**]

13. 答案：A

解析：为比较不同类型金属的电阻，应将其他变量条件（温度、直径等）均固定，只改变金属。只有 A 选项符合条件。

14. 答案：J

解析：由表 3 可看出，铝线的电阻与长度成正比，故 20 米长的导线电阻应为 10 米长导线的 2 倍，即 $35.5\times2=71$，选 J。

15. 答案：B

解析：根据公式 $R=pL/S$（R 为电阻，p 为电阻率，L 为导线长度，S 为横截面积），题干指根据某一个表计算出密度，根据公式可推知长度和横截面积，继而求出导线体积，但由于质量未知，无法求出，选 B。

16. 答案：H

解析：最低电阻应对应最低的电阻率、最大直径和最低温。故选 H。

17. 答案：A

解析：该题考查铝线的直径和电阻的关系图。根据公式 $R=pL/S$（R 为电阻，p 为电阻率，L 为导线长度，S 为横截面积），直径越大，横截面积越大，电阻越小，符合该条件的只有 A。

[**Passage IV**]

18. 答案：J

解析："无反应"应指从表面上看溶液未发生变化，即无沉淀或变色发生。选 J。

19. 答案：C

解析：根据题意，未知溶液与硫酸无反应，从表中可知只有钙和镁符合条件，其他两种离子会和硫酸根离子结合生成白色沉淀。故选 C。

20. 答案：F

解析：Sr 和 Ca 与硫酸反应的现象不同，前者产生白色沉淀而后者无反应，据此可区别开，故选 F。其他 3 种试剂与 Sr 和 Ca 反应产生的现象都相同，排除。

21. 答案：D

解析：题干要求未知溶液中只含有硝酸镁。排除 A、B、C，因为可能还含有钙离子，也符合条件；D 选项正确，因为若有其他离子存在产生的现象会不同，第一步会产生白色沉淀。

22. 答案：J

解析：要最佳分离四种离子，应让其分步沉淀，只有 J 符合条件。先加 Chromate 可沉淀 Barium，得到含有其他 3 种离子的上清液，再依次加入 Sulfate、Oxalate、Carbonate 等逐一分离。

[**Passage V**]

23. 答案：C

解析：由题表可看出钟摆周期与质量和角度均无关，只与长度有关。根据表 2，长度为 0.5 米的绳子对应周期为 1.40 秒，故选 C。

24. 答案：F

解析：由于实验 3 中钟摆周期均接近 1.40 s，由表 2 可知对应绳长为 0.5 m，选 A。

25. 答案：D

解析：实验者能控制的变量为绳长、质量和初始放置角度。振动周期是由这 3 个变量决定的，不能由实验者人为控制，选 D。

26. 答案：H

解析：记 50 次全振动的时间再除以 50 得到的周期相对于直接记 1 次全振动时间更为精确，因为实验者的反应时间所造成的人为系统误差由于测量时间变长而相对比例减小，简而言之就是系统误差减小，选 H。空气阻力影响与测量时间无关，排除 F、G。

27. 答案：D

解析：由题表 1、2、3 可看出钟摆周期与质量和角度均无关，只与长度有关。选 D。

28. 答案：F

解析：由于钟摆周期只与长度有关，故长度相等的两组试验得到的周期最接近，即 I、II。故选 F。

[**Passage VI**]

29. 答案：B

解析：找到题表中铁对应的功能——活化 porphyrins，选择 B 选项。

30. 答案：J

解析：题干要求被用作为开花植物酶组分的所需微量元素，锌为微量元素，且是催化含碳酸降解的酶的组成成分，符合条件，选 J。

31. 答案：B

解析：题目中的玉米每 100 蒲式耳需要 2.0 lb 的铁来活化，而新型的玉米利用铜替代铁，故推测需要 2.0 lb 的铜，选 B。

32. 答案：G

解析：从表中可看出钠离子和氯离子的功能未知，但它们都是植物生长必不可少的大量元素，G 选项符合题意。

33. 答案：A

解析：镁为大量元素，不符合要求。其他 3 种元素都为微量或痕量，故排除。选 A。

[**Passage VII**]

34. 答案：F

解析：根据原文，Gradualism 的观点是由祖先到后代逐步过渡不断发展变化不存在停滞的，符合要求的只有 F。

35. 答案：B

解析：Episodic 的观点是物种形成是阶段性的、大规模的，且在一定阶段内是较稳定的。根据

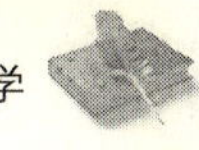

原文内容,能随变化的环境做出适应的种群会形成新种,而其他无法适应的种群将被淘汰。选择B选项。

36. 答案:H

解析:此题可用排除法解答。由示意图看出明显是阶段性的变化,为 Episodic 形式的进化,排除 F、G;进化的方向未发生改变,宽度逐渐增大,排除 J;正确答案为 H。对照原文内容也是一致的。

37. 答案:A

解析:考查世代间隔与进化速度的关系。对于 Gradualism(渐进主义学说)而言,进化是通过子代与祖先差异的积累而实现的,所以世代间隔越长,一定时间内代数就越少,差异积累也相应较小,进化速度慢。符合该逻辑关系的选项为 A。

38. 答案:F

解析:基因突变导致子代遗传物质较父代而言发生变化。根据渐进主义学说,进化是通过差异的积累逐步实现的,所以生物体基因突变造成的进化应为不符合自然规律的、有害的,不利于生物生存的,选 F。文中并未涉及到基因突变的频率及显隐性问题,故排除 H、J。

39. 答案:C

解析:题意要求按 Episodic 的观点分析,而 C 为 Gradualism 的观点,不合题意。要求选择不符合题干的选项,故 C 为正确答案。

40. 答案:F

解析:题述的单细胞生物生活在开阔海洋中,人们认为它主要通过循序渐进的方式进化而非插曲式的阶段进化。而 Episodic 的一个必要条件就是形成相对隔离的小种群,所以 F 符合要求,正确。其他选项都并非必要条件,原文也未涉及,应排除。

55C 解析

[**Passage I**]

1. 答案:D

解析:由于硝酸钙是由大理石被硝酸腐蚀而产生的,故时间越长,硝酸浓度越大,产生的硝酸钙也越多。而硝酸主要来自空气中的氮氧化物与水反应产生。按此逻辑应选 D。

2. 答案:H

解析:原文中提到 4 块大理石板的表面面积都相等,为 24 平方厘米,应选择 H。其他答案从表格比较中可明显排除。

3. 答案:A

解析:样品 1 和样品 3 的区别在于使用的酸不同,通过溶解的大理石量可看出硫酸的腐蚀性更强,腐蚀速率更快,A 符合要求。

4. 答案:G

解析:由于其他条件均相同,用 50 ppm 的硝酸溶解大理石的效果应介于 30 ppm 和 100 ppm 之间,即损失的大理石质量应在 4.0~4.3 mg 之间,只有 G 符合要求。

5. 答案:D

解析:表面积增大,反应速率应加快,同样时间里溶解的大理石质量也会增加,与使用的酸种类无关。D 选项正确。

6. 答案:J

解析：由于大理石受氮氧化物氧化腐蚀后会产生硝酸钙，故硝酸钙的质量可反映腐蚀程度，选 J。

[**Passage II**]

7. 答案：B

   解析：由表 2 可知，含相同碳原子数的直链烃比含支链烃的沸点高 8～12℃，选项中最接近的为 10℃，选 B。

8. 答案：G

   解析：密度最低的烃类由表 3 可推断出应为含 4 个碳原子的支链烃，从表 1 又可看出相应结构式。应选 G。

9. 答案：D

   解析：由表 2 和表 3 结合可看出，碳原子数增加，沸点也增加，密度也相应增大。D 选项符合条件。

10. 答案：F

    解析：由表 3 可看出，含 4 个碳原子的烃类环状结构密度最大，支链结构密度最小，F 为正确选项。

11. 答案：D

    解析：要求在 10℃时为气体，即沸点要低于 10℃，只有 3 个碳原子的烃类和含 4 个碳原子的链状烃符合要求，选 D。

[**Passage III**]

12. 答案：H

    解析：由表 1 可知，塑料球的降落时间约为 0.80 秒，故应选 H。

13. 答案：A

    解析：由题意可知，两球的半径、表面积和体积均相同，只有质量不同，故选 A。

14. 答案：G

    解析：要求证明球除了受到地心引力的影响，还受到空气阻力的影响，观测的最佳证据应该是实际加速度低于重力加速度 $9.8\ m/s^2$。G 选项正确。

15. 答案：A

    解析：根据表 1，2.5 米处降落时塑料球需花 0.80 秒到达地面，故从 1 米处降落所需时间应少于 0.80 秒，选 A。

16. 答案：H

    解析：由于两球的降落时间都少于 1 秒，所以精确到秒的秒表对于测定其降落时间不会有任何差别，没有意义。选择 H。

17. 答案：A

    解析：应加入对比实验充分证明空气阻力的影响。在真空条件下进行两球的降落实验，其他条件与原文相同，故选 A。

[**Passage IV**]

18. 答案：H

    解析：原文中提到后生动物的形成途径：多核细胞长出纤毛帮助运动，进化成类似现代蠕虫的水生的、两边对称的后生生物。但未提到其为中空的，故选择 H 选项。

19. 答案：D

解析：题干要求找出集群理论提出而细胞化理论未提出的方面。对照原文，二者都有提出身体对称、纤毛组织和多核细胞，只有D选项生殖细胞符合要求。故选D。

20. 答案：F

解析：3种理论的共同点就是认为后生动物由原生动物进化而成，文章详述了3种不同的进化理论和过程。选择F。

21. 答案：B

解析：根据原文，集群理论的重点是类似水母的尾部和中空结构，显然选项B最符合要求。

22. 答案：J

解析：文章中，分别进化理论指出两种不同对称形式的后生动物分别来源于相应的原生动物，且二者亲缘关系疏远，互不影响，只有J选项符合题意。

23. 答案：B

解析：题目要求找出集群理论提出但未回答的问题。B选项符合条件，文章指出了某些细胞更易于繁殖分裂，故分化成生殖细胞，但并未说明原因。C不是由集群理论提出的问题，排除；D选项不合题意，进化方向应为单细胞向多细胞进化，而非反之；A选项的答案文中有涉及，排除。

24. 答案：F

解析：要求找出三种学说的支持者都同意的结论。F正确，两边对称和辐射对称的后生动物演化于不同时间。G错误，因为只有集群学说才支持这一结论；H错误，后生动物的形成不会造成原生动物的灭绝，二者是相互独立的；J错误，文中未提及二者的高级程度差异。

[**Passage V**]

25. 答案：D

解析：实验1中选用含有网孔的玻璃屏障来模拟植被覆盖，其中所隐含的假设就是这种模拟方法与植被保护土壤免受水土流失的形式、过程一致。D符合要求。

26. 答案：F

解析：从原文的表中可看出，增加植被覆盖和减少动物踩踏能缓解水土流失。由于土壤2砂石含量较低，水土保持力更强，综合上述条件应选择A。

27. 答案：C

解析：由于50%的砂石含量介于土壤1和土壤2之间，故其储水能力和水土保持能力也应介于二者之间。结合原文中表格可得正确选项为C。

28. 答案：H

解析：两种土壤突然被30%踩踏后出水能力相同而水土保持能力不同，可能原因是砂石土更易遭受土壤破坏，H选项正确。其他选项均无法从原文推出，应排除。

29. 答案：C

解析：砂石含量为50%的土壤水土保持能力应介于土壤1和土壤2之间，结合表1对照70%植被覆盖情况下两种土壤的流失量可知只有C选项符合条件。

30. 答案：F

解析：为进一步探究植被覆盖对土壤的影响，应使用不同类型的植被进行再次试验，且无需动物踩踏这个新变量，故应重复实验1。正确答案为F。

[**Passage VI**]

31. 答案：B

解析：从图 2 可看出，当海拔达到 13.5 千米时两条线相交，即热带气团与极地气团的温度相等，故无法区分，选 B。其他选项对应的两条线温度都不同，故排除。

32. 答案：J

解析：从图 1 可看出中间层和光化层在海拔 50～72 千米处有部分重叠，故选 J。其他选项无重叠，不合要求。

33. 答案：C

解析：根据表 1 的趋势可以推断，气压随海拔升高而降低。故当海拔超过 13.7 km 时，气压应低于 13.7 km 处的气压，即 200 mb，C 选项正确。

34. 答案：G

解析：气压低于 5 mb，从图 1 可知，对应的海拔高度应在 32～50 km 之间，对应臭氧层，G 为正确选项。

35. 答案：C

解析：从表 1 可看出，第一天的温度随海拔升高先降低后又略有上升，而第二天温度随海拔升高始终处于降低状态，故只有 C 选项符合题意。

[**Passage VII**]

36. 答案：G

解析：抗菌剂的有效程度可由暴露时间和存活细菌百分比衡量——在最短的暴露时间年内杀灭最多的细菌对应的抗菌剂越有效。正确选项为 G。

37. 答案：A

解析：从图 1 可看出，与只用水和肥皂浸泡对比，加入酒精后杀菌剂的效果变强，相同暴露时间内杀死的细菌更多，存活百分比更低。A 选项正确。B 错误，70%酒精杀菌效果显著；C 错误，酒精浓度越高，杀菌效果应越好(斜率更大)；D 错误，酒精消毒机理文中提到过。

38. 答案：F

解析：从图 1 可看出，相同物质的水溶液与酊剂相比，后者的斜率绝对值更大，即杀菌效果更好。F 选项正确。

39. 答案：D

解析：从图 1 可知，用水和肥皂浸泡只能杀死约 10%的细菌，大部分细菌仍然存活，故 D 选项正确。

40. 答案：J

解析：60%酒精的杀菌效果应介于 50%和 70%酒精之间，从图 1 可看出 70%酒精杀死 90%的细菌需 120 秒，故 60%酒精应需大于 120 秒的时间，J 选项正确。

56B 解析

[**Passage I**]

1. 答案：B

解析：由题意可知，月球的组成物质大部分来自于地球表面，但由于来自太阳系另一部分的一个大型物体与地球碰撞并使地球表面上部分物质被撞入太空，可能造成了月球与地球组成的微弱差异。正确答案为 B。

2. 答案：J

解析：假说 1 认为月球的组成物质全部来自地球，月球受地球引力影响绕其公转，且月球刚形

成时地球的自转速度很快以致其无法吸附表面上任何物体。而现在地球自转速度为1年365次，所以过去地球自转远远超过1年365次。J选项正确。

3. 答案：A

解析：由观察3可知，现在月球几乎没有水分，而根据题意月球刚形成时含有大量水分，因此只能说明其形成之后水分含量逐渐下降，选择A选项。

4. 答案：F

解析：根据假说3，地球和月球来自于相同的气尘云，由此可推断它们的组成十分类似，而观察1、2都是表明地球和月球物质、成分的相似性，故F选项符合要求。

5. 答案：A

解析：结合4种假说很容易发现文中4种月球形成机制的共同影响因素是地球对月球的引力，正确选项为A。其他3个选项都是某一种假说的特定影响因素。

6. 答案：J

解析：根据观察1，月球与地球含有相同的同位素比例，故正确答案为J。

7. 答案：B

解析：假说1明确指出月球形成于地球物质，其中隐含的假设就是月球形成比地球晚，即月球比地球“年轻”，故正确选项为B。其他选项都可明显排除。C选项，假说1中并未提到火山运动；D选项，月球组成不应与地核等同，而是与地球表面物质相似。

［**Passage II**］

8. 答案：H

解析：从图1可看出夏季一天中不同时间段的郊区和城市温度，根据题意要求只要找出对应的虚线在实线上方的时间段即可，只有H选项符合要求。

9. 答案：B

解析：根据题干，水蒸气需要“凝结核”才能成云致雨，而城市中污染较严重，颗粒物排放较多，所以降雨量更大，选项B正确。其他选项都不能从题干及实验4推断得出。

10. 答案：H

解析：J选项明显错误，同一海拔高度处城市风速与郊区风速不同；从图3可看出，在海拔150 m以下时，同一高度处郊区对应的风速最大，H选项正确。

11. 答案：A

解析：从图1可看出，冬季一天温度的变化幅度低于夏季，故A选项正确，B错误。冬季农村的最大温度与城市、郊区显然不等，从冬季图中三线无交点即可判断，C、D选项错误。

12. 答案：G

解析：在图1的冬季图中找到下午6时的城市和农村曲线对应的温度，即可估算出两者大约相差4℃，正确选项为G。

13. 答案：D

解析：从图3可看出，风速从0增加到30 km/hr，城市区域的海拔增加得最多，即风速相对海拔增加的速度最慢，正确选项为D。

［**Passage III**］

14. 答案：F

解析：所有实验中加入的溶剂（水）的体积都是相同的，F选项正确；溶解固体的种类和总量是控制变量，随不同实验而调整改变。溶解固体百分比是因变量，不能人为控制，也不可能在不同实验中维持不变。

15. 答案：B

解析：对比表 2 和表 3 可知，相同百分含量的 KCl 与 NaCl 相比，前者的凝固点更低。故溶液 11 的凝固点应低于溶液 16 的凝固点，只有选项 B 符合条件。

16. 答案：H

解析：由实验 2 和实验 3 对比可知，溶质种类和溶质质量不同，对应溶液的凝固点也不同，正确答案为 H。

17. 答案：B

解析：由实验 3，百分含量为 7.5%的 $CaCl_2$ 溶液凝固点应在百分含量为 6%和 9%的 $CaCl_2$ 溶液之间，即 −2.93 和 −5.04 之间，只有 B 选项符合要求。

18. 答案：H

解析：根据实验 2 和实验 3，药剂师用干冰给溶液降温至其达到凝固点，其中隐含的要求就是干冰温度低于溶液凝固点，否则两者在温度降至溶液凝固点前就达到热量平衡，无法测得实际凝点。H 选项正确。

19. 答案：C

解析：从文中表格可看出，溶质的百分含量越高，对应溶液的凝固点越低。所以加水稀释最有可能使得凝固点升高。C 选项正确。

[**Passage IV**]

20. 答案：G

解析：培育时间 3 小时产生的菌落数应介于培养 1 小时和 6 小时之间，从表 3 中可获得使用药 C 培育 1 小时和 6 小时产生的菌落数，即可推断选项 G 正确。

21. 答案：A

解析：从表 1 可知，药 A 对应的渗透系数最大，故渗透能力最强。A 选项正确。

22. 答案：J

解析：由表 3 可知，未加任何药品的培养含有的菌落数最大且保持不变，排除 F、G 选项；且由于药品 D 的杀菌效果最差，曲线应在其他药品曲线上方，故可判断 J 选项正确。

23. 答案：B

解析：从表 1 可明显看出，分子量增大，渗透系数减小，渗透能力下降，B 选项正确。

24. 答案：F

解析：对比实验 2 和实验 3 可知，两者的培养时间相同，均为 1 小时，而每组的浓度有所改变，故 F 选项符合条件。

25. 答案：A

解析：从表 2 可看出，4 种药品的浓度越大，培养 1 小时产生的菌落数越少，即药品的杀菌能力越强，故 A 选项正确。

[**Passage V**]

26. 答案：J

解析：从图 2 可知，海脊的热流最大，深海平原次之，海渠最小，据此作出条形图可知 J 选项符合要求。

27. 答案：D

解析：从图 2 可看出，弧后盆地的热流输入与海脊、深海平原都相差较大，而接近于大洋岩石圈

的平均热流输入,(可从图中右方箭头看出),故D选项正确。

28. 答案:F

解析:由题干可知,水热排气口通常有最高的热量输入,而由图2可知海脊对应的热量输入最高,故正确选项为F。

29. 答案:D

解析:由正文可知,热量输入越高,温度升高越快。根据图2可判断,深海平原热流低于海脊,故A错误;同理可判断B、C错误,D选项正确。

30. 答案:G

解析:由图3可看出,深度低于10 km时,虚线始终在实线下方,即陆地岩石圈对应的温度高于海洋岩石圈,G选项正确。

[**Passage VI**]

31. 答案:C

解析:从图1可看出,生态系统D对应的曲线斜率绝对值最大,即石油含量下降的速度最快,故C选项正确。

32. 答案:H

解析:生物质包括活着的和死亡的鱼,而数量只包括存活的鱼类。污染环境可能对活着的生物造成负面影响但不致死,因此相较而言,使用生物质是一种更为精确的方法。H选项正确。

33. 答案:C

解析:结合图1和图3可知,随着石油浓度升高,污染程度加剧,生物质相应减少,只有C选项符合要求。

34. 答案:H

解析:由图1可看出,D组的石油降解率最高,故无需加入磷肥,只需加入蠕虫和鱼类。选项H最符合要求。

35. 答案:B

解析:由题意,要证明细菌仅依靠石油作为营养源,只需设置对照实验,在无石油存在时细菌无法生长(种群数量锐减至0)即可。选项B正确。

[**Passage VII**]

36. 答案:F

解析:由图1可看出,若处于轨道3,则无法释放近红外的光子。而4、5、6轨道可释放3种光子的任意一种,故选项F正确。

37. 答案:A

解析:由题干可知,氢原子只吸收了一个光子就从轨道1跃升到轨道5,符合这一要求的只有紫外光,其他两种光都无法使氢原子直接从能级1开始跃升。故正确答案为A。

38. 答案:J

解析:由表1可看出,随着光子波长降低,3种光子的能量都随之增加,J选项正确。

39. 答案:C

解析:由图1可看出,当光子从轨道6跃迁至轨道3时,放出红外光子;接着从轨道3跃迁至轨道1时放出紫外光子。选项C符合条件。

40. 答案:F

解析:电子的轨道能级越高,对应的电子能量越高,而氢原子由电子和质子组成,因此氢原子的能量也越高,F 正确。

57B 解析

[**Passage I**]

1. 答案:A
解析:从表 2 可看出,对同一除草剂浓度,土壤类型 1 和除草剂 A 对应的植物的平均高度最低。即 A 选项正确。
2. 答案:A
解析:在控制变量实验中,不应对对照组施加人为变量。此题中对照组应为未经任何除草剂处理的组,只有选项 A 符合要求。
3. 答案:B
解析:若直接向玉米苗上喷洒除草剂可能导致其死亡,而使实验无法继续进行。因此采用向土壤中加入除草剂的方法,B 选项正确。
4. 答案:J
解析:根据题意,植株的高度与质量成正比,而实验 2 中,施用的除草剂剂量越大,植株高度越小,由此可推断质量也相应越小,因此正确答案为 J。
5. 答案:D
解析:由题意,使用的杂交玉米和杀虫剂都与原文中的不同,故无法根据原实验推断出可能产生的结果,D 选项正确。A、B、C 不合题意,原文实验中施用的除草剂剂量越大,植株生长越受阻。
6. 答案:J
解析:由于土壤酸度是需要控制的变量,其他变量均为无关变量,应保持一致。只有 J 选项符合条件。

[**Passage II**]

7. 答案:B
解析:文中提到了许多影响地震短期预测的因素及不确定性,对其前景并未表示乐观态度,A 选项错误,B 正确。短期预报不准确,无法准确指出地震发生的地点和强度,C、D 错误。
8. 答案:G
解析:科学家 1 提到的都是短期地震预报的线索,而科学家 2 逐一对这些线索提出了反驳,并指出一个主要障碍——我们不能直接研究地震发生的区域(地表 10 km 以下),故 G 选项正确。
9. 答案:C
解析:两位科学家都指出氡气是在许多地方的岩石中都能发现的一种气体,当岩层破裂时也会释放出,但并不能凭此预测地震,因为可能其他与地震无关的活动也会放出氡气。故 C 选项正确。
10. 答案:F
解析:岩石受压力会造成体积膨胀,F 正确;地下水不是由于岩石受压导致的,其他因素也有可能造成,岩石受压只是导致地下水位升高,水流外溢,G、H 错误;断层面的不同位置压力不同,J 选项错误。
11. 答案:C

解析：科学家 1 指出，地震前岩石体积增加形成断层面，同时岩石内会形成很多裂缝，从而导致一种地震波的传播速度降低。为了证明她的假说，最适宜在地震活跃区测量岩石的体积变化和地震波速，才能检验其真实性，C 选项正确。

12. 答案：G

解析：文中，科学家 2 提出，前震几乎无法从持续不停的地壳振动中分离出来进行研究，故题干假设与之矛盾，正确选项为 G。科学家 1 未指出前震的分离问题。

13. 答案：A

解析：科学家 2 指出，岩石在压力下发生的许多物理变化随岩石种类或其断层面上周围岩石种类的不同而不同，而科学家 1 未考虑这些因素，把所有岩石受压变化当成是同质的，故选项 A 正确。

［**Passage III**］

14. 答案：F

解析：由表 1 可知，11 次太阳循环持续时间的平均值已知，其余 10 次太阳循环的持续时间也已知，据此可求出第 11 次太阳循环的持续时间远低于平均值。所以推断这次循环是不完全的，选项 F 正确。

15. 答案：B

解析：从图 2 可看出 1990 年的质子事件数柱形图中，3 月对应的柱最高，故正确答案为 B。

16. 答案：H

解析：结合图 1 和图 2 可看出，质子事件发生数与太阳亮度和黑子数基本呈正相关，当后两者都超过 90 时，对应的质子事件数最高，故 H 选项正确。

17. 答案：A

解析：由图 1 可看出某年对应的太阳黑子数与特定波长下的亮度基本趋势一致，在太阳处在最大亮度时对应的黑子数量也最多，A 选项正确。

18. 答案：G

解析：由表 1 可看出，太阳循环平均 11 年发生一次，第 11 个循环发生在 1986 年，据此可推断第 21 个循环应发生在 $10\times 11=110$ 年之后，即 2096 年，符合条件的选项只有 G。

［**Passage IV**］

19. 答案：D

解析：从图 1 可看出，物种 G 在两种阳光条件下的存活率都很高，超过 90%，而其他蛋受阳光的负面影响较大，存活率低。故 G 物种最可能在持续阳光曝晒下存活，D 选项正确。

20. 答案：H

解析：从图 1 柱形图可看出，物种 E 在两种阳光条件下存活率差异最大，两柱高度差距最明显，故 H 选项正确。

21. 答案：A

解析：由表 1 可看出，两栖物种 B 也是在掩护下孵蛋，与新发现的物种相似，而其对应的修复 DNA 损伤的相对能力为＜0.1，故推测新发现物种的修复能力也低于 0.1，A 选项正确。

22. 答案：G

解析：由表 1 可看出，按由物种 A 到物种 G 的顺序，蛋在阳光下的暴露程度越大，对 DNA 损伤的相对修复能力也越强。G 选项正确。

23. 答案：A

解析:由图 1 可看出,物种 A 暴露在未去除紫外线的阳光下时,其孵出的蛋存活率最低。由表 1 可知,物种 A 通常会埋它们的蛋,故选项 A 正确。

[**Passage V**]

24. 答案:H
解析:由图 1 结合图例可看出,离海岸 12 km 时对应的悬崖组成为泥岩,H 选项正确。
25. 答案:A
解析:由图 1 的图例可看出,区别悬崖组成的依据就是颗粒粒径,不同粒径范围对应不同种类的岩石。故 A 选项正确。
26. 答案:J
解析:由表 1 可知,悬崖高度越大,对应的海浪侵蚀比率越低,结合表中数据,由该趋势可推测当高度超过 4.0 m 时,对应百分比应低于 0.5%,即 J 选项正确。
27. 答案:A
解析:由图 1 可看出,悬崖 E、F 的岩石组成不同,而沿海岸线距离相似,A 选项正确,排除 C 选项。年均江水和海浪强度文中均未提及。故 B、D 选项错误。
28. 答案:F
解析:由表 1 可看出,悬崖高度越大,对应的海浪侵蚀比率越低,但降低的速率逐渐减小,故对应的斜率值也应相应减小,F 选项符合要求。

[**Passage VI**]

29. 答案:D
解析:从表 1 可看出,管 11 与其他管相比,未加入胰蛋白酶,与相同温度及培养时间的管相比沉淀质量明显增大。故缺少胰蛋白酶是造成大量沉淀的关键因素,D 选项正确。
30. 答案:G
解析:由表 1 和表 2 可看出,实验 1 考查温度对沉淀质量的影响,而实验 2 考查 pH 值对沉淀质量的影响。故在试验 1 中,温度为控制变量,而在实验 2 中为无关变量,应保持一致。G 选项正确。
31. 答案:C
解析:由表 2 可看出,随着 pH 值由 4 增加到 14,沉淀的质量先减少后增大,对应的胰蛋白酶的有效性应为先增大后减小,C 选项正确。
32. 答案:J
解析:由表 1 可知,培养时间越短,沉淀质量越大,故对管 16 而言,若培养时间为 0,得到的沉淀质量应大于 2.6 mg,只有选项 J 符合要求。
33. 答案:D
解析:由表 1 可看出,管 10 对应的沉淀质量最少,即未降解的蛋白质质量最少,胰蛋白酶催化分解的量最多,故选项 D 正确。
34. 答案:J
解析:结合实验 1 和实验 2 可看出,温度较高、pH 值接近中性时酶的活性最强,降解速率最快,残留的蛋白质质量越小,故选项 J 正确。

[**Passage VII**]

35. 答案:B

解析：结合表 1、2、3 即可看出，实验 2 对应的棒球速率最大，由于风速与棒球在空中的运动方向相同，合成的速度也相对增大。选项 B 正确。

36. 答案：F

解析：由于实验 2、3 的风速都相同，而风与棒球在空中的运动方向恰好相反，这是导致两者平均水平速度的唯一区别，故选项 F 正确。

37. 答案：B

解析：由图 1 可看出从投掷机到接收机的水平距离为 18 米，由 0.1 s 反应时间的相机抓拍刚好能得到 5 张图像。若减少投掷机到接收机的水平距离或增大投掷速度，都会导致图像数量少于 5 张。B 选项正确。

38. 答案：F

解析：实验 3 风速方向与投掷方向相反，而根据题干，调换了投掷机和接收机的位置，即自西向东投掷，故风速应为自东向西才能保证与实验 3 结果相同。F 正确。

39. 答案：D

解析：3 次实验中 D 间隔对应的水平速度相比 A、B、C 都较慢，而飞行的时间相同，故飞行的水平距离较短，D 选项正确。

40. 答案：H

解析：若风速更大，则顺风需要的时间更短，而逆风花费的时间更长。根据此结论可推知 H 选项正确。

59F 解析

[**Passage I**]

1. 答案：C

解析：由图 2 可看出，kyanite 只存在于中等变质等级，故其最可能只在中等变质等级中被找到。其他矿石在高、低变质等级中也存在。故选项 C 正确。

2. 答案：J

解析：由图 1 可看出，岩石 G 对应的压力大于 10 kb，温度范围为 200～1 000℃，只有选项 J 符合要求。

3. 答案：C

解析：从图 1 可看出，深度增加，对应的压力也逐渐增大，选项 C 正确。

4. 答案：J

解析：从图 2 可看出，plagioclase(斜长岩)在各种变质等级下都存在，所以无法根据其存在判断岩石的变质等级，即它对判断变质等级帮助最小，J 选项正确。

5. 答案：A

解析：题干中有两个关键词：molten 和 surface。由此可判断 Hornfel 这种岩石应该是高温并且深度较低的，最符合这两个条件的为 A 种类，故正确选项为 A。

[**Passage II**]

6. 答案：J

解析：两位科学家假说的主要论点差异就是科学家 1 认为摧毁森林的物体是彗星，而科学家 2 认为是小行星带，即两人认为进入地球大气层的物体不同。

7. 答案：B

解析：文中明显提出，科学家 2 认为计算显示直径在 10～100 m 之间的彗星会在远高于 8 km 的位置爆炸，故选项 B 符合题意。

8. 答案：G

解析：科学家 1 提出，组成彗星的大部分物质都是挥发性的，即容易蒸发的，故充分加热时能够变成气体，G 选项正确。

9. 答案：D

解析：科学家 2 认为星体撞击的地区多沼泽，因为大的星体碎片很难获得，而小的碎片都为玻璃状的，可能是融化后又重新凝结形成的。选项 D 正确。

10. 答案：H

解析：科学家 2 提到，小行星变平，并由于表面积快速增加而迅速减速。所以若小行星没有由于气压差异迅速变平，它的速度应该不会降低得那么快，H 选项正确。

11. 答案：A

解析：两位科学家均认为，物体爆炸导致森林毁坏主要是由于其爆炸产生的能量快速传至地表，A 选项正确。B、C、D 选项均不能说明森林破坏的原因，反而削弱了原文中爆炸危害的论述，故排除。

12. 答案：G

解析：题目要求选出最能削弱科学家 1 观点的论述。由于科学家 1 的观点是建立在爆炸物体直径在 10～100 m 范围之间的，若该条件不成立则科学家 1 的论述会被大大削弱。而 H、J 文中未提及，F 选项符合科学家 1 的描述，也应排除，故正确选项为 G。

[**Passage III**]

13. 答案：A

解析：由表 3 可看出，蚂蚁种植的种子相比手植的种子发芽数量更多，A 选项符合要求。B、C、D 均与表格推断相反，与手植的种子相比，蚂蚁种植的种子 1(或 2)年后植物存活量均增加，每株植物的种子产量应降低，故应排除。正确答案为 A。

14. 答案：G

解析：控制变量即为各组都一致且保持不变的变量，可看出 F、H、J 在各组实验中并不相同，为实验变量，只有每个地点放置的植株数是相同的，均为 20，G 选项正确。

15. 答案：C

解析：结合表 1、表 2、表 3 可迅速看出物种 A 和物种 B 的种子质量、发芽速率和 1 年后种子的产生速率均有较大差异，排除 A、B、D。而平均每颗种子含有油质体的百分含量基本相同，均为 6.2%，故 C 选项正确。

16. 答案：G

解析：在试验 2 中，地点 3 两种植物(A 和 B)都未种植，所以研究目的应为测定蚂蚁在空白区域的偏好，G 选项正确。

17. 答案：C

解析：实验 2 要研究的是蚂蚁将种子从碟中移走的数量，而实际测量时无法判断被移走的种子是否全都是蚂蚁造成的，故这是实验的一个漏洞，C 选项正确。

18. 答案：J

解析：由表 2 可看出，植物 A、B 都不在时，蚂蚁对两种种子的偏好无明显差别；而当只有其中一种植物不在时，蚂蚁的偏好明显改变，所以给定区域中植物的丰富度是造成蚂蚁对种子偏好

的主要影响因素。J 选项正确。其他选项的变量都不是实验 2 的研究内容。

[**Passage IV**]

19. 答案：A

解析：由表 1 和表 2 中数据可看出，随着胶带宽度增加，拉动胶带所需的力也逐渐增加，A 选项正确。

20. 答案：G

解析：使用 4 cm 宽的 X 型胶带，所需的拉力应大于 3 cm 宽的，即大于 5 N，根据表 2 中增加的趋势预计，拉力增加的幅度不会太大，应低于 8 N，故符合条件的只有 G 选项。

21. 答案：A

解析：比较不同类型胶带在实验 1(纸质拉环)和实验 2(塑料拉环)中的平均拉力，可发现只有 X 型胶带在试验 1 中所需拉力较大，即对纸质的黏附性更强，A 选项正确。

22. 答案：G

解析：Y 型胶带在两次试验中都使用了两次，而 X 型胶带都使用了 3 次，Z 型胶带在试验 1 中用了 2 次而在实验 2 中只用了 1 次，故 G 选项正确。

23. 答案：A

解析：根据力学知识，要能拉动胶带，必须使得夹子与胶带之间的静摩擦力超过胶带与包裹材料之间的粘附力，故 A 选项正确。

24. 答案：F

解析：根据题干信息，2.5 cm 宽的胶带与纸质的粘附力为 4.9 N，而与塑料的粘附力为 4.1 N。首先可排除 G 选项，因为 2.5 cm 宽的 Y 型胶带在两种材料下的对应拉力均为 5.4 N；而 Z 型胶带信息不足，难以推断其与塑料的粘附力。X 型胶带在 2.5 cm 宽时与两种材料的粘附力可根据表中数据推测出来，符合相应条件。故 F 选项正确。

[**Passage V**]

25. 答案：B

解析：题干要求热量由 T2 温度的墙向 T1 温度的墙传导，即要求 T2>T1，只有 B 选项符合条件。

26. 答案：F

解析：绝缘体是热的不良导体，即传导的热量很低，从试验 7～10 可看出，传导热量最低的是木头(0.072)，故最好的绝缘体为木头，F 选项正确。

27. 答案：D

解析：由实验 1 和实验 5 可看出，使用的砖头材料和结构均相同，但两个墙体的温度都不同，而温度差均为 30℃，对应的热量也相同。所以热量只由温度差决定，D 选项正确。

28. 答案：H

解析：从实验 6～11 的热量数据可看出，砖头的热传导性能高于玻璃棉和木头，F、G 选项正确；钢铁的热传导性能比混凝土更高，比铝更低，J 选项正确，H 选项错误。由于题干要求选择错误选项，故应选 H。

29. 答案：A

解析：实验 1 和 3 只有结构不同，而结构中的不同只有两块墙壁之间的距离不同，故 A 选项正确。

[**Passage VI**]

30. 答案：H

解析：由于当加入 0.125 mol 氯化钠时，溶液已达到沸点，再加入氯化钠也不可能使得溶液温度升高，虽然反应速率会加快，因此 H 选项正确。

31. 答案：A

解析：由表 2 可看出，加入的氯化钠量越大，15 分钟内温度的升高量也越大，即 A 选项符合题意

32. 答案：G

解析：若加入 0.060 mol 氯化钠，15 分钟内温度的升高量应介于加入 0.050 mol 氯化钠和 0.075 mol氯化钠之间，即 34～50℃之间，且更接近 34℃，故 G 选项正确。

33. 答案：D

解析：由原文图表可看出，实验 1 使用镁粉、镁片和镁条，探究表面积对温度升高速度的影响；而实验 2、3 分别探讨铁加入量和氯化钠加入量对温度升高速度的影响。故 D 选项正确。

34. 答案：F

解析：根据题意，工程师希望找到温度升高速度最快的实验条件，根据文中 3 个实验的研究结论，在溶液到达沸点前，加入的铁和氯化钠越多，镁的表面积越大，温度升高得越快。对比各选项可知 F 正确。

35. 答案：D

解析：根据题意，镁与水反应会生成氢氧化镁覆盖在镁的表面，阻碍了反应物(镁和水)的接触，使反应变慢。而向溶液中加入氯化钠能使反应速度加快，合理的推测应是氯化钠可以去除氢氧化镁，D 选项正确。A 选项显然不符合常识；B、C 选项都会使反应速度更慢，故排除。

[**Passage VII**]

36. 答案：F

解析：从图 2 可看出，A 曲线的最高峰对应 pH 在 5 附近，所以 F 选项正确。

37. 答案：B

解析：由图 2 可看出，A、B 曲线只有一个交点，即只在某一 pH 时两种酶对应的促进系数相同，横坐标在 pH 6.7 附近，故 B 选项正确。

38. 答案：J

解析：一科学家声称酶 B 的促进系数取决于酶浓度和底物浓度两个条件，由图 3、4 也可看出，当酶或底物浓度增加时，对应的促进系数先升高后保持不变，证实了科学家的观点。J 选项正确。

39. 答案：A

解析：由图 4 可知，A 曲线始终在 B 曲线上方，即在某一给定酶浓度下，酶 A 的促进系数始终大于酶 B，与题中所述结论相反，故 A 选项正确。

40. 答案：G

解析：由题图可看出，trypsin(胰蛋白酶)对应的 pH 范围比 pepsin(胃蛋白酶)更高，即小肠液比胃液更偏碱性，酸度更低，G 选项符合要求。

61B 解析

[**Passage I**]

1. 答案：C

解析：由 Table 2 可知，85℃位于 80℃和 90℃之间，Activity 位于 60 和 94 之间。

2. 答案：F

解析：由 Table 2 可知，随着温度增加，Activity 就会增加。

3. 答案：A

解析：比较 Experiment 1 和 Experiment 2，Experiment 1 有 3 种离子，Experiment 2 只有 1 种单一离子Co^{2+}。

4. 答案：H

解析：由 Table 1 可知，随着Mn^{2+}的量增加，Activity 先增加到最高值 100 再降低。

5. 答案：A

解析：由 Table 2 可知，随着温度的增加，Activity 增加，但是在 40℃时，Activity 都降到 0 了。

6. 答案：F

解析：由 Experiment 1 可知，前言中的 proline to produce a bright red color。

[**Passage II**]

7. 答案：D

解析：比较 1、3、4、5 的人口数量的增加量，simulation 5 的增加量最快。

8. 答案：F

解析：由图表可知，simulation 3 中的 b 和 d 相等，人口数量不变。

9. 答案：D

解析：由图表可知，simulation 10 中的出生率和死亡率的差值最大，b 和 d 的差值最大的就是 simulation 10。

10. 答案：H

解析：由图表可知，b 和 d 的差值最大的就是 H。

11. 答案：C

解析：由图表可知，找到 b 和 d 差值为 0.25，对应的 N = 8，N = 16，N = 10 的时候 N = 16 是 N = 8 的两倍，所以 N = 4 的时候是 N = 8 的时候的一半，即 97 的一半。

[**Passage III**]

12. 答案：H

解析：由 Table 1 可知，Seattle 的温度变化影响 Average Egg Production，可以看到 Production 随着温度的增加先增加后下降。

13. 答案：B

解析：由 Table 2 可知，直接数 Race B 的数量，找到了 Group 10。

14. 答案：J

解析：由 Table 1 可知，直接找到 Average Egg Production 最大的就是 Race B Humboldt 19C。

15. 答案：C

解析：由 Table 2 可知，找到所描述的 Group，找到 Average testis length = 480。

16. 答案：F

解析：观察 4 个选项，发现 F 选项的 Group 并没有出现在 Table 2 中。

[**Passage IV**]

17. 答案：C

解析：仔细阅读 Scientist 1 和 Scientist 2 的陈述，总结出了 dehydration 和 change。

18. 答案：J

解析：观察图片，左边的竖坐标一直延伸到 670 km。

19. 答案：A

解析：阅读 Scientist 1 的陈述，对于 Serpentine，Scientist 1 用的是"suchas"，说明不止一种，排除 B，保留 A；同时整个 0～640 km 都属于 lower mantle，不存在什么 Serpentine 只在 lower mantle，排除 D；C 属于 Scientist 2 的观点。

20. 答案：F

解析：阅读两位科学家，Scientist 1 支持脱水理论(dehydration)，Scientist 2 支持变化理论(change)，所以如果脱水就是变化的过程，那么两者就是同一个概念了，F 可以理解为脱水就是整个变化的过程。

21. 答案：B

解析：两位科学家都提到了 fractures，同时由于挤压生热和压缩，才会有能量。

22. 答案：J

解析：由于两位科学家的所有陈述都建立在岩石在下沉过程中温度不会立即降低，所以这个发现会削弱两位科学家的陈述。

23. 答案：B

解析：由于 spinel 是压缩得到的，所以它的密度更大。

[**Passage V**]

24. 答案：G

解析：由 Table 3 可知，同样是 1 m 的基础高度，反弹的高度却不一样，说明弹簧储存的能量是不同的。

25. 答案：D

解析：由 Table 2 可知，在最低点的时候，没有一个实验的 PE 和 KE 相等，说明无论如何能量是有损失的。

26. 答案：F

解析：由 Table 1 和 Table 2 可知，只有前 4 组的试验总能量是守恒的。

27. 答案：B

解析：由 Table 1 可知，PE 随着 H 的增加而增加。

28. 答案：H

解析：由题意可知，改变的是 mass，同时质量与高度并没关系，所以质量是和总机械能成正比的。

29. 答案：D

解析：Experiment 3 中的起始高度为 1 m，所以当能量守恒的时候，弹簧保留所有能量，然后返回到 1 m。

[**Passage VI**]

30. 答案：G

解析：由 Table 4 可知，11 个电子的原子核外电子排布为 G。

31. 答案：C

解析：由 Table 4 可知，s 层填补到两个电子，剩下的电子就排到 3p 层了。

32. 答案：G
解析：观察所有原子外电子排布，发现 1s 永远只有 2 个电子。
33. 答案：D
解析：由 Table 4 的拥有 22 个电子的原子电子层排布可知，4s 和 3d 分别有 2 个电子，根据 Table 3 的能量级，如果减掉一个电子，应该减在 3d 上。
34. 答案：G
解析：由 Table 3 和 4 推理到拥有 23 个电子的原子电子排布，然后进一步推理到 24 个电子的原子电子排布。

[**Passage VII**]
35. 答案：D
解析：由 Study 1 可知，94 大约是 31 的三倍。
36. 答案：G
解析：使用 Table 2 的数据进行分析，使用 Day = 50 的数据作图，所以选 G。
37. 答案：D
解析：由 Table 1 可知，Hay 和 Manure 的混合物的 dry density 明显比原来的 Hay 要高得多，所以 Manure 的 dry density 要比 Hay 高。
38. 答案：H
解析：由 Figure 2 和 Table 1 可知，carbon content 含量最高的是 leaf compost，但是它的转化效率并不是最高的。
39. 答案：A
解析：由题意可知，由于抽取的氧气是从 Straw 通过的，所以这些氧气反而会降低转化效率，导致S^{2-}的含量低于标准值 60 ppm。
40. 答案：J
解析：由 Study 2 的第一句话可知，AMD 的含量为 100 ppm。

61C 解析

[**Passage I**]
1. 答案：B
解析：文章 paragraph 3 可以看到一个 gene 的转换时间是 15 min，50/15 = 3。
2. 答案：J
解析：Student 3 的陈述就是无论从哪个开始，只要是顺时针就行。
3. 答案：C
解析：Student 1 和 2 都明确地说从 Gene X 或者 Gene F 开始，而 Student 3 和 4 只是陈述了方向，所以选 C。
4. 答案：F
解析：由 Student 1 的陈述来看，Gene X 是最先开始的然后紧接着是 R、S、A，45 min/15 min = 3，所以只有 Gene G 是复制不到的。
5. 答案：A
解析：由 Student 2 的陈述来看，无论开始的是 X 还是 F，一共有 4 种 Gene 可能被复制了，R、

X、F、G，所以 Gene A 是不可能的。

6. 答案：J

解析：这一题可以参考第三题，由于只有 Student 3 和 4 没有规定起始的 Gene，也只有 Student 3 和 4 能以 Gene A 结束。

7. 答案：D

解析：由 Student 1 的陈述可知，复制从 Gene X 开始到 Gene A 结束，经历 4 个 Gene，一共用时 60 min。

[**Passage II**]

8. 答案：G

解析：由 Figure 1 可知，随着 wave length 的增加，S 的曲线是上升的，而SO_2的曲线则是先上升再下降。

9. 答案：C

解析：由 Figure 4 可知，实线一直在虚线下方，也就是说 large plumes 的 reflectance 一直比 small plumes 要低。

10. 答案：H

解析：由 Figure 1 可知，当 wave length 在 0.40 时，对应的 white S 的 reflectance 是 0.2。

11. 答案：D

解析：由 Figure 3 和 Figure 1 的对比可知，Pele 和 Brown S 的曲线最为相近。

12. 答案：H

解析：利用 Figure 4 的曲线大约估计出 Large plumes 和 Small plumes 的 reflectance。

13. 答案：B

解析：由 Study 1 中的陈述可知，reflectance 指反射百分比，所以 0.98 指 98%的反射率。

[**Passage III**]

14. 答案：F

解析：由 Table 1 可知，当电压为 7.6 V 时，即 7.6 V 在 0～8.4 V 之间，说明时间比 12 sec 少。

15. 答案：C

解析：由 Table 2 可知，随着 Capacitance 的增加，时间也相应增加，同时当 Capacitance 增加到 1.5×10^{-6} F 时，时间可以直接用 1.2＋0.3 算出来。

16. 答案：J

解析：由 Table 3 可知，resistance 对时间的影响是由 resistance 的增加而增加。

17. 答案：A

解析：由 Figure 1 可知，如果要测 Capacitor 的电压就把 voltmeter 接在 capacitor 两端，同样要测 resistor 的电压，就把 voltmeter 接在 resistor 两端。

18. 答案：F

解析：由 Table 2 和 3 可知，时间随着 resistance 和 capacitance 的增加而增加，所以当这两个变量都为最小值时，时间最短。

19. 答案：B

解析：由 Table 2 可知，Experiment 2 是测量 capacitance 对于时间的影响的。

[**Passage IV**]

20. 答案：F

解析：由 Table 2 可知，随着加入的 sucrose 的质量增加，所放出来的热量 heat 也在增加；由 Table 1 可知，随着热量的增加，change in water temperature 也增加，所以 mass of sucrose 和 temperature 也是正相关。

21. 答案：B

解析：由 Table 1 可知，随着热量 heat 增加，change in water temperature 也在增加，所以是一条正相关的直线。

22. 答案：G

解析：由 Table 2 可知，mass of sucrose 和 heat 成正比，通过寻找两个质量和热量进行对比也能得到同样的结论。

23. 答案：A

解析：由 Table 1 可知，同样是 1 g 的 Food，放出的热量从小到大就是 Potato、Egg、Bread、Cheese。

24. 答案：H

解析：使用 Table 1 的数据 3.2 kJ 直接乘以 5。

[**Passage V**]

25. 答案：D

解析：由 Figure 1 可知，注意是从 10℃ 降低到 0℃ 所以从右到左，先上升再下降。

26. 答案：G

解析：由 Table 1 可知，mercury 的 density 最大，mercury 又是液体，这和题干中的陈述不符。

27. 答案：B

解析：由 Table 2 可知，density 随着温度的升高而降低。

28. 答案：F

解析：由 Table 2 可知，Ethylether 的密度最小，water 第二，而 Mercury 密度最大，按密度从小到大，最小的在最上面。

29. 答案：C

解析：由 Figure 1 可知，在 4℃ 时 density 到达最高 1.00 g/cm^3，即 100。

[**Passage VI**]

30. 答案：F

解析：由 Study 4 可知，frugivores 的曲线呈现下降趋势。

31. 答案：D

解析：由 Figure 3 可知，insectivores 的曲线呈现下降趋势，humming birds 处于略微上升的趋势。

32. 答案：G

解析：由 Figure 1 可知，当 distance 在 75 m 时，对应的 AGTB 在 −2.6 t/yr。

33. 答案：C

解析：这一题是常识题，对于平均值是 0 的数据，即有可能样本中所有数据都是 0，也有可能有正有负。

34. 答案：J

解析：分析所有 Study，只有 humming birds 的变化不符合常规，即其他动物都受到 Fragmentation 的影响而减少，只有这个增加。

35. 答案：C

解析：由 Figure 3 可知，Year 2 的时候，insectivores 的捕获量是 80，而题干中的时间为 10 000 hr，而 Figure 3 的纵坐标为 captures/1 000 hr，最终结果要乘以 10。

[**Passage VII**]

36. 答案：H

解析：由 Table 1 可知，对比一下图中的数据，发现这种 Sample 为 Gray C。

37. 答案：D

解析：由 Figure 1 可知，距离地表最深的就是年代最久远的。

38. 答案：G

解析：由 Figure 1 可知，sand and gravel 的 resistivity 是最高的。

39. 答案：C

解析：由 Figure 1 可知，bed rock 的 resistivity 在 50 左右，所以找到相近的 resistivity，为 Oliva green and gray till。

40. 答案：J

解析：由 Figure 1 可知，gray till 中CO_2含量最高的在 35 mL/g 左右，所以比这个更高就是 J。

61E 解析

[**Passage I**]

1. 答案：B

题干：判断 placoderms 的灭绝时间。

定位：Figure 1

解析：从 Figure 1 中可以看出，placoderms 所对应的图形在 235 mya 处消失，代表着物种的灭绝。

2. 答案：F

题干：判断哪个 period 最短。

定位：Table 1

解析：从 Table 1 中可以计算出，Triassic 对应的时间最短，为 35 million 年。

3. 答案：C

题干：判断 bonyfish、amphibians 和 reptile 之间的进化关系。

定位：Figure 1

解析：从 Figure 1 中可以看出，根据物种出现的时间先后排序为 bonyfish、amphibians、reptile，所以 reptile 从 amphibians 进化而来，amphibians 从 bonyfish 进化而来。

4. 答案：H

题干：判断 jawless vertebrate 的丰富度。

定位：Figure 1、Table 1

解析：从 Table 1 中判断出 Silurian 和 Devonian 代表的为 430～345 mya，从 Figure 1 上可找到对应的图形为先变宽后变窄。

5. 答案：B

题干：判断 flowering plant 出现的时期。

定位：Table 1

解析：从 Table 1 可以看到人类首先出现在 Tertiary，鸟类首先出现在 Jurassic，所以 flowering plant 出现在两个时期的中间，即为 Cretaceous 时期。

[**Passage II**]

6. 答案：G

题干：判断 25%海水蒸发时的盐度。

定位：Figure 1

解析：从 Figure 1 中可以看出，25%海水蒸发时的盐度介于 35 和 60 之间。

7. 答案：A

题干：判断沉淀中厚度最大的两种物质。

定位：Figure 2

解析：从 Figure 2 中可以看出，厚度最大的两种物质为 bittern salts 和 NaCl，分别为 2.5 m 和 12 m。

8. 答案：H

题干：判断 25%海水蒸发时的盐度。

定位：Table 1

解析：从 Table 1 中可以看出，4 种物质的密度分别为 2.7 g/cm^3、2.2 g/cm^3、3.1 g/cm^3、4.4 g/cm^3，即可判断。

9. 答案：D

题干：判断海水蒸发时何时发生沉降。

定位：Figure 1

解析：从 Figure 1 中可以看出，在海水蒸发接近 50%时才发生沉降。

10. 答案：G

题干：判断最早沉降的物质的性质。

定位：Table 1、Figure 1

解析：从 Figure 1 中可以看出，最早发生沉降的物质为 $CaCO_3$，从 Table 1 中可以看出，$CaCO_3$ 的溶解度最低。

[**Passage III**]

11. 答案：D

题干：判断从 0 开始到 180 分钟，E2 中 A1 的百分比曲线的变化趋势。

定位：Figure 3

解析：从 Figure 3 中可以看出，A1 对应的曲线先增加，然后保持水平不变。

12. 答案：H

题干：判断在 110 分钟 E1 和 A2 对应的百分比曲线为多少。

定位：Figure 2

解析：从 Figure 2 中可以看出，在 110 min 时 A2 所对应的值约为 70。

13. 答案：D

题干：在 60 分钟时，根据百分比曲线的大小将 A1～A4 从小到大排序。

定位：Figure 2

解析：从 Figure 2 中可以看出，百分比曲线的值从小到大排序为 A4、A2、A1、A3。

14. 答案：J

题干：判断在温度为 40℃时，E2 和 A4 在何时百分比曲线达到 100%。

定位：Figure 4

解析：从 Figure 4 中可以看出，随着温度的增加，达到 100%曲线的点逐渐左移，所以在 40℃的 100%曲线的点在 20℃和 50℃之间。

15. 答案：D

题干：判断 A4 是否会使 E1 和 E2 完全曲线。

定位：Figure 2、3

解析：从 Figure 2 中可以看出，A4 对应的曲线先增加，然后保持水平不变，所以不能使 E1 达到 100%曲线，但在 Figure 3 中，A4 对应的曲线在 80 分钟时达到 100%。

[**Passage IV**]

16. 答案：F

题干：判断在实验 2 中，当灯泡数量增加时，L 的变化规律。

定位：Table 2

解析：从 Table 2 中可以看出，点亮的灯泡数量增多时，L 逐渐变大。

17. 答案：A

题干：判断试验中关掉房间里面灯的原因。

定位：无

解析：试验中测量的是灯泡将 paraff in block 完全照明所用的距离，所以需要保证没有外界光源的干扰。

18. 答案：J

题干：在实验 2 中，判断同时打开 8 个灯泡时所测量的 L 的大小。

定位：Table 2

解析：从 Table 2 中可以看出，点亮的灯泡数量增多时，L 逐渐变大。所以在开 8 盏灯时，L 的距离应该要大于 0.446。

19. 答案：C

题干：判断实验 1 的目的。

定位：Figure 1

解析：从 Figure 1 中可以看出，几个灯泡的位置不同，而在实验 1 中每次实验只开 1 盏灯，说明实验是为了判断灯泡的位置对 L 的影响。

20. 答案：H

题干：判断如果将左边的灯换做 1 盏灯，要达到 L = 0.446 m 是完全照亮的目的，新的灯的亮度应该是原来每盏灯的几倍。

定位：Table 2

解析：从 Table 2 中可以看出，L = 0.446 m 时灯泡数量为 5 盏，所以新的灯泡的亮度应该为原来每盏灯亮度的 5 倍。

21. 答案：B

题干：判断在实验 2 中，如果将灯泡 F 换为亮度更大的灯泡 G，每组实验所测量的 L 会如何变化。

定位：Table 2

解析：从 Table 2 中可以看出，点亮的灯泡数量增多时，亮度越大，L 逐渐变大。当 F 换为 G 时，为了达到左右同样的亮度，左边的灯泡亮度需要增大，在左边灯泡数量保持不变时，只能通过缩短 L 达到此目的。

[**Passage V**]

22. 答案：H

 题干：解释实验 3 中无现象的原因。

 定位：无

 解析：此实验利用的是无机盐在溶液中水解的原理，如果没有溶于溶液，就不会存在自由电子，因此不会发生金属的电子析出。

23. 答案：C

 题干：判断 $Zn(NO_3)_2$溶解在水中的现象。

 定位：第 4 行

 解析：从文中第 4 行可以看到，当无机盐溶于水时，会分解为金属阳离子和无机阴离子。

24. 答案：G

 题干：判断 tin 所对应的 E°。

 定位：Table 1

 解析：因为 tin 所对应的 E°比 Fe 要大，比 Cu 要小，所以 tin 所对应的 E°介于 -0.44 和 0.34 之间。

25. 答案：A

 题干：判断实验 2 是否支持“金属条放在同一种金属的盐溶液中不会有金属析出”。

 定位：Table 2

 解析：从 Table 2 中可以看到，4 种金属条在放到它们对应的盐溶液中时均没有金属析出。

26. 答案：F

 题干：判断实验 1 是否支持“Zn 比其他几种金属更容易析出”。

 定位：Table 1

 解析：实验 1 的说明中有 E°的数值越高，金属离子越容易的电子后析出的论述，而 Zn 对应的 E°最低，所以最难析出。

27. 答案：A

 题干：判断当 lead 棒插在 $AgNO_3$和 $Zn(NO_3)_2$溶液中时的现象。

 定位：Table 1

 解析：从 Table 1 可以看出，E°小的金属棒插入 E°大的金属盐溶液中时，后者所对应的金属会析出，所以当 lead 插入两个溶液中时，因为 Ag 的 E°要大，所以 Ag 会析出。

[**Passage VI**]

28. 答案：F

 题干：判断无色素子代的亲代基因型。

 定位：Table 3

 解析：从 Table 3 可以看出，当亲代基因为 oobb 时，子代全部为无色素性状。

29. 答案：D

 题干：判断与 Cross 8 相同的杂交体。

 定位：Table 2、3

解析：从 Table 3 可以看出，Cross 8 的子代有 75%可以合成橙色和黑色色素，25%全部合成橙色色素，对照 Table 2 可以看出，Cross 5 与 Cross 8 表现的性状相同。

30. 答案：G
题干：判断可以产生 Cross 1 中 male parents 的基因型的基因组合。
定位：Table 1
解析：从 Table 1 可以看出，当 Cross 1 中 male parents 的基因型为 Oo，而选项 F、H、J 只能依次产生 oo、OO、OO 的基因型。

31. 答案：B
题干：判断 Cross 11 中能同时产生橙色和黑色色素的子代基因型。
定位：Table 3
解析：题目中已知基因 O 控制橙色色素的合成，基因 B 控制黑色色素的合成，所以能同时产生两种色素的基因型需同时含有 O 和 B。

32. 答案：J
题干：判断可以产生 50%橙色色素和 50%不能合成色素的子代的基因组合。
定位：Table 1
解析：F 会同时产生橙色和黑色色素的子代，排除；G 产生只合成黑色素的子代，排除；H 只能产生同时产生两种色素的子代，排除。

33. 答案：B
题干：判断可以 Cross 2 中 female parents 的基因型。
定位：Table 1
解析：从 Table 1 可以看出，Cross 2 中 female parents 的基因型为 Oo，并且由于所产生的子代都能合成黑色素，只有 BB 基因能确保所有子代都能合成黑色素。

[**Passage VII**]

34. 答案：H
题干：根据第一种模型，判断在哪种情况下原子核最不可能发生裂变。
定位：Liquid Drop Model L5
解析：从 L5 可以看出，球形的原子核相比水滴形更不容易发生裂变。

35. 答案：B
题干：当原子核内有 8 个中子时，需要有几个 shell 来容纳。
定位：Table 1
解析：从 Table 1 中可以看出，第一层的容量为 2，第二层的容量为 6，所以容纳 8 个需要两层。

36. 答案：F
题干：根据第一种模型，两个原子核结合时可与水滴做的类比。
定位：Liquid Drop Model L11
解析：从 L11 可以看出，两个原子核结合可类比为两个水滴的融合。

37. 答案：C
题干：两种模型在最稳定原子核上的共同点。
定位：Liquid Drop Model L4、The Shell Model L15
解析：两个模型都指出最稳定的原子核为球形。

38. 答案：H
题干：原子核中有 20 个质子和 19 个中子时，中子不能达到 magic 的原因。

定位：Table 1

解析：从 Table 1 可以看出，3 个层都充满时需要的数量为 20，所以当中子有 19 个时，有一层未达到充满状态。

39. 答案：D

题干：根据第二个模型，判断当原子核为球形时前两层的质子和中子数。

定位：Table 1

解析：原子核为球形时，各层需要达到充满状态，所以两层共需要包含 8 个质子或者中子。

40. 答案：G

题干：判断否定第一种模型的选项。

定位：Liquid Drop Model L11

解析：从 L11 可以看出，如果是符合模型的设定，低能量的中子在经过原子核时不会不受到阻碍。

63D 解析

[**Passage I**]

1. 答案：C

解析：抓关键词 shell diameter，看 Figure 2 最后一张图，30 000 年的厚度大约为 28 mm，选 C。

2. 答案：G

解析：看 Table 1，31 000 介于 30 000 和 32 000，所以 L、L、L、B 的比例在 72%～79%之间，选 G。

3. 答案：D

解析：Study 1 研究的是壳的条纹，Study 2 研究的是壳的 3 种特征，选 D。

4. 答案：G

解析：实验方法由实验目标决定，Study 2 要研究壳的特征，需要完整的壳，选 G。

5. 答案：B

解析：看 Study 1 的 L 和 B 的解释，L 是细的，B 是宽的，从壳顶部开始黑色的条纹应为宽、细、宽、宽，选 B。

6. 答案：H

解析：抓关键词 whorl 和 shell diameter，现在的蜗牛在最右端，40 000 年前的在最左端，可知 whorl 数量增加，diameter 减小，选 H。

[**Passage II**]

7. 答案：A

解析：生物遗传学，基本知识看导语，后代全部为白眼，配对应只含隐性性状 r，选 A。

8. 答案：F

解析：雌性为 XX，从 genotype 与 eye color 的表格可知，白眼为 XrXr，选 F。

9. 答案：D

解析：雄性为 XY，对照表格，只要后代的雄性性状为白眼，就有一个白眼基因，实验 2、3、4，都有白眼雄性后代，选 D。

10. 答案：G

解析：雄性和雌性概率各为 50%，实验 3 雄性后代中是红眼的概率是 50%，1 000 × 50% × 50% = 250，选 G。

11. 答案：D

解析：雄性和雌性概率各为 50%，后代为白眼概率为 50% × 50% = 25%，红眼 ∶ 白眼 = 3 ∶ 1，选 D。

12. 答案：J

解析：方法 1：排除法。F 选项所有雌性后代为 XrXR，全部红眼，排除。G 选项所有雌性后代为 XRXr，全部红眼，排除。H 选项雌性后代为 XRXr 或 XRXR，全部红眼，排除。选 J。

方法 2：倒推法(高手)。后代雄性两种性状都存在，Y 来自父方，X 来自母方，所以母方显性基因和隐性基因都有，是 XRXr。后代雌性两种性状都存在，X 来自父方和母方，因为雌雄白眼只有 XrXr，所以父方的 X 携带隐性基因，选 J。

［**Passage III**］

13. 答案：B

解析：看 Table 3，%Δp2.2 介于 2.0 和 2.4，air volume capacity 介于 0.50 和 0.55，选 B。

14. 答案：F

解析：看 Table 1，engine speed 与%Δp 正相关，engine speed 小于 1 000，%Δp 小于 0.3，选 F。

15. 答案：A

解析：由%Δp 的计算公式和导语可知，%Δp 越大，压力差越大，空气流速越快，看 Table 1，engine speed 与%Δp 正相关，选 A。

16. 答案：J

解析：Location A、B、C 压强近似相等，此时流速越快，半径越小，选 J。

17. 答案：B

解析：当实验 1 和实验 2 转速都是 3 000 时，实验 1 的%Δp 是 2.4，对应实验 2 中的 venturi radius 是 1.2 cm，说明实验 1 用的 carburetor 的 venturi radius 是 1.2 cm。因为实验 1 和 3 用同样的 carburetor，所以实验 3 用的 carburetor 的 venturi radius 也是 1.2 cm，选 B。

18. 答案：G

解析：因为%Δp 的值大于 0，所以 atmospheric pressure 大于 venturi pressure，由%Δp 的计算公式可知，值越小，atmospheric pressure 与 venturi pressure 的值越接近，选 G。

［**Passage IV**］

19. 答案：C

解析：每次物质升高 10℃扩大的体积不变的有铅、银、乙醇、水银，选 C。

20. 答案：F

解析：由 Table 1 可知，铅是热胀冷缩的，温度降低 10℃，体积缩小 0.000 9 L，选 F。

21. 答案：D

解析：Table 2 水从 0℃到 4℃时，水的体积缩小，选 D。

22. 答案：H

解析：铅受热膨胀，因为温度升高，原子具有的能量增大，原子间距变大，导致体积增大，选 H。

23. 答案：A

解析：由 Table 3 可知，Helium 的初始温度越高，升高相同温度膨胀的体积越小，初始温度 34℃高于 24℃，所以膨胀的体积小于 0.034 8 L，选 A。

[**Passage V**]

24. 答案：H

解析：横坐标代表温度，在 125～150 km 时横坐标变化最大，选 H。

25. 答案：A

解析：找 Table 1 中占火星大气比例最多且占地球大气比例最少的气体，是 CO_2，选 A。

26. 答案：J

解析：金星在 150～250 km 时横坐标不随纵坐标变化而变化，选 J。

27. 答案：D

解析：排除法，金星和火星没有氧气，地球有氧气，选 D。

28. 答案：H

解析：Table 2 中金星没有温室效应的温度为 280 K，Figure 1 中金星温度为 700 K，700－280＝420 K，选 H。

[**Passage VI**]

29. 答案：A

解析：导语中提到让两个原子核靠近发生核聚变需要大量能量，选 A。

30. 答案：H

解析：Lawson's criterionn $\times$ t $>10^{14}$，Magnetic Confinement Method 中的 $n=10^{14}$，所以 $t=1$ s，方法解释的最后也提到维持大约 1 s，选 H。

31. 答案：A

解析：从导语可知，因为原子核都带正电相斥，所以核聚变困难，选 A。

32. 答案：H

解析：Lawson's criterion 说明核聚变需要高温和释放大量产物，所以两种方法的目的都是升高温度和增大原子核在容器中的密度以增加产物，选 H。

33. 答案：B

解析：Magnetic Confinement Method 的密度小于 10^{14}，Laser Confinement Method 的密度大约 10^{23}，选 B。

34. 答案：G

解析：Laser Confinement Method 的解释中说 laser 是用来压缩原子核的，选 G。

35. 答案：D

解析：Lawson's criterionn $\times$ t $>10^{14}$，n 和 t 都应该增大选 D。

[**Passage VII**]

36. 答案：H

解析：横坐标是 internal head temperature，纵坐标是 evaporation heat loss，找到该点，在 skin temperature 弧线 31～32℃，选 H。

37. 答案：C

解析：Skin temperature 为 20℃ 的弧线斜率越来越小，所以 internal head temperature 值越大 heat production 减小的越多，internal head temperature 大于 37.2℃ 时，heat production 不再减小，选 C。

38. 答案：G

解析：Evaporation heat loss 在 36.2～36.9℃保持不变，在 36.9～37.0℃增加，选 G。

39. 答案：A

解析：Internal head temperature 在 36.6℃时的 heat production 比在 37.0℃的高，skin temperature 在 22℃时的 heat production 比在 28℃的高，选 A。

40. 答案：F

解析：29 在 28 到 30 之间，skin temperature 为 28℃，internal head temperature 为 36.8℃的 heat production 为 35，skin temperature 为 30℃，internal head temperature 为 36.8℃的 heat production 为 20，则在 20 到 35 之间，选 F。

63E 解析

[**Passage I**]

1. 答案：D

解析：从 Zone E～A，mice 数量增加，larvae/mouse 比例没有稳定变化趋势，选 D。

2. 答案：G

解析：有一个环节老鼠单独发挥作用，所以老鼠必不可少，选 G。

3. 答案：C

解析：算 5 个百分比的平均值，求出 53%，最接近 50%，选 C。

4. 答案：F

解析：Zone A 人的感染比例最高，看到鹿的数量也最多，传播途径多，选 F。

5. 答案：D

解析：看 Figure 2，8 月和 11 月 case 总数不同，选 D。

[**Passage II**]

6. 答案：G

解析：150 在 140～160 之间，OFC1 在 218～442 之间，OFC2 在 133～301 之间，选 G。

7. 答案：B

解析：看 Table 2，FeF_3 用的时间最短，选 B。

8. 答案：H

解析：实验 1 研究不同温度的影响，实验 2 研究不同化合物的影响，温度保持在 180℃，选 H。

9. 答案：D

解析：实验 1 的介绍中提到压力升高，测量的数据是压力到 0.20 atm 时的时间，选 D。

10. 答案：J

解析：实验 1 中测量的所有温度 OFC2 分解的时间一直比 OFC1 短，选 J。

11. 答案：A

解析：导语中介绍 OFC 只含 C、F、O，选 A。

[**Passage III**]

12. 答案：H

解析：Student 2 认为 50%花粉传播依靠昆虫，实验 2 排除了昆虫，所以只有 50%能传播，选 H。

13. 答案：B

解析：Wind tunnel 实验说明雌性 Zamia 产生气流方便花粉传播，选 B。

14. 答案：F

解析：Student 1 认为除了昆虫和风没有其他传播方式，选 F。

15. 答案：B

解析：Student 1 认为风授粉不常见，因为花粉很大很重，排除 D，可以推断出花粉不能靠风传播很远，A、C 与导语内容相反，选 B。

16. 答案：F

解析：不做任何改变的传播途径最多，授粉比例最高，选 F。

17. 答案：D

解析：控制组不对雌蕊做任何改变，选 D。

18. 答案：J

解析：Student 2 认为靠风和昆虫传粉的各占一半，所以如果排除昆虫后传粉的比例和排除风后传粉的比例一样，可以验证他的观点，选 J。

[**Passage IV**]

19. 答案：B

解析：Table 1 中 clay content 越多，water content 越多，选 B。

20. 答案：G

解析：Sand content 78%在 soil A 和 B 之间，water content 在 2.9～6.8%之间，选 G。

21. 答案：D

解析：没有 saturate 之前，soil C 的水含量已经大于 15%，选 D。

22. 答案：H

解析：从 Table 2 可知，Soil A、B、C 的临界风速大致相同，选 H。

23. 答案：A

解析：加了沙子后，临界风速从 0.31 降到 0.21，大约 1/3，选 A。

24. 答案：H

解析：Soil A 和 B 加沙子的临界风速在 0.21 左右，等量混合后应仍在 0.21 左右，选 H。

[**Passage V**]

25. 答案：B

解析：看 Table 1，两块 plates 的距离越远，电压越大，电容越小，选 B。

26. 答案：G

解析：看 Table 2 第一列，实验 2 改变的 plate 的面积，选 G。

27. 答案：C

解析：Table 1 可知距离越近，电容越大，Table 2 可知面积越大，电容越大，Table 3 可知用 titanium dioxide 电容最大，选 C。

28. 答案：H

解析：把 Table 3 的 K 值按从大到小排列，选 H。

29. 答案：A

解析：导语解释 −1×10^−8C 流向 B，有相反等量的电荷流向 A，选 A。

30. 答案：F

解析：负电荷流向 B，电子带负电，箭头指向 B，A 带等量相反电荷，箭头离开 A，选 F。

[**Passage VI**]

31. 答案:D

   解析:Figure 2 和 3 纵坐标不是一个级别,solubility 在任何温度都不等,选 D。

32. 答案:H

   解析:1 mole/L 的浓度是 0.5 mole/L 的两倍,在同一份溶液中体积相同,选 H。

33. 答案:B

   解析:Compound B 溶解放热,Figure 3 说明 B 的溶解度随温度升高而降低,选 B。

34. 答案:F

   解析:水温从 25℃降到 0℃,说明溶质溶解吸热,是 compound A,ΔH 是正数,选 F。

35. 答案:A

   解析:ΔH 为 +25.7 说明吸热比 compound A 少,选 A。

[**Passage VII**]

36. 答案:G

   解析:看 Figure 2 第一张图,eccentricity 为 0.10 的弧线有两段在 30 km/s 以上,选 G。

37. 答案:C

   解析:速度先减小后增大,选 C。

38. 答案:J

   解析:从第一张图可知,当 θ 为 0°时,速度远小于逃脱速度 44.2 km/s,不会脱离轨道,选 J。

39. 答案:A

   解析:eccentricity 越大,速度变化越大,当 eccentricity 为 0 时,轨道为正圆,速度不变,选 A。

40. 答案:F

   解析:eccentricity 为 0.05,θ 为 0°时的速度小于 eccentricity 为 0.10 时的速度,选 F。

63F 解析

[**Passage I**]

1. 答案:C

   解析:Figure 1 的 ionosphere 包括 mesosphere 和 thermosphere 的全部及 stratosphere 的顶部,选 C。

2. 答案:F

   解析:50~80 km 主要和 red sprite 重合,选 F。

3. 答案:B

   解析:125~150 peak current 出现 TLE 概率大于 100~125 peak current 出现 TLE 概率的两倍,选 B。

4. 答案:J

   解析:Peak current 越高,出现概率越大,选 J。

5. 答案:D

   解析:75~100 的概率是 21.1%,约 1/5,选 D。

[**Passage II**]

6. 答案：F

   解析：porosity 最高的能存最多的水，选 F。

7. 答案：B

   解析：25%在 10～34%，voidratio 在 0.11～0.52，选 B。

8. 答案：J

   解析：加热重量没减轻说明泥土含水少，选 J。

9. 答案：D

   解析：水会使泥土黏在一起，选 D。

10. 答案：J

    解析：导语解释泥土颗粒的直径范围小是分类好的，泥土 5 每种类别都有，直径范围大，分类不好，选 J。

11. 答案：A

    解析：沙子越粗糙，颗粒直径越大，渗透越快，选 A。

[**Passage III**]

12. 答案：F

    解析：Figure 2 混合时间越长，温度越高，Figure 3 混合时间越长，电流越大，温度越高，电流越大，选 F。

13. 答案：B

    解析：Figure 3 右边 viscosity 的箭头说明电流越大，viscosity 越大，选 B。

14. 答案：H

    解析：M2 混合 8 分钟电流为 1.50 A，选 H。

15. 答案：A

    解析：M1 电流到达 2 A 的混合时间最长，选 A。

16. 答案：F

    解析：Figure 2 中 icecream mixture 温度降低，salt/ice mixture 温度升高，说明 Figure 1 的装置示意图 salt/ice mixture 冷却 icecream mixture，热量从 icecream mixture 转移到 salt/ice mixture，选 F。

[**Passage IV**]

17. 答案：A

    解析：Table 2 中 x 代表可以生长，MM 全部不能生长，是控制组，选 A。

18. 答案：J

    解析：能在 MM + citrulline 上生长的可能是 Type 1、2、5，它们都能在 MM + argininosuccinate 上生长，选 J。

19. 答案：B

    解析：Precursor 的意思是反应物，看 Figure 1 生成顺序，选 B。

20. 答案：H

    解析：导语中解释 + 代表可以生成，- 代表不可以，对照 Table 1，注意题目问的是不能生成，选 H。

21. 答案：D

解析：不能生成 E4 会使 argininosuccinate 不断积累，选 D。

22. 答案：F

解析：Type 1 不能在 acetylornithine 上生长，却可以在后面几种媒介上生长，说明不能把 acetylornithine 转换成 ornithine，选 F。

[**Passage V**]

23. 答案：B

解析：Figure 1 中在下午 1:30 和下午 5:30，四组入睡时间最接近，选 B。

24. 答案：H

解析：下午 1:30 更老人群平均口腔温度高于青少年，选 H。

25. 答案：C

解析：Figure 1 显示青少年在下午 9:30 入睡时间最长，选 C。

26. 答案：F

解析：在上午 3:30 入睡时间最短的是 youth group，选 F。

27. 答案：A

解析：把这 4 个时间画在 Figure 1 中，youth group 夹在中间，选 A。

[**Passage VI**]

28. 答案：H

解析：抓关键词 Solvent 3，half、Component 时间最接近 35 分钟，选 H。

29. 答案：B

解析：3.9 最接近 Component B 的 4.2，选 B。

30. 答案：H

解析：0.7 在 0.4～1.1 之间，Component D 和 C 之间，看 Figure 2，顺序是 D、Z、C、B、A，选 H。

31. 答案：D

解析：看 Figure 2，normal phase 时间间隔最长的是 Solvent 3，看 Figure 3，reverse phase 时间间隔最长的是 Solvent 1，选 D。

32. 答案：J

解析：看 Figure 1，当 Belute 50%时，D 已经全部 elute，选 J。

33. 答案：D

解析：9.3 大于 Solvent 1 的 polarity，evolution time 比 Solvent 1 长，选 D。

[**Passage VII**]

34. 答案：F

解析：Student 1 认为木块受平面摩擦匀减速，最终静止，选 F。

35. 答案：B

解析：所有学生的解释都是基于老师对实验的描述，选 B。

36. 答案：G

解析：三人都认为木块受到反方向作用力，所以速度测量期间一直在减速，选 G。

37. 答案：B

解析：Student 3 认为是空气阻力减速，该试验排除空气最能证明他的观点，选 B。

38. 答案：H

解析：最高点动能全部转换为重力势能，此时重力势能等于机械能，选 H。

39\. 答案：D

解析：Student 1 认为受到恒定的摩擦力，摩擦力与速度无关，只与摩擦系数和压力大小有关，选 D。

40\. 答案：H

解析：动能全部转换成摩擦力产生的热能，重力势能没有增加，机械能不守恒，选 H。

65B 解析

[**Passage I**]

1\. 答案：C

题干：判断 $\theta=380^\circ$ 时，V 的值。

定位：Figure 2

解析：从 Figure 2 中可以看出，图形是有周期的，并且关于 $\theta=310^\circ$ 对称，有对称可得 $\theta=380^\circ$ 时，V 为 4.4。

2\. 答案：H

题干：判断 V 在哪个 θ 的变化区间内变化得最大。

定位：Figure 2

解析：从 Figure 2 可以判断得出。

3\. 答案：B

题干：判断当 I 接近 18 lux 时 θ 的值。

定位：Figure 2、3

解析：从 Figure 3 中可以看出 I 为 18 lux 时 V 为 3.6，再对应 Figure 2 可得 θ 为 70°。

4\. 答案：G

题干：判断 θ 为何值时光的强度最强。

定位：Figure 2、3

解析：从 Figure 3 中可以看出 I 与 V 成正比，再对应 Figure 3 可得 θ 为 40° 和 220° 时，V 取最大值。

5\. 答案：C

题干：判断在 $\theta=0^\circ$ 时 I 的值。

定位：Figure 2、3

解析：$\theta=0^\circ$ 时，V 为 3 volt，对应的 I 为 15 lux。

[**Passage II**]

6\. 答案：J

题干：判断在哪个时间段内发生了 2002 年全年规模最大的降水。

定位：Figure 3

解析：图 3 可以看出日均排场量在 Mar. 23 到 Mar. 30 之间达到最大值，所以最大规模的降水应该发生在前一周。

7\. 答案：D

题干：判断从 1 月 5 日到 3 月 30 日这段期间内哪个水流的历史日平均排水量逐渐增加。

定位：Figure 1～3
解析：观察三幅图中实线走势即可得出答案。

8. 答案：F
题干：判断对于 Stream 2 的日平均排水量与历史平均排水量之间的关系。
定位：Figure 2
解析：图 2 可以看出对于几乎全部的时间段，虚线一直在实线的下方。

9. 答案：D
题干：判断水流 3 在 3 月 23 日的最大日排水量。
定位：Figure 3
解析：图 3 可以看出日均排场量在 75 ft^3/sec，所以当天的最大值应该大于 75。

10. 答案：J
题干：判断排水流域总面积。
定位：Table 1
解析：文中提到 3 个水流处在同一排水流域中，所以 3 个水流的排数区域可能会有重合，因此整个排水流域的最小值为水流 1 的排水面积。

[**Passage III**]

11. 答案：A
题干：判断实验 3 中的对照组。
定位：Study 3
解析：实验 3 关心的是暴露在不同的气体中的发芽率情况，所以对照组为正常的气体，即空气。

12. 答案：G
题干：判断在 NO_2浓度为 675 mg/m^3时发芽率的范围。
定位：Table 1
解析：表 1 可以看到当 NO_2浓度从 50 增加到 790，再增加到 1 500 时，发芽率也逐渐增加，所以当浓度为 675 时，发芽率应该介于 0 和 93 之间。

13. 答案：C
题干：判断何种气体对于促进发芽最有效果。
定位：Table 1
解析：表 1 可以看到当 NO_2的浓度为 790 mg/m^3时，发芽率为 100%。

14. 答案：H
题干：判断实验 1 中在 10 分钟暴露下哪两个实验的发芽率最相近。
定位：Figure 1
解析：从 Figure 1 中可观察得出。

15. 答案：D
题干：判断暴露 5 分钟时的发芽率。
定位：Figure 1
解析：从表 1 中可以看到在同样的实验条件下，发芽率随暴露时间的增加而增加，所以暴露 5 分钟时的发芽率介于 75%和 100%之间。

16. 答案：F
题干：判断 NO_2因溶于水而对发芽率的影响。
定位：Figure 2

解析：在表 2 中可以看到在水中，当暴露时间从 1 分钟增加到 10 分钟时，发芽率大幅下降，结合题干中 NO_2溶于水产生酸性物质说明 10 分钟时 NO_2因大量溶于水而使得溶液酸性增强，不利于发芽。

[**Passage IV**]

17. 答案：B
题干：判断 maltose 的 RT。
定位：Figure 2
解析：根据图 2 可得。
18. 答案：G
题干：判断 maltose 的 RT。
定位：Table 1、Figure 3
解析：根据表 1 可知，苹果汁的 RT 出现在 4.7、6.4、7.6、12.8 min 处，对应图 3 可得所对应的物质为 sucrose、glucose、fructose 和 sorbitol。文中提到后缀为“ose”的是 sugar，后缀为“itol”为 sugar alcohols。所以答案为前三项。
19. 答案：C
题干：判断 FR = 1.5 mL/min 时，4～5 分钟内可收集到的物质数量。
定位：Figure 1
解析：根据图 1 峰值数量可得。
20. 答案：F
题干：判断何种物质最先离开分离管道。
定位：Figure 1、2、3
解析：RT 为一半的物质通过分离管道所用的时间，全部分离需要用的时间为 2 RT。根据 3 张图可得，sucrose 有最小的 RT。
21. 答案：D
题干：判断 FR 为何值时，sucrose 和 lactose 分离的 resolution 最高。
定位：Figure 1、2、3
解析：根据 3 幅图可以看到，在 FR = 0.5 时，两者 RTs 的差值最大。
22. 答案：F
题干：判断 FR = 2.0 mL/min 时，sorbitol 的 RT 值。
定位：Figure 1、2、3
解析：根据 3 幅图可以看到，sorbitol 的 RT 值随着 FR 的增大而减小，所以 FR 为 2.0 时，RT 应小于 9。

[**Passage V**]

23. 答案：D
题干：实验 3 中变化的量。
定位：Study 3
解析：实验中土壤发生了 4 次结冰和融化，说明实验者有意控制了土壤的温度以使其重复结冰与融化。
24. 答案：G
题干：判断上升的液体与下降的液体的相对密度。

定位：Figure 3

解析：根据图 3，液体上升部分是亮的，下降部分是暗的，说明上升部分的密度低，下降部分的密度高。

25. 答案：A

题干：判断在冬天泥土被冻住数月时所发生的岩石或土壤的移动情况。

定位：L4

解析：文中提到，泥土和岩石的移动是由于温度和密度的差异，当已被冷冻数月未发生融化时，不会发生移动。

26. 答案：G

题干：判断去除实验 3 中泥土中的水分后，测量得到的岩石位置变化。

定位：Figure 1、Study 3

解析：从图 1 可以看到，泥土的移动是伴随泥土中不同温度水的移动发生的，所以当泥土中没有水分时，泥土和被放入中央的岩石都不会发生位置的移动。

27. 答案：C

题干：判断哪个实验结果支持土壤表面的岩石原本被埋在土壤下的观点。

定位：Study 3

解析：实验中土壤发生 4 次结冰和融化后，岩石的位置提升了 3 cm。

28. 答案：J

题干：判断土壤位置的变动原因。

定位：Figure 1

解析：图 1 说明了土壤位置的移动是由于 4℃ 水向下移动，0℃ 水向上移动，这证明了 4℃ 水比 0℃ 水密度更大。

[**Passage VI**]

29. 答案：C

题干：判断基因突变发生的位置。

定位：Table 1

解析：基因突变发生在 DNA 上。

30. 答案：G

题干：判断 Tt 发生的概率。

定位：Table 3

解析：TT、Tt 和 tt 的概率总和应为 1。

31. 答案：C

题干：判断基因突变发生的位置。

定位：Table 1

解析：基因突变发生在 DNA 上。

32. 答案：C

题干：判断 p 与 AA 发生频率的关系。

定位：Table 2

解析：AA 发生的频率等于 p 的平方，所以曲线公式应为 y = x^2。

33. 答案：A

题干：判断显性形状对应的频率。

定位：Table 2
解析：显性性状的基因型为 AA 和 Aa。

[**Passage VII**]

34. 答案：J
题干：判断将圆柱体投入沸腾的水中会使圆柱体的哪种能量提升。
定位：Introduction
解析：将 25℃ 的圆柱体投入 50℃ 的水中，圆柱体会从水中吸收热量而升温。
35. 答案：C
题干：判断哪个圆柱体会先将热量传导另一端。
定位：Student 1、2
解析：根据学生 1 的说法，X 所花费的时间是 Y 的一半。根据学生 2 的说法，X 所花费的时间是 Y 的两倍。
36. 答案：F
题干：判断 Y 的 SH。
定位：Table 2
解析：根据表 2，Y 的 SH 是 X 的一半。
37. 答案：B
题干：判断学生 1 的认为影响热量传导速率的因素。
定位：Student 1
解析：学生 1 的观点中考虑了 X 和 Y 的 TC 和尺寸大小。
38. 答案：H
题干：判断 SH 的单位。
定位：Student 2
解析：根据学生 2 的说法，heat capacity = SH × mass，mass 的单位为 g，所以 SH 的单位为 cal/(g℃)。
39. 答案：B
题干：判断 X 的长度变为一半时 HC 的变化。
定位：Student 2
解析：HC = SH × mass，当长度变为一半时，mass 变为原来的二分之一，SH 不变，所以 HC 变为原来的二分之一。
40. 答案：G
题干：判断圆柱体降温的速度与升温速度相同所基于的假设。
定位：Student 1
解析：学生 1 考虑的是 TC，当升温降温速度相同时，说明升温和降温的 TC 相同。

65D 解析

[**Passage I**]

1. 答案：D
解析：先看 Figure 1 找到染色体 13，携带 ribosomal RNA 基因，再看 Table 1，可知 ribosomal

RNA gene 与 Protein synthesis 有关,选 D。

2. 答案:G
解析:tRNA proline gene 与 hexokinase gene 是否有关在于这两种基因是否在同一染色体上,在同一染色体上则有关,在不同染色体上则无关,从 Figure 1 可知,这两种基因不在同一染色体上,所以无关,选 G。
3. 答案:A
解析:看 Figure 1,找 Table 1 中 3 种与 Digestion 有关的基因是否在同一染色体上,结果在不同染色体上,选 A。
4. 答案:G
解析:从 Table 2 可知,neuro fibromatosis gene 在染色体 17 上,看 Figure 1 的染色体 17,该染色体同样含有 growth hormone gene,选 G。
5. 答案:D
解析:常识:男性的性染色体由一个 X 染色体和一个 Y 染色体组成,女性的性染色体由两个 Y 染色体组成,所以男性特有的基因是 Y 染色体,看 Figure 1 的 Y 染色体,含有 TSPY 基因,选 D。

[**Passage II**]

6. 答案:J
解析:看 Table 2 比较 Y-tocopherol percentage × tocopherol concentration 的大小,很明显 S4 最大,选 J。
7. 答案:B
解析:因为 Experiment 1 和 Experiment 2 用了同种 A. thaliana strains,所以 tocopherol concentration 应该都为 360 mg/kg,在实验 2 中对应的是 S2,选 B。
8. 答案:J
解析:题目问应比较哪两个研究来验证 vector 是否影响 tocopherol concentration。自变量为 vector,其他条件相同,在 Experiment 1 中符合要求的为 L5 和 L6,其中 L6 为对照组,选 J。
9. 答案:C
解析:某种基因比其他基因的转换效率低,则处理后的反应物 Y-tocopherol 含量应多于其他 3 种基因,而生成物 a-tocopherol 含量应少于其他 3 种基因,Table 1 中的 TMT3 与其他基因在反应物和生成物比例上有明显差距,选 C。
10. 答案:J
解析:某种转换不成功,说明处理后反应物没有转化成生成物,S4 的反应几乎没有进行,选 J。
11. 答案:B
解析:转基因说明某种基因能满足人类需要,能成功把 Y-tocopherol 转换成 a-tocopherol,选 B。

[**Passage III**]

12. 答案:H
解析:抓定位词 Figure 2 和 Figure 3,找到 H = 1.5 m 的坐标,横坐标表示角度,可知 X 先增大后减小,选 H。
13. 答案:A
解析:从导语可知 Figure 3 代表 sliding sphere,当角度为 10 度时,H 每减小 0.5 m,X 减小

0.10 m，H = 0.5 m 时大约为 0.55 − 0.10 = 0.45 m，选 A。

14. 答案：H

解析：题目问如果角度的变化为 2.5 度，则 X 的最高点是多少。由导语可知 sliding sphere 看 Figure 3，画一条弧线把 H = 2.0 m 的坐标连起来，X 最大的角度应该在现在 X 最大的两个角度之间，选 H。

15. 答案：B

解析：由导语可知 rolling sphere 看 Figure 2，角度大于 30 度后，角度越大，X 越小，H = 2.0 m，角度为 50 时，X 在 0.6～0.8 m 之间，选 B。

16. 答案：F

解析：随着 sphere 滚下斜坡，重力势能减少，动能会逐渐增大，动能和时间同时增加，选 F。

［**Passage IV**］

17. 答案：C

解析：看 Table 1 和 Table 4，Study 4 用的是 copper，所以在 Table 4 中找与 Table 1 的 copper 最接近的 V 和 R，此时温度为 20 摄氏度，选 C。

18. 答案：J

解析：看 Table 3，随着横截面的增大，R 逐渐减小，选 J。

19. 答案：D

解析：题目要求把材料按电阻从小到大的顺序排列，看 Table 1 材料电阻从小到大为 Copper、Tungsten、Platinum、Lead，选 D。

20. 答案：H

解析：从 Study 2 可知，导线长度与 V 基本成正比关系，导线从 100 m 变成 200 m，V 应为原来的两倍，60 摄氏度铜线的电阻应为 0.13×2 = 0.26 volts，选 H。

21. 答案：C

解析：抓关键词 electrical resistance，Table 2 可知长度越长，电阻越大，Table 3 可知横截面面积越小，电阻越大，选 C。

22. 答案：G

解析：实验测量的是导线两端的电压和通过导线的电流，am meter 是用来测量通过导线的电流，所以学生假设所有电流都经过导线，选 G。

［**Passage V**］

23. 答案：A

解析：Figure 1 的横坐标是 relative concentration，在 4 个选项中 oceanic basalt and continental basalt 的含量差距最大即横坐标差距最大是 Cerium，选 A。

24. 答案：H

解析：在 Figure 1 中找与这 3 种 REE 含量最接近的，是 Granite，选 H。

25. 答案：B

解析：比较 Table 1 中所有岩石 neodymium and samarium 的含量，所有岩石的 neodymium 含量都高于 samarium 含量，选 B。

26. 答案：H

解析：Lime stone 是 sedimentary rocks，Figure 1 中 sedimentary rocks 那块阴影的 terbium 含量是 15～20，选 H。

27. 答案：A
解析：题目问哪种岩石覆盖最小范围的 relative concentration，Oceanic basalt 的 relative concentration of REE 的极差最小，选 A。

[**Passage VI**]

28. 答案：F
解析：科学家 2 认为在 4BYA，大量二氧化碳来自火山活动，现在大部分二氧化碳成为 carbonate sin rock and sedimenton land，选 F。
29. 答案：A
解析：科学家 1 认为 CH_4 与 NH_3 反应生成的有机物阻挡大部分 UV radiation，使 NH_3 分子存在更长时间，有更强的温室效应，选 A。
30. 答案：H
解析：现在的 CO_2 含量是 360 ppm，NH_3 浓度只需 CO_2 浓度的 1/3，即 120 ppm，选 H。
31. 答案：A
解析：从导语可知，40 亿年前，地球表面温度本应该为 − 15℃，题目假设每种温室气体所占比例不变，所以使地球表面温度高于 0℃ 需要的 minimum total concentration 多于现在的 minimum total concentration，选 A。
32. 答案：F
解析：科学家 1 认为 CH_4 与 NH_3 反应保护了 NH_3，火山活动解释了 CH_4 的来源，科学家 2 认为大量的 CH_4 以前不存在，选 F。
33. 答案：B
解析：阻挡地球外的 UV radiation 要在 NH_3 存在大气层外侧，选 B。
34. 答案：J
解析：科学家 2 认为以前 CO_2 浓度比现在高 75%，只有 J 选项大于 360，选 J。

[**Passage VII**]

35. 答案：D
解析：由实验 1 可知，80℃ 的水的密度小于 10℃ 的水的密度，密度小的往上，密度大的往下，所以会混合，选 D。
36. 答案：F
解析：由实验 3 可知，盐水沸点高于蒸馏水沸点的 100℃，所以不加盐的溶液会在最低温度沸腾，选 F。
37. 答案：B
解析：看实验 2 的描述，常温的水一开始随着温度降低液面下降，说明体积减小，4℃ 时液面停止下降，然后液面开始上升，说明体积增大，对照图像，选 B。
38. 答案：F
解析：盐水到 − 6℃ 仍未凝固，说明冷却温度不够低，应该继续冷却，选 F。
39. 答案：C
解析：溶液 1 的沸点是 102℃，溶液 2 的沸点是 104℃，等体积混合后浓度在溶液 1 和溶液 2 浓度之间，沸点同样，选 C。
40. 答案：H
解析：液面改变说明水的体积改变，因为物体质量不可能改变，所以密度也改变，选 H。

65F 解析

[**Passage I**]

1. 答案：B

   题干：判断当温度降低时水的 specific volume 的变化。

   定位：Figure 1

   解析：从 Figure 1 中可以看出，温度降低时，specific volume 降低。

2. 答案：J

   题干：判断当 specific volume 为 1.03 时所对应的温度。

   定位：Figure 1

   解析：根据 Figure 1 可得。

3. 答案：C

   题干：判断当温度为 60℃时 2 g ethyl alcohol 的体积。

   定位：Figure 2

   解析：从 Figure 2 中可以看出，当温度为 60℃时，specific volume 为 1.32 cm^3/g，由此可算得体积。

4. 答案：F

   题干：判断 −117℃时的 specific volume。

   定位：Figure 2

   解析：文中已知密度与 specific volume 成反比，因为 −117℃时的密度高于 0℃时，−117℃时的 specific volume 要低于 1.24。

5. 答案：B

   题干：判断 specific volume 的另一种单位。

   定位：无

   解析：specific vloume 是密度的倒数，所以应该选择密度单位的倒数。

[**Passage II**]

6. 答案：F

   题干：判断使 B 取最大值时的 D 的最小值。

   定位：Figure 2

   解析：Figure 2 第一个峰值所对应的横坐标即为答案。

7. 答案：A

   题干：判断实验 1 中所用的到油对应的 index。

   定位：Figure 2、Table 3

   解析：从 Figure 2 可得实验 1 中用到的油在 B 取最大值时 D 的最小值为 89，对应 Table 1 可得此种油为 W。

8. 答案：G

   题干：判断光的频率增大时，使 B 取最大值时的 D 的最小值的变化趋势。

   定位：Table 3

   解析：从 Table 3 可以看出 D 是单调递减的。

9. 答案：C

题干：判断 445 nm 之后的下一个峰值位置。

定位：Figure 2

解析：Figure 2 中可以观察到曲线是呈周期性的，两个峰值之间的间隔为 178 nm。

10. 答案：H

题干：比较实验中使用的油与水的密度。

定位：Figure 1

解析：Figure 1 中可以看到油是漂浮在水的上方，说明油的密度要比水小。

11. 答案：F

题干：判断使 B 取最大值的 D 的最小值为 80 nm 时对应的油的 index。

定位：Table 1

解析：Table 1 中可以看到 index 与 D 的值是负相关的，所以当 D 取 80 nm 时 index 应居于 1.4 和 1.5 之间。

［**Passage III**］

12. 答案：J

题干：判断 lactose 可以与哪种物质结合。

定位：Figure 2、3

解析：Figure 2、3 都体现出 lactose 可以与 P1 结合。

13. 答案：B

题干：判断怎样可以使 LOO 失活。

定位：Student 3

解析：根据 Student 3 的观点，galacose 与 P1 结合后，会诱发 P1 的改变，使其与 LOO 结合从而激活 LOO，所以去除 galacose 后，上述反应即无法发生。

14. 答案：J

题干：判断 lactose 不存在时 LOO 的状态。

定位：Figure 2

解析：根据 Figure 2，当 lactose 不存在时，P1 无法与 LOO 结合从而激活 LOO，所以 LOO 处于未激活状态，也就无法合成酶。

15. 答案：C

题干：判断 Student 1 关于 P1 的观点。

定位：Figure 2

解析：根据 Figure 2，当 lactose 不存在时，P1 与 LOO 结合后会抑制 LOO 的活性。

16. 答案：F

题干：判断哪位学生认为 P1 会在 lactose 与 galactose 不存在时与 LOO 结合。

定位：Figure 1、2、3

解析：只有 Student 1 认为 P1 会在 lactose 与 galactose 不存在时与 LOO 结合。

17. 答案：A

题干：判断 LOO 是否处于激活状态。

定位：Figure 1、2、3

解析：Student 1 认为 P1 会在 lactose 存在时激活 LOO，Student 2 认为 P1 会在 lactose 存在时激活 LOO，Student 3 认为 P1 会在 galactose 存在时激活 LOO。

18. 答案：F
题干：判断哪位学生认为 P1 不存在时 LOO 会在激活状态。
定位：Figure 1、2、3
解析：只有 Student 1 认为 LOO 会因为与 P1 结合而失活。

［**Passage IV**］

19. 答案：C
题干：判断 Mass 随时间的变化趋势。
定位：Table 2
解析：Table 2 中可以看到 M1、M2、M3 的质量变化率是正值，说明质量随时间增加，NM1、NM2 的变化率是负值，说明质量随时间减少。
20. 答案：J
题干：判断哪一条在后 16 天质量的下降率最高。
定位：Table 2
解析：Table 2 中可以看到后 16 天 NM1 质量的下降率为 15%，NM2 为 34%。
21. 答案：B
题干：判断细胞质中水移动到高盐度水中需经过哪个细胞结构。
定位：L5
解析：细胞内水的流出需要经过细胞膜。
22. 答案：F
题干：判断高度随时间的变化规律。
定位：Table 2
解析：Table 2 中可以看到所有的实验植物高度都随着时间的推移而增加。
23. 答案：A
题干：判断实验 1 的目的。
定位：Table 1、2
解析：Table 2 中可以看到 M 系列和 NM 系列的生长率有较大的差异，而从 Table 1 中可以看到两个系列的生长率差异不大，所以实验者是希望从第一个实验中判断在正常的盐浓度情况下两个系列是否具有相同的生长率，以判断改变盐溶液浓度时对两个系列生长率的影响。
24. 答案：F
题干：判断解释变量。
定位：Table 1、2
解析：解释变量是实验中所控制的变量，而质量为实验的结果。

［**Passage V**］

25. 答案：C
题干：判断 cooling curve 在哪一个温度上是水平的。
定位：Figure 2
解析：Figure 2 中 cooling curve 在 120℃ 上是水平的。
26. 答案：H
题干：判断混合体从 900℃ 下降到 0℃ 时，温度随时间变化的趋势。
定位：Figure 2

解析：Figure 2 中可以看到曲线是先下降然后水平然后再下降的。

27. 答案：B

题干：判断 TI 的形态。

定位：Figure 1

解析：Figure 1 中在 160℃时，5%Au 中有 TI 固体存在，60%Au 中 TI 只呈液态。

28. 答案：J

题干：判断 70℃时 Au－TI 的形态。

定位：Figure 1

解析：Figure 1 中在 70℃时，混合体处于 IV 区域，全部为固态。

29. 答案：D

题干：判断 90%Au 混合体全为固态时的温度。

定位：Figure 1

解析：Figure 1 中该混合体在 950℃以上才会位于区域 I 中。

[**Passage VI**]

30. 答案：G

题干：判断在 1989 年末净水的爆发量。

定位：Figure 3

解析：Figure 3 中曲线的截距。

31. 答案：A

题干：判断北部与南部地区地面抬升度的变化趋势。

定位：Figure 1

解析：Figure 1 中前两幅图可以看出抬升度逐年提升，后两幅图可以看出抬升度逐年递减。

32. 答案：F

题干：判断地震的起因。

定位：Figure 3

解析：Figure 3 中可以看出，当井水的喷涌量达到最高峰时，发生了地震，所以说地震是由于井水喷涌所造成的侵蚀引发的。

33. 答案：D

题干：判断哪个 site 距离地震发生地最远。

定位：Figure 1

解析：Figure 1 中可以看出，Site D 的最高峰与最低谷之间的差值最小。

34. 答案：J

题干：判断线路中电流大小。

定位：Figure 2

解析：Figure 2 中可以看出，7 月份的电阻率要小于 5 月份，说明 B 的电阻要小于 A，所以电流要高于 A 所在的电路。

[**Passage VII**]

35. 答案：C

题干：判断 60%结冰时固体和液体部分的 conductivity。

定位：Table 2

解析：Table 2 中可以看到液体的 conductivity 随结冰率的提升而升高，固体的 conductivity 随结冰率的升高而下降。

36. 答案：G

题干：判断盐溶液的 NaCl concentration。

定位：Table 1

解析：Table 1 中可以看到液体的 conductivity 随 NaCl 含量的升高而增加，所以当传导率为 15.2 时 NaCl 含量应介于 0.5 和 1.5 之间。

37. 答案：B

题干：比较两个溶液的沸点高低。

定位：Table 1

解析：Table 1 中可以看到溶液 2 的 NaCl concentration 要低于溶液 4，而溶液浓度越高沸点越高，所以溶液 4 的沸点高于溶液 2。

38. 答案：J

题干：判断实验 2 设计中可能的缺陷。

定位：Table 2

解析：实验 2 中可以看到所有的结冰发生在 -20℃ 的条件下，但是如果某些溶液的结冰点低于 -20℃，则不能得到实验结果。

39. 答案：C

题干：判断 NaCl 含量。

定位：Table 1、2

解析：Table 2 中可以看到 Solution 3 在 75%结冰时液体部分的传导率约为 52.4，对照 table 1 可以看到 NaCl 含量接近 3.5%。

40. 答案：G

题干：判断溶液 1 和溶液 3 混合后的传导率。

定位：Table 1

解析：Table 1 中可以看到溶液 1 和溶液 3 各自对应的 NaCl 含量，所以混合后的溶液中 NaCl 含量约为 1.5%，对应的传导率要接近 25.8。

67A 解析

[**Passage I**]

1. 答案：D

解析：由 Figure 1 可知，找到 50 g H_2O 的直线，发现直线的斜率是正的，随着 LiCl 的加入 ΔT 逐渐变大且一直大于 0。选 D。

2. 答案：F

解析：由 Figure 1 可知，LiCl 的加入量和 ΔT 成线性关系，且斜率大于 0，所以随着 LiCl 的含量增加而增加。选 F。

3. 答案：C

解析：看 Figure 1 的图象，延长 75 g H_2O 的直线至横坐标等于 25 g，读取数据，发现纵轴在 30～40 度之间。选 C。

4. 答案：G

解析：由 Figure 1 可知，ΔT 一直是负的，并且 ΔT 和 NH_4NO_3 的加入量呈负相关，所以温度随着 NH_4NO_3 量的增加而减少。选 G。

5. 答案：A

解析：由 Figure 1 和 2 可知，加入 LiCl 温度会升高，加入 NH_4NO_3 温度会降低，所以排除 C、D，纵向比较得知，同时同等质量的 LiCl 随着加入的水增多，ΔT 减少。选 A。

[**Passage II**]

6. 答案：F

解析：仔细观察 Figure 3，观察发现只有 Gene A 和 Gene B 在 Map 上距离一样。选 F。

7. 答案：A

解析：读图 Figure 2，找到横轴等于 70 mu 的纵坐标，得到答案 0.377。选 A。

8. 答案：H

解析：由 Figure 3，Researcher 2 的图可知，D 在 B 左侧，所以要想 Gene G 距离 D 比距离 B 要大，那么 G 必须在 B 的左侧，同时 B 和 C 之间间隔 30 mu，所以 G 在 B、C 之间。选 H。

9. 答案：D

解析：结合 Figure 2，RF 等于 0.091，map distance 等于 10 mu，而 Gene A 和 B 之间的 map distance 等于 20 mu，所以 C 与 A 的距离要小于 A 和 B 的距离。选 D。

10. 答案：J

解析：基础题，F 神经细胞，G 皮肤细胞，H 红细胞，J 配子，这道题考察基因重组在什么时候发生。选 J。

11. 答案：A

解析：由 Figure 3 可知，A 和 B 之间距离大约是 20 mu，所以粗略估计 64 mu 是三倍 A 和 B 之间的距离。选 A。

12. 答案：F

解析：由 Figure 1 可知，在 crossing over 中，RRrrRrRr、TTttTTtt，根据题意得到了新的 Rt 和 rT。选 F。

[**Passage III**]

13. 答案：C

解析：读图可知，当 depth below ground surface 等于 2.5 m 时，conductivity 等于 600 μmho/cm。选 C。

14. 答案：H

解析：读图可知，当 depth below ground surface 等于 2.7 m 时，pH 约等于 7.0。选 H。

15. 答案：D

解析：由 introduction 和 Figure 3 分析可知，bog 的水深相差了 1 m，推测得旱季雨水量较第二年同期少。选 D。

16. 答案：J

解析：观察 Figure 2 和 3 图标右侧的 peat layer 长度，bog：3.75 m，fen：3.0 m，bog 中 peat layer 长度明显比 fen 中长。选 J。

17. 答案：C

解析：由 introduction 可知，1990 是干旱，而 1991 年是正常降雨，所以比较一下 CH_4 的曲线，发现两张图中 summer of 1990 的曲线都在右边，说明 CH_4 的含量比较高。选 C。

[**Passage IV**]

18. 答案：J

解析：由 introduction 可知，元素质量在元素左上角，元素中质子数在右下角（同时表示是几号元素）。选 J。

19. 答案：C

解析：由 introduction 可知，中子数 = 元素的质量-质子数：4 − 2 = 2。选 C。

20. 答案：G

解析：由 Figure 1 可知，经历一次 beta decay 后，Z 增加 1，且 A 不变，质子数增加 1，质量不变。选 G。

21. 答案：B

解析：由 Figure 1 可知，在经历一次 alpha decay 后，A 减少 4，Z 增加 2，质量减少 4，质子数增加 2，观察题目需求的两个元素。选 B。

22. 答案：J

解析：常识题：kinetic energy = $\frac{1}{2}mv^2$，所以在同等的 kinetic energy 下，m 越小，v 越大，而 e^- 的质量远小于 He 原子的质量。选 J。

[**Passage V**]

23. 答案：B

解析：结合 Figure 2 和 Figure 3，匹配两个峰值所在的 RT，发现 RT 在 7～8 min 的是 P3，在 12 min左右的是 P1。选 B。

24. 答案：F

解析：由 Figure 1 可知，RT 最长的是 P1。选 F。

25. 答案：C

解析：由 Table 1 可知，AMM 与 RT 呈反相关，随着 AMM 的升高，RT 越来越小，同时观察到 Figure 3 中 M2 的 RT 在 6～7 之间，说明 M2 的 AMM 小于 P4 和 P5。选 C。

26. 答案：G

解析：由 introduction 可知，smaller mole cules easily diffuse into the pores，比较 P3 和 P4 的 AMM，发现 P3 的 AMM 较小。选 G。

27. 答案：A

解析：由 Table 1 可知，P5 的 AMM 为 200 000，所以 M1 的峰值所在处的 AMM 远大于200 000。选 A。

28. 答案：J

解析：由 Table 1 可知，P2 的 AMM 比 P4 小，所以同等质量的 mole cule 中 P2 比 P4 数量要多。选 J。

[**Passage VI**]

29. 答案：A

解析：由 Table 1 可知，图例 Flame spread rate 增加，从 2.48 到 2.76。

30. 答案：J

解析：仔细看 Figure 1，下降最快的部分在 425～475。

31. 答案：B

解析：由 Table 1 可知，当 water content 增加到 61%以上，无论多少的氧气含量都是 F，意味着 Failed burn。

32. 答案：H

解析：由 Table 1 可知，当 water content 在 2～12%之间，燃烧时间就在 22.61～37.50 cm/min。

33. 答案：B

解析：由 Table 1 可知，flame spread rate 在 needles 部分的速度明显比 dowels 部分快多了。

34. 答案：H

解析：由 Figure 1 可知，percent of original mass of sample remaining 是 40%，说明烧掉了 60%。

[**Passage VII**]

35. 答案：B

解析：由 Figure 5 可知，100 feet 和 90 feet 发射后的距离分别是 630 和 530，差值就是 100 feet。

36. 答案：G

解析：在 Study 1 中，有 every 0.5 sec 这个措辞，意味着 two times per second。

37. 答案：C

解析：首先分析题目中的数据，有看到 37 ft 和 310 ft，所以首先观察图表 Figure 4，确定了 Height 大于 37 ft 的和 Range 大于 310 ft 的有 100 mph、110 mph、120 mph。

38. 答案：F

解析：由 Figure 4 可知，H 和 R 会随着 launch speed 增加而增加。

39. 答案：C

解析：由 Figure 5 可知，以 120 mph 的速度，时间会增加到 6 sec 之后。

40. 答案：F

解析：Round-trip 是来回所以是两倍，用 D 除以 c 再乘以 2。

67B 解析

[**Passage I**]

1. 答案：A

题干：哪一个图表示了实验 1～5 中 L 跟随 D 变化的规律。

定位：Table 1

解析：从表格 1 中可以看出，随着 D 从 10 逐渐增加到 50，L 从 44.7 先增加到 60.0，后减小到 44.7，所以图像应该是上凸的，根据 L 的具体数值可判断出是 A 选项。

2. 答案：H

题干：在实验 10 中为了保持圆柱体 Y 充满水并且不让水溢出，应该以多少的速率向圆柱中注水。

定位：Table 2

解析：从表格 2 中可以看出，实验 10 水从洞中流出的速率为 6.26 cm^3/sec，为了保持 Y 充满水，水从洞中流出的速率和注入水的速率需相等。

3. 答案：B

题干：根据实验 1、6 和 11 的结果，每个洞横截面 A 增加时 t 如何变化。

定位：Table 1、2 和 3

解析：从每个表格上方的说明可以看到，X、Y、Z 三个圆柱体洞的横截面大小逐渐增加，从每个表格的第一行数据可以看到，实验 1 的 t 为 71.4，实验 2 的 t 为 35.7，实验 3 的 t 为 23.8，因此 A 增加时 t 减小。

4. 答案：G

题干：求三个试验中的圆柱体高度。

定位：Figure 1

解析：从图 1 可以看出，D 衡量的是从圆柱体顶端到洞中心的距离，第五个洞距圆柱体上方 50 cm，圆柱体低端距上方 60 cm，即高为 60 cm。

5. 答案：D

题干：求三个试验中的圆柱体高度。

定位：Table 1

解析：根据压强公式 $p=\rho gh$，上方水的高度越高，下方压强越大，水的流速越快。也可以根据表 1，洞的高度越低，R 越大。当不向圆柱体中持续加水时，随着水的流出，水面逐渐降低，洞处的压强逐渐减小，R 随之减小。

6. 答案：J

题干：对于给定的 D，L 是否取决于 A。

定位：Table 1、2、3

解析：以 D = 10 cm 为例，从实验 1、6、11 的结果可以看出，虽然 A 不同，但 L 都为 44.7 cm，因此当 D 给定时，L 保持恒定，与 A 无关。

[**Passage II**]

7. 答案：B

题干：哪一种 gastropod 的壳被打洞的比例最高。

定位：Table 2

解析：从 Table 2 中可以看出，四种 gastropod 中 Lacuna 被打洞的比例最高，为 86.1%。

8. 答案：F

题干：根据被摄入的数量将四种 gastropods 从大到小排序。

定位：Table 2

解析：依据 Table 2 中“shellingested”一栏的数字从大到小将 gastropods 进行排序。

9. 答案：A

题干：科学家提出假说：如果不需要打洞就可以消化，A. taylori 就不会在壳上打洞，从 Table 2 中辨析是否有 gastropods 的数据符合这个假说。

定位：Table 2

解析：从 Table 2 中可以看出，前三种 gastropods 都有一定比例被打了洞，也都有 survivors，而 Limpets 没有被打洞，也没有 survivors，说明 Limpets 不需要被打洞就可以全部消化，符合假说。

10. 答案：J

题干：辨析哪个关于 hermitcrabs 的选项最符合 Table 1。

定位：Table 1

解析：从 Table 1 中可以看出，hermitcrabs 被打洞的比例仅为 9.1%，而并没有 survivor，说明 A. taylori 并不会在吃的大多数 hermitcrabs 上打洞，而 hermitcrab 也都被消化了。

11. 答案：C

题干：根据 Table 2 判断所有未打洞的 Alvinia 都幸存的可能性。

定位：Table 2

解析：从 Table 2 中可以看出，101 个 Alvinia 中未被打洞的约为 20 个，survivor 为 11 个，而标注说明所有 survivor 都是未被打洞的，所以有 9 个左右未被打洞的 Alvinia 也幸存了。

［**Passage III**］

12. 答案：H

题干：根据 Figure 2 判断 Na_2SO_4的 concentration。

定位：Figure 2

解析：从 Figure 2 中可以看出，在 Na_2SO_4对应的曲线上，纵坐标为 12 的点所对应的横坐标约为 75。

13. 答案：D

题干：根据 Figure 3 判断 100℃时，20%的 NaCl 的传导性最大值。

定位：Figure 3

解析：从 Figure 3 中可以看出，100℃ 所对应的曲线在 NaCl 浓度为 20% 时的点要高于600 mS/cm。

14. 答案：F

题干：15% NaCl 的传导性为 100 mS/cm，求溶液所对应的温度。

定位：Figure 3

解析：从 Figure 3 中可以看出，随着温度的升高，同一浓度的 NaCl 溶液的传导性逐渐升高，而 15% NaCl 溶液在 20℃时的传导性高于 100 mS/cm，所以溶液的温度应该低于 20℃。

15. 答案：A

题干：两种不同的溶液，在温度和浓度均相同时，传导性是否相同。

定位：Figure 2

解析：从 Figure 3 中可以看出，当溶液温度均为 18℃时，相同浓度的不同的溶液所对应的传导性不同。

16. 答案：J

题干：求解 100℃时传导率为 200 mS/cm 的溶液组成。

定位：Figure 3

解析：从 Figure 3 中可以看出，当溶液温度为 100℃，传导率为 200 mS/cm 时，对应的 NaCl 溶液浓度为 5%。浓度的计算公式为 NaCl 的质量除以溶液总质量，由此公示可计算出 J 选项符合 5%浓度。

［**Passage IV**］

17. 答案：B

题干：X 为 0.33 m^2，R_A为 2.9 N 时，求解 V 的值。

定位：Table 1

解析：从 Table 1 中可以看出，R_A与 V 是正相关的，当 R_A为 2.9 N 时，介于 1.7 N 与 5.8 N 之间，所以对应的 V 应介于 3.0 与 5.6 之间，运用排除法可得 B。

18. 答案：J

题干：辨析哪一个选项所对应的 P_A最大。

定位：Table 1

解析：从 Table 1 中可以看出，R_A为 5.8 N 时，所对应的 P_A最大，为 32 W。

19. 答案：C

题干：求解当 V 为 11.2 m/sec，车轮 27 inch，压力 80 lb/in^{2}时，对应的 P_{A+B}为多少 W。

定位：Figure 1、2

解析：从 Figure 1 中可以看出，V 为 11.2 m/sec，车轮 27 inch，压力 80 lb/in^{2}时，所对应的 P_{A+B}为 0.4 hp，从 Figure 2 中可以看出，0.4 hp 为 300 W。

20. 答案：H

题干：求解当 1 hp 的增加对应多少 W。

定位：Figure 2

解析：从 Figure 2 中可以看出，直线的斜率为 750，即每增加 1 hp 对应 750 W。

21. 答案：D

题干：判断当 V 为 11.2 m/sec，车轮 27 inch，压力 80 lb/in^{2}时对应的 P_{A+B}是否比压力为 140 lb/in^{2}时要小。

定位：Figure 1

解析：从 Figure 1 中可以看出，随着压力的增加，P_{A+B}逐渐减小，所以 80 lb/in^{2}时对应的 P_{A+B}比压力为 140 lb/in^{2}时要大。

[**Passage V**]

22. 答案：J

题干：当 pH = 9.0，波长由 375 nm 增加到 625 nm 时，吸收能力如何变化。

定位：Figure 2

解析：从 Figure 2 中可以看出，随着波长的增加，吸收能力先升高后降低。

23. 答案：C

题干：当 pH = 7.25，波长为 525 nm 时，吸收能力的范围。

定位：Figure 3

解析：从 Figure 3 中可以看出，随着 pH 值的增加，同一波长长度对应的吸收能力减小，当 pH = 7.5，波长为 525 nm 时吸收能力约为 0.4，pH = 7.0，波长为 525 nm 时吸收能力为 0.55，所以当 pH = 7.25，波长为 525 nm 吸收能力介于 0.4 与 0.55 之间。

24. 答案：H

题干：判断两个实验的所用的溶液组成。

定位：Figure 2、3

解析：第一个实验测量了两个不同 pH 值的溶液，第二个实验测量了五个不同 pH 值的溶液。

25. 答案：A

题干：判断 A、B 两个溶液的酸碱性。

定位：Figure 1

解析：A 溶液是红色的，说明 pH$<$6.8，溶液呈酸性，而 B 溶液无色，说明 pH 值介于 6.8 与 8.0 之间，说明溶液是 basic。

26. 答案：G

题干：在 525 nm 处，比较 pH 值为 6.0 的溶液和 7.0 的溶液的吸收能力。

定位：Figure 3

解析：从图中可以看出，pH 为 6.0 的溶液的吸收能力比 7.0 的溶液要高，这是因为文中所说的带颜色的物质对可见光的吸收能力强，pH 值为 6.0 的溶液因为 NRH^+ 含量高而呈红色且吸收能力强。

27. 答案：B

题干：判断实验一中的 pH 等于 9.0 的溶液性质。

定位：Figure 2

解析：pH 值为 9.0 时，溶液呈黄色，实验一的介绍中也说明 pH 为 9.0 时溶液的分子基本不带电。

[**Passage VI**]

28. 答案：F

题干：判断 Study 3 中三个样本的干质量。

定位：Table 3

解析：从 Table 3 中可以看出，随着 fly ash 的增加，plant dry mass 减少。

29. 答案：C

题干：判断 30% fly ash by mass 的样本所含有的 sand-size 比例。

定位：Table 1

解析：从 Table 1 中可以看出，随着 fly ash 的增加，sand-size 比例减少，所以 30% 比例 fly ash 所含有的 sand-size 比例应在 59%与 71%之间。

30. 答案：H

题干：判断含有 5 mgB/kg 的样本的 dry mass。

定位：Table 2

解析：从 Table 2 中可以看出，随着 B 含量的增加，plant dry mass 的质量减少，所以含有 5 mgB/kg的样本的 dry mass 介于 14.1 和 18.2 之间。

31. 答案：B

题干：在实验三中如果没有将测量的植物完全烘干，对实验结果产生的影响。

定位：Table 3

解析：因为实验 3 测量的是干质量，如果没有烘干，植物中还残留着水分，会增大实验结果。

32. 答案：J

题干：判断 pure fly ash 所含成分比例。

定位：Table 1

解析：从 Table 1 中可以看出，fly ash 含量为 100%时，silt-size 含量为 78%，sand-size 含量为 1%。

33. 答案：D

题干：判断 pure fly ash 样本的 B 含量。

定位：Table 2

解析：从 Table 2 中可以看出，随着 fly ash 比例的增加，B 含量增加，所以 pure fly ash 的 B 含量要高于 40% fly ash 的 B 含量。

[**Passage VII**]

34. 答案：H

题干：根据减数分裂后细胞中染色体数目判断生物类型。

定位：Table 1

解析：减数分裂后每个细胞中所含染色体数目表示为 N，当 N 为 32 时，Table 1 中对应的动物为 Horse。

35. 答案：B

题干：根据学生 1 的理论判断染色体数量。

定位：Figure 3

解析：在进入第一阶段时有 4 条四分体，按照 Figure 3，第一阶段结束后染色体数量减半，即为 2 条四分体。

36. 答案：H

题干：判断一个细胞在减数分裂后变为几个细胞。

定位：Figure 2

解析：由 Figure 2 可判断出一个细胞减数分裂后变为 4 个细胞，所以试管中会存留四个细胞。

37. 答案：A

题干：比较不同细胞染色体数目。

定位：Table 1

解析：Dog 细胞的 N 为 39，Human 细胞的 N 为 23，在刚进入减数分裂第一阶段时，细胞内染色体数目为 2 N，所以 Dog 的细胞在进入减数分裂时染色体数目最多。

38. 答案：J

题干：判断哪种细胞可发生减数分裂。

定位：Figure 1

解析：减数分裂只存在于生殖细胞当中，所以选择精子。

39. 答案：A

题干：判断减数分裂后基因数目。

定位：Figure 2

解析：从 Figure 2 中可以看出，四分体上的 4 个基因在减数分裂后分布到每个细胞中的一条染色体上，所以每个细胞中含有一个基因 X。

40. 答案：G

题干：根据学生 2 的理论判断染色体数量。

定位：Figure 4

解析：在进入第一阶段时细胞中染色体数目为 2 N，第一阶段结束时数目为 2 N，所以染色体数目不变。

67C 解析

［**Passage I**］

1. 答案：D

解析：实验总结类文章，此题为实验结果题。

抓住定位词 Study 1、highest、Island B、Island C，看 Figure 2 第 2 和第 3 张图，比例最高的 beak depth 分别是 10 mm 和 10 mm，选 D。

2. 答案：J

解析：实验总结类文章，此题为实验推断题。

抓住定位词 Island B 和 small seeds，看 Study 2，找到信息 Small seeds are abundant during wet years。题目问 most abundant 是哪年,也就是找哪年 most wet。看 Figure 3 图例可知,wet 为最矮的,是 1984 年,所以选 J。

3. 答案:B

解析:实验总结类文章,此题为实验对比题。

题目问 Study 1 与 Study 2 哪里不同,看选项。A 说 Study 1G. fortis finches 被抓,Study 2 没有,Study 1 和 Study 2 都提到 capture G. fortis,不选。B 说 Study 1 capture G. fuliginosa,Study 2 没有。因为 Study 2 的实验对象没有 G. fuliginosa,所以没抓,选 B。因为 Study 1 和 2 的 beak depth 都测量了,所以不选 C 和 D。

4. 答案:J

解析:实验总结类文章,此题为实验推断题。

题目问 Study 1 researcher tag the bird 的原因。F 说 beak depth 怎样被 rainfall 影响,Study 1 与 rainfall 无关,排除。G 说测量 average age,与 age 无关,排除。H 说确保 each finch 被多次测量,J 说被测量 1 次。实验是为了计算比例,重复测量 beak depth 会影响比例的平衡,tag 的目的是去捕捉未捉过的 finch,所以选 J。

5. 答案:C

解析:实验总结类文章,此题为实验推断题。

抓住定位词 Study 2,题目问是 9.4 mm 的 beak length 还是 9.9 mm 的更容易在 1977 年存活。看导语可知,shallower beak can only eat mall seeds。从 Figure 3 可知,1977 年是 dry year 所以 seeds 更大,所以 birds with deeper beak 更容易存活。选 C。

6. 答案:F

解析:实验总结类文章,此题为实验假设题。

题目问假设 G. fortis 要竞争,beak length 变化会更多,Study 1 是否验证该假设。看 Figure 2,Island A 中 G. fortis 与 G. fuliginosa 共存有竞争,Island B 中只有 G. fortis。G. fortis 在 Island A 的 beak depth 分布明显宽于 Island B,所以验证了假设。选 F。

[**Passage II**]

7. 答案:D

解析:题目问哪种离子和 Figure 1 一样,在 2 月最多,在 7 月最少。抓住定位词 Figure 2 和 Figure 3,发现硫酸根离子 2 月最多,7 月最少。选 D。

8. 答案:G

解析:抓住定位词 Study 1 和铜离子,看 Figure 2 的第 1 张图,估计平均 wet deposition。折线大部分时间在 50 上下,但 5 月到 7 月远高于 50,所以平均应该为 50~75,选 G。

9. 答案:A

解析:抓住定位词 Study 2 和氯离子,题目问氯离子的 wet deposition 在冬天和早春更高的假设是否被 Study 2 证实。看选项都是比较 11~4 月和 5~10 月。Figure 3 中 11~4 月的 wet deposition 比 5~11 月的高,选 A。

10. 答案:H

解析:题目问假设一个月没降雨,则那个月的 wet deposition 会怎样变化。从导语中可知,这四种离子到土地表层都通过降雨,所以没降雨就不会有 wet deposition,选 H。

11. 答案:C

解析:抓定位词 Study 3,看 Figure 4。Rural Site 1 离城市 50 km,Site 2 离城市 100 km,离城市越来越远。铜离子和锌离子的 wet deposition 都越来越少,所以选 C。

12. 答案：F

解析：抓定位词 Study 2，题目问什么因素是不变的。每月的降雨肯定不同，Figure 3 显示锌离子和氯离子的 wet deposition 每月都在变化，从 Study 1 所给的文字信息中可以看出实验数据都是从同一个样本中收集的，样本采集的位置不变，所以选 F。

［**Passage III**］

13. 答案：B

解析：抓定位词 Jan 1987 和 high clouds，找到 Figure 1 的虚线，读图发现最接近 13.5%，选 B。

14. 答案：H

解析：抓定位词 Table 1，发现 cosmic ray flux 每增加 20 000，cover of low clouds 增加 0.3%，440 000 比 420 000 大 20 000，所以 cover of lowc louds 应该比 29.0%大 0.3%，选 H。

15. 答案：A

解析：抓定位词 Figures 1 和 3，问两图是否证实 cover of low clouds 与 cosmic ray flux 的联系比 cover of high clouds 与 cosmic ray flux 的联系更大。看图发现 Figure 3 的实线和虚线联系比 Figure 1 的实线和虚线的联系更大，验证了假设，选 A。

16. 答案：G

解析：抓定位词 high、middle、low clouds 和 Jan 1992，看 Figure 1、2、3，High clouds 13%＜middle clouds 19.5%＜low clouds 28%，画出的图应符合 high clouds 最少，low clouds 最多，选 G。

17. 答案：D

解析：抓关键词 high clouds→ice，low clouds→water，从导语可知 low clouds 在 0～3.2 km，high clouds 在 6.0～16.0 km。常识：冰的形成温度小于 0 摄氏度，水大于 0 摄氏度 D。所以 0～3.2 km 的温度大于 0 摄氏度，6.0～16.0 km 的温度小于 0 摄氏度，选 D。

［**Passage IV**］

18. 答案：F

解析：抓定位词 Experiment 1 和 yellow，看图例可知短虚线是 yellow，在 0～1.00 mL 之间出现，选 F。

19. 答案：B

解析：抓定位词 Experiment 2 和 neutral，从导语最后一句可知：如果 pH 小于 6.0，Nitrazine 是 yellow，如果 pH 大于 7.0，Nitrazine 是 blue。中性的 pH 是 7.0，在图中是绿色到蓝色的交界处，此时添加了 1.00 mL，选 B。

20. 答案：J

解析：抓定位词 Experiment 1，当添加的大于 1.00 mL 时，导电率增加，如果加入 2.30 mL，导电率应大于 2.00 mL 时的 3.7 kS/cm，延长虚线后肯定也大于 3.80 kS/cm，选 J。

21. 答案：C

解析：抓定位词 Experiment 2，题目问哪个是样本溶液，哪个是溶质。Experiment 2 说 HCl 溶液换成 acetic acid，则样本溶液应为 acetic acid，选 C。

22. 答案：J

解析：从导语中第 2 句可知，实验能用两种方法操作，一种是加指示剂，另一种是测导电率。题目问在样本溶液中的探测器(probe)最可能做什么。探测器要测导电率，所以应该通电，选 J。

23. 答案：A

解析：题目问 Experiment 2 是否支持观点，加 0.2 mL 时的 pH 值比加 1.8 mL 时的 pH 值大。看 Figure 2 可知加 0.2 mL 时的指示剂是黄色，pH 小于 6.0，加 1.8 mL 时的指示剂是蓝色，pH 大于 7.0，不支持观点，选 A。

[**Passage V**]

24. 答案：H
解析：题目问 Student 2 认为 Algol B 变成 Algol System 的一部分因为哪种作用力。Student 2 认为 Algol B 的轨道相交于 Algol System 的轨道成为 Algol System 一部分，宇宙中万有引力是最普遍存在的一种力，选 H。
25. 答案：B
解析：从导语可知 Algol B 是 post-MS star，从 Fact 4 可知 post-MS star 产生的绝大部分能量来自核聚变 hydrogen 成 helium 在 shell，选 B。
26. 答案：G
解析：Student 2 认为 Algol B 原来不在 Algol System，Algol A 和 C 在 Algol System，所以可推断出 Algol A 和 C 的化学组成相同，选 G。
27. 答案：C
解析：由导语可知 Algol C 是 1.7-solar-mass star，即太阳质量的 1.7 倍，$1.7\times2.0=3.4$，选 C。
28. 答案：G
解析：从 Fact 3 可知，pre-MS star 变成 MS-star 通过核聚变 hydrogen nuclei(proton)，常识：质子带正电，同种电荷相斥，选 G。
29. 答案：B
解析：Student 1 认为 Algol B 的质量原本大于 Algol A，后来物质被 Algol A 吸引，所以现在质量小于 Algol A 且是唯一的 post-MS star。原来 Algol B 质量至少是现在 Algol A 和 Algol B 的平均值，$(3.6+0.8)/2=2.2$，Algol B 肯定大于 Algol C 的质量，根据 Student 1 的猜测，又大于 Algol A 的质量。从 Fact 5 可知，行星质量越大，进化越快，所以 Algol B 应该最先变成 MS star，选 B。
30. 答案：H
解析：Student 2 认为 Algol A 和 B 之间不存在质量传递，Algol A 现在的质量大于 Algol B，以前也是这样。从 Fact 5 可知，行星质量越大，进化越快，因为 Algol A 的质量大于 Algol B，所以 Algol A 的进化更快，从 MS star 进化成 post-MS star 的时间比 Algol B 短，选 H。

[**Passage VI**]

31. 答案：C
解析：抓定位词 Figure 2，找直线 Kr，13 g 大于图像横坐标最大值 10 g，延长直线 Kr 到 13 g，预估横坐标应该在 400～600，选 C。
32. 答案：G
解析：5 L 在 Figure 1 的 3 L 和 Figure 2 的 6 L 之间，从 Figure 1 可知，在 3 L 容器里 7 g CO_2 的压力为 1 000 torr，从 Figure 2 可知，在 6 L 容器里 7 g CO_2 的压力为 500 torr，所以在 5 L 容器里 7 g CO_2 的压力在 500～1 000 torr 之间，选 G。
33. 答案：A
解析：抓定位词 Figure 1 和 Figure 2，看直线 O_2，相同质量的 O_2 在 3 L 容器里的压力是在 6 L 容器里的两倍，常识：相同条件下气体压力与容器体积成反比，选 A。

34. 答案：J

解析：任选 Figure 1 或 Figure 2，比较直线 O_2 和直线 CO_2，O_2 的压力大于 CO_2 的压力，O_2 的质量数为 32，CO_2 的质量数为 44，所以同等质量 O_2 和 CO_2，O_2 分子的个数多于 CO_2 分子的个数，造成 O_2 的压力大于 CO_2 的压力，选 J。

35. 答案：A

解析：常识：同样条件下，温度越高，在容器体积不变的情况下，气体压力增大，成正相关。因为 14 摄氏度低于实验 22 摄氏度，所以 O_2 的压力更小，选 A。

[**Passage VII**]

36. 答案：G

解析：看图像，找 thresh old of hearing 最低点的纵坐标，为 20 Hz，选 G。

37. 答案：A

解析：从题目信息可知，随着年龄增长，听不到高频率的声音，所以 thresh old of hearing 的上限应该降低，选 A。

38. 答案：F

解析：题目问什么情况下声音的强度最大，看图像横坐标找最大的声音强度。在 S = 100%的水中的那条虚线最靠右，选 F。

39. 答案：C

解析：看线条 thresh old of hearing，声音的频率为 10 的 5 次方不在 thresh old of hearing 之内，所以人是无法听到这种频率的声音，选 C。

40. 答案：J

解析：看任意一条虚线，任何频率同样强度的声音不影响 S，所以 S 与声音的频率无关，选 J。

68A 解析

[**Passage I**]

1. 答案：C

解析：Based on Table 2，这里只要看 Table 2 一张表。题干中说影响 seedshape 的 gene，所以比较的时候要比较 flower color、pod color 和 stemlength 都一样的。这里保证 3 项都一样的是 purple (flower)、green (pod)和 tall (stem)，再比较 seed shape，分别是 round 和 wrinkled。基因型分别是 AABBDDEE 和 AABBddEE，二者唯一的区别在于 D 和 d，所以 gene D 决定 seed shape。答案选 C。

2. 答案：J

解析：Based on Table 2，依旧只看 Table 2。题干中的这个植物基因型中每种性状都带有一个显性基因，所以每一种表现型都是显性的。换言之 Genotype 那一栏底下每个字母代表的基因都有一个大写，所以就是 AaBbDdEe。对应的表现型即为 purple flowers、green pods、round seeds、tallstems。答案选 J。

3. 答案：C

解析：这里出现但是只出现了 Table 3，所以只看 Table 3。题目问的是子代性状的表现型对半分(split evenly)的情况下"父母"分别的基因型。既然是对半分，那就找 Table 3 里一行全为 50%与 50%的，也就是 Cross 3，得出"父母"的基因型 aaBbDdee 和 AabbddEe。答案选 C。

4. 答案：G
解析：这里没有特别说看那个表，所以综合 3 张表。题目问的是 Cross 4 子代全是 yellow pod 是因为“父母”的那个基因导致的。由 Table 2 可知，决定 pod color 的基因是 B 和 b。答案选 G。
5. 答案：A
解析：题目问的是 Cross 3 里子代基因型是 BB 的 percent。Cross 3 中“父母”的基因型(光看 B)分别是 Bb 和 bb，根据基因分离定律，一般子代是不会有 BB 这种基因型的，只有 Bb 和 bb，所以 BB 百分比只能是 0%。答案选 A。

[**Passage II**]

6. 答案：H
解析：Based on Figure 4，纵轴表示的是被吸引的蚊子。题目要求比较哪个阶段最容易招蚊子，选项只有 Subject 1 和 Subject 9，所以只比较这两个。Subject 9 的 before treatment 明显高于其他几项。答案选 H。
7. 答案：B
解析：主要看 Study 1。题目问在 Study 1 的结果上假设被 gametocytes 感染的人比被 sporozoites 感染的人和没有被感染的人更容易招蚊子。看 Table 1 和 Figure 3，X，Y，Z 分别代表 Uninfected、Sporozoites present 和 Gametocytes present。Figure 3 中，纵轴表示招到蚊子的平均数，明显 Z 即 Gametocytes present，最高。答案选 B。
8. 答案：G
解析：看 Figure 4，题目问的是治疗后比治疗前招了更多蚊子的有几个。就是柱状图中白色比黑色高的几个，有 1、3、4、8 一共 4 个。答案选 G。
9. 答案：A
解析：题目问的是为什么被 Gametocytes 感染的人治疗前后都要做测试。是为了确定蚊子是因为 Gametocytes 的感染而被吸引，而不是因为别的因素。答案选 A。
10. 答案：G
解析：综合来看。题目问的是 Group X 和 Group Y 哪一个更适合做 Group Z 在 Study 1 和 Study 2 之间的对照组。应该是 X，因为在 Study 1 和 Study 2 中 Group X 的条件不发生改变。答案选 G。
11. 答案：C
解析：题目问的是用什么方法使得蚊子被特定的 subject 吸引而不是一个特定的 tent。让每个 tent 里各个 Group 的 subject 随机分布(random)，这样可以确保蚊子是被 subject 的状态所吸引而排除了 tent 的干扰。答案选 C。

[**Passage III**]

12. 答案：J
解析：看 Scientist 1，注意 a long period，所以原油最可能在 an ocean had existed at sometime in the past。答案选 J。
13. 答案：B
解析：依旧看 Scientist 1，原油被发现在 5 km 的地下，这是否与 Scientist 1 的观点相符。是的，因为 at depths of less than 10 km below Earth's surface。答案选 B。
14. 答案：J

解析：看哪个提出了原油形成需要压力，但是两个都提到了。注意题干中说的是 higher。Scientist 1 说原油在距地表 10 km 以内的地下形成，而 Scientist 2 认为原油在距地表 100～200 km的地下形成。Scientist 2 提出的观点中需要的压力比 Scientist 1 观点中的更大。答案选 J。

15. 答案：D

解析：题目问原油可由二氧化碳和水反应形成与哪个 Scientist 的观点相符。Scientist 2 说“The process being saswater reacts with simple, in organic carbon compounds”。答案选 D。

16. 答案：F

解析：题目问哪个图跟 Scientist 2 的观点相符。Scientist 2 认为原油在地下 100～200 km 形成，并且“most petroleum deposits exist a long tectonicplate boundaries”也就是在浅层地下。答案选 F。

17. 答案：B

解析：要使得原油从它形成的地方运动到可以采集的地方，它需要具备的物理性质。两个 Scientist 都认为原油是从深入地表的地方运动到较浅的地方，所以它应当具有流动性，并且密度比它经过的地方低。答案选 B。

18. 答案：F

解析：只看 Scientist 2，文中提到且只提到了“methane”，即 CH_4。答案选 F。

[**Passage IV**]

19. 答案：C

解析：看 Figure 2，without a magnetic field 即是虚线，在横轴上 10 min 对应的是在 45 左右的%PM。答案选 C。

20. 答案：G

解析：Reaction 2，依旧看 Figure 2。with magnetic field 即是实线，当 10 min 后把磁场撤去，图像趋向于 without magnetic field 的图像，即向上偏但并不会达到 without magnetic field 的图像。15 min 时，图像应当在 with magnetic field 和 without magnetic field 之间，也就是 30% 和 60%之间。答案选 G。

21. 答案：D

解析：只看 Figure 3，20 min 时 without magnetic field 的%PM 为 50，而 with magnetic field 是将近 100%。后者大约是前者的两倍。答案选 D。

22. 答案：J

解析：虽然 Figure 1 和 3 是支持该观点(磁场会提高氢气还原金属氧化物的效率)的，但是 Figure 2 确实反对该观点的。答案选 J。

23. 答案：A

解析：在反应过程中金属氧化物减少，图像应当与 Figure 1 相反。答案选 A。

[**Passage V**]

24. 答案：H

解析：若要让光子从原子中踢出一个电子，光子的频率需要大于等于该原子频率的阀值。Table 1 中 Ca 的阀值为 6.55×10^14 Hz。光子的频率最小应当与之相等。答案选 H。

25. 答案：A

解析：看 Figure 1，将 f = 16.0×10^14 Hz 时的 Kmax 值从小到大排。依次是 Pt、Hg、Mg、Ca。答案选 A。

26. 答案：H
解析：Hg 的频率阀值为 10.9×10^14 Hz，对应 Figure 2 光子能量约在 7×10^(-19)J。答案选 H。
27. 答案：D
解析：做这道题的不需要计算的方法可以虚拟扩大图像，在横轴 28.0 时，纵轴是远大于 7.0 的。答案选 D。
28. 答案：G
解析：可以根据表格在 Figure 1 上简单画一下 MetalX 的图像，得出图像在 Ca 和 Mg 之间。查看 Table 1 中 Ca 和 Mg 对应的数值，选择在其之间的选项。答案选 G。

[**Passage VI**]
29. 答案：C
解析：看 Table 2，NO 增加时，NO_2 对应增加到 8 然后不变了。答案选 C。
30. 答案：G
解析：NO 全部转化为 NO_2，NO 体积为 0，而 NO_2 体积即为 Final volume，与 Trial 2 相符。答案选 G。
31. 答案：A
解析：Trial 1 中先反应完的是 NO，氧气还有剩余。所以 limiting reagent 是 NO。答案选 A。
32. 答案：J
解析：配平就好。答案选 J。
33. 答案：B
解析：pH 最低，酸性最强，NO_2 浓度最高。Table 1 中 Trial 2 NO_2 浓度最高。答案选 B。
34. 答案：F
解析：在 Syringe II 推入氧气时，Syringe I 尾端和针头的距离先增大。后来因为反应进行，气体体积减小，Syringe I 尾端和针头的距离又减小。答案选 F。

[**Passage VII**]
35. 答案：C
解析：看 Table 1，L = 0.030 m 在 Trial 1 和 2 之间，P 值也在 0.94 和 0.75 之间。答案选 C。
36. 答案：F
解析：看 Table 1、2、3 比较 L 和 I 的关系。L 增大时，I 增大。答案选 F。
37. 答案：A
解析：比较 Study 1 和 3，物体距离 support 越远，moment of inertia 越大。Object A 的小球距离 support 比 Object B 的远。答案选 A。
38. 答案：J
解析：周期和频率成反比，求频率最大只要找周期 P 最小的即可。P 最小的是 Trial 14。答案选 J。
39. 答案：A
解析：Table 1、2、3 之间同一 L 值比较 P 值。P 值最小是 Table 1，也就是 solidsphere，Student W 是对的。答案选 A。
40. 答案：H
解析：周期 P×20 圈 = 0.74×20 = 14.8 秒。答案选 H。

68C 解析

[**Passage I**]

1. 答案：B

解析：看 Figure 1，Drug A concentration 是横轴，percent colony formation 是纵轴，观察 Cell Line Z（斜线的柱状图）对应二者的相互关系。Drug A concentration 越大，percent colony formation 越小。答案选 B。

2. 答案：G

解析：看 Table 1，Cell Line W 对应的 organ of origin 是 colon，结肠属于消化系统，digestive system。答案选 G。

3. 答案：A

解析：看 Figure 1，Cell Line X 与 Drug A concentration 对应的 percent colony formation 是根据前者的递增而递减的。200 μg/L 的浓度对应的 percentcolony formation 一定比 100 μg/L 时的要少。所以是少于 40%的。答案选 A。

4. 答案：G

解析：看 Table 1 中哪个 Cell Line 对应的 LD 50 of Drug A 跟 Cell Line Y(70.0)是大约 10 倍的关系。是 Cell Line W(6.9)。答案选 G。

5. 答案：A

解析：找到 Figure 1 中 Cell Line V 的临界值。Drug A concentration 为 1 μg/L 时 Cell Line V 的 percent colony formation 开始变化。答案选 A。

[**Passage II**]

6. 答案：H

解析：看 Table 1，tall 和 short 的比是 154∶46。化简大约是 3∶1。答案选 H。

7. 答案：D

解析：Cross 2 中只提到了 Gene R，没有提到 Gene T。无法判断 Cross 2 子代有关 Gene T 的基因型。答案选 D。

8. 答案：H

解析：Cross 2 中 pink flowers 占总数的百分比。102/(46 + 102 + 52) × 100% = 51%。最接近的是 50%。答案选 H。

9. 答案：A

解析：看 Cross 3，同时 tall 和 pink 对应的 Genotype 是 TTRr 和 TtRr。要产生这样的子代，“父母”双方合在一起必须同时有 T 和 R。答案选 A。

10. 答案：J

解析：Cross 3 中是 tall white flower 的有 11 + 20 = 31 个，而 tall pink flower 的有 18 + 41 = 59 个。Tall white flower 并不是最多的。答案选 J。

11. 答案：C

解析：看 Table 3，shortred-flowered 对应的基因型是 ttRR，shortpink-flowered 对应的是 ttRr。这两种产生的子代基因型只有 ttRR 和 ttRr。所以 ttRr 占 50%。答案选 C。

[**Passage III**]

12. 答案：G

解析：Beam 的受力示意图。是边上两个 roller 的支持力和中间的杆子对它的压力。两边的力朝上，中间的朝下。答案选 G。

13. 答案：B

解析：看 Table 3，W = 25 N 时，D = (4.2 + 6.3)/2 × 10^(- 6) = 5.25 × 10^(- 6)m。答案选 B。

14. 答案：H

解析：选项中 W × D 的值分别是 42(Trial 2)、20(Trial 4)、84(Trial 6)、28(Trial 8)。最大的是 Trial 6。答案选 H。

15. 答案：D

解析：看 Table 1，图像的纵轴应该是 I，D 随 I 的增大而减小。答案选 D。

16. 答案：G

解析：Study 3 中 E = 50 × 10^(- 9)N/m^2。对应 Table 2 是 Metal T。答案选 G。

17. 答案：D

解析：越 stiff 说明 D 越小。根据 Table 1 和 2，I 和 E 值越大，D 值越小。答案选 D。

[**Passage IV**]

18. 答案：H

解析：看 Figure 3，concentration of TBHQ 对应 induction period 最小的是 BD 3。答案选 H。

19. 答案：C

解析：Figure 3 中 concentration of TBHQ 从 500 加到 1 000(mg/kg)时，只有 BD 3 减少，与题中的 claim 相违。答案选 C。

20. 答案：F

解析：看 Figure 1，BD 2 和 BD 3 在 115℃时对应的 induction period 分别大约为 25℃和 35℃。答案选 F。

21. 答案：A

解析：看 Figure 1，induction period 随 temperature 的增大而减小，要使 induction period 为 65 min，temperature 必须小于 100℃。答案选 A。

22. 答案：J

解析：能跟油反应的只有氧气。答案选 J。

23. 答案：B

解析：看 Figure 2，因为 BD 5 是 BD 1 和 BD 4 的混合物，它对应 induction period 应该在 BD 1 和 BD 4 之间但是更偏向 BD 4 一点。BD 5 在横轴上 TBCA 对应的 induction period 应该在 20 min到 100 min 之间但是更偏向 20 min 一点。答案选 B。

[**Passage V**]

24. 答案：F

解析：看 Figure 2，E2 在 120 天的 alachlor concentration 相较于刚开始的 25 g/L 只有大约 2 g/L。大约占 8%，不足 20%。答案选 F。

25. 答案：C

解析：看 Figure 1，50 天时的 S1 和 E1 的 atrazinecon centration 分别是大约 16 g/L 和 9 g/L。S1 比 E1 多 7。答案选 C。

26. 答案：F

解析：Figure 1 和 Figure 3 中 S1 对应的天数越多，atrazinec oncentration 越小，DEA concentration 越大。答案选 F。

27. 答案：D

解析：Figure 1 中 120 天后减到最少的是 E1，所以 statement 是错的。答案选 D。

28. 答案：G

解析：Figure 2 中 O2，S2，E2 的值始终相近是因为植物对酒精的吸收并不强。答案选 G。

[**Passage VI**]

29. 答案：A

解析：Student 1 认为球在 L 点的速度最大，KE = 1/2 mv^2。答案选 A。

30. 答案：J

解析：Student 3 认为是 string 的变化导球速度的改变。答案选 J。

31. 答案：D

解析：AM = mvr。Student 1 实验中 m 和 r 始终不变，但是 v 发生改变，AM 也改变。答案选 D。

32. 答案：F

解析：Student 2 认为 r 减小时 v 增大。所以 KE 增大。答案选 F。

33. 答案：C

解析：只有 Student 2 认为 v 是不停增加的，其他两个都认为 v 会减小并偶尔为 0。答案选 C。

34. 答案：G

解析：KE + PE = TME = 100。相加为 100 的只有 10 + 90。答案选 G。

35. 答案：B

解析：Student 2 认为 v 和 r 的乘积是一个定值。所以 $v' = 5 \times 20/15 = 20/3$ cm/sec。答案选 B。

[**Passage VII**]

36. 答案：G

解析：看 Figure 1，C = 0.20 mole/L 且 $\pi = 10$ atm 时，图像为 NaCl 在 310 K。答案选 G。

37. 答案：D

解析：看 Table 2，glucose 和 lactose 质量相比，lactose 更大。答案选 D。

38. 答案：F

解析：看 Table 2，HCl 的 i 值比 $MgCl_2$ 的要小。Table 1 中说 i 值代表物质溶于水时形成的颗粒数。答案选 F。

39. 答案：C

解析：$\pi = 0.0821 \times T \times i \times C$。T = 290 K，i = 2，C = 2 mole/L。代入。答案选 C。

40. 答案：F

解析：y-intercept 始终为 0，但是斜率要更大。答案选 F。

68G 解析

[**Passage I**]

1. 答案：D

解析：看 Figure 3，其实根本看不出来有多少 Species B。答案选 D。

2. 答案：G

解析：看 Figure 1 的 Species B，取水深 0.2 m 和 0.4 m 对应 average shoot length 的中间值。大约在 34 cm 到 42 cm 之间。答案选 G。

3. 答案：A

解析：看 Figure 3，dry mass 是 400 mg，shoot length 是 33 cm，对应的大约是 0.2 m 的线。答案选 A。

4. 答案：J

解析：对应 Figure 3 的 0.4 m 的图像，即是中间的那条。答案选 J。

5. 答案：C

解析：由 Figure 1 得，A 的 average shoot length 比 B 的短；由 Figure 2 得，A 的 average dry mass 比 B 的小。答案选 C。

6. 答案：F

解析：存活下来的 Species A seedlings 只有 6 个，由 Study 2 得 Species A 在 0.2 m 水深的 average dry mass 是 2.3 mg。所以用 2.3 mg×6。答案选 F。

[**Passage II**]

7. 答案：D

解析：看 Figure 2，在 No Leu 的情况下没有出现的 colony 是 Colony P。答案选 D。

8. 答案：J

解析：看 Table 1，在 No His 一栏下的 + 有 7 个。答案选 J。

9. 答案：C

解析：Table 1 中可以看出 Strain 4 可以 No Arg，No His，No Leu，而不可以 No Lys。对应 Figure 2 中是 Colony O。答案选 C。

10. 答案：J

解析：Table 1 中可以看出 Strain 2 colony 的形成不能没有 leucine。所以在没有 His 和 Leu 的情况下不能形成 colony。答案选 J。

11. 答案：B

解析：Strain 10 可以存在于每一个 EP，但 Strain 6 只能在后两个。对应 Figure 2 是 Mixed Culture F。答案选 B。

12. 答案：G

解析：该举措是消除 velvet cloth 上带有的外界杂质带给实验的干扰。答案选 G。

[**Passage III**]

13. 答案：B

解析：看 Figure 1，找纵轴上 55 units 对应横轴的值大约是 0.1 km。答案选 B。

14. 答案：F

解析：看 Figure 2，asteroid diameter 越大，average time elapsed between consecutive asteroid impacts 越大。答案选 F。

15. 答案：A

解析：看 Figure 3，Mars 的 percent of surface covered by impact craters 始终比其他两个要小。答案选 A。

16. 答案：J

解析：Figure 1 上面的文字里提到，impact crater 的直径约是 asteroid 直径的 20 倍。20 km 的 crater 说明是 1 km 的 asteroid。对应 Figure 1，在 30 000 energy units。答案选 J。

17. 答案：A

解析：找到 Figure 2 中直径 10 km 的 asteroid 对应的时间 100 000 000 年。减去 65 000 000 年。得到 35 000 000 年。答案选 A。

[**Passage IV**]

18. 答案：G

解析：液体流出滴定管，液面降低。答案选 G。

19. 答案：C

解析：Student 1 认为温度一定时，密度越小的液体越容易流动。由 Table 1 得，选项中密度最小的是 Nonane。答案选 C。

20. 答案：F

解析：Student 1 认为温度一定时，密度越小的液体越容易流动。Isopropanol 流动花时间比 Liquid A 长比 Liquid B 短，所以密度比 Liquid A 大比 Liquid B 小。答案选 F。

21. 答案：A

解析：Student 2 认为 molecular mass 大的更不容易流动。由 Table 1 得，Nonane 的 molecular mass 是 128.3 amu，acetone 的是 58.08 amu 比 nonane 的小，应该更容易流动。与题中的 claim 相违。答案选 A。

22. 答案：H

解析：Student 3 认为 molecular volume 越大的越不容易流动。而 viscosity 越大越不容易流动。由 Table 1 得，isopropanol 的 molecular volume 最大，DMSO 第二，水最小。答案选 H。

23. 答案：D

解析：由 Table 1 得，isopropanol 与 nonane 相比，密度更大，molecular mass 更小，molecular volume 更小。与 Student 2 和 Student 3 观点相符。答案选 D。

24. 答案：F

解析：由 Table 1 得，heptane 与 toluene 相比，密度小，molecular mass 大，molecular volume 大。会认为 heptane 在 20℃流动比 toluene 快的只有 Student 1。答案选 F。

[**Passage V**]

25. 答案：B

解析：看 Figure 3，30% EO 对应的 bubble point 是大约 25℃。答案选 B。

26. 答案：G

解析：mass per unit volume 就是密度，所以看 Figure 1。随 %EO 的增大，密度减小。答案选 G。

27. 答案：D

解析：melting point 和 freezing point 一般是同一温度，所以看 Figure 2。选项中对应的熔点最低的是 80%EO。答案选 D。

28. 答案：H

解析：Figure 3 中 bubble point 15℃ 对应的%EO 是大约 70%。Figure 2 中 70%EO 对应的 freezing point 大约是 7℃。答案选 H。

29. 答案：D
解析：看 Figure 2，水在一个标准大气压下凝固点是 0℃，对应的%EO 与选项中最靠近的只有 89%EO。答案选 D。

[**Passage VI**]

30. 答案：H
解析：看 Figure 1，seeding concentration 越大，average amount of rainfall 越小。答案选 H。
31. 答案：B
解析：cloud droplet 由 water droplet 聚集而成，raindrop 由 cloud droplet 继续吸收 water droplet 形成。从小到大排应该是，water droplet，cloud droplet，raindrop。答案选 B。
32. 答案：F
解析：看 Figure 2，unseeded clouds 的 mass of raindrops in clouds 比 seeded clouds 的更早达到最大值，而后者的最大值更大。答案选 F。
33. 答案：C
解析：Study 1 测量了下雨的量，而 Study 2 决定了 mass of raindrop in cloud（Figure 2）。答案选 C。
34. 答案：H
解析：超过 4 900 m 很难再有 liquid water content。答案选 H。
35. 答案：B
解析：看 Table 1，0.1～0.5 占有的 percent 最多。答案选 B。

[**Passage VII**]

36. 答案：H
解析：看 Figure 2，resonant angular frequency（ω0）为 1.00×10^7 radians/sec。答案选 H。
37. 答案：B
解析：看 Figure 3，L 增大时，ω0 减小。答案选 B。
38. 答案：H
解析：看 Figure 2，产热最大需要电流最大，即 ω0 时。答案选 H。
39. 答案：D
解析：看 Figure 2，ω0 始终为 1.00×10^7 radians/sec。不随 R 改变答案选 D。
40. 答案：J
解析：看 Figure 3，L 一定时，C 越大，ω0 越小。答案选 J。

69A 解析

[**Passage I**]

1. 答案：A
解析：Rider A 与 Rider B 运动方向相同，一开始 Rider A 速度比 Rider B 慢，但是后来超过了 Rider B。可以看出 Rider A 是 Rider 1，Rider B 是 Rider 2。答案选 A。
2. 答案：J
解析：从 P 点出发在图上表示即为从零点出发。没有从零点出发的有 Rider 3、4、5。答案选 J。

3. 答案：A

解析：看 Figure 2，Rider 4 在 t = 15 sec 时，D 为大约 350 m。D 从 600 m 到 375 m，即 Rider 4 运动了 225 m。答案选 A。

4. 答案：H

解析：看 Figure 1，Rider 2 在 35 sec 里的平均速度大约是 140/35 = 4 m/sec。答案选 H。

5. 答案：B

解析：看 Figure 2，Rider 5 在 t = 15 sec 到 t = 20 sec 间 D 没有变，说明 Rider 5 没有动。与题目中学生的观点相同。答案选 B。

［**Passage II**］

6. 答案：H

解析：看 Figure 1，pupa stage 和 larva stage、adult stage 各有一段重叠。产卵是在 pupa stage 结束以后的 adult stage，成虫通过完全变态形成是在 pupa stage，但 larvae 通过完全变态形成是在 pupa stage 以前。答案选 H。

7. 答案：D

解析：看 Figure 2，可以得出前一个 peak 在 1981 年，10 年后就是 1991 年。答案选 D。

8. 答案：G

解析：看 Table 1，yellow poplar trees 的 average percent defoliation 是 5%。它的 10 倍就是 50%，也就是 Scarlet oak。答案选 G。

9. 答案：A

解析：看 Figure 2，1981 年的饼图，所占百分比最大的是 light defoliation 53%。答案选 A。

10. 答案：F

解析：一共有 1 000 个 test plots，80 个占 8%。看 Figure 2，moderate defoliation 占 8% 的是 1980 年。答案选 F。

［**Passage III**］

11. 答案：B

解析：Student 1、3、4 都认为 CH_4 是在火星表面以下形成的。答案选 B。

12. 答案：H

解析：Student 3 认为一旦受到影响，CH_4 会从地下释放出来。答案选 H。

13. 答案：B

解析：Student 4 认为地球厌氧菌可以和火星厌氧菌一样将二氧化碳和氢气，或一氧化碳和水，转化为甲烷。答案选 B。

14. 答案：F

解析：Student 1 认为高温流体可以将玄武岩转化成蛇纹石，从而产生氢气，和二氧化碳反应生成甲烷。答案选 F。

15. 答案：C

解析：根据 Student 2 的想法，火星大气中的甲烷应该是均匀分布的。但是引言中提到火星大气中甲烷平均浓度是 10 ppbv，但是有的地方是 250 ppbv，与 Student 2 的观点不符。答案选 C。

16. 答案：J

解析：Student 1 的观点中高温流体将玄武岩转化成蛇纹石是变质作用（metamorphism）。答案选 J。

17. 答案：A
    解析：火星大气中甲烷平均浓度是 10 ppbv，$10\times10=100$。答案选 A。

[**Passage IV**]

18. 答案：G
    解析：看 Figure 3，427 nm 和 603 nm 分别的 exposure time 对应的 absorbance 最相近的时间是大约 3 min。答案选 G。
19. 答案：D
    解析：看 Figure 1，exposure time 为 0 时，603 nm 的 absorbance 比 427 nm 的要大。答案选 D。
20. 答案：G
    解析：Exposuretime 为 4 min 时，427 nm 在每种光照射下的 absorbance 分别约为 0.05(blue)、1.5(yellow)、0.9(green)。答案为 G。
21. 答案：B
    解析：绿光是黄光和蓝光混合而成的。答案选 B。
22. 答案：F
    解析：看 Figure 1，603 nm 的 exposure time 为 12 min 时的 absorbance 比 2 min 时的小。所以蓝光的浓度要更小。答案选 F。
23. 答案：D
    解析：看 Figure 1 和 2 603 nm 吸收蓝光始终比 427 nm 多，而对于黄光恰恰相反。答案选 D。

[**Passage V**]

24. 答案：H
    解析：看 Table 1，D 增加时，θ 减小。答案选 H。
25. 答案：D
    解析：3 个 Study 中，初始的 charge 都是一样的。答案选 D。
26. 答案：H
    解析：看 Table 3，R 越小，θ 越小。0.7 cm 在 0.95 cm 和 0.48 cm 之间，所以 θ 也在 11° 和 8° 之间。答案选 H。
27. 答案：C
    解析：因为异性相吸，Sphere B 会向 Sphere A 靠近。答案选 C。
28. 答案：G
    解析：看 Table 2，QB 增大时，θ 减小。答案选 G。
29. 答案：A
    解析：两个球相向而行时，线会变得更加的 twisted，势能增加。答案选 A。

[**Passage VI**]

30. 答案：H
    解析：看 Figure 2，图像从 25 Hz 到 175 Hz 先增大后减小。答案选 H。
31. 答案：B
    解析：看 Figure 2，140 Hz 在 125 Hz 和 150 Hz 对应的图像之间。大约在 22%。答案选 B。
32. 答案：H
    解析：Researcher 想要规避重复记录同一只青蛙导致数据不精确。答案选 H。

33. 答案：A

解析：在 mean PRR 时，最多的青蛙被吸引。与假设相符。答案选 A。

34. 答案：H

解析：实验中的 gravid frogs 是被求偶的带有未受精的卵子的 female frogs。答案选 H。

35. 答案：D

解析：实验开始时，青蛙距离两个 speaker 的距离相同。1.8/2 = 0.9 m。答案选 D。

[**Passage VII**]

36. 答案：J

解析：看 Table 2，2-iodo propanoicacid 的分子式是 $CH_3CIHCOOH$。与 Figure 1 结合可判断。答案选 J。

37. 答案：A

解析：通过 Figure 1 和 Table 2 可得出，该结构式的分子式是 $BrCH_2CH_2COOH$。答案选 A。

38. 答案：J

解析：对应 Figure 1 靠下的结构式，X 是 I。答案选 J。

39. 答案：B

解析：看 Table 2，acetic acid 和 propanoic acid 对应的 pH 值分别为 2.38 和 2.44。Acetic acid 的 pH 值更小，酸性更强。答案选 B。

40. 答案：F

解析：结合 Table 1 和 Table 2，EN 越大，pH 值越小。答案选 F。

69F 解析

[**Passage I**]

1. 答案：B

解析：看 Figure 2，随着 temperature 的增加，average CH_4 emission rate 增大。答案选 B。

2. 答案：G

解析：看 Figure 1，60℃ beech 对应的大约是 2 ng of dry leaves/hr。答案选 G。

3. 答案：C

解析：被太阳光照射，chamber 内温度升高。答案选 C。

4. 答案：J

解析：Study 3 中作为对照组的是 chamber without sweet grass。答案选 J。

5. 答案：A

解析：看 Figure 1 和 2，二者图像没有什么显著差异，所以 sterilization 对于 CH_4 emission rate for ash leaves 没有影响。答案选 A。

6. 答案：F

解析：average CH_4 emissionrate 与单位干叶子有关。答案选 F。

[**Passage II**]

7. 答案：C

解析：看 Figure 1 和 2，51～65 mm 的 flounder 的 prey 并不一样。Group 1 的食物种类多样，

Group 2 主要吃 malacostraca。答案选 C。

8. 答案：H

解析：看 Figure 2,31～40 mm 的 Group 2 flounder 不吃的有 calanoids 和 cirripeds。答案选 H。

9. 答案：C

解析：看 Table 1 和 2,Group 1 的 Percent with empty stomachs 比 Group 2 小的只有 51～65 mm,其他 3 组都要更大。答案选 C。

10. 答案：J

解析：Estuary 是淡水和海水的交界处,笼子放在 bottom of estuary。答案选 J。

11. 答案：C

解析：看 Figure 2,bivalves 占 20～30 mm Group 2 flounder 食物的大约一半。50 mg 的一半是 25 mg。答案选 C。

12. 答案：F

解析：看 Figure 1,40 mm 以下的 Group 1 flounder 食物主要是 harpacticoids(超过 75%),而以上的 Group 1 flounder 食物更加多样。答案选 F。

[**Passage III**]

13. 答案：A

解析：看图,900℃时 $CaC_2O_4 \cdot H_2O$ 已经转化为 CaO 了。$CaC_2O_4 \cdot H_2O$ 和 CaO 的质量比大约是 100∶40。有 50 g 的 $CaC_2O_4 \cdot H_2O$ 可以形成 20 g 的 CaO。答案选 A。

14. 答案：H

解析：质量变化最大的是 $CaCO_3$ 分解成 CaO。答案选 H。

15. 答案：B

解析：CaC_2O_4 大约在 350℃开始分解。答案选 B。

16. 答案：F

解析：$CaC_2O_4 \cdot H_2O$ 和 CaC_2O_4 的质量差就是水的质量,大约是 12 g。占 $CaC_2O_4 \cdot H_2O$ 的 12%。答案选 F。

17. 答案：D

解析：二氧化碳是碳酸钙分解的生成物。答案选 D。

[**Passage IV**]

18. 答案：G

解析：看图上的 lung volume 平均大约在 2.4 L。答案选 G。

19. 答案：B

解析：图上 inspiration 所用时间比 expiration 短。答案选 B。

20. 答案：G

解析：图中当 pleural pressure 最低时,air flow 对应的值最接近 0 L/sec。答案选 G。

21. 答案：D

解析：当 lung volume 和 air flow 都增大时,pleural pressure 和 alveolar pressure 都减小。答案选 D。

22. 答案：J

解析：expiration 时,alveolar pressure 大于 atmospheric pressure,空气流出肺部。答案选 J。

[**Passage V**]

23. 答案：B

 解析：看 Table 1，T = 112 K 时，Voltage 为 5.09 mV。答案选 B。

24. 答案：F

 解析：Table 1 中 voltage 减小时，T 增大。答案选 F。

25. 答案：C

 解析：看 Figure 1，Material X 在 6～8 mV 时几乎没有电阻，对应 Table 1 中的 T 即是 80～87 K。选项中最接近的是 88 K。答案选 C。

26. 答案：J

 解析：看 Figure 1，Material Y 在大约 5.5 mV 时开始有电阻，对应 Table 1 中的 T 即是 100 K。答案选 J。

27. 答案：A

 解析：T = 81 K 时，Material Y 电阻为 0，不产热。答案选 A。

[**Passage VI**]

28. 答案：H

 解析：高度相同时，Y 比 X 的重力势能大，所以 Y 的重力更大。答案选 H。

29. 答案：A

 解析：Student 2 认为 MOL 越大的滑上坡越远。VL 相同的情况下，Sphere S 的质量更大，MOL 更大，所以 Sphere S 滑上坡越远。答案选 A。

30. 答案：J

 解析：Student 1 认为是重力势能转化为动能使得球滑上坡。月球上的 g 比地球上的小，Sphere X 在月球上从同一高度滑下重力势能转化成的动能没有地球上的大。答案选 J。

31. 答案：B

 解析：只有 Student 3 认为球的质量与滑上坡的距离无关。答案选 B。

32. 答案：H

 解析：Student 3 认为两球滑上坡的距离是一样的，速度也是一样的，所以所花时间也是一样的。答案选 H。

33. 答案：D

 解析：因为球在 Point Q 的重力势能比在 Point P 要小，所以转化成的动能也更小。答案选 D。

34. 答案：H

 解析：一个球比另一个球滑的更远，与 Student 1 和 2 的观点相符。答案选 H。

[**Passage VII**]

35. 答案：A

 解析：看 Table 1，biphenyl 对应的最低温度是 69℃。答案选 A。

36. 答案：H

 解析：看 Table 1，选项中 Rrvalue 最大的是 acenaphthene。答案选 H。

37. 答案：A

 解析：Rr 是一个一定小于 1 的比值，如果 Rr 大于 1，那说明点的运动超过了溶剂。答案选 A。

38. 答案：G

 解析：Unknown B 的 MP range 最大。答案选 G。

39. 答案：D
解析：Unknown A 的 MP range 在 93～95℃，Rrvalue 在 0.02，与 m-toluamide 最相近。答案选 D。
40. 答案：F
解析：看 Table 1，Group II 的 Rr value 分别是 0.67、0.85、0.05。答案选 F。

70B 解析

[**Passage I**]

1. 答案：C
题干：判断 10 号试管和 18 号试管的实验条件差异。
定位：Table 2
解析：实验 2 是通过在同一温度下改变不同试管中 pH 进行的。
2. 答案：F
题干：判断当 pH 等于 2 时的相对活性。
定位：Table 2
解析：根据 Table 2，活性随 pH 值的增加而先升高后降低，所以当 pH = 2 时，活性要低于 10%。
3. 答案：B
题干：判断活性最大的温度和 pH。
定位：Table 1、2
解析：从 Table 1 中可以看出，当温度为 40℃时，活性为 100%，从 Table 2 中可以看到，当 pH 为 7 时，活性为 100%。
4. 答案：J
题干：判断实验 1 结果对应的图形。
定位：Table 1
解析：从 Table 1 中可以看到，实验自变量是温度，因变量是活性，所以横坐标应为温度，在 40℃时活性达到最高点，在 70℃时活性达到最低点。
5. 答案：D
题干：判断哪个试管中的 agarose 含量最多。
定位：Table 1
解析：Table 1 中可以看到试管 9 对应的酶活性最低，所以 agarose 分解最少，剩余最多。
6. 答案：H
题干：判断实验设计思路。
定位：Table 2
解析：实验 2 研究的是温度固定时 pH 值对酶活性的影响，所以研究 60℃下的酶活性，只需在 60℃条件下重复实验 2。

[**Passage II**]

7. 答案：D
题干：判断叶绿素 B 所对应的曲线。
定位：Figure 3

解析：从 Figure 3 可以看到色素 V 对应的曲线峰值出现在 450 nm 和 640 nm 处。

8. 答案：J

题干：判断色素 U 对哪个波长的光线吸收率最高。

定位：Figure 3

解析：从 Figure 3 可以看到色素 U 的峰值出现在 660 nm 处。

9. 答案：D

题干：判断色素位置。

定位：Figure 2

解析：第 5 种色素所对应的 R_f 小于色素 V，说明色素移动的距离小于色素 V。

10. 答案：G

题干：判断当纸条从层析液中提前取出时的现象。

定位：Figure 2

解析：如果实验进行了一半的时间就取出，色素分离的时间变短，所以移动的距离也会相应变短，但同时层析液移动的距离也会变短，所以不能确定 R_f 的变化情况。

11. 答案：A

题干：判断计算色素 U 的 R_f 的计算公式。

定位：Table 1

解析：Table 1 中可以看到色素 U 的移动距离为 62 mm，层析液的移动距离为 63 mm。

12. 答案：F

题干：判断实验 2 的设计思路。

定位：Figure 2

解析：实验 2 是将纸条上不同色素所对应的部分分开后溶解在溶剂中，然后再分别测量对可见光的吸收率。

[**Passage III**]

13. 答案：A

题干：判断温度降低时金属块长度的变化。

定位：Table 1

解析：从 Table 1 中可以看到，当温度由 40℃ 降低为 20℃ 时，长度由 5.002 降为 5.000。

14. 答案：F

题干：判断 30℃ 时金属块的长度。

定位：Table 1

解析：根据 Table 1，金属块的长度随温度的升高而增大，所以长度应介于 5.000 和 5.002 之间。

15. 答案：C

题干：判断水浴的作用。

定位：Study 1

解析：实验 1 关心的是温度和金属体长度的关系，通过改变水浴的温度来改变金属体的温度。

16. 答案：G

题干：判断实验 3 中金属体的相同之处。

定位：Table 3

解析：实验 3 关心的是不同的金属在温度升高后体积的变化程度，所以初始的体积需要保持一致。

17. 答案：D
题干：判断金属条下方的材质。
定位：Table 1、2、3
解析：如果让金属片向上弯曲，下方的金属条的体积变化应大于上方金属条，体积变化比 copper 小的只有 steel。
18. 答案：G
题干：判断每摄氏度温度的升高所带来体积变化的表达公式。
定位：Table 2
解析：体积变化值为 125.38～125.00，温度变化值为 80～20，每摄氏度温度变化所带来的体积变化即为两者相除。

[**Passage IV**]
19. 答案：A
题干：判断放大镜的选择。
定位：Table 1
解析：最开始观察生物体的时候需要使用观察视野大的放大镜来进行定位，然后再逐步增大放大倍数。
20. 答案：H
题干：判断哪个组织的大小所处的范围最大。
定位：Table 2
解析：Table 2 中可以看到 Volvoxes 大小所处的范围为 1.5，最大。
21. 答案：C
题干：判断生物体类型。
定位：Table 1、2
解析：Table 1 中 Len 2 对应的 FOV 为 1.6 mm，处于 amoebas 和 volvoxes 所处的范围内，因为观察到的组织内有叶绿体，而 volvoxes 可以进行光合作用，所以为 volvoxes。
22. 答案：J
题干：根据放大倍数判断所用镜片。
定位：Table 1
解析：总放大倍数为 Len 乘以 power，根据 Table 1 得出 Len 为 4。
23. 答案：C
题干：判断所用的 Len。
定位：Table 1、2
解析：从图中可以判断此生物体为草履虫，Table 2 中可以看到草履虫的大小范围为 0.05～0.35，所以 FOV 应该接近 0.35。

[**Passage V**]
24. 答案：G
题干：三种汽油所降低的 ON 量。
定位：Figure 1
解析：从图 1 中可以看到，50 ppm、70 ppm 和 100 ppm 对应的 ON 减少量依次递增。
25. 答案：B

题干：判断哪种汽油符合不会对发动机产生损坏的标准。

定位：Table 1

解析：Table 1 中可以看到，ON 值低于 88 的只有 A、B 和 D。

26. 答案：H

题干：判断降低硫含量后 D 与 F 哪个 ON 含量低。

定位：Table 1、Figure 1

解析：Table 1 中可以看到 D 的 S 含量为 75 ppm，F 的 S 含量为 100 ppm，根据图 1，当硫含量降低为 10 ppm 后，D 中 ON 减少 0.6，F 中减少 0.76，可根据最初的 ON 值确定 ON 的高低。

27. 答案：B

题干：判断通过方法 2 可将 C 中的 ON 降低多少。

定位：Table 1、Figure 2

解析：Figure 1 可以看到 C 中的 S 含量为 50 ppm，对应图 2 中最下方的虚线。

28. 答案：J

题干：判断 Z 的 ON 值。

定位：Table 1、Figure 1

解析：Table 1 中 A 的 S 含量为 14 ppm，Z 对应的 Figure 2 中的第 2 条曲线，当 S 含量降低为 14 ppm时，ON 约减少 0.6，所以 Z 的 ON 值为 83.6。

[**Passage VI**]

29. 答案：D

题干：根据学生 2 的说法判断 v_t的表达式。

定位：Student 2 L4

解析：L4 中提到速度是质量和半径比的平方根。

30. 答案：G

题干：判断 X 所受的摩擦力。

定位：Table 1

解析：根据 Student 2 的思路，速度会增加到 weight 和摩擦力相同的点，所以摩擦力等于 X 的重量。

31. 答案：D

题干：判断 3 个学生观点的漏洞。

定位：无

解析：学生 1 考虑了重力和浮力，学生 2 考虑了重力和摩擦力，学生 3 只考虑了重力，3 个学生均没有同时考虑重力、浮力和摩擦力。

32. 答案：H

题干：判断球体 U 的半径长度。

定位：Table 1

解析：根据 v_t的公式，半径和质量的比值决定了速度，所以球体 U 的比值应与 X 和 Y 相同。

33. 答案：C

题干：根据学生 1 的观点判断球体的受力图。

定位：Student 1

解析：学生 1 认为球体受到重力和浮力，重力大于浮力，合力向下。

34. 答案：F

题干：判断新的液体对球体施加的浮力。
定位：Student 1
解析：学生 1 认为球体受到的浮力等于球体排出的水的重量，所以当液体密度降低为一半时，重量也降低为一半，浮力相应减半。

35. 答案：D
题干：判断使 Y 所受合力为零的浮力值。
定位：Student 1
解析：Student 1 认为球体受到重力和浮力，所以为了使合力为零，重力应等于浮力。

[**Passage VII**]

36. 答案：F
题干：判断电子密度最强的时刻及位置。
定位：Figure 1
解析：从图中可以看出最右边实线可以到达密度最大值。

37. 答案：B
题干：判断 200 km 处在 minimum sunspot count 处所对应的图形。
定位：Figure 1
解析：从图中 200 km 处两条虚线所对应的横坐标大小可得。

38. 答案：H
题干：判断两条曲线相交的位置。
定位：Table 2
解析：根据图中两条曲线交点对应的纵坐标可得。

39. 答案：A
题干：判断丢失电子后的原子的电性。
定位：L2
解析：电子带负电荷，原子在丢失电子后，带正电。

40. 答案：J
题干：判断哪个纬度上方的电子密度最大。
定位：无
解析：题干提示太阳直射的地区上方的电子密度最大，所以纬度越低的地方所对应的电子密度最大。

70C 解析

[**Passage I**]

1. 答案：B
解析：抓关键词 double NaCl concentration，其他条件不变，选 B。

2. 答案：G
解析：抓关键词 42℃，5 g/L，看 Trial 3 和 9 的 ACD 可知，选 G。

3. 答案：A
解析：找 Trial 10～12 的自变量，只有 incubation temperature，选 A。

4. 答案：J

解析：找 ACD 的最大值为 2.1，是 Trial 11，选 J。

5. 答案：A

解析：比较 Trial 4 和 Trial 10 的不同，Trial 4 比 Trial 10 的 pH 低，选 A。

［**Passage II**］

6. 答案：G

解析：在 combination 5～8 中，T 增加，F 减小，选 G。

7. 答案：C

解析：在 combination 9～12 中，V 以 10 的倍数增长，F 比倍数增长快，所以应为弧线，选 C。

8. 答案：J

解析：从 combination 1～4 可知，D 越大，F 越大，从 combination 5～8 可知，T 越大，F 越小，从 combination 9～12 可知，V 越大，F 越大，选择 D 最大，V 最大，T 最小的，选 J。

9. 答案：D

解析：看导语，F depends on D，D 的改变引起 F 的改变，D 是自变量，F 是因变量，选 D。

10. 答案：H

解析：球一开始具有的重力势能在下落过程中转换成球的动能和热量，选 H。

［**Passage III**］

11. 答案：A

解析：抓关键词 conductivity、endofreaction，看 Figure 1 和 2 的 RC 点（反应完成点）的纵坐标，50%＜10%＜20%＜40%＜30%，选 A。

12. 答案：H

解析：45%介于 40%～50%，横坐标为时间，45%溶液的反应完成时间在 40%RC 的横坐标与 50%RC 的横坐标之间，时间最可能在 1 200～1 800 秒，选 H。

13. 答案：A

解析：反应完成时间最短找 RC 的横坐标最小，10%溶液 RC 的横坐标最小，选 A。

14. 答案：H

解析：先找到电导率最大的溶液，RC 纵坐标最大的是 30%溶液，看 figure 2 下的注释，concentration 是溶质占溶液的质量，选 H。

15. 答案：D

解析：最高的电阻也就是最低的电导率，找 RC 纵坐标最小的溶液，是 50%，选 D。

［**Passage IV**］

16. 答案：F

解析：看 Table 1，抓关键词 not trained for Seq Y，只与 Group 1 和 2 有关，Group 2 有睡觉，准确率高于 Group 1，选 F。

17. 答案：C

解析：抓关键词 immediately，Time between training sessions 为 0，只剩 Group 3 和 4，选 C。

18. 答案：G

解析：实验中所有的睡觉都是在学习后的，排除 F、H，比较 Group 1 和 2，Group 3 和 4，Seq X 和 Y 的准确率都有提升，选 G。

19. 答案：D
解析：看导语，Seq X 和 Seq Y 只是按键顺序不同，其他全部相同，选 D。
20. 答案：F
解析：因为 Group 3 Seq X 的正确率变化小于 0，所以再次测试后正确率降低，选 F。
21. 答案：D
解析：比较 Group 4 和 Group 5 的 Seq X 的正确率变化，变化差距很大，Group 5 正确率提高，Group 4 降低，选 D。

[**Passage V**]
22. 答案：H
解析：科学家 1 认为 planet core 为 10 ME 时，才开始形成，所以 core 至少 10 ME。科学家 2 认为不大于 6 ME，选 H。
23. 答案：A
解析：科学家认为 core 要足够重，地球不够重，选 A。
24. 答案：G
解析：导语介绍星云是环绕新形成恒星的气体和灰尘，科学家 2 认为当恒星形成后，星云继续存在不超过 700 万年，所以如果有星云存在时间超过 1 000 万年，则与科学家 2 矛盾，科学家 1 认为巨行星形成所需时间超过 1 000 万年，有星云存在时间超过 1 000 万年是前提条件，不矛盾，选 G。
25. 答案：C
解析：科学家 1 认为需要吸引至少 300 ME 的气体，选 C。
26. 答案：G
解析：科学家 2 认为巨行星在太阳年龄到达 700 万年之前形成，形成时间大约 100 万年，需要环绕年龄小于 700 万年的太阳的巨行星来证明，选 G。
27. 答案：A
解析：太阳系巨行星比所有类地行星远，比所有类地行星大，选 A。
28. 答案：G
解析：小于 6 ME 不在 GGPP 之内的会向恒星撞去，10 ME 的 core 大于形成巨行星所需的 6 ME，并且不在 GGPP 之内，所以最有可能不受恒星影响，选 G。

[**Passage VI**]
29. 答案：B
解析：看 Figure 3，在深度为 5 cm 和 7 cm 时，没有 calcite，选 B。
30. 答案：G
解析：把 Figure 2 的两条线继续往下画，硫酸根应该仍不存在，甲烷维持在 65 左右，选 G。
31. 答案：C
解析：硫酸根在深度大于 4 cm 时不存在，所以不是每层都有，选 C。
32. 答案：G
解析：在 Figure 3 中，calcite 含量在每层都比 aragonite 少，选 G。
33. 答案：B
解析：Aragonite 在深度为 10 cm 时的比例是 10%，50 g 样本大约有 5 g，选 B。
34. 答案：F

解析：Study 1 测量的是 AOM 的反应物，Study 2 测量的是 AOM 生成物的间接产物，选 F。

[**Passage VII**]

35. 答案：A
解析：Figure 3 中，x-half 与 ray energy 正相关，选 A。
36. 答案：J
解析：x-half 测量的是 I 变为初始值一半的 x 值，材料 3 使 I 从 8 000 变为 4 000 的 x 大约是 4.0 cm，选 J。
37. 答案：C
解析：看 Figure 3，材料 3 的线一直高于材料 1 的线，即材料 3 做到 x-half 所需厚度一直大于材料 1，所以使 I 降为 0 时，材料 3 会更厚，选 C。
38. 答案：G
解析：从导语可知，I 为 number of counts per minute，能量不变，材料能力增强，探测器感应到的次数少了，即 I 减小，选 G。
39. 答案：A
解析：看 Figure 1，I 为 1 000 时，材料 1 和 2 的厚度都小于 10.0 cm，选 A。
40. 答案：J
解析：I0 是无材料时的情况，看 Figure 2 材料厚度为 0 时 I0 为 8 000，选 J。

70G 解析

[**Passage I**]

1. 答案：B
解析：看 Figure 1，在 50～100 msec 的时间区间里，force 增加后减少。答案选 B。
2. 答案：F
解析：3 个 phase 的时间分别大约是 2 msec（Latent period）、85 msec（Contraction phase）、190 msec（Relaxation phase）。从小到大排就是 Latent period、Contraction phase、Relaxation phase。答案选 F。
3. 答案：B
解析：看 Figure 1，最大值在大约 90 msec。答案选 B。
4. 答案：G
解析：看 Figure 1，maximum force 大约是 7.5 N，两倍就是 15 N。答案选 G。
5. 答案：C
解析：看 Figure 1，开始有力的产生是在 2 msec。答案选 C。

[**Passage II**]

6. 答案：G
解析：看 Figure 2，October 15 的图像在 O_3 partial pressure 为 0 时对应的 altitude instratosphere 在大约 19～21 km。答案选 G。
7. 答案：B
解析：看 Figure 2，在 16～26 km 时，September 15 和 November 15 的 O_3 partial pressure 最大

值分别为 7 m Pa 和 20 m Pa。答案选 B。

8. 答案：J

解析：看 Figure 1，从 October 15 到 November 15 气温相差最小的是在大约 25 km。答案选 J。

9. 答案：A

解析：看 Figure 2，altitude instratosphere 为 18 km 时，O_3 partial pressure 对应在大约 1 左右。答案选 A。

10. 答案：H

解析：辐射最强，说明 O_3 pressure 最低，即 October 15。答案选 H。

[**Passage III**]

11. 答案：C

解析：Student 1、2 和 3 认为加热之前烧杯里存在不止一种物质。答案选 C。

12. 答案：J

解析：Student 1 认为溶剂在 12 min 里蒸发。答案选 J。

13. 答案：A

解析：因为白色固体漂浮在绿色液体表面，所以该固体的密度比绿色液体小。答案选 A。

14. 答案：G

解析：不存在绿色液体，与 Student 1 和 4 的观点相违。答案选 G。

15. 答案：D

解析：Student 1 认为溶液呈绿色是因为溶剂，Student 3 认为溶液呈绿色是因为溶质不相同。答案选 D。

16. 答案：J

解析：Student 4 认为液体没有蒸发，质量不变。答案选 J。

17. 答案：B

解析：Student 2 的观点既不需要绿色溶剂也不需要绿色溶质，而是白色溶质和无色溶剂，与题目相符。答案选 B。

[**Passage IV**]

18. 答案：J

解析：看 Figure 2，选项中第一天 percent surviving 下降最多的是 Group 7。答案选 J。

19. 答案：B

解析：结合 Table 1 和 Figure 2，dose of UV-B 越多，存活率越低。答案选 B。

20. 答案：F

解析：看 Figure 1，FB 和 FT 相差不到 5%的只有 H. regilla。答案选 F。

21. 答案：B

解析：看 Figure 3，H. regilla 和 B. boreas 相比 photolyase activity 要高很多。答案选 B。

22. 答案：G

解析：看 Figure 1，B. boreas 对应的 FB 和 Nofilter 分别是 0.9 和 0.6。因为每个类别有 4 组，每组 150 个 egg。所以 $0.9\times600-0.6\times600$。答案选 G。

23. 答案：A

解析：看 Figure 1，R. cascadae 和 B. boreas 的 FTs 比 FBs 的 percent hatched 低许多。而 H. regilla 的两者没有什么变化。答案选 A。

[**Passage V**]

24. 答案：F

解析：看 Table 2，RH 最低的是 Tank 1。答案选 F。

25. 答案：C

解析：看 Table 3，RH 越高，Aqueous tension 越大。氯化钾的 RH 在硫酸钾和氯化钠之间，所以 aqueous tension 也在二者之间，即 100～140 torr。答案选 C。

26. 答案：G

解析：综合 3 张表，随温度升高，RH 降低的有氢氧化钾，氯化镁，和硝酸镁。答案选 G。

27. 答案：D

解析：RH 相同时，比如 30℃时的氯化钠和 60℃时的氯化钠，aqueous tension 是不同的。答案选 D。

28. 答案：F

解析：防止一开始存在水汽对实验结果的干扰。答案选 F。

29. 答案：D

解析：RH 是测量值，并不是一开始决定好的。答案选 D。

[**Passage VI**]

30. 答案：J

解析：看 Table 1，将密度从小到大排是 ethanol、water、ethyleneglycol、carbon tetrachloride。答案选 J。

31. 答案：C

解析：看 Table 1，ethanol 的密度是 786 kg/m^3，carbon tetrachloride 的密度是 1,580 kg/m^3。看 Figure 1，carbon tetrachloride 的密度对应的 PL 是大约 150 kPa，ethanol 对应的是 75 kPa。前者大约是后者的两倍。答案选 C。

32. 答案：H

解析：看 Table 1，3 m^3 的 ethyleneglycol 的质量是 $3 \times 1,130 = 3,390$ kg。答案选 H。

33. 答案：A

解析：看 Figure 2，PL 和 D 的关系式写作 $PL = 9.8 \times D$。答案选 A。

34. 答案：H

解析：看 Figure 2，20 m 对应的 PL 和 PA 的和即是这时 PT 的值 300 kPa。答案选 H。

[**Passage VII**]

35. 答案：C

解析：看 Figure 2，5 个湿地的 organic detritus 的 average Se concentration 的平均值大约为 $(9+7+10+7+9)/5 = 8.4$ mg/kgdw。答案选 C。

36. 答案：G

解析：看 Table 1，什么都没种的湿地即为对照组，是 Wetland 2。答案选 G。

37. 答案：C

解析：Figure 1 中 1999 年 average annual Se concentration of outflow 最大的是 Wetland 2。看 Table 1，Wetland 的 average RT 恰恰最小，而 average RT 最大的是 Wetland 4。答案选 C。

38. 答案：H

解析：看 Figure 1，几个 Wetland 的 average annual Se concentration of outflow 都逐年下降，而 Wetland 3 的最低，且最有可能小于 5。答案选 H。

39. 答案：A

解析：Study 2 考察的是液体中的 Se 浓度，Study 3 考察的几种土壤中的 Se 浓度。答案选 A。

40. 答案：F

解析：看 Figure 2，在 Wetland 1、3、4 中，plant litter 对应的 average Se concentration 比 top 5 cm of soil 高。答案选 F。

71A 解析

[**Passage I**]

1. 答案：B

题干：判断不能确定灭绝风险的比例。

定位：Table 1

解析：实验 1 中可以看到因为缺少充足的数据而无法判断灭绝风险的样本比例为 4%。

2. 答案：G

题干：判断当 zebra mussel 数量丰富时 pearly mussel 的数量。

定位：Figure 1

解析：1992 年时 zebra mussel 数量丰富，所对应的 pearly mussel 的数量介于 1 000 million 和 1 200 million之间。

3. 答案：D

题干：判断除无法界定、灭绝和稳定之外的比例。

定位：Table 1

解析：从 Table 1 中可以看出，无法界定占 4%，灭绝占 7%，稳定占 24%，其余占 65%。

4. 答案：J

题干：判断 2002 年时将 zebra mussel 从该区域去除后，到 2005 年 pearly mussels 的数量。

定位：Figure 1

解析：从 Figure 1 可以看到，2002 年时的数量约为 225 million，去除 zebra mussel 后，数量应回升到高于 225 million。

5. 答案：A

题干：判断 zebra 和 pearly 两个哪个为入侵者。

定位：Table 1

解析：因为 zebra 的引入导致 pearly 数量骤减，所以 zebra 为入侵者。

[**Passage II**]

6. 答案：J

题干：判断 1.1 V 时 diode 对应的电流大小。

定位：Figure 1

解析：从图 1 可以看到，电流强度随电压的增大而增大，所以当电压为 1.1 V 时，电流强度应高于 1.0 V 时所对应的 130 mA。

7. 答案：A

题干：判断电流随电压变化的趋势。
定位：Figure 1
解析：从 Figure 1 中可以看出三条曲线都是单调递增的。

8. 答案：H
题干：判断那两个设备符合 Ohm’slaw。
定位：Figure 3
解析：电压和电流的比值为电阻，所以当图 3 中的曲线水平时，说明电阻恒定。

9. 答案：A
题干：判断 diode 的电阻为 60 Ω 时电流的大小。
定位：Figure 2、3
解析：根据图 3，R 为 60 Ω 时电压为 0.7 V，对应图 1 得电流为 12 mA。

10. 答案：J
题干：判断传导性最强时的电压大小。
定位：Figure 3
解析：传导性与电阻成反比，根据图 3 电阻与电压成反比，所以电压越强传导性越强。

[**Passage III**]

11. 答案：C
题干：判断 H 为 0.75 时 y 的大小。
定位：Figure 1
解析：图 1 可以看到当 H 为 0.75 时对应的 y 为 0.65 m。

12. 答案：H
题干：判断当测得的 C 大于 1.0 的原因。
定位：无
解析：C 的范围应介于 0 和 1 之间，当 C 大于 1.0 时，说明球不是自由落体而是掉落时被人为施加了外力。

13. 答案：A
题干：判断当球没有弹起时对应的 C 的值。
定位：Table 1
解析：C 的值等于 y 与 H 的比值，当 y 等于 0 时，C 也为 0。

14. 答案：F
题干：判断如何判断球撞击面的类型的方法。
定位：Table 1
解析：实验 1 中用到的球为 racquet ball，所以为了判断撞击面的类型，应该将实验 1 测得的 C 值与表 1 中 racquet ball 的 C 值比较。

15. 答案：C
题干：判断当从 2 m 高度落下时，两个不同撞击面上的反弹高度的差值。
定位：Table 1
解析：表 1 中可以得到两个撞击面的 C 值，从而可以得到两个撞击面对应的 y 值，即可求得。

16. 答案：G
题干：判断实验地点的选择原因。
定位：Table 3

解析：通过控制空气温度和空气的压强，可以减少空气阻力对球体的影响。

[**Passage IV**]

17. 答案：D
题干：判断哪个实验条件可使 Rp 产生最大的 average dry shoot biomass。
定位：Figure 1
解析：从图 1 可以看到，使 Rp 最大的实验条件为第四个。

18. 答案：H
题干：判断清洗 root 的原因。
定位：无
解析：因为后续需要测量 root 的重量，所以需要保证 root 上没有其他的物质附着。

19. 答案：A
题干：判断条件 3 下 T 类植株和 S 类植株 average dry root biomass 的大小差异。
定位：Table 1、Figure 2
解析：从图 2 可以看到基本所有的 T 类植株的 biomass 都比 S 类要高。

20. 答案：G
题干：判断得到图 2 数据所需要的仪器。
定位：Figure 2
解析：Figure 2 中的数据是质量，需要通过使用天平测得。

21. 答案：A
题干：判断 S 和 T 类植株 shoot biomass 和 root biomass 的差异。
定位：Figure 1、2
解析：从图 1 和图 2 对比可以看到 S 和 T 类植株的 shoot biomass 要普遍高于 root biomass。

22. 答案：G
题干：判断 6 种植株属于多少的属。
定位：Table 1
解析：从表 1 可以看出 6 种植株属于 3 种不同的属。

[**Passage V**]

23. 答案：B
题干：判断实验 1 中分离液体所用的器材。
定位：Experiment 1 L3
解析：从 L3 中可以看出所用的器材带有阀门。

24. 答案：H
题干：判断实验 1 和实验 3 的区别。
定位：L6
解析：从 L6 可以看到，titrant 是已知溶液，analyte 是未知溶液，而实验 1 和实验 3 的区别在于已知溶液都是氢氧化钠，未知溶液是不同的酸。

25. 答案：C
题干：判断 hydrazoic 的 pKa 值范围。
定位：Table 1
解析：酸性与 pKa 值负相关，所以 hydrazoic 的 pKa 值应介于 formic 和 acetic 之间。

26. 答案：J

题干：判断溶液呈中性时添加的 NaOH 量。

定位：Figure 2

解析：从图 2 中可以看到，当溶液的 pH 值为 6 时，添加的 NaOH 量约为 20 mL。

27. 答案：C

题干：判断 UAX 是否为 pyruvic。

定位：Table 1、Figure 1

解析：Figure 1 可以看到 half way point 对应的 pH 值为 4.8 左右，高于 pyruvic 的 pKa 值，而根据文中提到的，half way point 对应的 pH 值与酸溶液的 pKa 值相等。

28. 答案：F

题干：判断 NaOH 浓度提升后，达到两个点需要的 NaOH 含量的变化。

定位：Figure 3

解析：两个点对应的是 NaOH 和一半的酸和全部的酸反应所需的量，因为浓度提升，所以对应的量也相应减少。

[**Passage VI**]

29. 答案：C

题干：判断混合体的属性。

定位：L3

解析：老师提到 iodine 能溶解在 mineral oil 中，说明两者同质，而 iodine 和水不相溶，说明两者异质。

30. 答案：G

题干：判断水是否能溶于 mineral oil 中。

定位：Student 1

解析：根据 Student 1 的思路，分子小的物质可以溶解于分子大的物质中，而水分子的大小小于 mineral oil，所以能溶解。

31. 答案：B

题干：判断三种物质的分子大小。

定位：Student 1

解析：学生 1 认为水分子小于油分子，iodine 不能溶于水而能溶于油说明其分子大小介于两者之间。

32. 答案：F

题干：判断 iodine 分子的极性。

定位：Student 2

解析：学生 2 认为极性物质与极性物质吸引，非极性与非极性吸引，因为油分子和 iodine 分子都为极性，所以相互吸引能够溶解。

33. 答案：D

题干：根据分子大小对学生 3 观点的影响。

定位：Student 3

解析：学生 3 的观点只与分子极性有关，与分子的大小无关。

34. 答案：J

题干：判断非极性固体在极性溶液中的溶解程度。

定位：Student 3

解析：学生 3 认为极性分子之间的结合力度要高于非极性分子。

35. 答案：A

题干：判断非极性溶液溶于非极性溶液的结果与哪位学生的观点不符合。

定位：Student 1

解析：Student 1 认为大分子不能溶解在小分子中。

[**Passage VII**]

36. 答案：J

题干：判断沙漠 D 的 dune 间隔和面积的可能取值。

定位：Figure 2

解析：从图 2 可以看到 D 的间隔取值在 700 到 2 000 之间，高度的取值在 3 到 20 之间。

37. 答案：A

题干：判断 A 和 B 哪处的平均风速更高。

定位：Figure 2

解析：dune 高度与风速成正比，从图 2 中可以看到 A 处的高度要普遍高于 B 处的高度。

38. 答案：J

题干：判断 Titan 和沙漠 A 表面抬升值的差异。

定位：Table 3

解析：根据图 3，Titan 代表的实线时而高于 A 代表的虚线，时而低于 A。

39. 答案：D

题干：判断 Titan 的 tune 高度高于 C 的 tune 高度的次数。

定位：Figure 2

解析：通过计数图 2 中 Titan 代表的点纵坐标高于 C 的点的数量即可。

40. 答案：G

题干：判断可类比 dune spacing 和 dune height 的电磁波变量。

定位：Figure 1

解析：dune 间隔类似于电磁波的波长，dune 高度类似于电磁波的振幅。

71C 解析

[**Passage I**]

1. 答案：A

解析：在图 1 中，纵坐标是圆柱平均长度百分比变化。4 条平均长度变化曲线从上到下依次为 $MgCl_2$、$CaCl_2$、NaCl、$Ca(OH)_2$，因此圆柱长度平均百分比变化从大到小依次为 $MgCl_2$、$CaCl_2$、NaCl、$Ca(OH)_2$。所以正确答案选 A。

2. 答案：G

解析：CS 是圆柱体的压缩强度，定义为施加在圆柱体两端的，不使其被压碎的最大纵向压力。图 F 和 H 表现的是施加在圆柱体横向的力，图 J 表现的是纵向拉力，均不符合 CS 的定义。图 G 表现了施加在圆柱体两端的纵向压力。所以正确答案选 G。

3. 答案：A

解析：图 2 的横坐标是浸没时间，纵坐标是平均质量百分比变化。可以看出，在浸没时间为 250 d时，对应的浸没在 $MgCl_2$溶液中的圆柱体平均质量百分比变化最大。所以正确答案选 A。

4. 答案：H

解析：根据题意，每种除冰剂都是质量分数为 15%的盐溶液。因此准备 1 000 g NaCl 除冰剂需溶解固体 150 g NaCl。所以正确答案选 H。

5. 答案：D

解析：实验要求将圆柱体浸没在 4℃液态除冰剂中，因此 4℃不可能是 4 种除冰剂的凝固点，A 选项错误。水在正常大气压下的凝固点是 0℃，所以 B 选项错误。除冰剂应用在冬天，如果 4℃是夏天典型温度，则该实验没有实际意义，所以 C 选项错误。因此正确答案是 D。

6. 答案：J

解析：要保持道路表面的光滑、不开裂，要求混凝土的最低 CS 不能低于 25 MPa。从实验 2 的结果可以看出，在 600 天的浸没时间中，浸泡在 $MgCl_2$除冰剂中的混凝土圆柱体最低 CS 小于 25 MPa，而浸泡在 $CaCl_2$、NaCl、$Ca(OH)_2$除冰剂中的圆柱体最低 CS 均大于 25 MPa。所以正确答案选 J。

[**Passage II**]

7. 答案：D

解析：由图 2 可以看出，在 140 d 时，P－32 的数量为 0，Fe－59 的数量约为 100，S－35 的数量约为 320。所以正确答案选 D。

8. 答案：H

解析：在相同时间内，剩余原子越少，即 N_t越小，同位素的平均衰减率越大。从图 2 可以看出，前 200 天内 P－32 的数量总是小于 S－35，因此 P－32 的平均衰减率更大，因为它的 N_t较小。所以正确答案选 H。

9. 答案：C

解析：含有 1 000 个原子的 Ni－63 和 Sr－90 样品，衰减 20 年后剩余原子数约为 900 和 600。Ti－44 的衰变常数介于 Ni－63 和 Sr－90 之间，因此 1 000 个 Ti－44 原子衰减 20 年后剩余原子数介于 600 到 900 之间。所以正确答案是 C。

10. 答案：F

解析：某种同位素的半衰期指一定量该同位素原子衰减一半所需时间。由图 1 可以看出，1 000 个 Sr－90 原子衰减到 500 个大约需要 30 年，因此 Sr－90 的半衰期约为 30 年。所以正确答案选 F。

11. 答案：D

解析：2 000 个 Fe－59 原子衰减到 400 个所需时间与 1 000 个 Fe－59 原子衰减到 200 个所需时间相同。由图 2 可以看出，1 000 个 Fe－59 原子衰减到 200 的时间约 100 d，因此 2 000 个 Fe－59 原子衰减到 400 个大约需要 100 d。所以正确答案选 D。

[**Passage III**]

12. 答案：F

解析：使用色度计时应选取吸光度为 0 的溶液作为空白对照。溶液 1 的吸光度为 0。所以正确答案选 F。

13. 答案：C

解析：由图 1 和图 2 可以看出，实验 2 和实验 3 每隔 100 s 测量一次吸光度。所以正确答案选 C。

14. 答案：G

解析：因为只有与 Transferrin 结合的 Fe^{3+} 能吸收波长为 466 nm 的光，当溶液中与 Transferrin 结合的 Fe^{3+} 浓度降低时，被吸收的光减少，溶液吸光度降低。所以正确答案选 G。

15. 答案：C

解析：在各曲线中选取若干点进行比较。在相同时间点，TREN - HOPO 试验的吸光度值与 25℃下 Deferiprone 试验的吸光度值最接近。所以正确答案选 C。

16. 答案：G

解析：等量溶液 2 与溶液 4 混合，混合溶液中 Transferrin 与 Fe^{3+} 的浓度比为 1∶1，与溶液 3 中 Transferrin 与 Fe^{3+} 的浓度比相同。因此混合溶液的吸光度应与溶液 3 的吸光度 0.64 相近。所以正确答案选 G。

17. 答案：A

解析：作为吸光度测量时的容器，比色皿的材料不能对 466 nm 波长的光线有吸收，否则会对测量结果造成影响。因此正确答案选 A。

[**Passage IV**]

18. 答案：F

解析：由图 1 可以看出，同种液体不同线圈，随电流增大 ΔT 增大。从图 2 可以看出，同种线圈不同液体，随电流增大 ΔT 也增大。因此对于给定的液体和线圈，电流增大，ΔT 增大。所以正确答案选 F。

19. 答案：A

解析：由图 1 可以看出，当液体是水的时候，对于给定的 I 值，铜线圈产生的 ΔT 最小。由图 2 可以看出，当使用铝线圈时，液体为水产生的 ΔT 最小。比较这两条曲线，可发现对于任意 I 值，以水作为液体并用铜线圈加热产生的 ΔT 小于以水为液体用铝线圈加热产生的 ΔT。所以正确答案选 A。

20. 答案：G

解析：搅拌液体的作用在于使热量在液体中均匀分布，防止冷热不均匀产生的测量误差。所以正确答案选 G。

21. 答案：C

解析：根据图 1 曲线的规律，当 I = 1.5 A 时，金属 X 的 ΔT = 6℃，介于铝和钨之间。则当 I = 2.0 A时，金属 X 的 ΔT 也介于铝和钨之间，即 7～15℃之间。所以正确答案选 C。

22. 答案：G

解析：由图 2 可以看出，当 I = 1.5 A 时，vegetable oil 的 ΔT 为 10℃。ΔT 是 T 与初始温度 25℃的差值，因此 T 为 35℃。所以正确答案选 G。

23. 答案：D

解析：由图 1 可以看出，用钨线圈在 I = 2.0 A 条件下加热 400 mL 水，可将水加热到 15℃。当水的体积减少到 200 mL，在相同条件下加热，水的温度会大于 15℃。所以正确答案选 D。

[**Passage V**]

24. 答案：F

解析：根据题意，botulin 是人体吸收的一种毒素，不是由人体细胞合成的，因此 G 选项错误。Botulin 进入血液后扩散到突触间隙中，阻碍肌肉纤维与 NMJs 的联系，并没有在离开血液前被

破坏，因此 H 选项错误。Botulin 并没有在进入消化道之前被排放，因此 J 选项错误。假说 1 认为 botulin 被突触终端吸收，假说 4 认为 botulin 被肌肉纤维吸收，突触终端与肌肉纤维都是人体细胞。所以正确答案选 F。

25. 答案：D

解析：Ach 的作用是将信息从突触终端携带到肌肉纤维，因此选项 A、C 错误。Ach 是一种神经递质而不是激素，因此 B 选项错误。D 选项的描述符合 ACh 的作用所以正确答案选 D。

26. 答案：G

解析：Acetylcholin esterase 的作用是结合并破坏 ACh，假说 2 中认为 botulin 的作用是在 Ach 扩散通过突触间隙之前与 ACh 结合并破坏 ACh，与 acetylcholin esterase 的作用相同。所以正确答案选 G。

27. 答案：D

解析：假说 3 认为 botulin 阻碍了 ACh 感受器，即 ACh 的结合位点。假说 4 认为 botulin 破坏了 myosin，即一种组成肌肉纤维收缩结构的蛋白质，符合 D 选项的描述。所以正确答案选 D。

28. 答案：G

解析：假说 1 认为 botulin 进入了突触终端，假说 2 和假说 3 认为 botulin 留在突触间隙中，假说 4 认为 botulin 进入了肌肉纤维。因此只有假说 1 认为 botulin 进入了神经元。所以正确答案选 G。

29. 答案：A

解析：假说 3 认为 botulin 与 ACh 感受器结合阻碍了 ACh 的结合，假说 4 认为 botulin 与 myosin 结合并导致其被破坏。ACh 感受器与 myosin 都是肌肉纤维上的蛋白质。因此选项 A 的描述符合 botulin 的作用机理。所以正确答案选 A。

30. 答案：H

解析：Botulin 与 ACh 感受器具有高近似性，因此 botulin 很可能与 ACh 感受器结合，阻碍 ACh 作用与肌肉纤维，与假说 3 相符。所以正确答案选 H。

[**Passage VI**]

31. 答案：A

解析：由表 2 可以看出，第 1 组人群中的基因型为 TT 和 tt 的频率都是 0.25，因此基因型为 TT 和 tt 的人数相等。所以正确答案选 A。

32. 答案：J

解析：由表 2 可以看出，在 4 组人群中，表现型为 nontaster，即基因型为 tt 的人数所占频率最高的 1 组是第 4 组。所以正确答案选 J。

33. 答案：B

解析：由表 2 可以看出，第 3 组基因型 tt 的频率为 0.04。因为基因型 tt 的频率等于 q^2，所以第 3 组的 q 等于 0.2，小于 $p=0.8$。所以正确答案选 B。

34. 答案：F

解析：因为基因型 TT 的频率等于 p^2，根据表 2，第 2 组人群的 $p=0.4$，所以基因型 TT 的频率等于0.4^2，即 0.16。所以正确答案选 F。

35. 答案：C

解析：由表 2 可以看出，在 4 组人群中，第 1 组人群中基因型为 Tt 的人数所占频率最高，该组 $p=q$。所以正确答案选 C。

[**Passage VII**]

36. 答案：G
解析：由图 1 可以看出，对于每一种液体，随物体密度逐渐增大，物体超出液面部分逐渐减小。所以正确答案选 G。

37. 答案：C
解析：根据表 1，物体 6 的密度为 0.600 g/cm³。由图 1 可以看出，在原油中，密度为 0.600 的物体露出液面部分约占 0.30。所以正确答案选 C。

38. 答案：H
解析：根据图 1，在水中，密度为 0.200 g/cm³ 的物体露出液面部分约占 0.80。该立方体的体积为 1 000 cm³，因此露出液面部分的体积约为 800 cm³。所以正确答案选 H。

39. 答案：B
解析：在 15℃时，物体的密度与水的密度相等。由于物体随温度变化不膨胀或收缩，所以物体的密度不随温度变化。而当温度大于 4℃时，随温度升高水的密度减小。因此当物体和水的温度都升高到 90℃时，水的密度小于物体的密度，物体下沉，与选项 B 的描述相符。所以正确答案选 B。

40. 答案：J
解析：密度的定义是单位体积物体的质量。因此水银的密度为 13.6 g/cm³ 表示 1 cm³ 水银的质量为 13.6 g，与选项 J 相符。所以正确答案选 J。

71G 解析

[**Passage I**]

1. 答案：D
解析：图的右侧是估计的数量，1980 年 1～3 岁 cod 估计有 1 000 000，选 D。

2. 答案：F
解析：1～3 岁 cod 估计数量最多的年份是 1981，该年捉到的 crab 少于 500 metrictons，选 F。

3. 答案：A
解析：导语介绍 cod 捕食 crab，所以 cod 是 predator，选 A。

4. 答案：F
解析：1984～1986 捉到的 cod 总数很多，捉到的 crab 很少，1992～1994 捉到的 cod 总数很少，捉到的 crab 很多，选 F。

5. 答案：B
解析：500 metrictons = 500 000 kg，图中 1987 年捉到的 crab 重量最接近，选 B。

[**Passage II**]

6. 答案：G
解析：Figure 2 中 Group 2 雌性消耗的 caffeinated cola 比 Group 1 雄性多，选 G。

7. 答案：D
解析：Group 3 和 4 没有消耗 cola，是正常状态，起控制组的作用，选 D。

8. 答案：H
解析：计算的是平均值，与每组数量无关，Group 2 消耗更多的 cola 导致液体消耗总量增加，可

以猜测 Group 2 更倾向 cola，选 H。

9. 答案：D

解析：Figure 1 中纵坐标是 BMD，一个反应骨头健康的参数，不是人数，所以无法得出哪组人数最多，选 D。

10. 答案：H

解析：Figure 1 中的 BMD 值比 Figure 3 中所有的 BMD 值都高，选 H。

11. 答案：A

解析：Study 2 喂老鼠相同的食物，不存在吃不同食物这个影响，Study 1 的对象没有吃相同的食物，存在影响，选 A。

[Passage III]

12. 答案：J

解析：Tank X 底部的水温度先下降，然后温度不变，选 J。

13. 答案：C

解析：看 Figure 3，Tank Y 底部的水温度降到 0℃ 比顶部的水大约多用了 $23-7=16$ h，选 C。

14. 答案：F

解析：Figure 2 和 3 说明流动的水表面温度下降到 0℃ 以下比静止的水慢，Stream A 是流动的，选 F。

15. 答案：B

解析：盖子阻挡容器与外界低温的热交换，温度会高于不盖盖子的温度，低于初始温度 14℃，选 B。

16. 答案：H

解析：空气温度是 -12℃，达到热平衡时水温会与空气温度相同，选 H。

[Passage IV]

17. 答案：D

解析：没有科学家认为粒子互相吸引，选 D。

18. 答案：G

解析：科学家 2 认为如果加热，粒子间的排斥力会减小，所以气球体积会减小，选 G。

19. 答案：B

解析：科学家 3 认为粒子不会撞击，受排斥力影响会换一个方向运动，选 B。

20. 答案：H

解析：只有科学家 2 认为加热压强不会增大，选 H。

21. 答案：C

解析：Tank B 的原子多，科学家 4 认为原子间不存在排斥力，选 C。

22. 答案：G

解析：科学家 1 和 2 都认为粒子由于斥力均匀分布且不运动，选 G。

[Passage V]

23. 答案：F

解析：Figure 1 中，200 和 500 的浓度一直升高，选 F。

24. 答案：C

解析：350 在 200～500 之间，15 min 时浓度应该在 20～50 之间，选 C。

25. 答案：H

解析：每隔 5 分钟出现一个标记，说明每隔 5 min 测量一次，选 H。

26. 答案：A

解析：看 Figure 3，添加 ammonia 后，每个时间段的浓度都低于没添加 ammonia 的浓度，选 A。

27. 答案：J

解析：Study 2 改变的 pH 值，Study 1 的 pH 值没改变，选 J。

28. 答案：D

解析：Figure 2 中，酸性水产生该离子的浓度低于碱性水，选 D。

[**Passage VI**]

29. 答案：J

解析：看 Figure 1，纵坐标是 5.0×10^9 时，横坐标是 0.6，选 J。

30. 答案：B

解析：看 Figure 2，横坐标是 0 时，纵坐标是 10，选 B。

31. 答案：G

解析：从 Table 2 可知，Mv 越小，output 越大，Table 1 中 Mv 最小的 SC 是 SC2，选 G。

32. 答案：C

解析：Table 1 中 SC1 的 Mv = 1.5，Mb − Mv = 0，所以 Mb = 1.5，选 C。

33. 答案：J

解析：SC3 的 Mb − Mv 小于 SC4 的 Mb − Mv，所以 SC4 的表面温度更低，选 J。

[**Passage VII**]

34. 答案：D

解析：从 Table 1 可知，V 越大 R 越大，9 000>7 500，对应的 R>0.140，选 D。

35. 答案：H

解析：R = 0.047 是 Q 为 + 3 测量的值，R = 0.070 是 Q 为 + 2 测量的值，说明 Q 有 + 2 和 + 3 两种，选 H。

36. 答案：B

解析：看 Figure 1，从发射器到小孔，粒子速度增加，从小孔到探测器，粒子方向改变，选 B。

37. 答案：F

解析：从 Table 1、2、3 分别可知，R 与 V 正相关，R 与 Q 负相关，R 与 B 负相关，选 F。

38. 答案：A

解析：R 与 B 负相关，Trial 7 的 B 增大，则 R 应减小，选 A。

39. 答案：H

解析：粒子移动路程是个半径为 R 的半圆，选 H。

71H 解析

[**Passage I**]

1. 答案：D

题干：判断在 X 区域没有存活幼苗的树种。

定位：Figure 2

解析：图 2 可以看到 yellow birch 在 herbaceous layer 没有受到影响的 X 处存活率几乎为零。

2. 答案：F

题干：判断 X 和 Y 处幼苗数量占比最多的树种。

定位：Figure 3

解析：图 3 可以看到两个饼状图中面积最大的区域对应的树种都为 red maple。

3. 答案：C

题干：判断消除 herbaceous layer 对幼苗数量分布的影响。

定位：Figure 3

解析：从图 3 可以看到，两个区域 5 种幼苗的分布均发生了改变。

4. 答案：J

题干：判断两个区域幼苗萌发率差值最大的树种。

定位：Figure 1

解析：从 Figure 1 可以看到，两个柱体差值最大的为 yellow birch。

5. 答案：D

题干：判断在 X 处播撒的种子数量。

定位：Figure 1

解析：图 1 可以看到，X 处仅 red maple 就萌发了 7 个，说明播撒的种子数要高于 7。

[**Passage II**]

6. 答案：G

题干：判断 silt 和 clay 大小的颗粒占比随到火山口的距离而变化的规律。

定位：Figure 2

解析：从图 2 可以看到，离火山口距离越远，silt 和 clay 大小的颗粒占比逐渐减小。

7. 答案：C

题干：判断在哪个距离范围内 cummulative percent by mass 的增量最大。

定位：Figure 3

解析：从 Figure 3 中可以看到 0.5～1 mm 的范围内增量最大。

8. 答案：H

题干：判断直径大于等于 0.5 mm 的颗粒占比。

定位：Figure 3

解析：在图 3 中，横坐标为 0.5 的点所对应的纵坐标约为 63%。

9. 答案：D

题干：判断在 270 m 处占比超过 50% clastcom position 和 matrix particle size class。

定位：Figure 1、2

解析：根据图 1，270 m 处占比超过 50% 的为 andesite，根据图 2，270 m 处占比超过 50% 的为 sand。

10. 答案：F

题干：比较 clasts 和 matrix 的大小。

定位：L3

解析：clasts 的直径均在 16 mm 以上，matrix 的直径均在 8 mm 以下。

[**Passage III**]

11. 答案:D

    题干:根据 3 位同学的观点判断羽毛和砖块哪个会最先落在月球表面。

    定位:Student 1、2、3

    解析:学生 1 认为质量轻的会先掉落,学生 2 认为质量重的会先掉落,学生 3 认为两者会同时掉落。

12. 答案:F

    题干:判断哪位同学认为加速度会和质量有关。

    定位:Student 1、2、3

    解析:学生 1 和 2 都认为加速度与质量有关,学生 3 认为与质量无关。

13. 答案:A

    题干:判断当重力增大时木块的速度如何变化。

    定位:Student 2

    解析:学生 2 认为重力增大时,木块的加速度增大,所以平均速度也会增大。

14. 答案:J

    题干:根据学生 1 的观点判断木块 A 的加速度。

    定位:Student 1

    解析:学生 1 认为两个木块质量与加速度的乘积相等,所以当 A 木块质量是 B 的一半时,A 木块的加速度是 B 的两倍。

15. 答案:A

    题干:判断当两个木块的质量相等时,加速度的大小。

    定位:Student 1

    解析:学生 1 认为两个木块所受的力 F 相等,并且等于质量与加速度的乘积,当质量相等时,加速度也就相等。

16. 答案:J

    题干:根据学生 3 的观点判断 A 和 B 所受的重力。

    定位:Student 3

    解析:学生 3 认为加速度取决于所处的位置,所以两个木块的加速度相同,因为 A 的质量小于 B,所以 A 所受的力小于 B。

17. 答案:C

    题干:根据学生 1 的观点,判断当加速度提升时,木块移动到底部花费的时间如何变化。

    定位:Student 1

    解析:学生 1 认为,加速度越大,木块的平均速度也越大,所以花费的时间越短。

[**Passage IV**]

18. 答案:G

    题干:判断 soiltest N 含量为 200 时对应的 amin osugwar N 含量。

    定位:Figure 1

    解析:根据图 1 可得。

19. 答案:C

    题干:判断 aminosugar N 含量为 350 mg/kg 时土壤是否为 responsive。

定位：Figure 2

解析：从图 2 可以看到在 350 mg/kg 处的产量变化为 0，对应 L5，在 nonresponsive 土壤中产量不随 N 的变化而变化。

20. 答案：F

题干：判断烘干土壤的目的。

定位：Figure 1、2

解析：两个实验关心的是 N 含量，烘干是为了去除土壤中的水分。

21. 答案：C

题干：判断产量变化最大的值及其所对应的 amino sugar N 含量。

定位：Figure 2

解析：从图 2 可以看到产量变化的最大值为 122%，对应的横坐标为 125 mg/kg。

22. 答案：G

题干：判断实验中需要控制的变量。

定位：无

解析：amino sugar N content 是自变量不需要控制，降雨和日晒需要控制以保证两者不会影响产量的变化。

23. 答案：D

题干：判断 2.5 公顷土壤需要添加多少 N。

定位：Study 2

解析：实验 2 中每公顷土地添加 120 kg N，2.5 公顷对应 300 kg。

[**Passage V**]

24. 答案：G

题干：判断三个电池的总电压。

定位：Step 1

解析：3 个电池的总电压为三个电池的电压之和，每个电池的电压为 1.4 V，总电压为 4.2 V。

25. 答案：C

题干：判断 0.45 mL 氧气被完全反应所用的时间。

定位：Figure 2

解析：图 2 中可以看到实验 4 对应的曲线在 0.45 mL 氧气被完全反应的点所对应的横坐标介于 200 和 250 之间。

26. 答案：F

题干：判断实验 2 中所用到的 SLB 的数量。

定位：Experiment 2

解析：从实验 2 中可以看到，两个实验室重复的实验 1 中的第三个实验，用的是三个 ZAB。

27. 答案：A

题干：判断氧气反应的速度与 ZAB 数量的关系。

定位：Figure 1

解析：Figure 1 可以看到当电池组中 ZAB 的数量增多时，完全反应既定的量的氧气所用的时间减少。

28. 答案：J

题干：判断消耗 5 个氧分子时，消耗的 Zn 原子数量。

定位：L4

解析：根据公式，反应消耗的 Zn 的数量是氧分子数量的 2 倍。

29. 答案：A

题干：判断实验 1 在 10 mA 条件下进行的实验结果。

定位：Figure 1、2

解析：在图 2 中可以看到，随着电流的增加，氧气的消耗速度增加，所以当实验 1 的实验条件由 20 mA 变为 10 mA 时，所需要的反应时间增加，在 200 sec 时反应的氧气量要少于 20 mA 条件下。

[**Passage VI**]

30. 答案：G

题干：判断有 7 个 plate 的后代基因型和性状。

定位：Table 1

解析：根据 7 个 plate 可以定位到基因型为 ee。

31. 答案：D

题干：判断被捕捉的子代所处的年龄段。

定位：Figure 1

解析：图 1 可以看到三个年龄段内均有子代被捕捉。

32. 答案：J

题干：判断后代长 62 mm 时，基因型可能为 EE 还是 ee。

定位：Figure 2

解析：图 2 可以看到 EE 基因型的子代在 60～64 mm 范围内没有分布。

33. 答案：C

题干：判断哪个基因型对应的 SM 个体最多。

定位：Figure 2

解析：图 2 可以看到 ee 对应的 SM 个体有 12 个，数量最多。

34. 答案：F

题干：判断淡水环境是否会让 low phenotype 后代比例升高。

定位：Figure 1

解析：图 1 中可以看出，在淡水环境中生活了一段时间后，ee 基因型的子代占比约提高 0.13。

35. 答案：B

题干：判断在 marine stickle back 上做标记的原因。

定位：Study 1

解析：实验思路是在 200 条 marine stickle back 上标记，然后捕捉他们的子代来计算基因型占比，所以需要在捕获的 marine stickle back 中区分子代和亲代。

[**Passage VII**]

36. 答案：G

题干：判断 K 与 Fx 的变化关系。

定位：Table 1、2

解析：从图 2 可以看到当 K 的值增大时，Fx 单调递减。

37. 答案：B

题干：判断实验 1 和 7 里哪个实验中 X 可以获得更大的加速度。
定位：Table 2
解析：加速度与受到的力成正比，从表中可以看到，实验 7 中 X 受力更大。

38. 答案：H
题干：比较实验中 X 和 Y 所受力的大小。
定位：Table 2
解析：力的作用是相互的，从表 2 中也可以看到，X 与 Y 大小相同。

39. 答案：A
题干：判断 X 和 Y 带电的原因。
定位：Table 2
解析：实验 3 中 X 带负电，应是来自于电子，Y 带正电，应来自于质子。

40. 答案：G
题干：判断 X 和 Y 的受力方向。
定位：Table 2
解析：表 2 中可以看到，X 和 Y 带相同的电性，互相排斥。

72G 解析

[**Passage I**]

1. 答案：A
题干：判断 recovery sleep 数量最小的品种的寿命长度。
定位：Figure 2、3
解析：图 2 可以看到 recovery sleep 数量最小的品种的基因型为 S^-S^-，对应的寿命为 60 天。

2. 答案：F
题干：比较 S^+S^+ 和 S^+S^- 的 recovery sleep 数量。
定位：Figure 2
解析：图 2 可以看到 S^+S^+ 约为 110，S^+S^- 约为 60。

3. 答案：C
题干：判断 S^-S^- 寿命达到 35 天的比例。
定位：Figure 1、3
解析：从图 1 可以看到，平均有 12 次睡眠的品种基因型为 S^-S^-，对应图 3 可以判断寿命达到 35 天的比例。

4. 答案：F
题干：比较 S^-S^- 和 S^+S^+ 每天睡眠时间。
定位：Figure 1
解析：从 Figure 1 可以看出，S^+S^+ 睡眠时间约为 1 000，S^-S^- 睡眠时间约为 100。

5. 答案：C
题干：判断 S^-S^- 和 S^+S^+ 子代寿命长于 50 天的数量。
定位：Figure 3
解析：S^-S^- 和 S^+S^+ 子代的基因型为 S^+S^-，从图 3 可以看到，寿命长于 50 天的子代比例为 75%，$80\times75\%=60$。

[**Passage II**]

6. 答案：H
   题干：判断 H 为 12 时，y 的值。
   定位：Figure 3
   解析：从图 3 可以看到，当 H 为 12 时，y 约为 6。
7. 答案：D
   题干：判断对于一个更为 stiff 的弹簧，当 H 为 4 时 a/g 的值。
   定位：Figure 2
   解析：从 Figure 2 中可以看到弹簧越 stiff，a/g 的值越大，所以当 H 为 4 时，W 对应的 a/g 值要大于 Z 所对应的值。
8. 答案：J
   题干：判断当弹簧施加的力为 3 000 N 时物块的位置。
   定位：Figure 4
   解析：在图 4 中，当 F 为 3 000 N 时，y 取值为 4。
9. 答案：D
   题干：判断对于弹簧 Z，在 H 为 8 m 时 a 的值。
   定位：Figure 2
   解析：根据图 2，H 为 8 m 时，a/g 的值为 7，求得 a 为 70。
10. 答案：G
   题干：判断 a 与 F 的关系。
   定位：Figure 2、3、4
   解析：从三幅图可以看出 a 与 H 成正比，H 与 y 成正比，y 与 F 成正比，所以 F 越大 a 越大，而 g 是恒定不变的。

[**Passage III**]

11. 答案：C
   题干：判断在 45°N 处地表温度。
   定位：Figure 1
   解析：图 1 可以看到，在代表 45°N 的实线与横坐标的交点为 12℃。
12. 答案：G
   题干：判断 0°N 和 45°N 两处在哪个高度温度相同。
   定位：Figure 1
   解析：在图 1 可以看到，两条线相交于 13 km 处。
13. 答案：C
   题干：判断 30°N 处的 average tropopause altitude 范围。
   定位：Figure 1
   解析：从图 1 可以看到，average tropopause altitude 随纬度的升高而降低。
14. 答案：G
   题干：判断 air pressure 与 tropopause altitude 的关系。
   定位：Figure 2
   解析：从图 2 可以看到，当 tropopause altitude 升高时，air pressure 降低，所以两者是负相关的关系。

15. 答案：D

题干：判断在两个气层中温度与高度的变化关系。

定位：Figure 1

解析：图 1 可以看到，在 troposphere 里面，温度随高度升高而降低，在 stratosphere 里，温度随高度升高而升高。

[**Passage IV**]

16. 答案：H

题干：当糖溶液含量为 70%时，质量的变化百分比范围。

定位：Table 1

解析：表 1 可以看到，随着溶液浓度的升高，质量变化百分比也升高。

17. 答案：A

题干：判断不将袋子装满样品溶液的原因。

定位：无

解析：根据题干，袋子的材质能允许水分子穿过而糖分子不能穿过，实验利用的原理也是水分子从低浓度溶液移到高浓度溶液，所以需要在袋子中留出空间给进入袋子的水分子。

18. 答案：H

题干：判断 60%蜂蜜溶液的制备方法。

定位：Experiment 1

解析：根据实验 1，20%的蜂蜜溶液是通过 2 mL 100%蜂蜜溶液和 8 mL 水制备而成，所以 60%的蜂蜜溶液是通过 6 mL 100%蜂蜜溶液和 4 mL 水制备而成。

19. 答案：B

题干：判断 40%的蜂蜜溶液质量变化。

定位：Table 1

解析：从表 1 可以看到，40%的蜂蜜溶液质量增加，这是因为 40%蜂蜜溶液的浓度高于纯水，所以水分子会进入到袋中。

20. 答案：H

题干：判断 Y 公司产品的浓度。

定位：Table 1、2

解析：从表 2 得 Y 公司产品质量变化百分比为 85%，介于 80%蜂蜜溶液和 100%蜂蜜溶液之间。

21. 答案：D

题干：判断实验 3 袋中溶液质量减小时所浸泡的溶液浓度。

定位：Table 2

解析：只有当溶液浓度低于所浸泡溶液浓度时袋中溶液质量才会减小。

[**Passage V**]

22. 答案：F

题干：判断在实验 1 中当 I 增大时，移动的电子数目如何变化。

定位：Table 1

解析：从图 1 可以看到，当 I 增大时，V_H也增大，说明移动的电子数目增多。

23. 答案：B

题干：判断夹具绝缘的原因。
定位：Figure 2
解析：夹具绝缘是为了防止电子从金属条转移到夹具上，从而对实验结果造成误差。

24. 答案：G
题干：判断实验 1 中的因变量和自变量。
定位：Table 1
解析：实验 1 中，改变的变量值为 I，V_H随 I 变化而变化。

25. 答案：A
题干：判断当 B = 0.2 T 时实验 1 的结果。
定位：Table 1、2
解析：图 2 中可以看到 V_H与 B 成正比，所以当实验 1 中的 B 减小时，V_H也减小。

26. 答案：H
题干：判断图 3 中 N 的含义。
定位：Figure 3
解析：从图 3 中可以看到，金属条置于电磁铁的两极之间，所以 N 代表的是电磁铁的 N 极。

27. 答案：D
题干：判断 V_H的决定公式。
定位：Table 1、2、3
解析：从图 1 可以看到 V_H与 I 成正比，从图 2 可以看到 V_H与 B 成正比，从图 3 可以看到 V_H与 d 成反比。

[**Passage VI**]

28. 答案：J
题干：判断哪个学生认为蜡烛会立即停止燃烧。
定位：Student 1、2、3、4
解析：4 位学生均没有提到蜡烛会立即停止燃烧。

29. 答案：D
题干：判断哪位学生认为蜡烛会在耗尽蜡油之前停止燃烧。
定位：Student 1、2、3、4
解析：学生 1、2、4 认为蜡烛的燃烧需要罐中气体参与，罐中气体耗尽后蜡烛即停止燃烧。

30. 答案：F
题干：判断学生 1 理论中的燃烧方程。
定位：Student 1
解析：学生 1 认为蜡油气体与氧气反应。

31. 答案：B
题干：根据学生 2 的理论判断罐中氧气和氮气的含量变化。
定位：Student 2
解析：学生 2 认为蜡油气体和氮气发生反应，所以罐中氧气含量不变，氮气减少。

32. 答案：J
题干：判断燃烧产生 phlogiston 的理论与哪位学生的理论相似。
定位：Student 4
解析：学生 4 认为燃烧中产生的热量需要气体吸收燃烧才能继续进行，与 1 600 s 气体需要吸收

phlogiston 燃烧才能继续进行的理论相似。

33. 答案：A

题干：判断哪个学生的理论最科学。

定位：Student 1

解析：科学的解释是当罐中参与燃烧的氧气耗尽后，蜡烛即熄灭。

34. 答案：F

题干：判断哪个学生会认为燃烧后氧气的质量会减少。

定位：Student 1

解析：只有学生 1 认为氧气会参与到反应中。

[**Passage VII**]

35. 答案：B

题干：判断年降水量为 750 mm 时，shrub plot 的根长。

定位：Table 1

解析：从表 1 可以看到，根长与降水量成正比。

36. 答案：H

题干：判断 shrub root 的根长大于 1.5 m 的结论是否正确。

定位：Table 1

解析：从图 1 可以看到三个地点的 shrub root 都长于 1.5 m。

37. 答案：A

题干：判断实验 3 中哪个地点的 shrub plot 在 2.0 m 处的 N 含量最多。

定位：Table 3

解析：从图 3 中可以看到，三个地点对应的图中曲线与横坐标的交点在 X 处最大。

38. 答案：F

题干：判断在实验 2 中哪个 plot 的 C 含量变化最大。

定位：Table 2

解析：图 2 中第一幅图的 grass plot 对应的 C 含量变化最大。

39. 答案：C

题干：判断实验 1 中将 soilcore 干燥的原因。

定位：Experiment 1

解析：实验 1 的说明中提到将泥土干燥的原因是为了更加容易地将泥土和根部分开。

40. 答案：J

题干：判断将 grass plot 和 shrub plot 种植在一起的原因。

定位：无

解析：种植在一起是为了控制两者的气候条件相同，不受无关变量的影响。

73C 解析

[**Passage I**]

1. 答案：A

解析：相对反射比越大，代表表层泥土越亮。在距离为 0 km 处相对反射比最大，也就是能找到亮度最大的表层泥土。

2. 答案:H

解析:要找相对反射比为25%的地方,则60 km的点代表的相对反射比与25%最相近。

3. 答案:C

解析:由图1第一幅图的曲线可看出,在50~75 km处曲线下降的幅度最大,则代表相对反射比变化最大。

4. 答案:J

解析:由图1第4幅图的曲线可看出,150 km处代表的平均相对亮度接近0%,而0 km处接近100%,亮度越小越黑,则150 km处的更黑。

5. 答案:B

解析:因为皮毛颜色和土相近,所以容易隐藏自己不被捕食者发现,存活下来,也更容易把自己皮毛颜色的特性传到下一代。

6. 答案:J

解析:0 km处的点对应的相对反射比为75%左右,低于100%,而相对反射比越低就越黑,所以该处相比参照物更黑。

[**Passage II**]

7. 答案:B

解析:10分钟CNF值为6 mg/kg,3天CNF值为39 mg/kg,浓度随时间递增,则2天应该位于这两个数字之前。

8. 答案:F

解析:时间越短,浓度越低;相同时间下,标准方法比真空方法浓度低。所以选10 min,标准方法。

9. 答案:C

解析:因为连接真空泵,锥形瓶内气压会越来越高,又不能和外界大气压平衡,液体滴下来需要的力就更大。

10. 答案:G

解析:操作顺序:先让两种溶液充分混合反应,生成固体,然后将其滤除,得到液体,最后测得CNF值。

11. 答案:D

解析:真空过滤对应的是4~6组实验,其中10 min和3天分别对应第4组和第5组实验,第5组的值比第4组高。

12. 答案:G

解析:要求是标准过滤情况下至少反应3天,则一共两次,分别是第2组和第3组实验。

13. 答案:A

解析:一个$Ni(OH)_2 \cdot H_2O$中有2个OH^-,则6个OH^-可以生成3个$Ni(OH)_2 \cdot H_2O$。

[**Passage III**]

14. 答案:G

解析:根据原文,当靠近原恒星的中心时,重力场吸引气体粒子向内加速运动;而辐射压力排斥气体使之向外,并防止堆积。

15. 答案:B

解析：根据科学家 2 的说法，盘状气体会在原恒星的赤道平面处聚集，并降低赤道处的辐射压力，B 选项符合要求。

16. 答案：H

解析：题中说星球合并的现象目前尚未在银河系发现，而科学家 1 和 2 都认为星球之间会合并，与之不符。

17. 答案：C

解析：一共是 120 Ms，科学家 1 认为每个恒星是 20 Ms，则需要 6 个；科学家 2 认为每个恒星是 40 Ms，则需要 3 个，由这两个答案可以选出 C。

18. 答案：H

解析：根据题干可推断，支持科学家 2 的观点，但削弱了科学家 1 的观点，则答案应该比 20 Ms 大，比 40 Ms 小，即 H。

19. 答案：A

解析：两个人都同意是因为原恒星的自转才会形成盘状气体，A 选项正确。

20. 答案：H

解析：三者都同意恒星可以通过堆积气体来自我形成。科学家 1 指出原恒星的最大堆积质量可达 20 Ms，科学家 2 指出辐射压力的影响被削弱能导致盘状气体的积累，科学家 3 指出随着周围的云中气体被消耗，盘装气体的积聚还会持续，故 H 选项正确。

[**Passage IV**]

21. 答案：D

解析：在两幅图中，横轴表示 6 组混合物，他们的 Vermicompost 的含量依次增加，纵轴表示平均产量，我们不难法随，随着 vermicompost 的增加，纵轴的数值现增加后减小，所以选 D。

22. 答案：F

解析：6 组混合物中总质量，水和光照时间都一样，只有 vermicompost 的含量变化，第 1 组混合物中 vermicompost 的含量为零，故为参照组。

23. 答案：B

解析：第 5 组混合物种的纵轴数值是 3 500 g/plant，换算成千克为单位，为 3.5 kg/plant。

24. 答案：G

解析：根据题意，我们不难发现第 2 组由 158 天缩短到 149 天，所以 2 排除，故选 G。

25. 答案：A

解析：有图 1 图 2 中我们不难发现，图 1 中产量的峰值出现在 2 号混合物，vermicompost 的含量是 20%，而图 2 中产量的峰值出现在 3 号混合物，即 40%，故 A 的说法正确。

26. 答案：J

解析：根据题意的描述我们不难发现在生长初期后，都会讲种子移除，这是为了避免干扰生长，故 J 选项为正确选项。

27. 答案：D

解析：考察光合作用的反应方程式，二氧化碳加水加光生成氧气和葡萄糖。

[**Passage V**]

28. 答案：H

解析：我们不难发现研究 1 和研究 2 磁场和电场方向不一样，在研究 2 中，这些因素决定了随着电势高低的变化，粒子位置的变化。

29. 答案：B
解析：根据表 2 我们不难发现，随着 V 的增加，Y 减小，2.6 介于 2.1 和 3.2 之间，所以 Y 介于 1.0 和 1.5 之间。
30. 答案：J
解析：根据电场的方向和磁场的大小，我们不难发现图 2 只能说明实验 4 和实验 8。
31. 答案：C
解析：我们根据 V 和 Y 的正负关系，不难发现 C 选项为正确选项。
32. 答案：G
解析：我们发现研究 3 改变的是 L 的长度，每做一次实验就要改变一次 L 长度，所以要 5 词实验要准备 5 个不同的 CRT。
33. 答案：B
解析：我们发现随着 Y 的减小，E 是减小的，V 是增大的，且当 Y 时 0 时，E 会变为 0，所以 B 是正确答案。
34. 答案：J
解析：同种电荷互相排斥，所以应该选下方的板子。

[**Passage VI**]

35. 答案：D
解析：根据图 2 我们不难发现在横坐标相同的情况下，纵坐标的数值从小到大依次是 Xe、Kr、Ar、Ne，故 D 选项为正确答案。
36. 答案：G
解析：根据图 2，我们不难发现横坐标为 6 时，纵坐标为 200，横坐标为 12 时，纵坐标约为 100，减少了一半，故选 G。
37. 答案：C
解析：将图中表示 Kr 的曲线延长出去，我们不难发现当横坐标为 50 时，纵坐标的值约为 400，是横坐标为 25 时纵坐标数值的 2 倍，故选 C。
38. 答案：J
解析：当横坐标为 20 时，Xe 的纵坐标约为 200，Ar 的纵坐标约为 400，所以大于 200，故选 J。
39. 答案：A
解析：随着体积的增加，Xe 碰撞前飞行的距离也变长，所以碰撞的频率也会减小，反之亦然，故选 A。
40. 答案：F
解析：说明 Rn 的原子直径要大于 Xe，根据表 2 我们不难发现 Rn 的曲线应位于 Xe 的下方，所以当纵坐标为 320 时，横坐标明显小于 6，故选 F。

73G 解析

[**Passage I**]

1. 答案：B
解析：从遗传谱图可明显看出一共有 4 行，即分为 4 代。B 选项正确。
2. 答案：G

解析：首先，有亲缘关系的两人之间基因组的相似性肯定更大，可排除 F 选项（两人非近亲）。在有亲缘关系的人中，遗传越接近，基因组越相似。对比剩下的 3 选项可知 G 最符合要求。

3. 答案：D

解析：由图看出，14 号和 15 号都没有 G 特征，但生出的子女 22、23 有 G 特征，结合题意判断出境 G 特征为隐性遗传(gg)。而 23 号和 24 号基因型均为 gg，则其后代也必为 gg，即有 G 特征，D 选项正确。

4. 答案：H

解析：由遗传谱图可看出，1 号和 2 号的孙辈中，有 10 号和 16 号为隐性，即有 G 特征，H 选项符合题意。

5. 答案：D

解析：根据伴性遗传的特点，含有 G 特征的女性生的儿子必有 G 特征，而由图中 3 号和 4 号生育的 11 号并没有表现出 G 特征，故为非伴性遗传，D 选项正确。

6. 答案：J

解析：由题意和系谱图推断均可知，G 特性的遗传为隐性(gg)，所以 J 选项正确。

[**Passage II**]

7. 答案：A

解析：图 2 的纵坐标为种子的平均质量，而测定质量需要用到天平，A 选项正确，B、C、D 分别用于测定 pH、观测星象和测定温度。

8. 答案：G

解析：根据题意可知，实验设置了不同的处理组别，判断授粉方式对种子质量和开花概率的影响，G 选项正确。

9. 答案：A

解析：由表 1 可知，组 1 的处理方式是自花授粉，花粉来自同株植物的花药，而组 2 的处理方式是异花传粉，只有 A 选项符合要求。

10. 答案：H

解析：图 1 中纵坐标为花的结果率，计算方法应为用果实的数量除以花的数量，H 选项正确。

11. 答案：B

解析：花药中含有花粉，若不人为去除的话可能会导致植物直接自花传粉，而实验中组 1 需要控制这一变量，所以 B 选项正确。

12. 答案：G

解析：由题干可知，尼龙袋可阻止花被授粉，而由图 1 和图 2 可看出未被授粉的植物(组 4)结果率为 0，也不会产生种子，故 G 选项正确。组 1、2、3 都经过人工授粉，不需考虑尼龙袋作用。

13. 答案：D

解析：组 3 中植物的结果率约为 43%，种子平均质量约为 85 mg，而题中并未提供花或果实的总数，故无法算出种子的总质量。D 选项正确。

[**Passage III**]

14. 答案：H

解析：由于夏季的平均气温高于冬季，更有利于细菌进行呼吸作用（包括有氧呼吸和无氧呼吸），故 H 选项正确。

15. 答案：A

解析：由图 1 和图 2 均可看出相同的趋势，即当土壤深度逐渐降低时，CO_2 的产生量逐渐升高而 CH_4 的产生量逐渐降低，A 选项正确。

16. 答案：F

解析：每个槽都用盖子先密闭 3 个月是为了隔绝空气，并防止产生的气体外漏，保证测得的体积准确，F 选项符合要求，G 错误。由于盖子是由玻璃制成，所以还是能透过阳光，可排除 J 选项。原文未提及保留细菌的情况，可排除 H。

17. 答案：D

解析：从图 1 和图 2 对比可看出，泥塘区(bog)产生的 CO_2 和 CH_4 气体均明显多于沼泽区(fen)，故好氧细菌和厌氧细菌在泥塘中生长都更加迅速，得到的养分更多，D 选项正确。

18. 答案：F

解析：由题图可看出，当两种土壤都完全浸入水下时，仍有二氧化碳气体产生，说明好氧细菌依旧存在，只是数量减少了而已，F 选项正确。

19. 答案：C

解析：由图，3 个月内沼泽区(fen)中水下 10 cm 处的 CO_2 排放总量约为 50 molC/m^2，故平均每月的排放量约为 16 molC/m^2，C 选项正确。

20. 答案：J

解析：实验在户外靠近湿地处进行，主要是为了保证实验槽的日照时间与湿地相同，J 选项正确。所用的植物和土壤均为人为控制，与实验地点无关，可排除 H、G 选项。降雨对实验槽没有影响，因为其为有盖密封状态，F 选项错误。

[**Passage IV**]

21. 答案：B

解析：由题图可看出，实验 2 的门有质量为 71 lb 的，大于实验 1 和实验 3 的 61 lb，故最大质量的门的测试在实验 2 中，B 选项正确。

22. 答案：F

解析：由题可看出在研究 2 中，宽度 D 不变而门的质量 W 改变；而研究 3 中，门的质量 W 恒定为 61 lb 而宽度 D 改变，F 选项符合题意。

23. 答案：D

解析：由实验 2 的图可看出，当 W 为 76 lb，S 为 50 时，F 约为 45 lb，根据图中可看出趋势：随 W 增大，F 也相应增大，故当 W 为 90 lb 时，F 应大于 45 lb，D 选项正确。

24. 答案：H

解析：由实验 1 的图可看出，当 S 小于 30 时，Fh 代表的曲线在 Fv 代表曲线的上方，即 Fh 大于 Fv；当 S 大于 30 时，Fh 小于 Fv。可判断 H 为正确选项。

25. 答案：B

解析：根据图中可看出趋势：W 或 D 的增大均会导致 F 也相应增大，而 S 增大会使 F 减小，综合两种趋势可判断 B 选项正确。

26. 答案：J

解析：由图 1 可看出，随着 S 的增大，Fv 始终保持不变而 Fh 不断减小。说明 Fv 不受 S 的影响，J 选项正确。

27. 答案：C

解析：由题意可知，当净作用力为 57 lb 时铰链会折断，由实验 3 的图可看出，若门质量为 61 lb 时，净作用力为 57 lb 对应的 D 为 36 in，S 约为 20 in，故 C 选项正确。

［**Passage V**］

28. 答案：J

解析：空气中含有体积分数低于1%的氩气，而氩气对题述的4个实验都不会产生任何影响，故J选项正确。

29. 答案：A

解析：硅树脂可用于连接石英管和注射器，需具有良好的耐热性（实验需加热）和低化学反应性。硅在水中的溶解度很低，否则会严重影响实验结果，可排除III，A选项正确。

30. 答案：J

解析：实验4中，Fe与空气中所有的 CO_2 反应生成固体 $FeCO_3$，所以空气中原本体积分数约占20%的 CO_2 被固定在固体中，剩余约占80%的 O_2。故在反应过程中，CO_2 的含量不断降低而 O_2 含量不断升高，J选项正确。

31. 答案：C

解析：学生3明确提出空气中氧气的体积分数约为20%，低于氮气的百分数。而其他同学的反应中氮气的含量均高于氧气，故更可能同意题述观点。C选项正确。

32. 答案：H

解析：学生3认为Fe与空气中的 O_2 发生了反应，符合条件的反应式只有H选项。

33. 答案：B

解析：反应结束后仪器中 N_2 的体积分数至少为20%的只有学生2和学生3的实验。学生1的实验中 N_2 为反应物，基本全部消耗；学生4的实验中不包含 N_2，可排除。B选项正确。

34. 答案：G

解析：只有在学生2的实验中，铁为反应限制性因素的情况，因为反应结束后还剩余体积分数约为75%的 O_2，即 O_2 显著过量。而其他同学的实验中与Fe反应的气体都基本耗尽。

［**Passage VI**］

35. 答案：C

解析：表2中Lambda-zero对应有2个上旋夸克和1个下旋夸克，而Delta-zero对应3个上旋夸克，根据题意可计算出前者的自旋数为 $1/2h \times 2 - 1/2h = 1/2h$，而后者为 $3 \times 1/2h = 3/2h$，C选项正确。

36. 答案：G

解析：根据题意，一个仅有2个自旋方向相同的电中性的中子的夸克组成应为G。H、J有3个自旋方向相同，可排除；F选项不满足电中性，可排除。G选项正确。

37. 答案：D

解析：已知质子带电量为1个单位，根据表1和表2可得质子的夸克组成为uud，计算出来带电量也为1，故与已知一致，D选项正确。

38. 答案：F

解析：题干的 Ω^- 重子组成为sss，相应的带电量为 -1，分别计算出四选项对应夸克组成的带电量，可判断出F选项正确。（$dsb = -1/3 - 1/3 - 1/3 = -1$）。

39. 答案：A

解析：原子核由质子和中子构成，其中质子带一个单位电荷而中子不带电，由表2可知两者的夸克组成分别为uud和udd，A选项正确。

40. 答案：F

解析：根据题干陈述，带正电的夸克比带负电的夸克更重，而由表1可知，带负点的d比带正电的 u 质量更大,与陈述相反,故 F 选项正确。其他两类均符合题述条件,故排除。

OG2 解析

[**Passage I**]

1. 答案:B
   题干:判断前 6 周记录的最高空气温度。
   定位:Table 2
   解析:表 2 可以看到最高温度为 21.13℃。
2. 答案:F
   题干:判断平均温度的精确度。
   定位:Table 2
   解析:表 2 可以看到温度的值保留了两位小数,所以精确到 0.01℃。
3. 答案:A
   题干:判断 intensity-temperature 在坐标轴上的示意图。
   定位:Table 1、2
   解析:从表 1 和 2 可以看到,intensity 和 temperature 都是逐渐增大的,只有 A 符合这一变化趋势。
4. 答案:H
   题干:判断平均温度的变化趋势。
   定位:Table 2
   解析:从表 2 可以看到,从第一周到第六周温度一直是单调递增的。
5. 答案:D
   题干:判断根据表 1 能否确定第一组的 efficiency of illumination 更高。
   定位:Table 1
   解析:计算 efficiency of illumination 需要提供的光照强度和被吸收的光照强度两个变量,而图 1 中只有一个变量,不足以计算比较。

[**Passage II**]

6. 答案:G
   题干:比较新车和旧车释放的 CO 含量。
   定位:Table 1
   解析:从表 1 中可以看到,1978 Model X 和 Y 均比 1996 Model X 和 Y 释放的 CO 要多。
7. 答案:D
   题干:寻找可以判断 CO_2 是否会影响 CO 检测的方法。
   定位:无
   解析:检测已知 CO 含量的 CO_2 和 CO 混合气体,如果 CO 的检测结果与已知含量不同,则说明 CO_2 会影响 CO 的检测。
8. 答案:F
   题干:判断哪个城市在一月份的 CO 排量最大。
   定位:Table 1、2

解析：比较表 1 和表 2 的数值可以看到，-9℃时 CO 的排量要普遍高于 20℃的排量，说明温度越低，CO 排量越大，所以答案为一月份温度最低的 Minneapolis。

9. 答案：C
题干：判断实验 1 中改变的变量。
定位：Table 1
解析：从表 1 可以看到，实验 1 检测了 4 个不同年份或者不同型号的汽车的 CO 排量，所以变量之一为汽车生产的年份。

10. 答案：G
题干：判断 CO 排量最大的时间段。
定位：Table 1、2
解析：表 1 和表 2 中均可看出，CO 排量最大的时间段均在 5 min 左右。

11. 答案：C
题干：判断当气体中混入 CO-free 空气后对实验结果产生的影响。
定位：无
解析：如果气体中混入了不含 CO 的空气，将会对 CO 产生稀释作用，计算出的 CO 占比将减小。

[**Passage III**]

12. 答案：H
题干：判断 image size 为 30 mm 时的 M 值。
定位：Table 2
解析：从表 2 中可以看到，根据第一行数据可以求出 object size 为 0.01 mm，由此求得 M 为 300。

13. 答案：D
题干：判断哪个选项的 image size 最大。
定位：Table 2
解析：结合表 2 中 M 的数值和公式可以分别计算每个选项的 image size，求得 D 选项最大。

14. 答案：G
题干：判断在观察切片 3 时多少镜片可以观测到两个分离的线。
定位：Table 1
解析：从表 1 可以看到，3 号和 4 号镜片可以看到分离的两条线。

15. 答案：B
题干：判断计算 2 号镜片 R 的公式。
定位：Table 3
解析：从表 3 可以得到 2 号镜片对应的 NA 值，将波长和 NA 值带入 R 的公式可得到 B 选项。

16. 答案：F
题干：判断 R 为 1 830 nm 镜片的 NA 值。
定位：Table 3
解析：将 R = 1 830，波长 = 550 带入公式可得 NA = 0.15。

17. 答案：A
题干：判断 Activity 1 和 Activity 2 的区别。
定位：Table 1、2

解析：比较表 1 和 2 可以看到，Activity 1 用了 4 个不同的切片，而 Activity 2 观察的是同一个切片。

[**Passage IV**]

18. 答案：J

    题干：判断不同温度下 1 平方米 black body 每秒释放的能量。

    定位：Figure

    解析：曲线与横坐标围成的面积即为释放的总能量，曲线最高的围成的面积最大。

19. 答案：A

    题干：判断在 300 K 时波长为 30×10^{-6} m 的光线亮度。

    定位：Figure

    解析：从图中最下面的曲线可以看到，在 30×10^{-6} m 波长处亮度值要低于 5×10^{6}。

20. 答案：J

    题干：判断星体释放的辐射对应的曲线。

    定位：Figure

    解析：从图中可以看到曲线分布的规律是温度越高峰值越高，并且所有的曲线都是左偏的，符合此规律的只有 J。

21. 答案：C

    题干：判断曲线最大值为 75×10^{6}时对应的温度。

    定位：Figure

    解析：从图中可以看到，75×10^{6}介于 500 K 和 400 K 对应的曲线最大值之间，所以对应的温度应该介于 400 K 和 500 K 之间。

22. 答案：H

    题干：判断当辐射频率提高时，辐射的亮度如何变化。

    定位：Table 1

    解析：题目中提到频率越高波长越低，从图中看到，波长降低时，亮度先增大后减小。

[**Passage V**]

23. 答案：C

    题干：判断可以表示 20℃下蒸气压(vapor pressure)的柱状图。

    定位：Table 1

    解析：根据表 1 中数据可以判断。

24. 答案：G

    题干：判断实验 1 实验前后的汞柱形态。

    定位：Figure 1、Table 1

    解析：在反应之前汞柱两端的气压相同，两边的液面等高，在反应后，由于产生了 vapor pressure，所以会如图 1 中所示产生左低右高的高度差。

25. 答案：D

    题干：判断沸点是否和液体粒子的质量成正比。

    定位：Table 2

    解析：从表中可以看到乙酸乙酯(ethylacetate)的粒子质量最高，但从图 2 中可以看到其对应的沸点并不是最高，观察其他的液体也可以发现沸点和粒子质量并没有必然的关系。

26. 答案：G

题干：判断沸点和外部压力(external pressure)的关系。

定位：Table 2

解析：从图 2 中可以看到，当外部压力升高时，沸点也升高。

27. 答案：B

题干：判断实验 2 中用到的器材示意图。

定位：实验 2

解析：从实验 2 的描述来看，实验器材为插有温度计并油浴的试管，B 最符合。

28. 答案：J

题干：判断在连接压力计前等待 5 分钟的目的。

定位：Experiment 1

解析：等待 5 分钟是为了让锥形瓶中的气体温度调整到水浴的温度，从而使 hexane 被加入的环境温度达到水浴设定的温度。

[**Passage VI**]

29. 答案：D

题干：判断低能量蛋白质的形状特点。

定位：Introduction

解析：介绍部分提到 random coil 通常是高能量不稳定的蛋白质，排除 A；所有蛋白质都有初级结构，排除 B；只有高能量蛋白质会 denature，排除 C；低能量蛋白质是稳定的，可以保持形状不变，选 D。

30. 答案：F

题干：判断在 denature 过程中蛋白质保持不变的结构。

定位：Introduction

解析：介绍中说初级结构是氨基酸的排列结构，denature 只是折叠结构发生改变，不会影响到氨基酸的排列，所以初级结构保持不变。

31. 答案：C

题干：判断两位科学家观点的不同之处。

定位：Scientist 2

解析：科学家 1 认为 active shape 只与初级结构有关，科学家 2 认为除了初级结构还与 process of synthesis 有关。

32. 答案：F

题干：判断球的排列顺序对应蛋白质的第几层结构。

定位：Introduction

解析：球的排列顺序对应氨基酸的排列顺数，也即蛋白质的初级结构。

33. 答案：A

题干：判断当所有蛋白质都能重新折叠成为最低能量形态时，哪个科学家的观点正确。

定位：Scientist 1

解析：科学家 1 认为蛋白质的 active shape 与最低能量形态相同，所以当所有蛋白质都能保持最低能量形态时，他们即能保持 active shape。

34. 答案：J

题干：根据科学家 2 的观点判断不同形态蛋白质能量对应的柱状图。

定位：Scientist 2

解析：科学家 2 认为 active shape 含有的能量要高于最低能量形态，同时 random coil 是高能量形态，在三者中能量最高。

35. 答案：B

题干：判断哪个观点与科学家 2 的观点相悖。

定位：Scientist 2

解析：科学家 2 认为在蛋白质的合成过程中，通过 hydrogen bonding 建立了 local structure，从而产生了与最低能量不同的形态，如果在环境中存在足够的能量能够抵抗这些 local energy，则会将蛋白质带到最低能量形态。

[**Passage VII**]

36. 答案：J

题干：判断 4.9 km 深处的海底覆盖物质。

定位：Figure 2、3

解析：从图 2 可以看到随着深度的增加，$CaCO_3$ 含量减少，红泥含量增加，在图 3 可以看到 4.3 km深的太平洋海底中红泥的覆盖面积要高于 $CaCO_3$，说明比太平洋更深的北冰洋的海底也是红泥覆盖面积更高。

37. 答案：B

题干：判断厚壳生物的分布位置。

定位：Figure 2

解析：从图 2 中可以看到，在较浅的地方海洋生物的壳也较薄，在较深的地方海洋生物的壳也较厚。

38. 答案：H

题干：判断在浅海处 $CaCO_3$ 沉淀多的原因。

定位：Figure 1

解析：图 1 可以看到在浅海处的海水对于 $CaCO_3$ 是 super saturated。

39. 答案：C

题干：判断在哪个深度以上海水对于 $CaCO_3$ 是 super saturated。

定位：Figure 1

解析：图 1 可以看到曲线与 saturated 对应的虚线相交于 4 km 深处。

40. 答案：J

题干：判断 $CaCO_3$ 的溶解率在哪个深度范围内增长最大。

定位：Figure 1

解析：图 1 的横坐标为溶解率，纵坐标为深度，所以应该取曲线最为平缓的一段为溶解度增长最快的一段。

OG3 解析

[**Passage I**]

1. 答案：D

题干：比较两个初始速度对应的 R 值大小。

定位：Table 1

解析：表 1 可以看到两个初始速度对应的 R 值分别为 22 和 88，后者是前者的 4 倍。

2. 答案：F

题干：判断方法一中计算 D 的公式。

定位：Table 1

解析：表 1 可以看到 D 的值为 R 和 B 的和。

3. 答案：B

题干：判断两个方法得出的 D 值相同时对应的初始速度。

定位：Figure 1

解析：由图 1 中两曲线交点对应的横坐标可确定。

4. 答案：H

题干：判断初始速度为 60 mi/hr 时根据方法 2 计算的 D 值。

定位：Table 1

解析：从表 1 可以看到，初始速度为 60 mi/hr 时对应的 D 为 176 m。

5. 答案：D

题干：判断初始速度为 90 mi/hr 时对应的 D 值。

定位：Table 1、Figure 1

解析：结合图 1 和表 1，D 值与初始速度正相关，从图中可以看出当初始速度为 90 时对应的 D 值应大于 250 ft。

[**Passage II**]

6. 答案：J

题干：判断哪个样本中每毫升可能含有的水分最多。

定位：Table 1、2

解析：从表 1 和 2 中可以看到，D 同学下午 8 点的样本中 specific gravity 最小，同时悬浮固体的质量也最小，说明含有的水分最多。

7. 答案：D

题干：判断尿液量与颜色深度是否正相关。

定位：Table 1、2

解析：在两个表格中可以看到，尿液量最多的样本对应的颜色指数最低，说明颜色最浅。

8. 答案：F

题干：判断 suspended solids 和 specific gravity 的变化关系。

定位：Table 1、2

解析：比较表 1 和表 2 的数值可以看到，在 suspended solids 增加时，specific gravity 的数值也增大。

9. 答案：A

题干：判断因为流感而失水的学生。

定位：Table 1、2

解析：题目中提到学生因为流感而通过呕吐等途径失水，说明其尿液量要低于其他的样本，即为表 1、2 中尿液量最少的 A。

10. 答案：H

题干：判断哪个样本 1 mL 的质量最大。

定位：Table 1、2

解析：质量为 specific gravity×1 mL，即选择样本对应的 specific gravity 最大的样本。

[**Passage III**]

11. 答案：C

题干：判断当盐溶液的沸点为 104℃时 NaCl 的摩尔数。

定位：Table 2

解析：从表 2 可以看到，0.1 mole 的 NaCl 能降沸点提升 1℃。

12. 答案：J

题干：判断实验 2 中没有被直接控制的变量。

定位：Table 2

解析：溶液的沸点是实验中的因变量，不是直接控制的变量。

13. 答案：A

题干：判断沸点与溶液中加入的粒子摩尔数的关系。

定位：Table 2

解析：根据表 2，NaCl 的摩尔数越大，溶液的沸点越高。

14. 答案：J

题干：比较 0.2 mole NaCl 对凝固点和沸点的改变大小。

定位：Table 1、2

解析：根据表 1，溶液的凝固点下降 6.9℃，根据表 2，溶液的沸点上升 2℃。

15. 答案：B

题干：判断当溶液中粒子数目增多时凝固点的变化。

定位：Table 1

解析：从表 1 可以得到当粒子数增多时凝固点单调递减。

16. 答案：H

题干：判断 0.1 mole 的 $CaCl_2$ 对溶液凝固点的改变值。

定位：Table 1

解析：0.1 mole 的 $CaCl_2$ 可以产生 0.3 mole 的粒子，相当于 0.15 mole 的 NaCl，根据图 1，对凝固点的改变应该介于 0.1 mole 的 NaCl 和 0.2 mole 的 NaCl 之间。

[**Passage IV**]

17. 答案：C

题干：判断哪两个月份的平均气温最相近。

定位：Figure 1

解析：通过图 1 可判断。

18. 答案：G

题干：判断 $\delta^{18}O$ 与平均气温的变化规律。

定位：Figure 1

解析：从图 1 可以看到，$\delta^{18}O$ 与平均温度对应的曲线接近平行，变化趋势相同。

19. 答案：B

题干：判断选择南极和北极的原因。

定位：Figure 1、2、3

解析：实验中选取了多处的冰川来探测 $\delta^{18}O$,B 选项符合这一点。

20. 答案：J

题干：判断北极 150 m 到 200 m 处冰川形成时期的气候。

定位：Figure 2

解析：从图 2 中可以看到 150 m 到 200 m 处的冰川对应的 $\delta^{18}O$ 要大于 0 m 处的 $\delta^{18}O$,所以当时冰川形成的气候要比表面冰川形成的时期(即为目前的时期)的气候要温暖。

21. 答案：A

题干：判断 100 000 年的冰川积累在两处对应的深度不同的原因。

定位：Figure 2、3

解析：经过 100 000 年,北极的冰川积累了 500 m,而南极积累了 300 米,说明北极的冰川积累速度要比南极快。

22. 答案：G

题干：判断当 $\delta^{18}O$ 为零时,样本 $^{18}O/^{16}O$ 的值。

定位：Formula

解析：根据公式,当 $\delta^{18}O$ 的值为零时,分子为零,即样本的 $^{18}O/^{16}O$ 值与标准值相同。

[**Passage V**]

23. 答案：B

题干：判断科学家 1 提及紫外线的原因。

定位：Scientist 1 - L8

解析：大量的紫外线辐射会对生物的生存造成威胁。

24. 答案：F

题干：判断 SO_4-containing aearosols 能通过反射太阳辐射降低大气温度的现象会削弱哪个科学家的观点。

定位：Scientist 1 - L3

解析：科学家 1 认为火山爆发后增加了空气中的 SO_4-containing aearosols 和二氧化碳,但他只提到了二氧化碳会导致温室效应,提升大气温度,没有考虑 SO_4-containing aearosols 对大气温度的降低作用。

25. 答案：C

题干：判断科学家 2 认为的 vertical circulation 的推动因素。

定位：Scientist 2 - L4

解析：科学家 2 认为当今推动 vertical circulation 的主要是 continental icesheet。

26. 答案：G

题干：判断 oxygen-poor 的海水出现在何时。

定位：Scientist 2 - L6

解析：科学家 2 认为在没有 verticalcir culation 时的海水是 stagnant 并且 oxygen-poor 的。

27. 答案：D

题干：判断科学家 1 描述的火山爆发中产生的火山石的年龄。

定位：L2

解析：科学家 1 认为火山爆发发生在 250 million 年前海洋生物灭绝之前,所以火山石至少有 250 million 的年龄。

28. 答案：G

题干：判断大量的 SO_4-containing aearosols 会使选项中哪个变量下降。

定位：Scientist 1

解析：科学家 1 认为 SO_4-containing aearosols 的大量出现会导致酸雨的爆发，所以会使雨水的 pH 值降低。

29. 答案：C

题干：判断 inorganic carbonates 的存在支持哪个科学家的观点。

定位：Scientist 1、2

解析：科学家 1 认为火山爆发释放了大量的 CO_2 到空气中，并进一步升高了海水表面溶解的 CO_2 的含量；科学家 2 提到光合生物将 CO_2 带到了海水中并下沉到水底，vertical circulation 将深层富含了丰富的 CO_2 的海水带到了海面，这与 inorganic carbonates 的形成在海水表面条件相同。

[**Passage VI**]

30. 答案：H

题干：判断水分解为氧气和氢气的化学方程式。

定位：Formular 1

解析：水分解的方程式与合成的方程式方向相反。

31. 答案：A

题干：判断反应结束 syringe plunger 解锁之前容器内的气压。

定位：Figure 1

解析：实验结束之后，容器的容积不变，但由于气体参与了反应，导致容器内的压强减小。

32. 答案：J

题干：判断反应后剩余氧气的体积。

定位：Table 1

解析：由反应方程式可知参与反应的氢气量是氧气的两倍，所以反应中氧气只有一半参与反应，氢气完全反应。

33. 答案：D

题干：判断哪个关于实验 1 中化学反应的假设是在最终测量之前做出的。

定位：Experiment 1

解析：通过参与反应的氢气或氧气量来计算剩余的气体组成是建立在反应完全的假设之上的，如果没有完全反应，则不能判断有多少氢气和氧气参与反应，也就不能计算反应剩余气体的组成。

34. 答案：G 、

题干：判断反应完成后剩余氢气的体积。

定位：Table 1

解析：参与反应的氢气量是氮气量的 3 倍，所以当 10 mL 氮气发生反应时，参与反应的氢气量为 30 mL，剩余 10 mL。

35. 答案：A

题干：判断哪个错误不会对实验结果造成影响。

定位：Scientist 2

解析：如果 CuO 中混杂了参与反应的杂质，会对参与反应的 CuO 质量测量造成误差，排除 B；如果水没有完全被 $CaCl_2$ 吸收，则会对反应生成的水的质量造成误差，排除 C；如果其氢气与

CuO 发生了其他反应，会对参与反应的 CuO 的质量测量造成误差，排除 D；氢气中混杂了不参与反应的气体不会对实验结果造成影响，选 A。

[**Passage VII**]

36. 答案：J

题干：判断在月球上当 Y_0 为 5 cm 时的下落时间。

定位：Figure 3

解析：根据图 3 曲线的走势可以判断。

37. 答案：C

题干：判断在月球上当下落时间为 2 秒时的链条长度。

定位：Figure 4

解析：从图 4 中可以看到，月球对应的曲线在 2 秒时的点对应的横坐标约为 113 cm。

38. 答案：G

题干：判断链条在下滑之前在桌面部分的长度。

定位：Figure 1

解析：链条总长度为 L，垂直部分为 Y_0，则水平部分为两者之间的差值。

39. 答案：A

题干：比较下滑时间为 0.7 秒的链条在地球和月球的长度。

定位：Figure 3

解析：图 3 可以看到下滑时间为 0.7 秒时，在地球上的长度为 12.5，在月球的长度为 47.5，差值为 35。

40. 答案：G

题干：判断链条在不同星球上的滑落时间之间的关系。

定位：Figure 3、Table 1

解析：结合表 1 和图 3 可以看到，重力加速度越大，对于给定的 Y_0，链条下滑需要的时间越短，因为 Neptune 的重力加速度介于地球和 Jupiter 之间，所以其下滑时间要大于 Jupiter，小于地球。

OG4 解析

[**Passage I**]

1. 答案：B

题干：判断两个取样点何时不适于游泳。

定位：Figure 1

解析：图 1 可以看到只有 Site 1 在第 30 天的数值超过了 400，不适于游泳。

2. 答案：F

题干：判断哪个取样点的 water flow 和 E. coli 水平更高。

定位：Figure 1、2

解析：图 1 和图 2 可以看到两个变量都是取样地 1 处的取值高。

3. 答案：B

题干：判断两个取样点的海水质量。

定位：Table 1、2

解析：将表 2 中的 BI 值对应到表 1 的范围内可以看到取样点 1 处的海水质量是 excellent，取样点 2 处的海水质量是 fair，1 处的评分更高，stone fly larvae 数量更多。

4. 答案：F

题干：判断哪个图表说明取样点 1 的海水质量低于取样点 2。

定位：Figure 1

解析：从表 1 可以看到，1 处的 E. coli 数量有两次超过 100，一次接近 100，说明了海水质量较低。

5. 答案：D

题干：判断当海水中化肥增多时，BI 如何变化。

定位：Table 1、2

解析：结合图 1 和图 2 可以看到，BI 值越大海水质量越高，所以当海水被化肥污染后，BI 值将降低。

[**Passage II**]

6. 答案：G

题干：判断哪个图像表示了 AWP2 的氢气产生量。

定位：Table 1

解析：结合表 1 的第 2 行数据即可判断。

7. 答案：B

题干：判断 AWP1 第 10 天的氢气产生量。

定位：Table 1

解析：从表 1 中可以看到，AWP1 第 10 天的数据会高于 133，从前 4 个数据来看，增长速率是逐渐下降的，所以第 10 天的数据不会高于 461。

8. 答案：F

题干：判断 AWP1 在第 6 天和第 8 天之间产生的氢气量。

定位：Table 1

解析：前 6 天产生的氢气量为 81 mL，前 8 天产生的氢气量为 133 mL，两天之间产生的氢气量为两者的差值。

9. 答案：C

题干：判断通过氢气量可用于测量什么反应速率。

定位：Formula

解析：从公式可以看到，通过测量氢气的产量，可以用于测量 Al 转化为 $Al(OH)_3$ 的速率。

10. 答案：J

题干：判断含有 EDTA 的 AWP3 在哪一天产生的氢气量与不含有 corrosion inhibitor 的 AWP3 在第 2 天产生的氧气量相同。

定位：Table 1、Figure 1

解析：不含有 corrosion inhibitor 的 AWP3 在第 2 天产生的氧气量为 121 mL，根据图 1 可以判断是对应的 EDTA 的第 10 天。

[**Passage III**]

11. 答案：B

题干：判断在实验 2 中哪个实验组中的两个天平受力相等。

定位：Figure 4

解析：从图 2 可以看到，实验 5 中的两个天平读数相等，说明均匀分配了 10 N 的力。

12. 答案：G

题干：判断天平的重量。

定位：Figure 2

解析：实验 2 可以看出，90°的读数对应的是 5 N，所以实验 1 中测得的天平重量为 5 N。

13. 答案：C

题干：判断天平 A 中的弹簧在哪个实验中能量最大。

定位：Figure 2

解析：根据图 2，天平 A 在实验 1 中受力 0 N，在实验 3 中受力 10 N，所以在实验 3 中的能量最大。

14. 答案：F

题干：判断当天平 A 倒置在天平 B 上时两者的读数。

定位：Table 1、2

解析：天平 B 受的压力来自于天平 A 的重力，即 5 N，所以天平 B 的示数应该为 5 N，排除 G、J；A 天平中弹簧受到的力也来源于自身的重力，所以 A 的示数也为 5 N。

15. 答案：C

题干：判断当施力点距离 B 越远，B 的受力如何变化。

定位：Figure 4

解析：从图 4 可以看到，施力点越远，B 的读数越小，受力越小。

16. 答案：J

题干：判断实验 2 在进行实验前将天平对数调零的目的。

定位：Figure 3

解析：在放上铅笔和平板后再将读数调零是为了将这部分读数从未调整的读数中去除，从而之后的读数就代表后来添加的物体的重量。

[**Passage IV**]

17. 答案：B

题干：判断当引擎速度增大时，EOR 如何变化。

定位：Table 2

解析：从表 2 可以看到，引擎速度与 EOR 成反比。

18. 答案：G

题干：判断当引擎速度为 2 200 时，用于检测的燃料 A 和 B 的 octane number。

定位：Table 2

解析：从表 2 可以看到，随着引擎速度的提升，两者的 octane number 单调递减，所以 2 200 对应的 octane number 应介于 2 000 和 2 500 对应的数值之间。

19. 答案：C

题干：判断表 1 中 octane number 的计算公式。

定位：Table 1

解析：根据表 1 可以看到 octane number 取决于 isooctane 在总体积中的占比与 100 的乘积。

20. 答案：H

题干：判断加入 3 ml TEL 后混合物的 octane number。

定位：Table 1、Figure 1

解析：从表 1 可以看到混合物的 octane number 为 90，根据图 1，octane number 为 100 时在加入 3 mLTEL 后提升到 125，所以 octane number 为 90 的混合物提升后不会超过 125。

21. 答案：B

题干：判断 A 和 B 哪个更适合 1 500 到 3 500 rpm 速度范围的引擎。

定位：Table 2

解析：从表 2 可以看到，A 的 octane number 要大于 EOR，说明 A 不会对引擎造成损害。

22. 答案：J

题干：判断混合物的 octane number。

定位：Table 1

解析：根据 19 题中 C 选项的公式可以计算。

[**Passage V**]

23. 答案：C

题干：判断哪个选项符合 B 的观点。

定位：B - L1

解析：科学家 B 认为短周期彗星都是由长周期彗星转变而来的。

24. 答案：H

题干：判断 KB 的位置。

定位：A - L3

解析：科学家 A 认为 KB 距离太阳 30～50 A. U.，并且相对 ecliptic plane 有小的倾角。

25. 答案：D

题干：判断短周期彗星与 ecliptic plane 的倾角的可能取值。

定位：Introduction - L11

解析：介绍中说明倾角范围在 0 到 30°之间。

26. 答案：J

题干：判断太阳系中哪个星球能够改变长周期彗星的轨道。

定位：Scientist B - L3

解析：科学家 B 认为质量大的星球更能够吸引长周期彗星从而改变其轨道，4 个选项中土星的质量最大。

27. 答案：A

题干：判断科学家 B 对哈雷彗星的判断。

定位：Scientist B - L2

解析：通过哈雷彗星的轨道周期小于 200 yr 可以判断其为短周期彗星，科学家 B 认为所有短周期彗星都曾是长周期彗星，介绍中提到长周期彗星起源于 Oort Cloud。

28. 答案：J

题干：判断 KB 中的“much largeri cybody”的直径长度。

定位：Scientist A - L6

解析：科学家 A 认为 KB 主要包含了直径介于 10～30 km 之间的 icybody，而较大的冰体还未被望远镜观测到，说明较大的冰体为大于 30 km 的。

29. 答案：D

题干：判断在星球没有发现与 Oort Cloud 相近的物质这一现象会削弱哪位科学家的观点。

定位：Scientist B

解析：两个科学家均没有提到与 spherical shell 相关的内容。

[**Passage VI**]

30. 答案：J

题干：判断 21 cm 高并且无果实的植株可能来自哪一组样本。

定位：Table 1、2、3

解析：只有在 120 g NaCl 中生长的 L3 和 L4 的高度和果实质量的均值最接近题目的植株，因此答案为两者之一。

31. 答案：C

题干：判断发生渗透作用经过的半透膜是哪一种。

定位：L3

解析：渗透作用中水分子进出细胞经过的半透膜是细胞膜。

32. 答案：G

题干：判断当营养液中 NaCl 的含量提升时，植株平均质量如何变化。

定位：Table 1、2、3

解析：比较 3 个表格可以看到当 NaCl 含量提升时，植株质量单调递减。

33. 答案：A

题干：判断实验中的自变量。

定位：Scientist 1

解析：实验中用到的都是番茄植株，排除 B；植株质量和高度是实验的因变量，排除 C、D。

34. 答案：J

题干：判断植株高度和质量的变化关系。

定位：Table 1、2、3

解析：比较表格中高度和质量的数据可以看到植株高度与质量是正相关的，所以对应的图形斜率为正。

35. 答案：D

题干：判断实验中的对照组。

定位：L9

解析：在实验的介绍部分可以看到实验者对于 L1、2、3 的基因型均做了改变，对于 L4 没有进行改变，说明 L4 是对照组。

[**Passage VII**]

36. 答案：F

题干：判断与 R 成负相关的变量。

定位：Figure 2

解析：图 2 中曲线斜率为负，说明 R 与长度成负相关。

37. 答案：C

题干：判断截面为两倍时 R 的倍数。

定位：Figure 3

解析：从图 3 可以看到，当截面为 2 cm^2 时的 R 为 50，截面为 4 cm^2 时的 R 为 100，后者与前者的 R 值之比为 2∶1。

38. 答案：H

题干：判断实验中热量传播的途径。

定位：Figure 1

解析：实验中热量的传导是从铜棒的一端传导至另一端，符合热传导关于“热量通过直接接触的物体，从温度较高部位传递到温度较低部位的过程”的定义；热对流是指热量通过流动介质传递热量的现象，热辐射是指以电磁波形式传递热量的现象，两者均与本实验无关。

39. 答案：A

题干：比较哪组铜棒的 R 值最大。

定位：Figure 3

解析：图 2 可以看到当横截面积相同时，R 与长度成反比，所以长度最短的 A 选项的 R 值最大。

40. 答案：F

题干：判断哪一组的温度会产生最大的 R 值。

定位：Table 1

解析：通过表 1 可知，温度差越大，R 值越大；F 选项的温差为 30℃，最大。

OG5 解析

[**Passage I**]

1. 答案：D

题干：判断 5 g LiCl 溶于 50 g 水中时的温度变化及原因。

定位：Figure 1

解析：图 1 可以看到温度改变值为正，说明溶于水时从外界吸收热量从而导致温度升高。

2. 答案：F

题干：判断不同浓度的 LiCl 溶液的温度改变情况。

定位：Figure 1

解析：水的含量越低则 LiCl 溶液的浓度越高，图 1 可以看到随着溶液浓度逐渐升高，温度改变值也逐渐变大。

3. 答案：C

题干：判断 25 g LiCl 溶于水时温度的变化值。

定位：Figure 1

解析：根据图 1 第二条曲线的走势可以判断。

4. 答案：G

题干：判断 5 g NH_4NO_3 溶于 100 g 水中时温度的变化值。

定位：Figure 2

解析：从图 2 可以看到，温度的改变值为负，说明溶解过程中温度下降。

5. 答案：A

题干：判断哪个选项对应的反应温度提升值最大。

定位：Figure 1、2

解析：NH_4NO_3 溶于水时温度降低，排除 C、D；根据图 2，水的含量越少，温度的提升值越大，所

以选 A。

［**Passage II**］

6. 答案：F
题干：判断 4 个模型中的 map distance 的相同之处。
定位：Figure 3
解析：在表 3 中可以看到，4 个模型中 A 和 B 之间的距离在所有模型中均相等，即他们的 map distance 相等。
7. 答案：A
题干：判断 map distance 为 70 mu 时，RF 的值。
定位：Figure 2
解析：根据图 2 可以判断所求值应该在 0.35 和 0.4 之间，选 A。
8. 答案：H
题干：判断基因 G 在模型 2 中的位置。
定位：Figure 3
解析：G 离 B 的距离小于离 D 的距离，所以应该在 B 的右边，即在 B 和 C 之间。
9. 答案：D
题干：判断第五个科学家的研究结果与哪个模型相符。
定位：Figure 3
解析：在图 3 中可以看到 A 和 C 之间的距离在 1 和 2 中相同，在 3 和 4 中相同，可以排除 A、B、C，选 D；同时也可以通过结合表 1 中 A 和 B 之间的 RF 小于 A 和 C 的 RF，说明 A 和 C 之间的距离小于 A 和 B 之间的距离，从而排除 1 和 2。
10. 答案：J
题干：判断 crossing over 在合成哪类细胞的过程中发生。
定位：L1
解析：第一行介绍说 crossingover 发生在减数分裂的第一阶段，通过减数分裂产生的细胞即为 gametes。
11. 答案：A
题干：判断哪个模型中 C 和 D 之间的距离为 64 mu。
定位：Table 1、Figure 3
解析：从表 1 可以看到，A 和 B 之间的距离为 20 mu，以此为参照可以判断当 C 和 D 之间距离为 64 mu 时，只有模型 1 中所示的距离最为合适。
12. 答案：F
题干：判断在参与 crossing over 的染色单体的基因型。
定位：Figure 1
解析：根据题干描述，参与反应的一个染色体的基因型为 RT，另一个为 rt，根据图 1，两条 cross over 后的染色单体的基因型应为 Rt 和 rT。

［**Passage III**］

13. 答案：C
题干：判断 1990 年在 fen 处 2.5 m 深的 pore water 的传导率。
定位：Figure 2

解析：根据图 2 可判断。

14. 答案：H

题干：判断 1991 年在 fen 处 2.7 m 深的 porewater 的 pH 值。

定位：Figure 2

解析：根据图 2 中虚线的走势，在 2.7 m 处的取值约在 7 附近。

15. 答案：D

题干：判断导致 bog 处两年的 water table 深度差异的原因。

定位：L4

解析：第四行提到 bog 处的主要水源是降雨，由于 1990 年干旱，所以通过降雨得到的补水较正常年份要少。

16. 答案：J

题干：比较两处的 peat layer 和 water table 的深度。

定位：Figure 2、3

解析：从两图中可以看到 fen 处的 peat layer 要低于 water table 而 bog 处的 peat layer 要高于 water table，并且 fen 处的 peat layer 要比 bog 处浅。

17. 答案：C

题干：比较两个年份中两处 0～3 米处 CH_4 含量。

定位：Figure 1

解析：从图 1 可以看出，在两处沼泽中都是 1990 年干旱时期的 CH_4 含量要高于 1991 年的正常时期。

[**Passage IV**]

18. 答案：J

题干：判断 Ra 原子核的正确表示方法。

定位：L3

解析：文中提到 A 代表 Z 与中子的和，所以 A 需要大于 Z。

19. 答案：C

题干：判断表 1 中 He 原子核中的中子数。

定位：Table 1

解析：$A = Z +$ 中子数，由 $A = 4, Z = 2$ 得中子数为 2。

20. 答案：G

题干：判断 Th 在经过 β 衰变后的产物。

定位：Figure 1

解析：从表 1 可以看到 β 衰变后 A 值不变，Z 增加 1，当 Z 为 91 是原子为 Pa。

21. 答案：B

题干：判断同位素衰变的过程。

定位：Figure 1

解析：从图 1 可以看到，原子核经过 β 衰变后 A 值不变，经过 α 衰变后 A 值和 Z 值均减小，从 Pu 到 U 需要经过 α 衰变以减小 A 值。

22. 答案：J

题干：判断 He 原子核与电子在具有相同动能时谁的速度大。

定位：无

解析：根据动能定理，动能等于物体质量与速度平方乘积的 1/2，当动能相同时，质量越小速度越大，因为电子的质量小于原子核，所以电子的速度大。

[**Passage V**]

23. 答案：B
题干：判断 M3 是那种合成物。
定位：Figure 2、3
解析：将图 3 中 M3 的两个 RT 峰值分别与图 2 中的峰值对应可得 M3 由 P1 和 P3 混合而成。
24. 答案：F
题干：判断实验 1 中哪种分子被分离的时间最长。
定位：Figure 2
解析：由图 2 知 P1 的 RT 峰值出现最晚，说明分离时间最长。
25. 答案：C
题干：将 P4、P5、M2 的 AMM 从小到大排序。
定位：Figure 2、3、Table 1
解析：由图 2 和表 1 可知 RT 越大，对应的 AMM 越小，根据三者的 RT 大小关系可以判断 AMM 由小到大排序为 M2、P4、P5。
26. 答案：G
题干：判断 P3 和 P4 哪个更容易扩散。
定位：Table 1
解析：质量越小的颗粒，颗粒大小也越小，更容易扩散；根据表 1，P3 的质量小于 P4，所以 P3 扩散更容易。
27. 答案：A
题干：判断实验 2 中哪个混合物的 AMM 最可能超过 200 000 amu。
定位：Table 1、Figure 2、3
解析：根据表 1 和图 2，只有当 RT 值比 P5 对应的 RT 值要小时，其 AMM 才有可能超过 200 000 amu，实验 2 中只有 M1 符合。
28. 答案：J
题干：判断相同质量的 P2 和 P4 中谁的分子个数多。
定位：Table 1
解析：由表 1 得 P2 的 AMM 小于 P4，所以给定质量的两种物质，P2 的分子个数比 P4 多。

[**Passage VI**]

29. 答案：A
题干：判断当氧含量由 16%升高到 35%时，火焰传播速度如何变化。
定位：Table 1
解析：由表 1 可以看出火焰传播速度是单调递增的。
30. 答案：J
题干：判断树叶在 35%氧含量中燃烧时在哪个温度范围内质量损失最快。
定位：Figure 1
解析：图 1 中虚线斜率最大的部分对应的范围为 425～475℃。
31. 答案：B

题干：判断两类含水量超过 65%的树木在 28%和 35%氧含量的环境中是否会完全燃尽。
定位：Table 1
解析：表 1 可以看到在含水量超过 61%时，树木在所有氧含量环境中都不会燃烧。

32. 答案：H
题干：判断含水量 10%的 needles 在 28%的氧含量环境中燃烧的火焰传播速度。
定位：Table 1
解析：从表 1 可得火焰传播速度跟含水量负相关，10%含水量对应的数据应介于 2%和 12%对应的数字之间。

33. 答案：B
题干：判断两种林火哪种传播速度快。
定位：Table 1
解析：表 1 可以看到在给定氧含量下 needles 对应的传播速度要快于 dowels。

34. 答案：H
题干：判断在 21%含量的氧气中燃烧的纸片在 350℃时损失的质量。
定位：Figure 1
解析：根据图 1 可以判断 350℃时燃烧后剩余的质量为 40%，所以损失了 60%。

［**Passage VII**］

35. 答案：B
题干：判断两个发射速度的射程差值。
定位：Figure 5
解析：根据图 5，两个发射速度对应的 R 的差值约为 100 ft。

36. 答案：G
题干：判断照相机记录小球位置的频率。
定位：L11
解析：照相机每隔 0.5 秒记录一次球的位置，频率即为每秒两次。

37. 答案：C
题干：判断能让球越过围墙的发射速度。
定位：Figure 4
解析：球越过围墙需要让射程长于 310 ft，从图 4 可以看到只有 100 mph、110 mph 和 120 mph 3 个速度符合条件。

38. 答案：F
题干：判断当发射速度提升时，3 秒时观测到的 H 和 R 的变化规律。
定位：Figure 4
解析：由图 4 中 3 秒处链接的直线上的点可以看到，发射速度提升时，H 和 R 都增大。

39. 答案：C
题干：比较初始速度为 120 mph 时小球在空中飞行的时间。
定位：Figure 5
解析：根据图 5，在 6 秒时小球仍没有降落，而 7 秒时的图像没有体现，说明飞行时间介于 6 秒和 7 秒之间。

40. 答案：F
题干：判断雷达脉冲从发射到返回需要的时间。

定位：Figure 3

解析：雷达脉冲走过的往返路程为 2D，速度为 c，则时间为两者相除。

PT1 解析

[**Passage I**]

1. 答案：D

   题干：判断哪个观测点的硫酸盐含量最为稳定。

   定位：Table 1

   解析：图 1 可以在第 5 个观测点硫酸盐含量在 0.65～0.68 范围内波动，极差为 0.03，是 5 个观测点中波动最小的。

2. 答案：J

   题干：判断 1993 年到 2000 年 pH 的变化情况。

   定位：Figure 2

   解析：图 2 中 nonglacial lake 对应的黑点可以反映出在 2000 年的 pH 值要显著高于 1993 年的值，而 glacial lake 对应的两个白点中的一个可以反映出在 2000 年的 pH 值与 1993 年的值差异不大，所以 glacial lake 的 pH 值相对来说较为稳定。

3. 答案：A

   题干：判断 terrestrial deposit 和 lake 中硫酸盐的含量变化。

   定位：Figure 2、Table 1

   解析：从表 1 可以看到 terrestrial deposit 的硫酸盐含量没有明显的变化趋势，而图 2 中基本所有的点都能表明 2000 年的硫酸盐含量要高于 1993 年。

4. 答案：H

   题干：判断哪个假说符合实验数据。

   定位：Figure 2

   解析：从图 2 可以看到，在 100 年间，气温稳定地上升，glacial lake 中的冰川融化到湖水中，从而使得硫酸盐物质进入到了湖水中，实验 2 中硫酸盐含量的升高支持了这一假说。

5. 答案：B

   题干：判断实验数据支持哪个结论。

   定位：Figure 1、2

   解析：实验 2 说明，当两个 glacial lake 中的硫酸盐含量增时，pH 值并没有增加，在另一方面，在温度相对较高的 non-glacial lake 中，硫酸盐含量和 pH 值都升高；选项 B 提供了关于两种湖泊差异的解释。

[**Passage II**]

6. 答案：G

   题干：判断最符合表 1 中数据的选项。

   定位：Table 1

   解析：旋转周期越大，星球旋转的速度越慢，根据表 1 可以看到，表面温度与旋转周期正相关，说明旋转速度与表面温度负相关，选 G。

7. 答案：C

题干：判断表 1 数据支持的选项。

定位：Table 1

解析：地球的平均密度是水星的 5.5 倍，(按题目编写时间来看)在 8 大星球中最大；旋转周期 24 小时，是第 5 长的。

8. 答案：H

题干：判断平均密度与水星最接近的星球。

定位：Table 1

解析：表 1 中密度的表示方法是水星的密度的倍数关系，Pluto 的平均密度是 1.0，按定义与水星密度相等。

9. 答案：A

题干：判断水星在一水星年中自转多少圈。

定位：Table 1

解析：在表 1 中可以看到水星自转需要 59 地球日，所以在 88 地球日，水星自转 1.3 次。

10. 答案：F

题干：判断密度和直径的关系。

定位：Figure

解析：在图中，Mars、Venus 和 Earth 接近在一条斜率为正的直线上，说明密度和直径呈正相关关系。

11. 答案：D

题干：判断 Mercury 上的最高温的平均值比 Venus 要高的原因。

定位：Table 1

解析：从表 1 可以看到，Mercury 的 orbital eccentricity 远高于 Venus，相应地，Mercury 在接近太阳时表面温度会大幅提升，在远离太阳后大幅下降。

[**Passage III**]

12. 答案：G

题干：判断森林中营养物质的流失情况。

定位：Table 1

解析：表 1 中正的 percent change 代表 net gain，负的 percent change 代表 net loss，除了 ammonium 和 nitrate 之外其他的营养成分的 percent change 都是负的。

13. 答案：D

题干：判断最不符合实验数据的关于 clear-cutting 的作用的假说。

定位：Table 2

解析：表 2 体现了在每一年被砍伐的区域的 organic 和 inorganic 物质的流失都普遍高于未受影响的区域。

14. 答案：F

题干：判断表 2 的数据最支持哪个选项的观点。

定位：Table 2

解析：表 2 体现了对于 basin 和 filter，未受影响区域的物质流失从第 1 年到第 2 年间显著地提升，然后从第 2 年到第 3 年间又显著下降；在未受影响区域，run off 显著提升的合理解释是降雨的增多。

15. 答案：C

题干：判断 sodium 的流失量。
定位：Table 2
解析：表 2 注释中提到 fine material 是通过 net 来捕获，因此，sodium 是 net-caught material，表 2 中体现在 3 年中 net-caught material 的流失量变化很小。

16. 答案：J
题干：比较两区域流失值的未来变化趋势。
定位：Figure 2、3
解析：表 2 并未体现未受影响区域数值的明显变化，因此在长期推测没有显著的改变是合理的；尽管表 2 显示在砍伐区的营养流失是逐渐增多的，但并没有证据证明这一趋势会一直持续下去，相反，生态学家在此区域喷洒除草剂来阻止生命物质的生长可以证明生命物质之后会重新出现，因此会使营养流失值逐渐减小。

17. 答案：B
题干：判断整个森林的流失值。
定位：Table 1
解析：如果这 6 个实验区域每公顷降雨量都少于森林整体，则营养的流入会高于表中的数据，在此情况下，除非其他区域的平均营养流出也高于表中数据，净流失会比表中数据要小（净流入要更高）。

[**Passage IV**]

18. 答案：H
题干：判断削弱 anti-cancer 理论的事实。
定位：anti-cancer theory-L3
解析：anti-cancer theory 是建立在 imprinted gene 是为了组织有致癌性的胎盘产生的理论基础上的，如果在没有胎盘的植物中也发现了此类基因，则此观点会被削弱。

19. 答案：A
题干：判断关于 protein control theory 的论断。
定位：protein control theory-L2
解析：根据该理论第 1 句话即可判断 A 正确。

20. 答案：J
题干：判断关于 competing parental interest theory 的论断。
定位：competing parental interest theory-L13
解析：该理论认为雌性和雄性个体都希望将最大化基因传递给大量健康后代的可能性，与 J 相符。

21. 答案：A
题干：判断 3 个理论的共同点。
定位：无
解析：3 种理论都与繁殖相关。第 1 个理论考虑了繁殖过程中基因的传递，第 2 个理论考虑了与反之相关的胎盘的生长，第 3 个理论考虑了胚胎的生长。

22. 答案：H
题干：判断能被 competing parental interest theory 解释的理论。
定位：competing parental interest theory
解析：competing parental interest theory 只有在 non-monogamous 物种参与时才说得通，H 提

及 imprinting 在 monogamous 物种间不是必要的,符合此理论。

23. 答案:D
题干:判断 hydatidi formmole 被哪个观点支持。
定位:competing parental interest theory
解析:competing parental interest theory 里提到父代的基因型与过度生长有关,anti-cancer 理论提到 imprinting 是为了控制胎盘的过度生长,protein control 理论中提到当 disorder 出现时母亲的基因型是缺失的,这 3 种理论都能解释题目描述的现象。

24. 答案:G
题干:判断 competing parental interest theory 所期望的小鼠实验的结果。
定位:competing parental interest theory
解析:实验结果会与此理论相符,因为 A 的雌性基因不会 imprint 给体型小的后代,而 B 的雄性基因会 imprint 给体型大的后代,两者结合会繁殖出非常大的后代。

[**Passage V**]

25. 答案:B
题干:判断 3 个实验中的被控制的变量。
定位:Experiment 1、2、3
解析:在 3 个实验中,input amplitude 都被控制在了 2.0 V。

26. 答案:F
题干:判断使用第 3 种 filter 时的 output amplitude。
定位:Experiment 2
解析:只有实验 2 反应了第 3 种 filter 在 1 m Hinductance 下的效果,从图中可以看到,100 kHz 的输入频率大约对应 1.9 V 的 output amplitude。

27. 答案:C
题干:判断实验 2 和 3 选择第 3 种 filter 的原因。
定位:filter 示意图
解析:在示意图中可以看到只有第 3 种 filter 包含一个 inductor。实验 2 的设计中 inductance 是变量,同时,实验 3 的设计中 inductance 是控制变量,所以应该选用包含 inductor 的 filter。

28. 答案:G
题干:判断增加 inductance 水平的效果。
定位:Experiment 2
解析:根据实验 2 的表格,inductance 水平越高,frequency response curve 的峰值出现得越早,这表示在低频率处,sine wave 更可能穿过 filter,从而产生更高的 output amplitude。

29. 答案:D
题干:判断 capacitance 和 frequency response 曲线峰值的关系。
定位:Experiment 3
解析:只有在实验 3 中 capacitance 是变量,从图中可以看出,当 capacitance 增大时,曲线的峰值变窄。

30. 答案:F
题干:判断低 capacitance 水平和高 inductance 水平的作用。
定位:Experiment 2、3
解析:实验 2 中显示高 inductance 水平会通过频率频谱的小部分来产生最宽的峰值,相反,实

验3显示低capacitance水平会通过频率频谱的大部分来产生最宽的峰值，因此，结合两者的特点来获得频谱的高接收水平是合理的。

［**Passage VI**］

31. 答案：C

题干：判断子代2的亲代基因型。

定位：Figure 1

解析：即求图1中子代1的基因型，女性和男性都知包含一个疾病基因D。

32. 答案：F

题干：判断基因数量与疾病的关系。

定位：Figure 1

解析：图中唯一可能感染这个疾病的是子代3中的女性DD，她的父母都是健康人，即携带一个疾病基因。

33. 答案：D

题干：判断子代3中母亲将疾病传递给孩子的概率。

定位：Figure 2

解析：图2并没有提供孩子父亲的信息，如果父亲没有携带疾病基因，则他们将疾病传递给孩子的概率为0，否则此可能性会大于0。

34. 答案：G

题干：判断子代1的后代中有多少人有疾病。

定位：Figure 2

解析：图2显示了子代1的9个子代和孙代，在这些后代中，有4人有疾病基因D。

35. 答案：D

题干：判断疾病X是显性遗传还是隐形遗传。

定位：无

解析：在显性遗传的疾病中，如果一个人有至少一个疾病基因，这个人就一定会患病。因为Pamela的父母中没有人有基因X，因此这个疾病一定不是显性遗传的。

［**Passage VII**］

36. 答案：H

题干：判断水深、温度与盐度的关系。

定位：Table-Chemist

解析：除了夏天以外的季节，5米处的盐度都低于20米处，即使在夏天，盐度也在各个水平上都相等，并不矛盾。

37. 答案：D

题干：判断几个物种繁殖程度与盐度和水温的关系。

定位：Table-Biologist

解析：鲑鱼捕获量的季节性增减并不与水温的增减一致，从夏天入秋，鲑鱼捕获量大幅上升时，盐度水平大幅下降，说明在盐度水平低时鲑鱼繁衍旺盛。

38. 答案：G

题干：判断蛋白质缺失相关的疾病的成因。

定位：Table-Doctor

解析：G 表明当地人口并不全部依靠鲑鱼作为蛋白质来源，但是蛋白质缺失疾病的季节性变化很大，因此通过鲑鱼的丰富度来判断蛋白质缺失疾病是不合理的。

39. 答案：A

题干：比较 locusta 和 gammarus 对盐度改变的敏感程度。

定位：Table-Biologist

解析：盐度的季节性改变与 gammarus locusta 的样本数量有直接的关系。另外，gammarus locusta 的样本数量的改变受盐度的影响程度要远高于 gammarus duebent 的样本数量受盐度的影响程度。例如，从冬天到春天，locusta 数量改变 98%，而 duebent 数量只改变 50%，因此，locusta 对于盐度的改变更敏感。

40. 答案：G

题干：判断医生降低蛋白质缺乏相关的疾病人数的途径。

定位：Table-Doctor

解析：这些疾病发病主要集中在冬季和春季，并且考虑到秋天鲑鱼和熊的高捕获数量，说明村民在捕获后不久就吃了鲑鱼和熊的肉。通过将鱼肉和熊肉保存到冬季和春季，村民可以避免感染这类疾病。

PT2 解析

[**Passage I**]

1. 答案：B

题干：判断 25℃电流为 100 mA 时电压的值。

定位：Table 1

解析：表 1 中只有 resisitor A 有符合条件的数据，对应的电压为 1 V。

2. 答案：H

题干：判断在电压为 4.5 V，温度为 23℃时，resistor C 的电流值。

定位：Table 1

解析：根据表 1 数据可得。

3. 答案：A

题干：判断哪个 resistor 是电阻仪而不是电热仪。

定位：Table 1

解析：对于 A，1 V 的电压改变率可引起电流等程度的变化率，也就是电压和电流之间有线性关系，说明 A 是电阻仪。并且通过 A 可以测得 23℃的电流与 25℃的电流相等，说明 A 不是电热仪。

4. 答案：H

题干：判断对于 C，为了在温度为 25℃时产生 126 mA 的电流需要多大的电压。

定位：Table 1

解析：从图 1 最右面的一列可以看到，对于电压 0.05 V 的增加，电流增加 9 mA，呈现线性关系。因此，可以计算 126 mA 时的电压为 7 V。

5. 答案：D

题干：根据浸没 B 时水温上升的现象判断 B 的类型。

定位：无

解析：因为 B 对于不同的水温不敏感，所以 B 不能视为是电热仪。

[**Passage II**]

6. 答案：H
题干：判断哪个土壤样本中包含最多比例的 silt。
定位：Table 1
解析：从表 1 第 2 列数据可以判断。
7. 答案：A
题干：判断 loam 最可能包含的选项。
定位：Figure
解析：从图中可以看到被视为 loam 的区域都靠近 100% sand 对应的角，而不是 clay 和 silt。
8. 答案：G
题干：判断不同土壤中各类物质的含量。
定位：Table 1
解析：考虑到土壤样本的质量相等，只需考虑物质含量的百分比大小即可。对于 G，森林土壤的 clay 含量为 50% + 20% + 15% = 85%，草地土壤的含量为 33% + 6% + 11% = 50%，所以 G 不正确。
9. 答案：B
题干：判断土壤颗粒按照大小分组的原因。
定位：Table 1
解析：表 1 列出了不同的颗粒所占的比例，所以按照大小分组的目的是将不同的颗粒按照大小区分开来以比较在土壤中的含量。
10. 答案：J
题干：判断第 7 组样本的与哪组样本质感更接近。
定位：Table 1
解析：森林第 2 样本组和草地第 1 样本组都包含了比 sand 和 clay 更多的 silt。
11. 答案：C
题干：判断测量两个泥土样本的 perme ability 时需要采取的措施。
定位：无
解析：只要每个杯子中的颗粒比例已知并且不同，通过 perme ability 来比较 sand、silt 和 clay 是可行的。

[**Passage III**]

12. 答案：G
题干：判断实验 1 中最高效的机翼。
定位：Table 1
解析：从表 1 中的第 4 列数据可以得出答案：从 lift-to-dragratio 来看，机翼 2 的效率是 40 ∶ 1，所有机翼中最高。
13. 答案：B
题干：判断哪个机翼最适合乘用飞机。
定位：Table 1、2
解析：最适合的机翼应该是从 lift-to-dragratio 和燃油消耗量两部分考虑的最高效的机翼，表 1

和2都表明机翼 2 是最高效的。

14. 答案：J

题干：判断结冰对机翼的影响。

定位：Table 2

解析：在机翼上表面结冰会增加 lift，因为上表面曲线越高，机翼上下侧的空气流速的差异越大；同时也会增加 drag，这可以从表 1 第 3 列数据中看到，上表面高的机翼同时也会有更大的 drag。如果机翼下表面结冰，会降低下册空气流速并且降低 lift。因此，3 种影响均有可能发生。

15. 答案：D

题干：判断哪两组有一致的实验数据。

定位：Table 1、2、3

解析：在 D 中的两个实验中，实验条件是相同的，都是用的同一个机翼，并且风速都是 400 mph。

16. 答案：H

题干：比较 lift 和 drag 与风速的关系。

定位：Table 3

解析：efficiency 和 lift-to-drag 是相同的。表 3 体现了当风速增大时，efficiency 降低，所以我们可以判断 drag 的增大程度应该高于 lift。

17. 答案：A

题干：判断风速与机翼曲线的关系。

定位：Table 3

解析：在表 3 中，机翼 2 在低速时比机翼 1 要更高效，但是当速度达到 500 mph 时，机翼 1 要比机翼 2 表现好，因此，在高速时更扁平的机翼是更有利的。

[**Passage IV**]

18. 答案：H

题干：判断图 1 表示的意思。

定位：Figure 1

解析：当电子从一个能量状态转移到另一个状态时，原子通过光释放出两个状态能量差大小的能量，能量差通过光谱线的形式表现，能量的释放通过箭头表现。

19. 答案：B

题干：判断图 1 中哪个原子释放的能量最少。

定位：Figure 1

解析：在图 1 中，平行的直线表示了不同的能量状态，箭头长度表示释放的能量大小，可以看到原子 2 释放的能量是最少的。

20. 答案：F

题干：判断与原子 1 相似的原子的性质。

定位：Figure 1

解析：箭头的长度代表了每次状态转移的能量释放量，图 1 中的原子 1 的上面 3 条箭头长度相似，下面 2 条箭头长度相似，与 F 的描述一致。

21. 答案：D

题干：判断与表 1 观测数据最相近的原子。

定位：Figure 1、Table 1

解析：表 1 中列出的数据表示了光线能量的测度，图 1 中的箭头长度也表现了光能的大小，所以当表 1 数据的差值与图 1 中箭头长度的差值一致是，即代表同一种原子。在表 1 中，868 440 和 880 570 都是较大的数字并且相比其他两个频率两者非常接近，这与图 1 中原子 3 的两个非常长并且长度相近的箭头是相似的，因此应该选择原子 3。

22. 答案：G

题干：判断原子 forbidden transition 的数目。

定位：Figure 1

解析：图 1 中没有箭头链接的一组平行直线代表了一个 frobidden transition，原子 1 有 2 个，原子 2 有 1 个，原子 3 没有。

[**Passage V**]

23. 答案：D

题干：判断关于表 1 中数据的判断正误。

定位：Table 1

解析：iryantheragrandis 的年龄是 800 年，比 hymenolobium 的一个要老，比另一个要年轻。

24. 答案：G

题干：判断检验两株距离相近的树的树龄的方法。

定位：Table 1

解析：文中表明了通过年轮数量不是判断树龄的可靠方法，表 1 也表现了比较直径来判断树龄也是不可靠的，没有给出关于判断树高的方法，通过 C^{14} 来判断树龄是这其中最可靠的方法。

25. 答案：A

题干：判断表 1 中不同指标之间的关系。

定位：Table 1

解析：在表 1 的 12 棵树中，最老的树 3 和 11 的生长速度最小，然而最年轻的树 1、8、9 和 12 的生长速度最大，这说明了树龄越大，生长速度越慢。

26. 答案：G

题干：判断比较直径判断树龄可用于哪两种树种。

定位：Table 1

解析：树 11 比树 12 的树龄和直径都要大，所以科学家推断通过比较树的直径来比较 dipteryxodorata 和 sclerolobium 两种树的树龄是可行的。

27. 答案：C

题干：判断在灾难中幸存的树种数目。

定位：Figure、Table 1

解析：最近的两次灾难发生在 400 年前和 700 年前，12 棵树中的 4 棵要老于 700 年，因此他们至少在那两个灾难中幸存了。

28. 答案：H

题干：判断可以削弱 dipteryx odorata 比 carinian amicrantha 更容易在灾难中幸存的依据。

定位：Experiment 2

解析：一个样本对于判断其他 dipteryxodorata 的寿命来说样本量太少了，如果其他的 dipteryxodorata 寿命都很短，则 dipteryxodorata 很有可能没有 carinianamicrantha 那么易于幸存。

[**Passage VI**]

29. 答案：C

题干：判断天文学家 1 和 3 共同的观点。

定位：Astronomer 1、3

解析：两者都认为彗星是通过 aggregation 形成的；然而天文学家 3 认为这一过程发生在刚形成的彗星经过 cold dark space 当他们进入星云的时候被太阳的引力捕捉到。天文学家 1 认为，彗星形成过程中受到的压迫力与其他太阳系中的星球受到的力一样，这表明了彗星的形成不可能发生在星云外。

30. 答案：F

题干：判断天文学家 2 和其他两人观点的分歧之处。

定位：Astronomer 1、2、3

解析：天文学家 2 认为在太阳系的形成时期，太阳系的内部形成早且快，同时没有合并的其他物质会 blown out。据此可推断这个过程是从中心质量(现在是太阳)扩张的过程。在另一方面，天文学家 1 和 3 认为太阳系是由星云的瓦解形成的。

31. 答案：B

题干：判断符合天文学家 2 的观点。

定位：Astronomer 2

解析：选项 B 表达的是天文学家 3 的观点，并且与天文学家 2 关于形成 Oort Cloud 的彗星最初质量与太阳和行星的质量相同的观点是相反的。

32. 答案：J

题干：判断天文学家 1 同意的观点。

定位：Astronomer 1

解析：根据天文学家 1 的观点，有证据表明太阳系外围的巨形外部星体已经被干扰，这支持了关于彗星碰撞然后成为星体一部分的理论。然而，天文学家 1 并没有提到任何关于靠近太阳的小型星体之间的干扰。另外，从常识来看移动的物体更容易撞到一个大的物体而不是小的。

33. 答案：C

题干：判断天文学家 3 赞同的选项。

定位：Astronomer 3

解析：尽管是天文学家 1 提出在太阳系形成过程中一些彗星与行星合并的理论，天文学家 3 关于太阳系的彗星从太空外的某处来的观点并不与此观点相悖。

34. 答案：F

题干：判断两个小型的星体更靠近太阳这一事实会削弱哪位天文学家的观点。

定位：Astronomer 1、2、3

解析：天文学家 2 认为太阳系是产生于内核剧烈的扩张，合并后的大块的物质保留在中心附近，而没有有效合并的小型的星体被扔到离中心较远的地方。所以两个较大的星体分布在比两个较小的星体更远的位置削弱了此理论。然而这个现象并不与另两位天文学家的观点相悖。

[**Passage VII**]

35. 答案：A

题干：判断实验 1 的实验目的。

定位：Table 1

解析：表 1 没有明确地区分 urban、suburban、rural 的苯排放来源，因此，这个实验并不关心 3 种地区苯排放水平的对比。

36. 答案：J

题干：判断个体接触的苯占比最多的来源。

定位：Table 1

解析：在表 1 可以看到，香烟和汽车释放的苯占了一个个体接触的所有苯的 61%，比其他选项都要高。

37. 答案：B

题干：判断在室外接触最多的物质。

定位：Table 2

解析：在两个检测的地区，chloroform 的接触量相比其他 4 种物质是最低的。

38. 答案：H

题干：比较室内和室外燃烧水平。

定位：Table 3

解析：文章表明了实验 3 中测量到的物质是燃烧产生的，因此通过图 3 可以比较燃烧水平。H 比较了第 1 行和第 2 行的数据，尽管一些对应的水平是不同的，但是差别很小，并且没有哪一行的数据中的数值会一直大于或小于另外一行。

39. 答案：A

题干：判断哪个选项调和了实验 2 和实验 3 的结果。

定位：Table 2、3

解析：实验 3 测量了小于等于 10 微米的颗粒数量，两个区域的颗粒数量并没有显著的差别，而实验 2 显示了 New Jersey 和 Maine 两地的 5 种颗粒数目有显著的差别，如果表 2 中的颗粒是 10 微米以下的，则表 3 应该反映出此差异，最合理的解释是表 2 中的颗粒大小要大于 10 微米，因此不包含在实验 3 的观测对象中。

40. 答案：J

题干：根据室内数据判断室外数据。

定位：Table 3

解析：个体在夜间接触的颗粒总水平是 73 或 75 mg/m^3，当室内的暴露量为 45 时，室外的暴露量为 28～30。

ST1 解析

[**Passage I**]

1. 答案：D

解析：抓关键词 Streptococcuslactis 和 37℃，Generation Time 分别是 26 和 37，在 25～40 范围内，选 D。

2. 答案：G

解析：看 Figure 1，数量增长最快的阶段是 log phase，选 G。

3. 答案：D

解析：看 Table 1 中 growth medium 为 glucose broth 的 generation time，找时间最长的细菌，选 D。

4. 答案:F
解析:看 Table 1 中 growth medium 为 milk 的 generation time,找 generation time 最接近 60 min的细菌,选 F。
5. 答案:D
解析:排除法,A:细菌数量在生长期稳定增长,Figure 1 细菌数量没有一直稳定增长,B:细菌数量立刻增加,Figure 1 细菌有 lagphase,C:细菌转移后立刻减少,lag phase 数量稳定,没有减少,细菌需要适应时间,所以存在 lag phase,选 D。

[**Passage II**]
6. 答案:G
解析:看实验 1 和实验 2 的描述,实验 1 每天从 ground water 取样,实验 2 在下雨和融雪时从 stream water 取样,选 G。
7. 答案:B
解析:自变量应为 phosphates 和 nitrates 含量,因变量为植物生长情况,选 B。
8. 答案:J
解析:验证假设化肥也会污染地下水,应该改变化肥使用量并测量地下水,J 选项最完整,选 J。
9. 答案:A
解析:看实验 1 描述和导语,科学家 1 认为营养物的来源是 see page from waste water system,导致 lake plant growth,选 A。
10. 答案:F
解析:实验 1 房屋废水排放营养物,实验 2 化肥经雨水冲刷排放营养物,F 增加房屋数量会增加排放物,选 F。
11. 答案:D
解析:测量更接近来源,phosphates 被泥土吸收的更少,测的含量会高于 May 3 的 8.4,选 D。

[**Passage III**]
12. 答案:H
解析:看实验 3 的 Table 2,自变量是 distance from road way,选 H。
13. 答案:B
解析:看 Table 1,speed limit 越低,vehicle usage 越少,NO_2 level 越低,改变 ozone 与减少 NO_2 无关,选 B。
14. 答案:G
解析:从 Table 2 可知,越远离 road way,ozone level 越高,选 G。
15. 答案:C
解析:如果 CO 表现类似氮氧化物,从实验 2 可知,越远离 roadway,氮氧化物含量越低,实验没有氮氧化物变化情况,排除 AB,选 C。
16. 答案:J
解析:从实验 2 可知,远离 road way 时,NO_2 level 降低,从 Table 2 可知,ozone level 增加,选 J。
17. 答案:D
解析:从 Table 1 可以推测,speed limit 为 100,vehicle usage 为 100 000 时,NO_2 含量应该远大于 speed limit 为 100,vehicle usage 为 300 000 时的 22,选 D。

[**Passage IV**]

18. 答案：G

解析：从 Table 2 可知，r 越长，precession rate 越大，再看 Figure 1，r 包括 light weight stem，所以 stem 越长，precession rate 越大，选 G。

19. 答案：C

解析：从 Table 1 可知，随着 spin rate 增加，precession rate 减小，选 C。

20. 答案：F

解析：验证假设 precession rate 与重力有关，自变量是重力，因变量是 precession rate，实验应改变重力，选 F。

21. 答案：A

解析：实验 1 的 r 不变，实验 2 的 spin rate 为 500，在 Table 1 中 spin rate 为 500 的 precession rate 是 11，在 Table 2 中 precession rate 是 11 时，r 的长度为 3，选 A。

22. 答案：G

解析：从实验 1 的描述中可知，spin rate 用电动机控制，如果技术不完善，则每次实验的转速可能不一致，干扰实验 2 的结果，选 G。

23. 答案：B

解析：研究 top mass 对 precession rate 的影响，自变量是 top mass，改变 top mass，选 B。

[**Passage V**]

24. 答案：H

解析：排除法，F 是理论 1 的形成条件，G 是理论 2 的形成条件，J 是导语中的信息，选 H。

25. 答案：B

解析：理论 1 认为电荷一开始存在云中，理论 2 认为电荷由风带来，A 和 D 选项未提到，C 选项两个理论观点相同，选 B。

26. 答案：F

解析：理论 1 认为大的颗粒与小的颗粒摩擦，大的颗粒降到底部使底部带负电，所以当雨滴很大，才能发生摩擦，使底部负电最大，选 F。

27. 答案：B

解析：由导语可知，mature thunder storm cloud 底部带负电，顶部带正电，两个理论都是为了解释形成这种 cloud 的原因，正电应该在负电的上方，选 B。

28. 答案：H

解析：Convective theory 认为 up drafts 是电荷的来源，所以如果经常打雷，是 up drafts 出现频率高，选 H。

29. 答案：C

解析：Gravitational Theory 认为大的带负电的颗粒下沉，选 C。

30. 答案：J

解析：Convective circulation 的作用是把大气中的正电荷带到云的顶部，把云边缘的负电荷存在云的底部，所以云的底部不可能与大气中的正电反应，选 J。

[**Passage VI**]

31. 答案：C

解析：从 Table 1 可知，Z 相同时，n 增加，I 减小，选 C。

32. 答案：F
    解析：当 n = 5 时，I 应小于 0.85，选 F。
33. 答案：C
    解析：从导语可知，protons 带正电，electrons 带负电，原子带正电时，质子数量多于电子数量，选 C。
34. 答案：J
    解析：H 不带正电，He + 带一个正电，Li + 2 带两个正电，Be + 3 带 3 个正电，比较 n 相同时 r 的大小，r 减小当正电荷增加，选 J。
35. 答案：D
    解析：从 Table 1 前的解释可知，E 代表 photon 从原轨道到 n = 1 轨道释放的能量，找 E 值最大的，选 D。

[**Passage VII**]

36. 答案：J
    解析：题目问颠倒 H_2 和 I_2 的浓度生成同样浓度的 HI，实验 9 和 10 温度相同，颠倒了 H_2 和 I_2 的浓度，生成 HI 浓度相同，选 J。
37. 答案：D
    解析：比较 Trial 3 和 7，4 和 8，H_2 和 I_2 的初始浓度翻倍，HI 的浓度增加大于翻倍，选 D。
38. 答案：G
    解析：比较 Trial 1～6，随着温度升高，HI 浓度降低，选 G。
39. 答案：A
    解析：比较 Trial 1～6，温度升高，Keq 值降低，选 A。
10. 答案：J
    解析：Trial 3 反应温度为 400℃，H_2 和 I_2 初始浓度为原来 4 倍，由 Trail 3 和 7 可知，HI 浓度增加大于倍数增加，最终浓度会大于 0.788×4，选 J。

ST2 解析

[**Passage I**]

1. 答案：D
   题干：判断表示 Outlet 2 的铁含量的图表。
   定位：Table 1
   解析：根据表 1 中的数据即可判断。
2. 答案：G
   题干：判断 Outlet 2 处第 3 天的锰含量最小的原因。
   定位：Table 1
   解析：从表 1 第 2 列可以看出，5 天中只有第 3 天有降雨，因此锰含量的降低可以解释为雨水稀释的缘故。
3. 答案：A
   题干：判断 Outlet 1 和 2 的流速与降雨的关系。
   定位：Table 1

解析：从表 1 可以看到，在第 3 天降水之后，两者的流速较前两天都大幅提升。

4. 答案：H

题干：判断从 Outlet 2 流出的水会被哪种物质污染。

定位：Table 1、2

解析：从图 1 可以看到该处的铁含量和锰含量均大于图 2 中允许的水平，说明均被铁和锰污染，而 pH 值始终大于 6.0，说明未受 pH 的污染。

5. 答案：A

题干：判断降低铁含量的措施。

定位：Table 1

解析：从图 1 可以看到，Outlet 2 中的铁含量水平已显著高于 Outlet 1，Outlet 1 中的铁含量水平已显著高于 inlet，说明修建 marsh 可以显著降低水中的铁含量，因此可以再建一个 marsh 将铁含量水平降低到污染值以下。

[**Passage II**]

6. 答案：G

题干：判断哪个指示剂经历了 pH 变化最大。

定位：Table 1

解析：分别计算选项中的指示剂对应的最终 pH 与初始 pH 的差值，从 A 到 D 分别为 3、6、5、3。因此选 G。

7. 答案：C

题干：判断酸性最强的溶液。

定位：Figure 1

解析：酸性最强的溶液 pH 值最小，分布在图 1 的最左边部分。

8. 答案：G

题干：判断滴定前后 pH 的变化。

定位：Table 1

解析：从图 1 可以看到添加酸溶液滴定后溶液的 pH 均小于滴定前。

9. 答案：B

题干：判断两种溶液调换后滴定的实验结果。

定位：Table 1

解析：在 pH 小的酸溶液中加入 pH 大的溶液后，酸性会减小，pH 上升，与之前实验的变化方向相反，相应地，指示剂的颜色变化也相反。

10. 答案：H

题干：判断滴定过程中哪个指示剂变色时的 pH 最低。

定位：Table 1

解析：表 1 中最后一列的 final pH 即为指示剂变色时的 pH，red cabbage 对应的 pH 最低。

[**Passage III**]

11. 答案：A

题干：判断为了让 dietary hypothesis 成立，低血钙水平应是哪种现象的指示。

定位：dietary hypothesis

解析：dietary hypothesis 关心的是血液中钙的水平，为了能解释骨骼中钙水平的缺失，血液中钙水平应作为骨骼钙水平的指示。

12. 答案：H

题干：判断 estrogen hypothesis 更好地解释了 osteoporosis 在哪个群体中更为常见。

定位：estrogen hypothesis

解析：estrogen hypothesis 提到 estrogens 促进女性骨骼钙的积累，androgens 促进男性骨骼钙的积累，androgens 的水平基本保持不变，而 estrogens 的水平在女性 45 岁之后就会缓慢下降，从而让女性骨骼中的钙流失。

13. 答案：C

题干：判断移除 ovaries 的女性可能呈现的症状。

定位：estrogen hypothesis

解析：estrogen 主要由 ovaries 生成，如果移除掉 ovaries，estrogen 的含量会减小，从而导致骨骼中钙的流失。

14. 答案：G

题干：判断 dietary 假说支持者会对 exercise 假说的实验结果进行的批评。

定位：dietary hypothesis、exercise hypothesis

解析：dietary hypothesis 认为血液中的维生素 D 含量对于骨骼中钙含量的提升起重要作用，而 exercise hypothesis 只关注了负重训练对钙含量的作用，没有对实验组的维生素 D 的含量进行检测，因此有可能会忽略维生素 D 的作用。

15. 答案：C

题干：判断 estrogen hypothesis 支持者会如何解释 dietary hypothesis 的实验结果。

定位：dietary hypothesis、estrogen hypothesis

解析：estrogen hypothesis 认为骨骼中钙的含量主要是受 estrogen 和 androgen 水平影响的，dietary hypothesis 的实验中，受试者摄入了维生素 D 和钙后血钙含量升高，由 estrogen hypothesis 理论解释的话则是因为受试者体内的 estrogen 和 androgen 含量处于正常水平，因此可以将钙含量调整到正常值。

16. 答案：G

题干：判断 dietary hypothesis 支持者如何解释 estrogen hypothesis 中的 B 组实验。

定位：estrogen hypothesis-Table

解析：B 组中在补充钙后，骨骼的密度反而下降，dietary hypothesis 可能认同的一个原因是饮食中添加的钙含量不够充分，因此没能使骨头中的钙含量恢复到正常水平。

17. 答案：D

题干：判断 dietary hypothesis 与 exercise hypothesis 中进行的实验的相似之处。

定位：dietary hypothesis、exercise hypothesis

解析：两个理论中进行的实验样本都是绝经后的女性。

[**Passage IV**]

18. 答案：G

题干：判断实验 1 和实验 2 的区别。

定位：Table 1、2

解析：在实验 1 中，实验观测的是 acaciaant 寄居的树和没有寄居的树，实验 2 观测的是 acaciaant 和另一种蚂蚁。

19. 答案：A

题干：判断是什么特性保护了 non-antacacias 不被其他动物咬食。
定位：Table 2、3
解析：在表 3 下方说明 C 组的 non-antacacias 没有被其他动物咬食，而 A 组的树叶被咬食了，说明 non-antacacias 的树叶与 acacia 不同，从表 1 中可以看到，non-antacacias 的树叶中含有 bitter-tasing chemical 而 acacias 的树叶中没有此物质，因此有可能是此物质保护了其不被咬食。

20. 答案：F
题干：判断 antacacia 旁边很少有其他植被的原因。
定位：Table 2
解析：从表 2 中 diet 一行可以看到，acaciaant 以含蛋白质的物质为食，而 non-acaciaant 不吃活的植物。

21. 答案：B
题干：判断植物与昆虫的关系。
定位：Figure 1、Table 1
解析：通过实验 3 的结果可以看到有 acaciaant 寄居的树没有受到其他生物的咬食，而没有 acaciaant 寄居的树受到了咬食，说明了 acaciatrees 通过让 acaciaant 寄居同时保护了自己。

22. 答案：F
题干：判断树在移除昆虫前后叶子都没有被咬食的原因。
定位：无
解析：藤蔓的存在并不一定能够保证叶子不被咬食，排除 G；如果 H、J 正确，则移除后叶子应该受到咬食，排除 H、J。

23. 答案：D
题干：判断 protein body 和 extra floral nectaries 的用途。
定位：Table 2
解析：从表 2 可以看到，两种物质都是 acaciaants 的食物。

[**Passage V**]

24. 答案：G
题干：判断传导率随溶液浓度升高的溶质。
定位：Table 1、2
解析：比较表 1 和 2，溶液浓度升高前后，$C_{12}H_{22}O_{11}$ 的传导率都为 0。

25. 答案：C
题干：判断在哪个条件下 $Mg(C_2H_3O_2)_2$ 的传导性最高。
定位：Table 1
解析：比较 3 个图表，$Mg(C_2H_3O_2)_2$ 的传导性随溶液浓度和温度的升高而升高，A 的浓度小于 B，D 的浓度和温度都小于 B，首先排除 A 和 D；B 的温度小于 C，所以选 C。

26. 答案：H
题干：判断当 $C_{12}H_{22}O_{11}$ 和 KCl 同时溶解时电流表的读数。
定位：Table 1
解析：$C_{12}H_{22}O_{11}$ 的传导性为 0，根据表 3，KCl 溶液对应的电流为 7.4 毫安。

27. 答案：D
题干：判断温度在 80℃ 时溶液的传导性变化。

定位：Table 1、3

解析：结合两个表，只有 HCl 的传导性随温度的升高而降低，所以当溶液温度升高到 80℃ 时，除 HCl 之外的溶液的传导性都提高。

28. 答案：G

题干：判断水被检测的原因。

定位：Table 1、2、3

解析：水是每个溶液中的溶剂，检验水的传导性的原因是为了判断溶液的传导性中有多少是水贡献的。

29. 答案：D

题干：判断实验进一步可以探究的方向。

定位：Table 1、2、3

解析：3 个实验已经研究了温度和溶液浓度对传导性的影响，排除 A；研究溶质的颜色没有意义，排除 B；水的传导性为 0，排除 C；可以将水换为其他溶剂来探究溶剂对传导性的影响，选 D。

[**Passage VI**]

30. 答案：F

题干：判断当 momentary length 增加时，momentary weight 如何变化。

定位：Table 1

解析：在表 1 可以看到，两者呈现正相关的关系。

31. 答案：D

题干：判断哪一组实验支持保持长度不变，当质量翻倍时施加的力也翻倍。

定位：Table 1

解析：根据表 1 的实验数据即可判断。

32. 答案：J

题干：判断质量为 1 250 g，长度为 2 m 时，当 x 为 1.5 时，力的大小。

定位：Table 1

解析：从表中可以看到，保持长度和 x 不变时，质量越大，力越大，所以质量为 1 250 g 时的力要大于质量为 1 000 g(实验 14)时的力。

33. 答案：C

题干：判断哪个实验用的链条单位长度的质量最大。

定位：Table 1

解析：单位长度的质量为链条质量除以长度，从表 1 可以看到，实验 11 的单位长度质量最大。

34. 答案：J

题干：判断当整个链条都滑落时 momentary weight 的大小。

定位：Table 1

解析：从表 1 可以看到，从实验 1 到 4，momentary length 每增加 0.1 m，momentary weight 约增加 0.5 N，所以当整个链条都滑落时($x = 0.5$ m)，momentary weight 约为 2.5 N。

[**Passage VII**]

35. 答案：A

题干：判断削弱因为质量大小而分层的理论的选项。

定位：Study 2

解析：如果因为两者的密度不同而出现了分层，则密度大的 darker particle 会一直在底层，不会出现在上层。

36. 答案：G

题干：判断实验 3 中的变量。

定位：Study 3

解析：实验 3 研究的是火山与 Montana 西部地区连线上不同地方的火山灰颗粒大小，所以变量应该为火山灰的取样点。

37. 答案：A

题干：判断火山灰是否均匀地分布在以火山为中心的圆形区域内。

定位：Figure 1

解析：从图 1 可以看到，图中的环形曲线并不是以火山为中心的同心圆，环形曲线是向东延伸的，说明火山灰的厚度是不均匀的并且集中分布在火山以东的地区。

38. 答案：J

题干：比较颗粒直径和与火山的距离之间的关系。

定位：Figure 3

解析：根据图 3 中曲线的走势及对应的地理区域可以判断。

39. 答案：A

题干：判断当实验 2 中的南北走向的直线穿过 Ritzville 时的实验结果。

定位：Figure 1、2

解析：从图 1 可以看到 Ritzville 处的火山灰厚度要高于 25 mm，所以在图 2 上曲线的最高点要高于 25 mm。

40. 答案：F

题干：判断火山灰主要是由喷发中形成的新的岩石产生的还是之前存在的岩石产生的。

定位：Study 2

解析：实验 2 中提到 dark ash 是从最初的喷发中形成的，而 light ash 是最近的喷发中形成的，在图 2 中可以看出，大部分的火山灰都是 light ash；实验 1 和实验 3 均没有提到这两类的差别。

Princeton 1 解析

[**Passage I**]

1. 答案：A

题干：判断在实验 3 中当温度为 62.5℃时的角度大小。

定位：Table 3

解析：表 3 可以看到角度和温度成正比，62.5℃时的角度应介于 50℃和 75℃之间。

2. 答案：F

题干：判断在实验 1 中哪个物块移动需要的力最大。

定位：Table 1

解析：受力大小与角度成正比，从表 1 可得 brick 移动需要的角度最大，即受力最大。

3. 答案：D

题干：判断摩擦系数与物块质量的关系。

定位：Table 1、3

解析：从图 1 和图 3 中可以看出，摩擦系数与物块质量无关。

4. 答案：G

题干：判断使用不同材质物块的目的。

定位：Figure 1

解析：不同的物块与斜面之间的摩擦系数不同。

5. 答案：D

题干：判断 4 种材质物块的摩擦系数大小关系。

定位：Table 1

解析：摩擦系数大小与物块移动所需角度成正比，从表 1 即可得结论。

6. 答案：G

题干：判断实验 3 的实验目的。

定位：Table 3

解析：从表 3 可以看到实验 3 关心的是温度和木块与斜面之间的静摩擦系数的关系。

[**Passage II**]

7. 答案：B

题干：判断哪两个月份之间 polio 感染人数增长最多。

定位：Figure 1

解析：从 Figure 1 中可以看到 2 月和 3 月之间增长 25，最多。

8. 答案：J

题干：判断在 6 月份有多少人有感染的危险。

定位：Figure 1

解析：在图 1 中，6 月份感染的人为 80 人，所以有感染危险的人为 $80 \times 200 = 1\,600$。

9. 答案：A

题干：判断 7 月份和 8 月份感染人数有差异的原因。

定位：Figure 2

解析：根据图 2，7 月份降水量少，感染人数少，8 月份降水量多，感染人数多，说明降水量多时水污染的概率大，从而通过水污染染病的人数多。

10. 答案：H

题干：判断实验 2 所验证的假设。

定位：Figure 2

解析：从图 2 可以看出，实验 2 关心的是印度不同地区在 7 月和 8 月的发病率。

11. 答案：D

题干：判断蚊子对疾病传播的影响。

定位：Study 2

解析：实验 2 中提及 polio 的传播主要与人类的排泄物有关，所以蚊虫的增多不会对疾病的传播产生显著影响。

12. 答案：H

题干：判断在 Kolkata 7 月份和 8 月份的感染人数的关系。

定位：Figure 2

解析：在图 2 可以看到，8 月份的感染人数约为 7 月份的两倍。

［**Passage III**］

13. 答案：D

题干：判断哪个溶液具有最低的 osmotic pressure。

定位：Figure 1

解析：从图 1 可以看到，2.0 M 时对应的 sucrose 溶液的 osmotic pressure 最低。

14. 答案：J

题干：判断哪个溶液的 ionization 水平最高。

定位：Table 1

解析：从表 1 可以看到，$FeCl_3$溶液的 Hofffactor 最高，因此 ionization 水平最高。

15. 答案：C

题干：判断哪两个溶液的 osmotic pressure 最相近。

定位：公式

解析：从公式中可以看到，osmotic pressure = iMRT，当 RT 固定时，osmotic pressure 相等时 iM 乘积应相等。

16. 答案：G

题干：判断 M 和 pressure 之间的关系。

定位：Figure 1

解析：图 1 可以看到 pressure 与 M 成单调递增关系。

17. 答案：D

题干：判断高 ionization 水平的溶液是否可能有低 osmotic pressure。

定位：Table 1、Figure 1

解析：根据 Table 1 和 Figure 1，i 小的溶液所对应的 osmotic pressure 也小。

［**Passage IV**］

18. 答案：H

题干：比较样本 1 和样本 4 的 ESP。

定位：Figure 1

解析：根据图 1，在深度浅的地方，样本 4 的 ESP 要高于样本 1。

19. 答案：B

题干：判断样本 3 在 30～60 m 处的 ESP。

定位：Figure 2

解析：从图 2 可以判断。

20. 答案：J

题干：判断样本 4 的 EC 大小。

定位：Figure 1

解析：从图 1 可以看到样本 4 在 0～30 m 处的 EC 值最小。

21. 答案：C

题干：判断 5 个地点的 ESP 大小关系。

定位：Figure 2

解析：根据图 2 可以判断。

22. 答案：G

题干：判断 ESP 和 EC 是否与土壤距离水源的距离有关。

定位：Figure 1、2

解析：从图 1 和图 2 可以看到，两幅图中并没有明显有一致的变化关系。

[**Passage V**]

23. 答案：B

题干：判断选取第 6 组的原因。

定位：Table 1

解析：从表 1 可以看到，第 6 组为未受影响的栖息地，所以第 6 组为对照组。

24. 答案：F

题干：判断设置第 2 组的原因。

定位：Table 1

解析：在表 1 中可以看到，第 2 组关心的是北极熊捕食的海洋生物的食物数量是否会影响北极熊的数量。

25. 答案：C

题干：判断各个实验组对北极熊数量的影响作用大小。

定位：Figure 1

解析：average population density ratio 越大，对应的实验组的实验条件越有利于北极熊的生存。

26. 答案：G

题十：判断第 1 组中 significantly decreased population 所指的物种。

定位：Table 1

解析：从表 1 可以看到，significantly decreased population 指的是被北极熊捕食的海洋哺乳动物，选项中只有 seal 符合。

27. 答案：D

题干：判断哪两个组可以研究协同作用。

定位：Table 1

解析：从表 1 可以看到组 4 重复了组 1 和组 3 的条件，是为了研究两者的协同作用。

28. 答案：H

题干：判断哪个假说得到了实验结果的支持。

定位：Figure 1

解析：组 1 研究的是食物的减少对北极熊的影响，组 3 研究的是北极冰川融化的影响，从图 1 可以看到，冰川融化对北极熊数量的影响更大。

[**Passage VI**]

29. 答案：D

题干：判断两位科学家都赞同的产生甲烷的原料。

定位：Reaction 1

解析：两位科学家都认同前 4 个反应，从前 4 个反应中可以看到甲烷的产生需要臭氧。

30. 答案：F

题干：判断甲烷与 H_2CO 含量的变化关系。

定位：Scientist 1

解析：第 1 位科学家认为甲烷可以转化为 H_2CO，所以当大气中甲烷含量升高时，H_2CO 含量也

相应升高。

31. 答案：C

题干：判断反应 5 中反应物和产物的分子质量大小。

定位：Reaction 5

解析：反应 5 中一个 H_2CO 分子分解为一个 H_2 和一个 CO 分子，所以反应物的分子质量要大于产物。

32. 答案：H

题干：判断臭氧含量减少时 CH_3 和 H_2CO 含量的变化。

定位：Reaction 1～3

解析：反应 1、2、3 可以看到臭氧通过一系列反应产生 CH_3 和 H_2CO，臭氧减少会导致 CH_3 和 H_2CO减少。

33. 答案：D

题干：判断第 2 位科学家不会赞同的观点。

定位：Scientist 2

解析：第 2 位科学家说反应 1～4 会发生，这支持了 A 和 C，选项 B 是他的重心论点；然而他提到有些 H_2CO 可能会由甲烷和臭氧产生，他认为 H_2CO 会很快分解所以反应 2～4 的发生会受阻，因此他不会认为甲烷的增多会大幅提高 H_2CO 的含量。

34. 答案：G

题干：判断反应 3 会增加 CO 含量的原因。

定位：Reaction 3、5、6

解析：反应 3 会产生 H_2CO，H_2CO 会进一步在反应 5 和 6 中反应产生 CO。

35. 答案：B

题干：判断当反应 6 大量发生时第一位科学家的理论缺陷。

定位：Reaction 2、6

解析：反应 6 表示了 OH 会与 H_2CO 反应，这在两方面削弱了第 1 位科学家的理论：这个反应过程会降低 H_2CO 的含量，而他认为会提高，同时也会消耗 OH 从而阻止反应 2～4 的进行，而这是第 1 位科学家的核心假设。

[**Passage VII**]

36. 答案：G

题干：判断当 V 从最高点回落到 1.5 mL 时，P 的取值。

定位：Figure 2

解析：此过程对应环形中右下方的部分。

37. 答案：C

题干：补全 P－V 图像。

定位：Figure 1、2

解析：从两幅图中可以看到，P－V 的图像两部分走势相同。

38. 答案：H

题干：判断在引擎 A 中，P 取最小值时的 V。

定位：Figure 1

解析：图 1 可以看到当 P 取最小值时，V 约为 3.5 mL。

39. 答案：B

题干：判断图 1 中，V 的最大值和最小值的数量关系。

定位：Figure 1

解析：V 的最大值约为 2.25 mL，是最小值 0.75 mL 的 3 倍。

40. 答案：F

题干：判断 A 引擎的 reversible isothermal expansion step 对应的 V 值。

定位：Figure 1

解析：reversible isothermal expansion step 开始于 P 从最大值减小，同时 V 从最小值增大的时刻，对应图 1 即为 V 在 1.0 mL 处。

Princeton 2 解析

[**Passage I**]

1. 答案：D

题干：判断在 I 为 500 A 时 v 的大小。

定位：Table 1

解析：从表 1 可以看到，I 与 v 的关系式为 $I = 5/4 * v$，当 I 为 500 A 时，v 为 400 m/s。

2. 答案：F

题干：判断在实验 2 中 L 与 I 的变化关系。

定位：Table 2

解析：从图 2 可以看到，I 随 L 单调递增。

3. 答案：C

题干：判断当 I 为 570 A 时，B 的取值。

定位：Table 3

解析：从图 3 中可以看出，I 随 B 单调递增，所以当 I 为 570 A 时，B 应介于 9.84×10^{-4} 和 1.05×10^{-3} 之间。

4. 答案：J

题干：判断 4 个实验中哪个产生的电压最大。

定位：Table 3

解析：maglev track 的电阻保持不变，电压与电流成正比，因为实验 14 的电流最大，所以在实验中产生的电压最大。

5. 答案：B

题干：判断 4 个实验中的电流流向。

定位：Study 4

解析：前 3 个实验中 maglev train 都是从东向西移动，而第 4 个实验中是从西向东移动。

6. 答案：G

题干：判断实验 3 中 B 和 I 的关系图。

定位：Table 3

解析：从表 3 可以看到 B 与 I 成正相关，所以直线应有正的斜率。

[**Passage II**]

7. 答案：D

题干：判断 Bat IV 和 pipistrellus hesperusl 的不同之处。

定位：Table 1、2

解析：从两个表中可以看到 pipistrellus hesperusl 是 not heavily furred，而 Bat IV 是 heavily furred。

8. 答案：G

题干：判断 Bat I 和 II 在哪个判断步骤上相同。

定位：Table 1、2

解析：两者的耳朵长度都小于 25 mm，从第 1 步可以看到判断步骤 5 对两者均适用。

9. 答案：A

题干：判断 Vespertilionidae 属于哪类生物。

定位：L1

解析：蝙蝠属于哺乳动物。

10. 答案：G

题干：判断 Lasiuruscinereus 和 Lasiurusblossevillii 的共同点。

定位：Table 1

解析：从表 1 可以看到两者的判断路径为 Step 1、5、6，在第 1 步中，两者适用于耳朵长度小于 25 mm。

11. 答案：D

题干：判断与 Bat II 最相近的种类。

定位：Table 1、2

解析：判断路径为 Step 1、5、7、9，所以 Bat II 应为 Myotisthysanodes，与它最相近的为 Myotisvolans。

[**Passage III**]

12. 答案：J

题干：判断在 0℃设定下在 220 分钟时的温度。

定位：Figure 2

解析：在图 2 可以看到，倒三角形对应的曲线在 220℃时的温度介于 0℃与 10℃之间。

13. 答案：B

题干：判断在 37℃设定下，加热器在 8 到 10 分钟内温度的变化速度。

定位：Figure 1

解析：从图 1 可以看到，8～10 分钟内的温度变化约为 4℃，变化速度为 4/2 = 2℃/min。

14. 答案：F

题干：判断制冷器在设定为 0℃时在哪个温度段的变化最剧烈。

定位：Figure 2

解析：从图 2 可以看出，曲线逐渐平缓，在 0～100 min 内斜率最大，变化最快。

15. 答案：A

题干：判断在哪个时刻温度计里水银分子的动能最大。

定位：Figure 2

解析：从图 2 可以看到，温度随时间的推移而降低，而动能与温度成正比，所以在 150 min 时的温度最高，动能最大。

16. 答案：F

题干：判断将温度降低为 - 10℃所需要的时间。

定位：Figure 2

解析：图 2 可以看出当温度降得越低，需要的时间越长，所以温度降为 - 10℃需要的时间要多于 0℃。

[**Passage IV**]

17. 答案：C

题干：判断 pepsin 可能存在的器官。

定位：L1

解析：根据题干，pepsin 是用于分解蛋白质的消化酶，此类物质应出现在消化系统中。

18. 答案：F

题干：判断 pepsin 活性高的 pH 值。

定位：Table 2

解析：根据表 2，pH 越高，pepsin 的活性越高，pH 在 4.0 以上时的活性低或者无活性。

19. 答案：C

题干：判断实验 5 中，pepsin 无活性的原因。

定位：Table 1

解析：从表 1 可以判断，实验 4 和 5 的差异在于实验 4 中有 casein 而没有 anserine，实验 5 中只有 anserine，说明 pepsin 能分解 casein 而不能分解 anserine，同时因为实验 3 中两者都有，不能说明 anserine 阻止了分解的进行。

20. 答案：H

题干：判断哪个实验组中有未被消化的 casein。

定位：Table 1

解析：从表 1 可以看到实验 1 和 7 中 pepsin 无活性，同时实验中添加了 casein，所以 casein 无法被消化。

21. 答案：A

题干：判断实验 3 与哪个实验组的实验条件更相似。

定位：Table 1、2

解析：实验 3 的 pH 值为 3.0，选项中的实验组只有实验 9 是在 pH 为 3 的条件下进行的。

22. 答案：G

题干：判断 pepsin 活性最高的条件。

定位：Table 1、2

解析：通过比较实验 1、2、3、7 可以得出 pepsin 在 40℃ 活性最高的结论，通过表 2 可以看出 pepsin 在 pH 小于 4.0 是活性最高。

[**Passage V**]

23. 答案：C

题干：判断 3 幅图中哪些有溶液在 0℃时粘稠度大于 1.0 cP。

定位：Figure 1、2、3

解析：只有图 3 中所有溶液在 0℃时，粘稠度均小于 1.0 cP。

24. 答案：F

题干：判断 nitrobenzene 溶液在哪个温度范围内粘稠度下降最大。

定位：Figure 2

解析：在图 2 可以看到，nitrobenzene 对应的曲线在 0～10℃范围内的斜率最大，粘稠度下降值最多。

25. 答案：C

题干：判断 70℃的水的粘稠度。

定位：Figure 1

解析：从图 1 可以看到，水在 70℃时的粘稠度约为 0.4 cP。

26. 答案：G

题干：判断粘稠度随温度变化的规律。

定位：Figure 2

解析：从图 2 可以看到，随着温度的升高，粘稠度降低，因此溶液流出所需的时间也降低。

27. 答案：D

题干：比较 nitrobenzene + A 和 die thylether 的粘稠度大小。

定位：Figure 1、2、3

解析：从 3 幅图中可以看到，实验中并没有测量 nitrobenzene + A 的粘稠度，所以不能比较。

[**Passage VI**]

28. 答案：G

题干：判断当距离震中越远，地震波类型的变化。

定位：Figure 2

解析：沿图 2 的 X 轴可以观察到，随着距离震中的距离越远，地震波的强度逐渐减弱。

29. 答案：B

题干：比较强地震波和中等强度地震波的传播距离。

定位：Figure 1、2、3

解析：从 3 幅图中均可以看出，强地震波的传播距离均小于中等强度地震波的传播距离。

30. 答案：J

题干：判断不受直接控制的变量。

定位：L7

解析：第 7 行提到"Ground density and propagation duration were controlled in the experiment"，可以排除 G 和 H，几个实验的区别是通过改变 sound intensity 进行的，所以排除 F。

31. 答案：D

题干：判断哪种强度的地震波长可能小于 100 cm。

定位：Figure 1

解析：从图 1 可以看到，中等强度地震波的波长约为 150 cm，弱震波的波长约为 500 cm，所以没有地震波的波长可能小于 100 cm。

32. 答案：J

题干：判断当 sound intensity 为 70 dB 时，地震波可能的种类。

定位：Figure 1、2

解析：比较图 1 和图 2，图 1 的 sound intensity 为 60 dB，包含 3 种地震波和未影响的地区，图 2 的 sound intensity 为 80 dB，包含 3 种地震波，所以当 sound intensity 为 70 dB 时，地震波应包含 3 种。

33. 答案：A

题干：判断当 sound intensity 介于 75 dB 和 85 dB 之间时，根据强地震波传播的距离判断震中距离。

定位：Figure 3

解析：实验 2 中 soundintensity 为 80 dB，符合题中的范围，可以看到强地震波对应的震中距离介于 0～2.3 m，据此可判断答案为小于 2.5 m。

[**Passage VII**]

34. 答案：G

    题干：判断溶液 2 和 4 的颗粒量和凝固点。

    定位：Table 1

    解析：从表 1 可以看到，溶液 4 的 i 值大于溶液 2，说明溶液 4 中的颗粒量多，比较两者的凝固点，溶液 4 的凝固点要低。

35. 答案：A

    题干：判断颗粒电性对溶液凝固点的影响。

    定位：Student 1

    解析：科学家 2 认为凝固点的改变与溶质的性质无关，因此题干描述与科学家 2 的观点无冲突，科学家 1 认为凝固点的改变需要溶质粒子带电才可以产生，因此中性溶质粒子对凝固点产生的改变与科学家 1 的观点矛盾。

36. 答案：F

    题干：判断两位科学家都同意的观点。

    定位：Scientist 1、2

    解析：科学家 1 认为带电性的溶质粒子会降低凝固点，科学家 2 认为增加粒子密度会降低凝固点，所以选 F。

37. 答案：A

    题干：判断保持溶液粒子密度不变时，加入带正电的溶质会降低凝固点的现象与哪位科学家的观点相符。

    定位：Scientist 1、2

    解析：科学家 2 认为凝固点的改变与溶液粒子密度有关，所以题中现象不符合科学家 2 的观点，加入正电荷溶质粒子降低凝固点与科学家 1 的观点相符。

38. 答案：G

    题干：判断溶质和溶剂粒子的排列方式。

    定位：Scientist 1

    解析：科学家 1 认为溶质粒子会被溶剂粒子吸引并且会干涉溶剂粒子的规律排列，只有 G 表现了两种粒子间的吸引与不规则的排列。

39. 答案：A

    题干：判断两种观点是否考虑溶质粒子的物理性质。

    定位：Scientist 1、2

    解析：科学家 2 认为凝固点的降低与溶质粒子的物理性质无关。

40. 答案：J

    题干：根据科学家 2 的观点判断凝固点改变值的决定公式。

    定位：Scientist 2

    解析：科学家 2 认为凝固点的改变与 van't Hofffactor 成正比，并未提到与 i 的平方成正比。

Princeton 3 解析

[**Passage I**]

1. 答案：C

   题干：判断 P 点可以在何处观测到。

   定位：Table 1

   解析：从图 1 可以看到，P 点位于月球和地球的中间，由于月球的阻挡在太阳上并不能观测到 P 点。

2. 答案：F

   题干：判断在日食时太阳的光线能否到达地球。

   定位：Figure 1

   解析：从图 1 可以看到，日食时太阳发射的光线被月球阻拦，从而无法到达地球表面。

3. 答案：B

   题干：判断海平面最高水平出现的间隔时间。

   定位：Figure 2

   解析：从图 2 中可以看出，在第 1 天最高点出现在 0 时左右，在第 2 天最高点出现在 26 小时左右，选项 B 最为符合。

4. 答案：G

   题干：判断图 2 中利用的数据最可能取自哪个月份。

   定位：Figure 2、3

   解析：图 2 中海平面高度的最大值约为 6 feet，将 4 个选项与图 3 对应，只有 3 月的海平面高度在 6 feet 左右。

5. 答案：D

   题干：判断图 2 中 0～12 小时间海平面高度的变化。

   定位：Figure 2

   解析：图 2 中可以看到，海平面高度先降低后升高。

[**Passage II**]

6. 答案：G

   题干：判断何处的 shale layer 最厚。

   定位：Figure 2

   解析：从图 2 可以看到，Site 1 处的 shale layer 为四者中最厚的。

7. 答案：A

   题干：判断 Site 2 和 3 之间的 limestone layer 厚度如何变化。

   定位：Figure 2

   解析：从图 2 可以看到，从 site 2 到 site 3 之间的 limestone layer 逐渐增加。

8. 答案：H

   题干：判断表示 3 个地点处的 limestone layer 厚度的柱状图。

   定位：Figure 2

   解析：根据图 2 limestone layer 的厚度可以判断。

9. 答案：A
题干：判断哪个位置的 Uranium 含量更高。
定位：Figure 3
解析：根据图 3，地下深度越深，Uranium 含量越少，所以 Uranium 含量大的位置应与地表距离更近。
10. 答案：G
题干：判断 Site 2 中被检测到的最深处的岩石的年龄。
定位：Figure 3
解析：从图中可以看到 Site 2 处检测出了 8 个 Uranium，根据图 3 中的公式可以计算出结果。

[**Passage III**]
11. 答案：C
题干：判断实验 3 中选择塑料水枪的原因。
定位：Experiment 3
解析：从实验 3 的描述中可以看到，学生需要观察水枪中的气泡数量，所以选择透明的塑料水枪。
12. 答案：J
题干：判断在摇晃水枪前射程相同的实验组。
定位：Table 1、2
解析：从表 1 和 2 可以看到，实验组 1、3、5 在摇晃水枪前的射程相同。
13. 答案：D
题干：判断实验 2 的实验结果。
定位：Table 2
解析：从表 2 可以看到，装有可乐的水枪在摇晃后射程都减小。
14. 答案：H
题干：判断实验 5 中在摇晃水枪之前可乐中是否有大量的气泡。
定位：Experiment 3
解析：实验 3 中提到在摇晃后 1 小时后，可乐中的气泡基本没有，在进行实验 5 之前由于水枪已经放置了 1 小时，所以在摇晃前没有大量的气泡。
15. 答案：D
题干：判断在实验 5 后，将水枪静置 1 小时后的射程。
定位：Table 2
解析：从表 2 可以看到，实验 4 后将水枪放置 1 小时再射击时，射程与摇晃前一致(实验 3)，所以实验 5 后再放置 1 小时的射程也与摇晃前一致，即 6.42 米。
16. 答案：G
题干：判断摇晃后，可乐中气泡消散到不影响射程的程度需用的时间。
定位：Table 2
解析：表 2 可以看到，实验 4 中水枪在静置 10 分钟后的射程小于 6.42 米，说明 10 分钟后射程仍受气泡的影响，实验 5 中水枪静置 1 小时后射程等于 6.42 米，说明 1 小时后射程已不受气泡影响，结合两者可以得出所需时间应介于 10 分钟和 1 小时之间。

[**Passage IV**]
17. 答案：D

题干：判断蓝绿水藻反射的可见光的颜色。
定位：Figure 1、Table 1
解析：根据图 1，蓝绿水藻反射的光线波长主要集中在 550 nm 处，根据表 1，550 nm 波长为绿光。

18. 答案：H
题干：判断叶绿素 II 主要参与的反应。
定位：无
解析：叶绿素 II 主要参与光合作用。

19. 答案：A
题干：判断绿藻对于哪个波长的光线吸收量超过硅藻。
定位：Figure 1
解析：从图 1 可以看到，绿藻对与 400 nm 波长的光线吸收量超过了硅藻。

20. 答案：J
题干：判断绿藻属于哪个生物界。
定位：无
解析：绿藻属于原生生物界。

21. 答案：B
题干：判断哪个种类的藻类在湖水样本中密度最大。
定位：Figure 1、2
解析：图 2 可以看到湖水样本对于 550 nm 波长的光线反射比例最大，而硅藻对于 550 nm 波长的光线反射最多，所以湖水样本中硅藻的密度最大。

[**Passage V**]

22. 答案：H
题干：判断 40℃时密度为 1.018 g/mL 的溶液质量。
定位：Table 1
解析：溶液的质量等于密度乘以体积，在实验 1 中用到的溶液体积为 150 mL，可求得质量为选项 H。

23. 答案：A
题干：判断在 10℃时盐度为 2.5%的溶液的密度。
定位：Table 2
解析：从表 2 可以看到随着盐度的升高，溶液的密度也升高，所以 2.5%盐度的溶液的密度应介于 2.35%和 2.6%盐度的密度之间。

24. 答案：H
题干：判断 U3 和 X2 哪个适合 10℃2.35%盐度的环境。
定位：Table 2、3
解析：在表 2 可以看到 10℃2.35%盐度的环境对应的是 VII，在图 3 中可以看到 VII 下 U3 会下沉而 X2 会漂浮，说明 X2 更适合。

25. 答案：D
题干：判断模型在样本 IV 到 VII 环境中的状态。
定位：Table 2、3
解析：从表 2 和 3 中可以看到样本 IV 到 VII 的密度逐渐降低，模型应该在高密度的环境中漂浮,在低密度的环境中下沉,选项 D 违背了这个原理。

26. 答案:H

题干:判断实验 1 中将样本溶液转移到圆柱体容器中的目的。

定位:Experiment 1

解析:圆柱体容器的体积为 150 mL,通过将溶液转移到圆柱体中可以更精确地测量溶液的体积,从而计算溶液密度。

27. 答案:A

题干:判断 U3 模型的密度。

定位:Table 1、2、3

解析:从表 3 可以看到,U3 在溶液 V 中漂浮,而在溶液 VI 中下沉,说明 U3 的密度介于溶液 V 和 VI 的密度之间,对照表 1 和 2 可得结论。

[**Passage VI**]

28. 答案:J

题干:判断哪些细胞可以在绿光条件下存活。

定位:Table 1

解析:从表 1 可以看到,T5 和 T6 在绿光下均没有生命活动,而 T7 和 T8 有生命活动。

29. 答案:B

题干:判断 plant 和 haloarchaeal 细胞同时存在的试管的实验现象。

定位:Table 1

解析:由于 plant 和 halo archael 两者不互相干扰,从表 1 可以看到 plant 在红光下只产生 CO_2,haloarchaea 在绿光下只产生 acid,所以合并后的试管在红光下只产生 CO_2,在绿光下只产生 acid。

30. 答案:G

题干:根据描述判断细胞类型。

定位:Table 1

解析:根据描述对照表 1 可以进行判断。

31. 答案:C

题干:判断 haloarchaea 是否需要绿光来产生能量。

定位:Table 1、2

解析:从表 1 可以看到,在绿光下 haloarchaea 可以产生 CO_2,从表 2 可以看到,haloarchaea 在绿光下的 transmittance 小,两者结合可知 haloarchaea 吸收了大量绿光用以产生热量,并生成了 CO_2。

32. 答案:G

题干:判断 plant Rosa Carolina 在红光下的实验现象。

定位:Table 1

解析:plant Rosa Carolina 在红光下只产生 CO_2,当存在 CO_2 时,在溶液上方会有气泡,如果没有 acid,溶液会显色。

33. 答案:C

题干:判断 haloarchaea 和 bacterium 产能过程是否相同。

定位:Table 1

解析:从表 1 可以看到,haloarchaea 只在绿光下产生 acid,而 bacterium 在红光和绿光下都产

生 acid 和 CO_2。

[**Passage VII**]

34. 答案：G

题干：判断哪个选项最符合 3-domain 分类法。

定位：3-domain classification

解析：最后一段第 2 行表示 rRNA 基因序列的差异越大，两个群体的基因型在进化中分离的时间越早，所以相近的基因型说明了进化上更加紧密的关系，排除 F；文中没有提及 ester 和 ether 的关系和差异，排除 H 和 J。

35. 答案：D

题干：判断 2-domain 假说下 archaea 缺少哪个结构。

定位：2-domain classification

解析：phospholipids 有 membranes，但是非 organelles，排除 A；ribosomes 在文中说明不是 membrane-bound organelles，并且文中提到 Archaea 有 ribosomes，排除 B 和 C；Nuclei 是只在 eukaryotes 中发现的 membrane-bound organelles。

36. 答案：J

题干：判断 eukaryotes 和 prokaryotes 的相同点。

定位：Introduction

解析：最后一段说明 eukaryotes 和 prokaryotes 有 esterlinkages，排除 F；介绍部分将 eukaryotes 和 prokaryotes 的区别定义为是否存在 membrane-bound organelles，排除 G；在 2-domain 假说中，prokaryotes 无性繁殖，排除 H；文中提到的所有生物体都是由细胞组成。

37. 答案：C

题干：判断 2-domain 假说与 3-domain 分类的最大冲突。

定位：2-domain 假说

解析：2-domain 假说将 Archaea 定义为了 prokaryotes。介绍部分说明 Archaea 有 rRNA，排除 A；B 是 3-domain 假说的观点，排除 B；蛋白质合成发生在所有的生物体中，排除 D。

38. 答案：F

题干：判断题干描述与哪个假说冲突。

定位：2-domain 假说、3-domain 假说

解析：细胞新陈代谢与 eukaryotes 相似削弱了 2-domain 假说，排除 H 和 J；通过新陈代谢与 eukaryotes 相似可以排除 G。

39. 答案：C

题干：判断哪个选项可以削弱 2-domain 假说。

定位：2-domain 假说

解析：没有科学家认为 Archaea 有 membrane-bound organelles，排除 A；显微镜在精确描述生物体方面发挥了重要作用，这点在文中并没有提及，排除 B；eukaryote 和 Archaea 关系的远近并不是科学家的主要讨论点，排除 D。

40. 答案：G

题干：判断 phospholipid cell membrane 的示意图。

定位：Scientist 2

解析：phospholipid 由水溶的部分和不溶于水的部分组成，因此合理的表示方法是水溶的部分排列在外侧与水接触，不溶的部分在内侧不与水接触。

第二部分

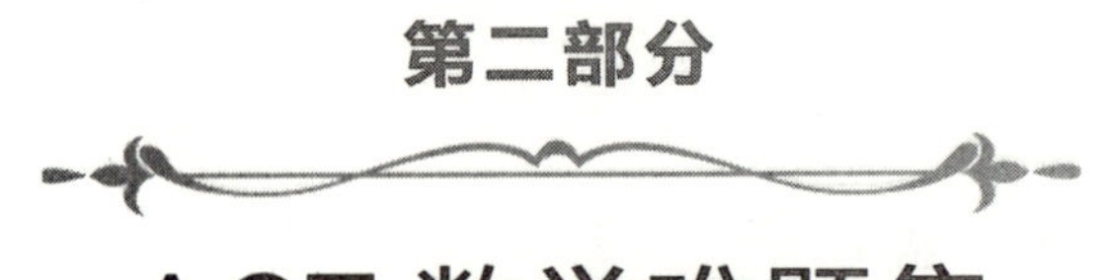

ACT 数学难题集

一、知识点梳理

(一) 算法

➢ 常见数学表达

Concept	Symbol	Words	Example	Translation
equality	=	is	2 plus 2 is 4	$2+2=4$
		equals	X minus 5 equals 2	$x-5=2$
		is the same as	Multiplying x by 2 is the same as dividing x by 7	$2x=\frac{x}{7}$
addition	+	sum	The sum of y and x is 20	$x+y=20$
		plus	X plus y equals 5	$x+y=5$
		add	How many marbles must John add to collection P so that he has 13 marbles	$x+P=13$
		increase	A number is increased by 10%	$x+10\%x$
		more	The perimeter of the square is 3 more than the area	$P=3+A$
subtraction	−	minus	x minus y	$x-y$
		difference	the difference of x and y is 8	$\|x-y\|=8$
		subtracted	x subtracted from y	$y-x$
		less than	the circumference is 5 less than the area	$C=A-5$
multiplication	· or ×	time	the acceleration is 5 times the velocity	$a=5v$
		product	the product of two consecutive integers	$n(n+1)$
		of	x is 125% of y	$x=125\%\cdot y$
division	÷ or /	quotient	the quotient of x and y is 9	$\frac{x}{y}=9$
		divided	if x is divided by y, the result is 4	$\frac{x}{y}=4$

➢ 重要概念

1. LCM and GCD

Least Common Multiple（LCM）最小公倍数

Greatest Common Divisor（GCD）最大公约数

2. Factors and Multiples 因数和倍数

Factor Theorem：

Let $f(x)$ be a polynomial. Then $x-h$ is a factor of $f(x)$ if and only if $f(h)=0$.

3. 自然数的整除特性：

能被 3 整除：所有数字之和能被 3 整除；

能被 4 整除：末两位数字能被 4 整除；

能被 5 整除：末位数字是 0 或者 5；

能被 8 整除：末三位数字能被 8 整除；

能被 9 整除：所有数字之和能被 9 整除。

4. Prime Number 质数

A positive integer P is a ***prime***, or a prime number, if $P\neq 1$ and its only positive divisors are 1 and itself.

5. Rational Number 有理数

A number that can be written in the form $\frac{a}{b}$, where a and b are integers, with $b\neq 0$.

6. Power and Exponent Functions 幂和指数函数

The fourth ***power*** of 3 is 3^4, the ***base*** is 3 and ***expoent*** is 4.

$$a^0=1;\ a^{-1}=\frac{1}{a};\ a^{\frac{1}{2}}=\sqrt{a}$$

7. Squares and Square Roots 平方和平方根

$$\sqrt{a}\sqrt{b}=\sqrt{ab}$$

$$\sqrt{\frac{a}{b}}=\frac{\sqrt{a}}{\sqrt{b}}$$

8. Scientific Notation 科学计数法

$$12\,340\,000=1.234\times 10^7$$

$$2.15\times 10^{-5}=0.000\,021\,5$$

9. Ratios, Proportions and Percents 比值、比例和百分比

A ***ratio*** is a quatient of two quantities: $\frac{x}{y}$

A ***percent*** is a ratio in which the sencond quantity is 100:

$$45\%=\frac{45}{100}=0.45$$

A ***proportion*** is an equation that sets two ratios equal to each other.

$\frac{3}{5}=\frac{12}{20}$

10. Permutations, Combinations, and Probability 排列组合以及概率

Permutations 排列

$$P_n^r = \frac{n!}{(n-r)!}$$

Combinations 组合

$$C_n^r = \frac{P_n^r}{r!} = \frac{n!}{(n-r)!r!}$$

The ***Probability***（概率）of an event E，P(E)，is given as follows. If E can occur in m ways out of a total of n equally likely ways，

$$P(E) = \frac{m}{n} = \frac{\text{number of outcomes in event } E}{\text{total number of possible outcomes}}$$

11. Simple Statistics 简单统计

Mean 平均数

The ***mean*** of the numbers a_1，a_2，…，a_n is equal to

$$\frac{a_1 + a_2 + \cdots + a_n}{n}$$

Median 中位数

将 n 个数据从小到大排序，中间的数(n = 奇数)或者中间两个数的平均数(n = 偶数)。

Mode 众数

出现频率最高的数。

Range 极差

数组中的最大值和最小值的差。

(二) 代数

1. Polynomials 多项式

$$y = a_0 + a_1 x + a_2 x^2 + \cdots + a_{n-1} x^{n-1} + a_n x^n$$

n：degree；a_n：leading coefficient；a_0：constant term

2. Basic Formula 基本公式

$$x^2 - y^2 = (x+y)(x-y)$$

$$(x+y)^2 = x^2 + 2xy + y^2$$

$$(x-y)^2 = x^2 - 2xy + y^2$$

3. Quadratic Equations 二次方程

$$ax^2 + bx + c = 0$$

$$x = \frac{-b \pm \sqrt{b^2 - 4ac}}{2a}$$

$$x_1 + x_2 = -\frac{b}{a}$$

$$x_1 \cdot x_2 = \frac{c}{a}$$

4. Functions 函数

A function f from S to T，where S and T are non-empty sets，is a rule that associates each element of S (the domain 定义域) with a unique element of T (the range 值域).

The linear function：

$y = kx + b$

The quadratic function

$y = ax^2 + bx + c$

Axis of symmetry：$x = -\dfrac{b}{2a}$

Transformations：函数变换

Related function	Resulting transformation of $f(x)$
$f(x)+k$	vertical shift，k units up
$f(x)-k$	vertical shift，k units down
$f(x+k)$	horizontal shift，k units to the left
$f(x-k)$	horizontal shift，k units to the right
$-f(x)$	reflection across the x-axis
$f(-x)$	reflection across the y-axis
$kf(x)$	vertical dilation along the y-axis by a factor of k
$f(kx)$	horizontal dilation along the x-axis by a factor of k

5. Matrices 矩阵

A rectangular array of entries displayed in rows and columns and enclosed in brackets.

$A = \begin{bmatrix} 2 & 7 & 1 \\ 4 & 3 & 5 \end{bmatrix}$；$B = \begin{bmatrix} 6 & 8 & 10 \\ 7 & 1 & 5 \end{bmatrix}$；$C = \begin{bmatrix} 1 & 2 \\ 2 & 1 \end{bmatrix}$

矩阵的加法：

$$A+B = \begin{bmatrix} 2+6 & 7+8 & 1+10 \\ 4+7 & 3+1 & 5+5 \end{bmatrix} = \begin{bmatrix} 8 & 15 & 11 \\ 11 & 4 & 10 \end{bmatrix}$$

矩阵的数乘：

$$2 \cdot A = \begin{bmatrix} 2\cdot 2 & 2\cdot 7 & 2\cdot 1 \\ 2\cdot 4 & 2\cdot 3 & 2\cdot 5 \end{bmatrix} = \begin{bmatrix} 4 & 14 & 2 \\ 8 & 6 & 10 \end{bmatrix}$$

矩阵的乘法：

$$CA = \begin{bmatrix} 1 & 2 \\ 2 & 1 \end{bmatrix}\begin{bmatrix} 2 & 7 & 1 \\ 4 & 3 & 5 \end{bmatrix} = \begin{bmatrix} 1\cdot 2+2\cdot 4 & 1\cdot 7+2\cdot 3 & 1\cdot 1+2\cdot 5 \\ 2\cdot 2+1\cdot 4 & 2\cdot 7+1\cdot 3 & 2\cdot 1+1\cdot 5 \end{bmatrix} = \begin{bmatrix} 10 & 13 & 11 \\ 8 & 17 & 7 \end{bmatrix}$$

行列式：

The ***determinant*** of $\begin{bmatrix} a & b \\ c & d \end{bmatrix}$ is denoted $\begin{vmatrix} a & b \\ c & d \end{vmatrix}$ and is defined as $ad - bc$.

6. Sequences 数列

Arithmetic sequence：等差数列

$a_1 = a$，$a_2 = a + d$，$a_3 = a + 2d$，…，$a_n = a_1 + (n-1)d$

$S_n = \dfrac{(a_1 + a_n) \cdot n}{2}$

Geometric sequence：等比数列

$a_1 = a$，$a_2 = ar$，$a_3 = ar^2$，…，$a_n = a_1 r^{n-1}$

$S_n = \frac{a_1(1-r^n)}{1-r}$

$S_\infty \overset{|r|<1}{\Rightarrow} \frac{a_1}{1-r}$

7. Complex Numbers 复数

$\sqrt{-1} = \mathrm{i}$

$\mathrm{i}^2 = -1$

$z = a + b\mathrm{i}$；$z^* = a - b\mathrm{i}$

$|z| = \sqrt{a^2 + b^2} = \sqrt{z \cdot z^*}$

8. Logarithms 对数

$y = a^x \leftrightarrow x = \log_a y$

$\log_a 1 = 0$；$\log_a a = 1$

$\log_a xy = \log_a x + \log_a y$

$\log_a \frac{x}{y} = \log_a x - \log_a y$

$\log_a x^m = m \log_a x$

(三) 几何

1. Distance 距离

$|AB| = \sqrt{(x_A - x_B)^2 + (y_A - y_B)^2}$

2. Midpoint 中点

$$\begin{cases} x = \frac{x_A + x_B}{2} \\ y = \frac{y_A + y_B}{2} \end{cases}$$

3. Slope 斜率

$k = \frac{y_A - y_B}{x_A - x_B}$

4. Slope-intercept Form of Lines 斜截式直线方程

$y = kx + b$

5. Point-slope Form of Lines 点斜式直线方程

$y - y_0 = k(x - x_0)$

6. Conics 圆锥曲线

Ellipse 椭圆：

$\frac{x^2}{a^2} + \frac{y^2}{b^2} = 1$

Parabola 抛物线：

$y^2 = 4px$

Hyperbola 双曲线：

$\frac{x^2}{a^2} - \frac{y^2}{b^2} = 1$

（四）三角函数

1. Right Triangle Trigonometry 直角三角形的三角函数关系

$\sin x = \dfrac{\text{opposite}}{\text{hypotenuse}}$

$\cos x = \dfrac{\text{adjacent}}{\text{hypotenuse}}$

$\tan x = \dfrac{\text{opposite}}{\text{adjacent}} = \dfrac{\sin x}{\cos x}$

$\csc x = \dfrac{1}{\sin x}$

$\sec x = \dfrac{1}{\cos x}$

$\cot x = \dfrac{1}{\tan x}$

2. Angles in Radians 弧度制

$\pi^{\text{radian}} = 180^{\text{degree}}$

Arc length 弧长

$l = r\theta$

Area of sector 扇形面积

$A = \dfrac{1}{2} r \cdot l = \dfrac{1}{2} r^2 \theta$

3. Graphs of Trig. Functions 三角函数图象

略。

4. Properties of Trig. Functions 三角函数性质

$y = A\sin(\omega x)$

Amplitude：振幅 A

Period：周期 $T = \dfrac{2\pi}{\omega}$

5. Trig Identities 三角恒等式

$\sin^2\theta + \cos^2\theta = 1$

$\sin 2\theta = 2\sin\theta\cos\theta$

$\cos 2\theta = 1 - 2\sin^2\theta = 2\cos^2\theta - 1 = \cos^2\theta - \sin^2\theta$

$\sin(A+B) = \sin A\cos B + \cos A\sin B$

$\sin(A-B) = \sin A\cos B - \cos A\sin B$

$\cos(A+B) = \cos A\cos B - \sin A\sin B$

$\cos(A-B) = \cos A\cos B + \sin A\sin B$

6. Solution of Triangles 解三角形

The law of sines：正弦定理

$\dfrac{\sin A}{a} = \dfrac{\sin B}{b} = \dfrac{\sin C}{c}$

The law of cosines 余弦定理

$a^2 = b^2 + c^2 - 2bc\cos A$

$b^2 = a^2 + c^2 - 2ac\cos B$

$c^2 = a^2 + b^2 - 2ab\cos C$

二、真题卷难题集锦

Session 1 Arithmetic 1 算术 1

1. What is the value of $\frac{2^2 - 1^4}{3^2 - 1^5}$?

A. 0　　B. $\frac{3}{10}$　　C. $\frac{3}{8}$　　D. $\frac{1}{2}$　　E. $\frac{5}{8}$

2. "Snake-eyes" occur when you roll two l's on a pair of regular, 6-sided dice numbered from 1 to 6. On any roll, what is the probability of rolling snake-eyes?

F. $\frac{1}{36}$　　G. $\frac{1}{25}$　　H. $\frac{1}{18}$　　J. $\frac{1}{6}$　　K. $\frac{1}{3}$

3. A line segment with length of $5\frac{1}{2}$ units is located on a number line with 1 endpoint fixed at coordinate $-3\frac{1}{2}$. What are the 2 possible coordinate locations of the other endpoint?

F. 9 and -2　　G. 9 and -9　　H. 2 and -8　　J. 2 and -9　　K. 2 and 9

4. At a certain store, all radios are discounted to 15% less than the radio's regular price. A customer brings a radio marked with a regular price of \$120 to the checkout counter. If a sales tax of 5% of the purchase price is added (rounded to the nearest cent), how much money does the customer owe?

A. \$102.90　　B. \$107.10　　C. \$108.00　　D. \$110.00　　E. \$110.25

5. On Family Day, attendance at the baseball game set a record. A reporter for the local paper asked how many adults had paid to see the game. The box office reported that exactly 450 tickets had been sold, and \$2,000 was collected. If adults' tickets were \$5 and children's tickets were \$3, how many adults' tickets were sold?

A. 75　　B. 125　　C. 325　　D. 375　　E. 400

6. $\frac{1}{3} \times \frac{2}{4} \times \frac{3}{5} \times \frac{4}{6} \times \frac{5}{7} \times \frac{6}{8} \times \frac{7}{9} \times \frac{8}{10} = ?$

A. $\frac{1}{90}$　　B. $\frac{1}{45}$　　C. $\frac{1}{5}$　　D. 1　　E. $\frac{9}{2}$

7. Which of the following is the least common denominator for the expression below?

$\frac{1}{13^2 \cdot 17 \cdot 23} + \frac{1}{17^2 \cdot 23} + \frac{1}{17 \cdot 23^3}$

F. $17 \cdot 23$　　G. $13 \cdot 17 \cdot 23$

H. $13^2 \cdot 17 \cdot 23$　　J. $13^2 \cdot 17^2 \cdot 23^3$

K. $13^2 \cdot 17^4 \cdot 23^5$

8. The Environmental Club selects its 3 officers by first selecting the president, then the vice president, and finally the secretary. If there are 20 members who are eligible to hold office and no member can hold more than 1 office, which of the following gives the number of different possible results of the election?

F. 17^3 G. 19^3 H. 20^3 J. $19 \cdot 18 \cdot 17$
K. $20 \cdot 19 \cdot 18$

9. Which of the following operations will produce the largest result when substituted for the blank in the expression: $2\square\frac{1}{3}$?

A. averaged with
B. divided by
C. minus
D. plus
E. multiplied by

10. A wheel 29 inches in diameter rolls along a line without slipping. How many inches does the wheel roll along its path in 25 revolutions?

F. 362.5 G. 725 H. 1,540 J. 210.25π K. 725π

11. One hot-air balloon is 10 kilometers (km) east and 3 km north of an airport tower while a second hot-air balloon at the same altitude is 2 km west and 5 km south of the same airport tower. Approximately how many kilometers separate the 2 hot-air balloons?

A. 8.2 B. 12 C. 14.4 D. 15.8 E. 20

12. The quantity $\sqrt[n]{2^p}$ is defined when n is an integer greater than 2 and p is any nonzero real number. Which of the following is a relationship between n and p that will always make $\sqrt[n]{2^p}$ a positive integer?

F. $\frac{p}{n}$ is a positive integer
G. $\frac{n}{p}$ is a positive integer
H. p is greater than n
J. n is greater than p
K. The sum of p and n is 1

13. Three distinct lines, all contained in a plane, separate the plane into distinct regions. What are all of the possible numbers of distinct regions of the plane that may be separated by any 3 such lines?

(Note: Do NOT include any of the points on the 3 lines in your count of distinct regions.)

A. 3, 4, 7 B. 3, 6, 7 C. 4, 5, 6 D. 4, 5, 7 E. 4, 6, 7

14. The balance in Joan's savings account tripled during the year. Joan then withdrew \$500, and the resulting balance was \$100. What was the balance in the account before it tripled?

A. \$200 B. \$300 C. \$400 D. \$500 E. \$600

15. Due to inflation, a car that formerly sold for \$15,000 now sells for 10% more. Which of the following calculations gives the current cost, in dollars, of the car?

F. 15,000 + 10
G. 15,000 + 15.000(0.01)
H. 15,000 + 15,000(0.10)
J. 15,000 + 15,000(10)
K. 15,000(0.10)

16. The number 0.005 is 100 times as large as which of the following numbers?

A. 0.5
B. 0.05
C. 0.000 5
D. 0.000 05
E. 0.000 005

17. The pattern shown in abbreviated form below is composed of squares that are arranged horizontally and surrounded by 4 hexagons. All the squares are congruent, and all the hexagons are congruent. How many of these congruent hexagons will there be if the pattern is

repeated until there are 20 squares?

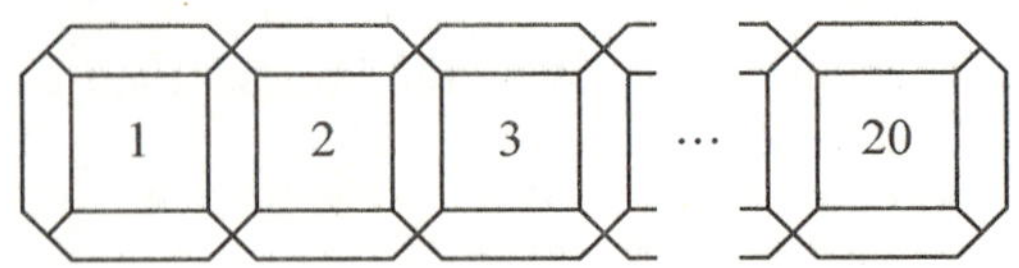

F. 44　　G. 61　　H. 70　　J. 79　　K. 80

18. This year, 75% of the graduating class of Harriet Tubman High School had taken at least 8 math courses. Of the remaining class members, 60% had taken 6 or 7 math courses. What percent of the graduating class had taken fewer than 6 math courses?

F. 0%　　G. 10%　　H. 15%　　J. 30%　　K. 45%

19. Kaylee is planning to purchase a car. She will need to borrow some of the money and has a chart, shown below, to use to approximate her monthly payment. The chart gives the approximate monthly payment per $1,000 borrowed.

Monthly payment per $1 000 borrowed for various annual rates and various numbers of payments			
Annual interest rate	Number of monthly payments		
	36	48	60
5%	$29.97	$23.03	$18.87
8%	$31.34	$24.41	$20.28
10%	$32.27	$25.36	$21.24
12%	$33.22	$26.24	$22.24

A local dealership is having an end-of-the-model-year clearance sale and is offering 5% annual interest on new-car loans for 36, 48, or 60 months. The maximum amount Kaylee can budget for her monthly car payment is $300. Of the following loan amounts, which one is the maximum Kaylee can borrow at 5% annual interest and stay within her budget?

A. $10,000　　B. $13,000　　C. $14,000　　D. $15,000　　E. $20,000

20. Pillar obtained estimates for cleaning her furnace from 2 heating companies. Lehman Heating's estimate was $30 for a service call plus $22 per hour for cleaning the furnace. A-1 Heating's estimate was $35 for a service call plus $20 per hour for cleaning the furnace. If the estimates were the same in both the total amount and the number of hours for cleaning Pillar's furnace, how many hours for cleaning the furnace were reflected in the estimates?

A. 2　　B. $2\frac{1}{2}$　　C. 3　　D. $3\frac{1}{2}$　　E. 4

21. As part of one day's training workout, 5 members of a track team ran for exactly 3 minutes each. The 5 runners ran the 5 distances given below, in miles. Which distance corresponds to the fastest speed?

F. $\frac{3}{5}$　　G. $\frac{3}{8}$　　H. $\frac{5}{8}$　　J. $\frac{7}{9}$　　K. $\frac{11}{16}$

22. Which of the following is an expression for the cubes of the sum of the first c consecutive counting numbers?

F. $(c+1)^3$　　G. $(c+1)^2$

H. $(1+2+\cdots+c)^c$　　J. $(1+2+\cdots+c)^3$

K. $(1+2+\cdots+c)^2$

23. On the first day of school, Mr. Vilani gave his third-grade students 5 new words to spell. On each day of school after that, he gave the students 3 new words to spell. In the first 20 days of school, how many new words had he given the students to spell?

A. 28　B. 62　C. 65　D. 68　E. 152

24. Diastolic blood pressure tends to increase linearly with age. Suppose that the average diastolic blood pressure of 20-year-olds is 120 and the average diastolic blood pressure of 60-year-olds is 140. Given this model, what would be the average diastolic blood pressure of 50-year-olds?

A. 120　B. 125　C. 130　D. 135　E. 140

25. Through how many degrees does a wheel rotate in 1.5 minutes at 45 revolutions per minute?

A. 24,300　B. 16,200　C. 12,150　D. 8,100　E. 4,050

26. The variables a, b, and c are all integers and $a+b+c=50$. If $a<0$ and $0<b<30$ then the minimum possible value for c is:

A. 16　B. 17　H. 21　J. 22　K. 25

27. A warehouse dispatcher is responsible for the immediate delivery of 75,000 condensers. She can use only 2 different sizes of trucks for the task. Each of the larger trucks will carry a maximum of 15,000 condensers. Each of the smaller trucks will carry a maximum of 12,000 condensers. The dispatcher has 2 of the larger trucks to use. If each truck makes only a single trip, how many of the smaller trucks must be used with the 2 larger size trucks to deliver this order?

A. 3　B. 4　C. 5　D. 7

E. Cannot be determined from the given information

28. The manager of a grocery store asks Kamara to construct a display consisting of 10 rows of cans stacked on top of each other. The manager wants the bottom row to have 25 cans and each succeeding row to have 1 less can than the row below it. Part of 3 rows of the display is shown in the figure below. How many cans will be in the top row of the display?

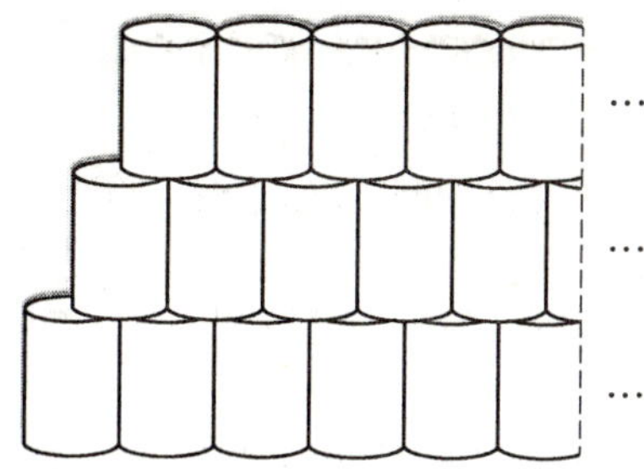

A. 14　B. 15　C. 16　D. 34　E. 35

29. The ratio of a to b is 3 to 1, and the ratio of b to c is 1 to 5. What is the value of $\frac{2a+3b}{4b+3c}$?

F. $\frac{3}{16}$　G. $\frac{9}{19}$　H. $\frac{1}{2}$　J. $\frac{5}{7}$　K. $\frac{18}{19}$

30. The probability that a specific event, E, happens is denoted P(E). The probability that this

event does not happen is denoted P(not E). Which of the following statements is always true?

F. $0 < P(\text{not } E) < P(E)$　　G. $P(\text{not } E) > 1$

H. $P(E) < P(\text{not } E)$　　J. $P(E) > P(\text{not } E)$

K. $P(E) + P(\text{not } E) = 1$

31. In basketball, when a player makes a basket, his or her team scores 3 points if the ball is shot from a distance of more than 6 meters from the basket. I point for a free throw. and 2 points for all other types of shots. During a recent game, Will's team scored a total of 26 points on Will's baskets, which consisted of 4 free throws and more 3-point baskets than 2-point baskets. How many 3-point baskets did Will make during the game?

A. 3　　B. 4　　C. 5　　D. 6　　E. 7

32. Two friends. Chris and Pat, joined a new 14-week program to lose weight through dieting and exercise. Chris set a goal to lose 10 pounds every 4 weeks, for a total of 35 pounds, while Pat's goal was to lose 7 pounds every 4 weeks, for a total of 24.5 pounds. Chris began the program weighing 200 pounds. and Pat began the program weighing 187.5 pounds.
Suppose that Pat loses 1.75 pounds each week. At the end of week k, where $k = 1, 2, \cdots, 14$, he calculates 1.75 pounds as a percent of his body weight and records the percent as $P(k)$. Which of the following best describes the values of $P(k)$?

A. They increase as k increases from 1 to 14.

B. They decrease as k increases from 1 to 14.

C. They increase as k increases from 1 to 7 and decrease as k increases from 7 to 14.

D. They decrease as k increases from 1 to 7 and increase as k increases from 7 to 14.

E. They are constant as k increases from 1 to 14.

33. A State's department of motor vehicles wants to issue licenses that contain 3 of 24 letters (the 26 letters of the alphabet except for O and I), followed by 2 of 10 digits. No single license should use any letter or digit more than once. Two such examples for licenses are AXL34 and ALX34. When the restrictions are followed, how many different licenses are possible?

A. $26^3 \cdot 10^2$　　B. $24^3 \cdot 10^2$

C. $22^3 \cdot 9^2$　　D. $26 \cdot 25 \cdot 24 \cdot 10 \cdot 9$

E. $24 \cdot 23 \cdot 22 \cdot 10 \cdot 9$

34. In the standard (x, y) coordinate plane, the points (600, 89.99), (1,000, 119.99), and (1,400, 149.99) are collinear. DigiPhone wants to offer a new plan that includes 400 minutes of calling time for a charge in line with those of its other plans. If \$$z$ represents the before-tax charge for this new plan. what should be the value of z so that $(400, z)$ is on the same line as the points representing the other plans?

A. 26.67　　B. 44.99　　C. 53.33　　D. 59.99　　E. 74.99

35. When x is divided by 8, the remainder is 5; and when y is divided by 6. the remainder is 1. If each of x and y is at least 20, what is the minimum value of $x + y$?

A. 40　　B. 46　　C. 52　　D. 54　　E. 60

36. The numbers a and b are real numbers and $|a| \cdot b = a \cdot |b|$. Which of the following must be true about the relationship between a and b?

F. $a = -b$　　G. $a = b$　　H. $ab \leqslant 0$　　J. $ab \geqslant 0$

K. $a = 0$ or $b = 0$

37. If k is an integer and $k > 2$. which of the following expressions is equivalent to $\frac{(k+1)!(k-1)!}{(k!)^2}$?

(Note: For any positive integer n, $n! = (n)(n-1)(n-2)\cdots(2)(1)$. Hence $5! = (5)(4)(3)(2)(1) = 120$.)

A. $\frac{k+1}{k}$　　B. k^2-1　　C. -1　　D. 0　　E. 1

38. As a fund-raiser, a local youth group sold boxes of regular popcorn for \$5 each and boxes of caramel popcorn for \$8 each. Altogether, they sold 160 boxes for \$1,010. How many boxes of caramel popcorn did they sell?

A. 20　　B. 32　　C. 70　　D. 80　　E. 100

Use the following information to answer guestions 39 - 40. Two trains travel the same route from Toronto to Montreal, a distance of 550 km. The Local leaves Toronto earlier than the Express, makes 3 stops at stations along the way, and arrives in Montreal later than the Express. Assume that the Local travels at a constant speed on each of the 4 parts of the route, but not necessarily at the same speed for all 4 parts, and that the Express travels at a constant speed. The schedule for the Local and a graph for the Local and the Express are shown below.

Schedule for the Local		
City	Scheduled arrival time	Distance (to the nearest kilometer) from Toronto
Toronto		0
Oshawa	10:45 A.M.	51
Kingston	12:30 P.M.	252
Lancaster	3:30 P.M.	451
Montreal	5:30 P.M.	550

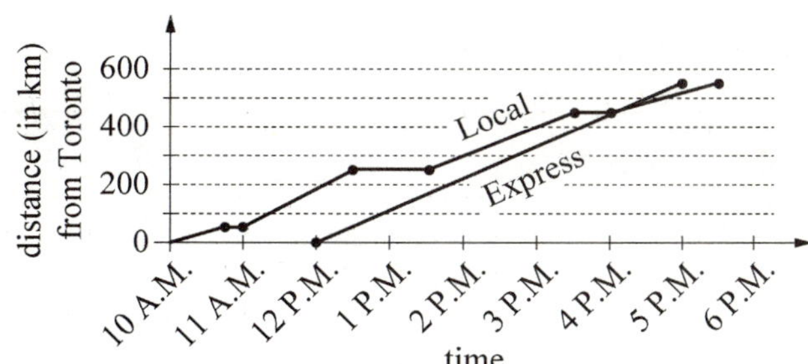

39. Over which of the following time intervals is the Local going faster than the Express?

I. 12:00 P.M 12:30 P.M.

II. 1:30 P.M 3:30 P.M.

III. 4:00 P.M 5:00 P.M.

A. Ionly　　B. III only

C. Iand II only　　D. II and III only

E. I, II, and III

40. One of the following gives the total amount of time that the Local spends at stops along the way. Which one is it?

F. 1 hour 45 minutes G. 2 hours 30 minutes

H. 2 hours 45 minutes J. 3 hours.

41. The integer a is 4 more than the positive integer b. The integer c is 4 less than b. The product of a and c is 84. What is the value of b ?

F. 6 G. 8 H. 10 J. 14 K. 42

42. Each of 6 historical events occurred in a different year. You are asked to arrange the 6 events in ascending order by the years they occurred. You know the earliest and the latest. You randomly order the other events. What is the probability that you order the 6 vents correctly?

A. $\frac{1}{720}$ B. $\frac{1}{120}$ C. $\frac{1}{24}$ D. $\frac{1}{6}$ E. $\frac{1}{4}$

43. The hours and minutes on a 12-hour digital clock are represented by 3 or 4 digits. Which of the following is the largest product that can be obtained by multiplying the digits in one of these representations?

(Note: If the time is 8: 45, the product of the digits is (8)(4)(5) = 160.)

F. 90 G. 162 H. 405 J. 708 K. 729

44. The difference of 2 integers is 4. The sum of the same 2 integers is 38. What is the greater of the 2 integers?

A. 17 B. 18 C. 19 D. 20 E. 21

45. If x is a factor of 35 and y is a factor of 16, the product of x and y could NOT be which of the following?

F. 1 G. 24 H. 40 J. 112 K. 560

46. For each positive integer n, let n_e the product of all positive even numbers less than or equal to n. For example, $6_e = (6)(4)(2) = 48$ and $7_e = (6)(4)(2) = 48$. What is the value of $\frac{12_e}{3_e}$?

A. 384 B. 1,280 C. 1,920 D. 15,360 E. 23,040

47. Three different logical operators are defined in the table below.

Symbol	Operator	Description
and	AND	If both impots are 1, then the output is 1. Otherwise, the output is 0
or	OR	If either imput is 1 or if both imput are 1, then the output is 1. Otherwise, the output is 0.
no	NOT	If the imput is 0, then the output is 1. Otherwise, the output is 0.

The logic diagram below uses the 3 operators. The only possible values for a, b, c, and d are 0 and 1. Which of the following (a, b, c, d) inputs will result in an output of 1?

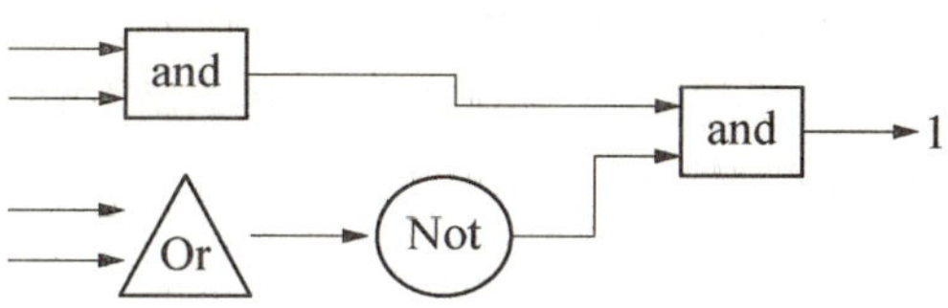

F. (0, 1, 0, 0)　　G. (0, 1, 1, 1)
H. (1, 0, 1, 0)　　J. (1, 1, 0, 0)
K. (1, 1, 0, 1)

48. Whenever $b>0$, which of the following real number line graphs represents the solutions for x to the inequality $|x|-b \geqslant 4$?

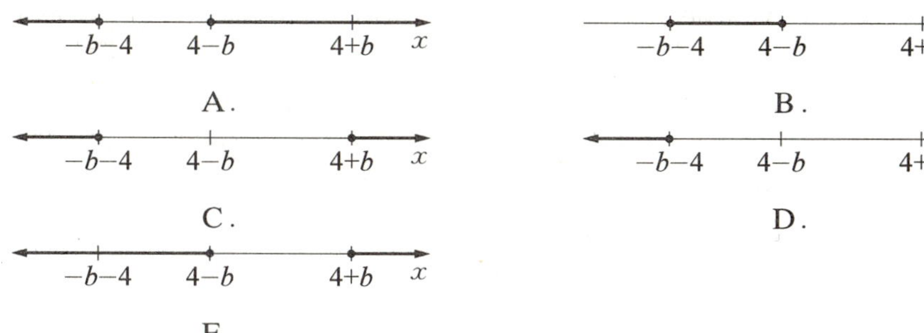

49. Mr. Gomez gave his class a test on 20 spelling words. Only one of the following percents is possible as the percent of the 20 words a student spelled correctly. Which one is it?

A. 77%　　B. 85%　　C. 88%　　D. 96%　　E. 99%

50. The first 5 terms of a geometric sequence are 0.375, −1.5, 6, −24, and 96. What is the 6th term?

F. −384.　　G. −126　　H. −66　　J. 126　　K. 384

51. As shown in the figure below, Mr. Thompson, who is standing at point A, needs to determine the distance from point C on the ground to point E at the top of one of the second-story windows of his house. He places a mirror on the ground at point B so that when he looks in the mirror, he can see the top of the window. Mr. Thompson's eye level, at point D, is 6 ft above the ground. He notes that $AB=4$ ft and $BC=14$ ft. Approximately how many feet above the ground is the top of the second-story window?

(Note: In $\triangle ABD$ and $\triangle CBE$, $\angle ABD$ is congruent to $\angle CBE$.)

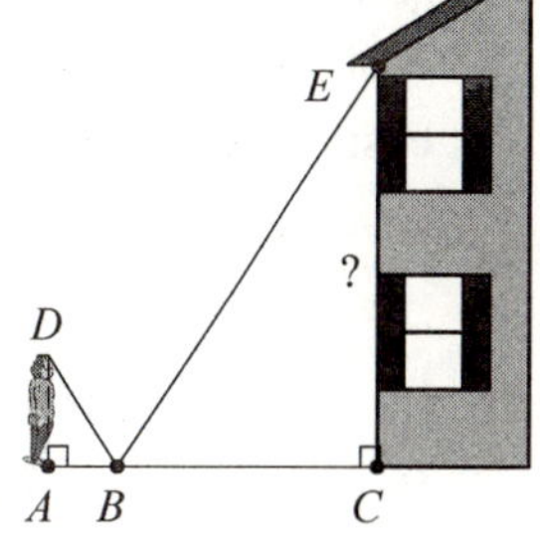

F. 2　　G. 10　　H. 16　　J. 21　　K. 24

52. The cheerleading squad wants to purchase new uniforms to wear at the regional championship competition. They decide to sell candy bars for \$1.00 each. The squad will receive \$0.40 for each of the first 200 candy bars sold. For each of the next 300 sold, the squad will receive \$0.50. For each additional candy bar sold, the squad will receive \$0.60. How many candy bars must the squad sell to reach their goal of raising \$350.00?

F. 350　　G. 584　　H. 667　　J. 700　　K. 875

53. At Brookfield High School, 55 seniors are enrolled in the sociology class and 40 seniors are

enrolled in the drawing class: Of these seniors, 20 are enrolled in both the sociology class, and the drawing class. How many of the 120 seniors enrolled at Brookfield High School are NOT enrolled in either the sociology class or the drawing class?

F. 5 G. 15 H. 20 J. 35 K. 45

54. How many 3-letter orderings, where no letter is repeated, can be made using the letters of the word GATORS?

A. 3 B. 6 C. 27 D. 120 E. 216

55. On the way to a family camping weekend, the Estradas stopped at a roadside stand to purchase firewood. The stand sold bundles of pine firewood for \$2 per bundle and bundles of hickory firewood for \$4 per bundle. The Estradas purchased a total of 25 bundles of pine firewood and hickory firewood for \$66. How many bundles of pine firewood did the Estradas purchase?

A. 8 B. 11 C. 17 D. 21 E. 22

56. For all positive integers n, which of the following is correct ordering of the terms n^n, $(n!)^n$, and $(n!)^{n!}$?

(Note: $n! = (n)(n-1)(n-2\cdots(2)(1)))$

A. $n^n \geqslant (n!)^n \geqslant (n!)^{n!}$ B. $(n!)^n \geqslant n^n \geqslant (n!)^{n!}$

C. $(n!)^n \geqslant (n!)^{n!} \geqslant n^n$ D. $(n!)^{n!} \geqslant (n!)^n \geqslant n^n$

E. $(n!)^{n!} \geqslant n^n \geqslant (n!)^n$

57. The sum of 2 positive numbers is a prime number. Which of the following prime numbers must be one of the original prime numbers?

A. 2 B. 3 C. 5 D. 7 E. 11

58. Vehicle A averages 14 miles per gallon of gasoline, and Vehicle B averages 36 miles per gallon of gasoline. At these rates, how many more gallons of gasoline does Vehicle A need than Vehicle B to make a 1,008-mile trip?

A. 25 B. 28 C. 44 D. 50 E. 72

59. Daisun owns 2 sportswear stores (X and Y). She stocks 3 brands of T-shirts (A, B, and C) in each store. The matrices below show the numbers of each type of T-shirt in each store and the cost for each type of T-shirt. The value of Daisun's T-shirt inventory is computed using the costs listed. What is the total value of the T-shirt inventory for Daisun's 2 stores?

$$\begin{array}{c} \\ X \\ Y \end{array} \begin{array}{c} \begin{array}{ccc} A & B & C \end{array} \\ \begin{bmatrix} 100 & 200 & 150 \\ 120 & 50 & 100 \end{bmatrix} \end{array} \quad \begin{array}{c} A \\ B \\ C \end{array} \overset{\textit{Cost}}{\begin{bmatrix} \$5 \\ \$10 \\ \$15 \end{bmatrix}}$$

A. \$2,200 B. \$2,220 C. \$4,965 D. \$5,450 E. \$7,350

60. Sergio plans to paint the 4 walls of his room with 1 coat of paint. The walls are rectangular, and, according to his measurements, each wall is 10 feet by 15 feet. He will not need to paint the single 3-foot-by-5-foot rectangular window in his room and the $3\frac{1}{2}$-foot-by-7-foot rectangular door. Sergio knows that each gallon of paint covers between 300 and 350 square feet. If only 1-gallon cans of paint are available, which of the following is the minimum number of cans of paint Sergio needs to buy to paint his walls?

F. 1 G. 2 H. 3 J. 4 K. 5

61. Which of the following is a rational number?

A. $\sqrt{2}$ B. $\sqrt{\pi}$ C. $\sqrt{7}$ D. $\sqrt{\frac{5}{25}}$ E. $\sqrt{\frac{64}{49}}$

62. An integer from 100 through 999, inclusive, is to be chosen at random. What is the probability that the number chosen will have 0 as at least 1 digit?

A. $\frac{19}{900}$ B. $\frac{81}{900}$ C. $\frac{90}{900}$ D. $\frac{171}{900}$ E. $\frac{271}{1,000}$

63. A fruit salad contains pineapples, apples, bananas, and andoranges. It contains twice as many bananas as apples, 10 times as many oranges as pineapples, and the same number of apples as oranges. Jeff made this fruit salad using 1 pineapple. How many of each of the other fruits did he use?

Apples Bananas Oranges

A. 10 20 10 B. 10 20 1 C. 10 2 10 D. 10 2 1 E. 1 2 1

64. A Little League baseball player has batted 120 times and has 25 hits. Starting now, if she gets a hit each time she is at bat, what is the least number of times she must be at bat to raise her batting average to at least 0.3?

(Note: batting average $= \frac{\text{number of hits}}{\text{number of times batted}}$)

A. 11 B. 16 C. 36 D. 61 E. 161

65. Suppose $0 < a < 1$. Which of the following has the greatest value?

F. $\frac{\pi}{a}$ G. $\frac{1}{a}$ H. a^2 J. a^3 K. $\log a$

66. Casey and 3 friends are snow sledding on a 4-person toboggan like the one shown in the figure below. Each time all 4 of them go down the hill on the toboggan, they sit in a different order, from front to back. What is the maximum number of times they can go down the hill without sitting in the same order twice?

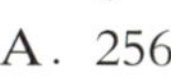

A. 256 B. 64

C. 24 D. 16

E. 10

67. A data set of integers has 5 members. The median of the data set is 6. The only mode of the data set is 2. The mean of the data set is 5. Which of the following statements must be true about the data set?

F. The sum of the 5 integers is 30.

G. The sum of the 5 integers is 10.

H. The median of the 3 largest integers is 6.

J. The largest integer is 9.

K. The largest integer is 8.

68. The student body at Julian High School consists of Sophomores to juniors, and seniors. only. The ratio of sophomores to juniors, to seniors on Julian High School's student council is 2 : 3 : 4. There are 15 juniors on the student council. How many students are on the entire student council?

F. 21　　G. 24　　H. 45　　J. 60　　K. 135

69. Mara is the timer for a road race. She is 200 feet from the starting gun. Using 1,120 feet per second for the speed of sound, which of the following is closest to how many seconds after the starting gun is fired that Mara will hear the starting gun?

A. 0.1　　B. 0.2　　C. 0.6　　D. 0.9　　E. 1.3

70. The Dow Jones Industrial Average (DJIA) is an index of stock values. The chart below gives the DJIA closing values from August 24 through September 30 of a certain year and the change in the closing value from the previous day. A minus sign indicates a decline (a losing value less than the previous day's closing value). A plus sigh indicates an advance (a closing value greater than the previous day's closing value).

Dow Jones Industrial Average Closing Values

Date	Closing value	Change	Date	Closing	Change
8/24	8 600		9/13	7 945	+150
8/25	8 515	−85	9/14	8 020	+75
8/26	8 160	−355	9/15	8 090	+70
8/27	8 050	−110	9/16	7 870	−220
8/30	7 540	−510	9/17	7 895	+25
8/31	7 825	+285	9/20	7 930	+35
9/01	7 780	45	9/21	7 900	−30
9/02	7 680	−100	9/22	8 150	+250
9/03	7 640	−40	9/23	8 000	−150
9/07	8 020	+380	9/24	8 025	+25
9/08	7 060	−160	9/27	8 110	+85
9/09	8 045	+185	9/28	8 080	−30
9/10	7 795	−250	9/29	7 845	−235
			9/30	7 630	−215

The chart shows 4 more declines than advances. All of the following statements are true. Which one best explains why the decline from the August 24 closing value to the September 30 closing value was relatively large?

F. The greatest change in the chart was a decline.

G. The least change in the chart was an advance.

H. The greatest number of consecutive declines was greater than the greatest number of consecutive advances.

J. The first change was a decline.

K. The average of the declines was much greater than the average of the advances.

71. What is the average closing value for the 5-day period from September 13 through September 17 ?

A. 7,895　　B. 7,920　　C. 7,964　　D. 7,980　　E. 8,090

72. In the figure below, both solids consist of 4 cubes, each 1 unit of a side. In the solid on the right, the 4 cubes form a rectangular prism that is 2 units long, I unit wide, and 2 units high. The solid on the left is the result of moving Cube D from its position above Cube C to beside. it so that Cubes B, C, and D form a rectangular prism 3 units long, 1 unit wide, and 1 unit

high. To the nearest percent, the total surface area of the solid on the right is what percent less than the total surface area of the solid on the left?

F. 0%　　G. 2%　　H. 6%　　J. 11%　　K. 13%

［**Session 1 答案**］

1 C	2 F	3 J	4 B	5 C	6 B	7 J	8 K	9 B	10 K
11 C	12 F	13 E	14 A	15 H	16 D	17 G	18 G	19 D	20 B
21 J	22 J	23 B	24 D	25 A	26 J	27 B	28 C	29 G	30 K
31 D	32 A	33 E	34 E	35 B	36 J	37 A	38 C	39 A	40 F
41 H	42 C	43 H	44 E	45 G	46 E	47 J	48 C	49 B	50 F
51 J	52 J	53 K	54 D	55 C	56 D	57 A	58 C	59 E	60 G
61 E	62 D	63 A	64 B	65 F	66 C	67 K	68 H	69 B	70 K
71 C	72 J								

［**Session 1 答案解析**］

1. 题干：$\frac{2^2-1^4}{3^2-1^5}$ 的值是多少？

   解析：注意 1 的任意次方都等于 1。

2. 题干：蛇眼的意思是两个骰子都为 1 点，求问蛇眼出现的几率？

   解析：一个骰子出现 1 的几率是 1/6，两个只要相乘即可。

3. 题干：一条线长 $5\frac{1}{2}$ 单位，如果其中一个端点位于 $-3\frac{1}{2}$，那么另一个端点的坐标可能是多少？

   解析：将第一个端点减去或者加上长度即可。

4. 题干：在一个商店里，所有的收音机降价 15%出售。一个顾客买了一个原价 120 的收音机，算上 5%的销售税，这位顾客要付多少钱？

   解析：注意销售税要根据降价后的价格来算。

5. 题干：一共售出 450 张票，总额 2 000 元，其中成人票 5 元一张，儿童票 3 元一张，求问一共卖出几张成人票？

   解析：设卖出 x 张成人票，则儿童票卖出了 $450-x$ 张，分别乘以票价得到方程。

6. 题干：$\frac{1}{3}\times\frac{2}{4}\times\frac{3}{5}\times\frac{4}{6}\times\frac{5}{7}\times\frac{6}{8}\times\frac{7}{9}\times\frac{8}{10}=?$

   解析：注意每隔一个数字，分子分母可以消去。

7. 题干：分子的最小公倍数是多少？

   $\frac{1}{13^2\cdot17\cdot23}+\frac{1}{17^2\cdot23}+\frac{1}{17\cdot23^3}$

   解析：要有 2 个 17，3 个 23，2 个 13。

8. 题干：环境俱乐部要选举，先选一个主席，然后一个副主席，最后一个秘书。每个人只能担任一个职位,从 20 个人里选举,一共有多少种可能?

解析:首先主席有 20 中可能;然后副主席有 19 种,因为主席不能同时担任副主席;同样的,秘书有 18 中可能。

9. 题干:在 $\frac{21}{3}$ 中间填入什么符号会使结果最大?

解析:逐一试验即可。

10. 题干:一个直径 29 英尺的轮子无滑动地滚动,25 圈后走了多远?

解析:求出周长的 25 倍即可。

11. 题干:一个热气球在机场向东 10 公里,向北 3 公里处,另一个热气球在这个机场向西 2 公里,向南 5 公里处,求问两个气球之间的距离?

解析:在纸上画出坐标系,以机场为原点,标出热气球然后再计算距离。

12. 题干:$\sqrt[n]{2^p}$ 在 n 为大于 2 的整数,p 为非零实数时有意义。什么时候 $\sqrt[n]{2^p}$ 会是正整数?

解析:正整数的正整数次方仍然是正整数。

13. 题干:三条直线可以把一个区域分成几份?

解析:分类即可。三条直线没有交点,一个交点,两个交点。

14. 题干:Joan 的银行账户里的钱变成原来的三倍,然后 Joan 取了 500,剩下 100。问最开始有多少?

解析:设最开始有 x 即可。然后 $3x - 500 = 100$。

15. 题干:由于通货膨胀,某车的价格贵了 10%,原来是 1 500,现在是多少?

解析:涨价的那部分等于原价乘以涨价幅度。

16. 题干:0.005 是哪个数的 100 倍?

解析:0.005 除以 100 即可。

17. 题干:正方形被六边形包围,然后该图案重复出现。所有正方形是全等的,六边形也是全等的。如果一共有 20 个正方形,那么有多少个六边形?

解析:先不考虑第第一个图案,考虑后面的重复单元,每一个正方形对应 3 个六边形。第一个是一对四。所以一共有 $3 \times 19 + 4 = 61$ 个六边形。

18. 题干:75%的学生上了 8 门数学课,剩下的里面的 60%上了 6 门或者 7 门。请问少于 6 门的百分比是多少?

解析:上了 6 或者 7 门的百分比为 25%×60%,即 15%。

19. 题干:买车,可以分 36、48,或者 60 期,年利率均为 5%。若某人一个月最多能拿出 300 块,那么他能买到的最贵的车是多少钱?

解析:设买到了 x 价格的车,易知 60 期可以买到最贵,即要花 5 年来还。题目要求的是在下列选项中能买得起的最贵的,所以不必求出精确值。

20. 题干:一家公司清理壁炉是 30 块起价,然后每小时再加 22,另一家是 35 起价,每小时再加 20。如果两家花费一样,那么多少小时?

解析:设 x 小时即可,分别算出费用令二者相等。

21. 题干:选项中是 5 个人跑的距离。所花的时间一样,请问哪个人跑得最快?

解析:找出最大的值即可。

22. 题干:1 到 c 连续整数的和的立方是哪一个?

解析:立方即 3 次方。

23. 题干:第一天老师教给学生 5 个词,以后每一天教 3 个。20 天后一共教了多少个?

解析:$3 \times 19 + 5 = 62$。

24. 题干：舒张压随着年龄线性增长。如果 20 岁平均舒张压是 120，60 岁平均 140，那么 50 岁平均多少？
    解析：可以看到每增长 10 岁，舒张压增长 5。
25. 题干：轮子一分钟转 45 圈，那么 1.5 分钟转了多少度？
    解析：一圈是 360 度。
26. 题干：a，b，c 都是整数，而且 $a < 0$，$0 < b < 30$，求问 c 的最小值？
    解析：a，b 均取最大即可。
27. 题干：要运 75 000 份物资，大车一次运 15 000 份，小车一次 12 000 份，每辆车只能运一次。有两辆大车，要用几辆小车？
    解析：把大车能运的算出来，然后剩下的除以小车的运力。
28. 题干：堆东西，最下面 25 个，每高一层少一个，第十层多少个？
    解析：$25 - 9$ 即可。
29. 题干：a 比 b 等于 3 比 1，b 比 c 等于 1 比 5。那么 $\frac{2a+3b}{4b+3c}$ 是多少？
    解析：全部换成 c。
30. 题干：时间 E 发生的概率是 P(E)，不发生的概率是 P(not E)，那么哪个选项是对的？
    解析：不发生和发生的概率加起来等于 1。
31. 题干：一共得了 26 分，其中 1 分的有 4 个，3 分的比 2 分的多。请问 3 分的有几个？
    解析：可以列出 3 分和 2 分的各种情况，最后符合总分 26 的只有一种。
32. 题干：某人每周减肥可以减掉 1.75 磅。那么 1.75 磅占他体重的比例怎么变化？
    解析：体重越来越轻，必然 1.75 占的越来越多。
33. 题干：驾照前三位是字母，然后是两位数字。所有的字母和数字只能出现一次，一共有几种情况？
    解析：因为不能重复出现，所以乘的时候要递减。
34. 题干：(600，89.99)，(1 000，119.99)，和(1 400，149.99)在同一条线上，(400，z)也在线上，z 是多少？
    解析：x 轴每少 400，y 少 30。
35. 题干：x 除以 8 余 5，y 除以 6 余 1。X 和 y 都大于等于 20，二者的和最小是多少？
    解析：x 最小是 21，y 最小是 25。
36. 题干：$|a| \cdot b = a \cdot |b|$，而且 a，b 都是实数。二者有什么关系？
    解析：二者相乘大于等于零。
37. 题干：$\frac{(k+1)!(k-1)!}{(k!)^2}$ 和哪个等价？
    解析：$k+1$ 的阶乘是 k 阶乘的 $k+1$ 倍。
38. 题干：普通爆米花一罐 5 块，caramel 爆米花一罐 8 块。一共卖了 160 罐，共 1 010 块。Caramel 爆米花卖了几罐？
    解析：设卖了 x 罐。
39. 题干：Local 在哪一段时间内走的比 Express 快？
    解析：看斜率即可。
40. 题干：Local 在站点上花了多少时间？
    解析：位移不变的就是在站点。
41. 题干：整数 a 比正整数 b 大 4，整数 c 比 b 小 4，$ab = 84$，$b =$？

解析：可以用 b 来表示 a。

42. 题干：6 个历史事件需要排顺序，你知道最早的和最晚的，其他的随机排，排对的概率是多少？
解析：中间一共有 24 种排法，只有一种是对的。

43. 题干：时间可以用四位或三位数字表示，这些数字的乘积最大值是多少？
解析：9∶59 乘积最大。

44. 题干：两整数的差是 4，和是 38，其中大的那个是多少？
解析：设大的为 x。

45. 题干：x 是 35 的因数，y 是 16 的因数，二者的乘积不可能是哪个？
解析：找出二者所有的情况。

46. 题干：n_e 等于所有小于或等于 n 的正偶数的乘积。那么 $\frac{12_e}{3_e}$ 等于多少？
解析：按照定义即可。

47. 题干：按照图示，输入 a，b，c，d 四个信号，与或非符号如图示。输入什么样的信号可以得到输出 1？
解析：1 and 1 = 1，0 or 0 = 0，not 0 = 1，1 and 1 = 1。

48. 题干：下面的数轴上哪一段表示 $|x|-b \geqslant 4$？
解析：即 x 的绝对值 >= $b+4$。

49. 题干：拼写 20 个单词，下面哪个概率可能是拼写正确率？
解析：一个概率是 5%，所以必须是 5% 的倍数。

50. 题干：一串几何数列前几位为 0.375，-1.5，6，-24，96。第六个是什么？
解析：前一位乘以 -6 等到后一位。

51. 题干：如图所示，$AB = 4$，$BC = 14$，$AD = 6$，求 BE？
解析：利用相似三角形。

52. 题干：前 200 个每个赚 0.4，接下来 300 个每个赚 0.5，再接下来每个赚 0.6。什么能赚到 350？
解析：先算出前 500 个能赚多少。

53. 题干：55 个人选了社会学，44 个人选了绘画，20 个人两个都选了。一共 120 人，有多少人都没选？
解析：可以先算出只选了一个的人数。

54. 题干：从 6 个字母里选 3 个按顺序排列，不重复，有几种情况？
解析：$6\times5\times4$。

55. 题干：第一种柴火一捆 2 块，第二种 4 块。一共买了 25 捆，花了 66 块，第一种买了多少捆？
解析：设为 x 即可。鸡兔同笼问题。

56. 题干：n^n，$(n!)^n$，and $(n!)^{n!}$ 按大小排顺序。
解析：最快的方法是代个数字进去。

57. 题干：两个质数的和是质数，问选项中哪个是原来这两个质数中的一个？
解析：除了 2 之外所有质数都是奇数(因为如果是偶数，必然能被 2 整除，与质数定义矛盾)，所以这两个质数的和必为奇数。那么这两个质数必然不能都是奇数(因为奇数与奇数的和为偶数)，所以必然有一个质数为偶数。同时是质数和偶数的数就只有 2。

58. 题干：第一种交通工具没加仑油可以跑 14 英里，第二种 36 英里。如果都跑了 1 008 英里，那么第一种多用了多少油？
解析：分别求出用的油。

59. 题干：衣服的库存如左边的矩阵所示，价格如右边所示。一共值多少钱？
解析：矩阵相乘即可。

60. 题干：刷四面墙，每个墙都是 10×15。其中有个 3×5 的窗户和 3.5×7 的门不用刷。每加仑的油漆可以刷的面积为 300 到 350，一罐一加仑，至少要买多少罐？
    解析：至少的话，则可以认为一加仑刷 350。
61. 题干：哪个是有理数？
    解析：化简即可。
62. 题干：从 100 到 999 选一个数字，选择的数字中含有 0 的概率是多少？
    解析：找出含有 0 的数字的个数然后除以总数。
63. 题干：香蕉是苹果的 2 倍，橘子是菠萝的 10 倍，苹果和橘子一样。菠萝 1 个，其他分别是多少？
    解析：从菠萝开始一个个入手即可。
64. 题干：某球员挥棒 120，击中 25 次。从现在起她每次都击中，那么至少要挥棒几次才可以让击中率达到 0.3？
    解析：设她又挥了 x 次棒即可。
65. 题干：$0 < a < 1$，哪个数值最大？
    解析：$1/a$ 大于 1。
66. 题干：四个人，按顺序排列有几种可能？
    解析：$4\times3\times2$。
67. 题干：五个整数。中位数是 6，公因数只有 2，平均数是 5。哪种说法正确？
    解析：由平均数求出总和 25，2 不是 9 的因数。
68. 题干：一年级、二年级、三年级的人数比是 2∶3∶4，二年级 15 人，一共多少人？
    解析：求出分别的人数再相加。
69. 题干：距离 200 英尺，枪响后多少时间能听到？声速 1 120 英尺每秒。
    解析：距离除以时间即可。
70. 题干：表格中可以发现下降的比上升的多。为什么？
    解析：下降的幅度都比较大。
71. 题干：913 到 917 的平均值。
    解析：和除以 5。
72. 题干：右边的表面积比左边的少了多少？
    解析：注意长宽高不同。

Session 2　Arithmetic 2 算术 2

Use the following information to answer questions 1 - 3.

The senior class at Figg High School is sponsoring a fund-raiser to raise \$1,250.00 for a graduation celebration. They can choose 1 of the 2 fund below.

Candy Bar option: After paying a start-up fee of \$15.00, the senior class can purchase candy bars for \$0.38 each and sell them for \$1.00 each.

Photo Prints option: After paying a start-up fee of \$25.00, the senior class can sell photo prints at prom. The film and flash for the camera cost \$1.00 per print. The senior class will sell each print for \$3.00.

1. For the Photo Prints option, at least how many prints must be sold to cover the start-up fee for the fund-raiser?

   F. 8　　G. 9　　H. 12　　J. 13　　K. 25

2. There are 510 students in the senior class at Figg High School. Abram suggests that instead of selling something, each senior donate \$3.00 toward the goal. If 80% of the senior class donates \$3.00, by what percent, to the, nearest whole percent of the goal, would the class fall short of the goal?

A. 1% B. 2% C. 3% D. 4% E. 5%

3. The senior class chose the Candy Bar option and met their fund-raising goal. They must have sold a minimum of how many candy bars?

F. 1,978 G. 2,041 H. 2,259 J. 3,250 K. 3,329

4. When using the quadratic formula, Monali found that an equation had solutions $x = 5 \pm \sqrt{-9a^2}$. where a is a positive real number. Which of the following expressions gives Monali's solutions as complex numbers?

A. $5 \pm 1ai$ B. $5 \pm 3ai$ C. $5 \pm 6ai$ D. $5 \pm 9ai$ E. $5 \pm 12ai$

5. When asked his age, the algebra teacher said, "If you square my age, then subtract 23 times my age, the result is 50." How old is he?

F. 23 G. 25 H. 27 J. 46 K. 50

Use the following information to answer questions 6 - 8.

Marcia makes and sells handcrafted picture frames in 2 sizes: small and large. It takes her 2 hours to make a small frame and 3 hours to make a large frame. The shaded triangular region shown below is the graph of a system of inequalities representing weekly constraints Marcia has in making the frames. For making and selling s small frames and l large frames, Marcia makes a profit of 30s + 70l dollars. Marcia sells all the frames she makes.

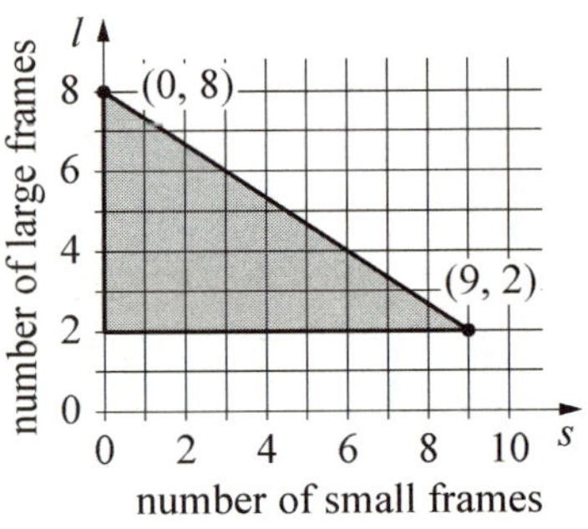

6. The weekly constraint represented by the horizontal line segment containing (9, 2) means that each week Marcia makes a minimum of:

F. 2 large frames. G. 9 large frames.

H. 2 small frames. J. 9 small frames.

K. 11 small frames.

7. For every hour that Marcia spends making frames in the second week of December each year, she donates \$3 from that week's profit to a local charity. This year, Marcia made 4 large frames and 2 small frames in that week. Which of the following is closest to the percent of that week's profit Marcia donated to the charity?

A. 6% B. 12% C. 14% D. 16% E. 19%

8. What is the maximum profit Marcia can earn from the picture frames she makes in I week?

F. \$410 G. \$460 H. \$540 J. \$560 K. \$690

9. What is the least common denominator for adding the fractions $\frac{4}{35}$, $\frac{1}{56}$, and $\frac{3}{16}$?

F. 80 G. 560 H. 1,960 J. 4,480 K. 31,360

10. Max bought several bags of organic lawn fertilizer. and each bag covers 5,000 square feet of lawn. He is fertilizing a lawn that is 50 feet wide. He pours 1 bag into the fertilizer spreader

and begins fertilizing. Before he needs to refill the spreader, Max can fertilize a rectangle that is the width of the lawn and is how many feet long?

F. 50　　G. 100　　H. 2,450　　J. 4,950　　K. 5,050

11. A supermarket soup can display consists of 5 levels of stacked cans. The figure below shows an overhead view of the top level of cans (circles shaded and with solid borders) and the level of cans below it (circles with dashed borders). In the display, each level has 4 more cans than the level above it. How many cans are in the display?

A. 60　　B. 100　　C. 116

D. 120　　E. 140

12. A greenhouse contained both 6-inch-high geraniums and 3-inch-high geraniums. The 6-inch-high geraniums were taken out of the greenhouse in early spring and grew at a rate of I inch per week. The 3-inch-high geraniums remained in the greenhouse and grew at a rate of $1\frac{1}{12}$ inches per week. After the 6-inch-high geraniums were taken outside, in how many weeks were both groups of geraniums the same height?

A. $7\frac{1}{2}$　　B. 6　　C. $4\frac{1}{2}$　　D. 3　　E. $1\frac{1}{2}$

13. A box contains 100 cardboard circles. Written on each circle is one of the following numbers, with no numbers repeated: $\sqrt{1}$, $\sqrt{2}$, $\sqrt{3}$, $\cdots$ $\sqrt{100}$. A circle is drawn at random from the box. What is the probability that the number on the circle is a rational number?

F. $\frac{0}{100}$　　G. $\frac{9}{100}$　　H. $\frac{10}{100}$　　J. $\frac{50}{100}$　　K. $\frac{74}{100}$

14. Reuben is standing 300 yards due east from the flagpole at his school and 400 yards due south from the oak tree in his front yard. What is the straight-line distance, in yards, from the flagpole to the oak tree?

F. $10\sqrt{7}$　　G. $100\sqrt{7}$　　H. 100　　J. 500　　K. 700

Use the following information to answer questions 15 - 17.

Kyla purchased 25 pieces of candy from Laszko's Candy Shop. Her purchase consists of 7 lollipops, 4 candy bars, 10 licorice sticks, and 4 gumballs. The unit price of each candy item is shown in the table below. Kyla's purchase, without sales tax, totaled \$10.30. Laszko's charges an 8% sales tax on each purchase, which is calculated by multiplying the purchase total by 0.08 and rounding to the nearest \$0.01.

Candy item	Unit price
Lollipop	\$0.90
Candy bar	\$0.60
Licorice stick	\$0.10
Gumball	\$0.15

15. Kyla gave the shop clerk \$15.00. How much change should Kyla have received?

A. \$3.88　　B. \$4.35　　C. \$4.62　　D. \$4.70　　E. \$5.08

16. Without sales tax, what was the average price Kyla paid per piece of candy, to the nearest \$0.01?

F. \$0.21　　G. \$0.25　　H. \$0.32　　J. \$0.41　　K. \$0.44

17. Kyla offers to sell 2 of the 25 pieces of candy to her brother Virgil. She lets Virgil have a choice of 2 pieces of the same candy item or 1 piece each of 2 different candy items. Kyla will have Virgil pay the same total cost for the 2 pieces that he would pay for the 2 pieces at Laszko's. How many different total costs (in dollars) are possible for Virgil's choice of 2 pieces?

A. 8　　B. 10　　C. 12　　D. 14　　E. 16

18. The marketing students at Fort Link Business Academy took a placement test for an accounting class. The mean of the test scores is 100 and the standard deviation is 15. In order to be accepted into the accounting class, a student must have attained a test score that is at least 1 standard deviation above the mean. What is the lowest test score a student could attain and still be accepted into the accounting class?

A. 15　　B. 16　　C. 101　　D. 115　　E. 116

19. The C & F Company manufactures cameras and rolls of film. The constraints on C & F's weekly production are shown on the coordinate plane below. The shaded region contains the feasible combinations of the number of cameras and the number of rolls of film produced in 1 week. Each vertex of the shaded region has integer coordinates (in thousands). The company makes a profit of \$3 per camera sold and \$1 per roll of film sold. Within the given constraints, what is the greatest possible profit, in dollars, from 1 week of C & F's production?

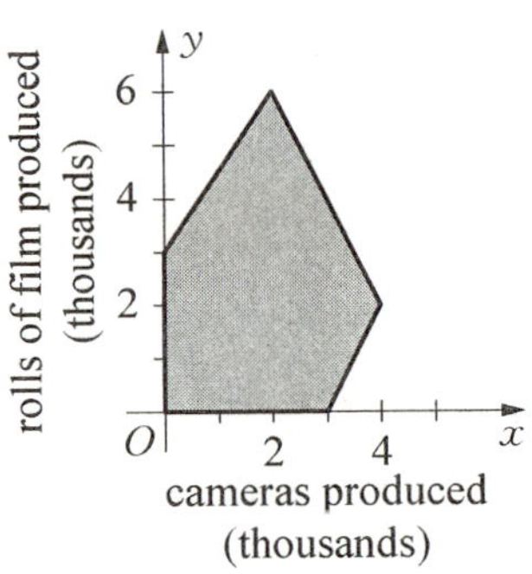

F. \$9,000　　G. \$10,000

H. \$12,000　　J. \$14,000

K. \$20,000

20. A high school band needs to make 3 sizes of flags—small, medium, and large—for an upcoming halftime show. The 3 sizes of flags are made by combining 1-foot squares of material that come in 2 colors. Four band members have agreed to make the flags. The information they will need is given to them in the tables below. The table with colors tells how many 1-foot squares of each color are needed for each size flag, and the table with names tells how many flags of each size that each person is to make.

	red	blue
small	2	2
medium	5	3
large	10	5

	small	medium	large
Jalinda	0	6	2
Lance	0	3	3
Hamako	2	6	0
Dakota	8	0	0

How many 1-foot squares of blue material does Lance need to make his flags?

A. 42 B. 24 C. 20 D. 15 E. 14

21. Ms. Johnson-purchased 1,000 prizes for the school carnival for \$90. Each prize costs either \$0.05 or \$0.25. How many of the less expensive prizes did she buy?

F. 200 G. 360 H. 500 J. 640 K. 800

22. In a large high school, some teachers teach only 1 subject, and some teachers teach more than 1 subject. Using the information given in the table below about the math, science, and gym teachers in the school, how many teachers teach math only?

Number of teachers	Subject (s) taught
12	at least 1 class of math
10	at least 1 class of gym
20	at least 1 class of science
6	both gym and science but not math
5	both math and science but not gym
2	gym only
1	math, gym, and science

F. 1 G. 2 H. 5 J. 16 K. 28

Use the following information to answerquestions 23 – 25.

The Environmental Club at Forrest Hills High School grows plants in the school's greenhouse. The members of the club sell the plants to raise money for the school, and Sami and Jacque are taking an inventory of the plants. The table below gives the numbers of packs of plants. For example, there are 60 packs of sunflowers with 1 plant per pack, 25 packs of petunias with 4 plants per pack, and 15 packs of tomatoes with 6 plants per pack. All of the packs have been counted except for the 6-plant packs of marigolds.

Plants	Number of 1-plant packs	Number of 4-plant packs	Number of 6-plant packs
Tomatoes	30	0	15
Marigolds	60	40	?
Petunias	0	25	100
Sunflowers	60	0	0

23. Jacque completes the inventory and later tells Sami that the number of marigold plants is the same as the number of petunia plants. How many 6-plant packs of marigolds are in the greenhouse?

A. 20 B. 25 C. 70 D. 80 E. 480

24. Mr. Mai bought $\frac{1}{10}$ of the sunflower plants for \$15.00. What was the price of 1 sunflower plant?

F. \$0.25 G. \$0.40 H. \$1.50 J. \$2.00 K. \$2.50

25. Helen takes all of the tomato plants in 1-plant packs and puts them together to make as many 4-plant packs as she can. How many whole 4-plant packs of tomato plants can Helen make?

A. 5 B. 7 C. 8 D. 15 E. 30

26. Mr. Cleary's algebra class is discussing slopes of lines. The class is to graph the total cost, C, of buying h hamburgers that cost 99¢ each. Mr. Cleary asks the class to describe the slope between any 2 points (h, C) on the graph. Devon gives a correct response that the slope between any 2 points on this graph is always:

F. zero.
G. the same positive value.
H. the same negative value.
J. a positive value, but the value varies.
K. a negative value, but the value varies.

27. A plane contains 11 horizontal lines and 11 vertical lines. These lines divide the plane into disjoint regions. How many of these disjoint regions have a finite, nonzero area?

A. 100 B. 110 C. 144 D. 156 E. 169

28. A warehouse dispatcher is arranging the delivery of 83,000 condensers. She will use 2 large-size trucks, each carrying a maximum of 18,000 condensers. The remaining trucks are small-size trucks, each carrying a maximum of 7,000 condensers. Each truck she uses will make exactly 1 trip. Along with the 2 large-size trucks, what is the minimum number of small-size trucks needed to deliver all the condensers?

F. 4 G. 6 H. 7 J. 9 K. 10

Use the following information to answer questions 29 – 31.

The table below gives the price per gallon of unleaded gasoline at Gus's Gas Station on January 1 for 5 consecutive years in the 1990s. At. Gus's, a customer can purchase car wash for \$4.00.

Year	Price	Year	Price
1	\$1.34	4	\$1.25
2	\$1.41	5	\$1.36
3	\$1.41		

29. What is the mean price per gallon, to the nearest \$0.01, on January 1 for the 5 years listed in the table?

F. \$1.25 G. \$1.33 H. \$1.34 J. \$1.35 K. \$1.41

30. The price for gas on January 1 of Year 6 was 3% higher than the price on January 1 of Year 5. To the nearest \$0.01, how much was the price per gallon on January 1 of Year 6?

A. \$1.39 B. \$1.40 C. \$1.66 D. \$1.77 E. \$2.39

31. On January 1 of Year 5, Anamosa bought gas and a car wash at Gus's. She put 11.38 gallons of

gas in her car and 1.85 gallons of gas in a container for her snow blower. To the nearest \$0.01, how much did Anamosa pay for the gas for her car and snow blower, and a car wash?

F. \$15.48 G. \$17.23 H. \$17.99 J. \$19.48 K. \$21.99

32. The decimal representation of 3.9×10^{-93} is:

F. a decimal point, followed by 92 zeros, then the digits 3 and 9.

G. a decimal point, followed by 93 zeros, then the digits 3 and 9.

H. a negative sign, followed by the digits 3 and 9, then 92 zeros, then a decimal point.

J. a negative sign, followed by the digits 3 and 9, then 93 zeros, then a decimal point.

K. a negative sign, followed by the digits 3 and 9, then 94 zeros, then a decimal point.

33. In how many distinct orders can 5 students stand in line to buy yearbooks?

A. 5 B. 15 C. 25 D. 120 E. 3,125

34. A teacher asked all the students in the junior class about the number of cats and/or dogs their family had. The results are given in the table below. How many students answered that their family had 1 or more cats?

		1 or more cats?	
		yes	no
1 or more dogs?	yes	48	84
	no	66	52

F. 48 G. 114 H. 132

J. 198 K. 250

35. Happy Soup Company stamps a 6-character product code on each can of soup it produces. Each product code consists of 5 letters (from the 26-letter alphabet) followed by a single digit (from the digits 0 to 9). The letters may repeat. How many such product codes are possible?

F. 5(26)(10) G. 5(4)(3)(2)

H. $1^5(10)$ J. 26(25)(24)(23)(22)(10)

K. $26^5(10)$

36. Which of the following complex numbers is a sum of $\sqrt{-48}$ and $\sqrt{-27}$?

A. $-5\sqrt{3}$ B. $-7\sqrt{3}$ C. $5i\sqrt{3}$ D. $7i\sqrt{3}$ E. $25i\sqrt{3}$

37. List B consists of all the integers in List A below and also 3 integers a, b, and c, where $a\leqslant 17$, $b=c$, and $b\geqslant 42$. What is the median of the integers in List B?

List A: 12, 16, 17, 29, 29, 35, 41, 42, 47, 47, 50

F. 29 G. 32 H. 35 J. 38 K. 41

38. The table below gives the heart rates, in beats per minute (bpm), for 8 participants in a fitness study after each participant completed 45 minutes of aerobic exercise. What is the mean heart rate of the 8 participants, to the nearest 0.1 bpm?

Participant	Heart rate (bpm)
1	130
2	155
3	162
4	148
5	177
6	162
7	170
8	156
Sum	1 260

A. 137.3

B. 153.5

C. 157.5

D. 162.0

E. 162.5

39. The first question on a 2-question quiz offers 2 answers, and exactly 1 answer must be chosen. The second

question offers 5 answers, and exactly 1 answer must be chosen. The quiz has how many possible combinations of answers?

A. 5 B. 10 C. 20 D. 25 E. 100

40. If cantaloupes sell at \$1.49 each or 3 for \$3.90, how much is saved, to the nearest cent, on each cantaloupe by buying them 3 at a time?

F. 12 ¢ G. 19 ¢ H. 31 ¢ J. 47 ¢ K. 92 ¢

41. When the owner of Pretty Pooches increases the price to have a small dog shampooed, the number of small dogs shampooed per day decreases. The expression $ax + b$ represents the number of small dogs shampooed in 1 day whenever the price is x dollars per dog. The number of small dogs shampooed per day was 12 when the price in the table was in effect. The number of small dogs shampooed per day decreases by 2 for every \$5 increase in price. What are the values of a and b ?

A.	$-\frac{5}{2}$	62	D.	2	200
B.	$-\frac{2}{5}$	20	E.	5	2
C.	$\frac{2}{5}$	4			

42. $\dfrac{1}{1+\dfrac{1}{1+\dfrac{1}{2}}}=?$

F. $\frac{5}{3}$ G. $\frac{3}{2}$ H. $\frac{3}{4}$ J. $\frac{2}{3}$ K. $\frac{3}{5}$

43. For all pairs of nonzero real numbers a and b, the product of the complex number $a+bi$ and which of the following complex numbers is a real number?

A. abi B. $a+bi$ C. $a-bi$ D. $b+ai$ E. $b-ai$

44. Which of the following fractions is equal to $\frac{1}{11^{20}}-\frac{1}{11^{21}}$?

A. $\frac{1}{11^{21}}$ B. $\frac{1}{11^{22}}$ C. $\frac{1}{11^{40}}$ D. $\frac{10}{11^{21}}$ E. $\frac{10}{11^{41}}$

Use the following information to answer questions 45 - 47.

Jason will have a rectangular concrete patio constructed beside his house, as shown below. The patio will have a length of 18 feet, and the top surface of the patio will have an area of 270 square feet. The patio will be constructed so that one side of the patio is against a side of Jason's house.

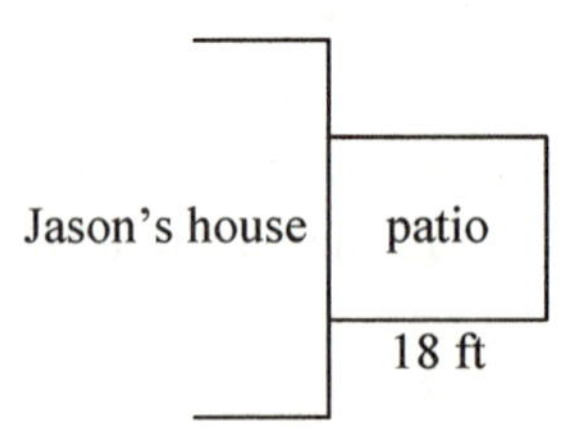

45. The patio will have a thickness of 6 inches. The patio will consist of how many cubic feet of concrete?

F. 45 G. 90 H. 108 J. 117 K. 135

46. Jason chooses Tully's Concrete Finishing to seal his patio. Tully's Concrete Finishing uses the

formula $C = 3.5A + 120$ to calculate the charge, C dollars, to seal a patio, where A square feet is the area of the top surface of the patio. What will be the charge for sealing Jason's patio?

A. \$483　B. \$945　C. \$1,065　D. \$1,128　E. \$1,365

47. Jason will plant shrubs along the portion of the perimeter of the patio that is NOT against his house. What is the length, in feet, of that portion?

F. 33　G. 43.5　H. 48　J. 51　K. 66

48. Sofia and Lance are contributing a total of \$2,500 per year to help their nephew pay for college. Each year, Lance contributes $1\frac{1}{2}$ times the amount Sofia contributes. What is the amount, in dollars, Lance will contribute over a period of 4 years?

A. \$1,250　B. \$1,875　C. \$4,000　D. \$5,000　E. \$6,000

49. A health club surveyed 175 members about which types of equipment they had used in the past month. Of the 175 members, 117 had used treadmills, 89 had used stationary bikes, and 53 had used both types of equipment. Some members had used neither type of equipment? Of the 175 members, how many had used treadmills, stationary bikes, or both?

A. 53　B. 81　C. 122　D. 134　E. 153

50. What percent of the even numbers from 2 to 50, inclusive, have a units digit that is twice the tens digit?

F. 4%　G. 5%　H. 8%　J. 16%　K. 20%

51. As a motivational speaker, Bree speaks at school assemblies, charging a school district for her travel costs and a fixed amount per assembly. Bree used the equation $C = 50a + 1,500$ to determine the charge of C dollars to speak at assemblies in the Escambia City School District. Bree charged the district \$4,250 to speak at school assemblies. How many assemblies did Bree speak at in this district?

F. 30　G. 54　H. 55　J. 85　K. 115

Use the following information to answer questions 52 – 54.

Miriam conducted a survey of the students in her 8th-grade class to determine which of 7 Olympic sports were the most popular. Each student who responded to the survey selected 1 Olympic sport as his or her favorite. The circle graph below shows the number of students who selected each of the 7 Olympic sports. A total of 40 students responded to the survey.

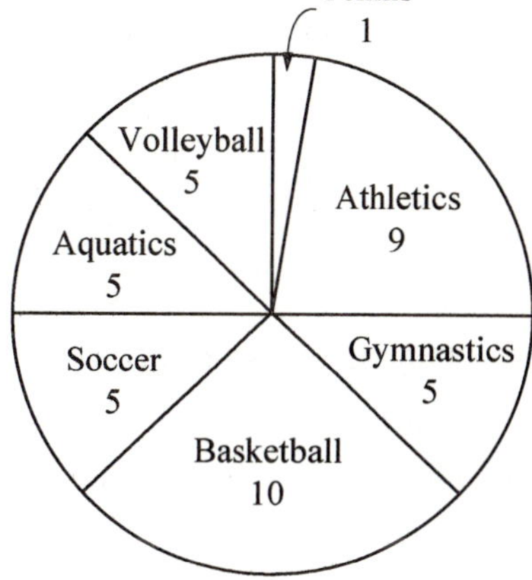

52. To the nearest 0.1%, what percent of the students who responded to the survey selected Basketball?

A. 10.0%　B. 12.5%　C. 22.5%
D. 25.0%　E. 30.0%

53. In this survey, what is the ratio of the number of students who selected Athletics to the number of students who selected Soccer?

F. 5 : 9　G. 5 : 14　H. 9 : 5　J. 9 : 14　K. 9 : 40

54. In the circle graph, what is the angle measure of the sector that represents the number of students who responded to the survey who selected Tennis?

A. 1° B. 4° C. 5° D. 9° E. 10°

55. A spinner dial from a game is shown in the figure below. Each numbered sector of the circle has the same central angle measure. If the arrow on the spinner dial is spun randomly, what is the probability the arrow will point to a sector whose number is both a multiple of 3 and a multiple of 4 ?

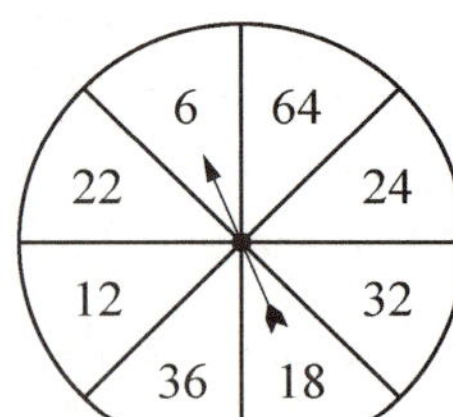

F. $\frac{3}{8}$ G. $\frac{1}{2}$ H. $\frac{5}{8}$ J. $\frac{3}{4}$

K. $\frac{7}{8}$

56. The counselors at Lakewood High School interviewed 200 students to determine placement in 3 different honors courses: Math, Chemistry, and Literature. The numbers of these students placed in these honors courses are shown in the Venn diagram below. Of these 200 students, 10% were placed into all 3 honors courses, and 35% were placed into exactly 2 honors courses. What percent of the students were placed into exactly 1 honors course?

Lakewood High School
Honors Course Placement

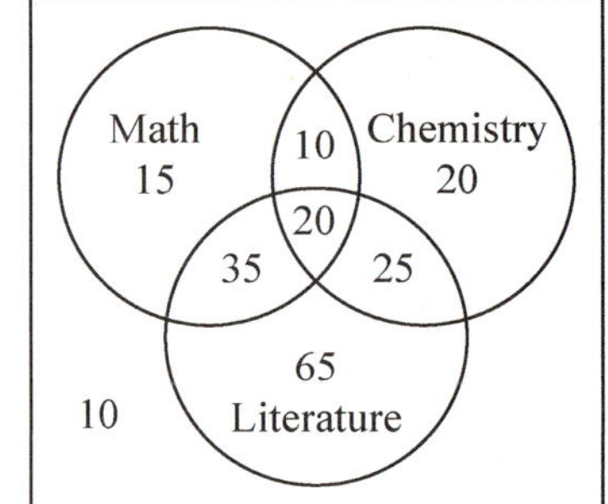

A. 7.5%

B. 10%

C. 32.5%

D. 45%

E. 50%

57. The equation $y =$ is graphed in the standard (x, y) coordinate plane below. No point on the graph has which of the following x-coordinates?

F. −3

G. −2

H. −1

J. 0

K. 1

58. The sum of a sequence of consecutive odd numbers, where the smallest term is 1, is always a perfect square. For example, $1+3=2^2$ and $1+3+5+7=4^2$. One of the sequences described above has a sum of 144. What is the largest odd number in the sequence?

F. 11 G. 13 H. 15 J. 23 K. 73

59. arry is paid a regular hourly wage of \$12.50 per hour for working up to and including 40 hours in 1 week. For each additional hour he works in a week, Harry is paid twice his regular hourly wage. Harry worked 46 hours this week. What is his pay for this week?

(Note: Amounts are before taxes and benefits are deducted.)

A. \$537.50 B. \$575.00 C. \$650.00 D. \$787.50 E. \$1,150.00

60. Send It Out mails advertisements for businesses. Two types of machines—stuffing machines and postage machines—are used to process envelopes. Each stuffing machine processes envelopes at the rate of 150 envelopes per minute, and each postage machine processes envelopes at the rate of 4 envelopes per second. Send It Out is currently using 24 stuffing machines. How many postage machines should be used so that the stuffing machines and the postage machines process the same number of envelopes in 1 minute ?

F. 6 G. 9 H. 15 J. 25 K. 60

Use the following information to answer questions 61 – 63.

Each of the 200 people in a random sample of the 2,500 people at the mall today was asked which, if any, of the following types of pets he or she owns: bird, cat, dog, or fish. All 200 people answered the question. The answers were tallied, and the exact percents of people who own the pets are shown in the diagram below.

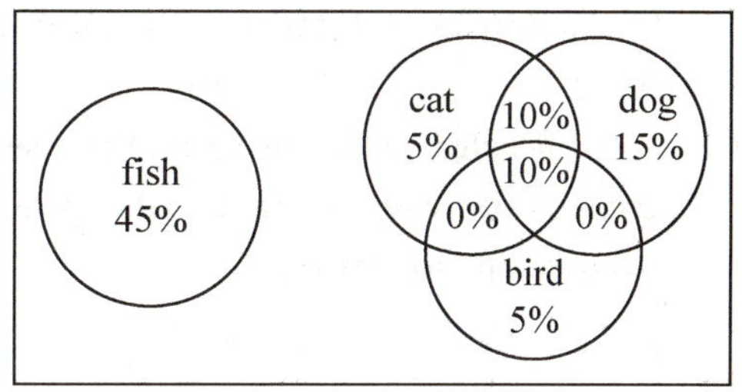

61. Because this was a random sample, the percents in the sample are the most likely estimates for the corresponding percents among all the people at the mall today. What estimate does this give for the number of people at the mall today who own dogs but none of the other 3 types of pets?

F. 125 G. 250 H. 375 J. 500 K. 875

62. What percent of the people in the random sample own exactly 1 type of the 4 types of pets?

A. 10% B. 25% C. 45% D. 70% E. 90%

63. Suppose 25 additional people at random were asked the question, with the following answers: 15 own fish only, 5 own a cat and a dog only, and 5 own a cat, a dog, and a bird only. Among all 225 people asked, what fraction own fish but none of the other 3 types of pets?

F. $\frac{105}{225}$ G. $\frac{105}{215}$ H. $\frac{105}{200}$ J. $\frac{115}{225}$ K. $\frac{115}{200}$

64. Each contestant at a math competition starts with 30 points. A contestant earns 10 points for each question answered correctly and loses 5 points for each question answered incorrectly. Sammi answered twice as many questions correctly as incorrectly, finishing with 150 points. How many questions did Sammi answer correctly?

A. 8 B. 12 C. 16 D. 20 E. 24

65. he stem-and-leaf plot below shows the number of daily credit card sales at Fancy Fabrics during a 34-day period. What is the median number of daily credit card sales?

Stem	Leaf
3	1 2 2 4 6 8
4	2 2 3 3 5 5 7 8
5	0 0 1 3 5 7 9 9 9
6	0 2 4 4 5 5 6
7	2 6 6 7

Key: 3 | 1=31

F. 52

G. 53

H. 54

J. 55

K. 59

66. Which of the following complex numbers equals $(6-7i)(\pi+6i)$?

F. $6\pi-42i$
G. $(6+\pi)-i$
H. $(6+\pi)+i$
J. $(6\pi+42)+(36-7\pi)i$
K. $(6\pi-42)+(36-7\pi)i$

67. The first term is 1 in the geometric sequence 1, −3, 9, −27, …. What is the. SEVENTH term of the geometric sequence?

A. −243
B. −30
C. 81
D. 189
E. 729

68. This month, Kami sold 70 figurines in 2 sizes. The large figurines sold for \$12 each, and the small figurines sold for \$8 each. The amount of money he received from die sales of the large figurines was equal to the amount of money he received from the sales of the small figurines. How many large figurines did Kami sell this month?

A. 20
B. 28
C. 35
D. 42
E. 50

69. A car accelerated from 88 feet per second (fps) to 220 fps in exactly 3 seconds. Assuming the acceleration was constant, what was the car's acceleration, in feet per second per second, from 88 fps to 220 fps ?

A. $\frac{1}{44}$
B. $29\frac{1}{3}$
C. 44
D. $75\frac{1}{3}$
E. $102\frac{2}{3}$

70. Mr. Dietz is a teacher whose salary is \$22,570 for this school year, which has 185 days. In Mr. Dietz's school district substitute teachers are paid \$80 per day. If Mr. Dietz takes a day off without pay and a substitute teacher is paid to teach Mr. Dietz's classes, how much less does the school district pay in salary by paying a substitute teacher instead of paying Mr. Dietz for that day?

A. \$42
B. \$80
C. \$97
D. \$105
E. \$122

71. The oxygen saturation level of a river is found by dividing the amount of dissolved oxygen the river water currently has per liter by the dissolved oxygen capacity per liter of the water and then converting to a percent. If the river currently has 7.3 milligrams of dis-solved oxygen per liter of water and the dissolved oxygen capacity is 9.8 milligrams per liter, what is the oxygen saturation level, to the nearest percent?

A. 34%
B. 70%
C. 73%
D. 98%

72. he number of students participating in fall sports at a certain high school can be shown by the following matrix. Tennis Soccer Cross-Country Football $[40\ 60\ 80\ 80]$ The athletic director estimates the radio of the number of snorts awards that will be earned to the number of students participating with the following matrix.

Tennis	0.3
Soccer	0.4
Cross-Country	0.2
Football	0.5

Given these matrices, what is the athletic director's estimate for the number of sports awards that will be earned for these fall sports?

A. 80
B. 88
C. 91
D. 92
E. 99

73. In decorating baskets for a retirement party, Rudy needs the following amounts of ribbon for

each basket:

number of ribbons	length (inches)
5	8
3	16
2	10

If the ribbon costs \$0.98 per yard, which of the following would be the approximate cost of ribbon for 10 baskets? (Note: 1 yard = 36 inches)

F. \$3 G. \$9 H. \$30 J. \$35 K. \$90

74. In the complex numbers, where $i^2 = -1$, $\frac{1}{1+i} \cdot \frac{1-i}{1-i} = ?$

F. $i-1$ G. $1+i$ H. $1-i$ J. $\frac{1-i}{2}$ K. $\frac{1+i}{2}$

75. Your friend shows you a scale drawing of her apartment. The drawing of the apartment is a rectangle 4 inches by 6 inches. Your friend wants to know the length of the shorter side of the apartment. If she knows that the length of the longer side of the apartment is 30 feet, how many feet long is the shorter side of her apartment?

A. 9 B. 20 C. 24. D. 30 E. 45

76. The median of a set of data containing 9 items was found. Four data items were added to the set. Two of these items were greater than the original median, and the other 2 items were less than the original median. Which of the following statements must be true about the median of the new data set?

A. It is the average of the 2 new lower values.
B. It is the same as the original median.
C. It is the average of the 2 new higher values.
D. It is greater than the original median.
E. It is less than the original median.

77. The normal amount of lead in a certain water supply is 1.5×10^{-5} milligrams per liter. Today, when the water was tested, the lead level found was exactly 100 times, as great as the normal level, still well below the Environmental Protection Agency's action level. What concentration of lead, ill milligrams per liter, was in the water tested today?

A. 1.5×10^{-105} B. 1.5×10^{-10} C. 1.5×10^{-7} D. 1.5×10^{-3}

E. $1.5 \times 10^{-\frac{5}{2}}$

78. A certain perfect square has exactly 4 digits (that is, it is an integer between 1,000 and 9,999). The positive square root of the perfect square must have how many digits?

F. 1 G. 2 H. 3 J. 4

79. On his first day as a telemarketer, Marshall made 24 calls. His goal was to make 5 more calls on each successive day than he had made the day before. If Marshall met, but did not exceed, his goal, how many calls had he made in all after spending exactly 20 days making calls as a telemarketer?

A. 670　　B. 690　　C. 974　　D. 1,430　　E. 1,530

80. Jennifer's best long jump distance increased by 10% from 1990 to 1991 and by 20% from 1991 to 1992. by what percent did her best long jump distance increase from 1990 to 1992?

F. 32%　　G. 30%　　H. 20%　　J. 15%　　K. 2%

81. When Angela was cleaning her refrigerator, she found 2 bottles of catsup. Looking at the labels, she noticed that the capacity of the larger bottle was twice the capacity of the smaller bottle. She estimated that the smaller bottle was about $\frac{1}{3}$ full of catsup and the larger bottle was about $\frac{2}{3}$ full of catsup. She poured all the catsup from the smaller bottle into the larger bottle. Then, about how full was the larger bottle? Then, about how full was the larger bottle?

A. $\frac{2}{9}$full　　B. $\frac{1}{2}$full　　C. $\frac{5}{6}$full　　D. Completely full

E. Overflowing

82. When Jeff starts a math assignment, he spends 5 minutes getting out his book and a sheet of paper, sharpening his pencil, looking up the assignment in his assignment notebook, and turning to the correct page in his book. The equation $t = 10p + 5$ models the time, t minutes, and Jeff budgets for a math assignment with p problems. Which of the following statements is necessarily true according to Jeff's model?

F. He budgets 15 minutes per problem.

G. He budgets 10 minutes per problem.

H. He budgets 5 minutes per problem.

J. He budgets 10 minutes per problem for the hard problems and 5 minutes per problem for the easy problems.

K. He budgets a 5-minute break after each problem.

83. Which of the following statements is true about rational and/or irrational numbers?

F. The product of any 2 irrational numbers is irrational.

G. The quotient of any 2 irrational numbers is rational.

H. The product of any 2 rational numbers is irrational.

J. The quotient of any 2 rational numbers is irrational.

K. The sum of any 2 rational numbers is rational.

84. If n is a positive integer, which of the following expressions must be an odd integer?

F. n^3　　G. 3^n　　H. $3n$　　J. $\frac{n}{3}$　　K. $3+n$

85. The value of $\log_5(5^{\frac{13}{2}})$ is between which of the following pairs of consecutive integers?

A. 0 and 1　　B. 4 and 5　　C. 5 and 6　　D. 6 and 7　　E. 9 and 10

86. The weight of a circular rod of a certain type is proportional to its length. A 15-foot circular rod of this type weighs 35 pounds. What is the weight, in pounds, of a 21-foot circular rod of this type?

F. 41　　G. 44　　H. 47　　J. 49　　K. 56

87. or a math homework assignment, Karla found the area and perimeter of a room of her house. She reported that the area of her rectangular living room is 180 square feet and that the perimeter is 54 feet. When drawing a sketch of her living room the next day, she realized that

she had forgotten to write down the dimensions of the room. What are the dimensions of Karla's living room, in feet?

F. 9 by 20　　G. 10 by 18　　H. 12 by 15　　J. 14 by 13　　K. 16 by 11

88. The degree measures of the interior angles of $\triangle ABC$, shown below, form an arithmetic sequence with common difference 10°. What is the first term of the sequence?

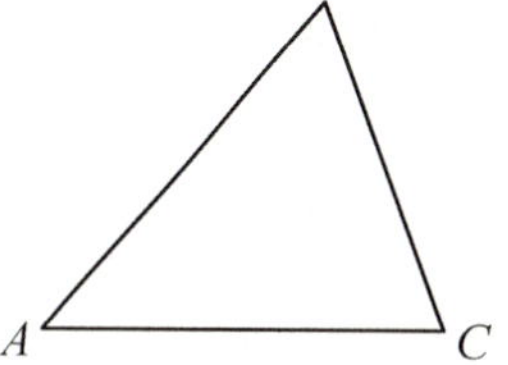

F. 80°　　G. 60°

H. 50°　　J. 40°

K. 30°

89. Chayton decides to save money in a savings account for a vacation. He deposits \$10 in his savings account the 1st month. Each month thereafter, the amount he deposits is \$10 more than the amount he deposited the previous month. Thus, Chayton's deposit is \$20 the 2nd month, \$30 the 3rd month, and so on. He makes his final deposit of \$360 the 36th month. What is the total amount of Chayton's 36 deposits?

F. \$710　　G. \$1,850　　H. \$6,300　　J. \$6,480　　K. \$6,660

90. M is P% of what number?

A. $\frac{100M}{P}$　　B. $\frac{100P}{M}$　　C. $\frac{M}{100P}$　　D. $\frac{P}{100M}$　　E. $\frac{MP}{100}$

91. How many different ways can you add four positive odd integers together for a sum of 10, without considering the sequence of integers?

A. Five　　B. Four

C. Three　　D. Two

E. One

PRICE OF COMMON STOCK OF XYZ CORP.AND ABC CORP. (YEAR X)

92. Referring to the graph below, what was the greatest dollar amount by which the share price of ABC common stock exceeded the share price of XYZ common stock during Year X?

A. \$1.80

B. \$2.60

C. \$3.00

D. \$3.60

E. It cannot be determined from the information given.

93. A certain cube contains 125 cubic inches. What is the surface area, in square inches, of each square face of the cube?

A. 5　　B. 10　　C. 15　　D. 20　　E. 25

94. A performance was rated on a 3-point scale by an audience. A rating of 1 was given by 30% of the audience, a rating of 2 by 60%, and a rating of 3 by 10%. To the nearest tenth, what was the average of the ratings?

F. 1.2　　G. 1.5　　H. 1.8　　J. 2.0　　K. 2.2

95. If A, B, and C are real numbers, and if $ABC = 1$, which of the following conditions must be true?

A. AB is equal to $\frac{1}{C}$
B. A, B, and C must all be positive
C. Either $A=1$, $B=1$, or $C=1$
D. Either $A=0$, $B=0$, or $C=0$
E. Either $A<1$, $B<1$, or $C<1$

96. Car A travels 60 miles per hour for $1\frac{1}{2}$ hours; Car B travels 40 miles per hour for 2 hours. What is the difference between the number of miles traveled by Car A and the number of miles traveled by Car B?

F. 0 G. 10 H. 80 J. 90 K. 170

97. Before his interview, Ben bought 1 suit and 2 shirts, all on sale. The suit, regularly $260, was 20% off, and the shirts, regularly $30 each, were 30% off. What was the total price of the 3 items Ben bought?
(Note: Assume there is no sales tax.)

F. $220 G. $229 H. $240 J. $250 K. $270

98. The specific gravity of a substance is the ratio of the weight of the substance to the weight of an equal volume of water. If 1 cubic foot of water weighs 62.5 pounds, what is the specific gravity of a liquid that weighs 125 pounds per cubic foot?

A. 1 B. 1.25 C. 2 D. 6.25 E. 125

99. The ratio of the lengths of the sides of a right triangle is $1:\sqrt{3}:2$. What is the sine of the triangle's smallest angle?

F. $\frac{1}{4}$ G. $\frac{1}{2}$ H. $\frac{\sqrt{3}}{2}$ J. $\frac{\sqrt{3}}{3}$ K. 1

100. For all non zero b and c, $\frac{(b\times10^4)(c\times0.001)}{(b\times10{,}000)(c\times10^3)}=?$

A. 1 B. 10 C. 10^{-6} D. $\frac{b}{c}$ E. $\frac{b^2}{c^2}$

[**Session 2 答案**]

1 J	2 B	3 G	4 B	5 G	6 F	7 C	8 J	9 G	10 G
11 E	12 B	13 H	14 J	15 A	16 J	17 B	18 D	19 J	20 B
21 K	22 H	23 D	24 K	25 B	26 G	27 A	28 H	29 J	30 B
31 K	32 F	33 D	34 G	35 K	36 D	37 J	38 C	39 B	40 G
41 B	42 K	43 C	44 D	45 K	46 C	47 J	48 E	49 E	50 J
51 H	52 D	53 H	54 D	55 F	56 E	57 G	58 J	59 C	60 H
61 H	62 D	63 F	64 C	65 F	66 J	67 E	68 B	69 C	70 A
71 C	72 D	73 H	74 J	75 B	76 B	77 D	78 G	79 D	80 F
81 C	82 G	83 K	84 G	85 D	86 J	87 H	88 H	89 K	90 A
91 C	92 D	93 E	94 H	95 A	96 G	97 J	98 C	99 G	100 C

［**Session 2 答案解析**］

1. 题干：卖多少件照片才能收回成本？
   解析：记得减去胶片等成本。
2. 题干：一共 510 名学生，80%捐 3 块，离 12 500 差多少？
   解析：(12 500 − 510×0.883)/12 500。
3. 题干：高年级选择了卖 candy bar 的方式来筹款，要卖多少才可以达到目标？
   解析：每卖一个赚 0.62。
4. 题干：$x = 5 \pm \sqrt{-9a^2}$ 用复数表示。
   解析：i 的平方等于 −1。
5. 题干：代数老师的年龄的平方减去其 23 倍等于 50。年龄是多少？
   解析：设年龄为 x。
6. 题干：包含(9，2)的水平线表示？
   解析：一周做两个大的。
7. 题干：做了四大一小，捐了 3 块，捐的比例是多少？
   解析：算出四大一小的价值。
8. 题干：一周一共能赚多少钱？
   解析：小的一个 30 块，大的一个 70。然后根据数量的约束关系即可得到最大利润。
9. 题干：$\frac{4}{35}$，$\frac{1}{56}$，and $\frac{3}{16}$ 的分母的最小公倍数是多少？
   解析：先找出所有的因数。
10. 题干：一包农药恩那个撒 5 000 平方英尺，宽 50 英尺的能撒多长？
    解析：相除即可。
11. 题干：如图，堆罐头，下一层比上一层多四个，可以堆几个？
    解析：等差数列求和。
12. 题干：一种植物一开始英寸，另一种一开始 3 英寸，拿出温室之后，第一种每周长 1 英寸，待在温室里，第二种每周长 1.5 英寸。几周之后一样高？
    解析：一周追上 0.5 英寸。
13. 题干：$\sqrt{1}$，$\sqrt{2}$，$\sqrt{3}$，… $\sqrt{100}$ 中选一个，选到有理数的几率是多少？
    解析：可以用列举法。
14. 题干：rueben 在旗杆 300 码往东，橡树 400 码往南。旗杆和橡树距离多少？
    解析：画出坐标轴。
15. 题干：kyla 给了收银员 15，应该找多少零钱？
    解析：数量乘以单价等于总价。
16. 题干：不计税费，每块糖果平均多少钱？
    解析：总量除以数量。
17. 题干：从相同的糖果中选两个，或者两种中各选一个，费用有几种不同情况？
    解析：列举法。
18. 题干：平均分 100，标准差 15。至少要比平均分高一个标准差，那么是多少？
    解析：100＋15。
19. 题干：相机和胶卷的产生量的约束关系如图。每个顶点都是整数，一个相机赚 3 块，一卷胶卷赚 1 块，怎么样生产最赚钱？
    解析：$z = 3y + x$，即 $y = (z - x)/3$。画出该直线族，与阴影相交，截距最大的即利润最大。

20. 题干：第一个表格列出了各种大小的旗子所需要的布料种类和数量；第二个表格列出了每个人需要做的各种颜色的旗子和数量。Lance 需要多少蓝色的布料？
解析：把两个表格看成矩阵，相乘即可得到各种所需数据。
21. 题干：1 000 个奖品价值 90，有两种奖品，要么 0.05，要么 0.25，0.05 的有多少个？
解析：设 0.05 的有 x 个。
22. 题干：左栏是教师的数量，右栏是这些教师所教的科目。有多少教师只教数学？
解析：只涉及到三种科目。可以用画图法来解决，简洁明了。
23. 题干：如表格，金盏花和矮牵牛数量一样多，那么 6 株的金盏花有多少袋？
解析：株数和袋数相乘即可。
24. 题干：某人买了 1/10 的向阳花，花了 15，每一株多少钱？
解析：算出株数。
25. 题干：海伦把所有的 1 株番茄凑成 4 株的，这样一共可以有多少袋 4 株？
解析：1 株的袋数除以 4，加上原来的。
26. 题干：h 是个数，c 是总价，单价 99。作图，y 轴是 c，x 轴是 h。下面哪个说法是正确的？
解析：斜率即单价。
27. 题干：11 条横线 11 条竖线把平面分割。其中有几块其面积非零且有限的区域？
解析：注意挑除最外边的，因为是无限大的。
28. 题干：83 000 个货物，大车拉 18 000 个，小车拉 7 000 个。每个车只能拉一趟，一共有 2 个大车，至少要用多少小车？
解析：总的减去大车能拉的，然后除以小车每个能拉的。
29. 题干：求平均值。
解析：加起来除以 5。
30. 题干：第 6 年比第 5 年高 3%，第 6 年是多少？
解析：第五年乘以 1.03。
31. 题干：加了 11.38 加仑的汽油，给除雪器存了 1.85 加仑的汽油，又洗了个车。一共花了多少钱？
解析：一共买了 13.23 加仑的汽油。
32. 题干：用小数的形式来表达 3.9×10^{-93}。
解析：小数点后面有 92 个零。
33. 题干：5 个学生按顺序排，可以有几种可能？
解析：$5\times4\times3\times2\times1$。
34. 题干：家庭养猫或狗的情况如下，有多少人家里至少有一只猫？
解析：把第一列加起来即可。
35. 题干：6 位的生产码，前 5 位是字母，可以重复，最后一位是数字。一共有几种可能？
解析：可以重复则 $26\times26\times26\times26\times26\times10$。
36. 题干：$\sqrt{-48}$ 和 $\sqrt{-27}$ 的和是多少？
解析：i 的平方是 −1。
37. 题干：B 列包含了 A 列和 a，b，c 三个数字，其中 b 列的中间值是多少？
解析：写出 b 列。
38. 题干：算出 8 个人心率的平均数。
解析：sum/8。
39. 题干：第一个问题 2 选 1，第二个问题 5 选 1，一共有多少种作答的可能？

解析：2×5。

40. 题干：一个 1.49，三个卖 3.90。三个一起买，每个省多少？
解析：3.90 除以 3 减去 1.49。

41. 题干：用直线方程来表示价格和数量的关系。斜率和截距是多少？
解析：斜率即数量变化除以价格的变化。

42. 题干：$\dfrac{1}{1+\dfrac{1}{1+\dfrac{1}{2}}}=?$
解析：先从最内层算起。

43. 题干：$a+b\mathrm{i}$ 和哪个相乘可以得到实数？
解析：和实数的乘法法则一样。

44. 题干：$\dfrac{1}{11^{20}}-\dfrac{1}{11^{21}}$ 通分。
解析：第一个分数上下同时乘 11。

45. 题干：露台长 10 英尺，上表面积为 270，厚 6 英尺。需要多少立方英尺的水泥？
解析：面积乘以厚度即可，注意单位。

46. 题干：价格与面积的公式为 $C=3.5A+120$，价格为多少？
解析：带入面积即可。

47. 题干：露台不与房间接触的部分的周长是多少？
解析：周长减去一个边。

48. 题干：s 和 L 每年一共捐 2 500，L 每年捐的是 s 的 1.5 倍。四年下来 L 捐多少？
解析：设 L 一年捐 x。

49. 题干：175 个人，其中 117 个人用了 a，89 个人用了 b，53 个人都用了。多少人至少用了一个？
解析：减去都没用的。

50. 题干：2 到 50 中(含)，多少比例的数字个位数是十位数的两倍？
解析：可以先把各个十位数列出来，然后填上复合条件的个位数。

51. 题干：$C=50a+1\,500$，$C=4\,250$，$a=?$
解析：按照上面简化的即可。

52. 题干：在接受调查的学生中，多少比例的选择了篮球？
解析：个数除以总数。

53. 题干：健身比去足球的是值是多少？
解析：9∶5

54. 题干：选择网球的占得角度数多少？
解析：比例乘以 360 度。

55. 题干：转盘如下，转到是 3 和 4 的公倍数的概率是多少？
解析：先找出有多少个是二者的公倍数。

56. 题干：如图，只有一节课的占多少比例？
解析：100 除以 200。

57. 题干：$y=$ 的图像如图。哪个横坐标是没有的？
解析：-2 和 2 是奇点。

58. 题干：连续正奇数的和总是完全平方数。如果和是 144，那么最大的奇数是多少？
解析：高斯法。

59. 题干：小于等于 40 小时，则每小时 12.5，大于这个数，每小时翻倍。46 小时赚多少钱？
解析：分段计算即可。
60. 题干：塞信封的机器每分钟 150 个信封，盖邮戳的每秒钟 4 个信封。24 个塞信封，要有多少个盖邮戳的？
解析：150×24/240。
61. 题干：2 500 人。调查了 200 人，结果如图。2 500 人中有多少人只有狗？
解析：可以用算出来比例直接乘总数。
62. 题干：只养一种的是多少比例？
解析：注意减去重叠部分。
63. 题干：又问了 25 人，数据如题。那么只养鱼的占多少？
解析：先把比例换成人数，然后相加，再换成比例。
64. 题干：一开始有 30 分，答对一题多 10，答错减 5。答对是答错的两倍，分数 150。那么答对了几题？
解析：设答对了 x 题。
65. 题干：如图中位数是多少？
解析：第一列是十位数，第二列是个位数。
66. 题干：$(6-7i)(\pi+6i)$ 等于什么？
解析：与实数的法则一样，i 的平方等于 −1。
67. 题干：1，−3，9，−27，…第七个是多少？
解析：连续乘 −3。
68. 题干：大的塑像卖 12 块，小的卖 8 块，一共卖了 70。两种的销售额一样，卖了多少大的？
解析：设大的 x 个。
69. 题干：从 88 加速到 220 花了 3 秒，加速度是多少？
解析：变化除以时间。
70. 题干：D 年薪 22 570，工作 185 天。代课教师一天 80。请代课老师一天省多少？
解析：算 d 的日薪。
71. 题干：河流的含氧量是水里的氧气浓度除以最高能溶解的氧气浓度然后乘以 100%。前者若为 7.3，后者若为 9.8，那么含氧量是多少？
解析：7.3 除以 9.8 即可。
72. 题干：网球 40 人，比例是 0.3 除以 0.3，0.4，0.2，0.5 的和，总数是多少？
解析：40 除以比例即可。
73. 题干：一个篮子所需的带子长度和数量如表，1 yard 花 0.98，5 个花多少钱？
解析：先算出总长度然后乘以单价。
74. 题干：$\frac{1}{1+i}\cdot\frac{1-i}{1-i}=?$
解析：通分。
75. 题干：蓝图上是宽 4 英寸长 6 英寸，实际上长 30 英尺，那么实际上宽多少？
解析：按照比例算即可。
76. 题干：已知九个数的中位数，现在多了四个数，两个比原先的中位数大，两个比原先的小，那么现在的中位数？
解析：不变。
77. 题干：正常的水中铅含量为 1.5×10^{-5} 毫升每升，超标 100 倍，那么检测的水铅含量是多少？

解析：了解科学计数法。

78. 题干：某四位数的完全平方数，其开方有几位数？
解析：取 1 000 为例。虽然不是完全平方数。

79. 题干：第一天 24 个，以后每天多 5 个，那么前 20 天一共多少个？
解析：等差数列求和。

80. 题干：1990 到 1991 增长 10%，1991 到 1992 增长 20%，1990 到 1992 增长多少？
解析：注意不是 30%，因为基数不同了。

81. 题干：小瓶装了三分之一满，大瓶装了三分之二满，大瓶是小瓶的两倍大。把小瓶倒到大瓶，大瓶多满？
解析：先把小瓶换算成大瓶的比例。

82. 题干：$t = 10p + 5$，t 为时间，p 为解决的题数。
解析：10 即每道题花的时间。

83. 题干：关于有理数和无理数，哪个说法是正确的？
解析：有理数之和还是有理数。

84. 题干：n 如果是一个正整数，那么哪个是奇数？
解析：3 的任意次方都是奇数。

85. 题干：$\log_5(5^{\frac{13}{2}})$的值在哪个区间？
解析：即 13 除以 2。

86. 题干：重量和长度正比，15 英尺的重 35，21 的重多少？
解析：算比例即可。

87. 题干：面积 180，周长 54，长宽多少？
解析：设长 x。

88. 题干：间隔 10，和 180。第三个多少？
解析：设第三个为 x。

89. 题干：第一个月存 10，以后每个月多存 10，36 各月共存多少？
解析：等差数列和。

90. 题干：M 是什么数值的百分之 P？
解析：按照定义即可。

91. 题干：四个正奇数的和为 10，不考虑顺序，有几种情况？
解析：1 117，1 135，3 331

92. 题干：xyz 最多比 abc 多了多少？
解析：找折线的最大差值即可。

93. 题干：立方体体积 125，一个面的面积多少？
解析：边长即 5。

94. 题干：1 占了 10%，2 占了 60%，3 占了 10%，平均多少？
解析：求平均数。

95. 题干：$abc = 1$，那么哪个是正确的？
解析：$ab = 1/c$。

96. 题干：a 时速 60，开了 1 个半小时，b 时速 40 开了 2 个小时。A 多开了多远？
解析：速度乘时间等于距离。

97. 题干：一套西服两件衬衫，西服原价 260，降价 20%，衬衫原价 30，降价 30%，花了多少钱？

解析：原价乘以(1－折扣百分比)＝买的价格。

98. 题干：1 立方英尺的水重 62.5 磅，一种液体重 125 磅每立方英尺。这种液体的比重多少？
解析：后者除以前者。

99. 题干：直角三角形的三个边比值为 $1:\sqrt{3}:2$，最小的角的正弦值是多少？
解析：最小角的正弦值等于对边除以斜边。

100. 题干：$\frac{(b\times10^4)(c\times0.001)}{(b\times10,000)(c\times10^3)}=?$
解析：化简，上下同时除以相同的数。

Session 3 Algebra 1 代数 1

1. If a is any real number, for what real value (s) of b does the equation $|x+a|=b$ have NO solutions for x?

F. All $b<0$　　G. Only $b=-1$
H. Only $b=0$　　J. All $b\neq0$
K. All $b>0$

2. To work properly, an engine part's diameter cannot be over the specified diameter of 3 centimeters by more than 05 centimeters, nor can it be under the specified diameter by more than 05 centimeters. If x is the diameter of a part, which of the following algebraic statements specifies these restrictions on x?

A. $x-3\geqslant0.5$　　B. $3-x\geqslant0.5$
C. $|x-0.5|\leqslant3$　　D. $|3-x|\leqslant0.5$
E. $|x|\leqslant0.5$

3. If $kx+k=0$, and $k>1$, then $x=$?

A. 0　　B. -1　　C. 1　　D. $-k$　　E. k

4. Three-ring notebooks are made in 2 steps. Machine A makes 180 covers per hour. Later, Machine B attaches the 3－ring paper holder and completes 150 notebooks per hour. How many hours should Machine A run in order to produce the right number of covers for Machine B to finish in exactly 8 hours of its operation?

F. 5　　G. $5\frac{1}{3}$　　H. 6　　J. $6\frac{2}{5}$　　K. $6\frac{2}{3}$

5. The trinomial x^2-x-6 can be factored as the product of 2 linear factors, in the form $(x+a)(x+b)$. What is the polynomial sum of these 2 factors?

A. $2x-1$　　B. $2x+1$　　C. $2x-5$　　D. $2x+5$　　E. $2x-6$

6. If $f(x)=3x^3-27x$, which of the following correctly describes the zeros of the polynomial? Note: Zeros arevalues of X where $f(x)=0$

A. No real zeros
B. Only 1 rational zero
C. Only 1 real zero, which is irrational
D. 1 number is a double zero
E. 3 different rational zeros

7. Which of the following expressions is NOT a polynomialfactor of x^4-4?

F. x^2-2　　G. x^2+2　　H. $x-\sqrt{2}$　　J. $x+\sqrt{2}$　　K. $x-2$

8. As a salesperson, Onawa travels to a variety of locations during a day. The graph shows the relationship between time and total distance traveled on a particular day. What was Onawa's average speed, in miles per hour, for the parts of the day when she was traveling from one, place to another?

A. 19　　B. 33　　C. 45

D. 55　　E. 110

9. If $\frac{x^a}{x^b} = x^3$ for all $x \neq 0$, which of the following must betrue?

F. $a - b = 3$　　G. $a + b = 3$　　H. $a \div b = 3$

J. $a \times b = 3$　　K. $\sqrt{ab} = 3$

10. If $b \neq c$, what are the real values of a that make the following inequality true?

$\frac{ab - ac}{2b - 2c} < 0$

A. 2 only　　B. $\frac{1}{2}$ only　　C. $-\frac{1}{2}$ only　　D. All positive realnumbers

E. All negative real numbers

11. An earring manufacturing company has fixed costs of \$10,000 per month and production costs of \$0.60 for each pair of earrings it makes. If the company produces x pairs of earrings in a month, which of the following expressions represents the total of the company's monthly costs?

A. \$10,000 x　　B. \$10,000 + x

C. \$10,000x + \$0.60　　D. \$10,000 + \$0.60x

E. (\$10,000 + \$0.60)x

12. Which of the following shows the solution set for the inequality $5x - 1 \geqslant 9$?

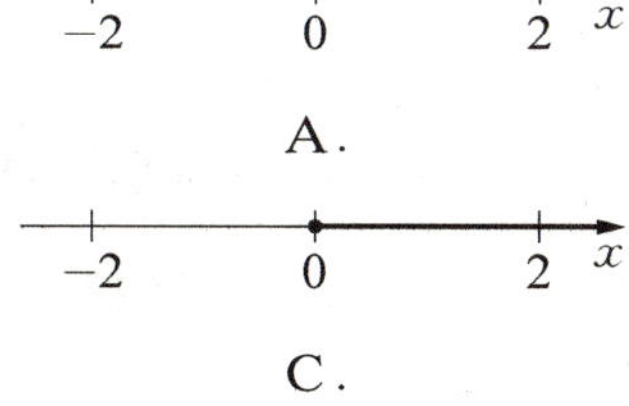

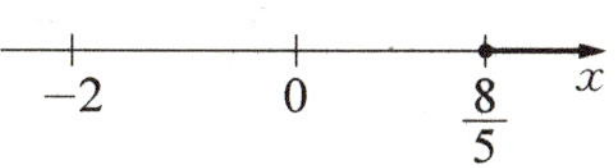

B.

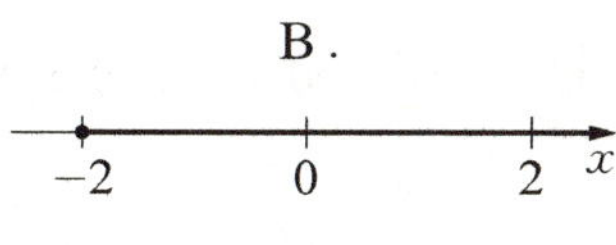

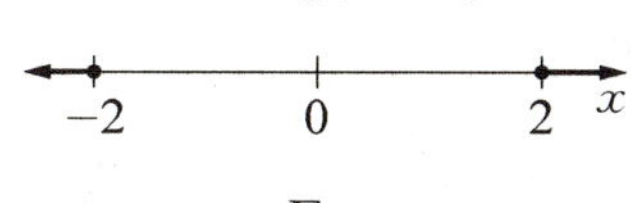

E.

13. If Mark works steadily he can complete a task in x hours. What portion of the task remains if he works steadily for y hours, where y is any value less than x ?

A. $\frac{(x+y)}{y}$　　B. $\frac{(y-x)}{x}$　　C. $\frac{(x-y)}{(x+y)}$　　D. $\frac{(x-y)}{y}$　　E. $\frac{(x-y)}{x}$

14. If the function f satisfies the equation $f(x+y) = f(x) + f(y)$ for every pair of real numbers x and y, what is(are) the possible value(s) of $f(0)$?

F. Any real number　　G. Any positive real number

H. 0 and 1 only　　J. 1 only

K. 0 only

15. It costs a dollars for an adult ticket to a reggae concert and s dollars for a student ticket. The difference between the cost of 12 adult tickets and 18 student tickets is \$36. Which of the following equations represents this relationship between a and s ?

A. $\frac{12a}{18s}=36$　　B. $216as=36$

C. $|12a-18s|=36$　　D. $|12a+18s|=36$

E. $|18a+12s|=36$

16. John Jones has decided to go into the business of producing and selling boats. In order to begin this venture, he must invest \$10 million in a boat production plant. The cost to produce each boat will be \$7,000, and the selling price will be \$20,000. Accounting for the cost of the production plant, which of the following expressions represents the profit, in dollars, that John will realize when x boats are produced and sold?

A. $13,000x-10,000,000$　　B. $27,000x-10,000,000$

C. $9,973,000x$　　D. $20,000x$

E. $13,000x$

17. As a class experiment, a cart was rolled at a constant rate along a straight line. Shawn recorded in the chart below the cart's distance (x), in feet, from a reference point at the start of the experiment and for each of 5 times (t), in seconds.

t	0	1	2	3	4	5
x	10	14	18	22	26	30

Which of the following equations represents this data?

A. $x=t+10$　　B. $x=4t+6$

C. $x=4t+10$　　D. $x=10t+4$

E. $x=14t$

18. If $\frac{A}{30}+\frac{B}{105}=\frac{7A+2B}{x}$ and A, B, and x are integers greater than 1, then what must x equal?

A. 9　　B. 135　　C. 210　　D. 630　　E. 3,150

19. The graph of the equation $h=-at^2+bt+c$, which describes how the height, h, of a hit baseball changes over time, t, is shown below.

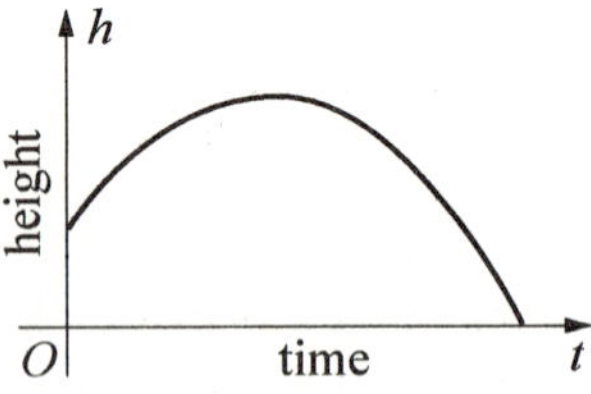

If you alter only this equation's c term, which gives the height at time $t=0$, the alteration has an effect on which of the following?

I. The h-intercept

II. The maximum value of h

III. The t-intercept

F. I only　　G. II only　　H. II only　　J. I and III only

K. I, II, and III

20. As shown below, rectangle $ABCD$ is divided into 2 large squares (labeled L) each x inches on a

side, 15 small squares (labeled S) each y inches on a side, and 13 rectangles (labeled R) each x inches by y inches. What is the total area, in square inches, of $ABCD$?

F. $2x+13xy+15y$

G. $6x+16y$

H. $2x^2+15y^2$

J. $2x^2+8xy+15y^2$

K. $2x^2+13xy+15y^2$

21. A function that is defined by the set of ordered pairs $\{(2, 1), (4, 2), (6, 3)\}$ has domain $\{2, 4, 6\}$. What is the domain of the function defined by the set of ordered pairs $\{(0, 2), (2, 2), (3, -2)\}$?

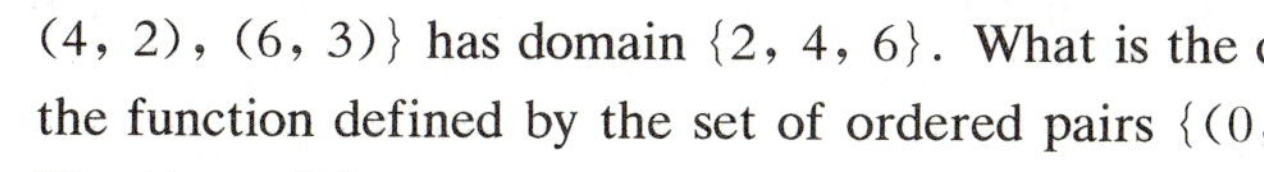

A. $\{2\}$　B. $\{-2, 2\}$　C. $\{-2, 0, 3\}$　D. $\{0, 2, 3\}$

E. $\{-2, 0, 2, 3\}$

22. If $f(x)=2x$ and $g(x)=x^2$, what is $f(g(3))$?

F. 6　G. 12　H. 18　J. 36　K. 54

23. What is the solution set of the equation $4x^2-9=0$?

A. $\{-\sqrt{2}, \sqrt{2}\}$　B. $\left\{-\frac{3}{2}, \frac{3}{2}\right\}$　C. $\{-\sqrt{3}, \sqrt{3}\}$　D. $\{-2, 2\}$　E. $\left\{\frac{9}{4}\right\}$

24. For all $x>0$, which of the following is equivalent to $\frac{1}{x+1}+\frac{1}{x}$?

F. $\frac{1}{x(x+1)}$　G. $\frac{1}{2x(x+1)}$　H. $\frac{2}{x(x+1)}$　J. $\frac{2}{x}+1$　K. $\frac{2x+1}{x(x+1)}$

25. Two enterprising college students decide to start a business. They will make up and deliver helium balloon bouquets for special occasions. It will cost them \$39.99 to buy a machine to fill the balloons with helium. They estimate that it will cost them \$2.00 to buy the balloons, helium, and ribbons needed to make each balloon bouquet. Which of the following expressions could be used to model the total cost for producing b balloon bouquets?

A. \$2.00b+ \$39.99　B. \$37.99b

C. \$39.99b+ \$2.00　D. \$41.99b

E. \$79.98b

26. Leticia went into Discount Music to price CDs. All CDs were discounted 23% off the marked price. Leticia wanted to program her calculator so she could input the marked price and the discounted price would be the output. Which of the following is an expression for the discounted price on a marked price of p dollars?

A. $p-0.23p$　B. $p-0.23$

C. $p-23p$　D. $p-23$

E. $0.23p$

27. For a population that grows at a constant rate of $r\%$ per year, the formula $p(t)=p_0\left(1+\frac{r}{100}\right)^t$ models the population t years after an initial population of p_0 people is counted.

The population of the city of San Jose was 782,000 in 1990. Assume the population grows at a constant rate of 5% per year. According to this formula, which of the following is an expression for the population of San Jose in the year 2000?

A. $782,000(6)^{10}$
B. $782,000(1.5)^{10}$
C. $782,000(1.05)^{10}$
D. $(782,000\times 1.5)^{10}$
E. $(782,000\times 1.05)^{10}$

28. For all x in the domain of the function $\frac{x+1}{x^3-x}$, this function is equivalent to:

F. $\frac{1}{x^2}-\frac{1}{x^3}$ G. $\frac{1}{x^3}-\frac{1}{x}$ H. $\frac{1}{x^2-1}$ J. $\frac{1}{x^2-x}$ K. $\frac{1}{x^3}$

29. What are the real solutions to the equation $|x|^2+2|x|-3=0$?

F. ±1 G. ±3 H. 1 and 3 J. −1 and −3 K. ±1 and ±3

30. A function P is defined as follows:

for $x>0$, $P(x)=x^5+x^4-36x-36$

for $x<0$, $P(x)=-x^5+x^4+36x-36$

What is the value of $P(-1)$?

A. −70 B. −36 C. 0 D. 36 E. 70

31. Consider the functions $f(x)=\sqrt{x}$ and $g(x)=7x+b$. In the standard (x, y) coordinate plane, $y=f(g(x))$ passes through (4, 6). What is the value of b?

A. 8 B. −8 C. −25 D. −26 E. $4-7\sqrt{6}$

32. What is the real value of x in the equation $\log_2 24-\log_2 3=\log_5 x$?

F. 3 G. 21 H. 72 J. 125 K. 243

33. Jan returned a library book that was 9days overdue. The library charged Jan s cents per day for the first 6 overdue days and 20 cents per day for each overdue day after 6 overdue days. Which of the following is an expression for the total amount, in cents, Jan was charged?

A. s + 180 B. 6s + 20 C. 6s + 60 D. 9s + 20 E. 9s + 60

34. Suppose that w, y, and z each stand for a digit from 0 through 9 and

$$\begin{array}{r} 5\ w\ 7 \\ +\ 9\ 2\ y \\ \hline 1,z\ 9\ 6 \end{array}$$

What is the value of the product $w\cdot y\cdot z$?

F. 19 G. 28 H. 216 J. 252 K. 270

35. The time, t seconds, required for a simple pendulum x feet long to make 1 complete swing can be modeled by $t=2\pi\sqrt{\frac{x}{32}}$. How many seconds are required for 1 complete swing of a simple pendulum that is 8 feet long?

F. Less than 1
G. Between 1 and 2
H. Between 2 and 3
J. Between 3 and 4
K. More than 4

36. If and,If $27\cdot 3^x=9^{y-6}$ and $y=6$, then what is the real number value of x?

A. −3 B. −2 C. −1 D. 0 E. 3.

37. Which of the following is a value for x that solves the equation $|x-2|=5$?

F. −3 G. $\frac{5}{2}$ H. 3 J. 10 K. 25

38. In Abraham Lincoln's 1863 Gettysburg Address, he refers to the year 1776 as "4 score and 7 years ago." Which of the following equations, when solved fors, gives the number of years a score refers to?

A. $4s+7=1,863-1,776$　　B. $4s+7=1,863+1,776$

C. $4s+7=1,776-1,863$　　D.. $4s+7=1,863$

E. $4s+7=1,776$

39. The function f shown in the graph below represents the projection of yearly profits for the Rip It Up toy company. The actual profits are represented by the graph of the functiong. Which of the following descriptions is the most accurate explanation for the variation between the graph of g and the graph of f?

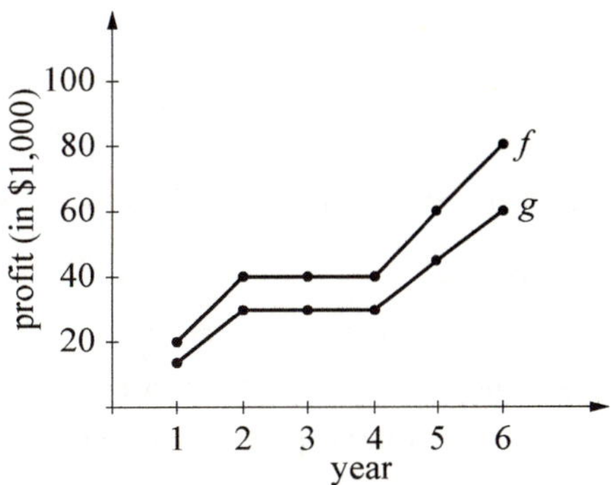

F. The yearly profits were only $\frac{3}{4}$ as large as projected.

G. The yearly profits were consistently \$10.000 less than projected.

H. The yearly profits were greater than projected.

J. The 2 graphs show no difference in the yearly profits.

K. The yearly profits started to decline after several years and continued to decline through the 6 the year.

40. Sven obtained the weight, y pounds, and shoe size, x, of 25 randomly selected male students at his school. He determined that the line best fitting his data was given by the equation $y=\frac{40}{3}x+\frac{110}{5}$. He used this line to predict the weight of a new male student who wears size $9\frac{1}{2}$ shoes. Compared to this student's actual weight of 165 pounds, the prediction of his weight from Sven's line was:

F. too high by less than 1 pound.

G. too high by more than 1 pound.

H. too low by less than 1 pound.

J. too low by exactly 1 pound.

K. too low by more than 1 pound

41. Consider the functions $f(x)=|x|$ and $g(x)=-x^2+a$. One of the following graphs is the graph of $y=f(g(x))$ in the standard (x, y) coordinate plane, for some $a>0$. Which graph is it?

A.

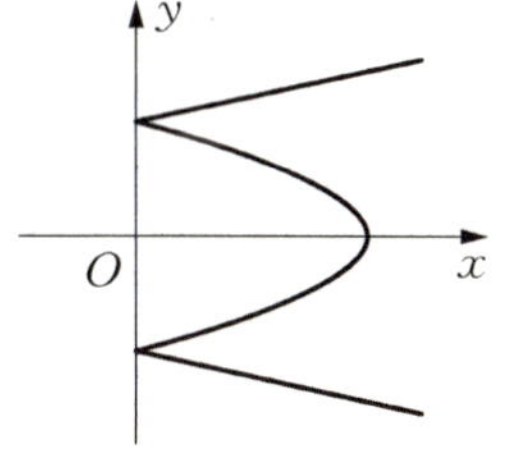

B.

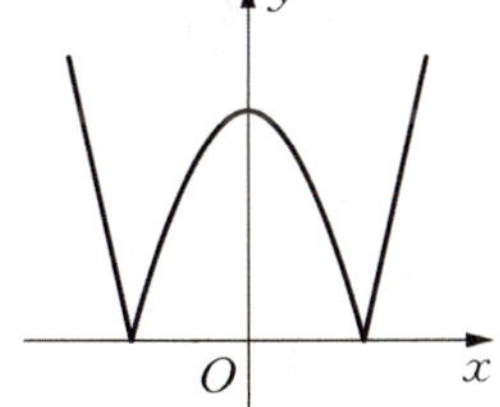

C.

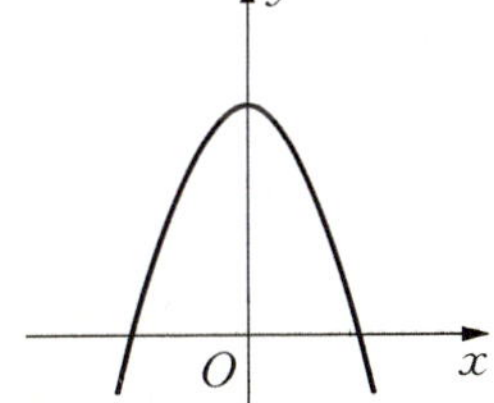

D.

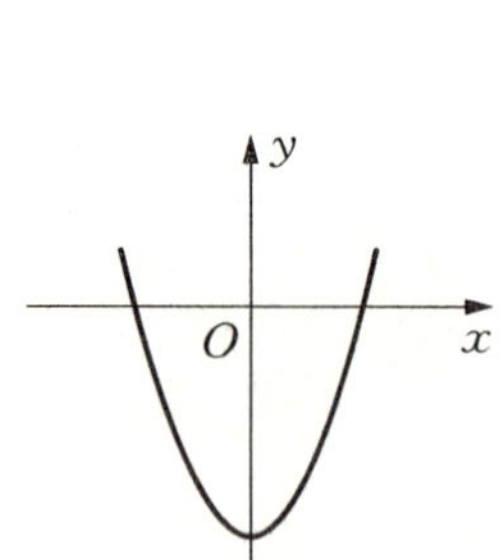

E.

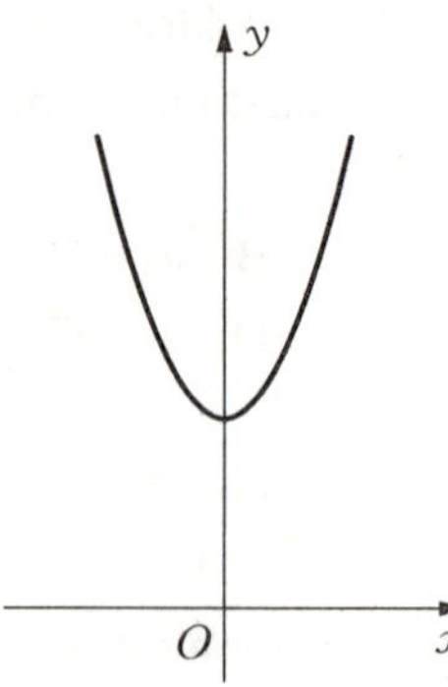

42. For positive real numbers a, b, and c such that $2a = \frac{b\sqrt{2}}{2} = \frac{c\sqrt{2}}{2.5}$, which of the following is true?

A. $a > b > c$ B. $b > a > c$ C. $b > c > a$ D. $c > a > b$ E. $c > b > a$

43. The filling machine in a cereal factory fills 1,200 boxes of cereal every 5 minutes. Which of the following proportions can be solved for t, the number of minutes it takes the machine to fill 2,000 of these boxes of cereal?

A. $\frac{1{,}200}{5} = \frac{2{,}000}{t}$ B. $\frac{1{,}200}{2{,}000} = \frac{t}{5}$

C. $\frac{1{,}200}{t} = \frac{2{,}000}{5}$ D. $\frac{1{,}200}{5} = \frac{2{,}000 - 1{,}200}{t}$

E. $\frac{1{,}200}{5} = \frac{1{,}200 + 2{,}000}{t}$

44. Given $x^3 = 38.7$ where x is a real number, the value of x is between which 2 consecutive integers?

F. 3 and 4 G. 6 and 7

H. 12 and 13 J. 38 and 39

K. 57,960 and 57,961

45. The functions $f(x) = x(x+3)(x+1)(x-3)(x-2)$ and $g(x) = -x(x+3)(x-3)(x-1)$ are graphed below in the standard (x, y) coordinate plane. How many solutions are there to $f(x) = g(x)$?

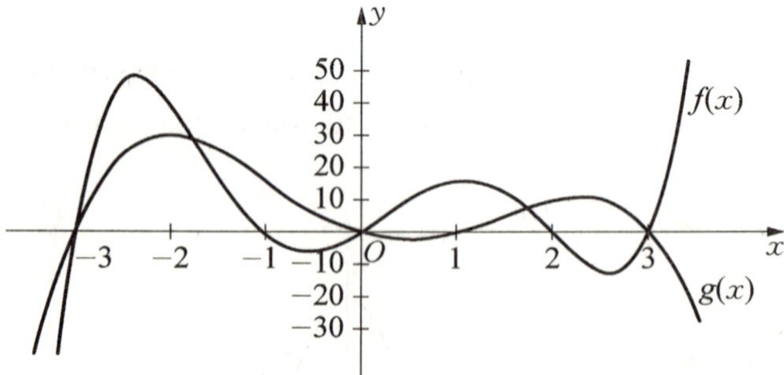

A. 2 B. 3 C. 5 D. 6

E. Infinitely many

46. What is the set of all integers in {5, 6, 7, 8, 9} that are also in the solution set of $2x+7<3x+1$?

A. {5, 6, 7} B. {6, 7, 8, 9} C. {7} D. {7, 8, 9} E. {9}

47. The shaded portion of one of the following graphs is the set of all x and y such that $-1\leqslant x-y\leqslant 1$. Which one?

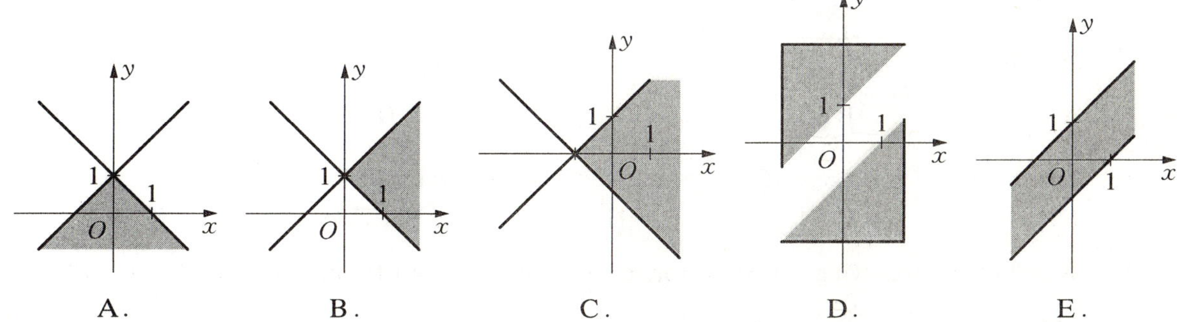

48. A formula that gives m, the recommended maximum heart rate, in beats per minute, while exercising, for a person a years old is $m=0.8(220-a)$: What is the recommended maximum heart rate, in beats per minute, while exercising for a person 20 years old?

A. 156 B. 160 C. 176 D. 192 E. 196

49. If $\frac{(n+2)(9-3)}{8(2)}=2$, then $n=$?

F. $-1\frac{1}{3}$ G. $1\frac{1}{3}$ H. $3\frac{1}{3}$ J. $5\frac{1}{3}$ K. $7\frac{1}{3}$

50. For which of the following values of a, will $\left(-\frac{1}{2}\right)^{a}$ represent a real number between -1 and 0?

F. -2 G. -1 H. 0 J. 1 K. 2

51. A flower pot fell from a windowsill. The graph below shows the distance, d feet, the flower pot was above the ground t seconds. after it fell. The graph shows that the flower pot fell 16 feet (from $d=256$ to $d=240$) during the 1st second of its fall and 48 feet (from $d=240$ to $d=192$) during the 2nd second of its fall. During which second of its fall, if any, was the average speed of the flowerpot, in feet per second, the greatest?

(Note: The average speed of an object over a given interval of time is the distance it traveled during the interval divided by the length of the interval.)

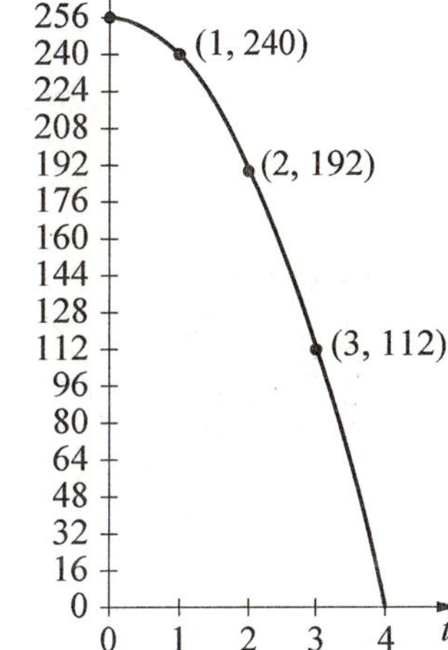

F. 4th

G. 3rd

H. 2nd

J. 1st

K. None; the speed of the flowerpot was constant during its fall.

52. If x and y are real, numbers such that $4\leqslant x\leqslant 12$ and $2\leqslant y\leqslant 4$, then the minimum value for

$\frac{x}{y}$ is:

F. 0 G. 1 H. 2 J. 3 K. 6

53. For $f(x) = 2x + 10$ and $g(x) = 3x^2$, what is the value of $f(g(-3))$?

F. 31 G. 48 H. 64 J. 108 K. 144

54. When $a = 2$ and $b = 3$, the expression

$\frac{ab}{25} + \frac{11}{10(a+b)} + \frac{1}{a+b} = ?$

A. $\frac{9}{40}$ B. $\frac{11}{20}$ C. $\frac{31}{50}$ D. $\frac{47}{75}$ E. $\frac{33}{50}$

55. The equation $\sqrt{x} + \sqrt{x-16} = 8$ is true for what real value of x?

F. 9 G. 16 H. 25 J. 36 K. 64

56. Which of the following is FALSE for some x and y that satisfy the equation $x\left(\frac{1}{y}\right) = 1$?

F. $y\left(\frac{1}{x}\right) = 1$ G. $y = x$

H. $x^2 + y^2 = 2xy$ J. $x^2 = y^2$

K. $x^5 + y^5 = 1$

57. For the first several months' after the Fiery Red Scooter arrived in toy stores, the rate of sales increased slowly. As this new scooter caught on, however, the rate of sales increased rapidly. After several more months, many people wneda Fiery Red Scooter, and the rate of sales decreased. Which of the following graphs could represent the total number of Fiery Red Scooters sold as a function of time, in months, after the scooter arrived in toy stores?

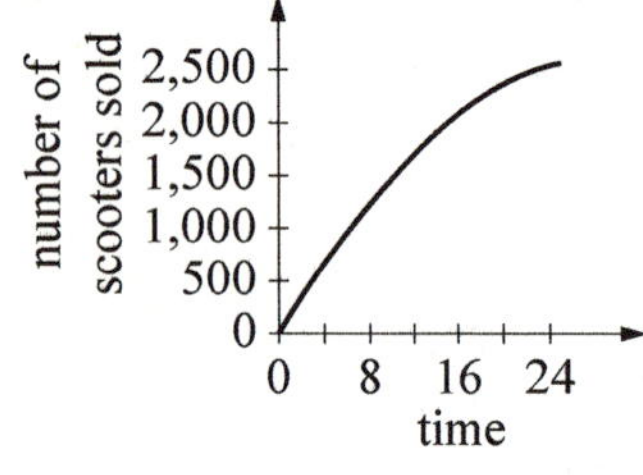

F.

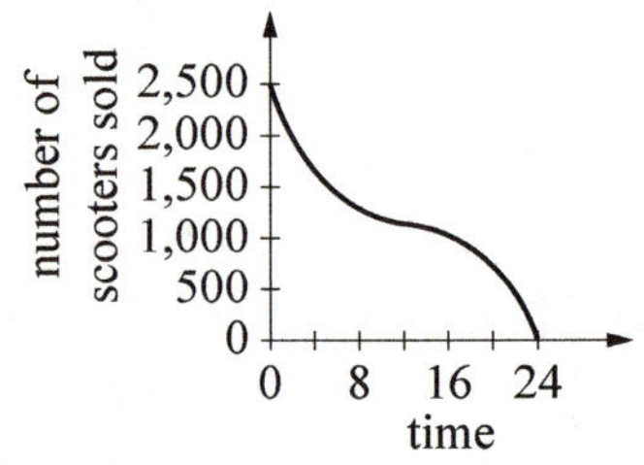

G.

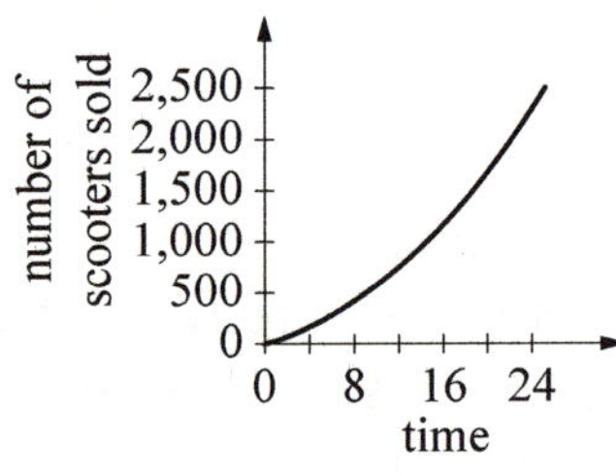

H.

J.

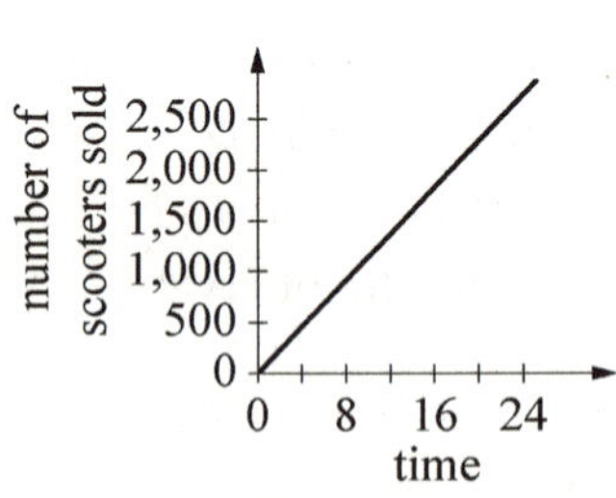

K.

58. $(4x^2 - 3x + 7) - (-1 + 5x + 2x^2)$ is equivalent to:

A. $2x^2 - 8x + 8$ B. $2x^2 + 2x + 8$

C. $2x^4 + 2x^2 + 6$ D. $6x^2 - 8x + 6$

E. $6x^4 - 8x^2 + 6$

59. In Intermediate Algebra class, Ms. Schimmack makes the statement "y varies directly as the product of w^2 and x, and inversel y as z^3 "and asks her students to translate it into an equation. Which of the following equations, with k as the constant of proportionality, is a correct translation of Ms. Schimmack's statement?

A. $y=\frac{kw^2x}{z^3}$ B. $y=\frac{kz^3}{w^2x}$

C. $y=\frac{w^2xz^3}{k}$ D. $y=\frac{z^3}{kw^2x}$

E. $y=kw^2xz^3$

60. If the following system has a solution, what is the x-coordinate of the solution?

$3x+6y=52$

$x+6y=24$

F. 19 G. 14 H. 6 J. 0

K. The system has no solution

61. Consider the exponential equation $y=Ca^t$, where C and a are positive real constants and t is a positive real number. The value of y decreases as the value of t increases if and only if which of the following statements about a is true?

F. $-1<a$ G. $0<a$ H. $0<a<1$ J. $1<a<2$ K. $1<a$

62. Whenever x, y, and z are positive real numbers, which of the following expressions is equivalent to $2\log_3 x+\frac{1}{2}\log_6 y-\log_3 z$

A. $\log_3\left(\frac{x^2y}{z}\right)$ B. $\log_3\left(\frac{x^2}{z}\right)+\log_6(\sqrt{y})$

C. $\log_3\left(\frac{z}{x^2}\right)+\log_6\left(\frac{y}{2}\right)$ D. $\log_3(x-z)+\log_6(\sqrt{y})$

E. $2\log_3(x-z)+\log_6\left(\frac{y}{2}\right)$

63. Which of the following is an equivalent expression for r in terms of S and t whenever r, S, and t are all distinct and $S=\frac{rt-3}{r-t}$?

A. $\frac{St-3}{S-t}$ B. $\frac{S-3}{S-1}$ C. $\frac{S-t}{S-3}$ D. $\frac{St-3}{S+t}$ E. $\frac{3}{t-S}$

64. Given $f(x)=\frac{x^3+\frac{5}{8}}{x+\frac{1}{4}}$, whatis $f\left(\frac{1}{2}\right)$?

A. $\frac{30}{32}$ B. 1 C. $\frac{36}{24}$ D. $\frac{20}{8}$ E. $\frac{7}{2}$

65. The table below lists the number (to the nearest 1,000) of Boy Scout units (packs, troops, posts, and groups) in the United States for 1994 through 1997. Of the following expressions with x representing the number of years after 1994, which best models the number of Boy Scout units (in

Year	Boy Scout units (in thousands)
1994	129
1995	132
1996	135
1997	139

thousands) in the United States?

Table adapted from U.S. Census Bureau, Statistical Abstract of the United States: 1998.

A. $\frac{3}{10}x+1,994$　　B. $\frac{10}{3}x+129$

C. $129x+1,994$　　D. $139x+1,997$

E. $1,994x+129$

66. The figure below shows a scatter plot for the data points in the table and 5 solid-line graphs that represent possible models for this data set. Among the 5 lines, which appears to be the best model for the data set?

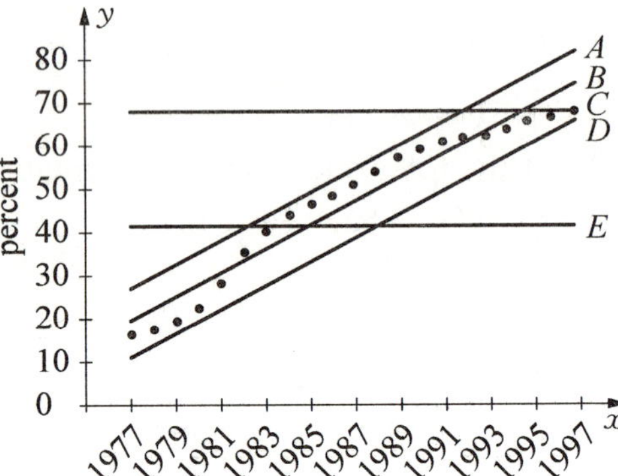

A. A

B. B

C. C

D. D

E. E

67. A ball is thrown upward toward a vertical brick wall. The ball hits the wall and bounces back down to the ground. Among the following graphs, which one best represents the relationship between the height, in meters, of the ball and the time, in seconds, from when the ball is thrown until it hits thc ground?

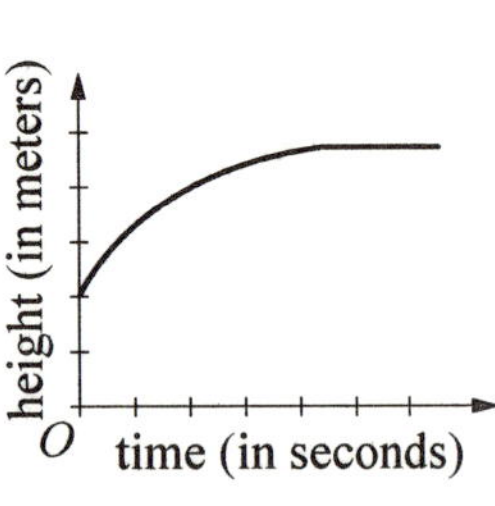

A.

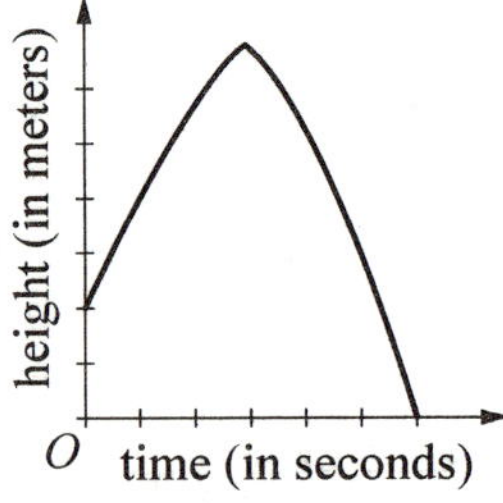

B.

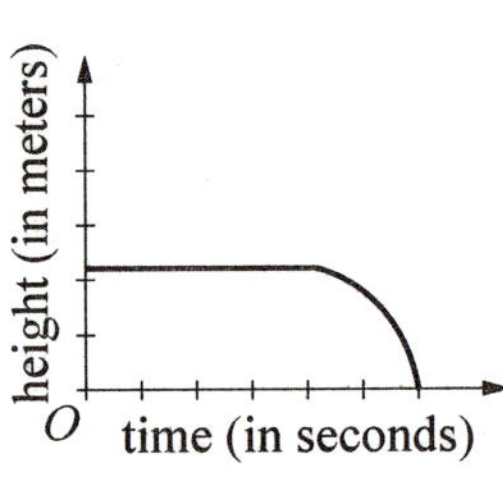

C.

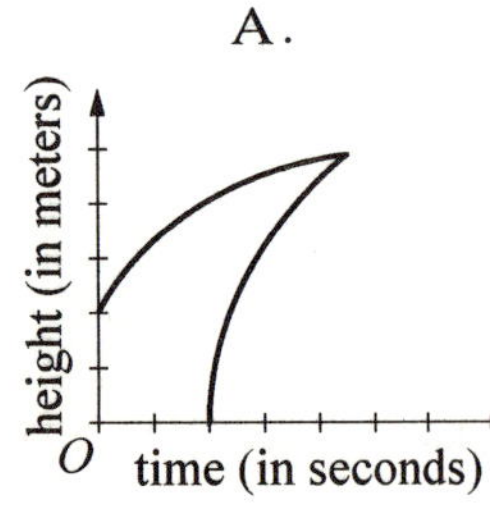

D.

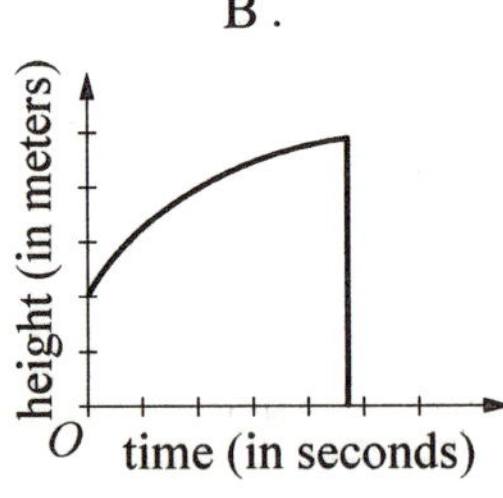

E.

68. If $h(x) = f(x) - g(x)$, where $f(x) = 5x^2 + 15x - 25$ and $g(x) = 5x^2 - 6x - 1$, then $h(x)$ is always divisible by which of the following?

A. 3　　B. 5　　C. 7　　D. 9　　E. 17

69. For all $a > 1$, the expression $\frac{3a^4}{3a^6}$ equals:

F. $\frac{1}{2}$　　G. $-a^2$　　H. a^2　　J. $-\frac{1}{a^2}$　　K. $\frac{1}{a^2}$

70. For every positive 2-digit number, x, with tens digit t and units digit u, let y be the 2-digit

number formed by reversing the digits of x. Which of the following expressions is equivalent to $x-y$?

F. $9(t-u)$ G. $9(u-t)$ H. $9t-u$ J. $9u-t$ K. 0

71. Let a function of 2 variables be defined by $f(x, y)=xy-(x-y)$. What is the value of f(9, 7)?

A. 16 B. 47 C. 61 D. 65 E. 79

72. If $a-b=5$ and $c=7a-9-7b$, then $c=$?

F. -4 G. -2 H. 26 J. 35 K. 44

73. The number of clients Galaxy Internet Company acquired in each calendar year can be modeled by the function $C(t)=750t+320$, where t = 0 corresponds to the 1999 calendar year. Using this model, how many clients would you expect Galaxy to acquire in the calendar year 2006?

F. 2,990 G. 4,070 H. 4,820 J. 5,570 K. 6,320

74. When $\frac{r}{s}=3$, $r^2-9s^2=$?

F. 0 G. 8 H. 9 J. -8 K. -9

75. What is the largest integer value of n that satisfies the in equality $\frac{12}{15}>\frac{n}{12}$?

F. 7 G. 8 H. 9 J. 10 K. 11

76. $\begin{bmatrix} a & b \\ c & d \end{bmatrix}+\begin{bmatrix} b & c \\ d & a \end{bmatrix}+\begin{bmatrix} \frac{1}{a+b} & \frac{1}{b+c} \\ \frac{1}{c+d} & \frac{1}{d+a} \end{bmatrix}=$?

A. $\begin{bmatrix} 1 & 1 \\ 1 & 1 \end{bmatrix}$

B. $\begin{bmatrix} \frac{ab}{a+b} & \frac{bc}{b+c} \\ \frac{cd}{c+d} & \frac{ad}{d+a} \end{bmatrix}$

C. $\begin{bmatrix} 2a+2b & 2b+2c \\ 2c+2d & 2d+2a \end{bmatrix}$

D. $\begin{bmatrix} \frac{1}{2a+2b} & \frac{1}{2b+2c} \\ \frac{1}{2c+2d} & \frac{1}{2d+2a} \end{bmatrix}$

E. $\begin{bmatrix} a+b+\frac{1}{a+b} & b+c+\frac{1}{b+c} \\ c+d+\frac{1}{c+d} & d+a+\frac{1}{d+a} \end{bmatrix}$

77. If $\frac{x}{y}=\frac{1}{9}$ and $\frac{y}{z}=\frac{9}{8}$, then $\frac{z}{x}=$?

A. $\frac{1}{648}$ B. $\frac{1}{8}$ C. $\frac{8}{81}$ D. $\frac{81}{8}$ E. 8

78. Last year, Tom earned an annual salary of \$S from which a total of \$D was deducted for taxes and insurance. The balance wasTom's-take-home pay, Tom's take-home pay represents what fraction of his annual salary?

F. $\frac{D}{S}$ G. $\frac{S}{D}$ H. $\frac{D-S}{D}$ J. $\frac{D-S}{S}$ K. $\frac{S-D}{S}$

79. For any non zero value of y, $(y^{-5})^3=$?

F. $\frac{1}{y^{15}}$　　G. $\frac{1}{y^2}$　　H. y^8　　J. y^{15}　　K. y^{125}

80. What are the possible values of y such that $xy^2 = 54$, $x < 10$, $y < 10$, and x and y are integers?

F. $-3, 3$　　G. $1, 3$　　H. $1, 9$　　J. $3, 6$　　K. $6, 3$

81. Whenever $(x+4)(x-3) < 0$, which of the following expressions always has a negative value?

F. $x-5$　　G. $x-2$　　H. $x+5$　　J. $2x$　　K. x^2-1

82. Which of the following is the graph of the solution set for $|x-c| \geqslant 2$?

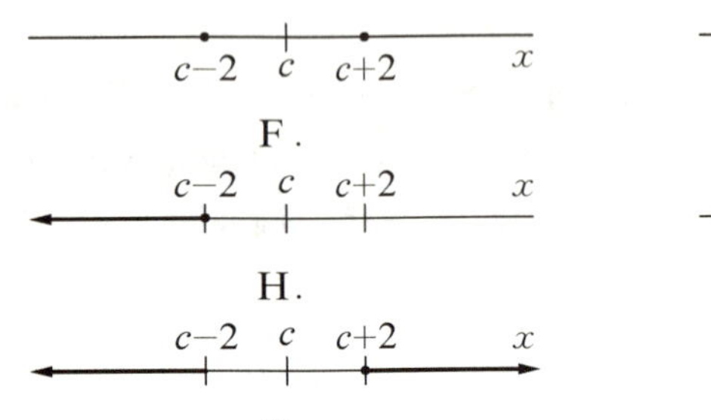

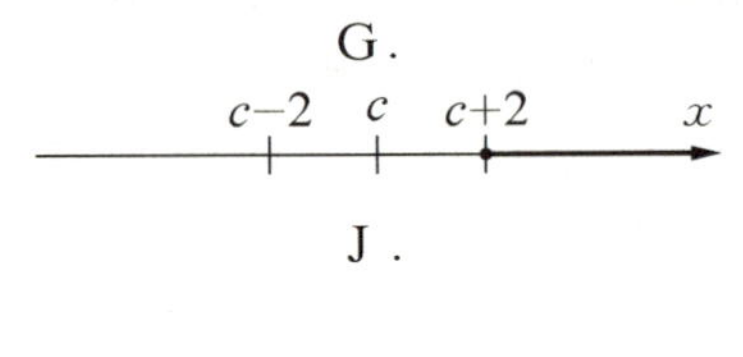

83. If $\log_3 2 = p$ and $\log_3 5 = q$, which of the following expressions is equal to 10?

F. 3^{p+q}　　G. $3^p + 3^q$　　H. 9^{p+q}　　J. pq　　K. $p+q$

84. How many ordered pairs (x, y) of real numbers will satisfy the equation $2x - 5y = 6$?

F. 0　　G. 1　　H. 2　　J. 3

K. Infinitely many

85. For any real number a, the equation $|x-a| = 7$ can be thought of as meaning "the distance on the real number line from x to a is 7 units." How far apart are the 2 solutions for x?

F. a　　G. $2a$　　H. $7+a$　　J. $\sqrt{7^2+a^2}$　　K. 14

86. What is the solution set of $|2z-1| \geqslant 5$?

A. $\{z: z \geqslant 3\}$　　B. $\{z: z \leqslant -2 \text{ or } z \geqslant 3\}$

C. $\{z: z \leqslant -3 \text{ or } z \geqslant 3\}$　　D. $\{z: z \leqslant -4 \text{ or } z \geqslant 6\}$

E. $\{\ \}$ (the empty set)

87. For $(x, y) = 5x + 4y$ what is the value of $g(x, y)$ when $y = \left(\frac{3}{x}\right)^2$ and $x = 2$?

F. $\frac{23}{2}$　　G. $\frac{49}{4}$　　C. 16　　D. 19　　E. 28

88. A certain fork lift can carry a maximum weight of 3,000 pounds. This fork lift will be used to carry boxes that weigh 65 Pounds each. Which of the following inequalities is true if and only if the forklift does not exceed its maximum weight limit when it carries b boxes, where b is a whole number?

A. $65b \leqslant 3\,000$　　B. $65b > 3\,000$

C. $65 - b \leqslant 3\,000$　　D. $65 - b > 3\,000$

E. $\frac{b}{65} > 3\,000$

89. For all non zero values of a, b, and c, which of the following a is the solution for X of the equation $ax + b = c$?

F. $\frac{c}{ab}$　　G. $\frac{c}{a} - b$　　H. $\frac{b-c}{a}$　　J. $\frac{b+c}{a}$　　K. $\frac{c-b}{a}$

90. How many (x, y) pairs of real numbers satisfy $xy = 3$ and $(x+y)^2 = 10$?

A. 0 B. 1 C. 2 D. 4

E. Infinitely many.

91. During their morning jog in the park, Jean stops at a drinking fountain. Sula continues to jog and gets 10 meters ahead of Jean. Sula is jogging at a constantrate of 2 meters per second, and Jean starts jogging at a constantrate of 2.4 meters per second to catch up to Sula. Which of the following equations, when solved for t, gives the number of seconds Jean will take to catch up to Sula?

F. $2t + 10 = 2.4t$ G. $2t - 10 = 2.4t$

H. $\frac{10+2.4t}{2.4}2t$ J. $2t = 10$

K. $2.4t = 10$

92. If $x + 22 = |-11|$, then $x = ?$

F. -33 G. -11 H. $\frac{1}{2}$ J. 11 K. 33

[**Session 3 答案**]

1 F	2 D	3 B	4 K	5 A	6 E	7 K	8 D	9 F	10 E
11 D	12 A	13 E	14 K	15 C	16 A	17 C	18 C	19 K	20 K
21 D	22 H	23 B	24 K	25 A	26 A	27 C	28 J	29 F	30 A
31 A	32 J	33 C	34 H	35 J	36 A	37 F	38 A	39 F	40 K
41 B	42 E	43 A	44 F	45 C	46 D	47 E	48 B	49 H	50 J
51 F	52 G	53 H	54 E	55 H	56 K	57 K	58 A	59 A	60 G
61 H	62 B	63 A	64 B	65 B	66 B	67 B	68 A	69 K	70 F
71 C	72 H	73 J	74 F	75 H	76 E	77 E	78 K	79 F	80 K
81 F	82 K	83 F	84 K	85 K	86 B	87 D	88 A	89 K	90 E
91 F	92 G								

[**Session 3 答案解析**]

1. 题干：$|x+a| = b$，a 是任意实数，b 为多少时无解？

解析：结合数轴。

2. 题干：x 表示直径，精确直径是 3，不能大于或者小于这个数值超过 0.5，用代数式如何表示？

解析：即 x 和 3 的差距的绝对值不能超过 0.5。

3. 题干：如果 $kx + k = 0$，$k > 1$，那么 $x = ?$

解析：$kx = -k$。

4. 题干：机器 a 处理步骤 1，b 处理 2。A 一小时处理 180 个，b 一小时处理 150 个。A 处理八个小时需要 b 处理几个小时？

解析：时间乘以效率一样即可。

5. 题干：x^2-x-6 因式分解为 $(x+a)(x+b)$，这两个因式的和是多少？
 解析：分解后即得到 a 和 b。
6. 题干：$f(x)=3x^3-27x$ 的零点是什么情况？
 解析：有三个不同的有理数零点。
7. 题干：哪个不是 x^4-4 的因式？
 解析：先看成平方。
8. 题干：路程时间图如题。换地点部分的平均速度是多少？
 解析：注意只算运动的部分。
9. 题干：$\frac{x^a}{x^b}=x^3$，对所有非零的 x 成立。哪个说法正确？
 解析：不为零意味着可以移到分母处。
10. 题干：$\frac{ab-ac}{2b-2c}<0$，$b\neq c$，a 的值是多少？
 解析：所有的负实数都可以。
11. 题干：生产耳环的公司，每月固定投入 10 000，一对耳环成本 0.6，如何表示每月的总成本？
 解析：x 是耳环的对数。
12. 题干：$5x-1\geqslant 9$ 在数轴上如何表示？
 解析：算出 x。
13. 题干：工作 x 小时能做完。那么工作了 y 小时的时候，还剩的比例怎么表示？
 解析：工作量和小时数成比例。
14. 题干：$f(x+y)=f(x)+f(y)$ 对实数成立，那么 $f(0)$ 等于多少？
 解析：令 x 和 y 都为零。
15. 题干：成人票 a 元，学生票 s 元，12 张成人票与 18 张学生票的差值是 36。如何表示？
 解析：注意绝对值符号。
16. 题干：x 表示生产和销售的船，初期投入 1 000 万，每艘船成本 7 000，售价 20 000，利润如何表示？
 解析：利润等于收入减去所有成本。
17. 题干：哪个式子和表格符合？
 解析：代入即可。
18. 题干：$\frac{A}{30}+\frac{B}{105}=\frac{7A+2B}{x}$，均为大于 1 的整数。$X$ 等于？
 解析：通分。
19. 题干：$h=-at^2+bt+c$ 的图像如下，如果调整 c 什么会改变？
 解析：截距和最大值都会变。
20. 题干：如图，大正方形的边长为 x，小的为 y。总面积是多少？
 解析：算出总的边长。
21. 题干：定义在{(2, 1), (4, 2), (6, 3)}上的函数有值{2, 4, 6}，那么在{(0, 2), (2, 2), (3, −2)}上的值是多少？
 解析：注意值都是取前者。
22. 题干：If $f(x)=2x$ and $g(x)=x^2$，$f(g(3))$ 等于多少？
 解析：复合函数。
23. 题干：$4x^2-9=0$ 的解集是什么？

解析：解方程。

24. 题干：$\frac{1}{x+1}+\frac{1}{x}$ 等于什么？

解析：通分。

25. 题干：给气球充气的机器花 39.99，原材料一个要花 2，如果做了 b 个，总成本怎么表示？

解析：$\$2.00b+\$39.99$。

26. 题干：市场价 p，降价 23%，现价多少？

解析：$p-0.23p$。

27. 题干：$p(t)=p_0\left(1+\frac{r}{100}\right)^t$，$p$ 是人口数，t 是时间 / 年，r 是增长速率。每年增长 $r\%$。1990 年有 782 000，每年多 5%，2000 有多少？

解析：t 为 10。

28. 题干：$\frac{x+1}{x^3-x}$ 分解。

解析：分解后可以约分。

29. 题干：$|x|^2+2|x|-3=0$ 的实数解是多少？

解析：可以先不管绝对值，算出正的零点。然后他们的共轭也是零点。

30. 题干：

对于 $x>0$，$P(x)=x^5+x^4-36x-36$

对于 $x<0$，$P(x)=-x^5+x^4+36x-36$

$P(-1)=?$

解析：$-1<0$。

31. 题干：$f(x)=\sqrt{x}$，$g(x)=7x+b$，$y=f(g(x))$ 经过(4，6)。$B=?$

解析：经过该点，则说明 $f=6$ 的时候 $g=4$。代入，列方程组即可。

32. 题干：$\log_2 24-\log_2 3=\log_5 x$，求 x？

解析：对数底数相同时可以进行加减。

33. 题干：还一本书，过期了 9 天，前 6 天滞纳金每天 5 分，6 天后每天 20 分。一共要交多少滞纳金？

解析：$6\times5+20\times3$

34. 题干：$\begin{array}{r} 5\ w\ 7 \\ +\ 9\ 2\ y \\ \hline 1,z\ 9\ 6 \end{array}$，其中 w，y，z 都是从 0 到 9 的整数，求 $w\times y\times z$？

解析：从个位数开始算起即可。

35. 题干：$t=2\pi\sqrt{\frac{x}{32}}$ 为单摆周期，x 为摆长。若摆长 8，那么周期是多少？

解析：代入即可，Π 约等于 3.14。

36. 题干：$27\cdot3^x=9^{y-6}$，$y=6$，$x=?$

解析：任何数的零次方等于 1，除了零。

37. 题干：求解 $|x-2|=5$。

解析：$x-2$ 等于 5 或者 -5。

38. 题干：林肯在 1863 年提到 1776 年，说是“4 score 又 7 年前”，如何表示这些关系？

解析：4s + 7 即时间差。

39. 题干：f 为预期利润，g 为实际利润。哪个说法是正确的？
解析：可以看出实际利润一直都是预期的 3/4。

40. 题干：$y=\frac{40}{3}x+\frac{110}{5}$ 是根据调查获得的预估曲线，Y 是体重，x 是鞋码。现在有个新学生，鞋码 $9\frac{1}{2}$，体重 165，和预估的有什么差别？
解析：把鞋码代入预估曲线。

41. 题干：$f(x)=|x|$，$g(x)=-x^2+a$，哪个是 $y=f(g(x))$ 的图像？
解析：即给 g 加上绝对值。

42. 题干：$2a=\frac{b\sqrt{2}}{2}=\frac{c\sqrt{2}}{2.5}$，均为正实数。哪个说法是对的？
解析：系数越大的越小。

43. 题干：五分中装 1 200 桶，那么 2 000 装满要花的时间怎么表达？
解析：速率是一样的。

44. 题干：$x^3=38.7$，x 的值介于什么之间？
解析：代入即可验算。

45. 题干：$f(x)=x(x+3)(x+1)(x-3)(x-2)$ 和 $g(x)=-x(x+3)(x-3)(x-1)$ 的图像如图。$f(x)=g(x)$ 有几个解？
解析：交点数。

46. 题干：$2x+7<3x+1$ 的解里面有哪几个在{5，6，7，8，9}里面？
解析：可以验算。

47. 题干：$-1\leqslant x-y\leqslant 1$ 的解是哪个阴影？
解析：可以解出两个直线方程，然后注意小于号大于号的方向即可。

48. 题干：$m=0.8(220-a)$，a 为年龄，m 为心率。A 为 20，$m=$？
解析：代入即可。

49. 题干：$\frac{(n+2)(9-3)}{8(2)}=2$，$n=$？
解析：移项。

50. 题干：$\left(-\frac{1}{2}\right)^a$ 什么时候表示 −1 到 0 的实数？
解析：一次方时等于本身。

51. 题干：如图，什么时候平均速度最快？
解析：速度等于位移时间图像的斜率。

52. 题干：$4\leqslant x\leqslant 12$，$2\leqslant y\leqslant 4$，$\frac{x}{y}$ 的最小值是多少？
解析：x 做出限制区域，求区域内的点与原点连线的斜率最大值。

53. 题干：$f(x)=2x+10$，$g(x)=3x^2$，$f(g(-3))=$？
解析：先算 g 的值。

54. 题干：$\frac{ab}{25}+\frac{11}{10(a+b)}+\frac{1}{a+b}=$？如果 $a=2$，$b=3$。
解析：代入即可。

55. 题干：什么时候 $\sqrt{x}+\sqrt{x-16}=8$ 对哪个实数值成立？
解析：验算法最快。

56. 题干：哪个不等价于 $x\left(\frac{1}{y}\right)=1$？

解析：移项，平方等操作可以采取。

57. 题干：一开始销售缓慢，然后销售速率变大，后来又变小。哪个图像体现了这一过程？

解析：斜率即速率。

58. 题干：$(4x^2-3x+7)-(-1+5x+2x^2)$ 等价于？

解析：把括号去掉。注意括号内的符号变化。

59. 题干：y 正比于 w^2 和 x 的乘积，反比于 z^3。如何表达？

解析：k 是系数，放在哪里无所谓。

60. 题干：$3x+6y=52$

$x+6y=24$ 的解是？

解析：上面的减去下面的，即可消掉 y。

61. 题干：$y=Ca^t$ 什么时候 y 随着 t 的增长而减小？a 是正数，C 是正数。

解析：幂函数性质。

62. 题干：$2\log_3 x+\frac{1}{2}\log_6 y-\log_3 z$ 等于？

解析：对数的底一样时可以进行加减运算。

63. 题干：r 等于什么？如果 $S=\frac{rt-3}{r-t}$。

解析：移项，把 r 移到一边。

64. 题干：$f(x)=\frac{x^3+\frac{5}{8}}{x+\frac{1}{4}}$，那么 $f\left(\frac{1}{2}\right)=$？

解析：代入。

65. 题干：数据如表，哪个函数最好地拟合了数据？

解析：注意单位的变化。

66. 题干：数据点和拟合曲线如图，哪个拟合地最好？

解析：最接近的那个就是最好的。

67. 题干：把气球径直砸向墙。哪个是气球高度与时间的关系？

解析：上升下降的速度和水平的速度无关。

68. 题干：$h(x)=f(x)-g(x)$，$f(x)=5x^2+15x-25$，$g(x)=5x^2-6x-1$，$h(x)$ 可以被什么整除？

解析：等于 $21x-24$，可以被 3 整除。

69. 题干：$\frac{3a^4}{3a^6}$ 等于？$a>1$。

解析：化简即可。

70. 题干：x 由十位数 t 和个位数 u 组成，交换位置变成 y。$x-y$ 等于什么？

解析：先把 x 和 y 用 t，u 表示。

71. 题干：$f(x, y)=xy-(x-y)$，那么 $f(9, 7)=$？

解析：代入即可。

72. 题干：$a-b=5$，$c=7a-9-7b$，$c=$？

解析：可以用 a 表示 b。

73. 题干：$C(t) = 750t + 320$，c 是人数，t 是年份，1999 年时 t 为 0，那么 2006 年时 c 为多少？
解析：2006 年时 $t = 7$。

74. 题干：$\frac{r}{s} = 3$，$r^2 - 9s^2 = ?$
解析：替换。

75. 题干：$\frac{12}{15} > \frac{n}{12}$，$n$ 为整数，最大是多少？
解析：移项。

76. 题干：$\begin{bmatrix} a & b \\ c & d \end{bmatrix} + \begin{bmatrix} b & c \\ d & a \end{bmatrix} + \begin{bmatrix} \frac{1}{a+b} & \frac{1}{b+c} \\ \frac{1}{c+d} & \frac{1}{d+a} \end{bmatrix} = ?$
解析：矩阵加法只要对应位置相加即可。

77. 题干：$\frac{x}{y} = \frac{1}{9}$，$\frac{y}{z} = \frac{9}{8}$，那么 $\frac{z}{x} = ?$
解析：乘积的倒数。

78. 题干：年薪 s，缴税和保险 d，剩下的占年薪多少比例？
解析：剩下的为 s - d。

79. 题干：$(y^{-5})^3 = ?$
解析：负次幂是倒数的形式。

80. 题干：$xy^2 = 54$，$x < 10$，$y < 10$，其中 x 和 y 都是整数。那么 y 的可能值是？
解析：因为是整数，所以只有几种情况，可列举。

81. 题干：$(x+4)(x-3) < 0$，那么哪个式子是负的？
解析：先解出 x 的范围。

82. 题干：$|x - c| \geqslant 2$ 怎么在数轴表示？
解析：这种情况一定是以 c 为中点的两段。

83. 题干：$\log_3 2 = p$ and $\log_3 5 = q$，那么哪个等于 10？
解析：对数相加，得到以 3 为底的 10 的对数。

84. 题干：有多少对实数 x，y 满足 $2x - 5y = 6$？
解析：相当于问这条线上有多少实数点，当然是无穷的。

85. 题干：$|x - a| = 7$ 可以理解为 x 到 a 的距离为 7。两个解之间的距离是多少？
解析：14。

86. 题干：$|2z - 1| \geqslant 5$ 的解集是？
解析：先把绝对值里看成正的，再看成负的，分别脱掉绝对值。

87. 题干：$g(x, y) = 5x + 4y$，如果 $y = \left(\frac{3}{x}\right)^2$，$x = 2$，那么 $g = ?$
解析：由 x 求出 y，然后代入 g。

88. 题干：最多可以叉起 3 000 磅，每个箱子 65 磅，箱子数为 b，如何表示其工作范围？
解析：不等式。

89. 题干：a，b，c 都是非负数，$ax + b = c$ 的解是什么？
解析：移项。

90. 题干：满足 $xy = 3$ and $(x+y)2 = 10$ 的点有几个？
解析：画图法。

91. 题干：a 在 b 前面 10 米，a 速度 2 米每秒，b 速度 2.4 米每秒。如何表示 b 追上 a？
解析：写出各自的跑步距离表达式，然后加上差距。

92. 题干：$x+22=|-11|$，那么 $x=$？
解析：分类，然后去掉绝对值。

Session 4 Algebra 2 代数 2

1. What is the largest value of x for which there exists a real value of y such that $x^2+y^2=324$?
A. 18 B. 162 C. 306 D. 324 E. 648

2. The expression given below is equivalent to which of the following expressions?
$(x^3+2x^2-6)-2(x^4-3x^3+2x^2+x-1)$
F. $x^{15}-7$
G. $-2x^4+7x^3-2x^2-2x-4$
H. $-2x^4-2x^3+4x^2-x-7$
J. $-2x^4-5x^3+6x^2+2x-1$
K. $-6x^{15}$

3. Which of the following number line graphs shows the solution set of $3(x+2)+1\leqslant 4x+15$?

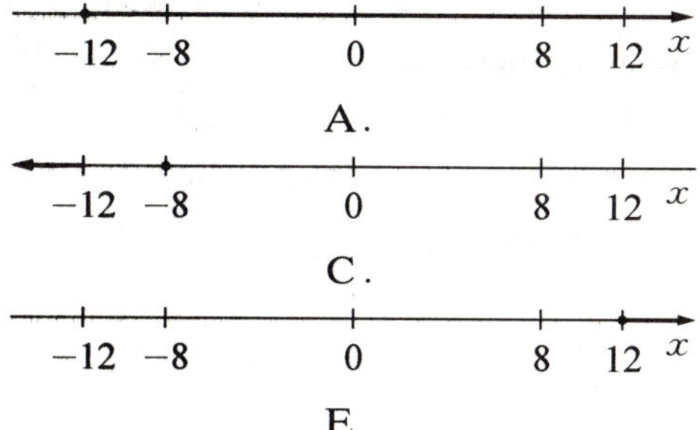

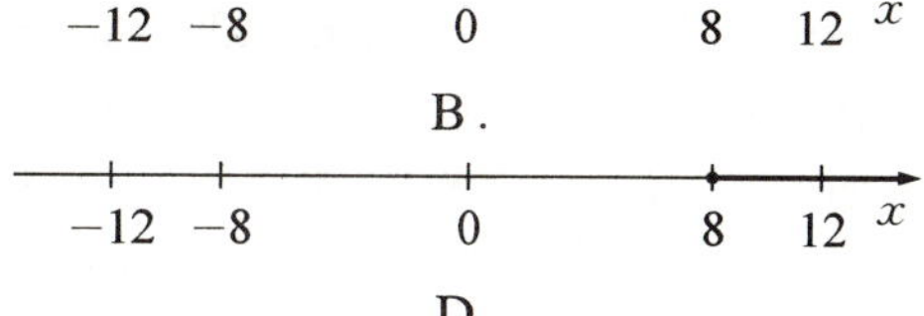

4. What is the solution set of $\sqrt[4]{x^2+6x}=2$?
A. $\{2\}$ B. $\{8\}$ C. $\{-8, 2\}$ D. $\{-2, 8\}$ E. $\{-3\pm\sqrt{13}\}$

5. Which of the following pairs of functions, $f(x)$ and $g(x)$, form the composite function $f(g(x))=\sqrt{2x^2+3}$?

	$f(x)$	$g(x)$
F.	$\sqrt{x}$	$2x^2+3$
G.	x^2	$\sqrt{2x+3}$
H.	$2x^2$	$\sqrt{x+3}$
J.	$\sqrt{x^2+3}$	$2x$
K.	$2x^2+3$	$\sqrt{x}$

6. Which of the following matrices, when substituted for T, satisfies the matrix equation below?
$T\begin{bmatrix}-3\\5\end{bmatrix}=\begin{bmatrix}5\\3\end{bmatrix}$
F. $\begin{bmatrix}1 & 0\\0 & -1\end{bmatrix}$ G. $\begin{bmatrix}0 & 1\\-1 & 0\end{bmatrix}$ H. $\begin{bmatrix}0 & -1\\1 & 0\end{bmatrix}$ J. $\begin{bmatrix}-1 & 0\\0 & 1\end{bmatrix}$ K. $\begin{bmatrix}-1 & 0\\1 & 0\end{bmatrix}$

7. If $\frac{n!}{(n-2)!}=30$, $(n-1)!=$?
A. 15 B. 24 C. 60 D. 120 E. 720

8. Let a function of. 2 variables be defined by $f(x, y)=xy-(x-y)$. What is the value of $f(10, 3)$?
F. 13 G. 17 H. 23 J. 37 K. 43

9. $8x^5 \cdot 12x^5$ is' equivalent to:

A. $20x^{10}$ B. $20x^{25}$ C. $96x^5$ D. $96x^{10}$ E. $96x^{25}$

10. If $\det\begin{bmatrix} a & b \\ c & d \end{bmatrix} = ad - bc$, then $\det\begin{bmatrix} -b & -c \\ -d & a \end{bmatrix} = ?$

F. $ad - bc$ G. $-ad + bc$ H. $ab - dc$ J. $-ab + bc$ K. $-ab - dc$

11. The amount of money, A dollars, in a savings account after f years is given by $A = P + Prt$, where P dollars is the amount of money in the account originally and r is the rate of simple interest. Which of the following expressions gives P in terms of A, r, and t?

A. $\frac{A}{1+rt}$ B. $\frac{1+rt}{A}$ C. $\frac{A-P}{n}$ D. $\frac{A}{2rt}$ E. $A - rt$

12. Consider the equation $\sqrt{b} - \sqrt{a} = 3\sqrt{a}$, where a and b are positive real numbers. What is b in terms of a?

F. $16a$ G. $9a$ H. $4a$ J. $3a$ K. $2a$

13. Two workers were hired to begin work at the same time. Worker A's contract called for a starting salary of \$20,000 with an increase of \$800 after each year of employment. Worker B's contract called for a staring salary of \$15,200 with an increase of \$2,000 after each year of employment. If x represents of the number of full year's employment (that is, the number of yearly increases each worker has received), which of the following equations could be solved to determine the number of years until B's yearly salary equals A's yearly salary?

A. $20{,}000 + 800x = 15{,}200 + 2{,}000x$

B. $20{,}000 + 2{,}000x = 15{,}200 + 800x$

C. $(20{,}000 + 800)x = (15{,}200 + 2{,}000)x$

D. $(2{,}000 + 800)x = 20{,}000 - 15{,}200$

E. $(2{,}000 - 800)x = 20{,}000 + 15{,}200$

14. An integer n is added to 4. That sum is then multiplied by 8. This result is 10 less twice the original integer. Which of the following equations represents this relationship?

F. $8(n+4) = 2n - 10$ G. $8(n+4) - 10 = 2n$

H. $8(n+4) = 10 - 2n$ J. $n + 4 \times 8 = 2n - 10$

K. $4 + 8 = 2n - 10$

15. The table below gives the values of 2 functions, f and g, for various values of x, One of the functions expresses a linear relationship. What is the value of that function at $x = 4$?

X	F(x)	G(x)
−2	1.4	0.6
−1	1.2	0.9
0		
1	0.8	1.3
2	0.6	1.6
3		
4		

A. 0.2

B. 0.4

C. 1.9

D. 2.0

E. 2.2

16. What is the sum of the 2 solutions of the equation $x^2 + x - 12 = 0$?

A. −12 B. −4 C. −1 D. 0 E. 3

17. Let a, b, c, and d be distinct positive integers. What is the 4th term of the geometric sequence below?

bcd，abc^2d，a^2bc^3d，…

F. a^3bc^4d　　G. $a^3b^2c^3d$　　H. $a^3bc^4d^2$　　J. a^4bc^6d　　K. a^4bc^9d

18. For all $x > 21$，$\dfrac{(x^2+8x+7)(x-3)}{(x^2+4x-21)(x+1)} = ?$

F. 1　　G. $\dfrac{9}{7}$　　H. $\dfrac{x-3}{x+3}$　　J. $\dfrac{2(x-3)}{x+1}$　　K. $-\dfrac{4(x-3)}{x+1}$

19. A trigonometric function with equation $y = a\sin(bx+c)$，where a, b, and c are real numbers, is graphed in the standard (x, y) coordinate plane below. The period of this function $f(x)$ is the smallest positive numbers p such that $f(x+p) = f(x)$ for every real number x. One of the following is the period of this function. Which one is it?

A. $\dfrac{\pi}{2}$　　B. π

C. 2π　　D. 4π

E. 2

20. Consider all pairs of positive integers w and z whose sum is 5. For how many values of w does there exist a positive integer x that satisfies both $2^w = x$ and $x^z = 64$?

A. 0　　B. 2　　C. 4　　D. 8

E. Infinitely many

21. Let $2x+3y=4$ and $5x+6y=7$. What is the value of $8x+9y$?

E. −10　　G. −1　　H. 2　　J. 7　　K. 10

22. The graph of $y = x^2$ is shown in the standard (x, y) coordinate plane below. For which of the following equations is the graph of the parabola shifted 3 units to the right and 2 units down?

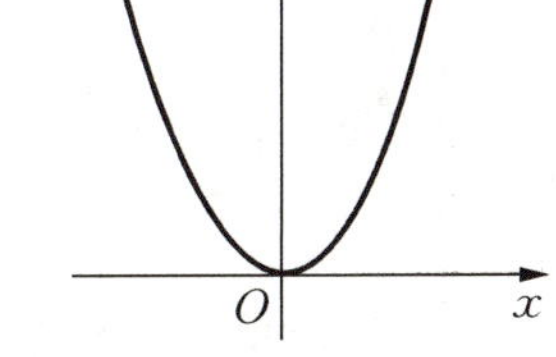

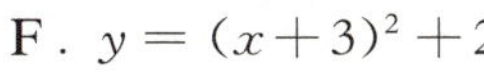

F. $y=(x+3)^2+2$　　G. $y=(x+3)^2-2$

H. $y=(x-2)^2+3$　　J. $y=(x-3)^2+2$

K. $y=(x-3)^2-2$

23. Whenever w is an integer greater than 1，$\log_w \dfrac{w^2}{w^6} = ?$

F. −4　　G. −3　　H. $-\dfrac{1}{3}$　　J. $\dfrac{1}{3}$　　K. 3

24. Alma's teacher assigned each student in class to draw a trapezoid using a segment of the line $y=x$ as one side. The interior of Alma's trapezoid is shown shaded in the standard (x, y) coordinate plane below. The equations of the lines that intersect to form the trapezoid are also shown.

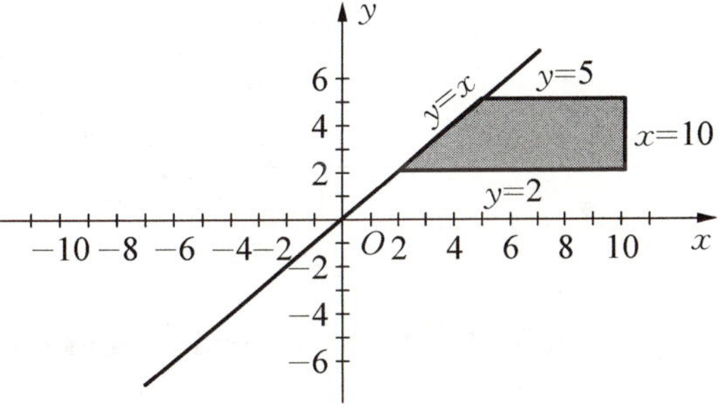

The next part of the assignment was to reflect the trapezoid across the x-axis and write a set of inequalities defining the reflected trapezoid and its interior. Which of the following sets of inequalities should Amal have written?

A. $x \leqslant 10$, $2 \leqslant y \leqslant 5$, $y \leqslant x$

B. $x \leqslant 10$, $-5 \leqslant y \leqslant -2$, $y \geqslant -x$

C. $x \leqslant 10$, $-5 \leqslant y \leqslant -2$, $y \leqslant -x$

D. $x \leqslant -10$, $2 \leqslant y \leqslant 5$, $y \leqslant -x$

E. $x \leqslant -10$, $-5 \leqslant y \leqslant -2$, $y \geqslant x$

25. Let the function f9 a, b) be defined as $f(a, b) = b^2 - a$. For all x and y, $f((x^2 + y^2), (x - y)) = ?$

F. $2y^2$　　G. 0　　H. $-2y^2$　　J. $-2xy + 2y^2$　　K. $-2xy$

26. If $3^x = 54$, then which of the following must be true?

A. $1 < x < 2$　　B. $2 < x < 3$　　C. $3 < x < 4$　　D. $4 < x < 5$　　E. $5 < x$

27. The inequality $6(x + 2) > 7(x - 5)$ is equivalent to which of the following inequalities?

A. $x < -23$　　B. $x < 7$　　C. $x < 17$　　D. $x < 37$　　E. $x < 47$

28. The graph of $y = -5x^2 + 9$ passes through $(1, 2a)$ in the standard (x, y) coordinate plane. What is the value of a.

F. 2　　G. 4　　H. 7　　J. −1　　K. −8

29. The determinant of a matrix $\begin{bmatrix} a & b \\ c & d \end{bmatrix}$ equals ad − cb. What must be the value of x for the matrix $\begin{bmatrix} x & 8 \\ x & x \end{bmatrix}$ to have a determinant of −16 ?

A. −4　　B. −2　　C. $-\frac{8}{5}$　　D. $\frac{8}{3}$　　E. 4

30. The solution set of which of the following equations is the set of real numbers that are 5 units from −3 ?

F. $|x + 3| = 5$　　G. $|x - 3| = 5$

H. $|x + 5| = 3$　　J. $|x - 5| = 3$

K. $|x + 5| = -3$

31. The graphs of and $f(x) = \cos x$ are $g(x) = \cos\left(x - \frac{\pi}{4}\right)$ shown in the standard (x, y) coordinate plane below. After one of the' following pairs of transformations is applied to the graph of $f(x)$, the image of the graph of $f(x)$ is the graph of $g(x)$. Which pair is it?

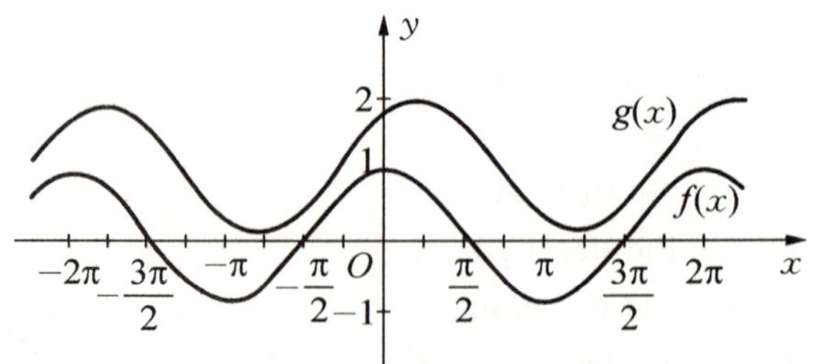

A. Shift $f(x)$ 1 unit left and $\frac{\pi}{4}$ units down.

B. Shift $f(x)$ 1 unit left and $\frac{\pi}{4}$ units up.

C. Shift $f(x)$ 1 unit right and $\frac{\pi}{4}$ units down.

D. Shift $f(x)$ $\frac{\pi}{4}$ units left and 1 unit up.

E. Shift $f(x)$ $\frac{\pi}{4}$ units right and 1 unit up.

32. If a is 25% of b, then 135% of b is what percent of a ?

A. 160% B. 210% C. 337.5% D. 540% E. 875%

33. If b is a positive number such that $\log_b\left(\frac{1}{81}\right)=-4$, then $b=$?

F. 3 G. 9 H. 85 J. $\frac{1}{3}$ K. $\frac{1}{9}$

34. Which of the following variable expressions would represent the area of a rectangle if its length is represented by $x+2$ and its width is represented by $x-1$?

A. $2x+1$ B. $4x+2$ C. x^2-2 D. x^2-x-2 E. x^2+x-2

35. On a map of Blueville in the standard (x, y) coordinate plane, where 1 coordinate unit represents 1 block, the middle school is at $(-8, 3)$ and the high school is at $(4, -2)$. What is the straight-line distance, in blocks, between the high school and the middle school?

A. 13 B. 17 C. $\sqrt{7}$ D. $\sqrt{13}$ E. $\sqrt{17}$

36. What real value of a satisfies the equation $16^a=\frac{1}{64^{a+1}}$?

A. -3 B. -2 C. $-\frac{3}{5}$ D. $\frac{1}{10}$ E. $\frac{1}{2}$

37. Which of the following equations given in factored form has roots at $\frac{1}{2}$, $\frac{3}{4}$, i, and $-i$?

A. $(2x-1)(4x-3)(x^2+1)=0$ B. $(2x-1)(4x-3)(x^2-1)=0$
C. $(2x+1)(4x-3)(x^2+1)=0$ D. $(2x+1)(4x-3)(x^2-1)=0$
E. $(2x+1)(4x+3)(x^2+1)=0$

38. Which of the following equations describes a line that is perpendicular to a line with equation $5x-6y=30$?

A. $5x-6y=15$ B. $5x+6y=24$
C. $6x-5y=12$ D. $6x+5y=10$
E. $7x-8y=32$

39. A test has 50 questions and is worth 130 points. It consists of x 5-point questions and y 2-point questions. Which of the following systems of equations, when solved, gives the number of each type of question that is on the test?

A. $\begin{cases}x+y=50\\x+y=130\end{cases}$ B. $\begin{cases}x+y=130\\2x+5y=50\end{cases}$

C. $\begin{cases}x+y=50\\5x+2y=130\end{cases}$ D. $\begin{cases}2x+5y=50\\2x+5y=130\end{cases}$

E. $\begin{cases}5x-y=130\\2x-y=50\end{cases}$

40. Which of the following is equivalent to $x^5 \cdot x^{-(3^2)}$?

F. x^{-45}　　G. x^{-4}　　H. x^{-1}　　J. x^{14}　　K. x^{45}

41. For what (x, y) pair is the matrix equation below true?

$$\begin{bmatrix} 3 & \frac{x}{2} \\ 0 & 1 \end{bmatrix} + \begin{bmatrix} x & 5 \\ 1 & 0 \end{bmatrix} = \begin{bmatrix} y & y \\ 1 & 1 \end{bmatrix}$$

F. (6, 0)　　G. (5, 5)　　H. (5, −2)　　J. (4, 7)　　K. (1, 4)

42. If $f(x) = \dfrac{3}{x^2 - 1}$ and $g(x) = x+1$, which of the following number lines shows the domain of $f(g(x))$?

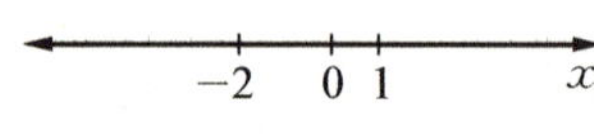

A.

B.

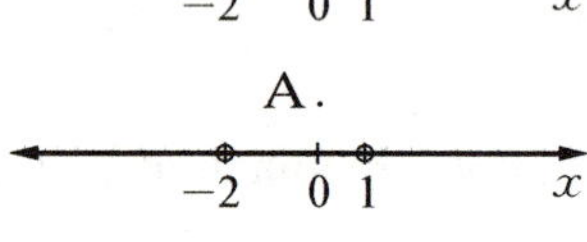

C.

D.

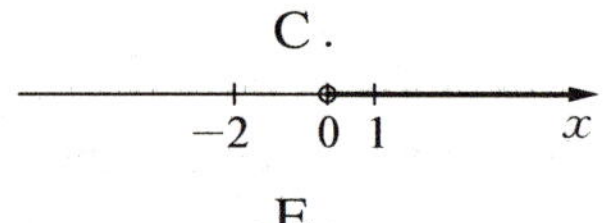

E.

43. The area, A, of a circle varies directly with the square of the radius, r. One of the following graphs shows the area, A, of *a* circle as the radius varies in the (r, A) coordinate plane. Which graph is it?

(Note: The (r, A) plane is the standard (x, y) coordinate plane with r along the horizontal axis and A along the vertical axis.)

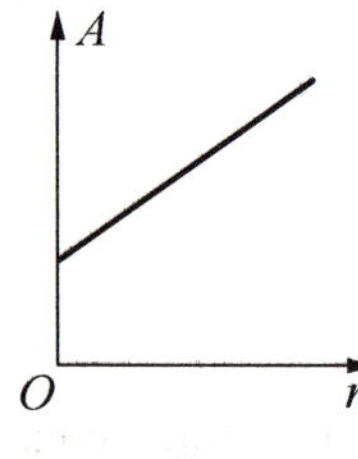

A.

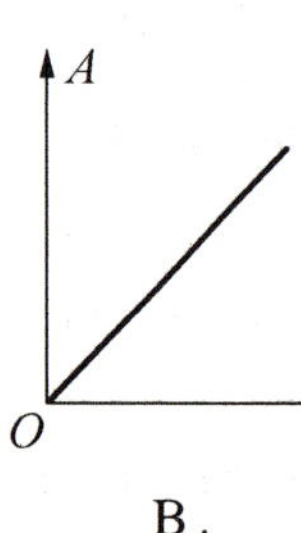

B.

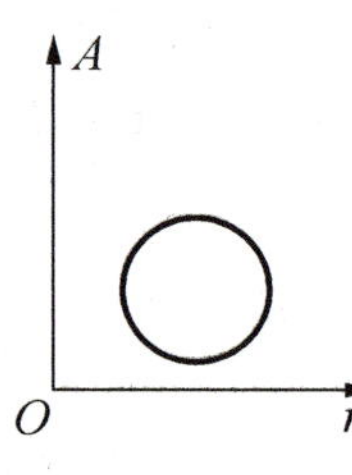

C.

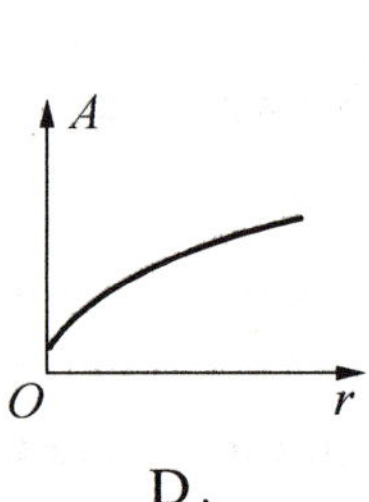

D.

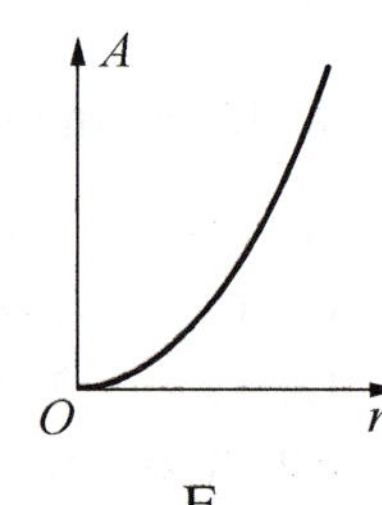

E.

44. Which of the following expressions is a factor of the expression $x^2 - 6x + 8$?

F. $x-3$　　G. $x-4$　　H. $x-5$　　J. $x-6$　　K. $x-8$

45. A new operation, ◆, is defined on pairs of ordered pairs of integers as follows: (a, b) ◆ $(c, d) = \dfrac{ac + bd}{ab - cd}$, What is the value of (2, 1) ◆ (4, 6)?

F. $-\dfrac{7}{11}$　　G. $-\dfrac{7}{4}$　　H. $\dfrac{7}{4}$　　J. 7　　K. 14

46. Which of the following equations shows a correct use of the quadratic formula to solve $x^2 - 5x + 3 = 0$?

A. $x = \dfrac{5 \pm \sqrt{25 - 4(1)(3)}}{2(1)}$　　B. $x = \dfrac{5 \pm \sqrt{25 + 4(1)(3)}}{2(1)}$

C. $x = \dfrac{-5 \pm \sqrt{25 - 4(1)(-3)}}{2(1)}$　　D. $x = \dfrac{-5 \pm \sqrt{25 - 4(1)(3)}}{2(1)}$

E. $x=\frac{-5\pm\sqrt{25+4(1)(3)}}{2(1)}$

47. When a, b, and c are real numbers and $ab^2c^4>0$, which of the following must be greater than 0 ?

F. ac^2　　G. ac　　H. ab　　J. abc　　K. bc

48. What is the value of $g(x)=(-3)^x+3$ when $x=2$?

F. −6　　G. −3　　H. 0　　J. 9　　K. 12

49. Given that m, n, and a are positive integers, which of thefollowing statements is true whenever $a^m<(-a)^n$?

F. $m=n$ and n is odd　　G. $m<n$ and n is odd

H. $m<n$ and n is even　　J. $m>n$ and n is odd

K. $m>n$ and n is even

50. Alexia knows that the height of an object propelled vertically from a height of 48 feet can be modeled by $h=-16t^2+32t+48$, where h is the height, in feet, and t is the time, in seconds. Using this model, how many seconds will it take the object to reach a height of 64 feet?

F. 1　　G. 2　　H. 3　　J. 16　　K. 64

51. If $r>0$ and $s>0$, $\sqrt{\frac{r}{s}}+\sqrt{\frac{s}{r}}$ is equivalent to which of the following?

F. 1　　G. $\frac{2\sqrt{rs}}{r+s}$　　H. $2\sqrt{rs}$　　J. $\frac{r+s}{rs}$　　K. $\frac{r+s}{\sqrt{rs}}$

52. Ty bought an equal number of 12d, 30d, and 40d nails. What is the minimum number of nails of each size that Ty could have bought?

A. 72　　B. 120　　C. 192　　D. 432　　E. 576

53. $(-mp)(mp^9)^4$ is equivalent to:

F. m^4p^{36}　　G. $-m^4p^{36}$　　H. $-m^5p^{37}$　　J. $-m^8p^{40}$　　K. $-m^{37}p^{37}$

54. Given the matrix equation shown below, what is $\frac{b}{a}$?

$$\begin{bmatrix}3!\\2!\end{bmatrix}+\begin{bmatrix}2!\\4!\end{bmatrix}=\begin{bmatrix}a\\b\end{bmatrix}$$

(Note: Whenever n is a positive integer, the notation n! represents the product of the integers from n to 1. For example, 3! =3 • 2 • 1.)

A. $\frac{13}{4}$　　B. $\frac{6}{5}$　　C. $\frac{4}{7}$　　D. 4　　E. 6

55. What is the value of c if $x+2$ is a factor of $2x^3+2x^2-2cx+4$?

F. −4　　G. −2　　H. 0　　J. 1　　K. 7

56. A formula used to compute the volume V, of a rectangular prism is V = lwh, where l i s the length of the base, w is the width of the base, and h is the height of the prism. What is the height, in centimeters, of a rectangular prism that has a volume of 510 cubic centimeters and a base that measures 5 centimeters by 12 centimeters?

F. 8.5　　G. 30　　H. 42.5　　J. 102　　K. 450

57. A formula for simple interest is $I=Prt$, where I is the interest in dollars, P is the principal in dollars, r is the annual interest rate expressed as a decimal, and t is the time in years the money

i s invested. Which of the following, expression s gives t when the annual interest rate is 5%?

F. $\frac{I}{0.05P}$ G. $\frac{I}{0.5P}$ H. $\frac{I}{5P}$ J. $\frac{0.5I}{P}$ K. $0.05IP$

58. Given the functions f and g defined by $f(x)=x+3$ and $g(x)=x^2+1$, what is the value of $f(g(1))$?

A. 2 B. 5 C. 6 D. 8 E. 17

59. What is the value of $x^2y^3-xy^2+x$ when $x=-3$ and $y=2$?

F. −63 G. −57 H. 57 J. 63 K. 81

60. In the standard (x, y) coordinate plane, what is the midpoint of the line segment with endpoints (1, 9) and, (7, −3)?

A. (−3, −6) B. (−1, 8) C. (4, 3) D. (5, 2) E. (8, 6)

61. In the plane shown in the figure below, lines m and n are cut by transversal line t. The 8 angles at the intersections of these lines are labeled. Which of the following statements, when it is true, CANNOT Always be used to prove that lines m and n are parallel?

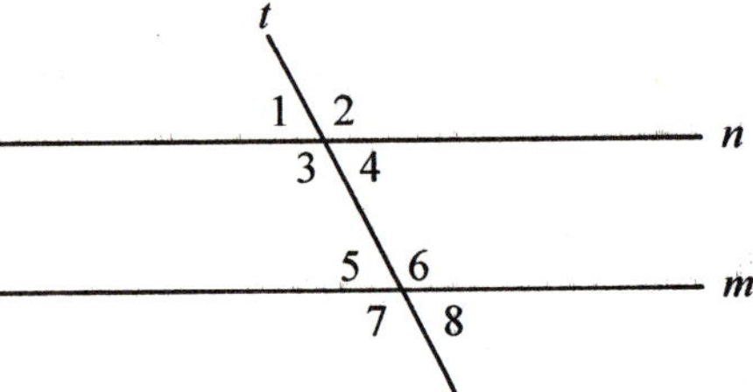

F. ∠1≅∠5 G. ∠1≅∠7

H. ∠1≅∠8 J. ∠2≅∠7

K. ∠4≅∠5

62. The dimensions of the right triangle shown below are in feet. What is the area, in square feet, of the triangle?

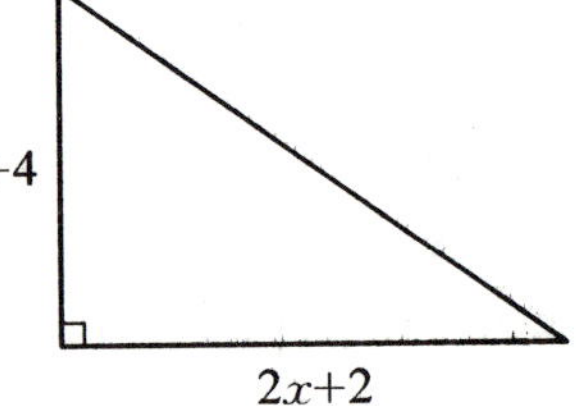

A. x^2+4 B. x^2+8

C. x^2+5x+4 D. $2x^2+8$

E. $8x^2$

63. For nonzero real numbers a, b, and c, the expression $\frac{a^3b^3c^4}{5a^2b^7c}$ is equivalent to:

A. $\frac{ac^3}{5b^4}$ B. $\frac{a^3c^4}{5b^4}$ C. $\frac{a^3bc^4}{5ab^4c}$ D. $\frac{(abc)^{12}}{(5abc)^9}$ E. $5a^7b^{10}c^5$

64. Which of the following is the least common denominator for $\frac{1}{x^2-4}+\frac{1}{4x-8}$?

F. $(x-2)$ G. $4(x+2)$

H. $(x-2)(x+2)$ J. $4(x-2)(x+2)$

K. $4(x-2)^2(x+2)$

65. The domain of the function $f(x)=\frac{1}{100-|x|}$ contains all real values of x EXCEPT:

F. 0 G. 0 and 100

H. 0 and $\frac{1}{100}$ J. $-\frac{1}{100}$ and $\frac{1}{100}$

K. −100 and 100

66. The graphs of $f(x)$ and $g(x)$ are shown in the standard (x, y) coordinate planes below. One of the following expressions represents $g(x)$ in terms of $f(x)$. Which one?

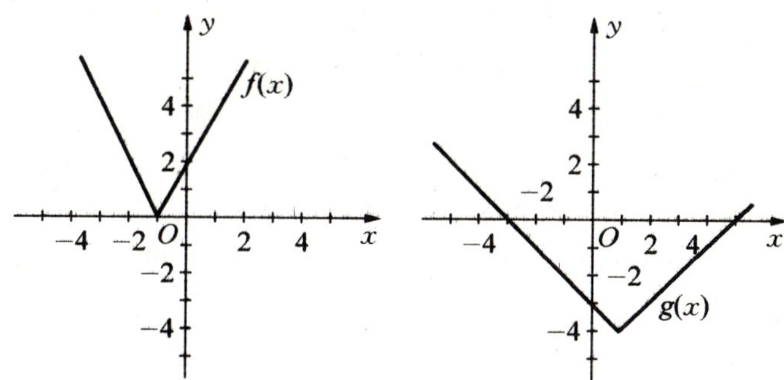

A. $\frac{1}{2}f(x-2)-4$　　B. $\frac{1}{2}f(x-2)+4$

C. $\frac{1}{2}f(x+2)+4$　　D. $f(x-2)-4$

E. $f(x+2)-4$

67. A vending machine only accepts quarters (\$0.25) and nickels (\$0.05). When the machine was emptied Friday afternoon, 325 coins were counted and had a value of \$56.25. Which of the following systems of equations, when solved, gives the number of quarters, \$, and the number of nickels, n?

F. $q+n=325$ and $0.25\$+0.05n=56.25$

G. $q+n=325$ and $0.25\$+0.50n=56.25$

H. $q+n=325$ and $25\$+5n=56.25$

J. $q+n=56.25$ and $0.25\$+0.05n=325$

K. $q+n=56.25$ and $25\$+5n=325$

68. Which of the following expressions is a factored form of x^2-5x+6?

A. $(x-3)(x-2)$　　B. $(x-3)(x-2)$

C. $(x-5)(x-1)$　　D. $(x-6)(x-1)$

E. $(x+6)(x-1)$

69. Which of the following values is *a* zero of $f(x)=2x^3-5x^2-12x$?

A. 3　　B. 2　　C. $-\frac{3}{2}$　　D. −4　　E. −6

70. A Ferris wheel is turning at a constant speed during 1 of its rotations. Let t represent the time that has elapsed since the wheel started turning and let h represent the height above ground level of a certain seat on the wheel. The seat is at its minimum height at $t=a$ seconds and is at its maximum height at $t=b$ seconds. One of the following graphs represents the relationship between t and h during this rotation.

Which one?

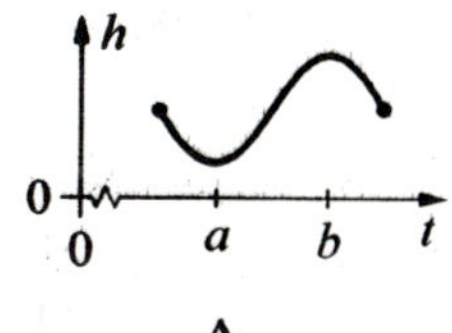

A.

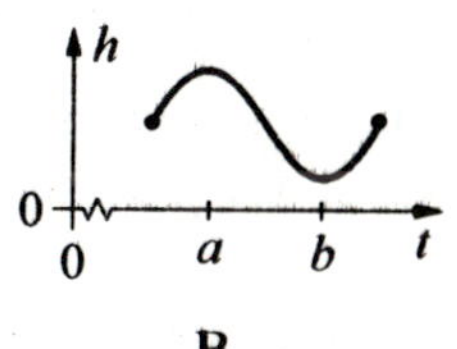

B.

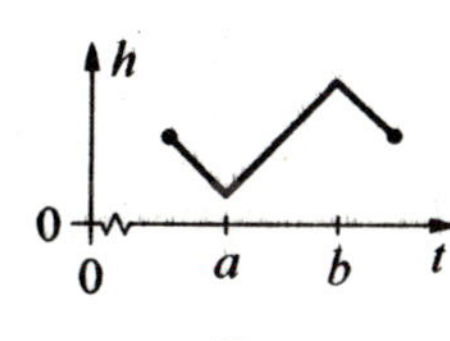

C.

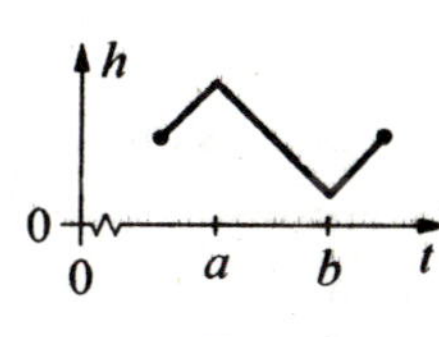

D.

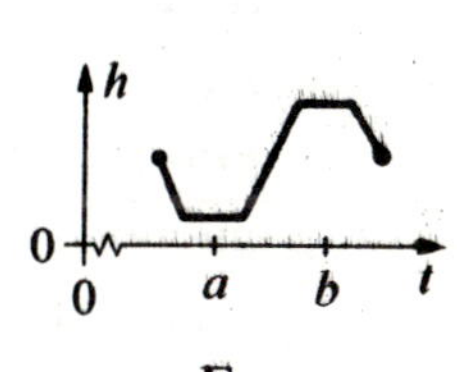

E.

71. For all $x>0$, which of the following expressions is equivalent to $\log((2x)^{\frac{1}{2}})$?

A. $\log x$　　B. $\log 1+\log\frac{x}{2}$

C. $\log 2+\frac{1}{2}\log x$

D. $\frac{1}{2}\log 2+\frac{1}{2}\log x$

E. $\frac{1}{2}(\log 2)(\log x)$

72. The graph below illustrates the normal distribution curve. The percent of the data that falls within each standard deviation from the mean is given to the nearest 0.1%.

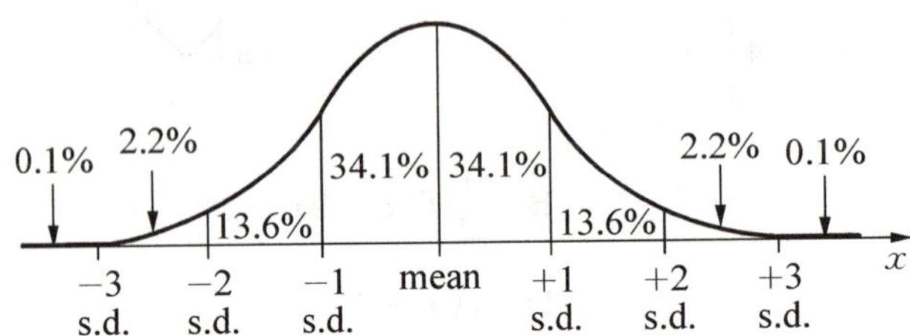

Suppose that the heights of men in a certain population are normally distributed with a mean of 69.0 inches and a standard deviation of 2.7 inches. To the nearest 0.1%, what percent of men in the population are at least 74.4 inches tall?

F. 2.3%　G. 2.7%　H. 4.6%　J. 47.7%　K. 54.4%

73. Let m and n be nonzero real numbers such that $2^{n+1}=2m$. Which of the following is an expression for 2^{n+3} in terms of m?

F. $\frac{1}{6m^3}$　G. $\frac{1}{4m}$　H. m^3　J. $4m^2$　K. $8m$

74. A new operation, ◆is defined on pairs of ordered pairs of integers as follows: (a, b)◆(c, d) $=\frac{ac+bd}{ab-cd}$ What is the value of (3,1)◆(4,5) ?

F. $-\frac{17}{11}$　G. -1　H. $\frac{17}{11}$　J. $\frac{17}{7}$　K. 17

75. What is the result of the subtraction problem below?

$(7x^2+5-(-4x^2+6x+3))$?

A. $3x^2+6x+2$

B. $3x^2-6x+2$

C. $11x^2+2$

P. $11x^2+6x+8$

E. $11x^2-6x+2$

76. On the real number line, -0.423 is between $\frac{n}{100}$ and $\frac{(n+1)}{100}$ for some integer n. What is the value of n?

A. −423　B. −43　C. −42　D. −5　E. −4

77. If $\sqrt{a}=b$ and $b=36$, $a=$?

F. 6　G. 18　H. 72　J. 324　K. 1,296

78. For trapezoid $ABCD$ shown below, $AB \parallel DC$, the measures of the interior angles are distinct, and the measure of $\angle D$ is x°. What is the degree measure of $\angle A$ in terms of x?

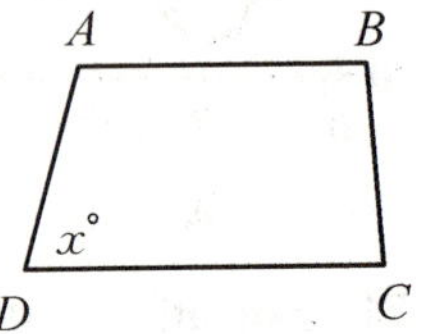

F. $(180-x)^\circ$

G. $(180-0.5x)^\circ$

H. $(180+0.5x)^\circ$

J. $(180+x)^\circ$

K. x°

79. Sara and Behzad are saving to make a down payment on a house. With an initial deposit of \$8,000, they have opened an account that compounds interest at an annual rate of 2.1%. Assuming that Sara and Behzad make no additional deposits or withdrawals, which of the following expressions gives the dollar value of the account 4 years after the initial deposit? (Note: For an account with an initial deposit of P dollars that compounds interest at an annual rate of r%. the value of the account t years after the initial deposit is $p\left(1+\frac{r}{100}\right)^t$ dollars.)

F. $8.000(1.021)^4$　　G. 8,000(1.21)4

H. $8,000(3.1)^4$　　J. $8,000(121)^4$

K. 8,000+8,000(0.21)4

80. The equation $y = ax^2 + bx + c$ is graphed in the standard (x, y) coordinate plane below for real values of a, b, and c. When $y = 0$, which of the following best describes the solutions for x?

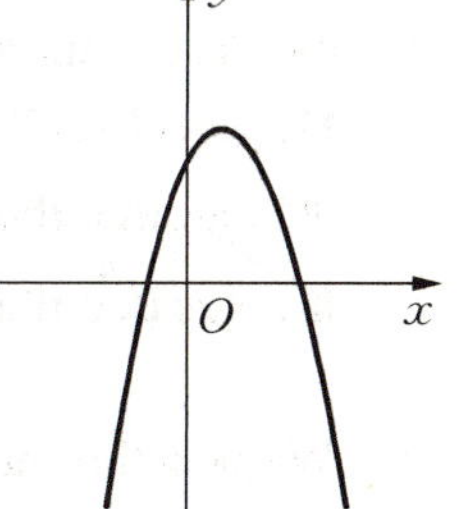

A. 2 distinct positive real solutions

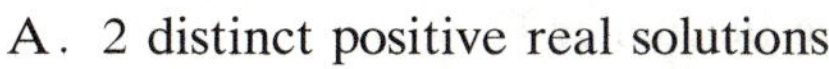

B. 2 distinct negative real solutions

C. 1 positive real solution and 1 negative real solution

D. 2 real solutions that are not distinct

E. 2 distinct solutions that are not real

81. Which of the following is a quadratic equation that has $\frac{2}{3}$ as its only solution?

A. $9x^2+12x+4=0$　　B. $9x^2-12x+4=0$

C. $9x^2+6x+4=0$　　D. $9x^2+4=0$

E. $9x^2-4=0$

82. For all values of x where the expression is defined.

$$\frac{\frac{3}{x-5}}{1-\frac{2}{x-5}}=?$$

A. -3　　B. $-\frac{3}{2}$　　C. $-\frac{3}{x^2-25}$　　D. $\frac{3}{x-7}$　　E. $\frac{3}{x-3}$

83. If x is a real number such that $x^3 = 64$, then $x^2+\sqrt{x}=?$

F. 4　　G. 10　　H. 18　　J. 20　　K. 47

84. What expression must the center cell of the table below contain so that the sums of each row, each column, and each diagonal are equivalent?

x	$8x$	$-3x$
$-2x$	?	$6x$
$7x$	$-4x$	$3x$

F. $6x$　　G. $4x$

H. $2x$　　J. $-2x$

K. $-4x$

85. If $f(x) = x^2-2$, then $f(x+h)=?$

F. x^2+h^2　　G. x^2-2+h　　H. x^2+h^2-2　　J. $x^2+2xh+h^2$

K. $x^2+2xh+h^2-2$

86. If $f(x) = x^2+x+5$ and $g(x)=\sqrt{x}$, then what is the value of $\frac{g(4)}{f(1)}$?

A. $\frac{2}{7}$　　B. $\frac{25}{7}$　　C. $\frac{2}{25}$　　D. 2　　E. 4

87. Tran wants to approximate the area underneath the curve $y = 0.005x^2 - 2x + 200$ for $0 \leqslant x \leqslant 200$, shown shaded in the graph below.

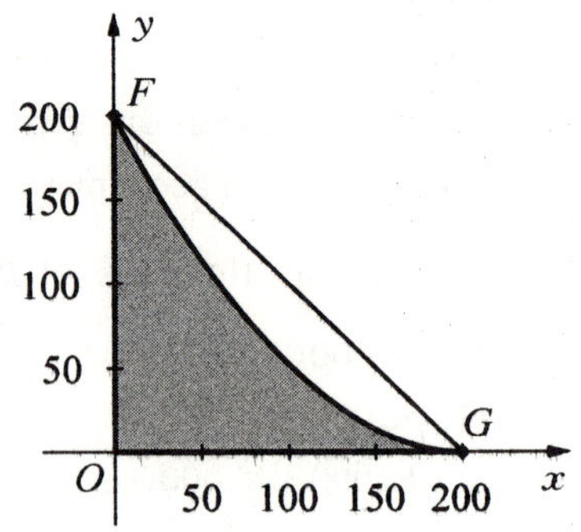

He finds an initial estimate, A, for the shaded area by using $\overline{FG}$ and computing $A = \frac{1}{2}$ (200 units)(200 units) = 20,000 square units. The area of the shaded region is:

F. less than 20,000 square units, because the curve lies under $\overline{FG}$.

G. less than 20,000 square units, because the curve lies over $\overline{FG}$.

H. equal to 20,000 square units.

J. greater than 20,000 square units, because the curve lies under $\overline{FG}$.

K. greater than 20,000 square units, because the curve lies over $\overline{FG}$

88. What is the matrix product $\begin{bmatrix} a \\ 2a \\ 3a \end{bmatrix} [1 \quad 0 \quad -1]$?

F. $\begin{bmatrix} a & 0 & -a \\ 2a & 0 & -2a \\ 3a & 0 & -3a \end{bmatrix}$　　G. $\begin{bmatrix} a & 2a & 3a \\ 0 & 0 & 0 \\ -a & -2a & -3a \end{bmatrix}$

H. $\begin{bmatrix} 2a & 0 & -2a \\ 6a & 0 & -6a \end{bmatrix}$　　J. $[6a \quad 0 \quad -6a]$

K. $[0]$

89. Which of the following is the graph of the function $f(x)$ defined below?

$$f(x) = \begin{cases} x^2 - 2 \text{ for } x \leqslant 1 \\ x - 7 \text{ for } 1 < x < 5 \\ 4 - x \text{ for } x \geqslant 5 \end{cases}$$

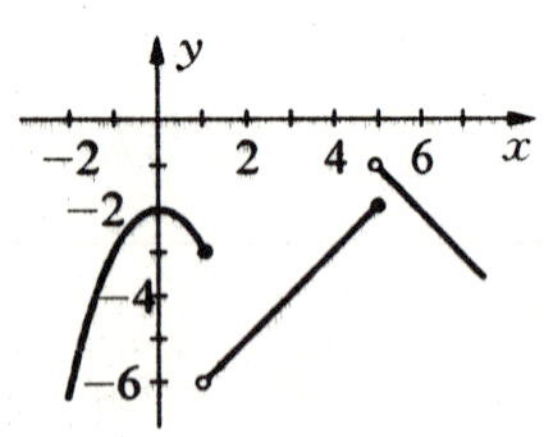

F.

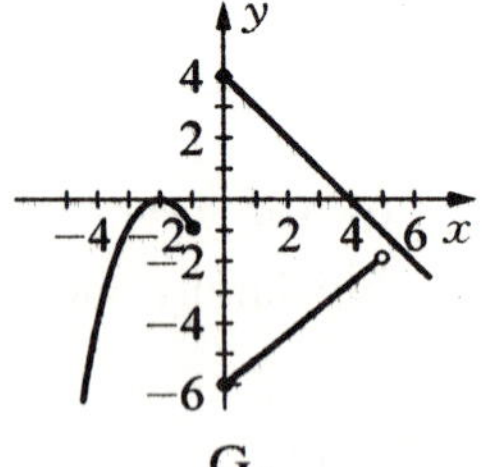

G.

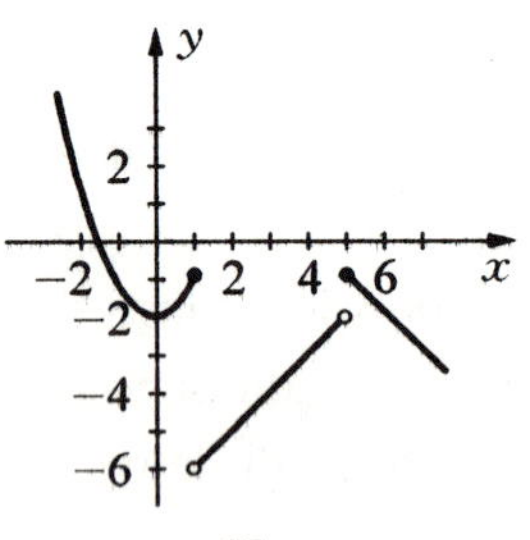

K.

H.

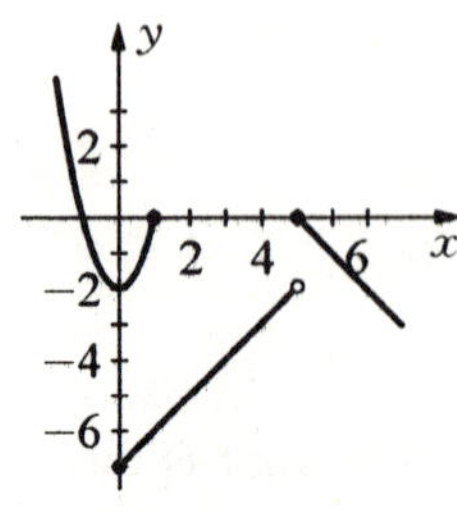

J.

90. In the standard (x, y) coordinate plane below, the vertices of the square have coordinates, $(0, 0)$, $(6, 0)$, $(6, 6)$ and $(0, 6)$. Which of the following is an equation of the circle that is inscribed in the square?

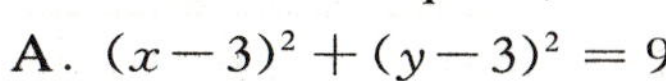

A. $(x-3)^2+(y-3)^2=9$
B. $(x-3)^2+(y-3)^2=3$
C. $(x+3)^2+(y+3)^2=9$
D. $(x+3)^2+(y+3)^2=6$
E. $(x+3)^2+(y+3)^2=3$

91. If $\log_a x = s$ and $\log_a y = t$, the $\log_a (xy)^2$?

A. $2(s+t)$　　B. $s+t$　　C. $4st$　　D. $2st$　　E. st

92. The electrical resistance, r ohms, of 1, 000 ft. of solid copper wire at 77°. F can be approximated by the model $r=\frac{10,770}{d^2}-0.37$ for any wire diameter, d mils (1 mil = 0.001 inch), such that $5 \leqslant d \leqslant 100$. What is the approximate resistance, in ohms, for such a wire with a diameter of 50 mils?

F. 1　　G. 4　　H. 17　　J. 215　　K. 430

93. For the function graphed below, the x-axis can be partitioned into intervals, each of length p radians, and the curve over any one interval is a repetition of the curve over each of the other intervals. What is the least possible value for p, the period of the function?

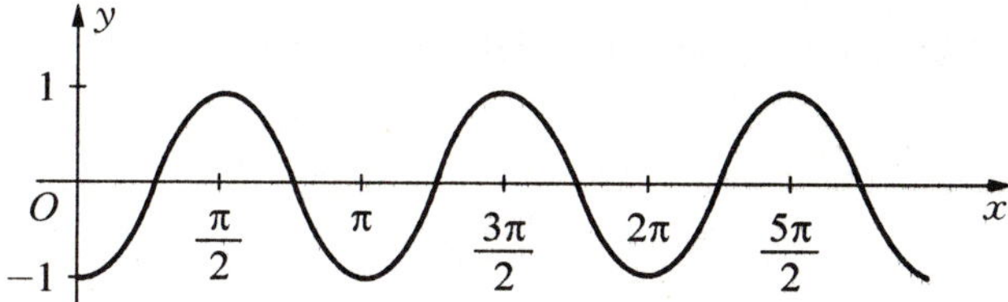

A. $\frac{\pi}{2}$　　B. π　　C. $\frac{3\pi}{2}$　　D. 2π　　E. 3π

94. As shown in the figure below, a clock has a minute hand that measures 5 cm from its tip to the center of the clock. To the nearest centimeter, what is the distance traveled by the tip of the minute hand between 2: 10 p.m. and 5: 30 p.m.?

A. 31　　B. 68　　C. 101
D. 105　　E. 173

95. The expression $\frac{2x+3}{12x^2}$ is equivalent to:

F. $\frac{1}{3}$　　G. $\frac{1}{x}$　　H. $\frac{1}{2x}$　　J. $\frac{x+1}{2x^2}$　　K. $\frac{1}{6x}+\frac{1}{4x^2}$

96. What is the set of all the values of b that satisfy the equation $(x^3)^{4-b^2}=1$ for all nonzero values of x?

F. {0}　　G. {2}　　H. {4}　　J. $\{-\sqrt{7}, \sqrt{7}\}$　　K. {−2, 2}

[Session 4 答案]

1 A	2 G	3 B	4 C	5 F	6 G	7 D	8 H	9 D	10 K
11 A	12 F	13 A	14 F	15 A	16 C	17 F	18 F	19 B	20 B
21 K	22 K	23 F	24 A	25 K	26 C	27 E	28 F	29 E	30 F
31 E	32 D	33 F	34 E	35 A	36 C	37 A	38 D	39 C	40 G
41 J	42 B	43 E	44 G	45 F	46 A	47 F	48 K	49 H	50 F
51 K	52 B	53 H	54 A	55 J	56 F	57 F	58 B	59 K	60 C
61 G	62 C	63 A	64 J	65 K	66 A	67 F	68 A	69 C	70 A
71 D	72 F	73 K	74 G	75 E	76 B	77 K	78 F	79 F	80 C
81 B	82 D	83 H	84 H	85 K	86 A	87 F	88 F	89 K	90 A
91 A	92 G	93 B	94 D	95 K	96 K				

[Session 4 答案解析]

1. 题干：$x^2 + y^2 = 324$ 要使 y 有实数值，x 最大可以是多少？
   解析：令 $y = 0$。
2. 题干：$(x^3 + 2x^2 - 6) - 2(x^4 - 3x^3 + 2x^2 + x - 1)$ 等价于？
   解析：去掉括号。
3. 题干：哪个是 $3(x+2) + 1 \leqslant 4x + 15$？
   解析：先化简。
4. 题干：$\sqrt[4]{x^2 + 6x} = 2$ 的解集？
   解析：可以同时四次方。
5. 题干：f 和 g 分别是什么函数可以使得 $f(g(x)) = \sqrt{2x^2 + 3}$？
   解析：f 可以是开根号。
6. 题干：$T\begin{bmatrix}-3 \\ 5\end{bmatrix} = \begin{bmatrix}5 \\ 3\end{bmatrix}$，$T$ 是什么？
   解析：矩阵乘法。
7. 题干：$\dfrac{n!}{(n-2)!} = 30$，$(n-1)! = ?$
   解析：2!即 1×2，3!即 $1 \times 2 \times 3$。
8. 题干：$f(x, y) = xy - (x - y)$。$f(10, 3) = ?$
   解析：代入即可。
9. 题干：$8x^5 \cdot 12x^5$ 等价于？
   解析：幂可以相加。

10. 题干：$\begin{bmatrix} a & b \\ c & d \end{bmatrix} = ad - bc$，$\begin{bmatrix} -b & -c \\ -d & a \end{bmatrix} = ?$

解析：按规律计算即可。即行列式。

11. 题干：$A = P + Prt$，A 是总的资金，P 是原始资金，r 是单利利率。T 是时间。如何表示 p?

解析：移项即可。

12. 题干：$\sqrt{b} - \sqrt{a} = 3\sqrt{a}$，$b$ 怎么表示?

解析：移项，然后平方。

13. 题干：a 起薪 20 000，每年增长 800，b 起薪 15 200，每年增长 2 000。如何表示二者工资相等的情况?

解析：x 表示年数。

14. 题干：n 加上 4，乘以 8，结果比 n 的两倍小 10。如何表示?

解析：按题意一步一步写即可，注意转化。

15. 题干：如表的，两个函数，其中一个是线性的，这个线性函数在 $x = 4$ 的时候函数值多少?

解析：看哪一个按比例变化。

16. 题干：$x^2 + x - 12 = 0$ 的两个解的和是多少?

解析：解一元二次方程。

17. 题干：bcd，abc^2d，a^2bc^3d，… 第四个是什么?

解析：乘上 ac。

18. 题干：$\dfrac{(x^2 + 8x + 7)(x - 3)}{(x^2 + 4x - 21)(x + 1)} = ?$当 x 大于 21。

解析：因式分解，然后化简。

19. 题干：$y = a\sin(bx + c)$ 如图，其周期是多少?

解析：找到最近的相同点之间的距离。

20. 题干：正整数 w 和 z 的和是 5，而且 $2^w = x$ and $x^z = 64$，x 是正整数。有多少种情况?

解析：可以列举。

21. 题干：$2x + 3y = 4$ and $5x + 6y = 7$，那么，$8x + 9y = ?$

解析：可以由前两个求出 x 和 y。

22. 题干：$y = x^2$ 如图。哪个是右移 3 个单位，下移 2 个单位的函数?

解析：左右移动对 x 操作。

23. 题干：$\log w \dfrac{w^2}{w^6} = ?w$ 是大于 1 的整数。

解析：幂可以提到对数前。

24. 题干：阴影部分如何表示?

解析：注意是大于还是小于。

25. 题干：$f(a, b) = b^2 - a$，那么 $f((x^2 + y^2), (x - y)) = ?$

解析：代入即可。

26. 题干：$3^x = 54$，哪个是正确的?

解析：可以验算。

27. 题干：$6(x + 2) > 7(x - 5)$ 等价于?

解析：去掉括号。

28. 题干：$y = -5x^2 + 9$ 经过$(1, 2a)$，$a = ?$

解析：把点带入方程。

29. 题干：$\begin{bmatrix} x & 8 \\ x & x \end{bmatrix}$行列式的值等于$-16$，$x=?$
    解析：x 的平方减 $8x$。
30. 题干：哪个表示到 -3 的距离为 5?
    解析：$x-(-3)$
31. 题干：如图，g 如何变到 f?
    解析：找到同相位的点。
32. 题干：a 是 b 的 25%，b 的 135% 是 a 的多少?
    解析：135 是 25 的多少。
33. 题干：$\log_b\left(\frac{1}{81}\right)=-4$，$b$ 是正数，那么 $b=?$
    解析：倒数和负号先消掉。
34. 题干：长 $x=2$，宽 $x-1$，那么面积 $=?$
    解析：相乘。
35. 题干：(-8, 3)和(4, -2)的距离是多少?
    解析：平面解析几何求两点距离。
36. 题干：$16^a=\frac{1}{64^{a+1}}$，a 是实数，那么 a 是多少?
    解析：利用 16 和 64 的关系，或者求出公因数。
37. 题干：哪个方程有解 $\frac{1}{2}$，$\frac{3}{4}$，i，以及 $-i$?
    解析：一一对应即可。
38. 题干：$5x-6y=30$ 的垂线是哪个?
    解析：斜率相乘等于 -1。
39. 题干：一共 50 题，130 分，有 x 道 5 分题，y 道 2 分题。x 和 y 的关系如何表示?
    解析：题数一个关系，分值一个关系。
40. 题干：$x^5\cdot x^{-(3^2)}$ 等价于?
    解析：化简。
41. 题干：$\begin{bmatrix} 3 & \frac{x}{2} \\ 0 & 1 \end{bmatrix}+\begin{bmatrix} x & 5 \\ 1 & 0 \end{bmatrix}=\begin{bmatrix} y & y \\ 1 & 1 \end{bmatrix}$，$(x, y)=?$
    解析：矩阵加法一一对应相加即可。
42. 题干：$f(x)=\frac{3}{x^2-1}$，$g(x)=x+1$，$f(g(x))$ 的定义域是什么?
    解析：分母不能为零。
43. 题干：A 是面积，r 是半径，$A-r$ 图是哪个?
    解析：二次函数。
44. 题干：哪个是 x^2-6x+8 的因式?
    解析：因式分解。
45. 题干：$(a, b)\blacklozenge(c, d)=\frac{ac+bd}{ab-cd}$，那么$(2,1)\blacklozenge(4,6)=?$
    解析：按照所给规律计算。
46. 题干：$x^2-5x+3=0$ 的根是什么?

解析：知道公式即可。注意正负号。

47. 题干：$ab^2c^4>0$，均为实数，那么哪个大于零？

解析：平方大于零，除以大于零的数对不等式符号没影响。

48. 题干：$x=2, g(x)=(-3)^x+3=?$

解析：代入即可。

49. 题干：$a^m<(-a)^n$，都是正实数。哪个是对的？

解析：从符号可以判断是偶次幂。

50. 题干：$h=-16t^2+32t+48$，$h=64$，$t=?$

解析：代入。

51. 题干：r 和 s 都大于零。$\sqrt{\frac{r}{s}}+\sqrt{\frac{s}{r}}$ 等价于？

解析：通分。

52. 题干：$12d$，$30d$，和 $40d$ 的钉子买了相同的个数，最小每种可以买多少？

解析：题意不明。应该是求公倍数。

53. 题干：$(-mp)(mp^9)^4$ 等价于？

解析：分别整理。

54. 题干：$\begin{bmatrix}3!\\2!\end{bmatrix}+\begin{bmatrix}2!\\4!\end{bmatrix}=\begin{bmatrix}a\\b\end{bmatrix}$，$\frac{b}{a}=?$

解析：向量相加。

55. 题干：如果 $x+2$ 是 $2x^3+2x^2-2cx+4$ 的因式，那么 $c=?$

解析：短除法。

56. 题干：$V=lwh$，l 是底面长，w 是底面宽。若体积 510。长 12，宽 5，那么高 $h=?$

解析：体积除以底面积即可。

57. 题干：$I=Prt$，$r=5\%$，那么 $t=?$

解析：移项。

58. 题干：$f(x)=x+3$，$g(x)=x^2+1$，那么 $f(g(1))=?$

解析：先算 g。

59. 题干：如果 $x=-3$，$y=2$。$x^2y^3-xy^2+x=?$

解析：代入。

60. 题干：(1, 9) 和(7, −3)的连线中点是什么？

解析：分别是 x 和 y 的平均值。

61. 题干：如图，哪个不能用来证明两直线平行。

解析：角 1 和 7 不是同位角。

62. 题干：如图，直角三角形的面积 = ?

解析：直角边的乘积的一半。

63. 题干：$\frac{a^3b^3c^4}{5a^2b^7c}$ 等价于？

解析：可以上下同除相同的数。

64. 题干：$\frac{1}{x^2-4}+\frac{1}{4x-8}$ 通分。

解析：先因式分解。

65. 题干：$f(x)=\frac{1}{100-|x|}$ 的定义域不包括？

解析：分母不能为零。

66. 题干：f 和 g 图像如图，用 f 表示 g。
解析：平移的问题。

67. 题干：325 个硬币，价值 56.25，只有 0.25 和 0.05 两种硬币，怎么列式求解？
解析：价值一个关系，个数一个关系。

68. 题干：x^2-5x+6 因式分解。
解析：因式分解可以用十字法。

69. 题干：哪个是 $f(x)=2x^3-5x^2-12x$ 的零点？
解析：代入。

70. 题干：哪个图像表示了轮子上某一点高度随时间的变化，转速为常数，而且 b 时刻最高。
解析：是三角函数的关系。

71. 题干：$\log((2x)^{\frac{1}{2}})=?$
解析：对数的加减法。

72. 题干：如图所示的正态分布，平均值 69，一个 sd 是 2.7，那么大于等于 74.4 的都是多少？
解析：把各部分加起来即可。

73. 题干：$2^{n+1}=2m$，如何用 m 表示2^{n+3}？
解析：多 2 的 2 次方。

74. 题干：$(a,\ b)\blacklozenge(c,\ d)=\dfrac{ac+bd}{ab-cd}$，那么 $(3,1)\blacklozenge(4,5)=?$
解析：按规律即可。

75. 题干：$(7\,x^2+5-(-4\,x^2+6x+3))=?$
解析：化简，去掉括号，注意正负的变化。

76. 题干：-0.423 介于$\dfrac{n}{100}$ 和$\dfrac{(n+1)}{100}$ 之间，$n=?$
解析：注意负号。

77. 题干：$\sqrt{a}=b$，$b=36$，$a=?$
解析：$a=36^2$

78. 题干：如图，如何表示角 a 的大小。
解析：同旁内角之和为 180。

79. 题干：本金 8 000，年利息 2.1%，4 年后有多少钱？
解析：四次方。

80. 题干：$y=a\,x^2+bx+c$ 如图，其解是怎么样的？
解析：和 x 轴交点即解。

81. 题干：哪个方程的唯一解是 $\dfrac{2}{3}$？
解析：可以代入，或者求根公式，或者因式分解。

82. 题干：$\dfrac{\dfrac{3}{x-5}}{1-\dfrac{2}{x-5}}=?$
解析：通分，化简。

83. 题干：$x^3=64$，那么 $x^2+\sqrt{x}=?$
解析：可以先求出 x。

84. 题干：表中每一行的和以及每一列的和都是一样的，求图中缺失处的值。
 解析：方程组。
85. 题干：$f(x)=x^2-2$，那么 $f(x+h)=$？
 解析：替换。
86. 题干：$f(x)=x^2+x+5$，$g(x)=\sqrt{x}$，$\dfrac{g(4)}{f(1)}=$？
 解析：代入。
87. 题干：如图，估算阴影面积，估值为 20 000，哪个说法正确？
 解析：正确值比估算的小。
88. 题干：$\begin{bmatrix} a \\ 2a \\ 3a \end{bmatrix}\begin{bmatrix} 1 & 0 & -1 \end{bmatrix}=$？
 解析：矩阵乘法。
89. 题干：$f(x)=\begin{cases} x^2-2 \text{ for } x\leqslant 1 \\ x-7 \text{ for } 1<x<5 \\ 4-x \text{ for } x\geqslant 5 \end{cases}$ 的图像？
 解析：分段函数图像。
90. 题干：正方形顶点坐标为(0, 0)，(6, 0)，(6, 6)，(0, 6)，那么如图所示的圆形方程是什么？
 解析：找出圆心和半径。
91. 题干：$\log_a x=s$，$\log_a y=t$，$\log_a(xy)^2=$？
 解析：对数加减法。
92. 题干：$r=\dfrac{10{,}770}{d^2}-0.37$，$d=50$，$r=$？
 解析：代入。
93. 题干：如图求周期。
 解析：找到相同的相位点。
94. 题干：如图的分针，长 5 cm，从 2：10 p.m. 到 5：30 p.m.，分针的针尖走了多少距离？
 解析：算出周长数，然后乘以周长。
95. 题干：$\dfrac{2x+3}{12x^2}$ 等价于？
 解析：分解，化简。
96. 题干：$(x^3)^{4-b^2}=1$ 的解集？x 非零。
 解析：幂的化简。

Session 5　几何

1. In the figure below, what is the value of x?
 A. 5°
 B. 30°
 C. 40°
 D. 55°
 E. 60°

2. One angle, LA, has 3 times the measure of its supplement, $\angle B$, as depicted below. What is the degree measure of $\angle A$?

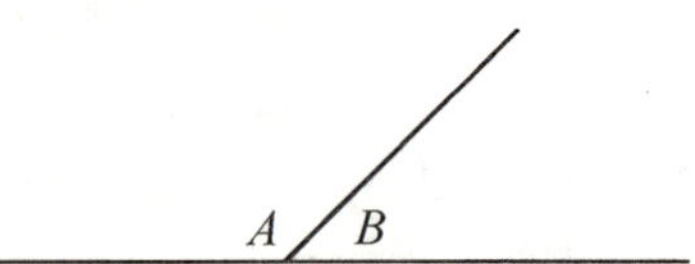

A. $112\frac{1}{2}°$　B. 120°　C. 135°

D. 150°　E. $157\frac{1}{2}°$

3. In the figure below, $\overline{AB}$ is parallel to $\overline{CD}$. What is the measure of $\angle ADC$?

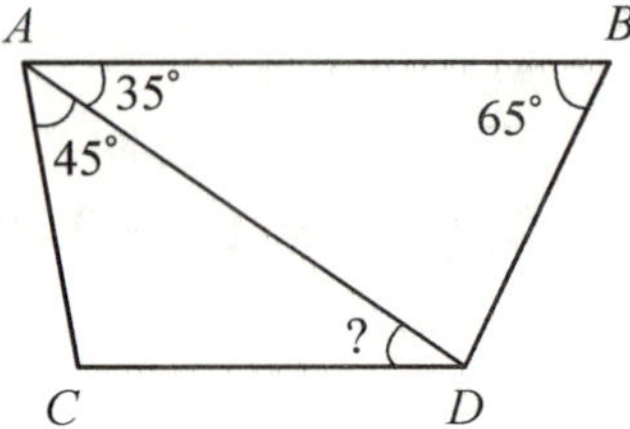

F. 35°
G. 40°
H. 45°
J. 65°
K. 80°

4. The 2 triangles below are similar, with $\angle A \cong \angle D$. What is the perimeter of $\triangle DEF$?

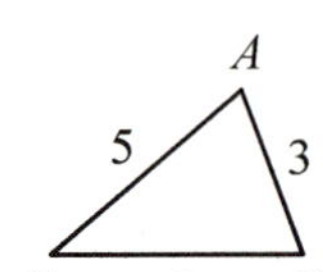

A. 14
B. 21
C. 29
D. 35
E. 42

5. What is the area, in square units, of the trapezoid graphed below?

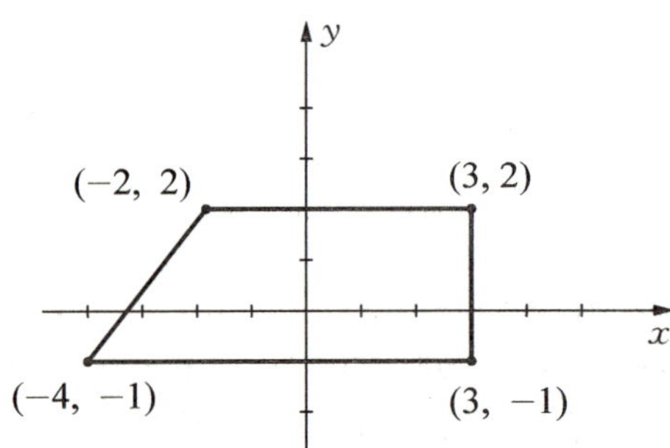

F. $16\frac{1}{2}$
G. 18
H. 24
J. 27
K. 33

6. If the total surface area, A, of a cylinder (including its ends) is given by the formula $A = 2\pi r^2 + 2\pi rh$, which of the following expresses h in terms of A and r?

F. $h = \frac{A}{2\pi r^2}$　G. $h = 2\pi rA - r$

H. $h = \frac{A}{2\pi r + r}$　J. $h = \frac{A + 2\pi r}{2\pi}$

K. $h = \frac{A - 2\pi r^2}{2\pi r}$

7. The area of a trapezoid may be found by using the formula $A = \frac{1}{2}h(b_1 + b_2)$, where h is the height and b_1 and b_2 are the lengths of the parallel bases. What is the area, in square inches, of the isosceles trapezoid below?

A. 15　B. 20　C. 27　D. 36　E. 45

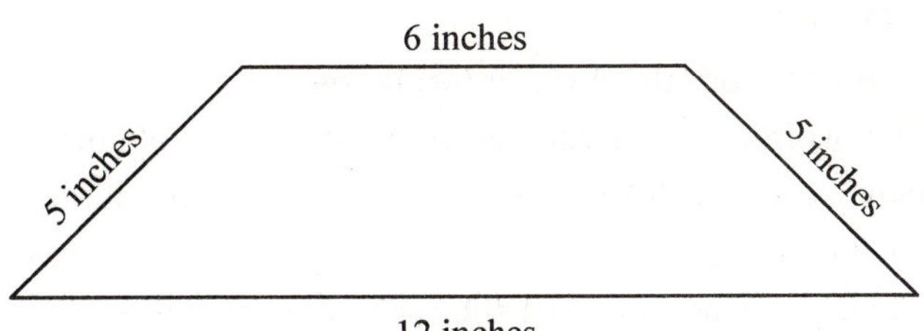

8. What is the center of the circle with equation $(x-2)^2+(y+2)^2=2$ in the standard (x, y) coordinate plane?

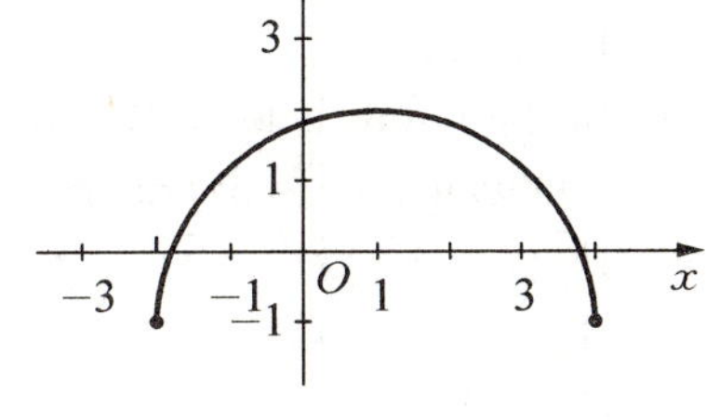

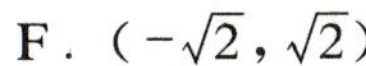

F. $(-\sqrt{2}, \sqrt{2})$

G. $(-2, 2)$

H. $(\sqrt{2}, -\sqrt{2})$

J. $(2, -2)$

K. $(2, 2)$

9. The ellipse shown below intersects any different ellipse in, at most, how many points?

A. 1

B. 2

C. 3

D. 4

E. Infinitely many

10. A circular fountain with a diameter of 20 meters is to be placed entirely within a rectangular plaza, 40 by 60 meters. Bricks will be laid on the entire plaza around thefountain (but not under it), making it accessible to pedestrians. What is the approximate area, insquare meters, of the plaza that will be brick?

F. 314　　G. 1 256　　H. 2 086　　J. 2 040　　K. 1 043

11. The volume, V, of the right circular cylinder below is given by the formula $V=\pi r^2 h$ where r is the radius of the base, and h is the height of the cylinder.

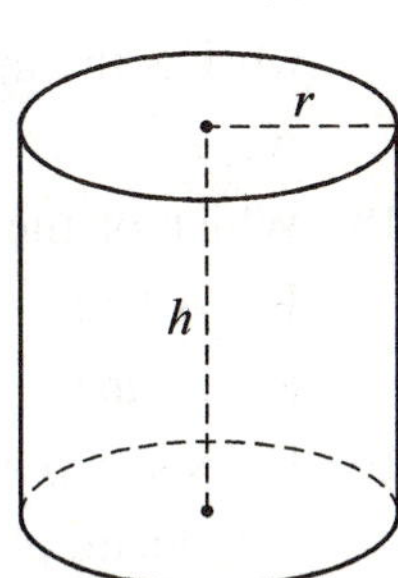

If r is doubled and h is halved, the new cylinder's volume, V, will be :

F. $\frac{1}{4}$ the original volume.　　G. $\frac{1}{2}$ the original volume.

H. the original volume.　　J. 2 times the original volume.

K. 4 times the original volume.

12. In the figure below, a square is inscribed in a circle. of radius r. What is the perpendicular distance from the center of the circle to a side of the square, in terms of r?

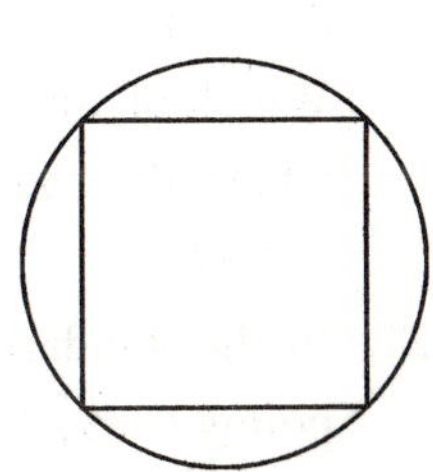

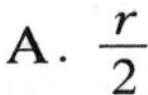

A. $\frac{r}{2}$

B. $\frac{r\sqrt{2}}{2}$

C. r D. $r\sqrt{2}$

E. Cannot be determined from the given information

13. To make a piece of jewelry, Aaron cuts out a circular piece of metal from a larger circular piece, as shown below. The radius of the larger circle is 2 inches. If the area of the cutout is to be the same as the area of the piece that remains, what should be the radius, in inches, of the inner circle ?

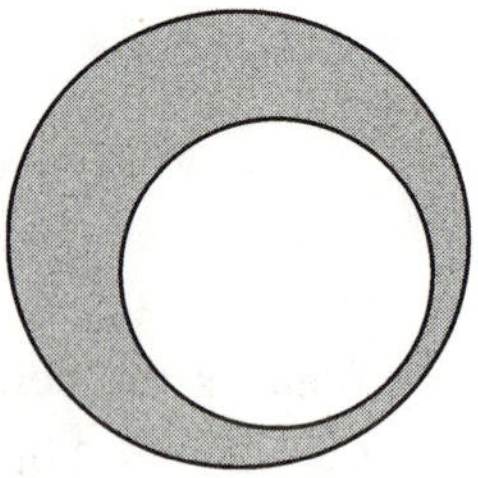

A. 1 B. π C. $\sqrt{2}$ D. $2\sqrt{2}$

E. $\pi\sqrt{2}$

14. In the figure below, B is on $\overline{DE}$ and $\overline{DE} \parallel \overline{AC}$. Which of the following angle congruences must hold?

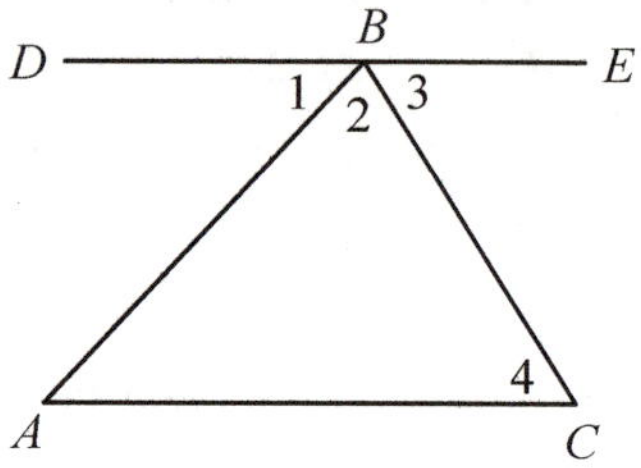

F. $\angle 1 \cong \angle 2$

G. $\angle 1 \cong \angle 4$

H. $\angle 2 \cong \angle 3$

J. $\angle 2 \cong \angle 4$

K. $\angle 3 \cong \angle 4$

15. In any parallelogram $ABCD$, it is always true that the measures of $\angle ABC$ and $\angle BCD$:

F. add up to 180°. G. add up to 90°.

H. are each greater than 90°. J. are each 90°.

K. are each less than 90°.

16. The lengths of the corresponding sides of 2 similar right triangles are in the ratio of 2 : 5. If the hypotenuse of the smaller triangle is 5 inches long, how many inches long is the hypotenuse of the larger triangle?

F. 2 G. 2.5 H. 7 J. 10 K. 12.5

17. Meg pounded a stake into the ground. When she attached a leash to both the stake and her dog's collar, the dog could reach 9 feet from the stake in any direction. Using 3.14 for π, what is the approximate area of the lawn, in square feet, the dog could reach from the stake?

A. 28 B. 57 C. 113 D. 254 E. 283

18. Which of the following figures in a plane separates it into half-planes?

F. A line G. A ray H. An angle J. A point

K. A line segment

19. For some real number A, the graph of the line $y = (A + 1)x + 8$ in the standard (x, y) coordinate plane passes through (2, 6). What is the slope of this line?

A. −4 B. −3 C. −1 D. 3 E. 7

20. Which of the following expresses the number of meters a contestant must travel in a 3-lap race where the course is a circle of radius R meters?

F. $3R$ G. $3\pi R$ H. $3\pi R^2$ J. $6R$ K. $6\pi R$

21. In the standard (x, y) coordinate plane, what is the slope of the line that passes through the points (−3, 5) and (7, 3)?

F. −5 G. −2 H. $-\frac{1}{5}$ J. $\frac{1}{2}$ K. 2

22. Which of the following is an equation for the line passing through (0, 0) and (4, 3) in the standard (x, y) coordinate plane?

A. $x-y=1$　B. $x+y=7$　C. $3x-4y=0$　D. $3x+4y=25$
E. $4x+3y=25$

23. Points P, Q, R, and S lie on a line in the order given. Point R is the midpoint of $\overline{QS}$, $\overline{PR}$ is 5 cm long, and $\overline{PS}$ is 7 cm long. How many centimeters long is $\overline{SQ}$?

F. 2　G. 3　H. 4　J. 5　K. 6

24. A rectangle that measures 4 cm by 6 cm is divided into 24 squares with sides 1 cm in length. What is the total number of 1 cm long sides in those 24 squares? (Note: If 2 squares share a side, the side should be counted only once.)

F. 24　G. 48　H. 58　J. 70　K. 96

25. The 2 legs of a right triangle measure 37 inches and 45 inches, respectively. What is the cosine of the triangle's smallest interior angle?

F. $\frac{37}{45}$　G. $\frac{45}{37}$　H. $\frac{37}{\sqrt{37+45}}$　J. $\frac{37}{\sqrt{37^2+45^2}}$
K. $\frac{45}{\sqrt{37^2+45^2}}$

26. Which of the following is an equation of the circle with center at (−2, 3) and a radius of 5 coordinate units in the standard (x, y) coordinate plane?

F. $x^2+y^2+4x-6y=5$　G. $x^2+y^2+4x-6y=12$
H. $x^2+y^2+4x-6y=25$　J. $x^2+y^2-4x+6y=12$
K. $x^2+y^2-4x+6y=25$

27. What is the length, in feet, of the hypotenuse of a right triangle with legs that are 6 feet long and 7 feet long, respectively?

F. $\sqrt{13}$　G. $\sqrt{85}$　H. 13　J. 21　K. 42

28. The slope of the line with equation $y=ax+b$ is greater than the slope of the line with equation $y=cx+b$. Which of the following statements must be true about the relationship between a and c?

F. $a\leqslant c$　G. $a<c$　H. $a=c$　J. $a>c$　K. $a\geqslant c+1$

29. In the standard (x, y) coordinate plane, the midpoint of $\overline{AB}$ is (4, −3) and A is located at (1, −5). If (x, y) are the coordinates of B, what is the value of $x+y$?

A. 19　B. 8　C. 6　D. −1.5　E. −3

30. In the figure below, $\angle A\cong\angle D$, $\angle B\cong\angle E$, and $\triangle ABC\cong\triangle DEF$. The measure of $\angle A$ is 20°. The measure of $\angle F$ is 75°. What is the measure of $\angle B$?

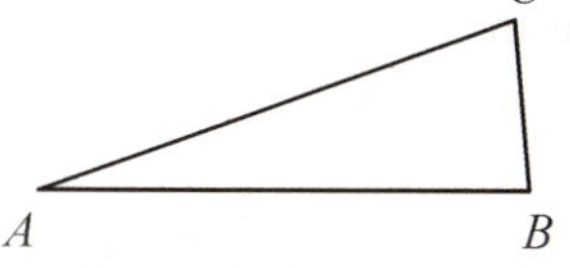

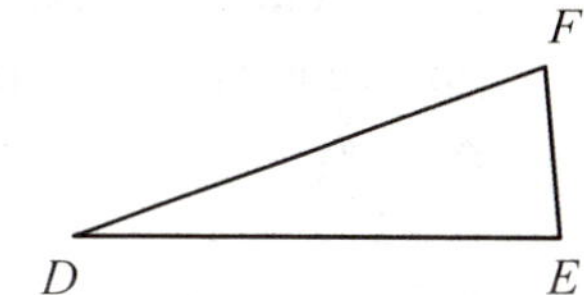

F. 20°　G. 75°
H. 85°　J. 95°　K. 105°

31. A regular pentagon P_1 has a perimeter of 25 inches, while another regular pentagon, P_2, has a perimeter that is 15 inches greater than the perimeter of P_1. The length of each side of P_2 exceeds the length of each side of P_1 by how many inches?

A. 3　B. 5　C. 8　D. 10　E. 15

32. Suppose that the measure of the larger of 2 supplementary angles is 5 times the measure of the smaller angle. What is the measure of the larger angle?
(Note：In the figure' below，∠ABD and ∠DBC are supplementary. The sum of their measures is 180°.)

F. 30°　　G. 36°　　H. $87\frac{1}{2}°$　　J. $92\frac{1}{2}°$　　K. 150°

33. A line in the standard (x, y) coordinate plane passes through the origin and the point $(-12, 6)$. An equation of this line is：

A. $y=-x-6$　　B. $y=-\frac{1}{2}x$　　C. $y=\frac{1}{2}x$　　D. $y=x+18$　　E. $y=2x$

34. A circle in the standard (x, y) coordinate plane has center $(3, 8)$ and is tangent to the *x-axis*. The point (x, y) is on the circle if and only if x and y satisfy which of the following equations?

A. $(x-3)^2+(y-8)^2=64$　　B. $(x-3)^2+(y-8)^2=9$
C. $(x+3)^2+(y+8)^2=64$　　D. $(x+3)^2+(y+8)^2=9$
E. $(x+3)^2+(y+8)^2=8$

35. The diagram below shows a quarter of each of 2 circles both having point C as their center. Point B lies on $\overline{AC}$ and point D lies on $\overline{CE}$. The length of $\overline{BC}$ is 5 inches and the length of $\overline{AB}$ is 3 inches. What is the area, in square-inches, of the shaded portion?

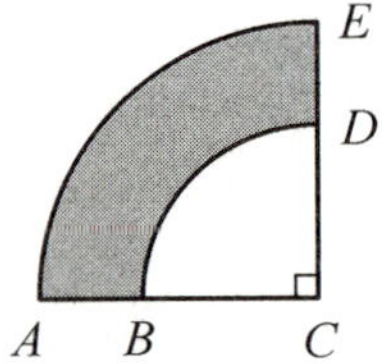

F. 4π　　G. $\frac{25}{4}\pi$　　H. $\frac{39}{4}\pi$　　J. $\frac{55}{4}\pi$

36. The radius of a right circular cone is doubled and its height is tripled to form a new right circular cone. What is the ratio of the volume of the original cone to the volume of the new cone?
(Note：$V_{cone}=\frac{1}{3}\pi r^2 h$ for radius r and height h.)

F. 1∶6　　G. 1∶12　　H. 1∶18　　J. 1∶36　　K. 1∶216

37. A polynomial function $P(x)$ has degree n. The graph in the standard (x, y) coordinate plane of $y=P(x)$ contains exactly 3 points on the *x-axis*. Which of the following could NOT be the value of n ?

A. 6　　B. 5　　C. 4　　D. 3　　E. 2

38. A solid block of wood has 6 rectangular faces. The length，width，and height of the block are a，b，and c inches，respectively. Which of the following expressions represents the block's surface area，in square inches?

A. $6abc$　　B. $4ab+2bc$　　C. $(a+b+c)^2$　　D. $2a+2b+2c$
E. $2(ab+ac+bc)$

39. In isosceles triangle $\triangle RET$，$\angle E$ and $\angle T$ are congruent and the measure of $\angle R$ is 94°. What is the measure of $\angle E$?

A. 43°　　B. 47°　　C. 48°　　D. 86°　　E. 94°

40. One side of square ABCD is 12 meters long. A rectangle with the same area as square ABCD has a length of 9 meters. What is the rectangle's width，in meters?

F. 3　　G. 16　　H. 21　　J. 108　　K. 144

41. Gerry is building a dollhouse that is to be a scale model of a house that is 36 feet high, 84 feet long, and 48 feet wide. What should be the dimensions, in feet, of the dollhouse Gerry is building if the scale of the model to the house is 1 : 12?

<u>Height Length Width</u>

F. $\frac{3}{12}$ $\frac{7}{12}$ $\frac{4}{12}$　　G. 3 7 4　　H. 36 7 4　　J. 432 84 48

42. Each of the 4 sides of the "IN" tray in an office has the shape of a trapezoid, as shown below.

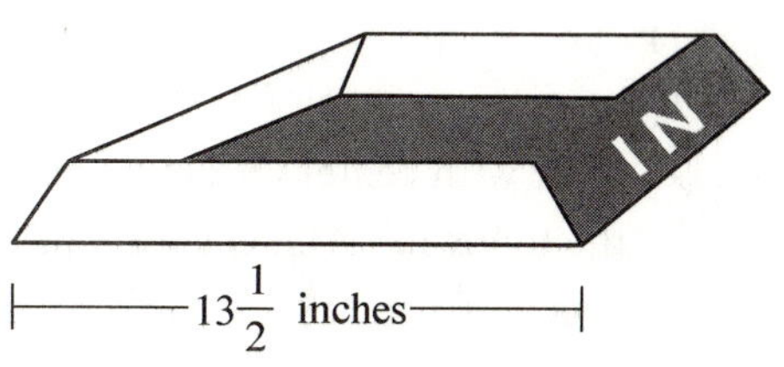

The length of bottom of each side is $13\frac{1}{2}$ inches and the length of the top of each side is 11 inches. What is the length, in inches, of the median of each trapezoid?

F. $6\frac{1}{8}$　　G. 12　　H. $12\frac{1}{4}$　　J. 14　　K. 16

43. To prepare 8 boxes of books for shipping, LaRonda will put 2 strips of strapping tape around each box, as shown below. Each strip of tape goes all the way around the box, and the strips of tape meet at right angles on the top and bottom of the box. Each box is 24 inches long, 18 inches wide and 20 inches high. What is the minimum number of inches of strapping tape LaRonda will need to prepare all 8 boxes for shipping?

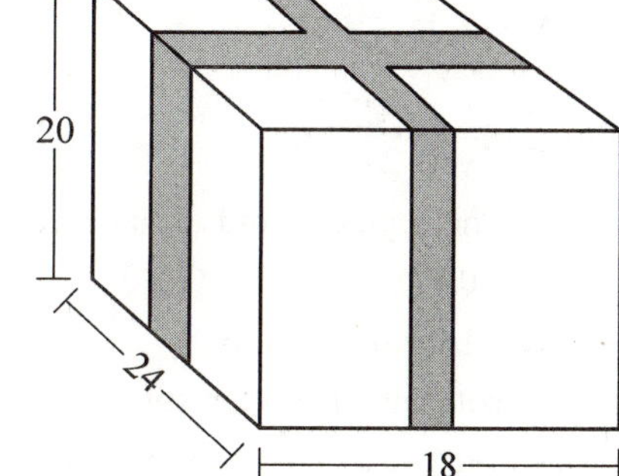

A. 164　　B. 496　　C. 656
D. 992　　E. 1,312

44. The graph of $\frac{x^2}{64}+\frac{y^2}{36}=1$ has an x-intercept at which of the following points?

A. (64, 0)　　B. (36, 0)　　C. (16, 0)　　D. (8, 0)　　E. (6, 0)

45. A circle with a diameter of 8 inches is inscribed in square ABCD, as shown below. What is the area, in square inches, of the shaded region?

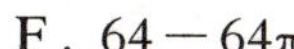
F. $64-64\pi$
G. $64-16\pi$
H. $16-4\pi$
J. $16-16\pi$
K. $4\pi-16$

46. The side lengths of $\triangle XYZ$, shown in the figure below, are in centimeters. One of the 5 points A − E is the center of the circle that goes through points X, Y, and Z. Which point is the center?

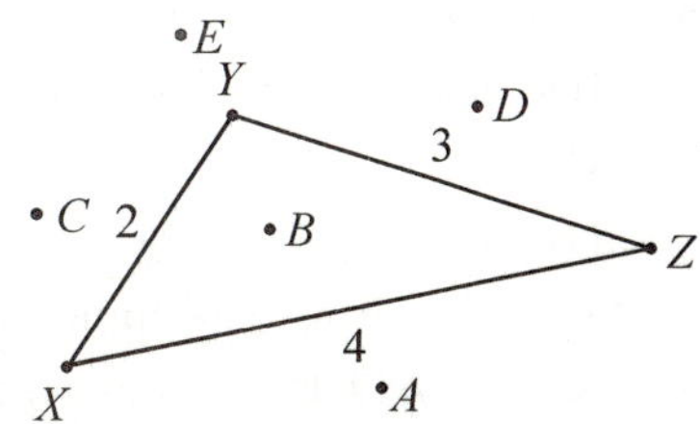

A. A　　B. B
C. C　　D. D
E. E

47. The triangle shown in the standard (x, y) coordinate lane below has vertices as marked. If each coordinate of each vertex is multiplied by 4, what will be the area, in square coordinate units, of the triangle with the resulting points as its vertices?

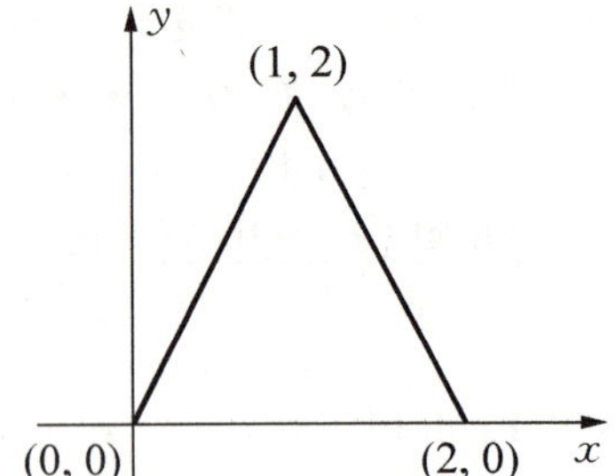

F. 4　　G. 8
H. 16　　J. 32
K. 64

48. A circle with center (−1, −4) is shown in the standard (x, y) coordinate plane below. Which of the following is an equation of the line that is tangent to the circle at the point (0, −2)?

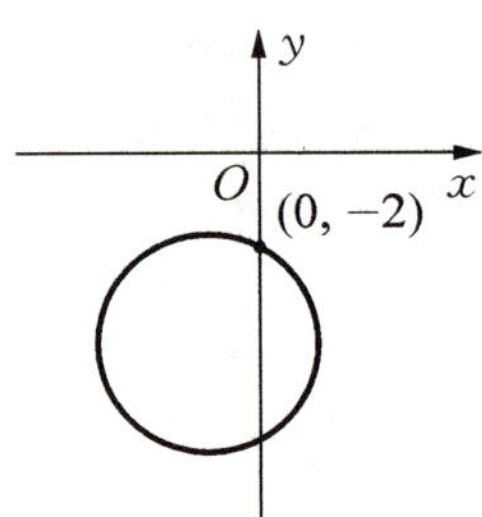

A. $y=-\frac{1}{2}x-2$

B. $y=-\frac{1}{2}x+2$

C. $y=\frac{1}{2}x+2$

D. $y=2x-2$

E. $y=2x+2$

49. A line segment and a plane can have at most how many points in common?

F. 0　　G. 1　　H. 2　　J. 3
K. Infinitely many

50. A rotating sprinkler sprays the entire area of a circular region with water out to 7 feet in every direction. as shown in the figure below. What is the area sprayed, to the nearest square foot?

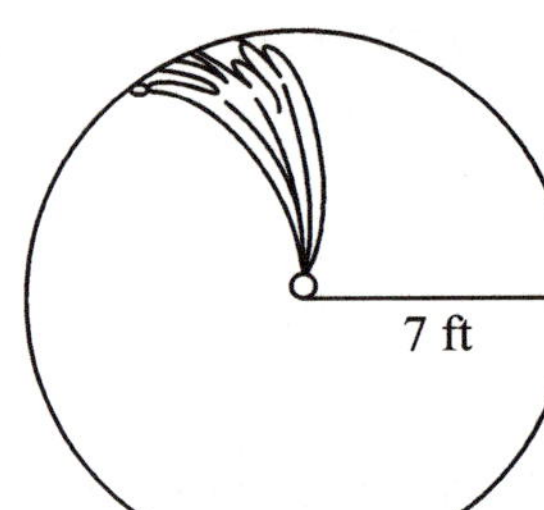

F. 22
G. 38
H. 44
J. 154
K. 616

51. Three lines intersect, as shown below, with angle measures as marked. Which of the following is NOT necessarily true?

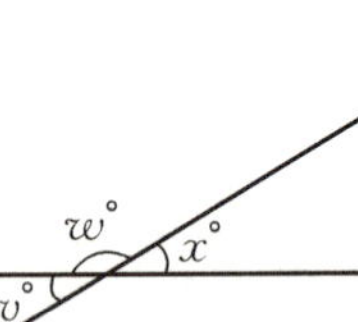

F. $v+y+z=180$　　G. $v+w=180$
H. $w+x=180$　　J. $x+z=y$
K. $y+z=w$

52. In rectangle $ABCD$ below, $\overline{AB}$ is 5 inches long and $\overline{BC}$ is 4 inches long. If point P lies on AB, what is the area of $\triangle PCD$, in square inches?

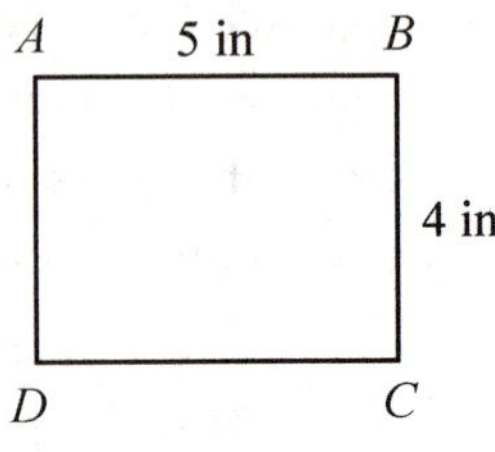

F. 5　　G. 9
H. 10　　J. 20
K. Cannot be determined from the given information

53. Square ABCD is shown below. in the standard (x, y) coordinate

plane. The line $y = ax + 2$ divides the square into 2 congruent regions if $a = ?$

A. $\frac{2}{3}$

B. $\frac{1}{6}$

C. $\frac{5}{6}$

D. $\frac{6}{7}$

E. 1

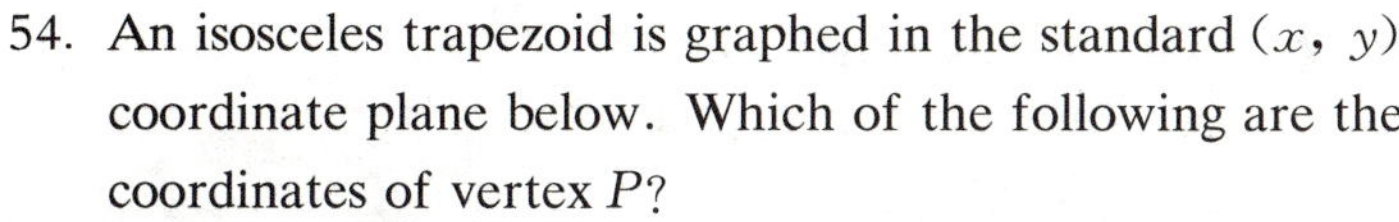

54. An isosceles trapezoid is graphed in the standard (x, y) coordinate plane below. Which of the following are the coordinates of vertex P?

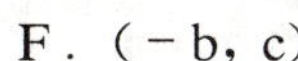

F. (−b, c) G. (−b, −a)

H. (b, −a) J. (b, −c)

K. (c, b)

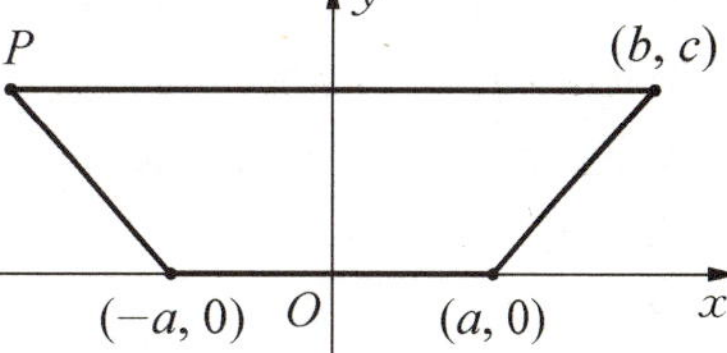

55. To the nearest foot, what is the length of a diagonal of a top of a rectangular cement slab 12 feet wide and 14 feet long?

F. 13 G. 18 H. 19 J. 20 K. 26

56. The hexagon shown below has 6 sides of equal length. What is the sum of the measures of the interior angles in this hexagon?

A. 900° B. 720° C. 540° D. 360°

57. When 2 chords of a circle intersect inside the circle, the product of the lengths of the 2 segments of one chord is equal to the product of the lengths of the 2 segments of the other chord. In the figure below, chords $\overline{EF}$ and $\overline{GH}$ intersect at I. The length of $\overline{GH}$ is 12 inches. The length of $\overline{FI}$ is 5 inches. The length of $\overline{EI}$ is 4 inches. The length of $\overline{HI}$ is less than the length of $\overline{GI}$. What is the length, in inches, of $\overline{GI}$?

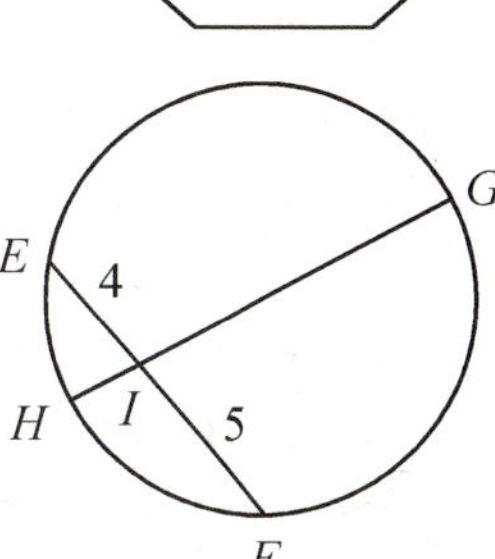

A. 3 B. 5

C. 7 D. 8

E. 10

58. The 7 congruent circles shown in the figure below are centered at points A through G, and each circle has a circumference of 24π cm. Points A through F are equally paced on the circumference of the circle centered at G. What is the sum of the lengths, in centimeters, of the 6 thicker arcs ($\overset{\frown}{AGC}$, $\overset{\frown}{BGD}$, $\overset{\frown}{CGE}$, $\overset{\frown}{DGF}$, $\overset{\frown}{EGA}$, and $\overset{\frown}{FGB}$)?

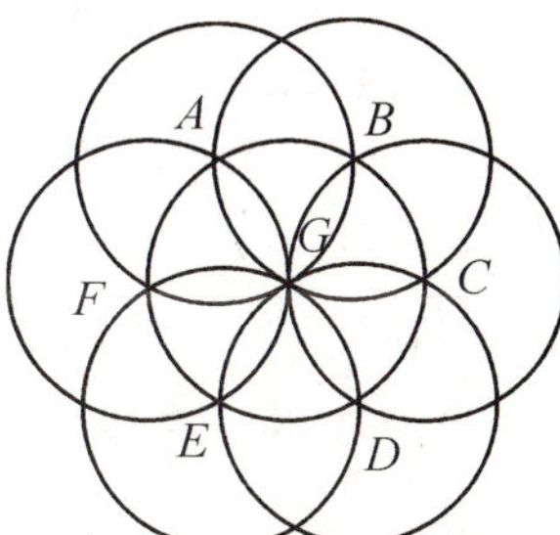

F. 48π G. 72π H. 96π

J. 144π K. 288π

59. Which of the following is an equation of the ellipse graphed below?

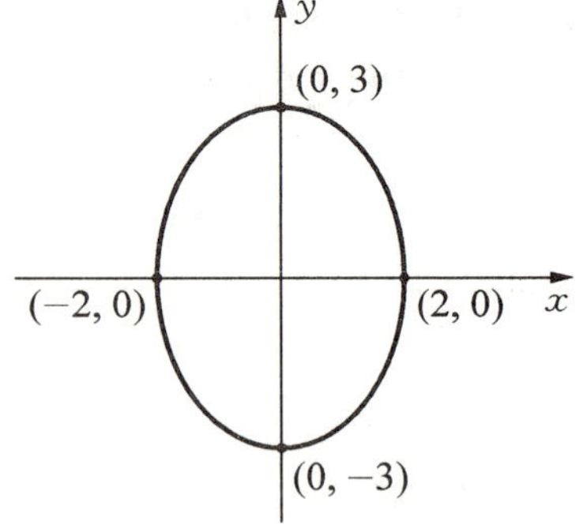

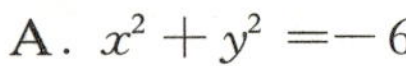
A. $x^2 + y^2 = -6$

B. $\frac{x^2}{2} + \frac{y^2}{3} = 0$

C. $\frac{x^2}{2} + \frac{y^2}{3} = 1$

D. $\frac{x^2}{4} + \frac{y^2}{9} = 0$

E. $\frac{x^2}{4} + \frac{y^2}{9} = 1$

60. Each small square on the grid shown below has a side length of 1 cm. Each vertex of the shaded region lies on a vertex of a small square. What is the area, in square centimeters, of the shaded region?

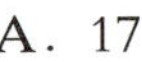
A. 17

B. 23

C. 28

D. 29

E. 39

61. In the figure below, lines l and m are tangent to the circle at points B and D, respectively. Points A and C are on the circle. The measure of $\angle ABC$ is 95° and the measure of $\angle BCD$ is 85°. The lines in which of the following pairs of lines are necessarily parallel?

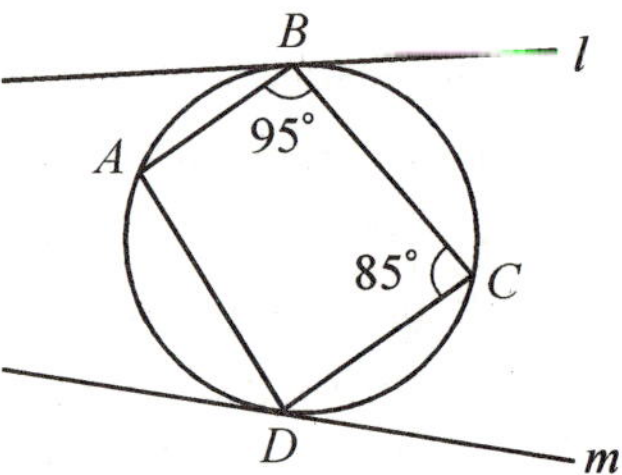

I. l and m

II. $\overline{AB}$ and $\overline{DC}$

III. $\overline{AD}$ and $\overline{BC}$

F. I only　G. II only　H. III only　J. I and II only

K. I, II and III

62. To measure the height of a smokestack, Ariel places a mirror on level ground 80 feet from the base of the smokestack. He then forms 2 similar triangles by looking into the mirror and backing up until he sees the reflection of the top of the smokestack, as shown below. Ariel's eyes are 6 feet from the ground and he is 5 feet from the image in the mirror. Which of the following is closest to the height, in feet, of the smokestack?

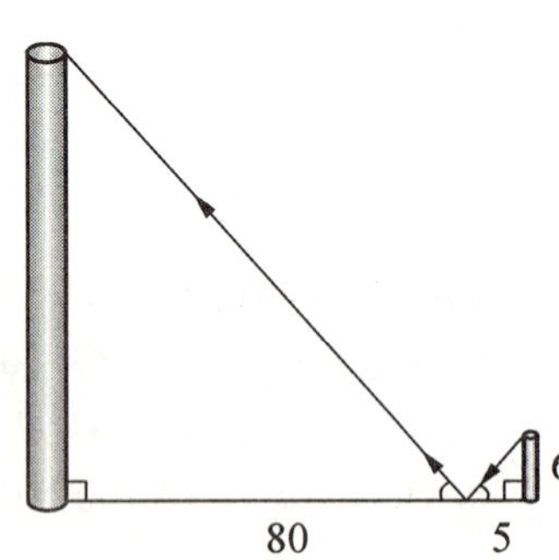

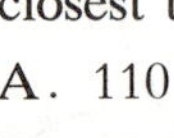
A. 110　B. 96　C. 91

D. 85　E. 67

63. A formula for the volume of a right circular cone with its top removed is $V = \frac{1}{3}\pi h(R^2 + r^2 + Rr)$, where R and r are radii and his height, as shown in the Figure below.

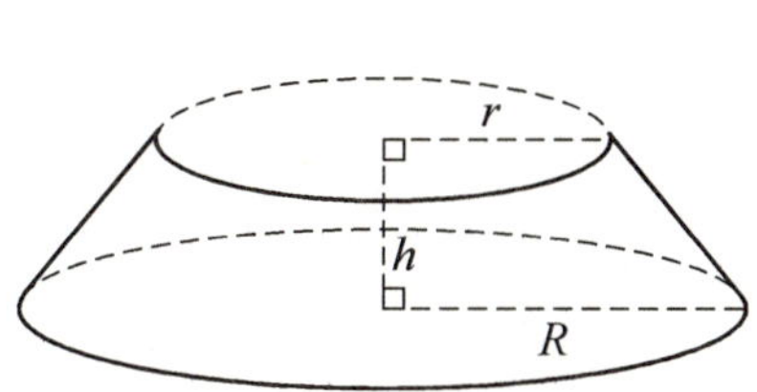

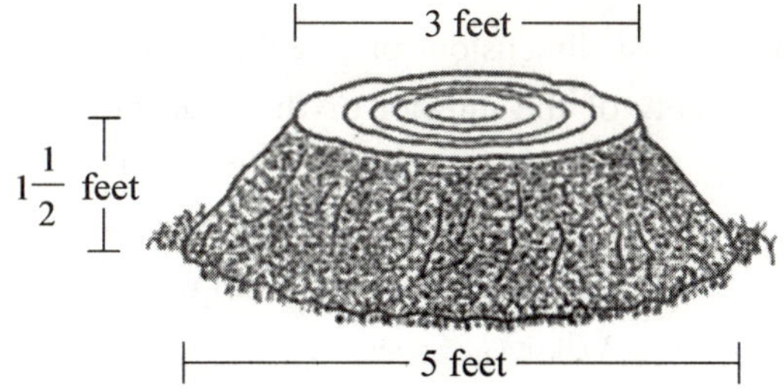

The number of cubic feet of wood in a tree stump can be estimated using the formula given. About how many cubic feet of wood are there in the tree stump shown below?

A. 12　　B. 18　　C. 19　　D. 38　　E. 77

64. What is the degree measure of an angle that measures $\frac{5\pi}{12}$ radians?

F. 15°　　G. 75°　　H. 150°　　J. $\left(180-\frac{5\pi}{12}\right)^\circ$

K. $\left(\frac{360-5\pi}{12}\right)^\circ$

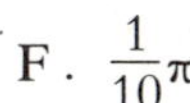

65. The circle shown below has a radius of 10 cm. A central angle with measure 18°. intercepts minor arc $\widehat{AB}$. How many centimeters longis minor arc $\widehat{AB}$?

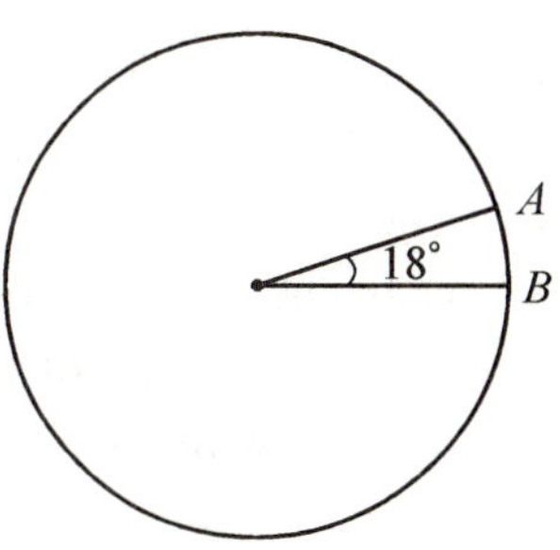

F. $\frac{1}{10}\pi$　　G. $\frac{1}{5}\pi$　　H. π

J. $\frac{100}{18}\pi$　　K. 180π

66. A square has sides that are the same length as the radius of a circle. If the circle has an area of 36π square units, how many units long is the perimeter of the square?

A. 18　　B. 24　　C. 36　　D. 72　　E. 324

67. In the standard (x, y) coordinate plane, (12, 3) is half-way between $(2a, a+3)$ and $(4a, a-5)$. What is the value of a?

F. 0　　G. 2　　H. 3　　J. 4　　K. 6

68. As shown in the (x, y, z) coordinate space below, the cube with vertices A through H has edges that are 1 coordinate unit long. The coordinates of F are (0, 0, 0), and H is on the positive y-axis. What are the coordinates of D?

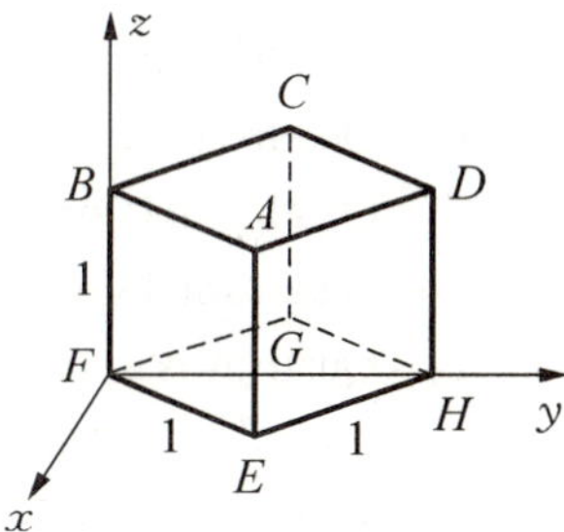

F. (0, 1, 1)　　G. $(0, \sqrt{2}, 0)$

H. $(0, \sqrt{2}, 1)$　　J. $(0, \sqrt{2}, \sqrt{3})$

K. (1, 1, 1)

69. In the figure below, lines l and m are parallel and angle measures are as marked, If it can be determined, what is the value of x?

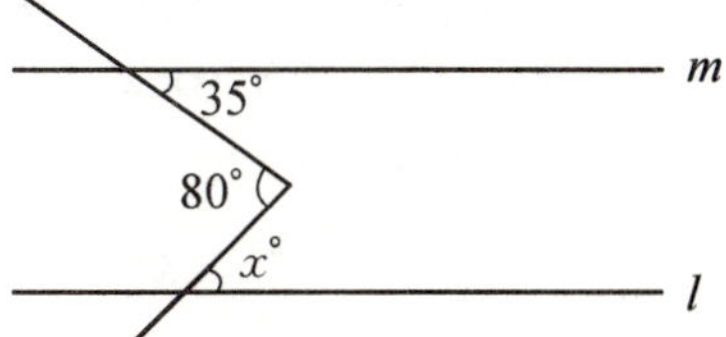

F. 35　　G. 45

H. 65　　J. 80

K. 75

70. The interior dimensions of a rectangular aquarium are 3 feet by 2 feet. What is the volume, in cubic feet, of the interior of the aquarium?

F. 7 G. 12 H. 24 J. 32 K. 36

71. In $\triangle ADE$ below, B lies on $\overline{AE}$; C lies on $\overline{AD}$; and r, s, t, and v are angle measures, in degrees. The measure of $\angle A$ is 40°. What is $r+s+t+v$?

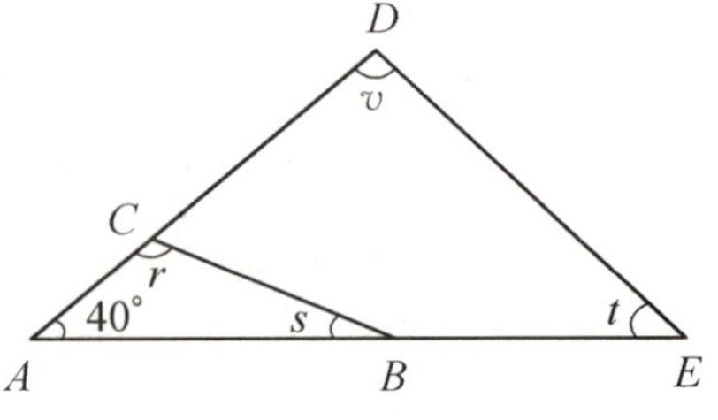

F. 100°

G. 140°

H. 240°

J. 280°

K. 320°

72. What is the area, in square feet, of a trapezoid with a height of 4 feet and parallel bases of 7 feet and 5 feet, respectively?

F. 16 G. 24 H. $27\frac{1}{2}$ J. 48 K. 55

73. Which of the following degree measures is equivalent to 3.75π radians?

A. 225° B. 337.5° C. 675° D. $1,350^\circ$ E. $2,700^\circ$

74. The angle opposite the 80-foot side measures about 28.1°. Hasan and Parvani are considering changing the shape of their flower bed. It will still be a right triangle with the 150-foot side as 1 leg, but they will extend the 80-foot side until the angle opposite that side is about 40°. By about how many feet would they need to extend the 80-foot side?

(Note: $\sin 40^\circ \approx 0.64$, $\cos 40^\circ \approx 0.77$, $\tan 40^\circ \approx 0.84$)

F. 12 G. 16 H. 36 J. 46 K. 51

75. What is the perimeter of quadrilateral $ABCD$ if it has vertices with (x, y) coordinates $A(0, 0)$, $B(1, 3)$, $C(4, 4)$, $D(3, 1)$?

F. $2\sqrt{10}$ G. $4\sqrt{10}$ H. $6\sqrt{2+2\sqrt{10}}$

J. 40 K. 100

76. The graph of the line with equation $3x-4y=24$ does NOT have points in what quadrant (s) of the standard (x, y) coordinate plane below?

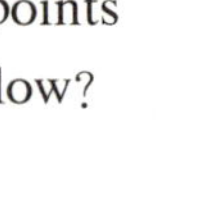

y
II I
O x
III IV

A. Quadrant I only

B. Quadrant II only

C. Quadrant II only

D. Quadrant IV only

E. Quadrants I and I only

77. A square, S_1, has a perimeter of 40 inches. The vertices of a second square, S_2 are the midpoints of the sides of S_1. The vertices of a third square, S_3, are the midpoints of the sides of S_2. Assume the process continues indefinitely. with the vertices of S_{k+1} being the midpoints of the sides of S_k for every positive integer k. What is the sum of the areas, in square inches, of S_1, S_2, S_3, …?

F. $\frac{40}{3}$ G. 20 H. 70 J. $\frac{400}{3}$ K. 200

78. Given the triangle shown below with exterior angles that measure $x°$, $y°$, and $z°$ as shown, what is the sum of x, y, and z?

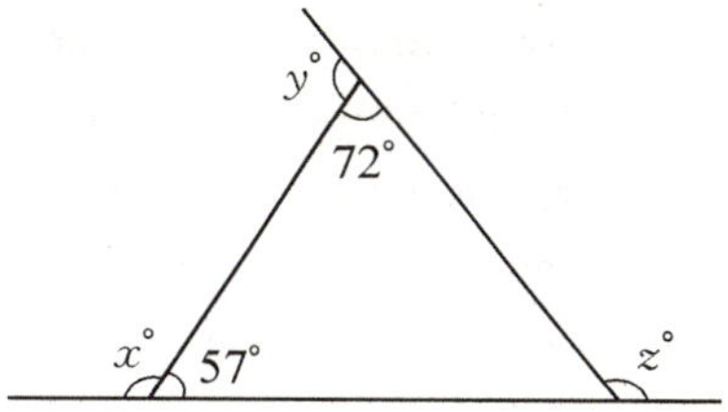

F. 180　　G. 231

H. 309　　J. 360

K. Cannot be determined from the given information

79. Cube A has an edge length of 2 inches. Cube B has an edge length double that of Cube A. What is the volume, in cubic inches, of Cube B ?

A. 4　　B. 8　　C. 16　　D. 32　　E. 64

80. A right circular cylinder is shown in the figure below, with dimensions given in centimeters. What is the total surface area of this cylinder, in square centimeters? (Note: The total surface area of a cylinder is given by $2\pi r^2 + 2\pi rh$ where r is the radius and h is the height.)

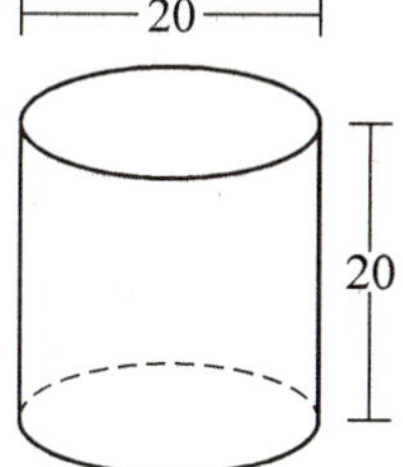

A. 300π

B. 400π

C. 500π

D. 600π

E. $1,600\pi$

81. Lines a, b, c, and d are shown below and $a \parallel b$. Which of the following is the set of all angles that must be supplementary to $\angle x$?

F. {1, 2}

G. {1, 2, 5, 6}

H. {1, 2, 9, 10}

J. {1, 2, 5, 6, 9, 10}

K. {1, 2, 5, 6, 9, 10, 13, 14}

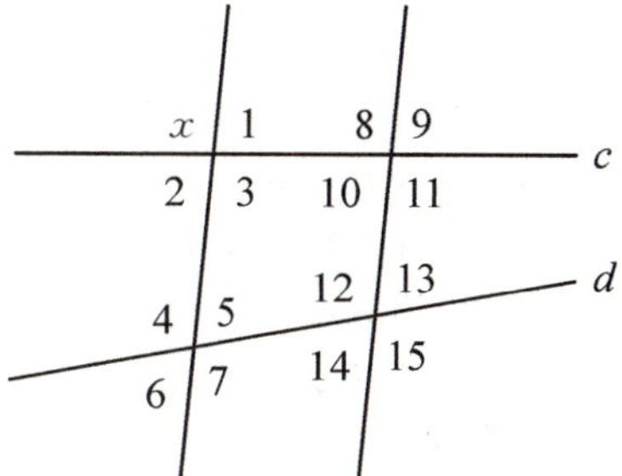

82. As shown in the standard (x, y) coordinate plane below, P (6, 6) lies on the circle with center (2, 3) and radius 5 coordinate units. What are the coordinates of the image of P after the circle is rotated 90° clockwise ( ) about the center of the circle?

A. (2, 3)

B. (3, 2)

C. (5, −1)

D. (6, 0)

E. (7, 3)

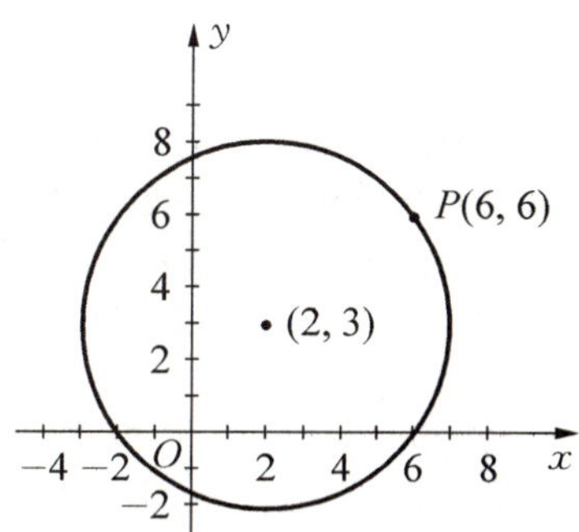

83. In isosceles trapezoid $ABCD$, $\overline{AB}$ is parallel to $\overline{DC}$, $\angle BDC$ measures 25°, and $\angle BCA$ measures 35°. What is the measure of $\angle DBC$?

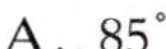

A. 85°　　B. 95°　　C. 105°

D. 115°　　E. 125°

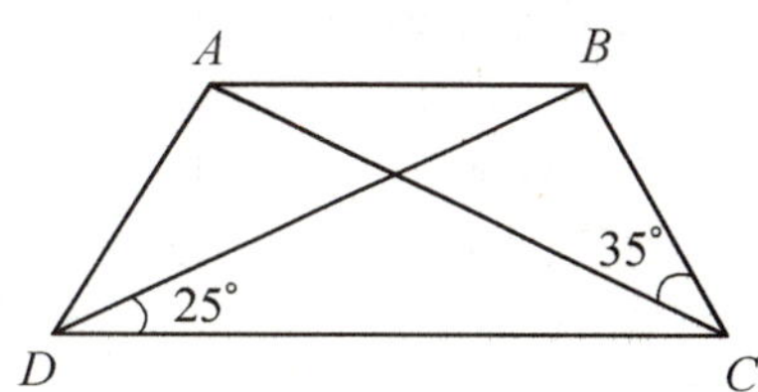

84. In the complex plane, the horizontal axis is called the real axis and the vertical axis is called the imaginary axis. The complex number $a + bi$ graphed in the complex plane is comparable to the point (a, b) graphed in the standard (x, y) coordinate plane. The modulus of the complex number $a + bi$ is given by $\sqrt{a^2 + b^2}$ Which of the complex numbers z_1, z_2, z_3, z_4, and z_5 below has the greatest modulus?

F. z_1 G. z_2 H. z_3

J. z_4 K. z_5

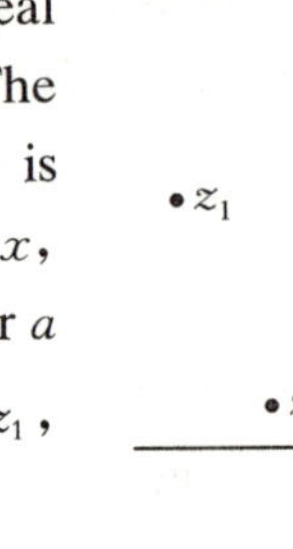

85. In the figure below, line q in the standard (x, y) coordinate plane has equation $-2x + y = 1$ and intersects line r, which is distinct from line q, at a point on the x-axis. The angles, $\angle a$ and $\angle b$, formed by these lines and the x-axis are congruent. What is the slope of line r?

F. -2 G. $-\frac{1}{2}$

H. $\frac{1}{2}$ J. 2

K. Cannot be determined from the given information

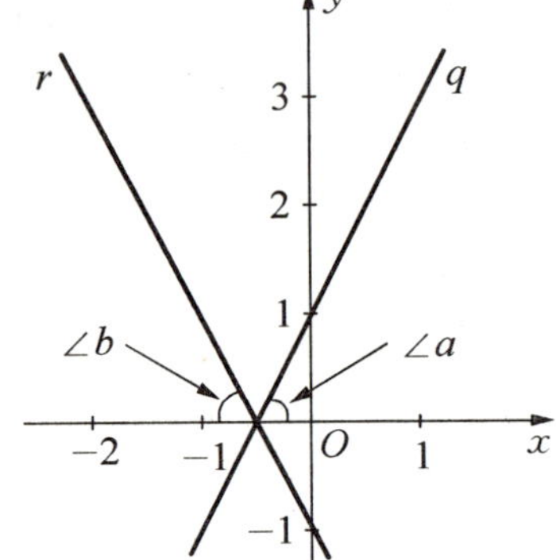

86. The graphs of the equations $y = x - 1$ and $y = (x - 1)^4$ are shown in the standard (x, y) coordinate plane below. What real values of x, if any, satisfy the inequality $(x - 1)^4 < (x - 1)$?

A. No real values

B. $x < 0$ and $x > 1$

C. $x < 1$ and $x > 2$

D. $0 < x < 1$

E. $1 < x < 2$

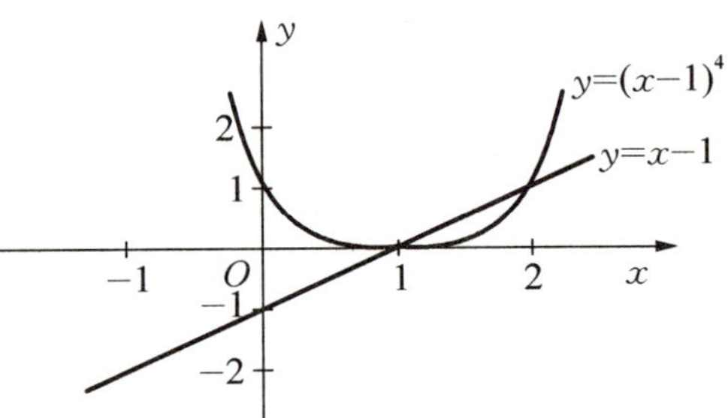

87. The measure of $\angle QOR$ in the figure below is 140°. The measures of 3 angles are given in terms of x, in degrees. What is the measure of $\angle QOS$?

F. 96° G. 100°

H. 120° J. 138°

K. 140°

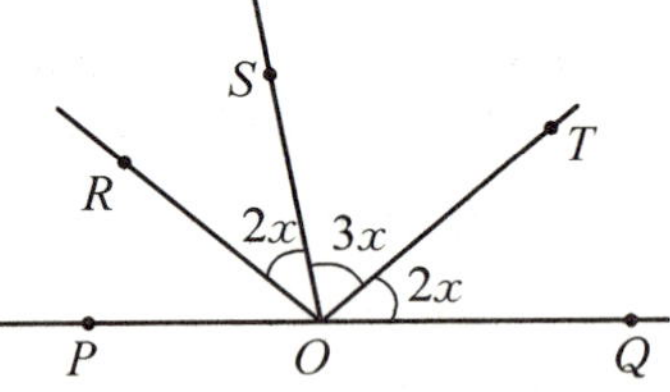

88. An 8-foot-square sheet of tin from which 4 identical circles are cut is shown below. Each circle is tangent to 2 other circles and tangent to 2 of the edges of the square. What is the approximate area, in square feet, of the remaining tin, as indicated by the shaded region below?

A. 51.4 B. 38.9

C. 19.4 D. 13.7

E. 6.9

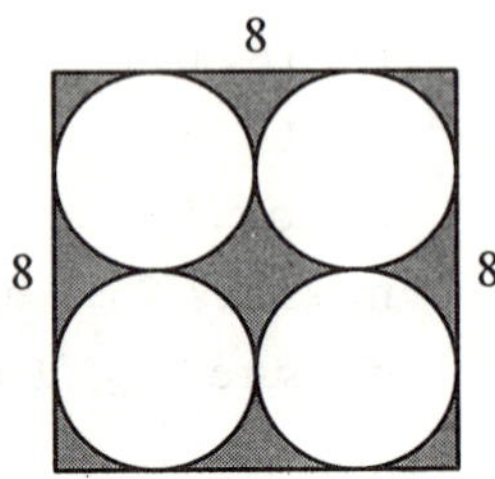

89. In $\triangle XYZ$, $XY = XZ$ and the measure of $\angle Y$ is 34°. What is the measure of $\angle X$?

F. 34° G. 56° H. 68° J. 73° K. 112°

90. In the figure below, $\angle ADC$ measures 50°, $\angle ACB$ measures 65°, and $\angle BAC$ measures 90°. What is the measure of $\angle BAD$?

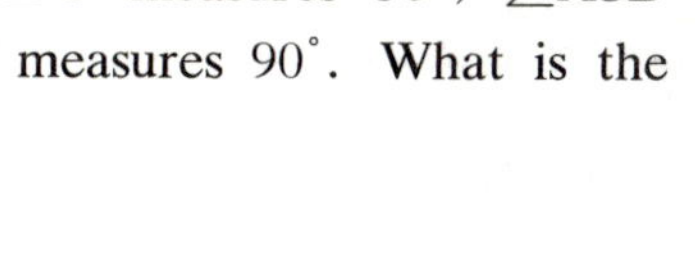

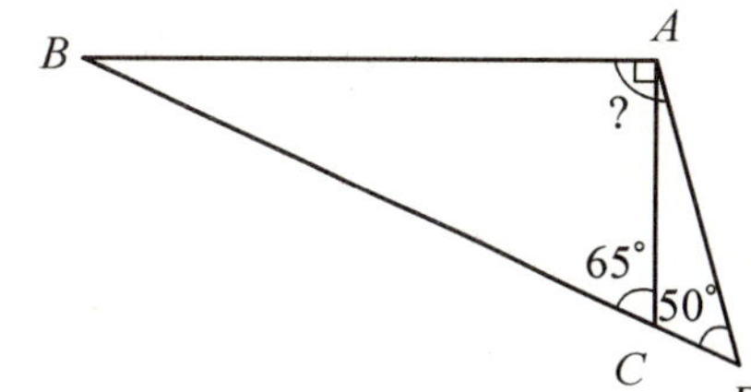

A. 105°

B. 115°

C. 130°

D. 140°

E. 155°

91. The graph of one of the following equations is the parabola shown in the standard (x, y) coordinate plane below. Which one?

F. $y-3=(x-4)^2$

G. $y-3=2(x+4)^2$

H. $y+3=2(x-4)^2$

J. $y-3=\frac{1}{2}(x+4)^2$

K. $y+3=\frac{1}{2}(x-4)^2$

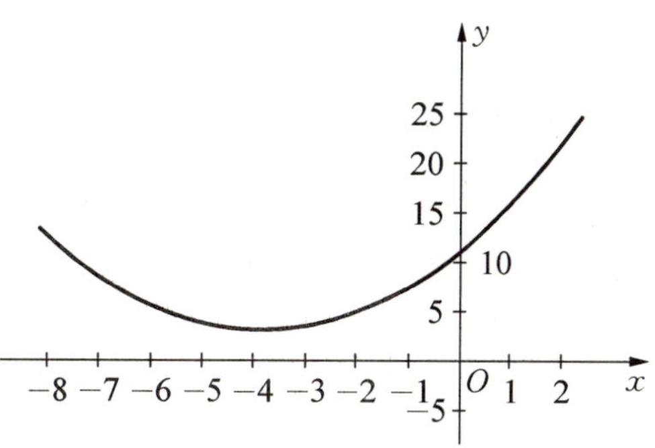

92. Rectangle $ABCD$ has vertices in the standard (x, y) coordinate plane at $A(-4, -2)$, $B(-4, 3)$, $C(2, 3)$, and $D(2, -2)$. A translation of rectangle $ABCD$ is a second rectangle, $A'B'C'D'$ with vertices $A'(4, -12)$, $B'(x, y)$, $C'(10, -7)$, and $D'(10, -12)$. What, are the coordinates of B'?

A. $(3, -6)$ B. $(4, 3)$

C. $(4, -7)$ D. $(4, -13)$

E. $(6, -5)$

93. A circle in the standard (x, y) coordinate plane has center $(7, -6)$ and radius 10 coordinate units. Which of the following is an equation of the circle?

F. $(x+7)^2-(y-6)^2=100$ G. $(x+7)^2-(y-6)^2=10$

H. $(x+7)^2-(y-6)^2=10$ J. $(x-7)^2+(y+6)^2=100$

K. $(x-7)^2+(y+6)^2=10$

94. Which of the following graphs in the standard (x, y) coordinate plane represents the solution set of the inequality $|x+y|>1$?

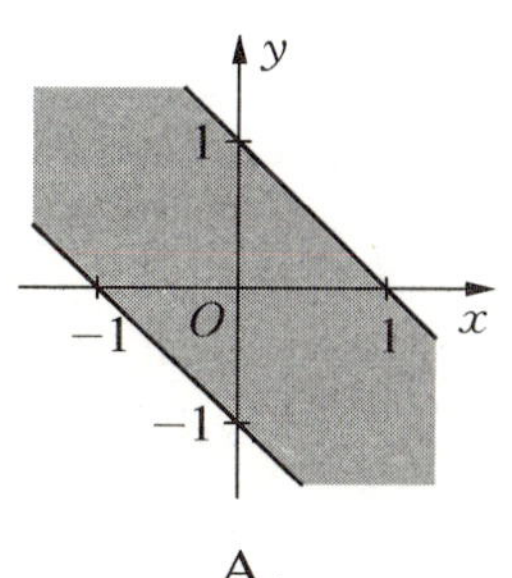

A.

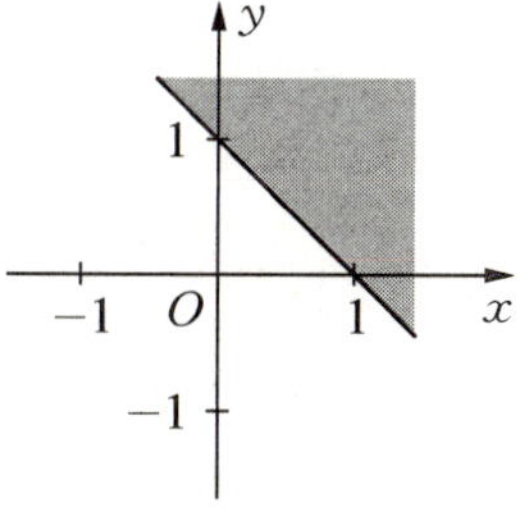

B.

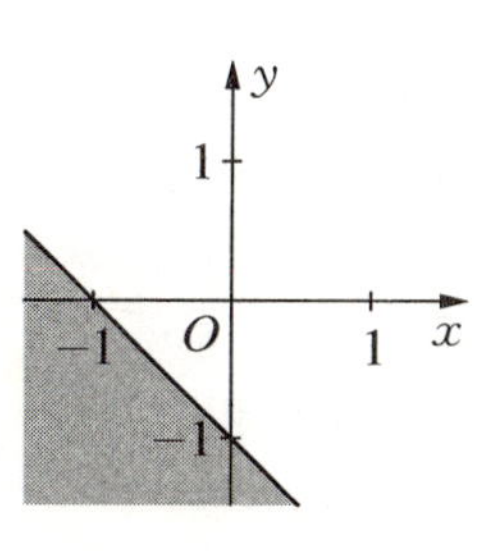

C.

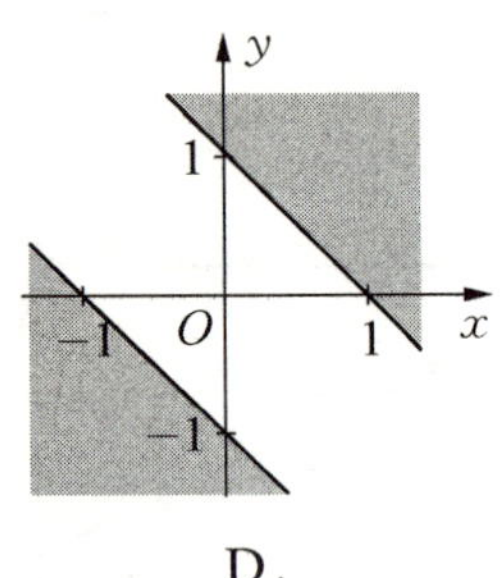

D.

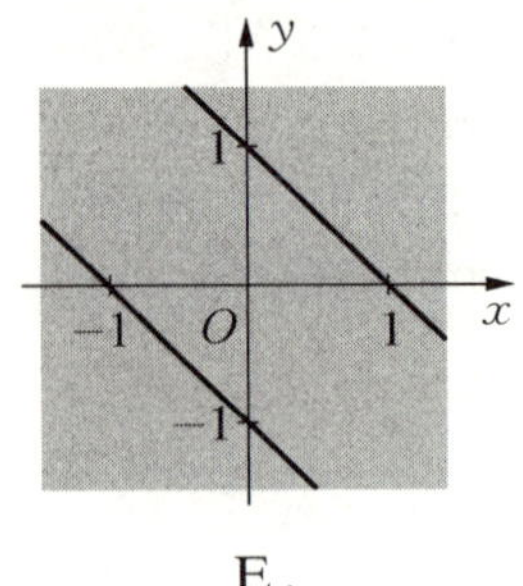

E.

[**Session 5 答案**]

1 B	2 C	3 F	4 D	5 G	6 K	7 D	8 J	9 D	10 H
11 J	12 B	13 C	14 K	15 F	16 K	17 D	18 F	19 C	20 K
21 H	22 C	23 H	24 H	25 K	26 G	27 G	28 J	29 C	30 H
31 A	32 K	33 B	34 A	35 H	36 G	37 E	38 E	39 A	40 G
41 G	42 H	43 E	44 D	45 H	46 A	47 J	48 A	49 K	50 J
51 J	52 H	53 A	54 F	55 G	56 B	57 E	58 F	59 E	60 B
61 G	62 B	63 C	64 G	65 H	66 B	67 J	68 H	69 G	70 G
71 J	72 G	73 C	74 J	75 G	76 B	77 K	78 J	79 E	80 D
81 H	82 C	83 B	84 F	85 F	86 E	87 G	88 D	89 K	90 A
91 J	92 C	93 J	94 D						

[**Session 5 答案解析**]

1. 题干：x 是多少度？
   解析：先求内角。
2. 题干：a 是 b 的三倍。A 是多少？
   解析：总和为 180。
3. 题干：ab 和 cd 平行，角 adc 多少度？
   解析：内错角。
4. 题干：三角形相似，大的周长是多少？
   解析：比例为 6∶15。
5. 题干：求面积。
   解析：上底加下底乘以高除以 2。
6. 题干：$A=2\pi r^2+2\pi rh$，$h=?$
   解析：移项。
7. 题干：计算梯形面积。
   解析：先算出高。
8. 题干：$(x-2)^2+(y+2)^2=2$ 的圆心？

解析：可以从方程中看出。即(2，－2)。

9. 题干：和另一个不同的椭圆形相交，最多几个交点？
   解析：四个。
10. 题干：矩形40乘以60，圆形直径20，圆形在矩形内，矩形其他部分要铺砖，砖的面积？
   解析：矩形面积减圆形面积。
11. 题干：底面半径翻倍，高减半，那么圆柱的体积怎么变？
   解析：底面积翻了四倍。
12. 题干：圆心到正方形边的距离是？
   解析：利用直角三角形来求。
13. 题干：阴影和白色部分面积一样，大圆半径2，小圆半径应该是？
   解析：阴影面积等于大圆减去小圆。
14. 题干：哪个是对的？
   解析：内错角。
15. 题干：在任意平行四边形 $ABCD$ 中，$\angle ABC$ 和 $\angle BCD$ 的关系是？
   解析：同旁内错角。
16. 题干：三角形相似，相似比是2∶5，小的斜边是5，那么大的斜边是？
   解析：5×2.5。
17. 题干：半径9英尺，面积？
   解析：圆的面积公式。
18. 题干：哪个把平面分成两部分？
   解析：直线。
19. 题干：$y = (A+1)x + 8$ 经过(2，6)，斜率是？
   解析：由经过的点可得到 A。
20. 题干：半径R，跑三圈是多远？
   解析：三倍的周长。
21. 题干：经过(－3，5)和(7，3)的直线斜率是多少？
   解析：可以直接根据两点来求。
22. 题干：经过(0，0)和(4，3)的直线是什么？
   解析：两点可同时确定斜率和截距。
23. 题干：有点 P, Q, R, S，一次排列在一条线上，R 是 qs 的中点，pr 长5 cm，ps 长7 cm。qs 多长？
   解析：画图。
24. 题干：4乘6的矩形分成24个正方形，有多少个边？
   解析：注意扣除共享的。
25. 题干：直角边分别是37和45，最小边的余弦值是多少？
   解析：余弦等于邻边除以斜边。
26. 题干：圆心为(－2，3)，半径5，方程是什么？
   解析：先写成圆心和半径的形式再转化为标准方程。
27. 题干：直角边6，以及7，斜边是？
   解析：勾股定理。
28. 题干：$y = ax + b$ 的斜率大于 $y = cx + b$，那么哪个正确？
   解析：斜率即 a 和 c。
29. 题干：$\overline{AB}$ 的中点是(4，－3)，$A(1，-5)$，那么 B 的坐标和是什么？

解析：可以反求出 B 的坐标。

30. 题干：

相似。$A = 20°$，$F = 75°$，B 多少度？

解析：相似三角形的角度不变。

31. 题干：第一个五边形周长 25，第二个周长多 15，那么第二个的边长比第一个多多少？

解析：周长除以 5 即边长。

32. 题干：两个互补角，一个是另一个的 5 倍，大的那个是多少？

解析：和为 180。

33. 题干：经过原点和(−12，6)的直线方程是？

解析：截距为零。

34. 题干：圆心(3，8)，和 x 轴相切，方程是什么？

解析：暗含了半径是 8 的条件。

35. 题干：如图，BC 长 5，AB 长 3，阴影面积是多少？

解析：阴影面积等于大圆减小圆的四分之一。

36. 题干：圆锥的半径翻倍，高翻三倍，体积为？

解析：$2 \times 2 \times 3 = 12$。

37. 题干：某多项式的曲线在 x 轴上有三个交点，那么它的最高次幂的秘书不可能是？

解析：至少为 3。

38. 题干：立方体边长为 abc，表面积是？

解析：分别求出六个面的面积。

39. 题干：等腰三角形，E 和 T 两个角相等，另一个角 94°，E 多少度？

解析：和 180。

40. 题干：正方形边长 12，另一个长方形面积与正方形相等，一边为 9，另一边是多少？

解析：面积除以 9。

41. 题干：高 36，长 84，宽 48，模型比例为 1∶12，模型的大小是？

解析：除以 12 即可。

42. 题干：梯形上底 11，下底 13.5，中位线是多少？

解析：平均值。

43. 题干：如图，包八个这样的箱子要花多长的带子？

解析：即两个侧面的周长之和的八倍。

44. 题干：$\frac{x^2}{64} + \frac{y^2}{36} = 1$ 在哪一点和 x 轴相截？

解析：有两点，取一点即可。

45. 题干：求阴影面积。

解析：正方形面积减去圆形面积除以 4。

46. 题干：三角形外接圆，哪一点是圆心？

解析：画出草图。

47. 题干：求面积。

解析：记得除以 2。

48. 题干：在所示点的切线是什么？

解析：点要在切线上，而且切线跟圆心的距离为半径。

49. 题干：线段和平面可以有多少点相交？

解析：无数多个。

50. 题干：求面积。

解析：近似即可。

51. 题干：哪个说法不一定正确？

解析：内角和为 180。

52. 题干：P 在 AB 上，求 PCD 的面积。

解析：底乘高除以 2。

53. 题干：$y=ax+2$ 把下图分成全等的两部分。$a=$？

解析：可以确定截距为 2。

54. 题干：P 的坐标？

解析：镜像。

55. 题干：长 14，宽 12，对角线多长？

解析：勾股定理。

56. 题干：六边形内角和？

解析：多边形的内角和有公式 $=(n-2)\times 180$。

57. 题干：两线段，各自的两部分长度之积相等，HG 总长 12，GI 多长？

解析：方程组。

58. 题干：如图，每个圆的周长是 24π，加粗部分的周长是多少？

解析：把交点连接起来可以得到多个正三角形，所以加粗部分的弧长每一条都等于弧长 BC。

59. 题干：求方程。

解析：根据半长轴和半短轴确定。

60. 题干：求面积。

解析：数格子。

61. 题干：如图哪一对线是平行的？

解析：内错角。

62. 题干：求左边柱子的高度。

解析：利用相似三角形。

63. 题干：锥台的体积为 $V=\frac{1}{3}\pi h(R^2+r^2+Rr)$，求体积。

解析：代入公式即可。

64. 题干：$\frac{5\pi}{12}$换成角度制。

解析：除以 π 乘以 180。

65. 题干：半径 10 cm。$\overset{\frown}{AB}$是多长？

解析：利用角度求弧长。

66. 题干：正方形的边长和圆的半径一样。圆的面积为 36π，正方形的周长是？

解析：求出圆的半径即正方形边长。

67. 题干：$(12, 3)$ 在$(2a, a+3)$ 和$(4a, a-5)$正当中，求 a？

解析：中点坐标分别是端点坐标的平均值。

68. 题干：求 D 坐标。

解析：注意 z 轴。

69. 题干：求 x 的值。

解析：把 80°分成两部分。

70. 题干：已知边长求体积。
解析：体积等于三边长之积。
71. 题干：求 $r+s+t+v$。
解析：三角形内角和为 180。
72. 题干：梯形高 4，上底 7 下底 5，面积为？
解析：上底加下底乘以高除以 2。
73. 题干：3.75π 的角度制值？
解析：除以 π 乘以 180°。
74. 题干：一个直角三角形，一个直角边是 80，对应角为 28.1°，另一个边是 180。保持 180 的不变，延长 80 的，延长多少能使得其对应的角边长 40？
解析：当成两个三角形分别计算，然后比较。
75. 题干：四边形有顶角 $A(0, 0)$，$B(1, 3)$，$C(4, 4)$，$D(3, 1)$，周长是多少？
解析：先画出草图，看是什么类型的。
76. 题干：$3x-4y=24$ 不出现在哪个象限？
解析：画图。
77. 题干：第一个正方形边长 40，其边的中点是第二个正方形的顶点，以此类推，面积的数列 S_1，S_2，S_3，… 和是多少？
解析：等比数列求和。
78. 题干：求 x，y，z 的和。
解析：z 等于另外两个内角的和。
79. 题干：立方体 a 的棱长为 2，b 棱长是 a 的两倍。B 的体积是多少？
解析：体积等于棱长的立方。
80. 题干：求表面积。
解析：分侧面积和两个底面积。
81. 题干：那些角和 x 互补？
解析：内错角互补。
82. 题干：圆关于圆心顺时针旋转 90°之后，P 的坐标？
解析：可以做垂线来求。
83. 题干：等腰梯形，求$\angle DBC$。
解析：利用平行线的内错角补上一些角然后再算。
84. 题干：哪个点的模最大？
解析：即与原点的连线最长。
85. 题干：q 即 $-2x+y=1$。角 a 等于角 b，求 r 的斜率。
解析：是 q 的相反数。
86. 题干：x 取什么值满足$(x-1)^4<(x-1)$？
解析：可以从图上直接看出来。
87. 题干：$\angle qor$ 等于 140°，求 $\angle qos$。
解析：平角等于 180。
88. 题干：求阴影面积。
解析：正方形减去四个圆即可。
89. 题干：$\triangle XYZ$，$XY=XZ$，$\angle Y=34°$ 那么 $\angle X=$？

解析：等腰三角形。

90. 题干：求 $\angle BAD$。
解析：某个内角的补角等于另外两个内角之和。

91. 题干：哪个函数表示下面的图像。
解析：注意对称轴。

92. 题干：矩形 $ABCD$ 的顶角为 $A(-4, -2)$，$B(-4, 3)$，$C(2, 3)$，$D(2, -2)$，平移后得到 $A'B'C'D'$，顶角为 $A'(4, -12)$，$B'(x, y)$，$C'(10, -7)$，$D'(10, -12)$。求 x，y。
解析：画出原来的矩形草图，就能发现点的关系。

93. 题干：原点为(7，-6)，半径 10，方程为？
解析：半径注意平方。

94. 题干：$|x+y|>1$ 表示了哪个阴影？
解析：分类讨论，然后去绝对值符号。

Session 6　三角函数

1. If A is the measure of an acute angle (that is, $0^\circ < A < 90^\circ$) and $\sin A = \frac{12}{13}$, what are the possible values of $\tan A$?

A. $\frac{5}{12}$ and $-\frac{5}{12}$　B. $\frac{12}{5}$ and $-\frac{12}{5}$　C. $\frac{5}{12}$ only　D. $\frac{12}{5}$ only　E. $\frac{13}{12}$ only

2. If $0^\circ \leqslant x^\circ \leqslant 90^\circ$, and $2\sin^2 x^\circ - 1 = 0$, then $x^\circ = ?$

A. 0°　B. 30°　C. 45°　D. 60°　E. 90°

3. Whenever $\frac{\tan\theta}{\sin\theta}$ is defined, it is equivalent to:

F. $\cos\theta$　G. $\frac{1}{\cos\theta}$　H. $\frac{1}{\sin\theta}$　J. $\frac{1}{\sin 2\theta}$　K. $\frac{\cos\theta}{\sin 2\theta}$

4. If $\sin\alpha = \frac{3}{4}$, and α is the measure of an acute angle, then $\cos\alpha = ?$
(Note: An acute angle has a degree measure from 0° to 90°.)

A. $\frac{1}{4}$　B. $\frac{4}{3}$　C. $\frac{\sqrt{3}}{2}$　D. $\frac{\sqrt{7}}{4}$
E. Cannot be determined from the given information

5. The radio station WEST is erecting a new transmitting tower that is 280 feet tall. A support wire will be attached to the ground at point A and to the tower 250 feet up at point B, as shown below. The wire must be at least as long as $\overline{AB}$. Which of the following expresses the length of $\overline{AB}$, in feet?

F. $250\cos 70^\circ$　G. $250\sin 70^\circ$
H. $250\tan 70^\circ$　J. $\frac{250}{\cos 70^\circ}$
K. $\frac{250}{\sin 70^\circ}$

6. Right triangle $\triangle ABC$ has angle measures α, β, and γ degrees and side lengths a, b, and c inches, as illustrated below. Which of the following is true about the value of the product $\tan\beta$

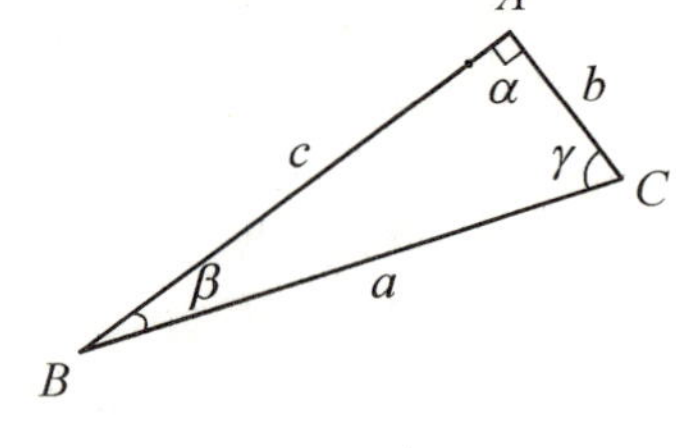

tan γ?

F. The value is 1.

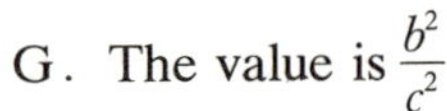

G. The value is $\frac{b^2}{c^2}$

H. The value is $\frac{b^2c^2}{a^4}$

J. The value is undefined.

K. The value cannot be determined from the given information.

7. The directions for assembling the pool state that the ladder should be placed at an angle of 75° relative to level ground. The depth of the pool is 6 feet. Which of the following expressions involving tangent gives the distance, in feet, that the bottom of the ladder should be placed away from the bottom edge of the pool in order to comply with the directions?

F. $\frac{6}{\tan 75^\circ}$　　G. $\frac{\tan 75^\circ}{6}$

H. $\frac{1}{6\tan 75^\circ}$　　J. $6\tan 75^\circ$

K. $\tan(6 \cdot 75^\circ)$

8. For x such that $0 < x < \frac{\pi}{2}$ the expression $\frac{\sqrt{1-\cos^2 x}}{\sin x} + \frac{\sqrt{1-\sin^2 x}}{\cos x}$ is equivalent to:

F. 0　　G. 1　　H. 2　　J. $-\tan x$　　K. $\sin 2x$

9. From a blimp 1,130 feet above the ground, the angle of depression to a marker on the ground is 52°, as shown in the figure below. Which of the following expressions gives the distance along the ground, in feet, from the marker to point P directly below the blimp?

52°

1,130 ft

?

P

A. 1,130 tan 38°　　B. 1,130 sin 38°

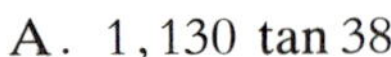

C. 1,130 cos 38°　　D. $\frac{1,130}{\cos 38^\circ}$

E. $\frac{1,130}{\tan 38^\circ}$

10. The quadrants of the standard (x, y) coordinate plane are shown in the figure below. Given that the vertex of $\angle\alpha$ is the origin, the positive is one side of $\angle\alpha$, its other side lies in Quadrant II, and $\sin\alpha = \frac{\sqrt{3}}{2}$, what is $\cos 2\alpha$?

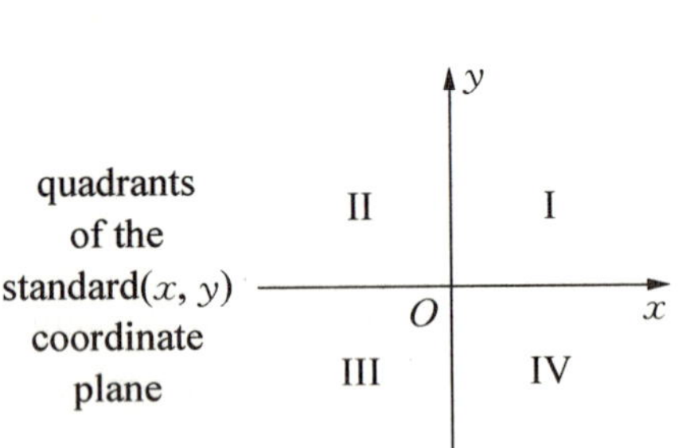

F. $-\frac{\sqrt{3}}{2}$　　G. $-\frac{1}{2}$　　H. $\frac{1}{4}$

J. $\frac{1}{2}$　　K. $\frac{\sqrt{3}}{2}$

11. For a specific nonzero value of b, the graph of $y = \sin bx$ in the standard (x, y) coordinate plane intersects the *x-axis* at k values of x in the interval $0 \leqslant x \leqslant 2\pi$. At how many values of x in this interval does the graph of $y = 2\sin bx$ intersect the *x-axis*?

A. k　　B. $k-2$　　C. $k+2$　　D. $\frac{k}{2}$　　E. $2k$

12. A small electric fan, shown below, has 3 blades. The angle between each 2 blades is 120°, and the tip of each blade is 5 inches from the center of the fan, as shown. To the nearest 0.1 inch, how many inches apart are the tips of 2 blades?

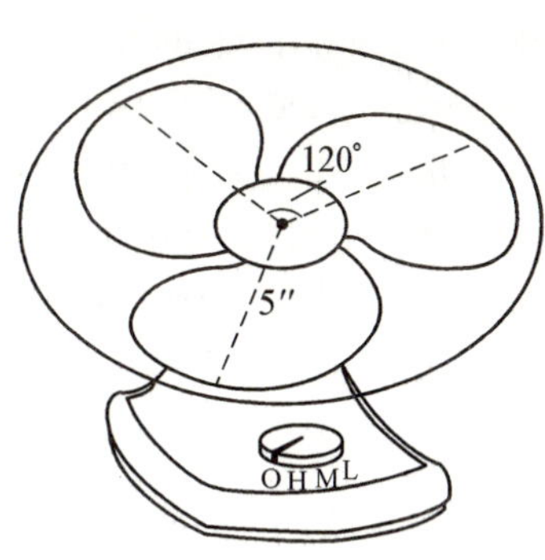

A. 8.7
B. 7.1
C. 5.0
D. 4.3
E. 2.5

13. The figure below shows the path of a certain projectile launched from the ground at an angle of θ. The horizontal range, r, of this projectile when launched from the ground at a speed of 20 meters per second is modeled by $r = 40 \sin(2\theta)$.

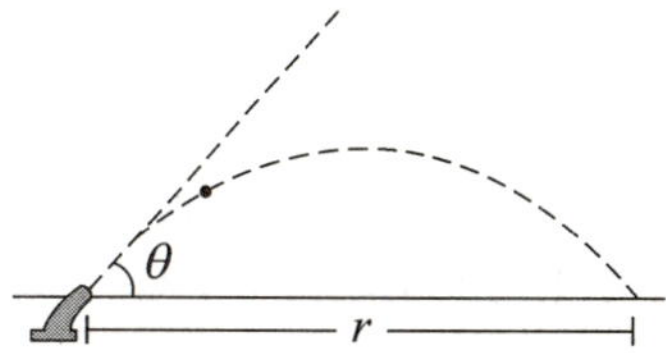

For this model, the angle measure θ that results in the greatest horizontal range, r, is 45° because:

F. $2 \sin\theta$ is greater than $\sin\theta$.
G. $\sin 90°$ is as large as sine can get.
H. $\sin 45°$ is as large as sine can get.
J. $\sin 45°$ is about 0.707.
K. $\sin 2\theta$ is greater than $\sin\theta$.

14. A surveyor needs to know the width of a flood control channel. From point A, she walks 100 feet to point B and sights to point C, as shown below.
From this sighting, the surveyor finds that the measure of $\angle ABC$ is 50°. Which of the following is closest to the width, in feet, of the flood control channel?
(Note: $\sin 50° \approx 0.766$
$\cos 50° \approx 0.643$
$\tan 50° \approx 1.192$)

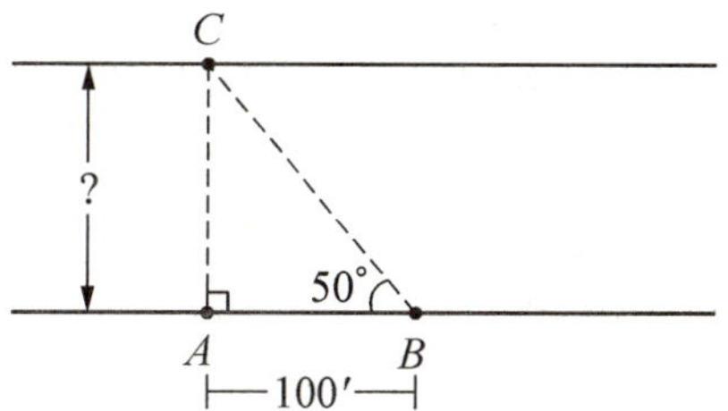

A. 64　　B. 77　　C. 119　　D. 131　　E. 156

15. Whenever $\cos x \neq 0$ and $\sin x \neq 0$, the expression $\sec^2 x + \tan^2 x$ is equivalent to:

F. $1 + \sin 2x$　　G. $1 + \cos 2x$　　H. $\frac{1+\cos^2 x}{\cos^2 x}$　　J. $\frac{2+\cos^2 x}{\cos^2 x}$　　K. $\frac{1+\sin^2 x}{\cos^2 x}$

16. The lengths, in inches, of all 3 sides of a triangle are positive integers. and 1 side is 7 inches long. If the area of this triangle is positive, what is the smallest possible perimeter for this triangle. in inches?

F. 9　　G. 10　　H. 14　　J. 15
K. 21

17. In the figure below, $\sin\alpha = \frac{4}{5}$. What is the value of h?

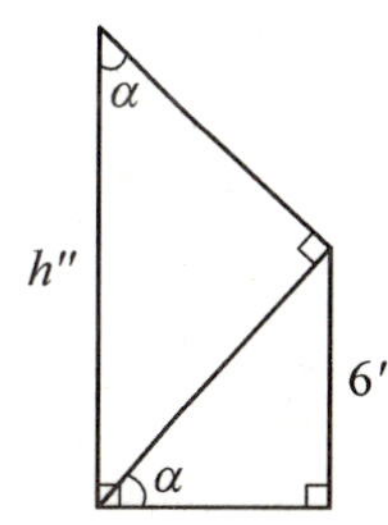

F. $\frac{24}{5}$　　G. $\frac{34}{5}$　　H. $\frac{36}{5}$
J. $\frac{75}{8}$　　K. $\frac{15}{2}$

18. A surveyor wants to approximate a river's width. As shown in the figure below, points A and C are located on the west bank of a river and point B is located on the east bank of the river such that $\angle ACB$ is a right angle. She measures and finds that the length of $\overline{AC}$ is 54 meters and the measure of $\angle BAC$ is 68°.
Given the trigonometric approximations in the tables below, which bf the following is closest to the river's width, in meters, represented by the length of $\overline{BC}$?

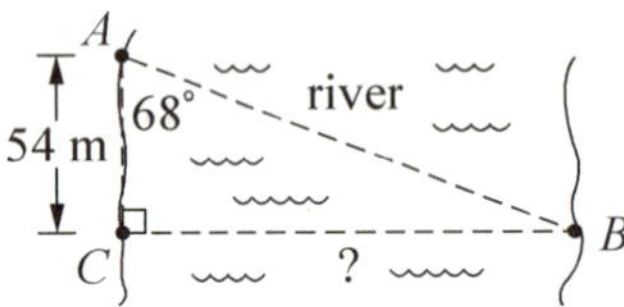

cos 22°	0.927
sin 22°	0.375
tan 22°	0.404

cos 68°	0.375
sin 68°	0.927
tan 68°	2.475

A. 58　　B. 108　　C. 134　　D. 136　　E. 144

19. In the figure below, $LM = MA$, and A, B, C, and Dare on $\overline{ME}$. Of the angles $\angle LAM$, $\angle LBM$, $\angle LCM$, $\angle LDM$, and $\angle LEM$, which one has the smallest sine?

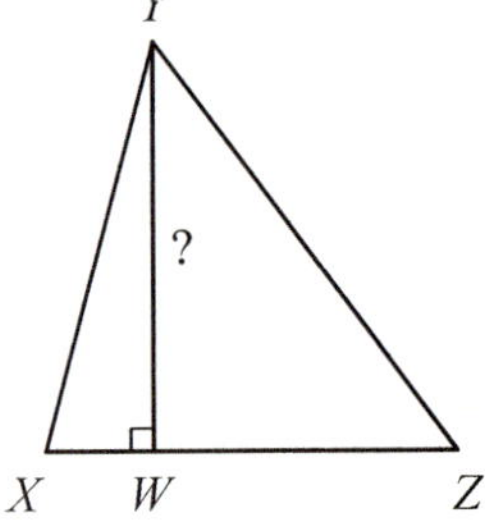

F. $\angle LAM$　　G. $\angle LBM$
H. $\angle LCM$　　J. $\angle LDM$
K. $\angle LEM$

20. The area of $\triangle XYZ$ below is 32 square inches. If $\overline{XZ}$ is 8 inches long, how long is altitude $\overline{YW}$ in inches?

F. 10
G. 8
H. 6
J. 4
K. 2

Use the following information to answer questions 21 – 22.

Hasan and Parvani have a flower bed that is shaped like a right triangle, as shown below.

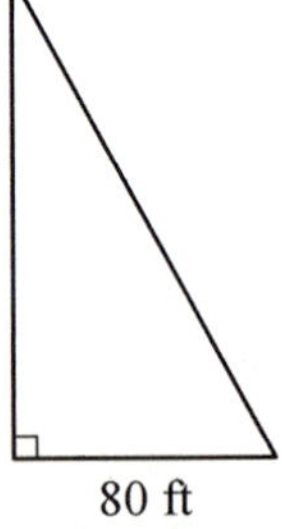

21. To determine how much fencing to buy to enclose their flower bed, Hasan and Parvani calculated the flower bed's perimeter. What is its perimeter, in feet?

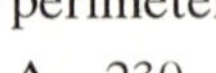

A. 230　　B. 310　　C. 380　　D. 400
E. 460

22. The angle opposite the 80-foot side measures about 28.1°. Hasan and Parvani are considering changing the shape of their flower bed. It will still be a right triangle with the 150-foot side as 1 leg, but they will extend the 80-foot side until the angle opposite that side is about 40°. By about how many feet would they need to extend the 80-foot side?
(Note: $\sin 40° \approx 0.64$, $\cos 40° \approx 0.77$, $\tan 40° \approx 0.84$)

F. 12　　G. 16　　H. 36　　J. 46　　K. 51

23. The sides of a right triangle measure 20 cm, 21 cm, and 29 cm. What is the tangent of the

angle opposite the side that measures 20 cm ?

F. $\frac{20}{21}$ G. $\frac{20}{29}$ H. $\frac{21}{20}$ J. $\frac{21}{29}$ K. $\frac{29}{20}$

24. In the figure below, a radar screen shows 2 ships. Ship A is located at a distance of 20 nautical miles and bearing 170°, and Ship B is located at a distance of 30 nautical miles and bearing 300°. Which of the following is an expression for the straight-line distance, in nautical miles, between the 2 ships?

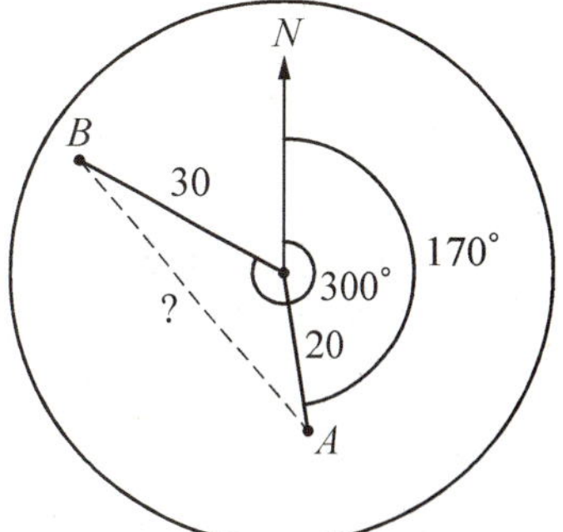

(Note: For $\triangle ABC$ with side of length an opposite $\angle A$, side of length b opposite $\angle B$, and side of length c opposite $\angle C$, the law of cosines states $c^2 = a^2 + b^2 - 2ab\cos\angle C$.)

A. $\sqrt{20^2 + 30^2 - 2(20)(30)\cos 60^\circ}$

B. $\sqrt{20^2 + 30^2 - 2(20)(30)\cos 130^\circ}$

C. $\sqrt{20^2 + 30^2 - 2(20)(30)\cos 170^\circ}$

D. $\sqrt{20^2 + 30^2 - 2(20)(30)\cos 300^\circ}$

E. $\sqrt{20^2 + 30^2 - 2(20)(30)\cos 470^\circ}$

25. In the circle below, O is the center. Chord $\overline{AB}$ is 12 inches long and is 8 inches from O. What is the area, in square inches, of the circle?

F. 36π G. 64π

H. 80π J. 100π

K. 208π

26. Suppose $0^\circ < x < 90^\circ$ and $\tan x = \frac{3}{7}$. What is the value of $\cos x + \sin$

x?

A. $\frac{7}{\sqrt{116}}$ B. $\frac{7}{\sqrt{58}}$ C. $\frac{10}{\sqrt{116}}$ D. $\frac{6}{7}$ E. $\frac{10}{\sqrt{58}}$

27. In $\triangle ABC$, shown below, angle measures are as marked and the length given is in meters. Which of the following is an expression for the length, in meters, of $\overline{AB}$?

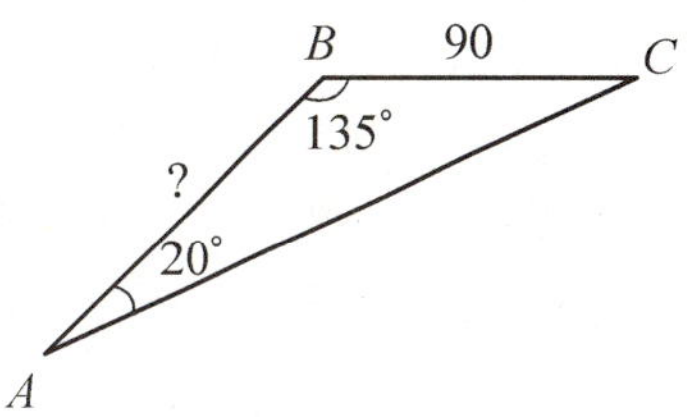

(Note: The law of sines states that for a triangle with sides of lengths a, b, and c opposite angles of measure α, β, and γ, respectively, $\frac{\sin\alpha}{a} = \frac{\sin\beta}{b} = \frac{\sin\gamma}{c}$)

A. $\frac{90\sin 20^\circ}{\sin 135^\circ}$ B. $\frac{90\sin 25^\circ}{\sin 20^\circ}$ C. $\frac{90\sin 25^\circ}{\sin 135^\circ}$ D. $\frac{90\sin 135^\circ}{\sin 20^\circ}$ E. $\frac{90\sin 135^\circ}{\sin 25^\circ}$

28. The expression $4\sin x\cos x$ is equivalent to which of the following?
(Note: $\sin(x+y) = \sin x\cos y + \cos x\sin y$)

F. $2\sin 2x$ G. $2\cos 2x$ H. $2\sin 4x$ J. $8\sin 2x$ K. $8\cos 2x$

29. The domain of the function $y(x) = 3\cos(5x-4)+1$ is all real numbers. Which of the following is the range of the function $y(x)$?

A. $-3 \leqslant y(x) \leqslant 3$ B. $-4 \leqslant y(x) \leqslant 3$

C. $-4 \leqslant y(x) \leqslant 2$ D. $-2 \leqslant y(x) \leqslant 4$

E. All real numbers

30. In the figure below, $\triangle ABC$ is a right triangle with all3sides of different lengths. What is the value of $\sin^2 A + \sin^2 B$?

F. 1　　G. 2　　H. $\sqrt{2}$　　J. $\frac{\sqrt{3}}{2}$　　K. $\frac{1+\sqrt{3}}{2}$

31. In isosceles trapezoid $ABCD$ below, E is the intersection of the diagonals. The length of $\overline{AB}$ is 6 inches, the lengths of $\overline{AE}$ and $\overline{BE}$ are 4 inches, the length of $\overline{CE}$ is 10 inches, and the measures of $\angle CDE$ and $\angle DCE$ are equal. What is the length, in inches, of $\overline{CD}$?

A. 10　　B. 14　　C. 15　　D. 16

E. 20

32. For ϕ, an angle whose measure is between 90° and 180°, $\tan\phi = -\frac{7}{24}$. Which of the following equals $\sin\phi$?

F. $-\frac{24}{7}$　　G. $-\frac{24}{25}$　　H. $-\frac{7}{25}$　　J. $\frac{24}{25}$　　K. $\frac{7}{25}$

33. In the standard (x, y) coordinate plane below, an angle is shown whose vertex is the origin. One side of this angle with measure θ passes through $(4, -3)$, and the other side includes the positive x-axis. What is the cosine of θ?

F. $-\frac{4}{3}$　　G. $-\frac{3}{4}$　　H. $-\frac{3}{5}$

J. $\frac{4}{5}$　　K. $\frac{5}{4}$

34. Triangles $\triangle ABC$ and $\triangle PQR$ are shown below. The given side lengths are in centimeters. The area of $\triangle ABC$ is 30 square centimeters. What is the area of $\triangle PQR$, in square centimeters?

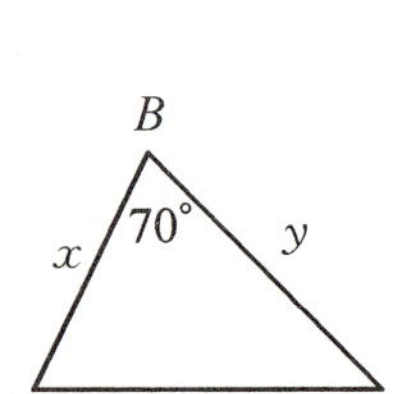

F. 15　　G. 19

H. 25　　J. 30　　K. 33

35. Consider the set of all points (x, y) that satisfy all 3 of the conditions below:

$y \geqslant 0$

$y \leqslant 2x + 4$

$y \leqslant -x + 4$

The graph of this set is $\triangle ABC$ and its interior, which is shown shaded in the standard (x, y) coordinate plane below. Let this set be the domain of the function $P(x, y) = 4x + 3y$.

What is the maximum value of $P(x, y)$ when x and y satisfy the 3 conditions given?

A. 4　　B. 8　　C. 12

D. 16　　E. 28

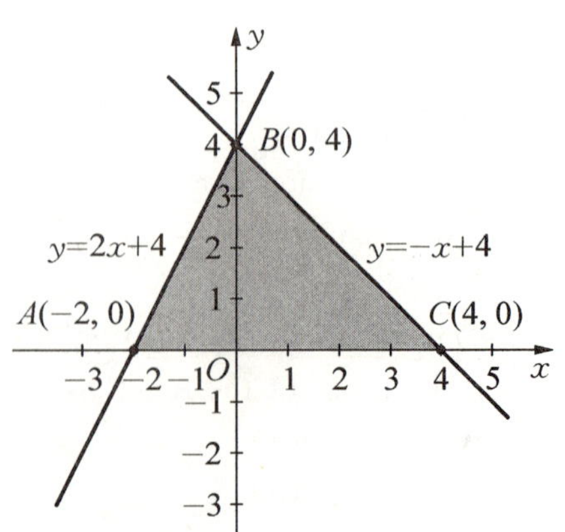

36. The quadrants of the standard (x, y) coordinate plane are labeled in the figure below. The domain of $P(x, y)$ contains points in which quadrants?

quadrants of the standard(x,y) coordinate plane

II I O x III IV y

F. I and II only
G. I and III only
H. I and IV only
J. II and III only
K. II and IV only

37. $\tan\angle BCA = ?$

A. 1 B. $\frac{2}{3}$ C. $\frac{\sqrt{5}}{3}$ D. $\frac{3}{\sqrt{5}}$ E. $\frac{3}{2\sqrt{2}}$

38. A right triangle is shown in the figure below. Which of the following expressions gives θ?

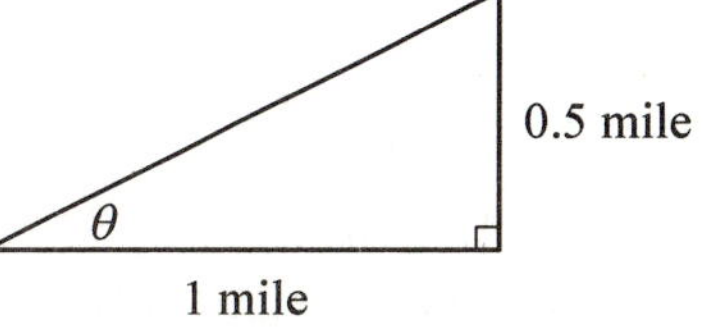

A. $\tan^{-1}\left(\frac{1}{2}\right)$ B. $\sin^{-1}\left(\frac{1}{2}\right)$

C. $\cos^{-1}\left(\frac{1}{2}\right)$ D. $\tan^{-1}(2)$

E. $\sin^{-1}(2)$

39. By the law of cosines, $a^2 = b^2 + c^2 - 2bc\cos\angle A$ for a triangle with sides of lengths a, b, and c opposite $\angle A$, $\angle B$, and $\angle C$. respectively. A boat travels 25 miles due east, makes a 40° turn toward the north, and then travels 30 miles, as shown below. To the nearest mile, what is the straight-line distance between the boat's starting position and its ending position?

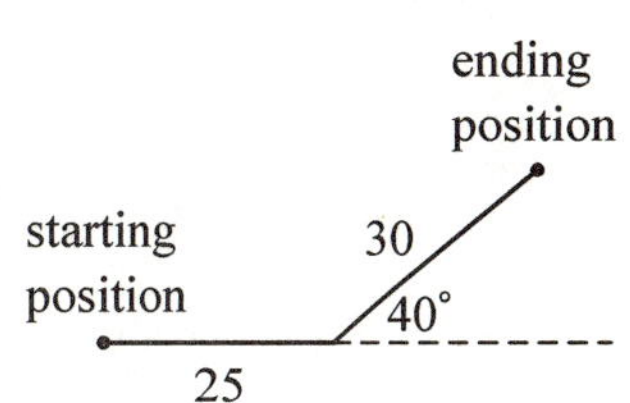

(Note: $\cos 40° \approx 0.766$, $\cos(180 - \alpha) = -\cos\alpha$)

A. 55 B. 52 C. 57 D. 31 E. 19

40. In $\triangle ABC$, the measure of $\angle A$ is 47°, the measure of $\angle B$ is 76°, and the length of $\overline{BC}$ is 18 centimeters. Which of the following is an expression for the length, in centimeters, of $\overline{AC}$? (Note: The law of sines states that for any triangle, the ratios of the lengths of the sides to the sines of the angles opposite those sides are equal.)

A. $\frac{\sin 47°}{18\sin 76°}$ B. $\frac{\sin 76°}{18\sin 47°}$ C. $\frac{18\sin 47°}{\sin 76°}$ D. $\frac{18\sin 76°}{\sin 47°}$

E. $\frac{(\sin 47°)(\sin 76°)}{18}$

41. If $\cos x = -\frac{1}{3}$, what is the value of $\cos 2x$?

(Note: $(\cos x)^2 = \frac{1 + \cos 2x}{2}$)

A. $-\frac{8}{9}$ B. $-\frac{7}{9}$ C. $-\frac{1}{6}$ D. $\frac{1}{9}$ E. $\frac{1}{6}$

42. For a certain angle with measure θ, $\sin\theta = 0.4$. What is $\cos\theta$?

F. $\frac{5}{2}$ G. $\frac{5}{3}$ H. $\frac{1}{4}$ J. $\sqrt{0.84}$ K. $\frac{1}{\sqrt{0.84}}$

43. For all values of x such that $\sin x > 0$ and $\cos x > 0$, which of the following expressions is equivalent to $\sin x > \frac{1}{2}\cos x$?

F. $\sin x + \cos x > \frac{1}{2}$　　G. $\sin x - \cos x > \frac{1}{2}$

H. $\cos x - \sin x < 2$　　J. $\tan x > \frac{1}{2}$

K. $\tan x < 2$

44. In the figure below, $\triangle ACD$ is a right triangle, B lies on $\overline{AC}$, and the measures of $\angle DAC$ and $\angle DBC$ are given. The length of $\overline{AB}$ is 10 yards. What is the approximate length, in yards, of $\overline{CD}$?

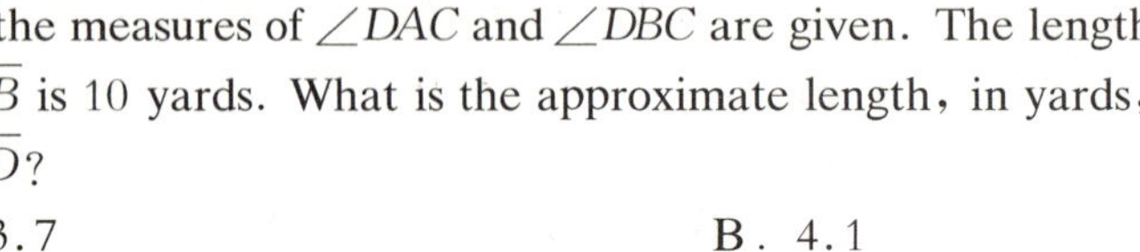

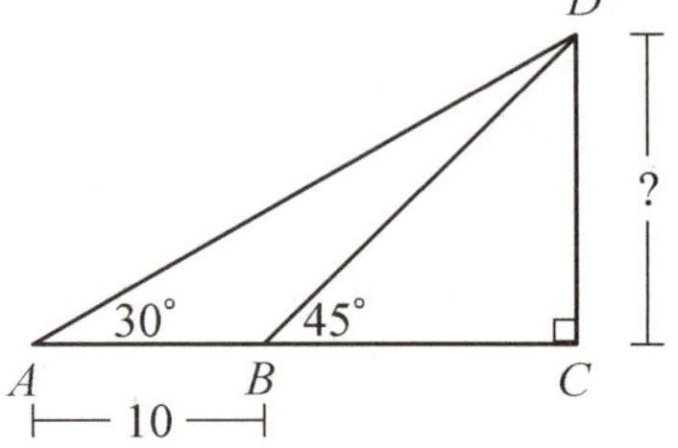

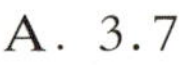

A. 3.7　　B. 4.1

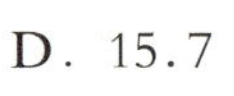

C. 13.7　　D. 15.7

E. 24.1

45. As shown in the figure below, a triangle has 2 sides each of length 5 feet and a 3rd side of length x feet. The degree measure of the angle? between the 2 sides that are 5 feet long is θ. In terms of x, $\cos\theta = ?$

(Note: For any triangle, if a, b, and c are the lengths of the sides opposite $\angle A$, $\angle B$, and $\angle C$, respectively, then $a^2 = b^2 + c^2 - 2bc\cos\angle A$.)

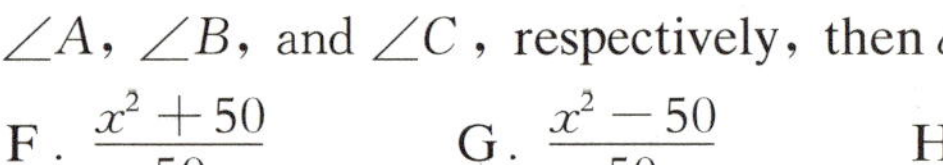

F. $\frac{x^2+50}{50}$　　G. $\frac{x^2-50}{50}$　　H. $\frac{x^2-10}{50}$　　J. $\frac{50-x^2}{50}$

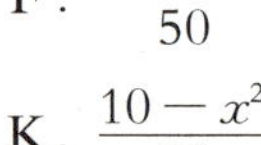

K. $\frac{10-x^2}{50}$

46. Which of the following is equal to $\tan\theta \cdot \cos\theta$ when $\sin\theta = \frac{2}{3}$ and $0 < \theta < \frac{\pi}{2}$?

F. $\frac{2}{3}$　　G. $\frac{2\sqrt{5}}{9}$　　H. $\frac{\sqrt{5}}{3}$　　J. $\frac{2\sqrt{5}}{5}$　　K. 1

47. Li is standing at point L on the north side of the small canyon shown in the figure below. As measured by line of sight, Li is 2 miles from an observation tower at T, and she is 3 miles from a scenic overlook at S. Li, the observation tower, and the scenic overlook are all at the same elevation. The measure of $\angle S$ is 28°. Which of the following equations, when solved, gives the measure of $\angle T$?

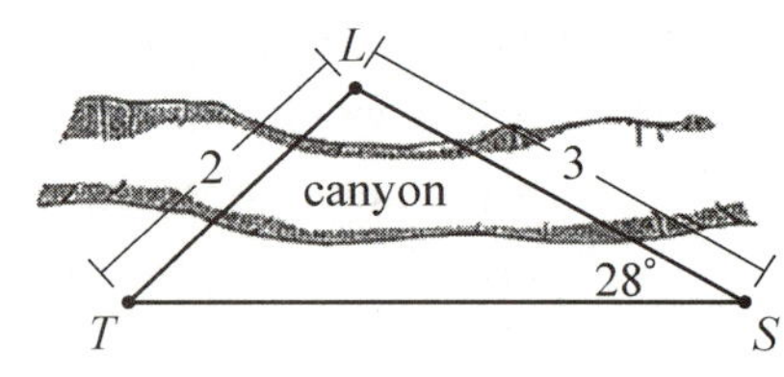

(Note: For a triangle with sides of length a, b, and c that are opposite $\angle A$, $\angle B$, and $\angle C$, respectively, $\frac{\sin A}{a} = \frac{\sin B}{b} = \frac{\sin C}{c}$).

F. $\frac{\sin T}{3} = \frac{\sin 28^\circ}{2}$　　G. $\frac{\sin T}{3} = 2$

H. $\frac{\sin T}{2} = \frac{\sin 28^\circ}{2}$　　J. $\frac{\sin 28^\circ}{T} = \frac{2}{3}$

K. $\sin T - \sin 28^\circ = 3 - 2$

48. The graph of $y = a\sin bx$ is shown below for certain positive values of a and b. One of the

following values is equal to a. Which one?

A. $\frac{1}{2}$

B. $\frac{2}{3}$

C. $\frac{3}{2}$

D. 2

E. 3

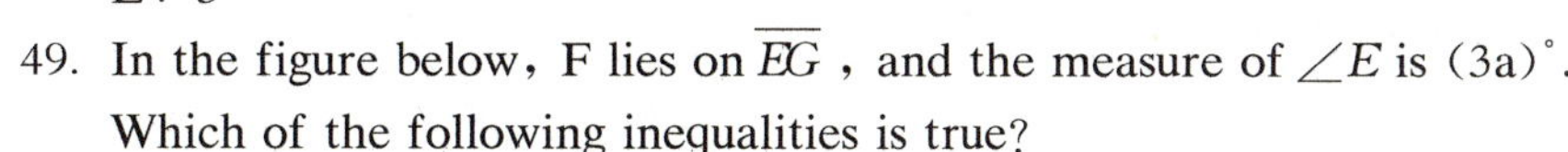
49. In the figure below, F lies on $\overline{EG}$, and the measure of $\angle E$ is $(3a)^{\circ}$. Which of the following inequalities is true?

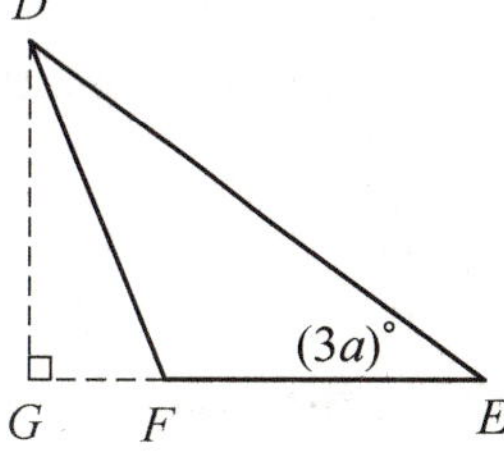

F. $0 < a < 30$　　G. $30 < a < 45$

H. $45 < a < 60$　　J. $60 < a < 90$

K. $90 < a < 180$

50. For all x such that $\tan x \neq 0$, the expression $\frac{\sec^2 x \cdot \sin x}{\tan x}$ is equivalent to which of the following?

(Note: $\sec x = \frac{1}{\cos x}$; $\tan x = \frac{\sin x}{\cos x}$)

F. 1　　G. $\cos x$　　H. $\cos^3 x$　　J. $\sec x$　　K. $\sec x . \tan^2 x$

51. The sides of an acute triangle measure 14 cm, 18 cm. and 20 cm, respectively. Which of the following equations, when solved for θ, gives the measure of the smallest angle of the triangle? (Note: For any triangle with sides of length a, b, and c that are opposite angles A, B, and C, respectively.

$\frac{\sin A}{a} = \frac{\sin B}{b} = \frac{\sin C}{c}$ and $c^2 = a^2 + b^2 - 2ab\cos C$.)

F. $\frac{\sin\theta}{14} = \frac{1}{18}$　　G. $\frac{\sin\theta}{14} = \frac{1}{20}$

H. $\frac{\sin\theta}{20} = \frac{1}{14}$　　J. $14^2 = 18^2 + 20^2 - 2(18)(20)\cos\theta$

K. $20^2 = 14^2 + 18^2 - 2(18)(20)\cos\theta$

52. What is $\sin\frac{\pi}{12}$ given that $\frac{\pi}{12} = \frac{\pi}{3} - \frac{\pi}{4}$ and that $\sin(\alpha - \beta) = (\sin\alpha)(\cos\beta) - (\cos\alpha)(\sin\beta)$?

(Note: You may use the following table of values.)

F. $\frac{1}{4}$　　G. $\frac{1}{2}$　　H. $\frac{\sqrt{3}-2}{4}$

J. $\frac{\sqrt{3}-\sqrt{2}}{2}$　　K. $\frac{\sqrt{6}-\sqrt{2}}{4}$

53. A trigonometric function with equation $y = a\sin(bx + c)$, where a, b, and c are real numbers, is graphed in the standard (x, y) coordinate plane below. The period of this function $f(x)$ is the smallest positive number p such that $f(x+p) = f(x)$ for every real number x. One of the following

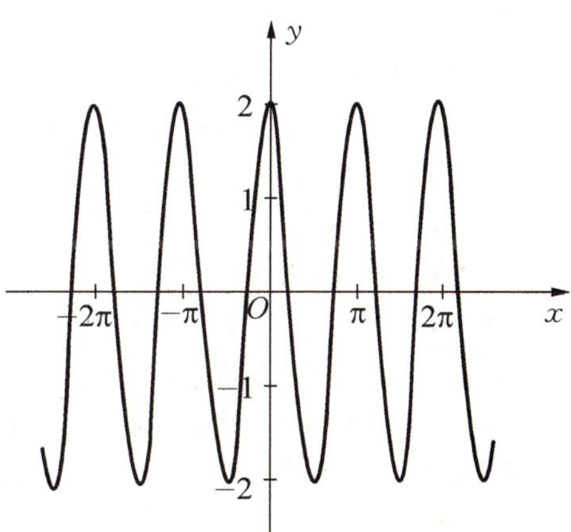

is the period of this function. Which one is it?

A. $\frac{\pi}{2}$　　B. π　　C. 2π　　D. 4π　　E. 2

54. A father and his son are standing near to each other on level ground late one afternoon so that their shadows end at the same place. The father is 75 inches tall, the son is 50 inches tall, and the father's shadow is 120 inches long, as shown in the figure below. Which of the following is closest to the distance, d inches, between the father and his son?

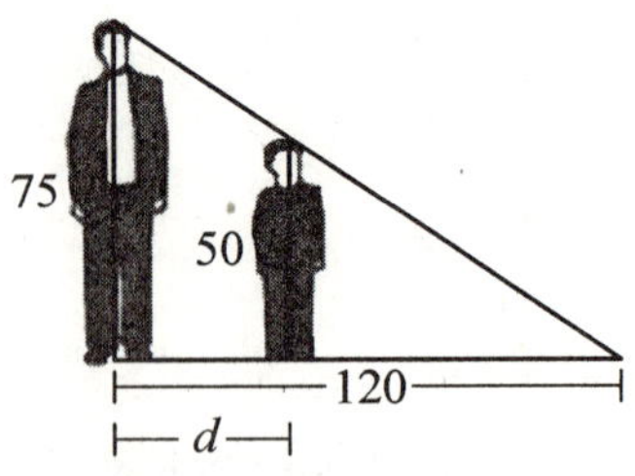

F. 25　　G. 40
H. 60　　J. 70
K. 80

55. In the figure below, $\triangle ACB$ is a right triangle with legs of length a units and b units, where $0 < a < b$, and hypotenuse of length c units. The triangles $\triangle YCA$, $\triangle ZBA$, and $\triangle XCB$ are equilateral. The area of an equilateral triangle with sides x units long is $\frac{\sqrt{3}}{4}x^2$ square units.

What is the perimeter of pentagon $AZBCY$, in units?

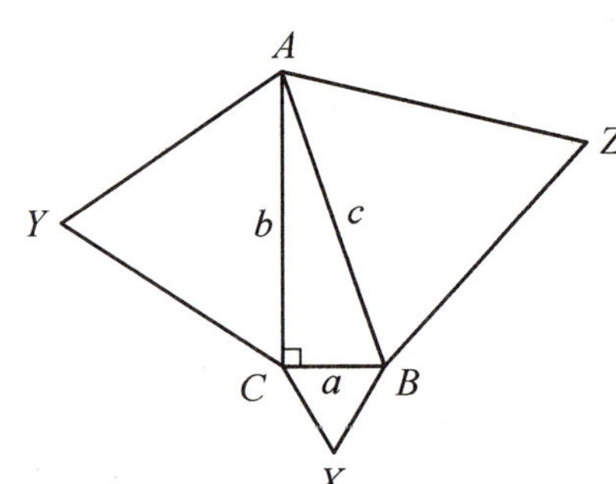

F. $a+b+2c$　　G. $a+2b+2c$
H. $a+3b+3c$　　J. $2a+2b+2c$
K. $3a+3b+3c$

56. For all values of a and b such that $0 < a < b$, which of the following lists the angles $\angle XCY$, $\angle CAZ$, and $\angle CBZ$ in order of their measures from least to greatest?

A. $\angle CBZ$, $\angle XCY$, $\angle CAZ$　　B. $\angle CBZ$, $\angle CAZ$, $\angle XCY$
C. $\angle XCY$, $\angle CAZ$, $\angle CBZ$　　D. $\angle CAZ$, $\angle CBZ$, $\angle XCY$
E. $\angle CAZ$, $\angle XCY$, $\angle CBZ$

57. If $b = 2a$, what is $\tan(\angle ABC)$?

F. 2　　G. $\frac{1}{2}$　　H. $\frac{1}{\sqrt{5}}$　　J. $\frac{2}{\sqrt{5}}$　　K. $\sqrt{5}$

58. If the sides of a triangle are 8, 15, and 17 units long, what is the measure of the angle formed by the two shortest sides?

F. 30°　　G. 45°　　H. 60°　　J. 75°　　K. 90°

59. $\triangle STR$ below has angle measures 90, θ, and β degrees as shown. Which of the following is true for all possible value of θ and β?

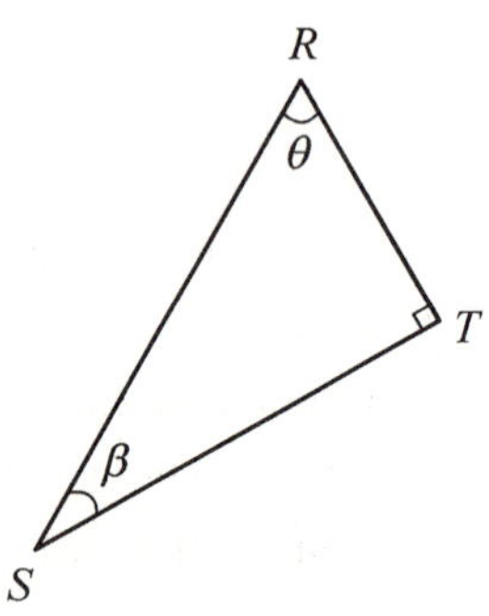

A. $\tan\theta = \tan\beta$
B. $\sin\theta = \cos\beta$
C. $\sin\theta \times \cos\beta = 1$
D. $\tan\theta \times \sin\beta = 1$
E. $\sin\theta\tan\beta = \cos\beta$

60. In $\triangle PQR$ below, if $\tan x > 1$, all of the following must be true EXCEPT:

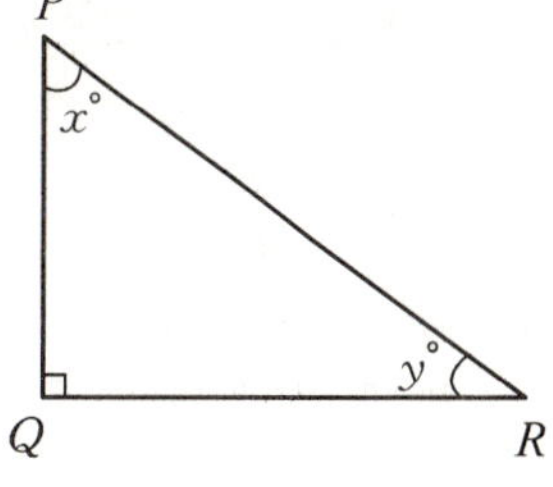

A. $x > 45$

B. $y > 45$

C. $\overline{PQ} \neq \overline{QR}$

D. $x + y = 90$

E. $x \neq y$

61. An isosceles triangle has two sides of length 3 feet each. The angle formed by the two 3-foot sides measures 32°. What is the length of the triangle's third side?

F. 3cos 32°　　G. 3sin 32°　　H. 3sin 16°　　J. 6tan 16°　　K. 6sin 16°

62. In the standard (x, y) coordinate plan, the amplitude of a graph is half the distance between the graph's minimum and maximum y-values. What is the amplitude of the graph of equation $y - 1 = 2\cos 3\theta$?

F. 6　　G. 3　　H. 2　　J. $\frac{3}{2}$　　K. 1

63. What is the smallest positive value for x where $y = \sin 2x$ reaches its maximum?

A. $\frac{\pi}{4}$　　B. π　　C. $\frac{3\pi}{2}$　　D. 2π　　E. $\frac{5\pi}{2}$

[**Session 6 答案**]

1 D	2 C	3 G	4 D	5 K	6 F	7 F	8 H	9 A	10 G
11 A	12 A	13 G	14 C	15 K	16 J	17 J	18 C	19 K	20 G
21 D	22 J	23 F	24 B	25 J	26 E	27 B	28 F	29 D	30 F
31 C	32 K	33 J	34 J	35 D	36 F	37 A	38 A	39 B	40 D
41 B	42 J	43 J	44 C	45 J	46 F	47 F	48 A	49 F	50 J
51 J	52 K	53 B	54 G	55 G	56 D	57 F	58 K	59 B	60 B
61 K	62 H	63 A							

[**Session 6 答案解析**]

1. 题干：A 是锐角，$\sin A = \frac{12}{13}$，$\tan A$ 的可能值是多少？

解析：根据同角正弦和余弦的平方和＝1，求出 $\cos A$。注意是锐角。

2. 题干：$0° \leqslant x° \leqslant 90°$，$2\sin^2 x° - 1 = 0$，$x° = ?$

解析：$\sin^2 x = 0.5$。

3. 题干：$\frac{\tan\theta}{\sin\theta}$ 等价于？

解析：即余弦的倒数。

4. 题干：$\sin\alpha = \frac{3}{4}$，a 是锐角，求 $\cos a$。

解析：利用同角正弦和余弦的平方和＝1。

5. 题干：怎么表示 AB 的长度？

解析：$\dfrac{250}{\sin 70^\circ}$

6. 题干：$\tan\beta\tan\gamma=$？

解析：可以全部用边来表示，然后会消掉。

7. 题干：梯子和地面成 75 度夹角，如何表示梯子底部和直角点的距离？

解析：画图。

8. 题干：$\dfrac{\sqrt{1-\cos^2 x}}{\sin x}+\dfrac{\sqrt{1-\sin^2 x}}{\cos x}=?0<x<\dfrac{\pi}{2}$

解析：同角正弦和余弦的平方和＝1。

9. 解析：余角之和等于 90°。

10. 题干：角 α 的顶点位于原点，一边是 x 正轴，另一边在第二象限。$\sin\alpha=\dfrac{\sqrt{3}}{2}$，求 $\cos 2\alpha$。

解析：同角正弦和余弦的平方和＝1，求出余弦值，然后利用倍角公式。

11. 题干：$y=\sin bx$ 在某区间内与 x 轴有 k 个交点，那么 $y=2\sin bx$ 在这个区间内与 x 轴有几个交点？

解析：周期没变。

12. 题干：求叶片顶点的距离。

解析：利用余弦定理。

13. 题干：$r=40\sin(2\theta)$。为什么角度为 45° 时 r 最大？

解析：注意 2θ。

14. 解析：利用 $\tan 50^\circ$。

15. 题干：$\sec^2 x+\tan^2 x$ 等价于？$\cos x\neq 0$，$\sin x\neq 0$。

解析：上下同时除以余弦的平方。

16. 题干：三角形一个边是 7 英寸，最小的可能周长是多少？边长都是整数。

解析：短边之和必须大于第三边。

17. 题干：$\sin\alpha=\dfrac{4}{5}$，求 h。

解析：可以根据右下角的三角形求出斜边，然后再算上面的三角形。

18. 解析：利用 $\tan 68^\circ$。

19. 题干：哪个角的正弦值最小？

解析：正弦值等于对边比斜边。

20. 题干：面积 32，$xz=8$，求 yw？

解析：三角形面积公式。

21. 题干：求周长？

解析：利用勾股定理。

22. 题干：一个直角三角形，一个直角边是 80，对应角为 28.1°，另一个边是 180。保持 180 的不变，延长 80 的，延长多少能使得其对应的角边长 40？

解析：分别计算前后两个三角形，然后比较。

23. 题干：直角三角形，三边 20 cm，21 cm 和 29 cm，20 cm 对应角的 tan 值是多少？

解析：先确定斜边是哪个。

24. 解析：余弦定理。
25. 题干：求圆的面积。
    解析：利用勾股定理求出半径。
26. 题干：$0° < x < 90°$，$\tan x = \frac{3}{7}$，求 $\cos x + \sin x$。
    解析：还有一个条件即同角正弦和余弦的平方和为 1。
27. 题干：求边长。
    解析：余弦定理或者正弦定理。
28. 题干：$4\sin x\cos x$ 等价于？
    解析：$\sin(x+y) = \sin x\cos y + \cos x\sin y$。
29. 题干：$y(x) = 3\cos(5x-4)+1$ 的定义域是实数范围。y 的函数值范围是什么？
    解析：单个三角函数的最大值是 1，最小值是 −1。
30. 题干：$\sin^2 A + \sin^2 B = ?$
    解析：小于 2。
31. 题干：求边长。
    解析：从三边都已知的三角形可以求出各角的大小。
32. 题干：$\tan\phi = -\frac{7}{24}$，ϕ 介于直角和平角之间。$\sin\phi = ?$
    解析：根据同角正弦和余弦的平方和为 1。
33. 题干：求 $\cos\theta$。
    解析：$360° - \theta$ 的余弦和 θ 的余弦是一样的。
34. 题干：第一个三角形面积为 30，求第二个三角形面积。
    解析：三角形面积等于两边之积乘以夹角正弦值。
35. 题干：$p(x, y) = 4x + 3y$。当点位于阴影内，P 的最大值是多少？
    解析：把 P 当成 y 函数的一个参数。做出 y 关于 x 的直线。
36. 题干：$p(x, y) = 4x + 3y$ 的点在哪些象限出现？
    解析：画图。
37. 题干：
    $\tan\angle BCA = ?$
    解析：4 除以 4。
38. 题干：如何表示 θ？
    解析：反函数。
39. 题干：求开始点和终点的距离。
    解析：利用余弦定理。
40. 题干：三角形中，角 a 是 $47°$，角 b 是 $76°$，BC 长 18，求 AC 的长度。
    解析：先画出草图，然后看用正弦定理还是余弦定理。
41. 题干：$\cos x = -\frac{1}{3}$，$\cos 2x = ?$
    解析：同角正弦和余弦的平方和 = 1。$(\cos x)^2 = \frac{1+\cos 2x}{2}$
42. 题干：$\sin\theta = 0.4$，$\cos\theta = ?$
    解析：同角正弦和余弦的平方和为 1。

43. 题干：$\sin x > \frac{1}{2}\cos x$ 等价于?

解析：移项。

44. 解析：先求出$\angle ADB$ 的值，然后求出边 BD 的值。

45. 题干：$\cos\theta = ?$

解析：先算 0.5θ 的余弦和正弦值。

46. 题干：$\tan\theta \cdot \cos\theta$ 等价于什么?$\sin\theta = \frac{2}{3}$，$0 < \theta < \frac{\pi}{2}$。

解析：$\tan\theta = \sin\theta/\cos\theta$。

47. 题干：角 T 等于多少?

解析：角 T 正弦值比 3，等于 $\sin 28^\circ$ 比 2。

48. 题干：$y = a\sin bx$，$A = ?$

解析：a 即振幅。

49. 题干：下列哪个不等式是正确的?

解析：已经有一个直角，所以$\angle E$ 不可能是直角。

50. 题干：$\frac{\sec^2 x \cdot \sin x}{\tan x}$ 等价于?$\tan x \neq 0$。

解析：先把 tan x 用 sin x 和 cos x 表示。$\sec x = \frac{1}{\cos x}$；$\tan x = \frac{\sin x}{\cos x}$

51. 题干：三角形边长分别为 14 cm，18 cm，20 cm，最小的边对应的角为 θ，哪个式子正确?

解析：$\frac{\sin A}{a} = \frac{\sin B}{b} = \frac{\sin C}{c}$，$c^2 = a^2 + b^2 - 2ab\cos C$

52. 题干：$\sin\frac{\pi}{12} = ?\frac{\pi}{12} = \frac{\pi}{3} - \frac{\pi}{4}$，$\sin(\alpha - \beta) = (\sin\alpha)(\cos\beta) - (\cos\alpha)(\sin\beta)$

解析：把角度拆开，按照提示拆分。

53. 题干：求周期。

解析：找到最近的同相位点。

54. 题干：求 d。

解析：利用相似三角形。

55. 题干：$\triangle YCA$，$\triangle ZBA$ 和 $\triangle XCB$ 相似，求 $AZBCY$ 的周长。

解析：相似三角形。根据比例求未知边。

56. 题干：$0 < a < b$，给 $\angle XCY$，$\angle CAZ$，$\angle CBZ$ 从小到大排序。

解析：大角对大边。

57. 题干：如果 $b = 2a$，$\tan(\angle ABC) = ?$

解析：tan 是对边除以邻边。

58. 题干：三边长 8，15，17。两短边组成的角是多少度?

解析：余弦定理。

59. 题干：哪个说法正确的?

解析：可以用 θ 来代替 β。

60. 题干：$\tan x > 1$，哪个说法错误?

解析：y 应该小于 45°。

61. 题干：等腰三角形，两腰长 3，夹角为 32°，底边长多少?

解析：余弦定理。

62. 题干：$y-1=2\cos 3\theta$ 图像的振幅？
    解析：振幅只跟三角函数前的系数有关。
63. 题干：$y=\sin 2x$ 有最大值，x 最小可以是多少？ x 为正数。
    解析：即 $2x=\pi/2$。

第三部分

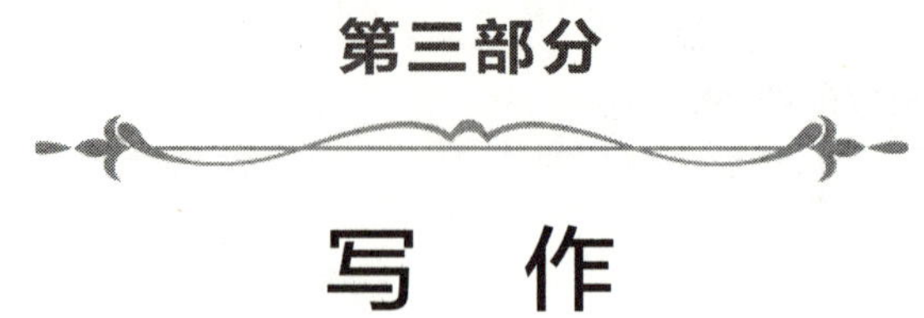

写 作

一、ACT写作总论

改革始末：在2015年9月，ACT对于写作部分做了一系列的变革。其中包括时间、话题范围、考试方式、评分标准和算分办法的改变。因为我们知道另外一个考试组织方Collegeboard对SAT也进行了变革，尤其是新SAT写作部分，变成了分析性写作，直接考查学生的阅读、分析和写作的综合能力，弱化了考试备考的技巧性和投机成分。迫于竞争对手的考试变革压力，ACT也相应地对其写作部分做了较大的变动。我们先具体看看其变化的细节。

新旧ACT写作对比：

1. 考试时间

[改革前]总时间长度为30分钟，文章体裁要求为议论文。

[改革后]总时间长度为40分钟，文章体裁要求为剖析性议论文。

2. 话题范围

[改革前]基本集中于考查教育类话题。

[改革后]考查更普遍多样的社会话题。

3. 考题方式

[改革前]试题提供正反两方观念供参考，需考生独立表达观点，可与题干观点不一致。

[改革后]试题提供三方观点，须对所给观点分别进行剖析，基本属于较复杂问题，必须与题干观点结合讨论。

4. 评分标准

[改革前]主要从考生文章谈论的复杂度、观点展开、文章组织及语言表达进行评分。

[改革后]四个范畴评价：观点和分析（Ideas and Analysis）、文章观点展开与论证支持（Development and Support）、文章组织（Organization）、语言应用和语法（Language Use and Conventions）

5. 算分办法

[改革前]两位阅卷人评分，分别依照1～6分评价，加和汇总。例如两位阅卷人的分数分别是6分、5分，考生最后的得分为11分。

[改革后]两位阅卷人评分，每人在4个范畴内依照1～6分评价，最后每个范畴加和汇总，即每个范畴得分区间2～12分。例如两位阅卷人分数分别是：3、3、3、3，3、3、3、3，最后得分为6、6、6、6。另外，除了每个范畴的得分外，考生还会取得一个最终换算的1～36分范围内的写作总分。

Session 1 评分标准

1. 详细评分标准

Score	Ideas and Analysis	Development and Support	Organization	Language Use and Conventions
6： 能够在写议论文中证明有效的写作技能。	作者写出跟题干相关的观点。作者观点要有一定的深度和思想。观点要确立并在深刻理解基础上使用原文，并且对不同观点进行分析。分析必须触及隐含意义、观点复杂性和张力，以及潜在的假设。	观点的展开要有见解和深度。整体推理过程要有效地传递观点的意义。让步和综合性会使得观点得以强化和润色。	作者文章要体现出很好的组织策略。文章要有一个核心观点和立场，组织观点的逻辑性会增加作者论述的有效性。段落间的起承转合能够加强各个观点的关系。	通过遣词造句增强论证。遣词要准确地道。句子结构要多变和清晰。风格和语域的选择要得当，包括态度语气。允许有少量语法错误存在，但是要做到不影响理解。
5： 能够在写议论文中证明很好的写作技能。	作者写出切合题干的观点，此观点要有一定深度，且对原文要有一定理解和分析。分析必须触及隐含意义、观点复杂性和张力，以及潜在的假设。	观点的展开要有一定的见解和深度。大部分推理过程要有效地传递观点的意义。让步和综合性会使得观点得以强化。	作者文章要体现出不错的组织策略。文章要有一个核心观点和立场，有较强的逻辑性来增强文章的叙述。段落间的起承转合必须流畅。	遣词造句需符合文章整体。用词要准确。句子结构要清楚和多变。风格和语言的选择要得当，允许一些语法错误存在，但不能影响理解。
4： 能够在写议论文中证明较好的写作技能。	作者写出符合题干的观点，此观点表明写作目的和中心思想，且要与原文的分析和理解相关。分析涉及隐含意义、观点复杂性和张力，以及潜在的假设。	观点的展开表明见解和深度。推理过程有效地传递观点的意义。让步和综合性能够传递观点。	作者文章能体现出一定的组织策略，有核心观点和立场，有不错的逻辑性来增强文章的叙述。段落间的起承转合能符合上下文。	遣词造句能符合文章整体。用词得当，句子结构要清楚，适当地进行结构的转变。风格和语言要适当，允许语法错误存在，但基本不能影响理解。
3： 能够在写议论文中证明尚可的部分写作技能。	作者能写出观点，此观点能表明部分写作目的和中心思想，且基本与原文的分析和理解相关。分析简单，有时不清晰。	观点能展开，但比较笼统和简单。推理过程能表明观点，但有重复和偏离。	作者文章能体现基础的组织策略。文章观点大致连贯，逻辑性尚可。段落间的起承转合偶尔能体现段落间的关系。	遣词造句基本能符合文章整体，用词基本得当，有基本的句型变化。风格和语言偶尔不适当，有明显的语法错误，但大体上不影响理解。

(续表)

Score	Ideas and Analysis	Development and Support	Organization	Language Use and Conventions
2：在写议论文中缺乏连贯性。	作者提出的观点不能充分符合题干，且此观点基本不能表明写作目的和中心思想。观点分析不到位，不相关，或者冗长重复。	观点和论点比较模糊或者不连贯。推理论证过程不充分，没有逻辑，无法清晰地证明观点。	作者文章能体现最基本的组织策略。文章观点不连贯，不清晰。段落间没有起承转合或运用得较差。	遣词造句不连贯，不清楚。用词不得当，句子结构不清晰。风格和语言不能体验文章主旨。明显的语言错误，且时常影响理解。
1：在写议论文中无任何写作技巧。	作者无法提出相对应的观点，且写作目的不明确。分析过程严重离题。	观点没有展开，且缺乏论点。推理论证过程不清楚，不连贯，或缺乏推理过程。	作者文章不能体现组织策略。没有文章观点。段落与段落间缺少联系。	遣词造句无法体验文章主旨，用词不准确，难以理解。句子结构不清楚，风格和语言不清晰，存在大量的语法错误，影响理解。

2. 官方范文分析

Intelligent Machines

Many of the goods and services we depend on daily are now supplied by intelligent, automated machines rather than human beings. Robots build cars and other goods on assembly lines, where once there were human workers. Many of our phone conversations are now conducted not with people but with sophisticated technologies. We can now buy goods at a variety of stores without the help of a human cashier. Automation is generally seen as a sign of progress, but what is lost when we replace humans with machines? Given the accelerating variety and prevalence of intelligent machines, it is worth examining the implications and meaning of their presence in our lives.

Read and carefully consider these perspectives. Each suggests a particular way of thinking about the increasing presence of intelligent machines.

Perspective One

What we lose with the replacement of people by machines is some part of our own humanity.

Even our mundane daily encounters no longer require from us basic courtesy, respect, and tolerance for other people.

Perspective Two

Machines are good at low-skill, repetitive jobs, and at high-speed, extremely precise jobs.

In both cases they work better than humans. This efficiency leads to a more prosperous and progressive world for everyone.

Perspective Three

Intelligent machines challenge our long-standing ideas about what humans are or can be. This is good because it pushes both humans and machines toward new, unimagined possibilities.

Essay Task

Write a unified, coherent essay in which you evaluate multiple perspectives on the increasing presence of intelligent machines. In your essay，be sure to：

- analyze and evaluate the perspectives given
- state and develop your own perspective on the issue
- explain the relationship between your perspective and those given

Your perspective may be in full agreement with any of the others，in partial agreement，or wholly different. Whatever the case，support your ideas with logical reasoning and detailed，persuasive examples.

［构思］

试卷上的笔记将不计分。

考生可以利用空白部分来列提纲，需要考虑以下几个方面：

(1) 试题中给出的三个观点的优缺点是什么。

- 它们所要表达的是什么，同时它们各自忽略了什么。
- 它们为何能说服别人，或者为何不能说服别人。

(2) 关于考生自己的知识，经验和价值

- 对于这个话题，考生自己的观点是什么。这些观点的优缺点各是什么。
- 考生将如何在自己的文章中支持自己的观点。

1 分范文

观点和分析：1 分

文章观点展开与论证支持：1 分

文章组织：1 分

语言应用和语法：1 分

Begin WRITING TEST Here.

Well Machines are good but they take people jobs like if they don't know how to use it they get fired and they'll find someone else and it's more easyer with machines but sometimes they don't need people because of this machines do there own job and there be many people that lack on there job but the intelligent machines sometimes may not work or they'll brake easy and it's waste of money on this machines and there really expensive to buy but they help alot at the same time it help alot but at the same time this intelligent machines work and some don't work but many store buy them and end up broken or not working but many stores gets them and end up wasting money on this intelligent machines' but how does it help us and the comunity because some people get fired because they do not need him because of this machines many people are losing job's because of this machines.

［**得分解析**］

观点和分析：1 分

文章缺少主旨，作者的写作意图难以体现。作者表达了一些观点，但是并没有展开论证。举个例子，“由于新科技的应用，人们开始失业”这个观点是很好的，但是作者并没有深入探究和分析。

文章观点展开与论证支持：1 分

作者没有展开观点，且文章中有大量的重复观点和缺乏论据的论点。这篇文章的很多问题都可以归纳为没有合理地展开。如果作者没有解释阐明观点，那么观点和问题或者论点之间的关系就会很模糊。

文章组织：1 分

这篇文章并没有一个明确的中心思想，并且两个观点之间也没有很好的逻辑衔接。文章以“由于科技，人们可能会失业”这样的观点来开头和结尾，但观点不连贯，整体没有清晰的结构。读者无法从过渡句来理解观点之间的关系，且连接词反而把不相关的信息联系起来了。

语言应用和语法：1 分

本篇文章没有运用恰当的语言来阐述观点。大量的用法、标点错误等影响了理解。用词重复单一，表达不到位。语言使用的缺乏使得文章更难以理解。

2 分范文

观点和分析：2 分

文章观点展开与论证支持：2 分

文章组织：2 分

语言应用和语法：2 分

Begin WRITING TEST Here.

Should machines be used to do good and services instead humans? I believe they should not for many reasons. Machines can not be smart unless a human is controling it. So it would not matter if its an intelligent machine or not a human is still controlling it to do everything.

When using a machine it could easily malfunction and it could be hard to fix the problem or it will just take a while to fix it. If a human is taking over instead of the machine there may be fewer problems. Machines have so many problems that it would not be worth having.

Also, the more machines you have the less jobs there are for people because everyone thinks it would be better to have machines instead of people. When less people are out of work that means less money for those people and sometimes they will lose their homes or cars because they can not afford anything.

Sometimes working with machines can be very stressful because they may not work at times or they could be running extremely slow and won't get anything done. Machines are not smart at all, only when people are controlling them they are but not all the time. It may seem smart but its really not.

In conclusion, I think machines should not be used to take over a human job because machines can not think only humans can think and make right or wrong decisions. Machines do not have brains, their not wired to think so why have them do stuff that we can do ourselves.

[**得分解析**]

观点和分析：2 分

观点切入点太窄，因此作者无法就 3 个观点展开分析。当作者无法提炼自己的观点时，就无法明确自己的观点和既定观点间的联系。作者只是简单地阐述了为什么机器不能代替人工的 3 个理由，而没有考虑成熟科技背后的潜在影响。并且，这 3 个理由之间关系疏松，和文章给出的观点之间的联系也不够紧密。总之，此篇文章没有清晰地表达观点和目的。

文章观点展开与论证支持：2 分

文章的展开方式没有清晰地表明论点的意思。在主体第一段中，作者通过对比表明了机器时常会坏掉，但人不会。但是，此段写作只是单纯地重复，并没有深入展开观点。同样地，第二段提出了合理的观点，却没有论据。第三段仅仅重复了作者的第一个理由。因此，文章的观点没有得到展

开,论证也没有得到支持。

文章组织:2 分

文章的分段形式体现了一定的文章结构,但段落之间缺乏连接性。第一段提出了一个重要的观点(machines are not intelligent; intelligent humans control them),但是在后文中却忽略了此观点,直到后来作者在解释为什么机器引发压力时才又重新阐述。文章的最后一段阐述了两个关系不明的观点。虽然作者使用了一些过渡词,但这些过渡词无法表明观点之间的联系。

语言应用和语法:2 分

用词不当,句子结构不明会影响理解,比如,"When less people are out of work that means less money for those people; Machines can not be smart unless a human is controlling it. So it would not matter if its an intelligent machine". 此外,一些用法的错误也会让读者困惑。此篇文章中,语言不连贯,观点表达不流畅。

3 分范文

观点和分析:3 分

文章观点展开与论证支持:3 分

文章组织:3 分

语言应用和语法:3 分

Begin WRITING TEST Here.

Intelligent Machines

Machines have taken a huge role in our day-to-day lives. They can either effect us in a good way or in a bad way. Granted, machines have impacted many people in the workplace but they help us finish the jobs. There are many ups and downs to the development of machines.

Some people have become so dependent on machines they start to lose their "humanity". Machines can take away the personal aspect of life. For example, we lose basic courtesy, respect, and tolerance for people due to using machines so much. Some machines that could make that happen are; cellphones, computers, and video games. When people purchase one of these machines they usually are on it and depend on it all the time. Due to the lack of self-motivation through machines we could lose our common courtesy.

In the workplace, machines have effected jobs dramatically. They can perform at low-skill repetitive jobs and at high-speed precise jobs. They mostly are better than humans because they are more precise within their work and they are less likely to produce an error. Although machines do help the workplace, they can also harm it as well. By the advancement of so many machines, an abundance of people are losing their jobs due to them. Machines can have a positive and negative effect in the workplace.

Although machines have a good amount of drawbacks, they also have a positive amount on us today. Due to the advancement of machines people are starting to push themselves to a whole new level. People are becoming more educated and precise in the workplace. Also, many people are starting to study machines and enter new, unimagined possibilties into the world! Machines can change the world in a positive way as well as a negative way.

In conclusion, machines effect the lives of everybody in our world today. Whether they effect us in our home or on the job they continue to change people's outlook on trying new ideas. The development of machines has its ups and downs. For example, they motivate people to work harder in order to compete with them. Although, they can demolish our common courtesy, machines play a huge role in technology today and will continue to shape the world's future.

[得分解析]

观点和分析：3 分

在第一段中，作者给出了一个中心论点，提示此篇文章将围绕一个主题展开："ups and downs to the development of machines"。但是，这个观点却不够正确。作者自己的观点很清晰，但分析过于简单。作者并没有辩证地去思考这些观点，因此没有有效地展开讨论。作者尝试着去理解论点潜在的含义，比如去讨论工作中使用机器的好处和坏处，但是这些分析并没有引出对更进一步的暗示和潜在的猜测。

文章观点展开与论证支持：3 分

文章观点过于笼统。在每个段落里，作者都进行了展开论述，但并没有更一步的阐明。一些有效的观点，比如对于工人的影响，都提到了，却没有得以展开。即使作者表明了观点，却没有阐述此观点的重要性，比如为什么了解智能机器很重要，更进一步的观点是什么。

文章组织：3 分

尽管 5 段式的结构表明了作者的观点，但过度依赖这样的文章结构也限制了文章的整体效果。文章围绕着优缺点展开，但段落与段落之间的联系很疏松，比如工作中机器的优缺点和个人生活中的优缺点，或者针对优缺点的讨论之间的联系。没有这些关联，文章也无法得到完全的展开。

语言应用和语法：3 分

文章运用了基础的语言。即使作者的观点表达得很清楚，语言上的问题还是存在着，比如语言不准确(Machines have taken a huge role, Due to the lack of self-motivation through machines)，词汇匮乏，句子结构拖沓等情况。

4 分范文

观点和分析：4 分

文章观点展开与论证支持：4 分

文章组织：4 分

语言应用和语法：4 分

Begin WRITING TEST Here.

As modern civilized society progresses into the future, the less civilized we have become. Though machines may benefit our society and growth, they also have important draw-backs. In relying on machines as employees, many human employees suffer negative economic consequences. Robots built entirely for the purpose of bringing the future of tomorrow into the present of today also eliminate opportunities of human-to-human interactions.

As the dream of tomorrow's future becomes ever closer, machines have become more refined and civilized where as humans have lost the ability to display even the most basic courtesy let alone show mutual respect to one another. A variety of machines such as self-checkouts can perform simple tasks. These usually offer convenience and time to their users, but the effect is lost opportunity for the human being to engage in civilized interaction. The more these opportunities disappear, the less understanding and respect we have for one another. Convenience also is taking on greater importance. As machines evolve and we devolve, there seems to be a greater push for

machines to become more innovative and precise, enabling their users to have everything at their finger tips. "Smart" phones, for example, have made it very easy to participate in "social networking" which has led people to believe they are being more social. But because interactions that require some "soul connection" are becoming harder and harder, this "social networking" seems to de-socialize us as people.

Machines are increasingly popular in the workplace. Though there are financial benefits to machine labor, they are restricted to a handful of people. And there are no benefits to those who lose their jobs. The increased job loss will effect the overall economy, but it will also create more tension between people in society and mean more de-socialization. Even though society itself has also benefited from advances in technology (from indoor plumbing to instant communication), pursuing it too hard leads to an obsession that is harming humanity.

With more and more machines "making our lives easier" and promoting "progress," there seems to be a decline of growth in humanity. The role of machines should maintain a focus on those that are used to "help" us as a whole, not "do" for us as individuals. Though machine have displayed superb ability for bringing us into the future, the loss of human jobs as well as ettiquitte should not be swept aside. Too much of a good thing can in the end become bad.

[得分解析]

观点和分析：4 分

此篇文章清晰地阐明了论点和观点。对于观点的分析遵循了一定的规则：我们赞成机器会促进发展(观点二)，新的科技会带给我们想象中的未来(观点三)，但是我们必须承认的是，科技带来的便捷是有消极作用的(观点一)。作者利用了一些假设来强调这些观点，并且表明了它的复杂性。作者没有明显地提到给出的三个观点，但这些观点和作者自己的观点联系清晰。

文章观点展开与论证支持：4 分

论证过程较为清晰。作者提供了两个观点，分别阐述了人和机器的关系是对社会有害的。作者阐述了新科技的几个方面，比如，作者认为社交网络鼓励了人们参加社会活动，然后通过讨论社交媒体提供的社交活动是否真正有用来进一步阐述观点。最后，作者总结得出机器得到更多的关注。

文章组织：4 分

组织结构清晰。开头段介绍了两个方面，智能机器的好处和经济结果。此后，作者引出了自己的观点，机器应该在某些特定的领域发挥它的作用。文章有转承启合，尤其是段落内的联接。比如："Convenience also is taking on greater importance; Even though society itself has also benefitted。"

语言应用和语法：4 分

语言清晰，选词多样，比如"civilized and social networking (alongside de-socialize)"。句子结构多变，增加了阅读的趣味，讽刺手法的使用，比如，"bringing the future of tomorrow into the present of today"，强调了作者的观点。

5 分范文

观点和分析：5 分

文章观点展开与论证支持：5 分

文章组织：5 分

语言应用和语法：5 分

Begin WRITING TEST Here.

It is no secret that today's workforce no longer consists entirely of people. Rather, machines are being developed to complete many of the tasks which humans have traditionally done. This can greatly increase productivity and efficiency of simple, repetitive tasks. Many people view this as a great positive and point out that it leads to a more uniform and less expensive product which is better for everyone. However, some people are more wary of this popular trend of automating the workforce and question whether this progress is truely positive. Their concerns, though, are outweighed by the benefits these machines offer.

It is the popular view among companies which are moving toward automation that robots can do many tasks better than humans. For example, in the automotive industry, most of a car's individual components are manufactured by pre-programmed robots which have much greater and more precise output than would be possible for a human. In addition, robots cut down the cost of production by a considerable amount. If a company hires an employee to complete a simple task for \$50,000 per year but could instead buy a machine for a one time purchase of \$30,000, it is far more cost effective to buy the machine. Lower cost of production means that the goods produced can now be sold at a lower pricepoint which passes the savings on to the consumer. Companies producing goods rightly contend that the use of machines to complete low-skill jobs has only positive impact for everyone.

Beyond these benefits for industry, some believe that machines will shape the future for the human race. Innovation and invention of new more intelligent machines can push us as humans toward new, unimagined possibilities. For example, before the first airplane was invented, people could only dream of human flight, but at the moment of takeoff, a whole new world of unimaginable possibilities was suddenly within our grasp. Through even just that one invention, an entire multi-billion dollar a year industry was born, and our lives improved and advanced in a multitude of ways. Who can know what great advancements may be brought about by a more intelligent machine than what we possess today? The possibilities are endless.

There are those who are less enthusiastic about all this progress and advancement. They argue that by not having to interact with fellow humans, we no longer are required to be courteous and have tolerance for others. While this may be true, this is a minor cost for a major increase in efficiency. Take the example of self checkout systems in grocery stores. Self checkout permits consumers to procure their goods and get out of the store quickly. This might seem like a small time-saver, but considering how often this experience is repeated reveals a cumulative effect. Across time, consumers end up saving hours, which improves the efficiency of their daily lives, allowing them to spend time on things that are of greater interest and meaning to them.

Whether humans like it or not, machines are becoming more and popular in the workplace and are decreasing the need for humans to work those jobs. This can lead to advancement of society, a greater end product or service, and even a lower consumer cost of goods. Many people are frightened of change, but unfortunately for them, the past is gone and now we must look to the future.

[得分解析]

观点和分析：5 分

有多样的观点，正反两方面分析充分到位，文章中，作者从对于工业的好处延伸到对于消费者

的好处。在阐述反方观点时，作者提出智能机器在某些地方，如杂货铺中，减少了人与人之间的交流，但是提出这也是一种好的现象，因为它更快捷便利了。作者通过阐述了这两个矛盾的观点，从而促使文章的展开。

文章观点展开与论证支持：5 分

全文主旨清晰。每段的论证过程逐步阐明了为什么作者认为智能机器的优点大于缺点。在阐述过程中，作者通过假设回答了之前的问题，比如，当作者提到使用机器人大大地减少了货品的价格，她回答了人工售卖和低于人工售卖三分之一价格的机器售卖之间的关系。之后作者进一步阐明了机器售卖的物品价格将更低，消费者将是最终获益者。一步步通过严谨的论证来支持和展开观点。

文章组织：5 分

文章结构合理。开头段中作者提出了总论点，且在下文中依次展开：作者首先描述了智能机器普及的好处，再逐步展开反方观点。文中适当地采用了过渡，使文章更流畅紧凑。

语言应用和语法：5 分

用词准确，句子结构多变，观点表达清晰。文章整体风格中不同的修辞手法，更好地阐述了主题。

6 分范文

观点和分析：6 分

文章观点展开与论证支持：6 分

文章组织：6 分

语言应用和语法：6 分

Begin WRITING TEST Here.

Advances in technology have become so widely accepted in today's culture that very few people are willing to pause to consider the consequences. People get so excited about what new technologies can offer that they forget to question whether there might be any negative effects. Without caution and deliberation, replacing the natural with the mechanical would undoubtedly be disasterous.

The economic implications of the potential mechanical takeover alone should be enough to dissuade anyone from moving too fast. In the event the robots are more widely used in the workplace, humans would surely be replaced. At first, businesses would benefit from the efficiency of robots, but eventually a depressed job market would lead to a population that struggles just to feed themselves and their families, let alone purchase the products these robots make. In the long run, society will suffer if it does not take care to prevent the economic consequences of giving everything over to machines.

Our careless use of automation has already taken a toll on our culture. People have been interacting with automation in nearly every aspect of their lives, whether it be shopping, banking, or the use of a telephone. The effect of this is obvious: basic respect for our fellow man is all but absent today because of increased interaction with automation. Why treat a machine with kindness? It suffers no emotional or psychological damage. In a culture saturated with automation, we get used to treating machines rudely, and we begin to treat each other rudely. This of course leads to all sorts of issues, like intolerence and incivility, and in the long run, results in the complete degradation of culture.

Even in the face of these obstacles, some people argue that the increasing intelligence of today's machines is a good thing. After all, machine power can decrease the human work load. Computer processers double in power and ability every year. Computers are projected to reach human intelligence by as soon as 2025. The implications of this shift are unknown, but one thing is for certain. We are moving into this change too fast to anticipate and prevent damage to the human species. We are approaching this change too quickly for any sort of safety net to be built. Because of this, it is important that we as a species slow down our technological development so that we might consider all the implications of a change this big. We must figure out how to handle negative societal and cultural consequences before we embrace total integration of automated, intelligent machines.

Decreasing the speed with which we incorporate mechanical influence is important because of the potential dangers that lurk in blind acceptance. Not only does the preference of the mechanical over the natural interfere with the job market and the economy, but its use also has the potential to seriously degrade our culture as a whole. In combination with the uncertainty surrounding the increasing intelligence of machines, it is most assuredly better for the human species that technological progress be slowed so that we can, if necessary, prevent additional damage.

[**得分解析**]

观点和分析:6 分

作者通过文章全面而深刻地讨论了盲目放弃科技这个问题和引文的三个观点,文章提供了十分准确的论点:即使我们拒绝接受机器的普及,在我们思考怎么去利用智能机器时,我们依旧需要小心谨慎,因为它背后隐藏着危机。在阐述这个观点时,作者从经济和文化转化太快两个角度切入,深入展开了讨论。

文章观点展开与论证支持:6 分

通过经济和文化两方面对于盲目使用智能机器的讨论,作者有效地展开了文章观点。通过假设的例子(In the event the robots are more widely used in the workplace)和有效的论证(The implications of this shift are unknown, but one thing is for certain. We are moving into this change too fast to anticipate and prevent damage to the human species),作者有效地阐述了它的重要性。最后一段通过讨论机器的优点和现在科技的成熟来阐述对于科技现代化的需要——当我们达到新的科技高度的时候,我们就更应该重视如何去应对潜在的一些后果。

文章组织:6 分

文章结构连贯,中心思想明确。作者在讨论未来的经济后果,到对于当前的文化情况,再到反对观点时,逻辑清楚。段落与段落之间过渡自然,体现了文章结构(The economic implications of the potential mechanical takeover; Our careless use of automation has already taken a toll on our culture; Even in the face of these obstacles, some people argue that the increasing intelligence of today's machines is a good thing)。段落中间的过渡起到了加强论证的效果(At first, but eventually, This of course, After all)。因此好的文章组织能有效地表达作者的论点。

语言应用和语法:6 分

用词准确(societal and cultural consequences, intolerence and incivility, emotional or psychological damage),句子结构多变,少有语言错误,文章风格统一,词汇丰富多样(degrade, depressed, damage 等)。在最后一段中,作者使用了排比的句型(We are, We are, We must)。这些修辞手法阐明了观点,极具说服力。

Session 2　写作技巧

1. 提升写作技能

(1) 审题

ACT写作要求考生在40分钟内写完一篇文章。对于考生来说，在限时写作中，审题、构思和检查是十分重要的。考试中时间非常紧张，考生是没有时间去打草稿、做修改或者誊抄作文的。

(2) 构思

拿到题目后，考生首先要仔细阅读和思考引用部分，确保能理解里面的问题、观点和写作任务。引用部分提供的问题和提示词能帮助考生分析观点和提炼自己的观点。考生需要辩证地去思考这些问题，构思如何能够有效地组织观点和展开分析。考试时，考生可以使用试卷上的空白部分去列写作提纲。

(3) 写作

写作的时候，考生要清晰地表明自己的观点和主旨大意，要有充分的论点和有效的例子来证明自己的观点。考生需要注意观点是否准确，内容是否得当，论点是否切题。写作过程中要注意逻辑是否清晰，论据是否有效，遣词造句是否得当。

(4) 检查

写完全文后，考生应花几分钟时间来检查文章，修正错误的地方，如字迹不清。在修改的时候，要注意卷面整洁，且不要写到划线以外空白的地方，阅卷官会体谅考生只有40分钟的时间来构思和写文章。在有限的时间内，考生应尽量地做到字迹工整。

(5) 练习

在备考时考生有多种复习方法可以选择，比如，阅读报刊杂志，多听时事评论，或者多参加讨论组和辩论赛。这些活动可以帮助考生来熟悉实事，拓宽不同的观点和角度，培养更好的写作策略来呈现观点。

其中，一种较好的方法是针对不同目的的文章多练习。比如思考面对不同的读者，针对不同的目的，怎么撰写不同形式的文章，英语课堂中的写作也能帮助考生提高写作技能。因此，考生可以多练习不同形式的写作，比如故事、评论、日记等等。因为ACT写作练习要求考生的观点具有说服力，给报社的主编写评论或者信件是十分有帮助的。同时，多练习不同种类的写作类型也能提高写作技能，来应对不同的写作任务。

同时，练习写作的时候要进行计时。进行写作练习能够帮助学生评估自己的水平。即使考生并不打算参加写作部分的考试，练习写作依旧有好处，因为在将来的大学学习和工作中，写作能力同样十分重要。

当然，一种较好的备考方法是针对不同的文章进行多练习。

以下有一些提升写作技能的方法

- 多读多写。尽可能多地阅读不同类型的文章，比如戏剧、散文、小说、诗歌、故事、商业文章，或者杂志专栏。
- 多了解社会事实，且培养自己的观点，练习使用自己的观点去说服别人。参加演讲和辩论也能有效地练习辩证思考。
- 多尝试用不同的形式，就真实情况去创作，比如通过写信给编辑或者某公司来索取信息。
- 在课外活动中进行写作。校报、年鉴，或者写作俱乐部都能提供写作机会来拓展思维。
- 和别人互相批改。别人的批改能帮助考生了解别人是如何看到文章的，能帮助考生更好地了解读者的想法。

- 把写作看成一个连贯的过程——构思、写作、修改。这样的过程适用于任何形式的写作。
- 多听取英语老师的意见。
- 不停地尝试去修改你的文章,使用更准确的词汇,更好的语言,构造更好的组织架构。
- 要相信每个人都能提升写作技能。熟能生巧,练习得越多,就能越来越自信和写得更好。

2. 新 ACT 写作实战技巧

(1) 开头段

观点

论点

(2) 主体第一段

描述第一个观点

描写它的优点/缺点

文章提供的观点/没有提供的观点

说服力

叙述你是否同意,或者部分同意这个观点

(3) 主体第二段

描述第二个观点

描写它的优点/缺点

文章提供的观点/没有提供的观点

说服力

叙述你是否同意,或者部分同意这个观点

(4) 主体第三段

描述第三个观点

描写它的优点/缺点

文章提供的观点/没有提供的观点

说服力

叙述你是否同意,或者部分同意这个观点

(5) 主体第四段

描述你的观点

提供准确、有关的论据

讨论你的观点的优点和缺点

比较对比你的观点和文章中的三个观点

总结句归纳整篇文章

写作过程中严格安排写作模板,中途不要随意改变文章思路

写作过程中不能跑题

3. 写作步骤

第一步:审题

(Example excerpted from Kaplan ACT 2016)

Bilingual Accreditation

While the United States has just one official national language, English is certainly not the only language in which Americans communicate. In fact, bilingual fluency is highly desirable in many professions, including business, education, and medicine. In an effort to ready students for success in their future careers, some high schools may consider instituting programs that would offer bilingual accreditation to students who successfully complete a significant portion of their schooling in a language other than English. Since bilingual certification is not a necessary component of traditional education, should schools be expected to explore this option for interested students? As American high schools aim to remain competitive as measured by increasingly rigorous international education standards, innovative programs such as bilingual certification may prove to be essential.

Read and carefully consider these perspectives. Each discusses relevant aspects of offering bilingual accreditation.

Perspective One

Schools should encourage bilingual fluency but should not be expected to offer special classes or programs. School administrators need to work on strengthening the existing curriculum rather than overcomplicating instruction by attempting to incorporate additional programs that do not reinforce traditional education.

Perspective Two

Offering bilingual accreditation weakens the core of high school curriculum. A large enough portion of the student population already struggles to maintain passing grades when taught in English, and adding other languages would likely add to that number.

Perspective Three

Bilingual accreditation should be offered, but it needs to be thoughtfully implemented. Courses taught in languages other than English need to be carefully selected to ensure that this program does not affect the integrity of the high school diploma.

写作任务：写一篇连贯完整的文章，体现对于双语证书的三个观点。在文章中，要有以下几个要素

分析三个观点

提出自己的观点

阐述文章观点和你自己的观点之间的关系

你的观点可以完全同意，部分同意或者完全反对文中任何一个观点。不管怎样，叙述自己观点的时候要有逻辑性，有细节的支持和有说服力的观点。

[**构思作文**]

在思考的时候考虑以下几点：

三个观点的优点和缺点：

- 它们所要表达的是什么，同时它们各自忽略了什么。
- 它们为何能说服别人，或者为何不能说服别人。

搜索自己的相关知识或经验：

- 对于这个话题，考生自己的观点是什么。这些观点的优缺点各是什么。
- 考生将如何在写作中支持自己的观点。

在阅读过程中，考生要清楚地理解这个论点。在这个例子中要讨论的是，学校是否需要向有兴趣的学生提供双语证书，即使这对于传统教学来说不是必要的。一般情况下，考生能清楚地找到这个问题，因为引文清楚地表达了这个问题。但有时候，问题并没有很明显，考生需要认真地阅读文章来提取观点，但不宜将观点复杂化。通过文章结构，考生可以利用三个观点来思考自己的立场。在这个例子中，考生可以表达，“高中应该提倡双语化，但是不应该要求双语教学”，“高中应该避免

双语现象”或者“在执行到位的情况下,高中应该提供双语教学”。在这个例子中,每个论点完全不同,因此考生无法讨论全部的论点,

第二步:大纲

考生可以利用8分钟的时间来分析引文,列出写作大纲。这一步骤很重要,好的大纲是得高分的前提。考生需注意选择论证方法和相应的例子。

提示:如果考生想到了更好的例子,则可以转换立场。

在写作之前,利用写作模板来确定文章结构。考生可以利用4～6分钟来构思,这个过程可以帮助考生在写作时更顺利。写作前,考生可以花几分钟的时间来分析引文,标注关键词,然后再用Kaplan里的写作模板来组织这些笔记。文章的大纲大致如下:

1. 开头段

介绍性论述。

论点——学校应该提供双语教学,只要学校能够谨慎地选择英语之外的第二语言。

2. 主体第一段

描述第一个论点——学校应该鼓励学生双语学习,但是学校并没有时间或者资源来提供双语项目。

此论点的优点和缺点——着重于现实生活中课程的设置。

它表达的和未表达的想法——没有考虑到双语设置也可以促进课程。

说服力:忽略了一些潜在的优点,因此没有说服力。

细致地陈述考生同意或反对——反对。

3. 主体第二段

描述第二个论点——双语教学不应该被接受,因为这将增加学校的教学难度。

此论点的优点和缺点——考虑学生将怎样看待这个项目。

它表达的和未表达的想法——并没有考虑到有部分学生的第一母语不是英语,因此他们学得很痛苦。

说服力——没有说服力,因为它并没有考虑到这个项目能够帮助学生。

细致地陈述考生同意或反对——反对。

4. 主体第三段

描述第三个观点——学校应该提供双语教学,但是学校必须合理安排才能有教学效果。

此论点的优点和缺点——考虑到了对学生的好处。

它表达的和未表达的想法——没有考虑到高中的课程都是经过严格删选的。

说服力——有说服力,因为在没有破坏教学整体性的前提下,它提供了额外的学习条件。

细致地陈述考生同意或反对——反对。

5. 主体第四段

描述你的论点——只要双语教学机会是传统课程所没有的,所有的学生都应该获得机会去追求双语教学。学校应该兼顾那些单语言学习的学生和多语言学习的学生。

提供详细且相关的论据——传统的外语教学课程给这个项目提供了基础。

讨论你的论点的优缺点——此项目对于学生来说是一个很好的机会,但却很难实施。

解释你的观点怎么对应到文章中的三个观点——同意第三个观点。

在第四段的结尾用一句话来概括全文。

[**实用技巧**]

- 使用新颖的开头来吸引读者
- 多使用过渡——这能很好地连接你的观点

- 使用让人印象深刻的结尾
- 不要偏离引用部分
- 使用恰当的例子，通常每个段落都要有
- 总结要到位

使用新颖的开头，避免千篇一律的开头，比如：in my opinion，... because...。对于阅文无数的考官来说，这样的开头毫无吸引力，因此要尝试使用更吸引眼球的开头。例如：

In today's global economy，students are looking for ways to ready themselves for an increasingly international future.

结尾需要简洁切题，可以重述观点或者例举恰当的例子，比如：

Enhancing instruction is always better than restricting learning，especially when the result is effective communication，desirable skills，and valuable experiences.

第三步：写作

考官不会按照写作字数来打分，但是考官们认为，一篇展开充分的文章写作需要时间和篇幅，是无法通过寥寥几句话或一两个段落就能表达强烈的观点或者展示所有论点。考生不需要去数文章的字数，但要考虑观点的篇幅。

考官以文章的结构来算分。如果考官能清晰地看懂文章的组织构架，这些文章的得分就会高很多。

字迹要清楚。如果考官无法辨认文章的字迹，则此篇文章很可能会得零分。如果考生的字迹不清楚，则要多练习。

坚持按照套路写作。即使临时想到新的表达方式去引入一个新的观点，无论多好，都不要采用，也不要跑题。

使用主旨句。每个段落都应该围绕一个主旨句展开。在写每个段落之前，构思好此段的主旨句。可以使用以下的句型：

- One example...
- Another example...
- Therefore，we can conclude...

当然，你不需要完全照抄这些句型，但是，预先构思好段落结构能确保你不偏题。

用词要谨慎。选择那些比较熟悉的词汇。使用新学的高级词汇和不熟悉的往往会适得其反，不但没有能使考官感到惊艳，反而偏离了中心思想。

还有一些需要注意的地方：

1. 避免过多地使用第一人称。当然，考生是允许使用个人例子的(At my school，we had this issue just last year，and I was very involved in the discussion...)，但要注意的是，避免使用个人观点(I really think...，I believe...，In my opinion...)。当你的论点是建立在主观想法上，而不是客观事实上时，则比较被动不利。

2. 避免使用俚语。语言风格应该是自然流畅且书面化的，毕竟这是一个书面性的文章，像平时短信中，网络上，或者个人邮件里使用的缩写，也不适用于写作中。因为它们不够规范，甚至考官很可能都无法理解你想要表达什么。

3. 注意起承转合。仔细地思考你所要表达的观点，且用清晰的语言方式表达出来，以便读者能够更好地理解你的文章。可以引用引文中或者文章中出现的表明观点、重要性、对比关系等的关键词。

4. 不要拘泥小节。不要因小失大。如果想不起某个单词的拼写，尽力绕过去。即便是满分作文也是有瑕疵的。评分员会理解考生文章是在未经过调查研究而仓促间写就的。

第四步：检查

要预留 2～3 分钟的时间去检查你的文章。大家都会犯拼写、漏写词等错误，快速地检查文章，确保文章大意清晰准确。

在修改文章时不要犹豫不决，毕竟这是一场限时考试，而不是期末论文。但是修改的时候要保证字迹清晰，可以适当地使用一些标志性的符号来标记加入的成分。在修改时要谨记已经没有时间来做大的调整，比如添加新的段落，或者改变观点等。在练习过程中也要练习修改的方法和习惯。

1. 常见错误：

漏写单词。

句子不完整。

修饰错位。

混词错误——尤其是同形同音异义词，比如 their，there 和 they're。

拼写错误。

2. 常见的句型错误：

太多短句——合并句子。

太多长难句——分离句子。

太多晦涩难懂的词——用一些简单词。

太多简单词——用一些大学水平的词。

总结：

在这一章里，我们讲解了在 ACT 写作中拿高分的写作方法。需要记住的是，文章的要求是写一篇文章分析三个既定的观点，同时阐述自己的观点。在阐述自己观点的时候，要立场明确、证据充分、逻辑清晰，要构思清楚。通过清晰地表达观点和合理地布局文章，考生就能够拿到一个理想的分数。写作前构思写作思路可以避免流水账。

合理的文章结构：第一段的时候就表明你的观点，并且用新颖的方式来展开论述。主体部分写四个段落，每个段落都要有分论点和论据。总结段落时要干净利落，不要引入新的论点。

最后留几分钟去检查文章。

二、解析

范文 1 解析

Public Health and Individual Freedom

Most people want to be healthy, and most people want as much freedom as possible to do the things they want. Unfortunately, these two desires sometimes conflict. For example, smoking is prohibited from most public places, which restricts the freedom of some individuals for the sake of the health of others. Likewise, car emissions are regulated in many areas in order to reduce pollution and its health risks to others, which in turn restricts some people's freedom to drive the vehicles they want. In a society that values both health and freedom, how do we best balance the two? How should we think about conflicts between public health and individual freedom?

Read and carefully consider these perspectives. Each suggests a particular way of thinking about the conflict between public health and individual freedom.

Perspective One

Our society should strive to achieve the greatest good for the greatest number of people. When the freedom of the individual interferes with that principle, freedom must be restricted.

Perspective Two

Nothing in society is more valuable than freedom. Perhaps physical health is sometimes improved by restricting freedom, but the cost to the health of our free society is far too great to justify it.

Perspective Three

The right to avoid health risks is a freedom, too. When we allow individual behavior to endanger others, we've damaged both freedom and health.

Essay Task

Write a unified, coherent essay in which you evaluate multiple perspectives on the conflict between public health and individual freedom. In your essay, be sure to:

- analyze and evaluate the perspectives given
- state and develop your own perspective on the issue
- explain the relationship between your perspective and those given

Your perspective may be in full agreement with any of the others, in partial agreement, or wholly different. Whatever the case, support your ideas with logical reasoning and detailed, persuasive examples.

[范文]	[点评]
The United States was founded on the principle that all citizens have the right to "life, liberty, and the pursuit of happiness." (1) As well known, lauded, and utopian as this phrase may be, there is an underlying issue with the first two rights allotted to Americans. Life and liberty can sometimes come into bitter conflict; and an example of said conflict is the restriction of so-dubbed "dangerous" activities in the name of the greater good. Therein lies a major quandary. Is it just to restrict liberty in the name of protection? The answer cannot be distilled down to a simple yes or no. There are those champions of Utilitarianism who argue for aggregate good. Others bang raucously on the battle drum of individual liberty; they state that Americans have the right to indulge in whatever they wish, as long as it resides comfortably within the confines of natural law. Yet another faction screams that the right to public health supersedes the right of the individual to partake in an activity deemed harmful by the lofty authorities. Not one of these stances is satisfactory in the least, and this is why the debate marches on, with different drummers tapping out syncopated, disjointed arguments. (2) The solution to the conflict between life and liberty is a glaring simple one, one that can be easily applied, thereby eliminating the need for argument. All individuals have the right to partake in self-destruction, such as consuming junk food, drugs, cigarettes, own a gun, and drive a specific type of pollutant spewing car et cetera. However, the government has the duty to protect the masses. The solution is, to put it bluntly, regulation. (3) Primarily, it is crucial to examine the problems with Utilitarianism and the rise of a	(1) 开篇引用了美国建国时提出的理念，主题紧密贴合，体现了深厚的积累，引出对life和liberty的讨论。 (2) 对比三种观点，完成了题目中分析三种观点的要求。表明自己的立场，引出下文自己的观点，结构清晰逻辑严谨。 (3) 切入点合理，中心句简洁明了，论证充足。

(续表)

nanny state in a country that touts the benefits of liberty. The 19th century fathers of Utilitarianism, such as John Stuart Mill had a lovely plan to minimize suffering, and distilling the problems of society to a simple, almost mathematical equation. (4) Their simple solution is as follows: the answer lies in whatever produces the highest rate of aggregate happiness. Lovely as this idea seems on the surface, there is a reason that it is flaccid and ineffective. The reason that it is inapplicable and unrealistic is obvious. How does one even to measure aggregate good? The simple answer is that one cannot. The happiness that a smoker gets from a rush of nicotine is perhaps equal to the amount of displeasure a non-smoker experiences as they traipse through a cloud of carcinogens. Hence, the argument for the greater good of all fails to consider this. Humanity cannot be simplified into a succinct mathematical formula.	(4) 通过举具体实例,使论证更有说服力,体现了深厚的积累。
There are three examples that support regulation instead of an outright ban. (5) These examples are former New York City mayor Bloomberg's jihad on large sodas, the War on Drugs, and, as hinted at above, the increased restrictions on smoking. Bloomberg, motivated by his own personal opinions on health, opted to ban king-sized carbonated beverages from being sold in "his" city. While it could be argued that Bloomberg's ban on big soda bottles comes from "a good place," it is not his right to tell people how much sugar they are allowed to drink. This was foolish because banning a big soda will not prevent someone intent on drinking sodas from skirting the ban by simply buying more small sodas. In addition, this action by Bloomberg monarchical, since he was the individual deciding what is best for the residents of New York City. How are a handful of human beings drinking large sodas harmful to the public at large? (6) The answer is that they are not. The War on Drugs is another example of illegalization of something deemed harmful and doing more harm than good. Since the illegalization of drugs, the nation has not seen a decline in drug use. What it has seen is an increase in prison overcrowding. Now, the regulations placed on tobacco use in public places are a wholly different matter. Second-hand smoke has been proven to harm others, yet cigarettes remain legal. It makes sense that something that poisons others should be banned within the confines of buildings or in certain areas, such as schools or parks. By regulating and taxing tobacco rather than criminalizing or banning it, people are still allowed to smoke, yet are permitted to do so without harming others. (7)	(5) 通过三个具体的实例支撑自己的观点,使论证更为严谨丰富。 (6) 运用设问的句型,进一步突出强调观点,增加了句式结构的多样性。 (7) 在两个反例之后举出一个正确监管的例子,进一步支持论点,举例论证也更形象具体。
If the same regulation were applied to the aforementioned issues, such as illegal drugs, cars that spout black CO2 emissions, firearms, and even the innocuous soda and candy that Bloomberg so fears, perhaps we could preserve freedom while also protecting the health of the masses.	

1. 经典单词

utopian 不切实际的

distill 提炼

raucously 刺耳地,喧闹地

supersede 取代

partake 参与

bluntly 直言不讳地

succinct 简明的

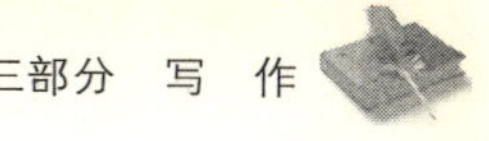

outright 完全的
monarchic 君主的
overcrowding 过度拥挤

2. 闪光句子

(1) Life and liberty can sometimes come into bitter conflict; and an example of said conflict is the restriction of so-dubbed "dangerous" activities in the name of the greater good.

(2) The answer cannot be distilled down to a simple yes or no.

(3) Not one of these stances is satisfactory in the least, and this is why the debate marches on, with different drummers tapping out syncopated, disjointed arguments.

(4) The War on Drugs is another example of illegalization of something deemed harmful and doing more harm than good.

3. 总体分析

整篇文章脉络清晰，立意深刻，引用了大量的例子，论据充分，很有说服力。开篇从美国建国时的理念入手讨论民主与自由的关系，分别指出三个观点的不足之处，并在此基础上提出自己的观点——政府对危害他人健康与利益的行为进行监管。利用前纽约市长的三个监管政策，从两正一反的角度进行论证，生动形象，富有说服力，进一步通过实例支持了自己的观点。

范文 2 解析

Intelligent Machines

Many of the goods and services we depend on daily are now supplied by intelligent, automated machines rather than human beings. Robots build cars and other goods on assembly lines, where once there were human workers. Many of our phone conversations are now conducted not with people but with sophisticated technologies. We can now buy goods at a variety of stores without the help of a human cashier. Automation is generally seen as a sign of progress, but what is lost when we replace humans with machines? Given the accelerating variety and prevalence of intelligent machines, it is worth examining the implications and meaning of their presence in our lives.

Read and carefully consider these perspectives. Each suggests a particular way of thinking about the increasing presence of intelligent machines.

Perspective One

What we lose with the replacement of people by machines is some part of our own humanity. Even our mundane daily encounters no longer require from us basic courtesy, respect, and tolerance for other people.

Perspective Two

Machines are good at low-skill, repetitive jobs, and at high-speed, extremely precise jobs. In both cases they work better than humans. This efficiency leads to a more prosperous and progressive world for everyone.

Perspective Three

Intelligent machines challenge our long-standing ideas about what humans are or can be. This is good because it pushes both humans and machines toward new, unimagined possibilities.

Essay Task

Write a unified, coherent essay in which you evaluate multiple perspectives on the conflict between public health and individual freedom. In your essay, be sure to:

- analyze and evaluate the perspectives given
- state and develop your own perspective on the issue
- explain the relationship between your perspective and those given

Your perspective may be in full agreement with any of the others, in partial agreement, or wholly different. Whatever the case, support your ideas with logical reasoning and detailed, persuasive examples.

[范文]	[点评]
Every Francophile knows the incomparable nature of fresh French bread and the unique tastes and textures of regional French cheeses. The French have opted to balk at the machine age in the areas where human hands and inherited recipes triumph over the loveless, mass produced loaves and plasticized cheese slices that explode from factory doors and materialize on grocery store shelves. (1) While those who enjoy the fruits of Frances's efforts to keep machines away from time honored artisanal foods, many seem nonplussed by the fact that machines are fast replacing human touch. This is evident in nearly every aspect of our modern lives. We champion quantity over quality; we praise efficiency and speed over care and meticulousness. (2) While machines are fast encroaching on the jobs of humans in nearly every arena, it is important to consider how intelligenly machines both help and harm us on a planet full of increasingly useless hands. The question that accompanies our increasingly existential existence is whether or not the machines will render all that we do inferior, imperfect, and imprecise. (3)	(1) 开头以法式手工面包和芝士为例进行对机械化的讨论,生动形象,贴合主题。 (2) 三个态度的对比,指出了问题的根本所在。 (3) 运用了三个形容词的排比,语句凝练,突出重点。
First, it is a beneficial thing that machines are able to perform the meaningless, tedious, and repetitive tasks once carried out by human hands. The image of Charlie Bucket's father in Roald Dahl's famous work on *Willy Wonka and the Chocolate Factory* comes to mind. (4) Mr. Bucket earns his meager pittance by screwing the caps onto toothpaste tubes. These menial tasks can now be allotted to emotionless, dreamless machines, allowing Mr. Bucket to either be out of a job and even more destitute, or there could be a silver lining. The removal of the human element from something as soul crushingly unstimulating as screwing the caps on toothpaste tubes allows a character like Mr. Bucket to seek employment in a more fulfilling career. Machines are unable to replace the human element in many service industry professions. For example, Mr. Bucket could mow lawns or become a personal shopper. He could walk dogs for extra income, and rent out the bed that Grandpa Joe left vacant on Airbnb. By freeing man from the shackles of the assembly line, machines have minimized injury and helped many find different, more fulfilling careers.	(4) 利用小说中人物以挤牙膏为生的例子,形象论证机器可以解放人类的双手,让人类去做更有意义的工作。
Another task that machines supersede human skill is the tiny, minute task of repairing arteries with laser precision, or cutting the infinitesimal gears destined to tick on in a timepiece. (5) Such high precision work is nearly impossible to be achieved by human hands alone, yet these highly refined machines are not able to create these things, to repair nerves or create tiny cogs without a human mind to guide them. The highly precise machines are not the enemy; these machines save lives and serve as tools of a highly specialized trade.	(5) 点明机器的另一个重要作用:帮助人类执行精密度高的任务,与上文相呼应,论证逻辑清晰,结构严谨。
Machines are a part of modern existence, and many jobs are rendered useless as mechanized labor increases. The challenge facing mankind is one of finding new	

（续表）

venues for two things the machines lack: creativity and heart. (6) These two aspects of the human mind are irreplaceable by a robotic hand or even by a highly intelligent computer. The reason French breads and cheeses are so adored and applauded is because of the human element that goes into artisanal bakeries and whipping milk into decadence. (7) There will always be demand for human elements, and machines can take on the mind numbingly menial and highly precise tasks that human beings assign them. This leaves humanity free to explore new, exciting venues never thought possible before machines began to work for us. Machines are not to be feared; they must also not be used as an easy replacement for a sentient creature with a beating heart and creative mind. It is our choice to use them wisely and honorably.	(6) 与中心观点相呼应，指出解决问题的重点：人类的创造力。 (7) 与开篇呼应，论证严谨，加强了观点的说服力。

1. 经典单词

incomparable 无可匹敌的
triumph 胜利，获得胜利
nonplussed 困惑的
meticulousness 谨小慎微
encroach 侵蚀
alllot 分配
destitute 贫困的
fulfulling 令人满意的，能实现个人抱负的
superdede 取代
irreplaceable 不可取代的

2. 闪光句子

(1) We champion quantity over quality; we praise efficiency and speed over care and meticulousness.

(2) The question that accompanies our increasingly existential existence is whether or not the machines will render all that we do inferior, imperfect, and imprecise.

(3) The reason French breads and cheeses are so adored and applauded is because of the human element that goes into artisanal bakeries and whipping milk into decadence.

3. 总体分析

全文结构严谨，脉络清晰，以法式面包和芝士的例子开篇，引出下文中人与机器关系的讨论，文中围绕机器可以帮助人类做低级重复性的工作和精密度高的工作来解放生产力，最终落脚到协调人类与机器关系的关键是增强创造力。

范文3解析

（作文题目同2）

[范文] As technology improves, and more and more tasks are completed by machines instead of humans, the question is no longer about what we can do with machines,	

(续表)

but rather what we should. Although the usage of machines increases efficiency and our standard of living, it detracts from the value of human life. (1) As machines increasingly perform all our basic tasks, society is able to produce more. The additional production adds material value to our society and frees people up from these low-skill tasks. This is in agreement with Perspective Two which claims that this industrialization leads to more prosperity. (2) For example, in the 18th century, short-staple cotton that was grown in the Southern United States required an immense amount of labor in order to seperate the seeds from the fiber to process the cotton to make it marketable. However, in the mid-19th century, Eli Whitney, an American entrepreneur, invented the cotton gin, which allowed automation of cotton processing. This machine replaced the need of a large work force for the process and greatly improved production. As a result of the cotton gin, short-staple cotton production skyrocketed, increasing by more than 10 times in the South while bringing prosperity to the region and setting in motion a new industrial era in America. This is in agreement with Perspective Three, which says that mechanization allows "unimagined possibilities". (3) Although there are clearly many advantages to industrialization, there are also some heavy drawbacks. The replacement of humans by machines leads to the loss of value to human life, an effect that outweighs the material gains of automation. The search to find human tasks that can be performed by machines inevitably leads to comparisons between the human and the machine. If a company executive wants to see if an inventory management team can be replaced by a robotic system, he will compare the two and determine which can do a better job. When this occurs, the people on the team are evaluated not for their worth as human beings, but for their effectiveness at performing a specific function—in essence, as we would evaluate a machine. In a larger sense, when we begin to think about humans in this way, the worth of a person's life becomes dependent on only what they can do and no longer has any intrinsic value. As Perspective One states, we begin to lose our humanity. (4) This new mindset and way of evaluating people, though seemingly harmless in the workplace, is devastating when it begins to pervade a society. If a person is judged only on his or her capability, there is no reason for a person to remain after they have served their function. This would warrant genocide against the elderly and the disabled because their burden on society would not be made up for by any production. Although the machines may seem to only fulfill the low skill jobs at the moment, there is no barrier to prevent the machines from replacing more. As the machines increase in intelligence, they will replace any tasks done by humans and render us unnecessary and worthless. Due to the risks of dehumanization, the material benefits of machines are not enough to justify their increasing presence. (5)	[点评] (1) 开门见山提出观点,论证清晰,点明问题的重点是人类是否应该让机器完成这些工作。 (2) 分析观点 2,机器可以将人类从低级工作中解放出来。 (3) 分析观点 3,机械化提供了更多的可能性。 (4) 对应观点 1,借助比较人类和机器生产力的例子来说明机器的存在会使人类丧失身为人类的尊严。 (5) 文末点题,总结全文。

1. 经典单词

immense 巨大的

skyrocket 飞涨

inevitable 不可避免的

intrinsic 内在的

devastating 毁灭性的

pervade 遍及
warrant 保证

2. 闪光句子

(1) Although there are clearly many advantages to industrialization, there are also some heavy drawbacks.

(2) This new mindset and way of evaluating people, though seemingly harmless in the workplace, is devastating when it begins to pervade a society.

3. 总体分析

文章论证脉络非常清晰,首先依次分析了观点 2 和 3,认可了这些观点和机器的积极作用,但进一步分析了机器的消极作用,支持了观点 1,并通过实例加以支撑,文末结合上述论证分析得出结论。

范文 4 解析

Can people be truely original?

Perspective One

Many newly created things today defy tradition and ignore history. The best ideas are often based on proven method and theories.

Perspective Two

People can live without creativity, but in order to thrive in the fast changing world, one needs to be creative.

Perspective Three

Creativity has no standard or set definition. It makes more sense for us to focus on other qualities that are productive and accurately defined.

Essay Task

Write a unified, coherent essay in which you evaluate multiple perspectives on the conflict between public health and individual freedom. In your essay, be sure to:

- analyze and evaluate the perspectives given
- state and develop your own perspective on the issue
- explain the relationship between your perspective and those given

Your perspective may be in full agreement with any of the others, in partial agreement, or wholly different. Whatever the case, support your ideas with logical reasoning and detailed, persuasive examples.

[范文]	[点评]
As the American education system strays from the liberal arts and rallies around mathematics and sciences, therein rises a dilemma. (1) This issue is one on the importance, or relevance of creativity. Some state that creativity must be limited to the confines of tested and proven methods. Some argue that the term is vague, nebulous, and lacks concrete classification. This viewpoint itself displays a lack of creativity, for lack of standard or set meaning in favor of the sterility of productivity and with a textbook definition. (2) The fact that the above arguments	(1) 首句通过教育制度切入,点明对主旨观点的理解。 (2) 体现了很好的逻辑分析能力,论证严谨清晰。

(续表)

even exist supports the dire need for increased creativity, for a society defined by strict, unforgiving lines and motivated by naught but production is contradictory to one of the most beautiful aspects of the human experience. (3) Although it is possible for some to live without creativity, but it is necessary for our increasingly math and science based world to encourage creative minds, for without creativity, there can be no innovation. The biggest fallacy in the flawed arguments in favor of structure and productivity is glaringly obvious; how are we, as innovative human beings, supposed to innovate and invent and put forward new methods and ideas without creativity? (4) An example of a modern hero who needed both creativity and productivity was Steve Jobs. The Apple co-founder, responsible for dreaming up the impossible and making it tangible and accessible, displayed creative thinking at every turn. First he brought American homes the PC; later he condensed our burgeoning music libraries to the size of a postage stamp; finally he placed iPhones in our ever-greedy hand. Jobs would have never achieved what he did if it were not for the massive doses of creativity. (5) Another creative mind that has made our lives much richer is J. K. Rowling. The author, blessed with heaps of creativity and a knack for turning words into rich, magical tomes, is capable of both productivity and creativity, and because of this combination of the aforementioned qualities, the world has Harry Potter. (6) Directors, cinematographers, writers, app developers, CEOs, designers, musicians, inventors, scientists, historians, graphic artists, and educators all need creativity to function fully. To decry something so integral to the human condition is not merely flawed thinking—it is horrifying. The most fantastic human achievements are not based on quantity, nor is history made by those who follow the rulebook to the letter, never straying from what has been written down by another. (7) We are not drones. We are beings who have been creative since before the Cro-Magnon painted beautiful, burning beasts on the walls of their caves. People have told stories, invented complex myths, solved complex problems through philosophy, and recorded their histories because of a desire to create as well as a desire to preserve. (8) For those poor advocates of soulless production instead of wrongly-labeled folly, for those who actually think that formulae and strict methodology trump a slightly out-of-the-box process, there is a question that must be posed. How is man so drastically altered now, in this present moment, that suddenly, he needs no creativity? When did creativity become a burden, an impediment, a problem? How does one logically conclude that there is no place for creativity in this world? (9) The rejection of creativity emphasizes following orders blindly, with nary a query. The spurning of creativity in favor of productivity reduces our world to a glorified assembly line. It is impossible to fully eradicate the burning need to create, to invent, to find new paths to explore. Advocates of snuffing out this flame are effectively supporting the dulling of humanity in favor of rules and results.	(3) 体现了对长难句的驾驭能力。 (4) 设问句式,突出强调创造性的重要意义,整句话体现出理解原文作者的推理论证过程。 (5) 引用苹果创始人乔布斯的事例,支持自己的论证观点,体现了深厚的素材积累和灵活运用的能力。 (6) 体现了深厚的写作功力和对复杂句式的运用能力。 (7) 总结论证观点,反驳观点 1 和 3。 (8) 从时间角度纵向分析,巩固了论点,体现了严谨清晰的逻辑分析能力。 (9) 三个连续的反问句,层层深入,体现出对原文作者推理论证过程的准确理解。

1. 经典单词

stray 偏离

nebulous 朦胧的

fallacy 谬论

tangible 切实的

burgeoning 生机勃勃的
decry 谴责
soulless 没有灵魂的
impediment 阻碍
query 疑问
spurn 蔑视

2. 闪光句子

(1) As the American education system strays from the liberal arts and rallies around mathematics and sciences, therein rises a dilemma.

(2) This viewpoint itself displays a lack of creativity, for lack of standard or set meaning in favor of the sterility of productivity and with a textbook definition.

(3) The fact that the above arguments even exist supports the dire need for increased creativity, for a society defined by strict, unforgiving lines and motivated by naught but production is contradictory to one of the most beautiful aspects of the human experience.

(4) The biggest fallacy in the flawed arguments in favor of structure and productivity is glaringly obvious; how are we, as innovative human beings, supposed to innovate and invent and put forward new methods and ideas without creativity?

(5) To decry something so integral to the human condition is not merely flawed thinking—it is horrifying.

3. 总体分析

全文脉络清晰,句式结构灵活,长短句交错,修辞、例证丰富,体现了深厚的写作功底和素材积累。论证过程由浅入深,层层深入,前后文相呼应,结构严谨,一环扣一环,体现了优秀的逻辑分析能力和语言组织能力,论证严谨清晰。

范文 5 解析

The Internet

In the rapidly developing modern society, the expansion of the Internet is so fast and prevailing that the Internet starts to cover almost every single corner of our lives. With just the touch of a few keys, people can communicate with others on the opposite side of the planet. In your point of view, do you think that the Internet has brought us all closer or driven us apart?

Read and carefully consider these perspectives. Each suggests a particular way of thinking about the increasing presence of the Internet.

Perspective One

Internet has brought people closer together and made the world a much smaller place.

Perspective Two

Not only is the reliability influenced, morality is also corrupted due to the massive amount of information.

Perspective Three

A problem that may be even more prevailing is that the efficiency of searching for information and the privacy-invading is considerably influenced.

Essay Task

Write a unified, coherent essay in which you evaluate multiple perspectives on the internet. In your essay, be sure to:

analyze and evaluate the perspectives given

state and develop your own perspective on the issue

explain the relationship between your perspective and those given

Your perspective may be in full agreement with any of the others, in partial agreement, or wholly different. Whatever the case, support your ideas with logical reasoning and detailed, persuasive examples.

[范文]

There is a prevailing fear and distrust of all things new and popular. Not so long ago, in the 18th and 19th centuries, people recoiled in fear at a dangerous new form of literature that was burgeoning in popularity, condemning it as vile, corrupting, and wholly dangerous; this wicked thing was the novel. In the first half of the 20th century, another demon reared its ugly head and set people to panic and debate; this new evil was the comic book. Comics were blamed for violence and decreased intelligence, labeled a waste of time, and even demonized by some. Video games—although many studies show that certain relationship and team-based games actually increase empathy and most games improve problem solving skills and hand-eye coordination—were the devil-du-jour. (1) However, our propensity as human beings to recoil in fear at a new, omnipresent, and ever-expanding form of popular media or technology is now laser-focused on the internet.

One argument against the internet is that morality is compromised due to the internet, and reliability is conceded as well. (2) Whereas there is sound reason to believe that there is a dearth in reliability, the argument that morality is eroded by the internet is as tired as can be. As noted earlier in this essay, the novel, now one of society's most treasured creations, was once presaged as a harbinger of moral depravity. Comic books, films, popular music, and video games were all labeled similarly. Some people tend to be afraid of change; this is to be expected. The internet is broad in scope to put it mildly. In fact, it touches nearly every sliver of this planet. This sends those who fear new things to trembling, just as those who once believed that the novel would lead to mass depravity and libertinism. This argument for the loss of morality is as worn and tattered as the pages of one's favorite novel, as scratched as one's favorite RPG disk, as decrepit as a shared comic book. (3)

Another stance against the internet is the destruction of personal privacy and the ability for one's personal information to be disclosed with a few keystrokes and mouse-clicks. Truthfully, this concept of disintegrating privacy is troublesome; however, all who have access to the internet are able to search for information on others. This has proved highly helpful to many, since background checks and checkered pasts can be found with a bit of online shrewdness. (4) This gaping hole in this argument is crystalline: the internet is here, and it cannot be simply deleted. Knowing full well that one's information can be discovered leads to heightened awareness, and there are myriad methods one can utilize in order to protect one's identity, assets, and information. It simply takes a bit of effort and research to protect your most important data.

The most fantastic aspect of the internet that the dissenters fail to acknowledge is

[点评]

(1) 以小说、科幻小说、电子游戏为例说明人们总是对新出现的事物存在恐惧,有力地支持了自己的观点。

(2) 针对观点 2 进行论证,思路清晰,结构布局合理。

(3) 利用比喻的修辞,形象生动,突出了自己的观点,丰富了句式结构,与上文的论证紧密对应,体现了出色的论证能力。

(4) 针对观点 3 进行论证,从反面论证 3 的错误性,思路清晰,体现了灵活的思路和出色的论证能力。

（续表）

how it has led to increased global connection. Although the omnipresence of the internet may have led to less eye-to-eye, face-to-face, legitimate human connection, it has allowed its users to remain in contact with friends and family, no matter how scattered they may be. Students can connect with educators worldwide, and the academic world now has millions of scholarly articles and historical documents archived online for all to access. (5) This allows humanity to reach out and almost touch one another, and these connections could lay the foundation for a more connected, accepting world. Through social media, the Arab Spring rose from the ashes of a ruined regime and caused a massive change in the Middle East. People can use hashtags to express opinions on a trending topic to the entire world. The internet gives connection of new sort, and allots a voice to the once voiceless, and for those two reasons alone, it should be cherished more than feared.	(5) 在反驳完观点 2 和 3 后，论证对观点 1 的支持，思路清晰，举例进一步支持了观点，论证严谨，思路灵活。

1. 经典单词

distrust 不信任

recoil 畏缩

demonize 妖魔化

propensity 倾向

omnipresent 无所不在的

concede 让步

dearth 缺乏

depravity 堕落

shrewdness 精明

crystalline 透明的

2. 闪光句子

(1) In the first half of the 20th century, another demon reared its ugly head and set people to panic and debate; this new evil was the comic book.

(2) However, our propensity as human beings to recoil in fear at a new, omnipresent, and ever-expanding form of popular media or technology is now laser-focused on the internet.

(3) Whereas there is sound reason to believe that there is a dearth in reliability, the argument that morality is eroded by the internet is as tired as can be.

(4) This argument for the loss of morality is as worn and tattered as the pages of one's favorite novel, as scratched as one's favorite RPG disk, as decrepit as a shared comic book.

(5) Knowing full well that one's information can be discovered leads to heightened awareness, and there are myriad methods one can utilize in order to protect one's identity, assets, and information.

3. 总体分析

全文结构非常清晰，首段论证人们总是对新出现的事物感到恐惧，并利用三个实例支持自己的观点，之后的两段分别反驳了后两个观点，思路清晰，论证严谨，句式灵活，列举了诸多实例，体现了良好的素材积累功底和论证能力。最后一段论证对观点 1 的支持，表明自己的观点并加以升华，层次清晰，体现了深厚的逻辑推理能力。

范文 6 解析

Animal Dissection

A student activist group is protesting the use of animals for dissection in science classes. The group claims that animals have the basic rights of life and happiness and that purposely destroying them for use in classes is cruel. Many of the science students disagree, stating that animals are useful in educating people about important medical and health issues and that eliminating their use in the classes would severely harm students' education. Is it necessary for human beings using animal for dissection? If not, what should people do with the experiment?

Read and carefully consider these perspectives. Each suggests a particular way of thinking about the animal dissection.

Perspective One

Animals have the basic rights of life and happiness and that purposely destroying them for use in classes is cruel.

Perspective Two

Animals are useful in educating people about important medical and health issues and that eliminating their use in the classes would severely harm students' education.

Perspective Three

The characteristics of animals and human beings are similar. Using animals for dissection is necessary.

[范文]

The writer vividly recalls recoiling, roiling with the onset of a violent wave of nausea as she was forced to cut into the pale belly of the frog. She winced as the sound of squishing assaulted her ears; her mouth began to salivate uncontrollably as her nostrils processed the stench of chemicals that preserved the moment of death in a sickening suspension. She knew that she had to peel back the amphibious skin to reveal the innards, yellow fat cells wrapped around organs like tallow hands. She wondered, as she tried in vain to hold back the stinging tears, why she had to do this. (1) She wanted to be a historian. She had no desire to change the world through science. She enjoyed Biology, and the state required her to take a science every year, whether or not her future lay in the realm of lab reports and anatomy. She would never use dissection in her life, except to recount the extreme sadness she felt that day in Ms. Neil's lab. How many frogs sat in sad jars, and for what purpose? Why must it be a rite of passage to desecrate the corpse of a little animal, when the dissector has no desire to pursue the sciences past what is required by the government and institutions of higher learning? (2) Her lab partner tapped her shoulder, and whispered cruelly, "Just wait until we dissect rabbits." The tears came in onslaughts, and she ran into the hallway, accepting a poor grade and a possible drop in class rank as opposed to peering inside the belly of a dead frog.

What is the point of dissection? There is a reason for it, to be sure. It does help students understand the workings of animal bodies and gives them a deeper understanding of the wonders of anatomy. This is all well and good for students who wish to study science after high school, but what is the point of forcing students

[点评]

(1) 对学生的心理描写和动作描写非常细腻，已例证开头，生动形象，可以吸引读者的注意力。

(2) 连续运用两个反问句式，气势强烈，层层逼近，有力地支持了论据，体现了良好的写作功底和灵活的句式运用。

（续表）

who are either ethically opposed to the process of dissection to slice open an animal? What is the point of ordering a future English major, musician, or sociologist to perform this task, when there are ample interactive resources that can teach them the same thing? (3) Dissection should not be wiped from the curriculum simply to pander to sensitive souls like the writer of this passage. Even though she was traumatized by her experience with the frog, she sees the enormous value of dissection, albeit for those who are interested in pursuing the sciences. In addition, it is hard to reconcile the argument for animal rights and welfare when the majority of the world relies predominantly on a diet of meat. However, the writer's teacher provided a simple solution to this ethical dilemma, one the writer will not forget. Ms. Neil came out into the hallway, and spoke to the crying student. She offered an alternative option to her, one that would still test her knowledge of the anatomical apparatuses of frogs, yet one that did not force her to handle a dead animal. This kindness and understanding displayed by Ms. Neil could and should be replicated. Since the issue of animal rights is one of the paramount importance to many young people, educators must take this into account. Alternative assignments can be given to students who are highly empathetic and sensitive, as well as to those students who have no desire to pursue a science-based career after graduating high school. There are resources online that can serve as valuable tools, but tools that are not scalpels and pins. Math and science are already stuffed down the unwilling throats of more artistically inclined students; there is no reason to force these children to engage in something so disturbing and unnecessary to them. (4) However, an outright ban on the process of dissection is unwise, as it prepares future biologists and doctors for their careers. Perhaps it is not dissection itself that should be called into question, but the biased, formulaic curriculum as a whole. (5) Humans are individuals, with specific goals. If dissection will not help the students attain their goal, they should be allowed the courtesy to complete an alternative assignment.	(3) 表现出对原文作者推理论证过程的准确理解。从写作角度也体现出对于复杂句型的运用能力。 (4) 提出替代解决方案，进一步支持了观点，论证思路灵活，脉络清晰。 (5) 提出问题的关键不是解剖本身，而是课程的设计问题，能够透过现象看本质，体现了较强的逻辑分析能力。

1. 经典单词

wince 畏缩

assault 攻击

suspension 暂停

pander 迎合

traumatize 使受精神创伤

albeit 虽然

empathetic 同感的

inclined 倾向于……的

outright 完全的，彻底的

courtesy 礼貌，好意

2. 闪光句子

(1) This is all well and good for students who wish to study the sciences after high school, but what is the point of forcing students who are either ethically opposed to the process of dissection to slice open an animal?

(2) Perhaps it is not dissection itself that should be called into question, but the biased, formulaic curriculum as a whole.

(3) If dissection will not help the students attain their goal, they should be allowed the courtesy to complete an alternative assignment.

3. 总体分析

文章从原文作者的经历入手,通过细腻的心理和动作描写,突出了解剖对于学生所产生的心理影响的严重性,由此入手讨论解剖课程存在的合理性。作者没有一概而论地认为应该取消解剖课程,而是主张针对之后不会从事生物研究专业的学生取消课程,有力地反驳了观点 2 和观点 3,并透过现象看本质,指出问题的本质不是解剖课程本身,而是僵化的课程制度,论证严谨脉络清晰。

范文 7 解析

The Internal Clock

Numerous scientific studies have shown that teenagers have a different internal clock than young children or adults. Because of these differences, they naturally sleep in late and stay up late. In response to this new information, some junior high and high school systems have considered changing the time that schools start in the morning. In your point of view, what are the ramifications when school schedules alter?

Read and carefully consider these perspectives. Each suggests a particular way of thinking about the internal clock.

Perspective One

By starting late, students will be more alert and learning will be easier and quicker.

Perspective Two

It will result in getting out too late in the afternoon and causing problems with job schedules.

Perspective Three

Good habits can be shaped by having the original school schedule.

[范文]	[点评]
There is an issue with studying the nuances of the mercurial teenage brain. (1) While on one hand, it is fascinating to learn more about what makes the brain of an adolescent—not a child, not fully adult, different. The troubled, difficult teenager is as old as civilization. In fact, there is a little story, written in cuneiform, pressed by wedged stylus on to ancient clay. The Sumerians addressed one of the issues with teenagers thousands of years before the Common Era. The Sumerian father asks the teen something along the lines of, "Where were you last night?" The surly son replies with words that are strangely familiar to modern ears, "Whatever, dad. I didn't go anywhere. Why can't you just leave me alone?" (2) This brings us to the question at hand: should the school schedule be changed so that classes begin at a later hour? This proposition to alter the schedule, raised by those who have been studying the teenage physiology and psychology, is based on the theory that teenagers are governed by a different internal clock than younger children and adults. One may wonder why the writer spoke of the Sumerian teen, and how this is applicable to a modern question, one that Sumerians would never have tackled. (3) The reason the Sumerian teen applies is as follows: for	(1) 首句精炼地概括了话题的重点,体现了对文章主旨观点的理解。 (2) 用苏美尔人的例子支撑讨论,支持了论点,体现了深厚的素材积累。 (3) 与首段相呼应,体现了结构的严谨,通过古今对比,支持论点,思路严谨逻辑清晰,体现了很好的论辩能力。

（续表）

millennia, teenagers have rebelled, arrived at school or to the fields groggy and grumpy, and have confused their elders with their quixotic and difficult nature. The difference is that modern science has led some bleeding hearts to plead for a change to cater to teens. Although there is nothing wrong with a bit of understanding, the coddling of a young person by adjusting their schedule is in no way conducive to producing a productive, fully developed member of society. (4) There are many more solutions to the issue of a teenager's internal clock, and these do not involve pandering nor do they infringe on the schedules of parents, siblings, and teachers alike. First and foremost, there is no proven benefit to be gleaned from changing the schedule. If teenagers are truly governed by a different internal clock, then this does not explain how teens of the past somehow pulled themselves out of bed before daybreak to head to school, work, or even war. The modern teen is handled with kid gloves, reared by helicopter parents who tend to place blame on all but their little jewel of a child. This is a terribly problematic development in the realm of parenting, and it is not surprising that many are rallying around a change that caters to the child. Children and teens, while precious, should not be catered to in this fashion, even if there is some scientific evidence that they are less productive in the morning due to a different internal clock. (5) The reason they should adjust to their schedule and accept their 8 AM classes with grace is that the current schedule serves a purpose. By showing up on time to class, teens are being trained to show up on time to work. This teaches much more than math, science, or shop class ever could. This teaches responsibility. This teaches the teenager how to function in the "real-world," where there are deadlines, schedules, and repercussions. Imagine a lawyer showing up to court late, and excusing himself with such an impotent excuse as, "My internal clock is different than yours." (6) Here is an unpopular solution to the tired teenager problem: tell them to adapt and learn to adhere to an adult schedule. With all of the extracurricular activities and volunteer hours desired by universities, how on earth is a teenager supposed to find the time to feed the homeless, run cross-country, attend a student council meeting, plow through gobs of busy work, write an essay, and have a semblance of a social life? By changing the schedule, the number of hours left in the day is slashed substantially, which poses a problem for teachers, parents, and the teenagers who would rather rise early so that they can achieve as much as possible during daylight hours. In short, the arguments for changing the schedule in favor of a new study is not going to ultimately help anyone. If anything, it coddles the teenager, and causes conflicts with extra-curricular activities and the work schedules of parents. Teenagers have suffered through this phase in their life, internal clock notwithstanding, since the first cities began to take root. Why is it necessary to pander to the teen now, instead of teaching them the values of responsibility, punctuality, and time management? The answer is that it is not. The internal clock does not justify pandering, and ultimately will not help the young adult who yawns through first period.	(4) 论证过程抓住了重点，层层深入，脉络清晰，也体现了对复杂局势的驾驭能力。 (5) 从反面论证改变时刻表的危害，论据合情合理，切入角度独到，见解深刻。 (6) 正面论证现存时刻表的积极意义，运用例证支持观点，有效地支撑了论点。 (7) 结尾点题，总结概括全文，进一步加强论证，结构完整，思路清晰。

1. 经典单词

mercurial 善变的

rebel 反抗

groggy 无力的
grumpy 脾气暴躁的
plead 辩护
coddle 溺爱
pander 迎合
infringe 侵犯
slash 削减
notwithstanding 虽然

2. 闪光句子

(1) Although there is nothing wrong with a bit of understanding, the coddling of a young person by adjusting their schedule is in no way conducive to producing a productive, fully developed member of society.

(2) This teaches the teenager how to function in the "real-world," where there are deadlines, schedules, and repercussions.

(3) With all of the extracurricular activities and volunteer hours desired by universities, how on earth is a teenager supposed to find the time to feed the homeless, run cross-country, attend a student council meeting, plow through gobs of busy work, write an essay, and have a semblance of a social life?

3. 总体分析

整篇文章脉络结构清晰,切入点合理,见解独到深刻。首尾呼应,论证严谨,从正反两面进行辨证分析,通过例证和对比的手法,进一步支撑观点,完善文章结构。用词贴切,句式灵活多变,体现了对复杂句式的驾驭能力。

范文 8 解析

The Skill of Writing

Text messages, emails and letters are everyday communication tools, although nowadays, text messages and emails appear to gain popularity while letters are used less frequently. The fears that writing skills will be attached with less importance are rooted mainly in the concern that the growing popularity of mobile phones and computers is about to make emails and text messaging much more popular. Such worries are unsupported.

Read and carefully consider these perspectives. Each suggests a particular way of thinking about that the skill of writing will disappear.

Perspective One

The prevalence of emails and text messages will not change the purposes, contents and conventions of communication, but merely medium, font or sentence length.

Perspective Two

Another fact to note is that all communication is interpersonal and interactive, thereby requiring information senders to use language properly and convey messages clearly and precisely.

Perspective Three

Time is money. People now focus less on the conventions of language. With the development

of mobiles, the proportion of oral communications increased.

[范文]	[点评]
Little girls at Camp Arrowhead, an idyllic Hill Country retreat in Central Texas, usually spent the inaccurately dubbed "rest hour" scribbling away on personalized stationary, drawing careful loops and rounding the corners of their cursive words with a love and dedication now lost. When the mail arrived, it was better than even the most anticipated Christmas morning. The envelopes would tumble from burlap or canvas mail sacks, and their little hands would excitedly rip apart the letters they received; some were from family, some were from friends, but all were akin to treasure. Camp Arrowhead is now gone, a victim of internal squabbling over property values, mineral rights, and stipulations and loopholes in a wilted will. The camp is gone, and so are the days where those little girls wrote letters. That activity has been replaced by text speak, rapid-fire emails, and LOL's. (1) The scene described was commonplace not that long ago, and was by no means exclusive to the now dead Camp Arrowhead.	(1) 对在 Camp Arrowhead 中写信的女生的细腻描写,突出了如今信件礼节的缺失。
In the 1990s, the art of writing was still something to be valued. Elementary school students were taught how to write a formal and informal letter, with the correct headings, salutations, capitalization, punctuations, and appropriate closing remarks. Today, email etiquette is encouraged, yet no one can come to a reasonable consensus on what exactly that entails. (2) The old guard still signs off with a "Kind Regards," the new guard offers "Peace, yo, TTYL" if anything at all. Once upon a time, kids practiced their Hancock inspired signatures; now kids perfect their pout on their smart phone camera. This all sounds quite tragic, especially to those who value the English language. The internet has created a new breed of neurotic, the "grammar Nazi," who brutalizes those poor unfortunate souls who confuse your and you're. This shift in how we use language to communicate has changed us irrevocably, and it can either be viewed as a sad devolution or a mere evolution.	(2) 对比论证,体现对原文主旨的理解,加深了论证力度。
Language is not a permanent thing. Languages die completely, and often. Languages evolve to suit the needs of those who speak and write them. If the English language were immune to evolution, we would still refer to sheriffs as shire reeves, we would call our female children Aelfgifu or Aedgith instead of Heavyn or Abcd; our boys would be Aelle or Aethelbert as opposed to Jaydyn or Caidyn. We would not call our cousins "cousins" nor our uncles "uncles." We would speak in Shakespearean riddles, referring to light that shatters windows and our paramours as avatars of stars. We would spell things differently, and vastly so. The British and Americans would have no need to squabble over "color" versus "colour," "ostracize" versus "ostracise." (3) The fact is simple. Languages, especially English, change despite the threnodies of those who love Keats more than Kanye.	(3) 运用大量例证,支撑观点,体现了作者深厚的素材积累以及对复杂句式的驾驭能力。
Technology changes things. This is something on which we all agree. The advent of the information age has carried with it enormous benefits, like vacuum cleaners for cats to ride on as they clean our floors for us. On a more intellectual note, one can see English in its first incarnation online, browsing every Anglo-Saxon charter by Sawyer number via a convenient, searchable interface. With the flood of information at our fingertips, we can choose to resurrect the greats of the past and read Gerard Manley Hopkins from a little screen, while responding to our peers with a quick "brb." (4)	(4) 本段这三句体现了对于高级词汇的使用能力,也说明了对作者的深度论证方式的理解。
We are not the first to abbreviate for the sake of time and effort. OMG is older than you realize. Latin manuscripts from the Middle Ages read like an adolescent	

(续表)

group text to the unschooled eye, covered in shortened versions of "episcopus," "ealdorman," and "sacerdote."(5) While this may be seen as feeble justification for devolution, one must realize that languages experience great change over time, no matter how strongly opposed one may be to this. This recent explosion of too-busy-to-care speak is merely another incarnation of the English language. What must be done to remedy complete evaporation of beautiful metaphors and complex syntax is to continue to teach children how to write a letter without reliance on emojis or reaction gifs. (6) Schools must continue to stress the glory of iambic pentameter, and not discount the English of Shakespeare, More, and Marlowe. Poetry should be honored, and Beowulf should serve as a lesson in how the words employed to tell a story might change, but storytelling remains the same. There is a way to preserve the excitement that came from opening letters at that now ghostly girls' camp in the hills. The question is less whether or not English is changing, but whether or not the elation that comes with writing thoughtfully has become a relic of the not-so-distant past. (7) The challenge we face is based more on disconnection, on thoughtlessness, on a dearth of carefully selected words. We can preserve the beauty of English, the excitement that bubbles up internally when receiving word from another. We can still communicate with meaning despite the memes that both stunt us and stoke us. It is our choice whether the written word lives or dies from a wilted will.	(5) 利用古代的例子支撑自己的观点,体现了丰富的素材积累,由古及今,论证清晰合理。 (6) 指出问题关键所在,体现了清晰的论证思路与逻辑。 (7) 文末点题,归纳总结全文观点,前后相呼应,逻辑架构清晰严谨。

1. 经典单词

scribble 乱写

stipulation 条款

salutation 问候

etiquette 礼节,规矩

tragic 悲剧的

brutalize 变残忍

irrevocable 不可改变的

abbreviate 缩写

wilt 枯萎

thoughtlessness 欠考虑

2. 闪光句子

(1) This shift in how we use language to communicate has changed us irrevocably, and it can either be viewed as a sad devolution or a mere evolution.

(2) The advent of the information age has carried with it enormous benefits, like vacuum cleaners for cats to ride on as they clean our floors for us.

(3) With the flood of information at our fingertips, we can choose to resurrect the greats of the past and read Gerard Manley Hopkins from a little screen, while responding to our peers with a quick "brb."

(4) Poetry should be honored, and Beowulf should serve as a lesson in how the words employed to tell a story might change, but storytelling remains the same.

(5) The question is less whether or not English is changing, but whether or not the elation that comes with writing thoughtfully has become a relic of the not-so-distant past.

3. 总体分析

本文例证丰富，逻辑清晰，结构严谨，由古及今，由浅入深，横纵两个方向进行对比论证，有力地支撑了观点，丰富了文章的架构。在语言层面，运用了大量的复杂句式，长短句交错，富有节奏感。在结构方面，前后呼应，篇尾点题，脉络清晰。

范文 9 解析

The Working Hours

In recent years, working hours have become a controversial issue, at a time when employees' benefits have been given serious thought. Although the extension of working hours is believed to have an impact on general well-being and result in work-family conflict and job stress, this practice is remarkably popular in many countries. Long working hours have a negative impact upon individuals, the organizations they work for, and ultimately upon the national economy and society as a whole.

Read and carefully consider these perspectives. Each suggests a particular way of thinking about the working hours.

Perspective One

It is not only to damage personal relationships (with families particularly), disrupt social lives and impede community activities but also to cause a feeling of stress, a psychological disturbance that is experienced by many working people.

Perspective Two

To employers, long working hours, although promising maximum benefit from limited resources every now and then, have destructive effects in the long term.

Perspective Three

It is reasonable for an employer to expect some degree of flexibility during a particularly busy period, but to those employers, reliance on the jobs with extended hours has the tendency to become a regular event.

[范文]	[点评]
Picture all that was wrong with the 19th century. What images arise in the mind's eye? Odds are that pictures of filthy, exhausted children with empty gazed drift about like sooty apparitions, black bristling brooms in hand, ready to risk their lives and health for a half-penny. Perhaps the mangled hands of young immigrant women come to mind, only to burst into flame in the tragedy of the Triangle Shirt Waist Factory disaster. Workhouses, with sad broken bowls of near inedible slop, materialize, and the black and white faces of the downtrodden, the overworked, and the destitute stare back at you from a comfortable divide, the divide of time. It	(1) 从19世纪的现实入手，运用多重修辞进行了细腻的描写，表现了作者深厚的文字功底。
seems almost barbaric, unthinkable that so recently it was permissible to risk the lives of workers in the name of industrial revolution. After all, is this world not modern, fair, riddled with unions that champion the rights of workers, with laws that protect children from the toils of child labor, and the desperate from meeting death by bad business practice? Do we not have leisure, paid vacations, health insurance, and the almighty weekend to keep us well? (2)The answer is not as cut and dry as one would think. In fact, businesses the world over are surreptitiously	(2) 运用多重问句，层层深入，突出强调了重点。从语言来看增强了句式的多样性，也体现了对复杂句式的驾驭能力。

(续表)

<table>
<tr><td>increasing hours, although many agree on the fact that a longer workday is ultimately detrimental to well being. If this is the case, then why do employers continue to enforce longer workdays?
Some argue that longer workdays cause a massive increase in stress and the crumbling of a family. While accurate in some ways, one must realize that in times endless labor, such as harvest season or any of the aforementioned 19th century scenarios, people mended the rifts in their relationships. It can be surmised that the breakdown in relationships is not due to longer hours logged in an office, nor due to stress. If it were, then how did our predecessors, who had no enforced weekends, no guarantees, no minimum wage, no severance pay, manage to muddle through? (3) These symptoms are not exclusively due to the sneaky increase in hours logged. It can be argued that these are symptoms of a societal malady as opposed to one related strictly to workload.</td><td>(3) 结合 19 世纪的情况进行论证,论据充分,条理清晰,结构严谨,富有说服力,体现了作者深度论证的能力和对主旨的把握能力。</td></tr>
<tr><td>There are more believable stances on the issue; these address both employer motivation and employee productivity. (4) It is expected in times of increased production or labor is required, that more hours must be worked to achieve the goals of a business. The quandary arises when an employer, pleased by the increased production, begins abusing this policy, increasing hours motivated by greed or success. However, this is not the best policy. It has been observed that while short spans of increased work is beneficial to the business, it has been shown that over time, increased hours actually impact the production capabilities of the business negatively. Therefore, it is permissible, even expected, to work longer hours at certain, crucial times. Albeit, it is inadvisable to employers and employees alike to overwork; the aggregate effects are ultimately detrimental. Why then would an employer continue to hold his employees hostage, per se, in order to chase a goal that may remain out of reach due to lack of employee energy, increased stress, and less time to exist outside of the walls of the modern day workhouse.</td><td>(4) 从雇员和雇主两个角度进行论证,思路清晰,结构严谨,分析全面,支持了观点 2。</td></tr>
<tr><td>In short, employees should realize that extra hours might sometimes be part of the job. (5) It is one of the truths of employment. However, no one benefits from being whittled down to little more than a work horse dragging the company along with a bit in the mouth and a whip to the hindquarters. The dirty faces of the Industrial Revolution may seem far in the past, cracked photographs and Dickensian characters, but no more. However, if employers continue to value products and quarterly earnings over their employees, our progress is invalid. We are no different than the sooty chimney sweeps of a not so bygone age.</td><td>(5) 最后一段总结全文观点,调和加班对于雇主和雇员的影响,体现了对文章主旨的把握和论证的严密逻辑性。</td></tr>
</table>

1. 经典单词

filthy 肮脏的
apparition 幻影
bristling 发怒的
mangle 损坏
barbaric 野蛮的,原始的
almighty 全能的
surreptitiously 不正当地
detrimental 有害的
crumbling 破碎
aforementioned 前面提及的

2. 闪光句子

(1) It seems almost barbaric, unthinkable that so recently it was permissible to risk the lives of workers in the name of industrial revolution.

(2) It can be surmised that the breakdown in relationships is not due to longer hours logged in an office, nor due to stress.

(3) If it were, then how did our predecessors, who had no enforced weekends, no guarantees, no minimum wage, no severance pay, manage to muddle through?

(4) There are more believable stances on the issue; these address both employer motivation and employee productivity.

(5) However, if employers continue to value product and quarterly earnings over their employees, our progress is invalid. We are no different than the sooty chimney sweeps of a not so bygone age.

3. 总体分析

全文思路清晰,主旨明确,从19世纪的历史情况入手分析,论据有多个实例支撑,具有说服性。从雇员和雇主两方面入手,论证全面,分析透彻,说理清晰,逻辑严密,体现了对文章主旨的精准理解和深厚的写作功底。从语言角度,文中多处运用了反问句,层层深入,增强了论证的说服力。

范文 10 解析

Bilingual Accreditation

While the United States has just one official national language, English is certainly not the only language in which Americans communicate. In fact, bilingual fluency is highly desirable in many professions, including business, education, and medicine. In an effort to ready students for success in their future careers, some high schools may consider instituting programs that would offer bilingual accreditation to students who successfully complete a significant portion of their schooling in a language other than English. Since bilingual certification is not a necessary component of traditional education, should schools be expected to explore this option for interested students? As American high schools aim to remain competitive as measured by increasingly rigorous international education standards, innovative programs such as bilingual certification may prove to be essential.

Read and carefully consider these perspectives. Each discusses relevant aspects of offering bilingual accreditation.

Perspective One

Schools should encourage bilingual fluency but should not be expected to offer special classes or programs. School administrators need to work on strengthening the existing curriculum rather than overcomplicating instruction by attempting to incorporate additional programs that do not reinforce traditional education.

Perspective Two

Offering bilingual accreditation weakens the core of high school curriculum. A large enough portion of the student population already struggles to maintain passing grades when taught in English, and adding other languages would likely add to that number.

Perspective Three

Bilingual accreditation should be offered, but it needs to be thoughtfully implemented. Courses taught in languages other than English need to be carefully selected to ensure that this program does not affect the integrity of the high school diploma.

[范文]	[点评]
There is little on earth that provides as much satisfaction as bilingual fluency. Being able to communicate without a hitch in more than one language expands one's cultural horizons as well as one's potential employment opportunities. (1) In centuries past, speaking more than one language was seen as an essential part of one's education. In today's technological, mathematical, business, and scientifically minded world, some do not see the validity in implementing bilingual accreditation at the high school level, even though employers hope that potential employees have fluency in either Spanish or Mandarin. Others claim, with no factual evidence to bolster their claim, that bilingual accreditation weakens the high school curriculum. This stance would be more believable if the high school curriculum was effective. Sadly, due to increased government meddling and a rampant addiction to measuring merit via the ineffective method of standardized testing, the education system and the core curriculum have already been damaged, rendered impotent and ineffectual. By implementing bilingual accreditation, the feeble education system may yet be able to give its students an opportunity to learn an applicable skill that will serve them in life much more than a passing a standardized test. (2)	(1) 开篇强调了双语的重要性,开门见山地表明态度。 (2) 在反驳反对双语的观点后,点明主旨,再一次强调双语的重要意义。
If a student wishes to pursue a curriculum that includes bilingual accreditation, then that student should be afforded that option as a right. Just as students who would prefer to pursue a career instead of college, this nation's education system should seriously consider expanding the choices available to students. (3) By implementing bilingual accreditation, the school system is fostering the growth of a special individual. Bilingualism helps with pattern recognition. Bilingualism also has been shown by some preliminary studies to reduce the chance of dementia and Alzheimer's disease later in life. Not only are bilingual people more employable, they are at the forefront of our new, much smaller world. The methods by which foreign languages are taught in most high schools are ineffective. Most students, despite years of education in a foreign language, are even able to order food or ask for direction. If a bilingual accreditation programs were implemented nationwide with care and consideration, the amount of students classified as bilingual would increase exponentially.	(3) 进一步补充观点,逻辑严谨,论证充分,体现了深度论证的能力和对文章主旨的把握能力。
The only issues that could possibly arise from the implementation of bilingual accreditation programs are principally of a monetary nature. (4) It costs vast amounts of money, all generated by the tax-paying public, to implement changes of this sort on a grand scale. Also, framers of the new curriculum to include bilingual accreditation should choose which classes are taught in another language and to what extent. It is crucial for the students desiring a bilingual education to be fully educated, and not miss important topics due to overzealous bilingual instruction. The program must be artfully tailored to maximize fluency in more than one language while not compromising the purpose and integrity of the lessons being taught. However, this is not an argument that is exclusive to bilingual accreditation programs. This attention to curriculum should be given to all programs, regardless of their ultimate goals. The courses should be selected with attention and care, and each student graduating with bilingual accreditation should possess the same skills as	(4) 引出双语制度可能存在的阻碍及解决办法,进一步补充论点,层层深入论证,使文章结构更为完整,论证更为严谨。

（续表）

their peers，yet with an added boon，the boon of bilingualism. Our world shrinks ever smaller by the minute as technology connects us to the most far-flung reaches of the globe. Now is the time to encourage effective learning of a second language. The students who benefit from these programs will be the shapers of the future，and denying them the opportunity to gain fluency in another language is backwards indeed. We should look forward，and rethink our curriculums，remodeling them to offer bilingual accreditation.（5）	（5）篇末点题，总结全文的主要观点，语言凝练，逻辑清晰，体现了很好的归纳总结能力。

1. 经典单词

stance 立场
meddling 干预
rampant 蔓延的
impotent 无效的
feeble 无力的
forefront 最前线
overzealous 过分热心的
monetary 财政的
artfully 巧妙地
boon 恩惠

2. 闪光句子

（1）Being able to communicate without a hitch in more than one language expands one's cultural horizons as well as one's potential employment opportunities.

（2）Sadly，due to increased government meddling and a rampant addiction to measuring merit via the ineffective method of standardized testing，the education system and the core curriculum have already been damaged，rendered impotent and ineffectual.

（3）The courses should be selected with attention and care，and each student graduating with bilingual accreditation should possess the same skills as their peers，yet with an added boon，the boon of bilingualism.

（4）Our world shrinks ever smaller by the minute as technology connects us to the most far-flung reaches of the globe.

（5）We should look forward，and rethink our curriculums，remodeling them to offer bilingual accreditation.

3. 总体分析

整篇文章立意独到，分析深入透彻，逻辑清楚，从必要性、重要性入手分析，没有局限于问题的表层，而是深入探究了潜在的问题，并提供了解决方案，层层深入，结构完整，论证严谨，语言凝练，说服力强。

范文 11 解析

High School-Based Career-Readiness Programs

High school curriculum is designed to ready students for future career paths，many of which include higher education. Whether or not students choose to attend college, a comprehensive high school education provides an essential foundation. Some educators argue that high schools have an obligation to provide career readiness training for students who do not intend to pursue a college degree. Should high schools invest time and money to develop programs for students who do not wish to continue their education beyond 12th grade? Given the many factors that students weigh when considering if, where, and when to attend college, it is prudent for educators to explore programs that contribute to a better-skilled workforce.

Read and carefully consider these perspectives. Each offers suggestions regarding high school-based career-readiness programs.

Perspective One

Rather than concentrating solely on students who may not pursue higher education, high schools should help all students develop valuable skills for the workforce. Requiring students to complete classes that focus on key cognitive strategies, content knowledge, and relevant skills and techniques will help them enter the workforce, either immediately after high school or later in their lives.

Perspective Two

Career-readiness training should be provided for students who do not wish to pursue college, and should be particularly targeted at students who are at risk for dropping out. By reframing their high school experience as training for successful careers rather than government-mandated learning, students can succeed where they may previously have failed.

Perspective Three

Students who do not want to pursue higher education should not be given additional accommodations in high school because they should not be provided any incentives to not attend college. College is the best way to learn how to be productive in the workforce, and students should be encouraged to attend, since it is in their best interest.

[范文]

American youth has been force-fed a terrible lie. This lie, while well intentioned, is that college is for everyone. It is a sad American pattern to sell something as essential to the masses, such as white picket-fence dreams and two car garages. This myth, this utter falsehood, that it is a part of the American Dream to own one's own home led to the housing crisis and the collapse of the market not so many years back. (1) As the once starry-eyed dreamers watched impotently as their homes, their cars, their dreams were repossessed, snatched up by banks or towed off by repo-men, the reverie of the white picket-fence self-immolated, leaving many destitute and devastated, and our economy limping. A similar lie is being told to high school students the nation over, and that lie is that college is the best and only route to success in the workforce. Attending university is in the best interest of the young adult, and other paths to careers are ill advised, foolish, and fruitless. (2)

Simply put, college is not for everyone. The Europeans seem to realize this, offering options of trade-based education as opposed to penalizing those who do not have a college degree. The irony is that requiring college for all does not simply hurt those who are not interested in higher education; it hurts the millions of

[点评]

(1) 通过美国梦的弊端,深入分析现象的本质,体现了出色的思辨能力和对主旨的深入理解。

(2) 从反面观点入手,突出此观点的错误性,欲扬先抑,为下文的论述做铺垫。

（续表）

college students who do wish to pursue higher education. There are many who simply wish to practice the art of motorcycle maintenance, and these people should not be shamed and cajoled into the not so comforting arms of a university. The inclusion of more trade-minded students in colleges has watered down the pool of bachelors and masters alike, leading to a glut of graduates who struggle to find employment. The other downside is the leviathan that is student debt. (3) Why must those who champion college for all ignore the fact that it is economically idiotic for many to pursue this? This issue can be resolved by simply offering trade-based options earlier; career-based programs should be implemented in public schools nationwide to discourage dropping out as well as thinning the pool of applicants to college, thereby benefitting both parties in question. (4) By providing career-based training early, dropping out is discouraged. Many at-risk teens do not see the value in annotating *The Scarlet Letter*, nor do they wish to struggle through English 101 or Music Appreciation at the college level. Many possess a different kind of intelligence, one that can be fostered and grown by career-based programs in high school. Some schools offer these sorts of programs, yet many others are cutting classes such as shop in order to make way for more math, more science. (5) When will the powers realize that math and science are not the only paths to take? When will the defunding of arts and career-based programs in favor of an insane goal desist? Not everyone is cut out to be a nanotechnologist, a molecular biologist, an astronaut, or a petroleum engineer; some people just want to repair light fixtures, and the world needs those people more than they need a college degree and insurmountable debts. It seems as if our country cannot make up its mind, preaching science while cutting funding to NASA, preaching college for all but doing precious little to make it affordable for all. This is wholly illogical, coming from a country that has been championing logic over creativity, science over skill, for decades now. By implementing career-based education in high schools across the nation, everyone can win. Perhaps it is time to rethink the importance placed on a college diploma, and start thinking about a different path for different minds.	(3) 通过对比分析的手法，以两类学生的经历为例证，支持观点，增强了说服力，丰富了论证结构，体现了灵活的论证思路与方式。 (4) 提出解决方案，完善论证结构，承上启下，引出下文的具体探讨，同时体现了对复杂句式的驾驭能力。 (5) 补充论据，完善了论证结构，条理清晰，在探究问题本质后继而提出解决方案，体现了对主旨的精准把握与严密的论证。

1. 经典单词

intentioned 有……意图的

falsehood 错误的信仰

repossess 收回

reverie 幻想

fruitless 徒劳的

cajole 哄骗

annotate 注释

defunding 撤销资助

desist 停止

insurmountable 不能克服的

2. 闪光句子

(1) This myth, this utter falsehood, that it is a part of the American Dream to own one's own home led to the housing crisis and the collapse of the market not so many years back.

(2) Simply put, college is not for everyone.

(3) The irony is that requiring college for all does not simply hurt those who are not interested in higher education; it hurts the millions of college students who do wish to pursue higher education.

(4) Not everyone is cut out to be a nanotechnologist, a molecular biologist, an astronaut, or a petroleum engineer; some people just want to repair light fixtures, and the world needs those people more than they need a college degree and insurmountable debts.

(5) This is wholly illogical, coming from a country that has been championing logic over creativity, science over skill, for decades now.

3. 总体分析

整篇文章观点明确,论证清晰,布局合理。从语言来看,措辞合理,长短句结合,对复杂句式的应用也比较到位,句式结构也较为多样。从内容来看,本文论述清晰,论据严谨,例证丰富,有较强的说服力,可以层层深入,不局限于问题表面,能够对问题实质做到精准的把握。

范文 12 解析

(题目同范文 11)

<table>
<tr>
<td>[范文]
Children are often asked, "What do you want to be when you grow up?" Little do they know whether or not they go to college has a huge impact on their career choices. The issue under discussion is whether or not schools should develop dual curricula to serve both those students who are college-bound, and those who intend to forego college and enter a career directly after high school graduation. (1) The fundamental concern is how to best serve all students, which I believe should be through two curricula working together. (2)
The first point of view supports having all students pursue the same curriculum, one primarily directed at college-bound students. (3) It essentially states that an academic-only curriculum is valuable for all students, regardless of their future plans. It is true that the ability to think critically, have a wide range of content knowledge, and be adept at the skills and techniques required to live a full and productive life, are important to all students. A well-rounded person is able to take advantage of many more opportunities than those with limited skills.
Furthermore, should a career-bound student change his mind and decide to go to college, he will have the basic requirements for a successful college experience. However, if a student is determined to start his career directly after high school, the college curriculum could be a waste of his time, and he would be better served by taking courses which prepare him for his career. I am in partial agreement with option one, since a broad, basic education is important for all students. However, it is similarly important to prepare students for their future lives which may begin immediately after high school.
The second option supports career-readiness education. (4) As stated above, it is important to recognize that some students are set on embarking on a career after high school rather than on going to college. High school is the place to prepare these students, since it can offer the courses which are most applicable to them. Furthermore, students in danger of dropping out of high school are generally those who are uninterested or bored by the academic curriculum. Such students would be</td>
<td>[点评]
(1) 精准把握问题的实质,对于文章主旨的总结清晰凝练,体现了良好的理解能力和逻辑分析能力。
(2) 开门见山,重点明确,引出下文,逻辑清晰。
(3) 从 college-bound 入手分析,脉络清楚,结构严谨。体现了清晰的思路和严谨的论证结构。
(4) 在第二方面,分析 career readiness 教育,补充前文观点,使文章结构更为丰满,论据更为充分,体现了开阔的思路。</td>
</tr>
</table>

（续表）

more engaged and successful if they were able to take classes which fit their goals and interests, and would be more likely not only to stay in school, but also to be well-prepared for their careers. This option purposes a dual curriculum, one for the college-bound and one for career readiness, and thus provides the best education for both. On the assumption that non-college-bound students are also taking an adequate number of general education classes, and supplementing them with courses designed to provide them with the skills they need for their careers, these students will now have a solid academic foundation as well as career skills. College-bound students will still have the option to take more academic classes, thus I support this option because it provides the best solution for both groups. Those who agree that students who are not planning on going to college should not be offered career-centered classes are denying the fact that not all students go to college, even if given incentives to do so. This option does not take into consideration the numerous facts which can affect whether or not a student goes to college. Some students cannot afford college fees, even with scholarships, some have a low GPA which would prohibit their acceptance at college, and some do poorly on pre-college tests such as the ACT.（5） Encouraging students to go to college is not enough to ensure that they will. Though it may be true that college teaches how to be productive in the workforce, it is also true that being a fully-qualified mechanic or electrician after high-school is extremely productive to those who choose these careers. This option is an elitist one which would disregard those for whom college is not a goal, and is one with which I completely disagree. It is vital to all students that high schools prepare them for their future, whatever that may be. Those who choose college are well served by an intensive academic curriculum which gives them a solid foundation for college. On the other hand, for those who choose, or are forced by circumstances to forego college in preference to immediate entry into the workforce, it is important that, along with a sufficient academic foundation, they also receive training in their intended careers. Thus the second perspective that of providing both an academic and a career-oriented curriculum, serves the needs of both and is the most effective one for all students.	（5）进一步补充论点，体现了论证的严谨和思考的周密，完善了文章的结构。

1. 经典单词

forego 放弃

adept 熟练的

well-rounded 全面发展的

embark 从事

elitist 优秀人才

2. 闪光句子

（1）Little do they know whether or not they go to college has a huge impact on their career choices.

（2）I am in partial agreement with option one, since a broad, basic education is important for all students.

（3）This option is an elitist one which would disregard those for whom college is not a goal, and is one with which I completely disagree.

3. 总体分析

文章整体脉络清晰，例证充足，主旨明确，分论点充分，结构严谨，能够从多角度进行论证，环环相扣。从语言来看，句式较为简单，没有太多的复杂句式，并且语言简洁，直白易懂，逻辑清楚，说服力强。

范文 13 解析

Student Feedback in Lesson Planning

Studies show that students not only retain more information but also enjoy learning more when they actively participate in the classroom. Teachers therefore strive to optimize engagement to foster a positive, effective instructional environment. In an effort to increase student interaction in the high school classroom, some educators argue that curriculum should take into account the interests and suggestions of students. Since teachers cannot allow students to choose every aspect of a lesson, is it worth the time and effort to actively seek relevant student feedback? As high schools aim to improve the quality of the education they offer to students, studeats' opinions may prove to be valuable.

Read and carefully consider these perspectives. Each discusses the relevance of student feedback in lesson planning.

Perspective One

Many colleges require students to complete a course survey before they are eligible to receive their semester grades. Colleges use students' responses to evaluate course materials to ensure quality education. High schools would benefit from implementing a similar system of regular feedback on classroom lesson plans by students.

Perspective Two

Students are not qualified to provide insight regarding lesson planning or curriculum design. Improving education quality is the responsibility of educators, and they are rightfully in charge of making effective changes.

Perspective Three

Many school districts evaluate teachers using students' test scores and conducting in-classroom observations. Information gathered from student surveys could not only inform lesson design, but also provide another source of evaluation by which to measure teacher effectiveness.

[范文]	[点评]
Teenagers know everything. This is an undeniable truth to them. However, adults have it in their minds that they know best, but one never knows as much as a high school student. Sarcasm aside, there is massive value in listening to students instead of simply assuming that designers of a curriculum know more about the most effective way to teach students. (1) In case the framers of curriculums forget, they are supposed serve the students, and the students are not on this planet to merely follow their orders. How can the department of education claim that students have no valid input when they are seventeen, yet college campuses world over alter their lesson plans and teaching methods based on student feedback?	(1) 表明观点，指出问题所在，表现了对文章主旨的精确理解。

（续表）

What massive shift takes place from seventeen to eighteen, from high school to university? The answer is that no great change takes place, but what occurs is an increase in respect and a willingness to be more malleable. College professors respect the feedback that students give. Online resources allow students to rate professors, on silly scales such as physical attractiveness; these include but are not limited to understandability, clarity, fairness, teaching style, and other factors. Many college professors encourage and even require students to fill out a survey so that they can better influence future students with their lessons. Why is this right simply denied to many high schoolers? (2)	(2) 由大学制度推及到高中，支持中心论点，逻辑清晰，论证合理，说服力强。
An example of how student feedback can drastically improve education is the following hypothetical situation. (3) Imagine an AP Anatomy class, populated by seniors who are more than ready to escape the bonds of high school and run straight to on-campus housing and Biology 101. The teacher, adhering to a prescribed lesson plan, asks them to construct a model of a DNA molecule out of random materials. It must be free standing. It may not use pipe cleaners, clay, cardboard, or paper. It must be pleasing to the eye. If it is not original, their grade will suffer. The students care about their grades, so they undertake the project with a sigh. William begins the project, but every attempt fails miserably. He began the project early in the morning on a Saturday, and it is now 11:43 PM on Sunday. William has spent a grand total of fourteen hours cutting up felt, twisting coat hangers, and screaming ineffectually as every model collapses. He puts homework for his other courses on the backburner, since the DNA model is a major test grader. It is now 4:11 AM on a Tuesday, and he has finally found a way to make the model stand up unassisted. William felt as if he was the only one who had trouble with this assignment that actually taught him nothing about anatomy. When he asked his classmates how they fared, they responded with similar tales of time lost, fingers sliced, and feeble frustrated yelps as the models buckled in front of them. This scenario could continue to play out year after year. However, if the anatomy teacher were encouraged to ask for end-of-the-year feedback by the school, and then allowed to apply student feedback to his lesson plan, his future students may never experience the frustration of a needlessly complicated, time consuming project that does nothing but irritates his students. (4)	(3) 利用虚构的故事进行论证，描述细腻，逻辑清晰，形象生动，富有说服力。 (4) 论证贴合主题，体现了对主旨的精确把握以及对原文作者推理论证过程的准确理解。
The above story is invented, but if one asks a high school student whether or not they have learned something, they are more than capable of providing an honest answer. Their youth does not render them incapable of constructive feedback. After all, they are the recipients of the lesson, and they are well aware whether a lesson is effective. Implementing student feedback would benefit students and teachers alike. (5)	(5) 文末点题，再次强调高中生反馈的重要性，使全文结构更加完整，说理清晰。

1. 经典单词

undeniable 不可否认的

sarcasm 讽刺

malleable 有延展性的

drastically 彻底地

adhere 坚持，依附

prescribed 规定的

ineffectually 无益地

backburner 不重要的
unassisted 无助的
frustration 挫折
irritate 激怒

2. 闪光句子

(1) Sarcasm aside, there is massive value in listening to students instead of simply assuming that designers of a curriculum know more about the most effective way to teach students.

(2) However, if the anatomy teacher were encouraged to ask for end-of-the-year feedback by the school, and then allowed to apply student feedback to his lesson plan, his future students may never experience the frustration of a needlessly complicated, time consuming project that does nothing but irritates his students.

(3) The above story is invented, but if one asks a high school student whether or not they have learned something, they are more than capable of providing an honest answer.

3. 总体分析

本文的论证方法很有特色,通过比较高中和大学的教育反馈制度,来强调高中生反馈的重要性,主题的论证部分利用虚构的事例来说理,形象生动,贴合主旨。整体脉络清晰,结构严谨,论证层层深入,体现了对主旨的精准理解和优秀的逻辑推理能力。

范文 14 解析

(题目同范文 13)

[范文]	[点评]
Teenagers have lots of opinions, many of which we share rather loudly. Taking into consideration the students' feelings about the courses they study in high school has both pros and cons. (1) Some argue that schools should provide students a way to make their preferences known, others feel students are too young to make good decisions about what to study, and others argue that surveying students can help make the curriculum more relevant to them and provide another way to evaluate a teacher's effectiveness. I agree that students' interests should be surveyed as long as they are not, in and of themselves, the basis for creating a curriculum.	(1) 开门见山地提出观点,引出下文从优缺点两方面进行论证,脉络清晰,论证全面透彻。
From the first perspective, it is argued that high schools should do what colleges do and survey students to see how they feel about their classroom lessons. Studies show that when high school students are engaged because they enjoy their studies, and understand the relevance of what they are learning, they are more participatory in class and remember more of what they have learned. However, one problem is that schools cannot let students create the lessons, since this would lead to chaos with so many students expressing different opinions. (2)	(2) 反驳观点 1,逻辑清晰,论证合理,体现了对原文主旨的良好把握和灵活的论证思路。
However, if it were made clear that not all suggestions would be used but that there would be some way to pare down the suggestions, and implement only those with most students' support, it would be possible for the students' preferences to be included in a lesson. (3) Schools could survey students, compile a list of five top suggestions, then have students vote on them. In this way, at least some student suggestions, and hopefully the most popular ones, would be part of the curriculum and promote more interaction and learning in a classroom. Surely this is the goal of	(3) 对观点 1 的缺陷进行补充论证,完善论证结构,体现了较好的论证思路和技巧。

（续表）

education, and therefore I believe that it should be encouraged. On the other hand, there are those who think that only teachers should be in charge of the curriculum because students are not qualified to make those changes. It's true that students don't have the education, knowledge and maturity to design lessons, but the argument doesn't say that the curriculum would be totally in the hands of students, but only that students' preferences should be considered. (4)	(4) 进一步补充论证，并且指明论证观点的关键缺陷，体现了对主旨的精准理解和较好的思辨能力。
Those who argue that students aren't capable of designing the curriculum have misunderstood the statement. Everybody can benefit from suggestions, including educators, so there is nothing wrong with finding out what students want and trying to incorporate at least some of it into the curriculum. Any good teacher does this already, and tries to make her examples relevant to what the students are interested in, such as teaching math by using basketball or baseball examples. So the argument is already partially in force, and those who misread it by thinking that the entire curriculum would be made up by students are misinterpreting the argument and coming to a wrong conclusion. (5)	(5) 指出观点的关键失误，洞察力强，论证严谨，结构清晰。
Finally, some argue that allowing student surveys could make lessons more interesting and also be a way of evaluating a teacher's effectiveness. I personally think that this would be a better way to evaluate teachers than using test scores, which don't always reflect the actual learning. But surveys are completely subjective, and it would be very difficult to tell which responses really reflect students' satisfaction and which are just written because the student needs to write something. So I somewhat support this option because it is better than cold test scores, but I also see problems in it, so can't support it fully. (6)	(6) 分析最后一个观点，表明自己的立场，论证严谨，观点明确，体现了良好的深度论证能力。
If a school administration makes it really clear that, just because students are asked to make lesson plan suggestions, it doesn't mean that all suggestions will be used, and that students are not in charge of making the curriculum, then the first perspective, allowing students to give their opinion about what they would like to study, is a good one. This one will make at least some lesson plans more interesting and relevant, and that will lead to better learning.	

1. 经典单词

undeniable 不可否认的

sarcasm 讽刺

chaos 混乱

pare down 削减

compile 汇编

misread 误解

2. 闪光句子

(1) Taking into consideration the students' feelings about the courses they study in high school has both pros and cons.

(2) I agree that students' interests should be surveyed as long as they are not, in and of themselves, the basis for creating a curriculum.

(3) So I somewhat support this option because it is better than cold test scores, but I also see problems in it, so can't support it fully.

3. 总体分析

文章脉络清晰，结构布局合理，开篇开门见山表明自己的观点，并对文章主题进行简要的论证，下文依次论证三个观点，表明自己的立场并对观点进行分析，简明扼要地指出观点的缺陷之处。

范文 15 解析

Experiential Education

Experiential education is a philosophy which recommends that students learn best through direct experience. Hands-on learning is said to promote deeper understanding because students are able to apply concepts and theories to physical situations. Rather than memorizing facts, students who are given the opportunity to create physical evidence of logical reasoning are better equipped to apply the same reasoning to new situations. Since all teachers aim to impart critical thinking in their classrooms, should they be expected to provide more hands-on learning opportunities? As educators aim to continuously improve the quality of the education they offer to students, consideration should be given to better incorporate hands-on learning.

Read and carefully consider these perspectives. Each suggests a particular approach regarding experiential education.

Perspective One

Some argue that to accept a theory without experiencing it is to learn nothing at all. Teachers need to provide opportunities for experiential involvement if they expect students to truly comprehend each lesson plan.

Perspective Two

Experiential education is an integral part of readying students to pursue careers in the science, technology, engineering, and math fields, but not all disciplines. If students are expected to perform skill-based tasks in these fields after they graduate, they should be provided with a strong foundation on which to build their careers. But teachers should not be expected to supply experiential learning where it is not appropriate.

Perspective Three

Schools cannot be expected to offer hands-on learning for students. Not only is it costly, but also it may not be effective for all learners. Students will be better served if schools invest their money in other educational models and opportunities.

[范文]	[点评]
Hands-on learning is excellent if one is a tactile learner. Some individuals learn exponentially better through experiential learning, and many argue that application of a theory is the best way to learn. These champions of the hands-on, experiential approach have valid points; however, they are forgetting that many other learning styles actually exist and possess a validity of their own. Since pioneers of education have pointed out these different learning styles, teachers have been encouraged to cater to all learning styles. This is a herculean task, and it is economically unfeasible for most school districts. Teachers who are wholeheartedly determined to implement lessons that cater to all learning styles often must pull from their own coffers, and this is unfair to say the least. (1) While experiential learning has shown to be highly effective in teaching science, mathematics, engineering, and technology, there is no evidence that it helps in other subjects that are just as important as the more logic-and reason-based subjects. In fact, attempts to apply	(1) 表明立场和观点，反驳所列观点，论证清晰，结构严谨，层层深入，体现了对主旨的精确理解。

（续表）

this fad to all subjects falls flat. Not all higher thought, not all careers, and not all learning styles need to have hands-on application of ideas. Therefore, teachers should attempt to implement experiential learning in the fields where it is most beneficial and applicable, but should not waste their time and resources attempting to apply it to subjects where it is unnecessary. (2)	(2) 总结上文观点，为下文做铺垫，条理清晰，也体现了对复杂句式的把握能力。
For example, imagine a World History teacher attempting to explain Kantian philosophy to a group of students while applying this new-fangled idea that experiential learning is the best procedure. (3) How would this teacher explain Kant to his students using a hands-on approach? Kantian philosophy is a theory, but it is not a theory that can be addressed using this method. Imagine the same teacher is teaching his students about the American Revolution and the French Revolution. To apply a hands-on experience, he taxes the students without their consent, attempting to replicate the emotions felt by colonists under the Stamp Act. Surely, a revolution of sorts would result. Hopefully the teacher will have learned his lesson before attempting to provide experiential learning to the Reign of Terror. These last two scenarios are partially in jest, but they serve to illustrate how this method is not feasible in some arenas. Other disciples where experiential learning fails to educate are classes where literature is analyzed, and grammar taught.	(3) 采用例证方式进行论证，形象生动，说服力强，体现了灵活的论证思路。
However, some classes outside of the realm of math and science could possibly benefit from experiential learning. Foreign language is a prime example. Many students will study Spanish for years, only to realize that they are incapable of speaking and understanding it in the real world. The old methodology of memorizing conjugations, rules for verb tenses, and bizarre vocabulary that has little place in actual conversation, is simply not serving the students. Applying more hands-on approaches to foreign languages and retiring tired methodology is clearly an excellent idea. Experiential education need not be restricted to math and science classrooms. (4)	(4) 进一步补充论证，完善了论证结构，使整个论证更为严谨合理。
Ergo, there is a time and a place for hands-on, experiential education. However, subjects that cannot seem to apply this newly popular method should not be pressured, cajoled, or ordered to alter their methods in order to pander to an educational fad, of which there are myriad. Educators must, first and foremost, attempt to educate as many different learning styles as possible. This style caters to but one of the many styles of learning, whereas lecture-based classes are fantastic for auditory learners. In order to maximize the amount of information processed by students, teachers should consider creative ways to reach different learning styles, and save experiential learning for when it would be most effective. (5)	(5) 文末点题，总结全文观点，体现了良好的总结概括能力和对主旨的把握能力。

1. 经典单词

tactile 能触知的

exponentially 以指数方式

cater to 迎合

herculean 困难的

wholeheartedly 全心全意地

experiential 经验上的

consent 同意

prime 最好的

bizarre 奇异的

ergo 因此

2. 闪光句子

(1) These champions of the hands-on, experiential approach have valid points; however, they are forgetting that many other learning styles actually exist and possess a validity of their own.

(2) These last two scenarios are partially in jest, but they serve to illustrate how this method is not feasible in some arenas.

(3) In fact, attempts to apply this fad to all subjects falls flat. Not all higher thought, not all careers, and not all learning styles need to have hands-on application of ideas.

(4) Many students will study Spanish for years, only to realize that they are incapable of speaking and understanding it in the real world.

(5) However, subjects that cannot seem to apply this newly popular method should not be pressured, cajoled, or ordered to alter their methods in order to pander to an educational fad, of which there are myriad.

3. 总体分析

全文脉络清晰,论证严谨,多处采用了例证的方式,形象生动,描写细腻,对主旨观点进行了强力的支撑,说服力强,论证透彻。在语言方面,没有用大量的复杂句式,但是用词贴切,语言凝练。

范文 16 解析

(题目同范文 15)

[范文]	[点评]
Teachers often tell us that learning is fun, and the best way to convince us that learning is enjoyable is to give us activities that keep us engaged (and awake.) The issue here is if teachers should provide more hands-on learning experiences because it helps all students learn and remember better. On the other hand, others say that it's possible to learn without doing and that schools should use their money for other educational purposes and not try to make everything hands-on learning. I agree that the best learning comes from hands-on work. (1)	(1) 开门见山表明观点,理清文章脉络,引出下文的讨论,体现了对文章主旨的准确把握。
I know from experience that I learn better when I can actually do something myself. When students do projects such as growing plants, they really learn about the science because they are part of making that science work. This is analogous to learning how to ride a bike. (2) A child can read, watch videos above it and even watch someone actually ride one, but he doesn't learn how to do it until he gets on a bike and pedals away. Thus, it is important that teachers provide opportunities for students to do as much hands-on learning as possible. However, those who think that students don't learn anything unless they actually do it are wrong. There are ideas that can't be experimented with. How can students recreate the Big Bang, or evolution? But just because they can't actually do this, it doesn't mean students don't learn. There is a lot that can be learned from reading and learning from experts. However, if there is a choice between learning by doing and not having that opportunity, learning by doing is the best way to teach and learn. (3)	(2) 利用骑自行车的例子进行论证,形象生动,有力地支撑了主旨观点,体现了灵活的写作手法。 (3) 补充论点,使论证更为严谨,结构更为完整,体现了良好的思辨能力。
On the other hand, other people think that experiential education is important only	

（续表）

for students who will work in a career that requires that they do things themselves, such as engineering and technology. It is important that students who will enter careers which are skill based have the opportunity to practise this in school. School is supposed to teach what is needed for students later in life, and knowing how to do experiments or re-create what others have done should be part of this. But the people who argue for this say it is important only for students who will need it in their future careers.（4） This means that some students, particularly those who don't know what career they want, will not get the benefit of hands-on experiences. That splits students into two groups; those who learn by doing and those who don't. All students learn well by doing, so it would not be fair to offer it only to some students. How can teachers know what is appropriate for students in their future careers if even the students don't yet know? This solution is not a good one because it assumes things that can't be supported.	（4）进一步补充论点，反驳文中观点，准确找到观点缺陷，体现了优秀的论证能力。
Finally, it is to argue that rather than create opportunities for hands-on learning, schools should spend their money on other things because learning by doing is expensive and may not be good for all students. There's always the problem that not all students learn in the same way so there's no one kind of learning that is best for everyone. But that doesn't mean teachers shouldn't provide hands on opportunities. Actually, this is a good way to reach all students because it involves working with your hands, maybe some reading and talking too, and critical thinking, and uses lots of ways of learning.（5） It is foolish to have the opportunity to do something important and not do it just because some people may not benefit from it or it will cost money. Teachers should give students the opportunity to learn in a hands-on way as much as possible.	（5）进一步论证观点，体现了严谨的论证思路，也体现了对复杂句式的驾驭能力。
In the real world, when we need to learn something new, like how to cook or use a computer program, if it's possible to learn by doing while having someone help and direct us, that is the best way to learn and the way that schools should teach. Studies, and my own experience, show that everyone can benefit from hands-on education; that is the way we learn and remember best.（6）	（6）文末点题，总结全文。

1. 经典单词

analogous 类似的

shortsighted 目光短浅的

2. 闪光句子

（1）However, if there is a choice between learning by doing and not having that opportunity, learning by doing is the best way to teach and learn.

（2）School is supposed to teach what is needed for students later in life, and knowing how to do experiments or re-create what others have done should be part of this.

（3）That splits students into two groups; those who learn by doing and those who don't.

（4）Actually, this is a good way to reach all students because it involves working with your hands, maybe some reading and talking too, and critical thinking, and uses lots of ways of learning.

3. 总体分析

全文论证严谨，说理透彻。在语言方面，没有用过多的复杂句式，选词恰当，直白易懂，并且逻辑清晰，环环相扣，能够切中论点要害，语言精练，结合自身的经验进行论证，更具说服力。

范文 17 解析

Truancy

Students are required to be in attendance during the school day unless they are ill, have a doctor's appointment, or need to attend a funeral. Parents are allowed to take students out of school for other reasons, but prior approval is often required. Truancy, or unexcused absenteeism, is a problem that many schools have yet to solve. Since reducing truancy increases student success, should schools be doing more to prevent unexcused absences? Considering that students rely on educators to offer guidance and support, it is wise for schools to assist students in attending school as regularly as possible.

Read and carefully consider these perspectives. Each suggests a particular approach regarding truancy.

Perspective One

Schools should contact law enforcement officers to report students who skip school regularly. In addition to receiving detention for unexcused absences, students' truancy should be noted in criminal records. This additional consequence will help discourage students from missing school.

Perspective Two

Truancy is a symptom rather than a core issue. Students who skip school regularly often do so because of transportation difficulties, social problems, violence concerns, or lack of interest. Addressing the core issues is the key to increasing student attendance, and schools should develop programs to help students overcome obstacles that prevent them from coming to school.

Perspective Three

Schools should offer helpful alternative instruction for students who regularly miss school. Whether students are allowed to attend school on the weekends or are required to take classes online, schools should provide students every opportunity to complete their courses and graduate.

[范文]

I was a semi-professional surfer throughout high school. I managed to simultaneously juggle contracts with sponsors and weekend tournaments, most of which were in far-flung locations. My sponsors would pay for my travel expenses and entry fees, and I excelled in the amateur and pro-am circuit in my sport of choice. The only issue with my athletic and professional achievements was that I was attending a public high school, and the issue of truancy reared its irritating, ugly head. I was an athlete, competing at a much higher level than the demigods of the football field. I was not merely attempting to beat the Wildcats from the next town over. I was attempting to win nationals. I was competing against international competitors as well. I managed to perform on the circuit, please my corporate sponsors, train four hours daily, and, staggeringly, maintain my position as salutatorian. Why was I being persecuted by the obsessive officers of truancy, when I clearly completed my work and excelled in school and sport alike? They pursued me with Chabert-like intensity, and with the same illogical, frothy mouthed addiction to a law, a law intended to help students who were in danger of failing. I clearly was not. I was Jean Valjean, and the truant officers did not care

（续表）

that my GPA was hundredths shy of perfect; they merely wanted to punish. (1) Rabid persecution of the truant misses the point entirely. Those who hope to make the world a better place by arresting, prosecuting, and destroying the futures of the truant miss the point of keeping children in school. Truant officers also fail to take into account extenuating circumstances. Sometimes, the student in question is a semi-professional athlete, as I was. As long as the schoolwork is completed, why should there be an issue? Why are high school athletes afforded a pass, but those on a national circuit penalized? It is nonsensical. (2) Other causes of truancy are altogether tragic. Perhaps the student is unable to come to school due to domestic horrors. Perhaps a parent is stricken with cancer or addiction, and the student must not only fend for themselves but for other family members. Bestowing the mark of criminal on these children only exacerbates their bad lot in life. Instead of criminalizing truancy, truant officers would be wise to have a heart and investigate the root cause of truancy itself. Perhaps, just perhaps, if truancy were viewed as a symptom of a greater issue, the world would see fewer children giving up hope. The number of teenage criminals would be reduced.	[点评] (1) 从个人经历入手讨论，形象生动，富有说服力。 (2) 运用两个连续的反问句，层层逼近，有力地支撑了论点，使论证更具有说服力。
Draconian policies involving truancy fail to see the big picture, simply to fulfill some law that does not care about the student's situation. I was fortunate to have been given an option. I attended Saturday school as often as I could on the weekends when I was not competing. This is a means to make up the hours missed, yet some students with no means of transportation nor support from their families cannot even take advantage of this option. (3) Instead of focusing on the "crime," perhaps more options should be given to students who have an insurmountable amount of unexcused absences. Why are they not allowed to make up their work at home? Is the goal of education simply having bodies in a classroom, or is the goal to educate? The idea of truancy is based on ideals that it does nothing to support. It merely carries out orders, and unknowingly destroys the lives of children who may benefit from other options. Simply slapping a criminal record on those who are already disenfranchised, discouraged, downtrodden, and at-risk is absolute folly. More options should be provided to those unfortunate students, who may have no means to abide by the law. Let us not forget that truants are mere children, and it is not always the child who is culpable.	(3) 进一步补充论证，运用自身经历进行论证，使论证更具说服力，体现了严谨的逻辑和良好的主旨把握能力。

1. 经典单词

simultaneously 同时地

excel 超过，擅长

irritating 使气人的

demigod 受崇拜的人

staggeringly 蹒跚地

persecute 烦扰，返客

frothy 空洞的

rabid 偏激的

persecution 迫害

extenuating 情有可原的

2. 闪光句子

(1) Those who hope to make the world a better place by arresting, prosecuting, and

destroying the futures of the truant miss the point of keeping children in school.

(2) Draconian policies involving truancy fail to see the big picture, simply to fulfill some law that does not care about the student's situation.

(3) Simply slapping a criminal record on those who are already disenfranchised, discouraged, downtrodden, and at-risk is absolute folly.

3. 总体分析

全文脉络清晰,结构清楚,运用了大量的自身经历进行例证,使文章更加生动形象,增强了说服力。句式结构方面,用了大量的复杂句式和形容词副词,多处采用了反问句式,层层深入剖析,增强了说理效果。

范文 18 解析

(题目同范文 17)

[范文]	[点评]
"Be cool; stay in school," is the type of saying that may sound silly to high school students. Even though that phrase isn't really sophisticated, it does provide very wise advice. Attending school is incredibly important, and some people argue that unexcused absences should be reported to the police. Other people want focus on treating the underlying causes of truancy rather than doling out harsh punishments. Still others think that schools should provide alternative instruction options for students who have trouble getting to school on a regular basis. (1) All three options have the same goal, which is to help students most at risk for missing school, and I think that schools should incorporate the best parts of all three approaches into their truancy-reduction policies.	(1) 简洁概括三个不同的观点,引出下文的主旨句,结构清晰,体现了良好的总结归纳能力和主旨把握能力。
The idea of having a police record because I have skipped school is extremely scary and would certainly prevent me from missing school. If students know that their school will report them to the police after a specific number of excused absences, they will be more likely to find a way to get to school. Teenagers don't always do the right thing because it's a good idea but rather because not doing the right thing will get them in a lot of trouble. (2) For example, many high school students turn in their assignments on time because they don't want teachers to deduct points for late submissions. The fear of consequence can promote good behavior in both homework habits and school attendance.	(2) 简明扼要指出问题的关键所在,思考透彻,逻辑清晰,体现了对深度辩论的把握能力。
While avoiding a harsh consequence is a good reason to get to school, it's sometimes not compelling enough for students who are struggling with issues that make attending school very difficult. The best way to increase attendance for these students is to address the underlying problems. (3) If students have transportation trouble, schools should help coordinate carpools and bus schedules. School counselors should be available to help students who have social issues or violence concerns. As for lack of interest, schools can offer before and after school activities such as intramural sports and social clubs to give students a reason to stay throughout the day.	(3) 进一步补充论证,提出问题的解决方案,使论述更加完整,更具说服力。
Even with the best efforts, some students will invariably struggle with attendance. For those students, schools should offer as many opportunities for them to complete their coursework as possible. It is in society's best interest to facilitate education, especially for at-risk youth. Now that technology allows students to	

（续表）

learn from nearly anywhere, schools should offer students the option to study remotely. Students will benefit from a high school diploma, of course, and they will be able to say that their teachers have done everything they could to give them the best chance at a good life. Attending school isn't just about learning facts. The school environment provides students with the opportunity to learn how to employ necessary social skills, collaborate with peers, and communicate effectively. The only way for students to develop these skills is to actually attend school. Every measure should be taken to reduce truancy, including the threat of a criminal record, the mitigation of underlying causes, and the option to pursue alternative instruction. (4) That way, students don't have to just take our "be cool; stay in school" word for it-they'll show up because, really, with all those measures in place, how could they not?	(4) 文末总结观点，再次强调中心论点，与上文相呼应，使文章架构更为完整。

1. 经典单词

sophisticated 复杂的
incredibly 难以置信地，非常地
harsh 严厉的
intramural 校内的
invariably 不变地

2. 闪光句子

(1) All three options have the same goal, which is to help students most at risk for missing school, and I think that schools should incorporate the best parts of all three approaches into their truancy-reduction policies.

(2) Teenagers don't always do the right thing because it's a good idea but rather because not doing the right thing will get them in a lot of trouble.

(3) Even with the best efforts, some students will invariably struggle with attendance.

(4) It is in society's best interest to facilitate education, especially for at-risk youth.

(5) Attending school isn't just about learning facts. The school environment provides students with the opportunity to learn how to employ necessary social skills, collaborate with peers, and communicate effectively.

3. 总体分析

全文思路清晰，立论合理，正确把握了文章的主旨，透过现象看到了问题的实质，能够简明地概括中心思想，并层层论证，善用实例进行支撑，环环紧扣主题，体现了严谨的辨证思路和技巧。

范文 19 解析

Endangered Species

Conservation status systems help governments and policy organizations prioritize and allocate resources to support the survival of imperiled species. In the United States, laws such as the Endangered Species Act provide a policy framework for implementing efforts to protect at-risk wildlife and ecosystems. These laws are often directly focused on mitigating the negative manmade effects of commercial expansion and land use. However, some activist groups support the broader goal of preventing the extinction of any species, regardless of whether or not humans are the cause of endangerment. Should regulatory efforts to protect endangered species be limited to offsetting the role of humans in placing wildlife at risk? Considering the global scope of conservation issues, the careful consideration and coordination of advocacy priorities could lead to improved policy outcomes.

Read and carefully consider these perspectives. Each suggests a particular way of thinking about the protection of endangered species.

Perspective One

Humans have the unique ability, through technological capability and scientific progress, to benefit the environment through the protection of wildlife and ecosystems. Conservation efforts should be open to any at-risk species, regardless of the known causes of endangerment.

Perspective Two

Conservation policies are regularly met with the challenge of an ever increasing number of species to save. With limited conservation resources available, funding priorities are too often biased in favor of publicly well-known animals and plants. Conservation decisions should instead be driven by scientific models that pinpoint sources of risk and identify high-value targets for species protection.

Perspective Three

To shape effective policy, a distinction should be drawn between species at risk due to human and nonhuman factors. Well intentioned conservation programs often carry unintended consequences that can create new environmental hazards despite successful species protection. Conservation policy should therefore be focused in a narrow way to repair the known negative effects of human activities on an ecosystem.

[范文]

Recently, the internet has been awash with stories about a species of black rhino vanishing to the realm of extinction. In the recent uproar of the death of Cecil the Lion, it appears that conservation of animals has come to the forefront of many a debate. In fact, one would think that the issue of protecting animals in danger of extinction is one easily resolved, given the number of people who complained about the loss of one lion. The issue is that even though people cry over the loss of an animal species for eternity, many do precious little to support conservation efforts. (1) This is not because they are incapable of action. This is not for desire to help. This is a tragic situation, because never before in human history have we had more capability to stem extinction. We have a gift that we can give the animal kingdom, and that gift comes from the very demon that many are quick to blame for the increasing numbers of extinctions. We can use the very science and technology that has harmed animals to actually save them. We have the capability and we have the resources to preserve our ecosystems. What we must do is harness these abilities and apply them.

The problem with people crying about extinction online is that it turns them into armchair activists. (2) Many feel as if they have more than done their part in the conservation effort by simply clicking the button that reads "share." No matter how many times someone cries foul, blames global warming, blames hunters, and

[点评]

(1) 简明扼要地指出问题的关键,体现了对原文主旨的精准理解和把握。

(2) 准确剖析问题的关键,透过现象看到了问题的本质,体现了深刻的洞察力和对文章主旨的把握。

（续表）

blames poachers, the wickedness of our encroachment on the homes of animals does not further conservation efforts. More must be done. This can be achieved in so many different ways. Some are frustratingly simple, and others are more wide reaching. To start, small donations add up. Instead of donating to PETA, an association that is vocally in support of animal rights and welfare while not doing much to conserve wildlife, one can research the most effective venues. Contributing to scientific research programs is a means to help. Recycling plastics and reducing the amount of trash that reaches our oceans is another way to contribute. Recently, a Swedish billionaire bought a swathe of land in the Amazonian Rain Forest for the sole purpose of conserving it. Discouraging businesses that destroy fragile environments by boycotting them entirely can also make a dent. However, more funding must be funneled into scientific research and legitimate conservation efforts. By our scientific advancement and increased understanding of the root causes of extinction, we can ultimately triumph. (3)	(3) 列举了诸多可以采取的解决措施，体现了对主题深入的剖析和开阔的写作思路。
Another aspect of conservation is preserving the animals that are not as adorable, popular, or majestic. Insects and amphibians and arachnids all are worthy of preservations. In fact, bird extinctions are rising drastically, yet there has been little outcry on social media outlets regarding our dying birds. (4) Despite our sadness at the loss of rhinos and lions, we have not contributed to the cause. We must get out of our armchairs and raise funds for legitimate research and valid preservation efforts. Only when something is irrevocably lost can we truly appreciate its value. Perhaps efforts should be undertaken earlier in order to best conserve our fragile, intricate ecosystems. Technology and progress have severely wounded our planet's animals. However, the same technology that can be blamed for their demise can also be used to preserve. The solution lies in science, technology, and concerted human effort, not simply shouting expletives online. We must fund the most effective methods of preservation, and support further research on the subject in order to protect the unique creatures that may be gone forever. (5)	(4) 从另一个角度进行论点的补充，完善了论证结构，体现了作者灵活的写作思路。 (5) 进一步总结全文，提炼主要观点，体现了对复杂句式的驾驭能力。

1. 经典单词

awash 充斥的
vanish 消失
uproar 骚动
forefront 最前部
eternity 永世
incapable 不能的
harness 利用
frustratingly 令人沮丧地
vocally 口头地
triumph 胜利

2. 闪光句子

(1) In the recent uproar of the death of Cecil the Lion, it appears that conservation of animals has come to the forefront of many a debate.

(2) This is not because they are incapable of action. This is not for of desire to help. This is a tragic situation, because never before in human history have we had more capability to stem

extinction.

(3) The problem with people crying about extinction online is that it turns them into armchair activists.

(4) No matter how many times someone cries foul, blames global warming, blames hunters, blames poachers, and or the wickedness of our encroachment on the homes of animals do not further conservation efforts.

(5) Only when something is irrevocably lost can we truly appreciate its value.

3. 总体分析

全文脉络清晰,语言凝练,思路开阔,逻辑架构完善。对于问题的剖析非常深刻,分析角度很独到,能够从多个角度进行论证,并且能够以具体事例加以佐证,增强了说服力,也使文章更具有可读性。文末针对问题提出的措施非常多样,体现了开阔的写作思路和灵活的论证手法。

范文 20 解析

(题目同范文 19)

[范文]	[点评]
Most people have heard politicians argue about global warming and environmentalists ask for donations to help save the rainforest. Some people believe that humans should be responsible for assisting any and all plants and animals that are at risk for extinction. Since it is impossible to save every species, I think it makes more sense to use scientific reasoning to determine which plants and animals should be saved. (1) While it is helpful to know which species are affected by purely human factors and which are affected by non-human influences, I don't believe that such a determination should affect environmental policy.	(1) 开门见山提出观点,立意合理,说服力强,体现了对文章中心思想的准确把握。
The idea of saving the rainforest is a noble one, and there are plenty of plants and animals close by that could use our help, but trying to help every at-risk species is costly, time-consuming, and will ultimately prove unsuccessful. Some organisms are more important to the overall ecosystem than others, and that should be taken into account. (2) If polluted water is affecting animals at the top of a food chain like alligators, it makes sense to work to protect the alligators rather than a species at the very bottom of the food chain like earthworms. If the alligators die out, the entire food chain will deteriorate quickly. If earthworms become extinct, it will certainly create problems, but it is more likely that other animals can adapt to take the place of earthworms than alligators.	(2) 指出问题的核心所在,体现了对问题的深入剖析,逻辑清晰,论证严谨。
Just like zoological observations that demonstrate that alligators are at the top of the food chain, we can use other scientific evidence to guide our choices. Currently, scientists are studying the naked mole rat because it is said to be immune to cancer. Since the naked mole rat may provide information that can lead to medical breakthroughs, we should protect that particular species. Protecting the earth is a great responsibility, and we should do so wisely. (3)	(3) 举例论证,进一步支撑观点,具有说服力,体现了丰富的素材积累。
As we act responsibly to repair some of the damage we may have done to the environment, we should focus on efforts that will provide the most benefit for both humans and the overall ecosystem. (4) Whether an issue arises due to manmade or natural causes, we should work to save species that we can confidently say are highly important to maintaining a global balance between human progress and	(4) 进一步补充论点,完善行文逻辑架构,体现了严谨的论证思路与技巧。

（续表）

natural wildlife. If the bee population suddenly declined due to an unexpected gene mutation, we shouldn't refrain from saving the species just because humans didn't cause the mutation. Bees are responsible for extremely important pollination efforts, and their demise should not be dismissed lightly. Humans should embrace the fact they can change the environment around them for the better. No matter what the reason-human or natural-if scientists determine that a species should be saved, money and time should be spent to make that happen. We can't wait until after alligators, naked mole rats, or bees are gone to try to do something. We need to plan ahead, use scientific reasoning, and allocate resources so that the world that sustains us continues to do just that. (5)	(5) 总结全文，简洁地归纳了中心思想，体现了对复杂句式的驾驭能力。

1. 经典单词

noble 高尚的
deteriorate 恶化
zoological 动物学的
mutation 突变
refrain 节制
pollination 授粉
demise 死亡
dismissed 不予理会
sustain 支撑
wisely 明智地

2. 闪光句子

(1) While it is helpful to know which species are affected by purely human factors and which are affected by non-human influences, I don't believe that such a determination should affect environmental policy.

(2) The idea of saving the rainforest is a noble one, and there are plenty of plants and animals close by that could use our help, but trying to help every at-risk species is costly, time-consuming, and will ultimately prove unsuccessful.

(3) Whether an issue arises due to manmade or natural causes, we should work to save species that we can confidently say are highly important to maintaining a global balance between human progress and natural wildlife.

(4) Humans should embrace the fact they can change the environment around them for the better.

(5) We need to plan ahead, use scientific reasoning, and allocate resources so that the world that sustains us continues to do just that.

3. 总体分析

全文行文流畅，语句简洁，思路清晰，结构完整。对文章的主旨进行了精准把握，从多个角度进行了论证，并且加以例证，增强了说服力。作者没有局限在问题表面，而是从多个角度进行深度剖析，分析到了问题的本质并对可能存在的问题进行补充论证，整个结构非常清楚，说理也非常透彻。